D1711182

Banned in Berlin

Monographs in German History

BANNED IN BERLIN

Literary Censorship in Imperial Germany
1871–1918

Gary D. Stark

Berghahn Books
New York • Oxford

Published in 2009 by

Berghahn Books

www.berghahnbooks.com

©2009 Gary D. Stark

Library of Congress Cataloging-in-Publication Data

Stark, Gary D., 1948–
    Banned in Berlin : literary censorship in imperial Germany, 1871–1918 / Gary D. Stark.
        p. cm. — (Monographs in German history ; v. 25)
    Includes bibliographical references and index.
    ISBN 978-1-84545-570-5 (hardback : alk. paper)
    1. German literature—19th century—Censorship. 2. German literature—20th century—
Censorship. 3. Theater—Censorship—Germany—History. 4. Literature and state—
Germany—History. 5. Censorship—Germany—History. I. Title.

PT345.S73 2009
363.310931'09034—dc22

                                                                        2008052671

British Library Cataloguing in Publication Data

A catalogue record for this book is available from the British Library

Printed in the United States on acid-free paper

ISBN: 978-1-84545-570-5 hardback

For Kathleen and Karl

CONTENTS

TABLES

FIGURES

ACKNOWLEDGEMENTS

When I began work on this topic toward the end of the last century, before periodically wandering off down twisting pathways of academic administration, I never imagined it would take so long to complete. It has been a labor of love, but a protracted one. Were it not for the patience (and impatience), prodding, suggestions, inspiration, and support of friends, colleagues, and family, I would be laboring still.

In Germany, Rainer and Rita Jagmann, Robert Brokopp, and Gaby Moll were always welcoming and generous hosts willing to listen tolerantly to tales from the archives. Though they may no longer remember it, at the University of Texas at Arlington my colleagues Don Kyle, Evan Anders, Robert Fairbanks, and Tom Porter read early drafts or encouraged me onward, while the university supported my initial research with grants and summer stipends from the Organized Research Fund. A German Academic Exchange Service Study Visit Grant and National Endowment for the Humanities Summer Stipend made possible additional visits to archives and libraries, while a National Endowment for the Humanities Fellowship in 1985–1986 underwrote a year of research, reflection, and writing. I was able to complete a major part of the manuscript during a glorious semester as a Visiting Fellow at the Institute for Advanced Study, where I benefited from Peter Paret's generous advice and encouragement and from the assistance of the library staff. A sabbatical and travel grants from Grand Valley State University have provided me the time necessary to complete the manuscript. My colleague Jason Crouthamel and the Faculty Writing Group read various chapters and offered valuable suggestions for improving and clarifying them, while the members of the colloquia of the History Department and the College of Liberal Arts & Sciences listened patiently and asked useful questions as I honed my arguments. Elaine Eldridge helped me wrestle some of the more lengthy segments into a more manageable, and readable, form.

Throughout my career Vernon Lidtke has been a most supportive and inspiring mentor. For many years Robert J. Goldstein, Peter Jelavich, Andrew Lees, Charles E. McClelland, and especially Leslie Moch have also followed this project with interest, heartened me when I needed it, read drafts of various chapters, and offered perceptive critiques.

My deepest debt, however, is to my wife Kathleen Underwood and son Karl Underwood Stark, who have lived with this topic nearly as long as I and are as happy as I am to see it completed. Their patience, support, and presence made that possible.

ABBREVIATIONS

BHStA	Bayerisches Hauptstaatsarchiv
BOP	Brandenburgische Oberpräsident (Brandenburg Provincial Governor)
BPP	Berlin Police President (Polizei-Präsident Berlin)
BZA	Bezirksausschuß (District Administrative Council)
FM	Foreign Minister (Außenminister)
GStA PK	Geheimes Staatsarchiv Preußischer Kulturbesitz, Berlin-Dahlem
GStA PK/1000	Geheimes Staatsarchiv Preußischer Kulturbesitz, Rep. 77: Ministerium des Innern, Tit. 1000
GStA PK/ZK	Geheimes Staatsarchiv Preußischer Kulturbestiz, 2.2.1., Königliches Geheime Zivilkabinett
HHStA/407	Hessisches Hauptstaatsarchiv, Abt. 407: Polizeipräsidium Frankfurt
HStA	Hauptstaatsarchiv
IM	Interior Minister (Innenminister)
JM	Justice Minister (Justizminister)
KK	Ludwig Leiss, *Kunst im Konflikt. Kunst und Künstler im Widerstreit mit der `Obrigkeit'* (Berlin, 1971)
LAB	Landesarchiv Berlin
LAB A/74	Landesarchiv Berlin A: Pr. Br. Rep. 030 Berlin C: Polizei-präsidium Berlin, Tit. 74-Theatersachen
LAB C/A	Landesarchiv Berlin, Pr. Br. Rep. 30 C/a: Theater-Zensur
MPD	Munich Police Director (Polizei-Direktor München)

OK	Oberkommando (Supreme Command)
OP	Oberpräsident (Provincial Governor)
OVG	Oberverwaltungsgericht (Supreme Administrative Court)
PD	Police Director (Polizei-Direktor)
PP	Police President (Polizei-Präsident)
Pr	Prussian (Preußische)
PrIM	Prussian Interior Minister (Preußischer Innenminister)
PrJM	Prussian Justice Minister (Preußischer Justizminister)
PrRM	Prussian Religion Minister (Preußischer Minister der geistlichen, Unterrichts- und Medizinal-Angelegenheiten)
PrWM	Prussian War Minister (Preußischer Kriegsminister)
RA	Regierungs-Assessor (Assistant Administrative Councilor)
RG	Reichsgericht (Imperial Supreme Court)
RP	Regierungspräsident (District Administrative President)
RR	Regierungsrat (Administrative Councilor)
StAH	Staatsarchiv Hamburg, Pol.S.: Polizeibehörde--Politische Polizei
StAL	Staatsarchiv Ludwigsburg
StAM/PDM	Staatsarchiv München, Pol.Dir. München
StAM/SA	Staatsarchiv München, St.Anw.
StA Bremen	Staatsarchiv Bremen
StBM	Stadtbibliothek München, Literaturarchiv
StenBer/Bav	*Stenographische Berichte über die Verhandlungen der bayerischen Kammer der Abgeordneten*
StenBer/Pr	*Stenographische Berichte über die Verhandlungen des preußischen Haus der Abgeordneten*
StenBer/RT	*Stenographische Berichte über die Verhandlungen des Reichstages, Haus der Abgeordneten*
VL	Heinrich Houben, *Verbotene Literatur. Von der klassischen Zeit bis zur Gegenwart. Ein kritisch-historisches Lexikon über verbotene Bücher, Zeitschriften und Theaterstücke, Schriftsteller und Verleger.* 2 vols. (Berlin, 1924. Reprint: Hildesheim, 1965)
WM	War Minister (Kriegsminister)

INTRODUCTION
Censorship, Society, and Literary Life in Imperial Germany

> Then the first thing will be to establish a censorship of the writers of fiction,
> and let the censors receive any tale of fiction which is good, and reject those bad.
> —Plato, *The Republic*, Book II

> There was, besides, full freedom of thought,
> Enjoyed by the masses of the nation;
> Restrictions applied to only a few—
> Those who wrote for publication.
> —Heinrich Heine, *Deutschland. Ein Wintermärchen* (1844), XXV

"**N**obody these days holds the written word in such high esteem as police states do," remarks a character in Italo Calvino's 1979 novel *If on a winter's night a traveler.* "What statistic allows one to identify the nations where literature enjoys true consideration better than the sums appropriated for controlling and suppressing it? Where it is the object of such attentions, literature gains an extraordinary authority, inconceivable in countries where it is allowed to vegetate as an innocuous pastime, without risks."[1] Calvino is certainly not the first writer to suggest that when artists enjoy total freedom of expression they are not being taken seriously. Alfred Döblin, remarking in the 1920s on demands by some in Germany for absolute artistic freedom, maintained that artists and writers were part of society and had a right to be treated like everyone else; allowing them to say whatever they want is to ignore or dismiss them as one would a child or idiot. "Art is not sacred, and artworks should be allowed to be banned," he said; "We [writers] want to be taken seriously. We want to have an impact, and thus we have—a right to be punished."[2]

Notes for this section begin on page xxv.

As the proverbial land of *Dichter und Denker* (poets and thinkers), Germany in the imperial era (1871–1918) devoted enormous resources to creating, editing, publishing, distributing, marketing, reading, interpreting, and reviewing serious (and not-so-serious) literature. In 1900, for example, the German Empire published nearly twenty-five thousand book and journal titles, with an average run of about one thousand copies each—nearly twice as many titles as published in France, nearly three and a half times as many as in England, and nearly four times as many as in the US. Of these titles, one in nine were classified as "*Schöne Literatur*" (belles lettres), a portion that had risen to one in seven by 1908.[3] With an estimated six hundred theaters, Germans were also heavily invested in producing, staging, directing, rehearsing, and performing drama.[4] At the same time state and local authorities—right up to the final days of World War I—expended much time and money prosecuting and trying writers; supervising, controlling, regulating, and censoring literature and the public stage; and hearing and arbitrating frequent appeals of their censorship decisions. The national Reichstag, several state parliaments, various government commissions, and the press, meanwhile, studied and debated at length the empire's censorship decisions, policies, and laws. And legions of private citizens within and outside of the literary community mobilized and organized to protest the nation's censorship practices and agitate for their change. Although some, like the liberal-left journalist Bernhard Kellermann, believed no country disdained literature and everything spiritual more than did the German Empire,[5] in Germany literature in general—and theater in particular—clearly enjoyed true consideration, was the object of great attention, and commanded an extraordinary authority. Writers there were taken seriously indeed and several were punished for what they wrote. Whether or not imperial Germany would have qualified as a "police state" in Calvino's eyes, it certainly went to great lengths to control and suppress some of its literature and drama. This is a study of how and why that literary censorship occurred and what consequences followed.

Imperial Germany and Modernist Literature

Historians have long argued about the nature of the German Empire, and since the 1960s their conflicting interpretations have often been vehemently debated. Many scholars characterize the *Kaiserreich* as a backward, rigid, pseudoconstitutional, semiabsolutistic and militaristic autocracy—a solidly authoritarian society where a strong interventionist *Obrigkeitsstaat* (a state based on monarchical, authoritarian principles) repressed or restricted civil rights and freedoms, including freedom of expression. Germany's weak, illiberal, and semifeudalized bourgeoisie (these observers argue) was unable to establish the kind of liberal, modern, middle-class political system their British and French counterparts had. Instead, the empire was controlled by a narrow, premodern, antiliberal, reactionary elite of agrarian-military aristocrats and archconservative industrialists who protected their domination by coercing opponents, manipulating political life and public opinion, and successfully blocking all progressive elements.

This "orthodox" view has been increasingly challenged by revisionists who argue imperial Germany was in many ways as liberal and "normal" as its Western neighbors. According to this school, the German bourgeoisie was actually strong and growing in influence; liberal bourgeois values had triumphed in many areas, and in the political realm had created a genuine *Rechtsstaat* (a state based on a rule of law). In some respects, such as its social security system, universal male suffrage, world-class universities, and exemplary municipal administration, Germany was more advanced than any other nation. New populist movements and ideologies within the lower middle classes were not fostered and manipulated by the elites from above, but rather arose from below through the autonomous political self-mobilization of previously subordinate social groups. After the 1890s, revisionists argue, modernizing and reformist forces in the empire were making headway; German society was becoming more progressive and pluralistic; the liberal public sphere, civil liberties, and freedom of the press were all expanding; and elections were fair and political culture was becoming more democratic. "[D]efenders of the 'people's rights' were clearly more numerous and more powerful than scholars once believed."[6]

Whether one believes traditional, antimodern forces still overpowered those of modernity, or that the latter were prevailing over the former, it is clear imperial Germany was a society in "restless movement"[7] undergoing fundamental and at times overwhelming economic, social, and cultural changes. The rapid shift from an agrarian to an industrial economy, while making Germany Europe's leading industrial power, also brought greater social stratification, class conflict, and industrial strife. A population explosion was accompanied by massive internal and external migration and rapid urbanization. Secularization, the modernization of the school curricula, and greatly expanded access for the middle and lower middle classes (and women) to a university education were altering many worldviews. New forms of mass entertainment, from the popular press and *Schundliteratur* ("trashy" pulp fiction) to the cinema, were rapidly changing popular culture. The growth of Europe's strongest socialist movement and of a middle-class feminist movement, as well as the growing assertiveness of various ethnic and religious minorities, heightened the level of social, religious, cultural, and political conflict. Everywhere traditional norms and values seemed to be colliding with newer, more modern ones.

This was true especially of art, where defenders of the traditional clashed with avant-garde proponents of new styles, techniques, and subject matter. The conventional, idealistic view of art and literature prevalent in imperial Germany was a conservative, backward-looking one that worshipped classical notions of the true, the good, and the beautiful and viewed innovation with profound suspicion. Artistic and literary traditionalists preached adherence to certain eternal, unchanging principles, including order, harmony, regularity, and a disinterested enjoyment of beauty. Rejecting notions of elite aestheticism, traditionalists also believed art had a social mission—indeed duty—to ennoble and uplift the broader populace, to elevate the spirits of common men and women and inspire them with noble, idealistic sentiments. For art to fulfill its social responsibilities required that artists and writers represent recognizable and potentially inspiring subjects in an intelligible and uplifting way.

No better articulation of this idealist conception of art can be found than in the pronouncements of Emperor Wilhelm II, especially his famous December 1901 speech at the dedication of the Berlin Siegesallee, at which he lectured the assembled sculptors about the nature of true art and the dangers of artistic modernism. Art, Wilhelm II proclaimed, takes its models from nature and God's eternal laws and the artists of classical antiquity expressed most perfectly these eternal, unchanging laws of beauty, harmony, and aesthetics. "[D]espite all our modern feelings and knowledge, we are proud when it is said of a particularly fine artistic achievement: 'that is nearly as good as the art of 1900 years ago.' But only nearly!" Warning against the corruption of pure art by "so-called modern tendencies," the emperor implored German artists not to be led astray by passing fads or to abandon the principles on which art is built. "*An art that transgresses the laws and limits I have outlined ceases to be art,*" he proclaimed. Artists who march behind the seductive banner of "freedom" frequently fall into unbounded license and overweening presumption. For Wilhelm II, "Whoever strays from the law of Beauty and from the feeling for the aesthetic and harmonious … sins against the fountainhead of art."

Finally, Wilhelm II expounded on art's social mission: art should help educate the nation:

> [Art] should make it possible even for the lower classes, after their toil and hard work, to lift themselves up and be inspired by ideals, … to elevate themselves to the beautiful and rise above the constraints of their everyday thoughts. But when art, as so often happens today, shows us only misery and shows it even uglier than misery is anyway, then art sins against the German people. … [Art must] hold out its hand to *raise people up, instead of descending into the gutter.*[8]

The emperor's notion that art should elevate and show only the beautiful reflected and reinforced attitudes widely held in imperial Germany. His conservative conception of art also became the semiofficial one because his opinions—and many of his stock platitudes on the subject—were in turn dutifully repeated in the reports of the empire's censors, the arguments of its public prosecutors, and the verdicts of its judges. Whether this was done out of genuine conviction or out of a desire to avoid the kind of royal reprimand given to a few of their more liberal-minded colleagues is largely irrelevant; contemporary observers were convinced that had Wilhelm II taken a less-hostile stance toward modern German drama, "then surely many actions by the censorship authorities—who have proven to be genuine enemies of art, shackles on the mighty, rushing development of our artistic life—would not have taken place."[9]

This conservative artistic idealism stood in sharp, even irreconcilable conflict with modern artists' conception of the function of their art and their relation to society. Like their counterparts elsewhere, avant-garde German artists and writers rejected traditional aesthetic norms, repudiating the classical conception of art in which some timeless beauty was the revered touchstone and artists strove for the ennoblement and uplift of the human spirit. For modernist writers especially, truth now became the central axiom of art and the artist's task was to make art conform to real life. Rather than glossing over unpleasant realities or attempting to beautify and idealize what was base or unattractive in life, mid-nineteenth-century German Realists (and the Naturalists who soon followed them) believed that truth in art demanded the acknowledgement and examination of the negative as well as the positive in nature. Using scientific observation and objective analysis in order to portray and reproduce reality as exactly and naturalistically as possible, they hoped finally to lay bare the raw, naked truths about modern society and human existence. Moreover, beginning with Naturalism, and becoming ever more pronounced in the avant-garde movements that followed it, modernist artists proclaimed the autonomy of art and the absolute independence of the artist. In fin de siècle Germany, as elsewhere, many modernist artists and writers embraced a vaguely anarchistic, extremely subjectivist cult of elite aestheticism and commitment to "art for art's sake" that emphasized the creative artists' spiritual and intellectual superiority over ordinary people and insisted on their immunity from normal social conventions and obligations.

As the remarks of Wilhelm II illustrate, these new conceptions of art met with strong resistance from wide segments of the general public as well as from state officials. Imperial authorities, for example, confiscated the work of some writers and artists, prosecuted others for violating the laws against obscenity, blasphemy, or lèse majesté, and police in most cities regularly prohibited the performance of certain dramas. Accordingly, some historians have argued that modernist writers, at least in the short term, were "effectively bridled and isolated" by legal and administrative controls; that legal penalties exerted an effective "restraining influence on writers" by "punishing or preventing the expression in literature of facts or opinions that demanded expression"; or that writers, satirists, and other cultural figures in Wilhelmine Germany existed in some "no-man's land between repression and liberality."[10] Others maintain that "ideas flowed freely" and the empire's "arts and literature were flourishing"; pointing to the "great latitudes of freedom and protection" artists and writers enjoyed, they argue the state's efforts at literary censorship were "largely ineffectual" and "official attempts to exert influence on the theater repertoire and on modern literature came to naught."[11] A leading textbook on twentieth-century European history flatly declares individual rights in the empire were carefully protected and "[t]here was no censorship."[12]

To determine what role formal state controls did in fact play in the literary and political life of imperial Germany, this book examines the laws, institutions, personnel, and everyday practices of literary censorship at both the central/national and the local/regional level. Taking a comparative perspective—noting where the empire's literary censorship resembled and where it differed from that of other

European nations—it can also shed light on the issue of Germany's relative "back-wardness" or "normalcy," particularly in its response to modernist literature.

Censorship

The study of censorship is an interdisciplinary field where political, legal, religious, and literary histories intersect with those of the book trade, libraries, the press, theater, and film. Traditionally, studies of censorship have focused on efforts to muzzle particular authors, artists, publications, or ideas, or on the censorship policies and practices of particular regimes or time periods. Since the late 1960s, however, "censorship studies" has expanded considerably and now flourishes as never before. Seminal systematic analyses by Ulla Otto, Hans Fügen, Dieter Breuer, Klaus Kanzog, Annabel Patterson, Reinhard Aulich, and others have explored the theoretical, historical, sociopolitical, and literary dimensions of censorship as a concept and as an institution.[13] Other scholars (including Annette Kuhn, Sue Curry Jansen, Richard Burt, Michael Holmquist, Michael Levine, Robert Post, and Beate Müller), drawing on new insights from literary, communication, and media theory; on a growing interest in the external determinants and social dimensions of literary life broadly defined; and on theories about the evolution of the public sphere (*Öffentlichkeit*), have turned from the study of explicit acts of "repressive intervention" by identifiable regulatory authorities to more latent, generalized structural processes of communications control and cultural regulation. These newer approaches see censorship not as a series of discrete acts by specific institutions and external agents to silence a subject, but rather as an ongoing process or system of power relationships between a variety of censorious forces and agents that transcend time and place. Censorship is omnipresent and inescapable, an inherent structural necessity, they argue, because *all* expression is constrained by underlying psychic and social forces, internalized perceptions and inhibitions, diverse and dispersed techniques of domination, and by discursive practices of exclusion, selection, differentiation, or demarcation.[14] The vast reach of contemporary censorship research is reflected in the recent four-volume *Censorship: A World Encyclopedia,* which defines censorship as any process, "formal and informal, overt and covert, conscious and unconscious, by which restrictions are imposed on the collection, display, dissemination, and exchange of information, opinions, ideas, and imaginative expression." Its entries range from the areas of ethics, law, languages, media studies, and philosophy to politics, psychology, the physical sciences, religion, and sociology.[15]

As censorship studies have expanded, however, the term has been so broadly applied that scholars no longer agree on what censorship is. When the term is used so freely that it includes any attempt by any group or individual, public or private, to "control communication between people" (Berger) or anything, including free market forces, that limits what we can read, hear, or know (Jansen), or any "discourse control" or "use of semantic domination" (Kienzle and Mende)—including the use of professional or expert language (Schauer)[16]—then the term is virtually devoid of meaning. As Peter Dittmar observed even before the field's postmodern turn: "The inflation of the word 'censorship' into a meaningless term of vilification [*Allerweltschimpfwort*] has become irreversible. Since 'censorship' has come to serve as an excuse for every rebuff that can befall an author, including those that are self-inflicted, that word can hardly be used rationally any more."[17]

In this study, the term *censorship* will be used in its narrower conventional sense, for acts of "repressive intervention": those formal, overt, and conscious attempts to control the public expression of opinions. It is an institutionalized, usually legally sanctioned form of social control involving systematic state examination and judgment of expressions intended for public dissemination. Preventive or prior censorship (*Vorzensur*) occurs when authorized agents of the state claim the prerogative of inspecting expressions and either approving or prohibiting them (or approving them provided they are altered) before they are publicly disseminated. Since expressions cannot legally circulate publicly until they receive explicit official permission, this is the most rigorous form of censorship, for it theoretically bans everything except what the censors approve. Punitive, repressive, or ex post facto censorship (*Nachzensur*), by contrast, controls expressions and imposes sanctions only after the expressions have been made public, for example by confiscating, prohibiting, destroying, or mandating the alteration of the offending material and/or by punishing those responsible for the expression or for its public dissemination. Since under punitive censorship materials may presumably circulate freely before a decision is made to permit or ban them, this is a more permissive form of censorship in that all public expressions are tolerated until they are expressly banned. In imperial Germany most theatrical performances were subject to preventive censorship, while printed literature had to contend only with punitive censorship.

Though I approach censorship from a conventional perspective, I hope to avoid some shortcomings of traditional (and contemporary) censorship studies. Like the satirist who characterized it as "the younger of two sisters, the older of whom is Inquisition,"[18] those who live from the expression and open exchange of ideas and opinions detest censorship. Artists, scholars, writers, and other people of letters decry censorship as a crude weapon wielded by the forces of ignorance to silence courageous heralds of truth and progress. One of its pioneering historians deemed the struggle of literature against censorship "the eternal conflict of two world views, the struggle of light against darkness, of enlightenment against obscurantism," while a recent scholar observes "it has become all but impossible to discuss censorship in anything other than pejorative terms."[19] Literary scholar Dieter Breuer notes that many studies of repressive interventions by censors become simplistic "censorship polemics" that reduce the story to a Manichean collision between rigid petty functionaries and unyielding evangelists of freedom. Censors and authors, he points out, actually have considerable latitude in deciding how best to exercise their respective prerogatives: the former to assert the state's need for security in the interest of the common good, the latter to stake out and maintain some free space for the individual.[20] Rather than a one-dimensional harangue, this study offers instead a nuanced examination of the motives, practices, limits, and consequences of state censorship of literature in Germany. Such an analysis demands that we look both at the censored and the censors, taking the latter seriously and seeking to understand the complexity of their motives and situation, and it requires us to consider the frequent gap between the intent and the effect of literary censorship. And although focusing on traditional institutional forms of state censorship rather than on broader impersonal processes of cultural regulation and discourse control, I draw on insights from recent literary and social theory (especially reader-response and reception theory and the social control of deviance) to explore some structural features of censorship—without, I hope, succumbing to the tendency of many such analyses to conflate or ignore the significantly different kinds of experiences of those who are subject to censorship.[21]

One such feature that has intrigued many recent scholars is the inclination of the subjects of censorship to internalize the mechanisms of control. Michael Foucault brilliantly analyzed the implicit systems of power and the constraining mechanisms embedded in modern social institutions (for example, prisons, factories, hospitals, or schools) that serve to discipline, control, and determine our behavior without our knowing it.[22] Drawing on his work, many modern studies emphasize how writers and artists are conditioned by constant, omnipresent scrutiny and surveillance to exercise a self-discipline and self-control that makes overt censorship unnecessary. Anxiously anticipating the censor's judgment and hoping to avoid a conflict with the law, some authors may become hesitant or uncertain and may come to practice, either consciously or unconsciously, an inhibiting self-censorship—to write with what one observer has cleverly called a "scissors in the head."[23] Leo Tolstoy, for example, remarked that the "horrible czarist censorship question" always tormented him and caused him involuntarily to abandon many projects he wanted to write; Diderot noted that censorship instills in writers a reticence, uncertainty, and self-doubt so that in the end an author himself no longer knows what he thinks; and John Galsworthy, testifying before a parliamentary committee in 1909 about Britain's theater censorship, quoted letters from many authors who claimed, because of the censor, to have been deterred from writing about something.[24] Censorship can thus ultimately create and sustain a power relationship semi-independent of the censors who exercise it: authors and artists caught up in this power situation can themselves become its bearers. Perhaps, as some observers suggest, censorship actually aims at "the internalization of the claims of domination": regimes seek "to build the secret police into the individual's brain itself and have it assume the position of censor within him," so that the result of successful censorship is ultimately self-censorship. As the French poet and essayist Paul Valery lamented, "In every way we are circumscribed, dominated by a hidden or obvious regimentation extending to everything, and we are so bewildered by this chaos of stimuli obsessing us that we end by needing it."[25] In examining the experiences of censored German authors, I will look closely at the various ways they responded to, sometimes internalized, and occasionally ended up "needing" censorship.

Even when narrowly defined as formal, overt, and conscious intervention by state authorities, censorship exerts a potent effect upon authors. Whether or not internalized self-censorship actually determines how or what authors think or write privately, it is clear censorship can profoundly influence what they produce for the public, including what subjects they choose and what genres and language they use. Censorship affects if and how their work is disseminated to a wider public and which groups or individuals have access to it. Censorship can have significant personal and financial consequences not only for writers and playwrights but also for the publishers, editors, and booksellers who help distribute their works or the theater owners, directors, and actors who stage them. Finally, censorship can influence how the public reads or understands an author's work or how theatergoers and dramatic critics respond to it. Censorship, in short, must be considered as a constitutive factor of literary life. And so it was in imperial Germany, where official efforts to censor literature and drama had a significant impact on the literary life of the period: as the writer Herbert Ihering observed, until censorship was abolished in November 1918, German police regulations were "an aesthetic principle" that shaped the language and themes of literature and the theater.[26]

In Germany, as elsewhere, state censorship was a form of social control employed by governing authorities to defend and secure conformity to the shared political, social, religious, and moral norms and values that, in their view, were essential for communal integration, social cohesion, and civic order. While all sociopolitical systems guard their norms and many use censorship to do so, censors must nevertheless permit some modification and adaptation of those norms over time. For norms are historically relative, not eternally fixed: as new existential circumstances emerge in a society, as conditions governing communal interaction and the satisfaction of basic human needs change and evolve, the norms on which the society's identity, cohesion, and stability depend must also change and evolve. New situations demand new norms; no social order will remain stable unless it adapts to changing circumstances and no code of norms will remain viable unless it, too, evolves to meet the changing conditions of social life. A continual dialectical tension thus exists between society's need to defend and uphold its norms on the one hand, and its need to adapt or creatively reformulate its norms to changing circumstances on the other.

Censorship plays a central role in this larger process of the evolution or reformulation of norms (*Normenwandel*). Any viable social order has—indeed, must have—people, institutions, and processes that promote the evolution and modernization of its norms: by questioning, challenging, and deviating from established norms and by exposing reigning conventions as outmoded, indefensible, or no longer tenable, they encourage the development of new values better suited to the social needs created by new circumstances. As one authority on social norms has observed, "All social change commences as deviant behavior."[27] Since the function of the censor is to uphold existing norms by suppressing public expressions that endanger or subvert them, an inevitable, perpetual conflict exists between the norm-preserving efforts of censors and the efforts of those, especially imaginative writers and artists, who promote norm evolution and adaptation. Confrontations between censors and writers are part of the larger, ongoing process of norm-conflict and norm-evolution that occurs in all societies and in all historical periods.[28]

The decisions of censors are clearly an important factor influencing the rate at which norms will evolve. The more rigidly censors interpret and defend existing norms and the more intolerant they are of deviations from reigning standards, the more norm evolution will be retarded; the more flexible and tolerant they are of expressions that depart from the traditional, the easier the process of norm adaptation and evolution will be. Censors who perform their function too well—that is, those who suppress *all* nonconformist expressions and thus block any change in the reigning code of norms—actually pose a threat to a society's long-term stability, especially in periods of rapid social transformation such as imperial Germany was experiencing. For when members of a community begin questioning or dissenting from traditional norms, it usually indicates prevailing norms have not adapted to changing social conditions. Nonconformist expressions, especially of a literary nature, are frequently symptoms of deeper social transformations taking place or that have already occurred. Unless these new underlying circumstances, needs, or problems are recognized and the society's norms are allowed to evolve to meet them, those norms will become unviable and will no longer provide a source of social integration, cohesion, and stability.

If seen simply as a means of preserving a social or political system's indispensable code of norms, censorship seems a justifiable and even beneficial social institution. But it also has a profoundly ideological dimension, both in the stricter sense of reflecting the interests of a particular class, and in the broader sense of being intimately involved with the dynamics of power and domination. Political sociologists and others have persuasively argued that all censorship is simply a method used by politically dominant elites to defend their interests and preserve their sociopolitical dominance by protecting and upholding the code of values on which that dominance is based.[29]

Self-protection, to be sure, is hardly how censoring authorities conceive of or characterize their actions. Those who exercise censorship or support its use have traditionally claimed they do so for the welfare and protection of others. Censorship is necessary, they maintain, to defend society's weaker, more susceptible, and more easily misled elements: women; the young; the less-educated, naïve, or susceptible readers or theater-goers; certain religious or ethnic groups; a particular social class—the list is extensive. Such justifications for censorship are based on two paternalistic-authoritarian assumptions: first, that some (or most) people, being weak and corruptible, can be saved from evil only by strict rules imposed by external authority; and second, that some social elements, because of their immaturity, inferiority, or some peculiar corruptibility, are not competent to defend themselves against harmful ideas or influences and are thus in need of the censor's tutelage. ("Censorship is guardianship," observed the Hungarian-German writer Ödön von Horváth; "for guardianship, one needs police; for police, one needs the penitentiary."[30]) As guardians or wardens for others, censors of course assume they and a circle of colleagues are safely immune to the moral dangers and corrupting influence of the materials they examine in order to declare them harmful to someone else. The "unsafe," vulnerable audiences they usually identify are people with no power to answer back: young, uneducated, or politically impotent groups that must accept the status of being unable to make their own decisions.[31]

Censorship, in other words, protects not society's most defenseless and least powerful members but its most secure, influential, and dominant ones. The prevailing system of values and social norms censors uphold and defend are defined by and serve the interests of that society's most powerful, dominant groups. Attempts to censor public expressions that conflict with, challenge, or violate established norms are, quite simply, attempts to defend and preserve the status quo, the system of relationships, attitudes, and conditions on which the primacy of the dominant elite rests. The institution of censorship, one early analyst observed, existed primarily to defend the established order against dissidents and critics. The most enthusiastic advocates of censorship are defenders of the status quo, those who feel most in harmony with and depend most upon established institutions and values and whose interests would be most harmed if these were radically altered. By contrast, it is those least attached to the status quo—maladjusted outsiders, the underprivileged, radicals, and heretics—who, because of their susceptibility to dangerous notions, are regarded as the greatest threat to the established order. Precisely these groups, because they cannot be trusted with dangerous ideas, are the real targets of censorship; in "protecting" these social outsiders from contact with certain "dangerous" expressions, censors are ultimately protecting the existing social order. As Goethe noted: "The powerful demand and exercise censorship, the underlings want freedom of the press. The former want neither their plans nor activities obstructed by a cheeky, contrary force, rather they want to be obeyed; the latter want to express their reasons in order to legitimize their disobedience."[32]

Despite their protestations to the contrary then, censoring authorities use censorship to defend not the weak and vulnerable but rather the strong and powerful. By suppressing challenges to the reigning code of norms—a code that is defined by and serves the interests of the dominant social group—from dissidents, critics, and opponents of the status quo, censorship is a coercive political weapon used to preserve the established sociopolitical order and the dominant elite's primacy within it. From the standpoint of political sociology, the history of censorship is "the history of the struggle for power of dissident groups against the existing interests in politics, religion, and morality, and the banned book is often only a symbol for a more comprehensive struggle over authority." What is at stake in this struggle is consensus over a system of norms and social rules that promote conformity beneficial to those in authority.[33] As one influential censorship scholar notes, all censorship (whether narrowly or broadly defined) is inextricably linked to the control of power and knowledge: it is "a mechanism for gathering intelligence that the powerful can use to tighten control over people or ideas that threaten to disrupt established systems of order" and "a strategy used by the powerful to deny the powerless access to power-knowledge."[34]

Interpreting censorship as an instrument of elite or class domination reveals and explains much about its motives, functions, and consequences in imperial Germany, but such an approach is not without its problems. In practice, the sorts of expressions censors attempt to suppress (and the severity of their coercive sanctions) vary greatly. In the late nineteenth and early twentieth century this was true not only among different nations with similar social norms, sociopolitical systems, and ruling elites, but also, as we shall see in Germany, among different regions or cities within the same nation. Moreover, different members of the "dominant elite" and different branches of the state apparatus, even at the local level, often disagreed vehemently over whether a particular expression should be prohibited. Identifying a coherent national or local ruling elite, its interests, and a particular code of norms crucial to its social and political power, whether in Germany or elsewhere, can be a dubious undertaking. The picture is further complicated by the fact that conservative segments of the broader German populace frequently pressured governing authorities to censor or prohibit things the latter would have preferred to ignore or tolerate.

As with many human institutions, censorship often produces ironic outcomes that are contrary to, even in mockery of, the intended, expected, or appropriate results. This study will show how in imperial Germany an array of important restraints to state power thwarted the efficient exercise of censorship and made it highly unpredictable. While efforts to censor literature proved effective in some settings, it also had consequences quite different from what the imperial authorities intended.

Notes

1. Italo Calvino, *If on a winter's night a traveler,* trans. William Weaver (San Diego and New York, 1981), 234–35.
2. Quoted in Peter Jelavich, "Paradoxes of Censorship in Modern Germany," in *Enlightenment, Passion, Modernity. Historical Essays in European Thought and Culture,* ed. Mark S. Micale and Robert L. Dietle (Stanford, 2000), 277–78. See also Michael Knoche, "Einführung in das Thema," in *Der Zensur zum Trotz. Das gefesselte Wort und die Freiheit Europa,* ed. Paul Raabe (Wolfenbüttel, 1991), 23–39.

3. Hans Widman, *Geschichte des Buchhandels. Vom Altertum bis zur Gegenwart,* rev. ed. (Wiesbaden, 1975), 154; Ernst Umlauff, "Zur Struktur der europäischen Kulturwirtschaft. Der deutsche Buchhandel bis 1930," *Europa-Archiv* 2 (Sept. 1947): 891–93.

4. One leading authority estimated in 1896 there were approximately six hundred theaters in Germany. (Adolph L'Arronge, *Deutsches Theater und deutsche Schauspielkunst* [Berlin, 1896], 24); another estimate on the eve of the war claimed over 460 (Eugen Schöndienst, *Geschichte des deutschen Bühnenvereins. Ein Beitrag zur Geschichte des Theaters 1846–1935* [Frankfurt, 1979], 229).

5. Bernhard Kellermann, "Der Schriftsteller und die deutsche Republik," in *An alle Künstler!* (Berlin, 1919), reprinted in *Weimarer Republik. Manifeste and Dokumente zur deutschen Literatur 1918–1933,* ed. Anton Kaes (Stuttgart, 1983), 30–31.

6. For brief overviews of the historiography of imperial Germany see Roger Chickering, "The Quest for a Usable German Empire," in *Imperial Germany: A Historiographical Companion,* ed. Roger Chickering (Westport, CT, 1996), 1–12 and James Retallack, *Germany in the Age of Kaiser Wilhelm II* (New York, 1996), 1–15 (quote from 42).

7. Volker R. Berghahn, *Imperial Germany, 1871–1914: Economy, Society, Culture and Politics* (Providence, RI and Oxford, 1994), 123.

8. Johannes Penzler, ed., *Die Reden Kaiser Wilhelms II. in den Jahren 1901—Ende 1905* (Leipzig, 1907), 60–62. My translation is based on that in Gerhard Masur, *Imperial Berlin* (Devon, UK, 1973), 211 and Peter Paret, *The Berlin Secession: Modernism and its Enemies in Imperial Germany* (Cambridge, MA, 1980), 25, 26–27. For similar statements see his speeches of 2 May 1896 to the Berlin Kunstakademie, 16 Jun. 1898 to the personnel of the Königliche Schauspielhaus, 25 Jan. 1902 to the Berliner Kunstgewerbemuseum and 2 Nov. 1902 to the Hochschulen der bildenen Künste und für Musik, as well as Paul J. Seidel, ed., *Der Kaiser und die Kunst* (Berlin, 1907), 14–16.

9. Hans von Hülsen, "Der Kaiser und das Theater," *Die Tat* 5, Heft 6 (Sept. 1913): 588; Paret, *Berlin Secession,* 162; Gerhard Schulz, "Naturalismus und Zensur," in *Naturalismus. Bürgerliche Dichtung und soziales Engagement,* ed. Helmut Scheuer (Stuttgart, 1974), 109.

10. Arno J. Mayer, *The Persistence of the Old Regime: Europe to the Great War* (New York, 1981), 190; Roy Pascal, *From Naturalism to Expressionism: German Literature and Society, 1880–1918* (London, 1973), 256, 261; Edgar Feuchtwanger, *Imperial Germany 1850–1918* (London and New York, 2001), 128.

11. Jack. R. Dukes and Joachim Remak, eds., *Another Germany: A Reconsideration of the Imperial Era* (Boulder, CO, 1988), 210; Peter Jelavich, "Literature and the Arts," in Chickering, *Imperial Germany,* 400; Wolfgang Mommsen, *Bürgerliche Kultur und künstlerische Avantgarde. Kultur und Politik im deutschen Kaiserreich 1870 bis 1918* (Frankfurt, 1994), 45–46.

12. Felix Gilbert and David Clay Large, *The End of the European Era: 1890 to the Present,* 5th edition (New York, 2002), 79.

13. Ulla Otto, *Die literarische Zensur als Problem der Soziologie der Politik* (Stuttgart, 1968) and "Zensur—Schutz der Unmündigen oder Instrument der Herrschaft?" *Publizistik* 13 (1968): 5–15; Hans Norbert Fügen, "Zensur als negativ wirkende Institution," in *Lesen—Ein Handbuch,* ed. Alfred C. Baumgärtner (Hamburg, 1974), 623–42; Dieter Breuer, *Geschichte der literarischen Zensur in Deutschland* (Heidelberg, 1982), 9–22; Klaus Kanzog, "Zensur, literarische," in *Reallexikon der deutschen Literaturgeschichte,* 2. Aufl., ed. W. Kohlschmidt, et al., *Band IV,* ed. K. Kanzog and A. Masser (Berlin, 1984), 998–1049; Annabel Patterson, *Censorship and Interpretation: The Conditions of Writing and Reading in Early Modern England* (Madison, WI, 1984); Reinhard Aulich, "Elemente einer funtionalen Differenzierung der literarischen Zensur. Überlegungen zur Form und Wirksamkeit von Zensur als einer intentional adäquaten Reaktion gegenüber literarischer Kommunikation," in *"Unmoralisch an sich…" Zensur im 18. und 19. Jahrhundert,* ed. Herbert G. Göpfert and Erdmann Weyrauch (Wiesbaden, 1988), 177–230. On the evolution of traditional censorship research through the late 1980s, see Dieter Breuer, "Stand und Aufgaben der Zensurforschung," in *"Unmoralisch an sich…",* 37–60

and Kanzog, "Textkritische Probleme der literarischen Zensur. Zukünftige Aufgaben einer literaturwissenschaftlichen Zensurforschung," ibid., 309–31.

14. Annette Kuhn, *Cinema, Censorship and Sexuality, 1909–1925* (London and New York, 1988); Sue Curry Jansen, *Censorship: The Knot That Binds Power and Knowledge* (New York, 1988) and "The Censor's New Clothes: Censorship in Liberal Societies," in *Patterns of Censorship Around the World,* ed. Ilan Peleg (Boulder, CO, 1993), 189–202; Richard Burt, ed., *The Administration of Aesthetics: Censorship, Political Criticism and the Public Sphere* (Minneapolis, 1994); Michael Holmquist, "Corrupt Originals: The Paradox of Censorship," *PMLA* 109, no. 1 (1994): 14–25; Michael Levine, *Writing Through Repression* (Baltimore, 1995); Robert C. Post, ed., *Censorship and Silencing: Practices of Cultural Regulation* (Los Angeles, 1998); Beate Müller, ed., *Censorship and Cultural Regulation in the Modern Age* (Amsterdam and New York, 2004). Two overviews of recent censorship research are Beate Müller, "Censorship and Cultural Regulation: Mapping the Territory," in *Censorship and Cultural Regulation,* 1–31; and Helen Freshwater, "Towards a Redefinition of Censorship," ibid., 225–45.

15. Derek Jones, ed., *Censorship: A World Encyclopedia,* 4 vols. (London and Chicago, 2001) (quotation from "Editor's Note," 1:xii) .

16. Melvin Berger, *Censorship* (New York, 1982), 1; Jansen, "Censor's New Clothes," 192–93; Michael Kienzle and Dirk Mende, eds., *Zensur in der BRD. Fakten und Analysen* (Munich, 1980); Frederick Schauer, "The Ontology of Censorship," in Post, *Censorship and Silencing,* 162.

17. Peter Dittmar, *Lob der Zensur. Verwirrung der Begriffe, Verwirrung der Geister* (Cologne, 1987), 183–84.

18. Eberhard Ultra, in Johann Nestroy's *Freiheit in Krähwinkel* (1849), Act I, scene 14 (Johann Nestroy, *Komödien,* 3 vols., ed. Franz H. Mautner [Frankfurt, 1970], 3:47).

19. Heinrich H. Houben, *Hier Zensur—Wer dort?* (Leipzig, 1918), 3; Freshwater, "Towards a Redefinition," 237.

20. Breuer, "Stand und Aufgaben," 59–60.

21. Freshwater, "Towards a Redefinition," 225, 240–42.

22. Michael Foucault, *Discipline and Punish: The Birth of the Prison,* trans. Alan Sheridan (New York, 1977).

23. Henryk M. Broder, ed., *Die Schere im Kopf. Über Zensur und Selbstzensur* (Cologne, 1976).

24. Eli Oboler, *The Fear of the Word: Censorship and Sex* (Metuchen, NJ, 1974), 138; George R. Scott, *"Into Whose Hands": An Examination of Obscene Libel in its Legal, Sociological, and Literary Aspects* (London, 1945), 180.

25. Kienzle and Mende, *Zensur in BRD,* 231; Walter Bückmann, ed., *Kunst vor dem Richter* (Frankfurt, 1964), 102; Valery as quoted in Jascha Kessler, "The Censorship of Art and the Art of Censorship," *The Literary Review* 12, no. 4 (Summer 1969): 421.

26. Quoted in Pascal, *From Naturalism to Expressionism,* 257.

27. Jack P. Gibbs, *Norms, Deviance, and Social Control: Conceptual Matters* (New York, 1981), 4.

28. Breuer, *Geschichte der literarischen Zensur,* 12–17, 201.

29. Otto, *Die literarische Zensur,* 19, 67–112, 129, 137–47, and "Zensur." See also Dieter Richter, "Literaturfreiheit und Zensur," *Buch und Bibliothek* 31, H. 4 (Apr. 1979): 323–30, and Sue Curry Jansen's work.

30. Ödön von Horváth, "Zensur und Proletariat," in *Gesammelte Werke,* 8 vols., ed. Traugott Krischke and Dieter Hildebrandt (Frankfurt, 1972), 3:667.

31. Oboler, *Fear of the Word,* 239.

32. Johann Wolfgang von Goethe, *Wilhelm Meisters Wanderjarhe,* quoted in Breuer, *Geschichte der literarischen Zensur,* 145–46.

33. Otto, *Die literarische Zensur,* 46, 71, and "Zensur," 11.

34. Jansen, *Censorship,* 14, 203.

Chapter 1

THE LAW

The police want to know everything, everything.
—Der Wirt, in Lessing, *Minna von Barnhelm*, Act II, scene 2

Before the law, all citizens are equal—but not, it seems, before the censors.
—Otto Brahm, director of the Berlin Freie Bühne,
Deutsches Theater, and Lessing-Theater

*L*ike their counterparts throughout Europe and North America in the nineteenth century, anyone engaged in literary or theatrical life in the German Empire did not enjoy absolute freedom to say, publish, or publicly perform whatever they wished. The law limited what subject matter writers could treat and the language they could use; it shaped and restricted institutions that mediated between writers and the public, such as the theater, press, and book trade; and it helped determine which audiences had access to which literary works or performances, and under what conditions. Some legal constraints were enacted by a popularly elected legislature, some were simple administrative (or, after 1914, military) edicts, and some, surprisingly, were requested by publishers or theater managers seeking more predictability, economic security, or legal protection. The laws restraining imperial literary life were uneven and at times confusing: different laws applied to different media, while the empire's federal structure ensured wide local variation in their nature, enforcement, and consequences. For these reasons and others, censorship laws were the subject of much public debate, especially after 1890, as popular and official forces struggled to standardize, broaden, narrow, tighten, or loosen them. Only war in 1914 and revolution in 1918 brought substantial changes to Germany's patchwork censorship system.

Notes for this section begin on page 32.

Control of the Printed Word

During the first half of the nineteenth century, the printed word was one of the most ruthlessly censored forums of public expression in Germany and other European states; by the last quarter of the century it was one of the freest from state control. Extensive government restrictions such as licensing and prior censorship shackled the press and book trade in most nations until 1848, but thereafter liberal reformers progressively dismantled these controls, especially prepublication censorship. By the 1860s there was substantial (but not total) freedom of the press and book trade in Great Britain, Sweden, Norway, Denmark, the Netherlands, Belgium, Switzerland, and several German states (including Prussia), while France abolished the last vestiges of state press control in 1881, and Russia not until 1905.

Prior censorship of books had ended in the German states with the revolution of 1848. Freedom of the periodical press was guaranteed in the new German Empire by the Imperial Press Law of 7 May 1874, which abolished government licensing of the press and all prepublication censorship of printed material. Although government retained the right to be informed about the contents of most periodical publications (except for artistic, scholarly, or commercial publications, publishers were to submit a copy of each issue to local police as distribution began), the Press Law placed few significant legal restraints on printed materials. (The exceptional Anti-Socialist Law, which did prohibit a wide range of socialist publications from 1878 to 1890, is discussed in Chapter 4.)

The state, however, did exercise a punitive or postpublication control over the printed word through other means. Under the Imperial Criminal Code of May 1871, for example, it was illegal to incite others, in print or speech, to disobey the law or commit criminal acts; to incite social classes to violence against each other; to knowingly fabricate or distort facts in order to incite in others contempt for state institutions or the law; to slander or libel officials, clergymen, or members of the armed forces who were carrying out their professional duties; or to maliciously slander or libel other citizens.[1] In the absence of prior press censorship, the government frequently used the Criminal Code to prosecute press opponents, especially for libel. Creative writers on the other hand were most affected by the paragraphs pertaining to lèse majesté (§§94–101), blasphemy (§166), and obscenity (§184). Because literary works dealing with the three sensitive areas of politics, religion, and sex were those most likely to put writers in legal peril, each of these offenses will be examined more closely in subsequent chapters.

Writers violating the Criminal Code could be subject to legal action. Local state prosecutors, either on their own initiative or in response to a citizen's complaint, could, within six months of its appearance, order the immediate confiscation of any publication thought to violate the law. (Only the remaining, undistributed copies could be seized; those already in citizens' hands were beyond the law's reach.) While local police also had authority to confiscate a work, such actions had to be reviewed by the state prosecutor within twelve hours; usually, police simply marked and forwarded to the prosecutor anything they considered actionable. In keeping with the general principle in the empire that administrative actions were subject to judicial review (of which more below), if a publication were confiscated, within five days a local district court had to either uphold the action or release the work for distribution. If the court affirmed the seizure, the prosecutor had two weeks to file criminal charges against those responsible for the offending publication. (Under German law, others involved in the distribution of an illegal publication, such as publishers, printers, editors, or booksellers, were also liable to prosecution.) The fact that a work had been published abroad did not protect a defendant from prosecution or punishment; and if a specific culprit could not be tried—for example, if the identity of the author could not be determined or a defendant fled abroad or died before the trial—the publication could still be permanently prohibited.[2]

In Prussia and other north German states, depending on the nature of the offense, defendants in criminal cases were tried either before a local district court (*Amtsgericht*), where a panel of one judge and two lay people heard the case, or by a superior court (*Landgericht*), where a panel of judges presided. However in Oldenburg and Braunschweig and in the south German states of Bavaria, Württemberg, and Baden, crimes committed in print had to be tried in public before twelve lay jurors (*Schwurgericht*). (It is perhaps no accident that of the five largest book production centers, two—Munich and Stuttgart—were located in the south.) Some indicted writers thus had the opportunity of being judged by their peers rather than professional jurists, though as we shall see below, for those accused of blasphemy a jury trial in the conservative Catholic south was not necessarily an advantage. If convicted of violating the Criminal Code, a defendant was fined or imprisoned and all remaining unsold copies of the offending publication (as well as the plates used to produce it) were destroyed; if only a portion of the work were judged illegal, only that was proscribed. Courts also could acquit the defendant of any crime yet rule the publication did indeed contain illegal material and must be destroyed. All verdicts, including acquittals, could be appealed to a court of appeal (*Oberlandesgericht*) and ultimately to the Imperial Supreme Court (*Reichsgericht*); while the latter occasionally nullified a writer's acquittal and ordered a retrial, it does not appear ever to have struck down a writer's conviction.

Could authors receive fair treatment from the German criminal justice system? Some historians, pointing to the empire's massive disregard of statutory guarantees of equality before the law, have disputed its reputation as a state based on the rule of law (*Rechtsstaat*). Justice in the imperial era, they argue, was far from impartial; rather, there existed a socially biased, frequently manipulated system of class justice heavily influenced by the partisan interests and ideologies of the ruling classes. Most contemporaries on the other hand saw the empire as a just, liberal state with progressive criminal and civil codes and judicial procedures and as a nation where citizens' rights were protected because administrative power, including police actions, was subject to the rule of law and independent judicial review. A growing body of recent scholarship also supports this view.[3]

German civil servants and jurists, it is true, were recruited from a narrow social elite and most were conservative supporters of the established order. University students preparing for administrative or legal careers came from elite upper and upper-middle class backgrounds and received a narrow, practical, professional training that, by focusing almost exclusively on law and its application to practical cases, largely insulated them from all "general cultivation" and humanistic subjects, not to mention art and literature. Because the number of law graduates far exceeded the judicial and administrative positions available, the government could be selective, and selection was closely linked to political orientation. The lengthy (and costly) probationary apprenticeship through which all aspiring civil servants and judges had to pass was used as much to screen out social and political undesirables as to assess their professional competence. It is hardly surprising, therefore, that most law graduates and civil servants emerged from their illiberal training as uncritical supporters of the imperial system and its policies.

Yet this same training also produced many nonconformists and even the empire's harshest critics acknowledge the system was a training ground for thousands of liberal attorneys.[4] Several authors whose writings later brought them into conflict with the law were, in fact, themselves products of the judicial training system: Ludwig Thoma, Hermann Bahr, Ernst von Wildenbruch, Frank Wedekind, O. E. Hartleben, Max Halbe, Carl Sternheim, and Herbert Eulenberg, for example, were either trained (and sometimes practicing) jurists or one-time legal students. And although candidates who lacked the requisite social background or political outlook had little chance of receiving an administrative post, the criteria were more relaxed for the judicial branch, which was more hospitable to liberals, Catholics, and even Jews. Furthermore, members of the German judiciary enjoyed far more independence and job security than their colleagues in administration. The Imperial Justice Laws of 1877–1879 established a modern, independent, and substantially liberal court system in Germany based on clear, fair, and uniform civil and criminal procedures. Judges were appointed for life with fixed salaries and were well insulated from political pressure. They could not be relieved of office, transferred, or pensioned against their will except by means of a judicial decision and in accordance with the law, and so they were answerable only to their fellow jurists, not to the political administration. Whereas administrative civil servants were fundamentally conservative and staunchly loyal to the monarch and his government, the German judiciary comprised a broader range of political viewpoints, including many moderate liberals; among judges "the separation of professional duty and private conviction was more normal, here there was more pluralism, here [logical] predicates and specialized professional judgments played a greater role."[5]

Within the judicial establishment, state prosecutors were responsible for initiating legal proceedings (although after 1879 in most German states victims of crimes and other citizens could also instigate legal action). In some smaller north German states, prosecutors came from the judiciary and returned to it after leaving the prosecutor's office, so were able to act fairly independently. But in Prussia and the larger states they were state officials responsible to the Ministry of Justice and thus subject to political pressure; if they failed to prosecute certain offenses aggressively enough they could be disciplined or removed by the government. Their literary ignorance, a result of their narrow legal training, could sometimes be embarrassing. Ambitious prosecutors sometimes resorted to questionable legal maneuvers and manipulations when dealing with censorship cases. Because most hoped one day to be appointed as judges, they were often eager to compile an impressive record of prosecutions and convictions; frequently this meant finding ways to circumvent the south German requirements that all press offenses be tried before a jury, where cases were about twice as likely to end in acquittal as those tried before a panel of judges.[6] One popular tactic involved the principle of "ambulatory venue" (*fliegender Gerichtsstand*), which, until its use was curtailed after 1902, allowed prosecutors some latitude in deciding where an alleged offense was to be tried. In cases involving a book or periodical for example, a defendant could be made to stand trial either in his or her place of residence, in the place the publication in question was edited or printed, or in any locality where the work was distributed. Because of this last possibility, zealous prosecutors could sometimes force south German defendants to stand trial in north German cities where there was no jury trial, or in more conservative regions where the chances of conviction were thought to be higher.[7] In 1899 for example, the defendants charged with lèse majesté in the famous *Simplicissimus* "Palestine Affair" (see chapter 3) were tried and convicted in Leipzig, where the satirical journal was printed, rather than in Munich, where its editorial offices were located and all the defendants resided. The *Simplicissimus* staff realized if the journal continued to be printed in Leipzig, they would remain highly vulnerable: "As long as we [publish] in Leipzig, we always face the danger of being destroyed. The gentlemen there can do that, if they want to be stubborn. It would not be hard for them, if they wanted, to lock us all up, one after the other."[8] This was one reason the journal changed printers; after 1899, *Simplicissimus* was printed in Stuttgart, where Württemberg law, like Bavarian law, required jury trials for all press offenses.

Some south German prosecutors sought to avoid jury trials by charging defendants under a vague and controversial paragraph of the Criminal Code (§360, sect. 11) that levied a fine of up to 150 marks or six weeks imprisonment on anyone "who, in an unseemly manner, creates loud, disturbing noises or commits a public nuisance (*grober Unfug*)." Originally intended for use against street urchins and malicious mischief makers who harassed passersby, disrupted traffic, released mice in crowded theaters, or otherwise created a public annoyance, some aggressive state prosecutors stretched this statute to cover behavior that caused psychological as well as physical annoyance to the public. In south Germany, where juries were sometimes reluctant to convict defendants charged under the strictly worded laws regarding obscenity, blasphemy, or lèse majesté, and where the government itself sometimes balked at prosecuting writers unless it was confident a jury would convict, frustrated police and prosecutors occasionally charged offensive publications with "public nuisance" instead, since no jury trial was required in such cases. For example, in April 1898 the Munich prosecutor charged Maximilian Harden with public nuisance rather than lèse majesté for an article in which he openly discussed the tragic insanity of the Bavarian King Otto I, a subject considered taboo during the regency of Otto's uncle Prince Luitpold. Harden was quickly sentenced to a fourteen-day jail term.[9] And after several unsuccessful efforts in the late 1890s to prosecute *Simplicissimus* for obscenity, the Munich police tried to confiscate the journal and prosecute its writers and editors for public nuisance instead. Although the state prosecutor had at first resisted such attempts, he eventually relented and in 1903 used that law to ban an offensive *Simplicissimus* political cartoon and fine the artist and editor thirty marks each.[10] In subsequent years, whenever a jury trial seemed unlikely to result in a conviction, enraged conservatives pressured the Bavarian government to apply the public nuisance paragraph against offensive publications like *Simplicissimus*.[11]

Finally, to avoid jury trials in press cases where an acquittal was likely, south German prosecutors at times misused the Criminal Code's "impersonal process" (*objektive Verfahren*) provision, whereby a publication could be permanently banned even if those responsible for it could not be convicted of violating the law. At the turn of the century the Imperial Supreme Court ruled that in press cases where a defendant had been acquitted on grounds of mental incompetence, a second hearing should be held to determine whether the contents of the publication in question was indeed illegal and should be banned by means of an impersonal process. Soon, some unscrupulous prosecutors began encouraging courts to declare defendants incompetent to stand trial, for this was a way to avoid a possible jury acquittal yet leave the door open for a permanent ban of the offending publication. Bavarian authorities, frustrated by their inability to obtain jury convictions against the writers and editors of *Simplicissimus,* once resorted to this ploy. After police confiscated an issue of the journal in 1904 for satirizing the Bavarian Catholic Center Party and charged Ludwig Thoma and Julius Linnenkogel with blasphemy, at the preliminary court hearing the prosecutor persuaded the presiding judge to dismiss all charges against the two defendants on the grounds their "mental incompetence" absolved them of any legal responsibility for their actions. Thoma, a former lawyer, immediately saw through this scheme: "All this means is that they don't want to bring me before a jury," he complained; "Perhaps I should be grateful that I have been acquitted? … I'm sorry that I can't appreciate this kind of mercy."[12]

In court, defendants were represented by private lawyers who were equals to the state's judges in terms of legal training, preparation, and professional admission requirements. Members of neither the judiciary nor the civil service, defense lawyers were free from any disciplinary oversight from courts or ministries of justice. After the legal reforms of the late 1870s opened admission to the bar to anyone meeting the professional requirements, German lawyers came from increasingly diverse social backgrounds. Compared to the state judiciary, by the later years of the empire the private bar consisted of more sons of middle-class commercial and industrial families and a much higher proportion of Jews. (Before the Weimar republic, Jews were virtually excluded from the judiciary, and women from both the judiciary and the bar.) These lawyers, who in the courtroom enjoyed certain procedural advantages over the prosecution (especially after 1900), often skillfully mounted tenacious defenses of their clients and mobilized public opinion on their behalf. In several literary trials defense attorneys called prominent scholars or writers as expert witnesses to bolster the defendant's case and discredit the prosecutor's interpretation of the work in question. Such testimony was often reported prominently in the press, which regularly covered controversial censorship trials.

Whether because of press reporting of courtroom proceedings, adroit defense by lawyers in private practice, or the impartiality of German judges, attempts by overzealous police and unscrupulous prosecutors to manipulate the law against writers rarely succeeded. The German judiciary generally made an earnest effort to safeguard defendants' rights and courts displayed a surprising independence from, and even resistance to, government efforts to stifle freedom of expression through the printed word. Indeed, after resisting efforts by the state in the 1890s to make the judicial system more repressive, in the years before the war German judges began acquitting a higher percentage of defendants (especially in cases they believed to be politically motivated) and they became increasingly lenient in their sentences (issuing more fines rather than prison sentences, and shorter rather than longer incarceration). Independent jurists frequently revoked confiscations initiated by police or prosecutors, threw out indictments against authors, acquitted defendants, or imposed lighter punishments than prosecutors demanded. For the government the outcome of a censorship trial was unpredictable and frequently disappointing. (Even during the anti-Catholic *Kulturkampf* and the years of the harsh Anti-Socialist Law, when the Bismarckian state used the most ruthless legal weapons and exceptional laws against its opponents and the judicial system was most politicized, in over two-thirds of all press trials judges imposed significantly lighter sentences than had been requested by the prosecutor and in 20 to 30 percent of all cases they acquitted the defendants completely.) Although police, prosecutors, and even the emperor sometimes railed against such decisions, there is no evidence the administration ever exerted pressure on judges to find defendants guilty; and while judges who freed confiscated material or acquitted indicted authors were occasionally scolded, they could not be punished or disciplined by the state. The evidence is strong, therefore, that throughout most of the imperial era authors who clashed with the law because of their work could generally receive fair treatment in court.

The outbreak of war in 1914 radically altered the legal rights of writers and the press in Germany, as it did in all belligerent nations. State control of printed material expanded enormously during World War I while judicial restraints on censors all but disappeared. On 31 July 1914, Emperor Wilhelm II declared a state of war to exist in the empire and with his constitutional power formally imposed a legal state of siege (*Belagerungszustand*). As long as the state of siege remained in force, the military enjoyed extraordinary power over civil life: deputy commanding generals assumed executive authority in each of the twenty-five Army Corps districts. Slicing through preexisting state and regional boundaries or lapping over several hitherto independent small states, the arbitrary borders of these military districts bore little relation to the peacetime government's bureaucratic structure. While civilian administrators and communal officials continued their normal functions, they were now obligated also to obey the instructions of the district's deputy commanding general, who, in turn, was responsible only to the emperor. As Wilhelm II became an increasingly peripheral and distant figure during the war, the deputy commanding generals were virtually autonomous: they were "like rulers of independent satrapies, and they could—and to the extent they wished—resist attempts from above, from civilian or military agencies, to impose common policies or institutional constraints on them."[13] In the interests of public security they could issue formal police ordinances under their own authority or through the regular civilian police; failure to obey a commander's orders or his police ordinances was punishable by up to a year in prison. During the state of siege, special military courts were established to handle serious offenses (spying, treason, sabotage), the punishment for certain criminal offenses was dramatically increased, and several constitutionally guaranteed rights were suspended, including freedom of association and freedom of assembly.

Freedom of the press also ended, for all nonscientific publications were now subject to military censorship. Initially the Press Office of the Acting Army Corps Headquarters (*stellvertretende Generalkommando*) was responsible for censorship; after February 1915 it came under the authority of a specially created Central Censorship Office (*Oberzensurstelle*) attached to the acting general staff. Although these offices established policies and guidelines and issued detailed directives, local police handled day-to-day military censorship. All military-related newspaper articles and, after April 1915, other publications dealing with military issues had to be approved prior to publication; one copy of all other printed material (including periodicals, books, and pamphlets) had to be submitted to local police immediately upon publication. Early in the war some publishers voluntarily submitted materials, especially books, to the military for prepublication censorship, for they found it less expensive to have a manuscript vetted before it went to print than to risk having it banned or changes ordered afterwards. The head of the Stuttgart publishers' union claimed in 1916, "Preventive censorship lies in the interest of publishers, since its exercise protects them from penalty and great economic damage."[14]

Police censors were instructed by military authorities to intervene against any printed matter that undermined the war effort by "disturbing the civil peace (*Burgfrieden*)." This granted them extremely broad powers, for during the war the civil peace was officially defined as "the effort to preserve the spirit of solidarity and submission to the great national goals, to prevent any endangerment of the unity of the German *Volk*, and never to allow the impression to arise that the determined popular will for victory is wavering." In the interests of the civil peace, wartime censors would permit "an objective, even if pointed, representation of one's own standpoint in political and economic questions ... [and] a calm discussion of the mistakes and errors of those who think differently." But they would not allow "any insults to others, ... especially any terms of abuse, derogatory comparisons, or degrading insinuations, ... any attempts to impute to others selfish or base motives in the pursuit of political goals, any needless rekindling of old quarrels, or any insults between social classes, occupational groups, or religious confessions."[15] Unlike before the war, when the press often lambasted them, it was now forbidden to publish any criticism of the censors that might undermine public confidence in their activities.

To control printed materials during the war, police wielded a variety of special weapons: besides refusing to allow publication of military-related material, they could also issue formal warnings to the writers, editors, and/or publishers of material already in print; they could require that in the future certain nonmilitary publications also be submitted for prior censorship; they could issue temporary or permanent bans against all future publications of specific periodicals or publishing houses; and, in extreme cases, they could fine or imprison journalists or writers who regularly violated official directives. Decisions of the military or police censors could be appealed only to the Prussian minister of war, who seldom overruled his subordinates. Only in Bavaria did the press retain some of its prewar freedom. Because of Bavaria's special legal status in the empire, the state of siege and press censorship system there was less harsh and press offenders still enjoyed the right to a jury trial.

As authorities attributed military importance to an ever-widening circle of political issues, such as the debates over war aims or food rationing, and as the vague concept of the "civil peace" expanded to include ever more aspects of public opinion and civil life, the scope of military censorship during the war expanded enormously. As one writer complained, "Every political issue could be made into a military one, if the censor wanted. He could even transform issues of a general scholarly or artistic nature into military ones in order to bring them under his sphere of influence."[16]

Censorship also became increasingly centralized and geographically uniform after 1914, as deputy commanding generals in the various Army Corps districts exchanged information and coordinated their policies concerning publications.[17] This near absolute control over printed materials continued until 12 November 1918, when Germany's new republican government lifted the official state of siege, abolished all censorship, and restored the civil rights suspended during the war.

Control of the Theater

Theaters were central to the empire's cultural life; they received generous support from local rulers and municipalities and were enthusiastically attended by a broad spectrum of the populace. The English writer Henry Vizetelly, a frequent visitor to Berlin in the 1870s, observed, "The Berlinese of to-day are steady playgoers, and pass much of their time at the theatres, which, on Sunday evenings especially, are filled to overflowing."[18] On the eve of World War I the nation's theater association listed a total of 463 theaters in Germany. Along with 116 privately owned commercial theaters (the majority of which were founded after 1871), 132 were operated by city or town governments, serving as a source of civic pride. German princes sponsored some twenty royal or "court" theaters (*Hoftheater*) that functioned as dynastic showcases and prominent centers of social life, especially in the smaller princely residences; some sovereigns, such as Duke Georg II of Saxe-Meiningen, devoted their lives and resources to their beloved theaters. In addition to the many permanent theaters, there were also 84 traveling troupes and 112 that operated only in the summer or showed films.[19] At the turn of the century, Berlin, with a population of 1.9 million and the "theater capital" of the nation, hosted three royal theaters and over twenty-five conventional commercial theaters (not counting scores of less-reputable vaudeville and variety halls) while its primary rival Munich (population nearly six hundred thousand) claimed two royal and fourteen commercial theaters.[20]

In contrast to the relative freedom enjoyed by print media, most theaters were subject to a number of special legal restraints including stringent prior censorship. Because of the powerful and potentially dangerous impact of the spoken word upon an audience, governments have always regarded the stage with particular concern.[21] In nineteenth-century Germany, however, state interest in theater was all the more pronounced because of a widespread "cult of the theater" that ascribed to this medium a unique moral, spiritual, educational, and even political mission. In his famous 1784 address "The Stage Considered as a Moral Institution," Friedrich Schiller venerated the theater as a source of moral enlightenment and civic education for the broad populace, an agent of social progress, and a source of national self-consciousness and unity. Its unique power and appeal was comparable to that of religion, he believed, and he foresaw a day when the stage would replace religion as a moral force in public life.[22] Popular enthusiasm for the theater flourished and spread in the nineteenth century. While local theaters may not have become sites of public worship (as the dramatist Franz Grillparzer once predicted), in many places they did become centers of public life. Prior to 1848, when political assemblies and associations were forbidden or tightly regulated, theaters provided one of the few arenas outside the church where regular mass gatherings were allowed; for middle-class audiences theaters were not merely vehicles of entertainment but sometimes served also as substitute parliaments or places where ideas and news could be exchanged.

By the imperial era, Schiller's idealized cult of the theater as an institution of personal cultivation and national consciousness was so pervasive that nearly every social stratum expressed reverence for the stage's uplifting spiritual power and national mission. At the pinnacle of the social pyramid, for example, Emperor Wilhelm II, whose aesthetic values were notoriously conservative, aggressively endorsed the "noble, idealistic viewpoint" of Schiller's famous essay. The Hohenzollern monarchy, he affirmed, had always regarded theater as a powerful weapon in the "struggle against materialism and un-Germanness (*undeutsche Wesen*)"; Wilhelm II believed the function of the stage, like the school and university, was to cultivate idealism and character in the younger generation, to ennoble their moral views, and to "prepare them for their task of preserving the highest spiritual values of our wonderful German fatherland."[23] The educated bourgeoisie that formed the backbone of imperial culture held similar views. Left-liberals like Ernst Müller-Meiningen viewed the stage as a powerful political tribune comparable to parliament where, when parliamentary discourse is blocked, the popular spirit resorts to "the sharpest, most dangerous weapons of political battle: parody, travesty, satire, in short, to scorn and mockery."[24] At the same time various cultural outsiders—Naturalist critics of the established culture, radical avant-garde modernists, and committed Social Democrats—also acknowledged the theater's unique spiritual power and rhapsodized over its importance as an institution that could help spark a national cultural, social, and political transformation.[25] This idealistic cult of the theater was regularly invoked to justify extensive state controls over theatrical productions. Prussian ministers of the interior regarded it their duty to protect the stage as "a place of cultivation and spiritual uplift for wide segments of the population" and to prevent "any performance that the uneducated 'common man' might misconstrue"; similarly, Munich's police director considered police censorship of theaters "a positive, state-sustaining, national, and monarchical institution."[26]

But authorities in Germany (and elsewhere) were especially vigilant toward the theater because live theatrical performances, unlike dead printed texts, could stir an audience's emotions and thus posed a more immediate threat to public order and security. Schiller had noted how spoken dialogue on stage exercised a more profound impact and lasting influence on the senses of theatergoers than even morality or law, especially when combined with physical action and when actors directly address the audience. Dramatic art, and especially tragedy, also has a cathartic element: for centuries, dramatists have sought to create an illusion of reality that arouses the audience's empathetic identification with the characters on stage and stimulates and vicariously satisfies spectators' emotions. Viewing a theatrical production can be an intense emotional experience and a skillfully staged piece can provoke strong audience reaction. This experience, moreover, takes place within a public, social setting. Unlike the private, solitary act of reading, which the reader ultimately controls (if enraged or disturbed by what he or she reads, the experience can be immediately terminated), people who attend the theater are not isolated individuals but members of an assembled public group participating in a collective experience over which they have little control. Above all, as members of an assembled group—as part of a crowd—theatergoers are susceptible to the powerful influences of crowd psychology.

After the Paris Commune of 1870, the psychology and behavior of crowds worried many in fin-de-siècle Europe because crowd behavior was governed by potent, largely unconscious forces that easily overpower the individual personality. Gustave Le Bon articulated these fears in his influential 1895 study *La psychologie des foules* (*The Psychology of the Crowd*), where he argued an assembled group assumes new, entirely different characteristics than those of the individuals who compose it. Members of a crowd lose their individual identities, inhibitions, and the rational self-control exercised by their conscious personality, becoming automatons whose behavior is now governed by larger, irrational, unconscious forces. According to Le Bon, crowds are highly impulsive, excitable, impressionable, and sentimental; simplistic in their thinking, incapable of logical thought, they can no longer distinguish between illusion and reality. The anonymity of the crowd often gives its members a sense of unlimited power that inspires them to attempt the immediate realization of the most fantastic ideas or schemes suggested to them: "To the solitary individual, it is clear that alone he cannot burn down palaces or plunder shops, and he hardly even dreams of doing so. But as a member of a crowd, he is overcome by a sense of omnipotence that the group lends him, and he will immediately succumb to the first incitements to murder and plunder." [27] To political reactionaries like Le Bon who feared the emergence of mass or crowd politics after 1870, the crowd represented an ominous threat not only to public order and security, but to civilization itself.

The theater was a particularly fertile and dangerous breeding ground for unpredictable, irrational crowd behavior. Le Bon was convinced crowds think only in images, which are able to horrify, inspire, or incite a crowd to action. Theatrical performances present images in their clearest form: "Nothing arouses the fantasies of people as strongly as a theater piece. The assembled spectators simultaneously feel the same emotions … [and] sometimes the feelings suggested by these images are strong enough to … translate themselves into action. … The unreal is in their eyes nearly as important as the real. They have a remarkable inclination not to distinguish between the two." [28] Indeed, Le Bon and other observers could cite examples of nineteenth-century theater audiences who had been incited to disorderly, even violent behavior by what they saw on stage: enraged lower-class theatergoers attacking actors who had depicted villains on stage; pitched verbal and physical battles between supporters and opponents of Victor Hugo's daring romantic style after his *Hernani* premiered in February 1830; how the opera *La Muette de Portici*, which depicted a seventeenth-century Neapolitan uprising against Spain, sparked demonstrations and riots that ultimately led to the Belgian revolution of 1830; and the 1896 near-riot that erupted when Jarry's absurdist *Ubu Roi* premiered in Paris.

German observers often cited these incidents as evidence of the unique power live theater exercised over its audience and the dangerous excesses to which theatergoers were sometimes prone. Theaters are collective enterprises in a public space; because the nature, function, and effect of that medium differed so radically from that of the press, government officials, local police, many legal scholars, and even some dramatists generally agreed it must be more stringently controlled. State supervision of the stage was considered necessary not only to safeguard the theater's special moral and national-political mission, but also to protect society against theatergoers who might, after viewing a particularly stirring performance, be transformed into a disorderly, even violent mob. [29]

Special legal restrictions were therefore placed on playwrights, theater operators, performers, and theatergoers, the two most important of which were licensing and prior censorship. While the Press Law of 1874 had established freedom
of the press by ending state licensing and censorship of that medium and created
uniform regulations for the journalism profession, no comparable national law
was ever passed for theaters and other public entertainments. Theaters continued
to be governed by a complex, uneven patchwork of laws and ordinances that predated the empire. Some aspects of theatrical life, such as licensing, were regulated
by the Imperial Commercial Code (*Reichsgewerbeordnung*); others, such as theater censorship, were governed by state and local ordinances that varied widely.

Germany's liberal Commercial Code, adopted by the North German Confederation in 1869 and extended two years later to the new empire, proclaimed,
"The practice of an occupation is permitted to everyone." It removed corporative
restrictions and established freedom of enterprise in most occupations, but not
for the theater industry. Those who wished to operate a privately owned theater anywhere in Germany (with the exception of Alsace-Lorraine[30]) were still
required to apply to district or county authorities for a license (*Konzession*), although royal theaters, theaters owned and financed by municipalities, and those
holding only private performances not open to the general public were exempted
from this requirement. Applicants could be denied a license only if authorities
had evidence of their "unreliability."[31]

During the 1870s local officials judged applicants' reliability primarily in ethical terms. As Cologne's district administrative president pointed out to officials
in his district: "Since theatrical performances, especially those geared to the lower
classes, can be very detrimental from a moral standpoint, it appears necessary to
impose the strictest demands when considering the reliability of those who are
seeking a theater license. Licenses should be granted only when the lifestyle of
the applicant has been completely beyond reproach and provides no grounds
for censure from a moral standpoint."[32] Even so, an enormous number of new
theater licenses were granted in the years after 1869.[33]

But since theater attendance lagged well behind the proliferation of new theaters and the growing number of aspiring actors, the industry soon suffered from
serious overcrowding and murderous competition, a condition many observers
believed was responsible for an alarming decline in the quality of theatrical life.
Drama critics and officials alike lamented that easy admission into the theater
industry after 1869 had turned dramatic art into the crassest kind of speculation.
Many new licenses, they charged, had gone to inexperienced and undercapital-
ized entrepreneurs who entered the business with dreams of quick fortunes; to
survive they had to pander to the crudest instincts of the masses, thereby ruining
the dramatic tastes of the public.[34]

Economic depression in the late 1870s created additional problems. Facing
stiff competition, many new theaters went bankrupt, especially those whose owners lacked theatrical experience or sufficient financial resources. Several older,
established houses were also driven out of business or encountered serious finan-

cial difficulties. In some cases fly-by-night theater operators simply disappeared, leaving behind huge debts and a troupe of unpaid employees and actors; many of the latter turned to busking, peddling, and begging or became a burden to local poor relief systems.

Responding to overcrowding in the theater industry and to local complaints about a growing "artistic proletariat," in 1880 the Reichstag amended the Commercial Code, placing tighter restrictions on the granting of theater licenses. Because local officials were now expected to consider an applicant's moral, artistic, and financial qualifications, before approving a new license they began routinely checking with the theater industry's professional associations and with the Berlin police force's special theater division regarding an applicant's professional qualifications and general reputation. To further limit competition and ensure theaters did not attempt expensive productions beyond their financial means, after 1880 authorities could restrict a theater's license to one genre of performance—to light drama, for example, but not expensive operatic productions.[35] These measures dramatically reduced the number of new theaters licensed after 1880. In Berlin, for example, where 146 licenses had been granted during the 1870s, during the decade 1881–1890 only twenty-seven applications were approved, while fifty were denied. Most applicants rejected by Berlin authorities in the 1880s and 1890s were actors, writers, or musicians lacking the financial means or businessmen lacking the artistic experience considered necessary to operate a theater.[36]

Originally, a license entitled one to operate a theater anywhere in the nation, but because of frequent abuses a theater license after 1896 was valid only within the state or specific district where it had been issued. Licensees were obligated to observe all local laws and ordinances; in Munich, police also admonished new theater operators to respect "religion and decency." Licenses could be revoked if a theater failed to comply with the terms and restrictions of its license or the operator no longer met the necessary financial, artistic, or moral qualifications.[37] While the most common grounds for revocation was financial, this weapon was also used against theaters whose repertoire authorities found objectionable.

Besides deciding who could operate theaters, German authorities were also able to decide what was performed on stage. In most of the empire, especially in the larger cities of Prussia, Bavaria, and Saxony, the local laws and ordinances that theater operators pledged to obey required them to obtain prior police permission for any drama to be performed publicly.

State censorship of the theater was hardly unique to Germany. By the eighteenth century, monarchs throughout Europe had brought theaters under strict regulation and required a central or local censor to approve each piece before it was performed. Although the democratic revolutions of 1848 temporarily abolished prior censorship of theaters in some states (including Prussia), it was usually quickly restored after the revolutions collapsed. By the late nineteenth century only a few smaller, peripheral states (Sweden, Belgium, and Portugal) did not censor dramatic works before they were performed—although authorities there, as in every nation, had the right to stop performances that violated the criminal code or caused a public disturbance; everywhere else some system of prior censorship still existed. In Russia and Denmark, for example, all dramas had to be approved by a special central censor, while in Austria-Hungary, Spain, and Italy each work had to be submitted to and passed by the local governor or prefect. Staging a drama without approval could result not only in the loss of a theater's license but also, in Russia at least, in a stiff fine and up to three months imprisonment. Even liberal England and the Third French Republic subjected theaters to prior censorship. The English Licensing Act of 1737 and Theatres Act of 1843 required that all privately owned theaters be licensed and all new plays be submitted to the lord chamberlain for approval before being performed. The lord chamberlain—a minister of the Crown and member of the House of Lords who was neither accountable for his actions to the House of Commons nor need give any reason for his censorship decisions—could prohibit or demand deletions in any drama if he believed "it is fitting for the preservation of good manners, decorum, or public peace to do so." This system of theater censorship remained in force until 1968. In republican France the prior censorship imposed on all Parisian theaters in March 1871 was extended to the entire nation in 1874. Before a public theater in France could announce or perform a new drama, it first had to be submitted to a special dramatic censorship commission for approval; any work banned from the Parisian stage was also prohibited throughout France. Commission decisions could be appealed to the minister of public instruction, cults, and fine arts, but his decision was final. France's censorship system functioned until 1905 when the senate suspended it because the volume of submitted scripts was more than the censors could keep up with. Beginning in 1906 French theaters were free to perform any work they wished, although local police inspectors who regularly visited the performances could close down any that endangered public order and morality, and the theater manager could be prosecuted under the regular provisions of the criminal code.

Because of its federal structure the German Empire had no uniform, national system of theater censorship like England, France, Denmark, or Russia. In the free cities of Hamburg, Bremen, and Lübeck, in the medium-sized states of Württemberg, Baden, Braunschweig, and Hesse, and in all the tiny states, privately owned theaters were not subject to any prior censorship, although in Baden theaters had to notify police in advance of works they intended to stage. (Authorities in these areas could of course halt performances that contravened the Criminal Code or whose highly offensive content presented a danger to public peace. On rare occasion, authorities in Württemberg requested a script beforehand and then forbade the theater from performing the piece.) While there were thus several localities where theaters were virtually free of censorship, these liberal regions comprised only a fraction—about 15 percent—of the empire's population, and in the tiny states there were in any case few cities and commercial theaters. Prussia, Bavaria, and Saxony—the three largest states, which between them contained over 80 percent of the nation's population and in 1900 twelve of Germany's fifteen largest cities—each subjected their theaters to some form of formal or de facto prior censorship, as did Alsace-Lorraine. [38]

Prussia's system of theater censorship, which was the most comprehensive in Germany and served as a model for the other major states, dated from the reactionary 1850s. Like Schiller, Berlin police president Carl von Hinckeldey regarded the theater as a "moral institution, a school … [that] the state can use as a lever for furthering general morality and all its other objectives." In July 1851, responding to complaints from exasperated theater operators about arbitrary and unpredictable police meddling, von Hinckeldey ordained that henceforth "no public theatrical performance may take place within the greater Berlin police district without the express approval of the Police Presidium."[39] All commercial theaters were required to submit to the police, fourteen days in advance, the text of any new theatrical work they wished to perform; permission was granted only if police had no objections "from a commercial or moral standpoint or for reasons of [public] security or order." Police could immediately halt any unauthorized performance and the operator could have his theater license revoked and be fined or imprisoned for "insubordination."

Berlin's system soon became a model for other Prussian cities. Before and during the imperial era, ministers of the interior continually urged local police throughout Prussia to adopt Berlin's theater censorship ordinance, and some cities like Breslau and Cologne complied.[40] Although police in Frankfurt, Düsseldorf, Hanover, and Aachen never formally promulgated a censorship ordinance, they nevertheless exercised a de facto prior censorship under which theaters "voluntarily" submitted works for approval; police then decided what excisions or alterations had to be made in the text or whether the work had to be dropped from the repertoire altogether.[41] Berlin's method of prior censorship was also adopted in Saxony and Bavaria. After 1871 police in Dresden, Leipzig, and Munich issued ordinances nearly identical to Berlin's and these, in turn, were soon imitated by authorities in many smaller Saxon and Bavarian municipalities.[42]

If police would not allow a drama or authorized its performance with certain conditions (for example, that portions of the text be excised or altered), a theater manager could appeal. Two avenues were open: a plaintiff had the right to appeal to a higher level within the administration (*Beschwerderecht*), or, in most states, could initiate a civil suit in a special external administrative law court (*Klagerecht*). Appeals up the administrative hierarchy—first to the county prefect (*Landrat*), then to the district administrative president (*Regierungspräsident*), the provincial governor (*Oberpräsident*), and even ultimately to the minister of the interior himself—were relatively fast and inexpensive. Unfortunately, they also had little chance for success since each administrative official generally relied on the judgment of his subordinates and upheld their decisions. Moreover, the administrator who heard and ruled on a complaint did not have to state the reasons for his decision.

Those with the time and money therefore usually appealed through the administrative law court system. These independent, nonpartisan courts were established in nearly every German state in the 1870s to protect citizens against the administrative abuse of power. Using formal civil court procedures (open sessions, representation by counsel, written briefs, oral testimony, cross examination, etc.) these bodies adjudicated citizens' complaints over administrative actions and ensured that administrative orders, decrees, and decisions conformed to the law. After reaching a decision these courts issued a written verdict citing the precedents and statutory bases for their ruling and billed the losing party for court costs (which could reach as high as five thousand marks).[43] Although practices varied, in most states the appeal of first instance was to the local district administrative council (*Bezirksausschuß*) or its equivalent—a partially appointed, partially elected board of administrators and lay people that handled some aspects of local self-administration and sat as an administrative law court when the need arose.[44] The council's decision could be appealed to the state supreme administrative law court (*Oberverwaltungsgericht*), the highest instance. These bodies were composed of judges trained as administrative officials and judges from the regular court system, who were all appointed for life and enjoyed the rights and status of other judges—that is, they were completely independent from the state legislature, the regular administration, and the ordinary civil and criminal court system. Recent studies of the Prussian Supreme Administrative Law Court confirm that it achieved a meaningful (if still somewhat limited) rule of law in Germany, was relatively liberal and citizen-friendly, and ruled surprisingly often against the police and for the individual rights of plaintiffs.[45]

Because of their independence and strict adherence to legality, administrative law courts effectively safeguarded citizen's rights from arbitrary or discriminatory actions of overzealous state officials. In Prussia, Saxony, and Baden, where their jurisdiction was fairly broad, the district administrative councils and the supreme administrative law courts set important limits on the powers of the police and freed numerous dramas local police tried to ban. In Bavaria, however, the competence of the administrative law court system was more limited, especially before 1900; since judges there had no jurisdiction over what were considered purely administrative censorship decisions, censorship appeals took place entirely within the Bavarian administrative hierarchy, where they were invariably rejected. (For example, none of the censorship decisions of the Munich police director were ever reversed by his superiors.[46]) Given the unlikelihood of success, few Bavarian theaters bothered to appeal the censor's decisions. And since theater licenses in Munich and other Bavarian localities were granted on the express condition that censorship ordinances be observed, any theater that sought publicly to perform a new work without first obtaining police permission could have its license revoked; moreover, under the Bavarian Police Code the theater operator could also be fined fifteen thaler or imprisoned for eight days, slightly stiffer punishments than in Berlin.

Some theaters were exempt from these punctilious controls. Royal court theaters (of which there approximately two dozen in the empire) were financed by the local king, duke, prince, or count but still normally open to the public. They were not subject to government licensing or censorship, but the royal intendants who operated them carefully avoided controversial modern works, filling their repertoires with safe classics instead. These officials (most of whom were high nobility with military or bureaucratic but little or no theatrical experience) also exercised their own careful prior censorship over scripts: Botho von Hülsen, for example, while serving as intendant of the Royal Theater in Berlin from 1869 to 1886, spent hours at night scrutinizing scripts word-by-word, eliminating anything that might be remotely offensive or carry a double meaning. It was no wonder the acerbic critic Maximilian Harden, surveying theatrical life in the capital, considered the Royal Theater boring and its "shameful repertoire" to be "simple artistic bankruptcy and the complete renunciation of any leading position in German theater life."[47] Not all court theaters were so stuffily conservative, however. In small Saxe-Meiningen, Duke Georg II developed one of Europe's most innovative and influential theaters and laid important groundwork for the modern, realistic theater; in 1886 his Meininger Players held Germany's first public performances of Ibsen's controversial *Gespenster* (*Ghosts*). Munich's royal Residenztheater had performed Ibsen's *Stützen der Gesellschaft* (*Pillars of Society*) in 1878 and *Ein Puppenheim* (*A Doll's House*) in 1880, while the Hoftheater of Stuttgart premiered his *Wenn wir Toten erwachen* (*When We Dead Awaken*) in 1900.

The more than one hundred municipal or state theaters owned and operated by a local government were also not subject to police censorship, although since the municipal government oversaw their repertoires and operations, they too exercised a self-censorship that resulted in inoffensive, noncontroversial offerings. Thus in Münster the director of the municipally owned theater had to receive permission from the city council for every work to be performed, while in Mannheim the city's National Theater established a standing subcommittee of board members to "ensure that no uncensored works are performed, and no offense against religion, good morals, and also no politically inflammatory material takes place."[48]

"Private" theaters on the other hand, which were also exempt, posed constant headaches for the authorities. The licensing requirements of the Commercial Code and local ordinances requiring prior censorship of theatrical works applied only to commercial (*gewerbmäßig*) theaters operated for a profit—that is, those charging admission—and to public performances. Clubs or associations whose members staged informal performances solely for their own enjoyment or for educational purposes were not required to obtain an operating license, provided they did not charge admission and used only amateur performers who received no pay. Likewise, any private theatrical performance that was closed to the general public did not need any prior police approval. Thus church and educational organizations, amateur theatrical clubs, literary societies, and various other "closed" (that is, private) associations could freely stage theatrical productions for their own members or for a small circle of invited guests as long as the general public was excluded.

To avoid or evade state censorship, many authors and theater directors naturally claimed their works or productions were private in nature, not intended for public consumption or dissemination, and so immune from censors. German authorities thus continually faced the problem of defining the boundary between public and private, distinguishing between the public literary and theatrical activities that were legally censorable and the "private" ones that were not.

There were a surprisingly large number of private, amateur theatrical societies theoretically exempt from all state control. Munich contained over forty such groups in the period between 1890 and 1914. In Berlin, the police reported some 393 associations of this kind in 1871 and 889 in 1880; by 1890 a total of 1,301 private theatrical associations had been registered in the capital, although, as police noted, "it can probably be assumed that a large number of these have since been dissolved or no longer exist in reality."[49]

Some of these groups were legitimate private, nonprofit undertakings with praiseworthy educational or artistic goals, such as Otto Brahm's Freie Bühne Verein (Free Stage Association). Founded in 1889 and modeled on Andre Antoine's Théâtre Libre in Paris, the Freie Bühne held private performances on a subscription basis for members only and was created to stage Naturalist plays banned (or unlikely to be approved) by the censor or new works that commercial theaters were unlikely to produce for financial reasons. (Julius Hart, one of the founders, maintained the creation of the Freie Bühne was "above all a way of rapping the nose of the police censor."[50]) Within a year it attracted over one thousand members from the educated middle class (primarily writers, artists, academics, journalists, and members of the free professions) and soon spawned a number of imitators in other cities (Hamburg-Altona, Leipzig, Hanover, Munich, Nuremberg) and even a working-class Freie Volksbühne (Free People's Stage, discussed in chapter 4).

Many private theaters, however, were really attempts to evade licensing and censorship regulations (as well as fire and safety ordinances) by exploiting the legal confusion over the distinction between public and private, amateur and commercial. For example, many so-called nonprofit theaters did in fact charge admission for their performances by selling mandatory programs at the door, charging everyone a stiff coat check fee, or requiring "voluntary contributions" from everyone in the audience. And some groups that claimed to be staging only private performances for their members were openly catering to the general public: the performances were often widely advertised beforehand and club memberships were sold at the door. Operators of legitimate theaters frequently complained about the unfair competition they faced from these unlicensed, uncensored enterprises masquerading as private or amateur theatrical associations.

To curb such abuses and evasions, police in Berlin, Munich, and other cities continually scrutinized uncensored private performances to ensure they were indeed closed to the general public; if a supposedly nonprofit theater was collecting admission in some other guise, vigilant police required it to obtain an operating license under the Commercial Code.[51] More importantly, authorities suspected private theatrical societies like the Freie Volksbühne not only of holding public performances but also of being outlets for subversive, socialist ideas and so waged a long struggle to force these theaters to submit to the same censorship as commercial ones (see chapter 4). Throughout the imperial era the state continually sought to broaden the legal definitions of "public" and "commercial activity" in hopes of thwarting those theatrical playhouses that tried to escape state control by claiming private or nonprofit status. Originally the administrative law courts resisted such attempts, but after the 1890s the judiciary supported a more circumscribed definition of what constituted a noncensorable private performance, especially where socialist organizations were involved.[52]

Local Discretion or National Uniformity? Theater Law Between Left and Right

The extensive controls local authorities wielded over the public stage and the wide regional variations in such laws became an increasingly contentious issue after 1890. Politicians on both the Right and the Left challenged the right of local authorities to regulate and censor theaters—the Right because they considered local police too lax, the Left because they considered them too severe. After 1890 both Right and Left attempted to remove jurisdiction over theatrical life from individual cities and states and place it instead under uniform federal law, be it the Criminal Code or the Commercial Code. To do so, however, involved a transfer of power not only from the separate German states to the federal government but also from the appointed administrative bureaucracy (police and government) to the popularly-elected Reichstag, which wrote federal law, and to the independent judiciary, which interpreted it. Because such changes would have upset the delicate constitutional balances of the Bismarckian empire—where every pressure was neutralized by a counterpressure and substantial barriers blocked any fundamental changes to the system, either progressive or reactionary—any attempts to reform German theater law were staunchly opposed and effectively blocked by the imperial government.

During the 1880s and early 1890s theater managers and liberals who opposed any form of prior theater censorship repeatedly questioned the legality of the censorship ordinances of Berlin and other cities. Arguing such regulation violated both the Prussian constitution of 1850 (which guaranteed freedom of expression and assembly and forbade imposing censorship or other limitations on the press except by legislative act) and the Press Law of 1874 (which guaranteed freedom of the press), they appealed first to the regular courts, then to the administrative law courts to invalidate all censorship ordinances. Prussian, Saxon, and Bavarian courts, however, repeatedly upheld the police's right to exercise prior censorship over theatrical performances. Such control, courts ruled, was part of the police's legitimate duty to "protect public peace, order, and security"; and because police banned only a work's public performance, not its publication or circulation in print, these prohibitions did not violate freedom of the press or other constitutionally guaranteed rights.[53]

The imperial government, like the states and courts, regarded police censorship ordinances as a strictly local matter and refused to become involved. Several influential groups, however, wanted censorship placed under central, imperial control. Soon after courts affirmed the right of local authorities to censor theater performances, the Right attempted to legislate more uniform national standards that could check the independence of local theater censors. In the mid- and late 1890s a right-wing coalition of Catholics, Conservatives, anti-Semites, and moral purity associations, angered over the complete lack of theater censorship in some regions and the laxity of censors where it did exist, made a concerted effort to standardize and toughen theater censorship by bringing it under the provisions of the national Criminal Code. To do this, they sought to attach a special "theater paragraph" to the government's controversial "Lex Heinze".

Shocked by revelations about urban vice and moral corruption that surfaced during the recent notorious murder trial of a Berlin pimp named Heinze, in February 1892 the imperial government introduced a bill in the Reichstag proposing stiffer punishments for a wide range of morally offensive activities, from prostitution to advertising contraceptive devices. During initial debate over this bill (which was quickly tagged the "Lex Heinze") the Catholic Center Party complained that despite police censorship many German theaters performed shamelessly immoral and indecent works that were as harmful to the nation's moral fiber as prostitution and pornographic literature.[54] In the Reichstag commission to which the bill was referred, anti-Semites like Adolf Stöcker joined Centrists in charging that theater censorship as currently practiced in Berlin and other large cities was "intolerable" and "not worth a penny." Not only were censors far too lenient, but once they approved a work a theater could then point to the authorities' permission as a defense against anyone who later complained about the material. To goad police into exercising tighter control, the commission's Center and anti-Semitic members proposed adding a special clause to §184 of the Imperial Criminal Code making it a criminal offense for anyone to stage (*veranstalten*) an indecent theatrical performance. Under this statute any citizen whose sense of shame and morality had been grossly violated by a performance, even one approved by police, could initiate criminal proceedings against the theater owner.[55] A Prussian Interior Ministry representative objected that involving the Criminal Code and public prosecutors in administrative matters such as theater censorship would create endless conflicts between police and the courts. Although the commission defeated the Center's proposed theater paragraph by one vote, the bill that did emerge was so extreme in other regards that it proved unacceptable to the government. After declining to promote it in the Reichstag, in 1894 the imperial government allowed the Lex Heinze to die.

But the issue lived on. Infuriated that existing laws could not keep Hauptmann's *Die Weber* (*The Weavers*), Sudermann's *Sodoms Ende* (*Sodom's End*) and other modernist works off public stages (see chapters 4 and 6), Centrists, private morality associations, and other conservatives continued to complain about the debasement of the theater's noble spiritual and social mission. One Center delegate lamented in the Prussian parliament in early 1895 that the theater had sunk from a place of cultivation and spiritual uplift "to a place for depicting immorality and misconduct, offering sensual stimuli and subversive tendencies, and for mocking religious belief. I think that [in combating such developments] one cannot be too strict." Rather than providing people with harmless entertainment or literary and artistic stimulation—which was the theater's true purpose—modernist works instead "are promoting and reinforcing wanton ideas about morality and order, irreligion, and various impulses in the state directed toward dissatisfaction, disorder, and revolution." [56]

In January 1895 the Center and its allies in and out of parliament revived the campaign for more repressive theater censorship by reintroducing the Lex Heinze into the Reichstag, but no action was taken on it during the 1895–1897 session. A new draft bill, with an even tougher version of the theater paragraph that had just barely been rejected by the Reichstag commission in March 1893, was submitted by the Center in December 1897. This proposal would add to §184 a clause (§184b) stating: "Whoever stages (*veranstaltet*) or directs (*leitet*) public theatrical performances, operettas, choral or declamatory recitals, exhibitions of people, or similar presentations that are capable of provoking a scandal by grossly violating the sense of shame and morality, shall be punished by up to one year imprisonment or by a fine of up to one thousand marks."[57] The Center's demands for a drastic reform of theater censorship laws were seconded by hundreds of citizens, who in January 1898 signed a petition to Emperor Wilhelm II calling for "stricter censorship of theatrical performances, stricter censorship of publications that report on the theater, ... passage of the Lex Heinze, and a tightening up (*Verschärfung*) of the Criminal Code concerning the entire area of immorality."[58]

The Center's new Lex Heinze was again submitted to a parliamentary commission, but one now dominated by Center Party members. During deliberations the government's representatives once more objected to dragging judges and the courts into an arena that was the sole prerogative of the police, while the commission's liberal and socialist members warned that placing theaters under the Criminal Code posed a serious threat to modern drama in Germany and to many "classical" works as well. The Centrists and their allies, although claiming the statute was directed primarily against low music halls and vaudeville theaters, indicated they would not mind if it were also applied to certain modern dramatists like Hermann Sudermann and even some immoral classics. In the end the rightist majority on the commission not only refused to exempt serious, legitimate theatrical performances from the proposed law but broadened its provisions still further to punish any performer who appeared in an indecent performance. This law, Center delegates reiterated, was intended to safeguard against the "hardened [police] officials" (*abgebrühten Beamten*) who were not doing their duty to keep objectionable works off the stage; at the least, they hoped it would persuade the government "to proceed more energetically in this area."[59]

When presented to the Reichstag in January 1900, the commission's bill was vehemently opposed by Liberals, Progressives, and Social Democrats. (Social Democratic delegates used several clever obstructionist tactics to prevent quick passage of the bill, allowing its other opponents time to organize.) The measure also provoked a powerful extraparliamentary mass-protest movement that reached well beyond the intellectual and artistic community and soon became one of the broadest-based fronts of public protest ever to arise in the prewar empire. In February and March writers, artists, publishers, journalists, academics, progressive politicians, and even members of the business community hastily organized "Goethe Leagues for the Protection of Free Art and Learning" (*Goethebund zum Schutze freier Kunst und Wissenschaft*) in Berlin, Hamburg, Munich, Breslau, Dresden, Düsseldorf, Stuttgart, Bremen, and four smaller cities. Goethe Leagues sought to unite intellectuals of all political persuasions and intellectual outlooks in order "to protect freedom of art and learning in the German Empire against attacks of every kind"; their immediate task was to combat the "unprecedented repressive attempts against the free spirit" proposed in the Lex Heinze.[60] To defeat the bill, throughout the spring of 1900 these liberal pressure groups enlisted prominent representatives of the artistic and scholarly communities, including the heads of respected art academies, against the Lex Heinze; they staged mass protest meetings attended by thousands of citizens; they sent to the Reichstag petitions signed by nearly all the nation's leading writers, artists, musicians, scholars, publishers, book dealers, and a few industrialists; they published numerous appeals and declarations in the liberal press; and they met with Chancellor von Hohenlohe, the imperial minister of justice, and other government representatives and party leaders to lobby their case.[61]

The imperial government had never liked the bill: Chancellor Hohenlohe, a moderately liberal Bavarian Catholic once described as "an artist in the avoidance of catastrophe,"[62] found the theater paragraph too extreme and favored passage of a more moderate bill. So too did the Bavarian government's delegate to the Bundesrat, the parliament's upper house that represented the individual state governments and that had to confirm any bill passed by the Reichstag. He and other members of the Bundesrat were suspicious of the bill because it shifted power from the states to the central imperial authorities. Some prominent leaders in Bavaria were also concerned that a rigid national law would stifle Munich's rich artistic and intellectual life, undermining its reputation as a lively cultural center that equaled Berlin and in some areas (such as its innovative, modernist theatrical life) even surpassed the nation's capital. The Center and the bill's other supporters on the Right slowly realized that to retain the imperial government's lukewarm support, to overcome the Social Democrats' obstructionist tactics and win Reichstag approval for other provisions of the bill, and to assure its approval by the Bundesrat, the controversial theater paragraph would have to be sacrificed. In April, therefore, they reached a compromise with the government and the Lex Heinze's liberal opponents under which the theater paragraph and other repressive clauses were dropped. The remainder of the bill was then approved by the Reichstag in late May and became law in June 1900.

The battle over the Lex Heinze and its defeat in 1900 marked an important turning point in imperial Germany's polices of literary censorship. As subsequent chapters will show, since approximately 1890 a loose but influential coalition of politically and culturally conservative forces had been profoundly disturbed about the direction being taken by modern art, and by the theater in particular. Largely in response to their pressure and complaints, state and local authorities had been exercising—or attempting to exercise—an increasingly stringent censorship over German literary life, especially over the theater, and the 1890s witnessed the empire's most dramatic and controversial confrontations between writers and the state. The fight over the Lex Heinze that ended in 1900 was a showdown between antimodern cultural conservatives and an unusually diverse and broad-based coalition of forces united in opposition to the designs of the cultural Right, albeit for different reasons. That coalition included artists and intellectuals who enthusiastically supported artistic modernism, but also more moderate members of the educated middle class as well as Social Democrats who, while perhaps unsympathetic toward artistic modernism, nevertheless feared a victory for the Right would also endanger more traditional, classic art and literature. These groups, in turn, were joined by some conservative authorities in states like Bavaria who wanted to preserve states' rights against further centralization. The unprecedented political cooperation over this issue between middle-class liberals and the hitherto isolated Social Democrats—a partnership in which the Socialists often played a leading role and were accepted on more-or-less equal terms—also opened up new political possibilities for the future and helped further integrate Social Democrats into the imperial political system. Finally, the dramatic mobilization and politicization of the German artistic and intellectual community over the Lex Heinze was itself a significant new development and signaled a shift in the balance of cultural power. Whereas the political power of the cultural Right and state intervention against modernist literature had been in the ascendant before 1900, after that date both began to recede. To be sure, liberals failed to abolish theater censorship and state intervention into literary life continued after 1900, but censors now intervened in fewer areas, on a more modest scale, and with less effectiveness than in the 1890s. This softening of state opposition to modernist culture corresponded to what some have argued was a general "civilizing of power relationships" throughout the empire after 1900: the authorities, more concerned about avoiding criticism and scandal, used their powers more cautiously and relations between the police and citizenry became less tense.[63]

Their successful campaign to defeat the Right's efforts to bring dramatic art under tighter censorship again emboldened the Left, which immediately launched a countercampaign to free theaters completely from the burdens of the law. Having failed in their earlier judicial challenges to local theater censorship ordinances, after 1900 the coalition of liberal intellectuals, the Progressive Party, and Social Democrats that emerged during the Lex Heinze controversy adopted a new strategy to eliminate theater censorship and licensing by means of nationwide legislation.

Rather than disbanding after defeating the Lex Heinze in the spring of 1900, the Goethe Leagues redoubled their efforts to defend the nation against what one prominent league spokesman called any "muzzling or subjugation of spiritual and intellectual life." Another leader compared the movement to a national guard that takes up its weapons whenever needed to defend the borders of free artistic creativity.[64] Having beaten back the most immediate threat to freedom of art and learning, leaders of the Goethe Leagues pledged themselves to keep watch against any new attacks on intellectual freedom: "Our task is also to exercise a sharp, eternal, ever-ready vigilance against the silent and not-so-silent work of the Reaction, to train the German nation to exercise this vigilance for itself, and to educate the nation about the meaning and incalculable importance of a free national culture, of an independent scholarship and art."[65] When representatives of local Goethe Leagues met in November at a national conference in Weimar, they approved a resolution condemning censorship of theatrical performances by local authorities and demanding its abolition everywhere in Germany. German dramatic art, they declared, was an expression and manifestation of the German national spirit and it was time to treat it as a national, not local matter. The existing uneven patchwork system of local theater censorship contravened a truly national German culture, the resolution continued: it placed in the hands of local authorities, whose decisions frequently contradicted each other, important dramatic and artistic questions that should really be decided on a nationwide basis by the German people itself. The Union of German Goethe Leagues, condemning theater censorship as an antiquated and "unworthy tutelage [for] the German nation," announced it would petition the Reichstag to abolish censorship by means of a national law and called upon "all friends of a free German art" for support.[66]

In November 1900 the Progressive Party presented the Goethe League petition to the Reichstag and two months later introduced a motion to abolish all local theater censorship by amending the Commercial Code. To the paragraphs of the code that required the licensing of all theater and music hall operators, Progressives proposed adding a clause clearly stating that no prior approval is necessary to stage an individual dramatic work in a legitimate theater or to hold declamatory, musical, pantomimic, or plastic performances on the popular stage.[67]

In Reichstag debates early the next February, Progressives condemned the confusing, haphazard hodgepodge of local censorship ordinances that were both unconstitutional (in Prussia) and violated the spirit of the nation's Commercial Code, which established freedom of occupation. They cited numerous instances where local police censors had recently issued irrational, arbitrary, and contradictory decisions (works banned in one locale but not others, important works by respected authors that should not have been forbidden at all but were, etc.), and argued if Germany were to have a truly national, rather than a local, particularistic literature, then the issue of prior theater censorship must be settled on a uniform, national basis. "Are we not *one* people, with *one* language and *one* literature?" a Progressive speaker asked. Yet from the illogical system of local censorship "one would almost conclude that we don't even have a local state literature, but rather simply a city literature! This is an abomination!" Theater censorship, Progressives maintained, was an area where the Reichstag and federal government must—and legally did—have ultimate jurisdiction. They called upon the Reichstag to undertake the difficult but necessary task of "finally looking into the Augean stables of particularistic police law—to examine it closely in regard to its legal compatibility vis-à-vis the provisions of the imperial constitution and the Imperial Commercial Code." If one wanted a true state of law (*Rechtsstaat*) rather than an arbitrary police state, the Reichstag had to ensure local police power did not contravene national legal norms; and the place to start was by affirming the supremacy of the national Commercial Code over all individual, local police ordinances and arbitrary rulings. To Progressives, prior censorship of theatrical performances was an unnecessary form of police tutelage; the existing provisions of the Criminal Code were adequate to deal with any theater excesses, for if a performance did indeed violate the law, police always had the authority to halt it and prosecute those responsible. Dramatic art should enjoy the same freedom enjoyed by writers who published their work and who were subject only to the controls of the Criminal Code: "We want every author, every theater director, every actor to assume his own direct responsibility before the common Criminal Code; we want the actor and the director to bear responsibility for his work, just as authors [now] do for the contents of their books. And if state authorities take energetic measures under the provisions of the existing criminal statutes, then surely we have no more need for any [prior] censorship."[68]

The Progressive's bill received enthusiastic support from Social Democrats (SPD), who expressed pleasure that bourgeois liberals had finally joined them in the fight against arbitrary, monopolistic police power. All forms of censorship, the SPD agreed, were to be condemned and art and intellectual inquiry must be liberated from censorship and other restrictions.[69]

The parties of the Right, however, staunchly opposed the bill. Both Conservatives and Free Conservatives, who customarily defended the status quo and resisted any attempt to reduce Prussian state rights or strengthen either the central (imperial) government or the Reichstag, urged the bill's rejection. Prior censorship of theatrical performances was needed now more than ever, they argued, to protect the more susceptible elements of the population from immoral, subversive, and harmful works. Relying simply on the Criminal Code and intervening only after a performance had taken place was foolhardy and dangerous, for by then the harm would already have been done. What was needed was stricter, not looser state control over theaters; and because local police were most familiar with their own city and were in the best position to judge what works may be harmful there, it was they who were in the best position to exercise prior theatrical censorship.[70]

Like Conservatives, the Center Party of course also wished to tighten, not abolish prior theater censorship. With delicious irony the Catholics pointed out that Progressives were now arguing the antithesis of what they had argued during the recent Lex Heinze debate. To prevent passage of the Center's theater paragraph, Progressives had earlier maintained that the "prophylactic actions" of local police censors and their legal authority to prevent immoral performances from taking place were more than sufficient to control excesses in theatrical life; indeed, Progressives had just argued that prior censorship was far preferable to and more efficient than invoking criminal penalties against theater directors. Yet if the Progressives had reversed themselves on this issue, so too had the Center, which now returned to its traditional position of defending state's rights and opposing any extension of central or federal authority. Regulation of the theater industry and censorship of theatrical performances were state and local matters, the Center speaker declared, one in which the Reichstag and imperial government should not interfere. Indeed, the Center reminded other parliamentarians how during the Lex Heinze debate the government had resisted any judicial and legislative encroachment on administrative matters; even if the Progressives' proposed bill were passed by the Reichstag, the Center warned, it would undoubtedly be vetoed in the Bundesrat, which represented the individual state governments. The Center maintained that rather than preventing local authorities from exercising prior censorship over theaters, the Reichstag should be encouraging them to exercise it more stringently.[71]

National Liberals were conflicted about the Progressives' bill. On the one hand they agreed police censorship of serious drama was often excessive and ultimately harmful to German culture, and many proscriptions by local authorities had been senseless and unnecessary. Like the Progressives, Liberals objected to the lack of uniform censorship ordinances throughout the Reich and desired a single nationwide standard. But while favoring abolition of prior censorship for the legitimate, serious stage, Liberals insisted it be retained for more popular entertainments such as music halls, vaudeville, and cabarets; and in those states where no censorship currently existed, they wished to see it instituted. Because the Progressives' bill would have abolished all forms of prior stage censorship, National Liberals in the end opposed it.[72]

Throughout the debate the government maintained the same position as during the controversy over the Center's theater paragraph. Using a concurrent debate in the Prussian Landtag as an opportunity to address the issue, the Prussian minister of the interior defended the legality of existing police censorship ordinances and reiterated that jurisdiction over theater censorship belonged to individual states, not the central government. Centralization or standardization of theater censorship was ill advised, he warned, for conditions varied from locality to locality and only local authorities were in a position to decide what would be harmful in their area. While admitting many mistakes had been made in individual censorship decisions and there was, perhaps, the need for improvement in how censorship was actually practiced, the minister warned that abolishing prior censorship altogether would endanger public order, security, and morality. Moreover, he pointed out to Progressives that a system of prior police approval actually protected theater operators from later arbitrary police intervention.[73] (This was precisely what had disturbed the Center about prior censorship and why they had pushed for a special theater clause in the Criminal Code.)

At the end of the lively debate, in late February 1901 the National Liberals moved that the Progressives' bill be sent to a commission for study. After two extremely close and inconclusive votes on this motion produced a deadlock, it was discovered the Reichstag lacked a quorum. No further action was taken on the Progressives' bill, which died on the floor.[74]

Despite parliamentary defeat of the Right's theater paragraph and of the Left's bill to end all theater censorship, the movement to fundamentally reform and standardize the laws governing the theater industry persisted for another decade and a half. Concerned over fierce competition, declining revenues, strained management-labor relations, and a host of other problems, after the turn of the century representatives of the entertainment industry mounted a campaign for new legislation to eliminate abuses, raise the national status of the theatrical profession, and protect their economic interests. Although disagreeing on specifics, the various associations and unions representing Germany's actors, playwrights, theater owners, theatrical agents, and stage employees were united in their desire for a comprehensive, national theater law, similar to the Imperial Press Law of 1874, which would govern all aspects of the entertainment business—from licensing, censorship, royalty rights, and taxation to actors' contracts, pensions, and the legal status of cinemas, vaudeville, and other forms of popular entertainment.[75] As a result of their constant lobbying for a comprehensive reform of theatrical law, beginning in early 1909 the Reichstag formally and regularly petitioned the imperial chancellor to draft and submit to parliament an imperial theater law (*Reichstheatergesetz*).

While the theater industry campaigned for a centralized codification of theater law, artists and liberal intellectuals renewed their efforts to abolish theater censorship nationwide. Each spring between 1901 and 1904 delegates to the national congress of German Goethe Leagues resoundingly condemned local theater censorship and petitioned the Reichstag to end, by means of national legislation, the "particularistic" local censorship ordinances. Such ordinances, they charged, subverted not only intellectual and artistic freedom but also national unity: one league leader argued the current system encouraged antinational particularism by dividing the empire into a series of isolated police districts, separated from one another by a "Chinese Wall." These annual Goethe League petitions, although widely and sympathetically reported in the liberal press, were routinely rejected by the Reichstag on the grounds jurisdiction over theater censorship rested with individual states, not the Reichstag.[76] As the movement for a comprehensive national theater law grew, however, the Left began to see it as another vehicle for finally abolishing theater censorship in the various states. In 1903 Progressives again condemned the use of theater censorship as a "hideous chapter in the narrow-minded, particularistic, reactionary spirit." In the Reichstag they expressed hope for a bold new imperial theater law that, besides rectifying other civil and legal problems plaguing theaters, would also bring a uniform, nationally legislated settlement to the censorship question.[77] Between 1903 and 1911 Progressive delegates in the Reichstag and in the Prussian and Bavarian state parliaments regularly attacked the irrationality and futility of local theater censorship. By 1911 their calls for a new theater law that would end censorship throughout the empire were also being seconded by the Social Democrats.[78]

Although government ministries had been discussing a comprehensive theater law internally since 1906, it was not until late 1911 that a formal commission consisting of representatives of government and of the theater industry was established to draft such a law. Throughout 1912 and 1913 the commission met, circulated drafts, solicited industry reaction, and refined its proposals. Much to the dismay of liberals, who hoped it would repeal both licensing and censorship, the final draft of the theater law presented to the imperial government in February 1914 did neither. It not only retained licensing of theater operators but imposed even more stringent requirements on applicants for certain kinds of entertainments. And it left the issue of prior theater censorship in the hands of each state, as before.[79] The bill (actually a series of amendments to the Commercial Code) was to be submitted for Reichstag approval in July 1914, but with the outbreak of war the nation immediately turned to more pressing matters and the theater law was shelved.

Once the deputy commanding generals assumed authority over all civil administration under the wartime state of siege, legal restraints on theaters became both more stringent and more uniform. On 4 August 1914, immediately after Germany's declaration of war against France, public theaters (and many other amusements) in Berlin and most other German cities were ordered closed. When allowed to reopen a week or two later, their hours were curtailed and theaters had to conclude performances by 11 PM (after 1916, by 10 PM). In many localities authorities began refusing all applications for theater licenses on the grounds such undertakings were "not in keeping with the seriousness of the present times."[80] Where prior censorship of theaters existed, police censors were now not to make any but the most routine decisions on submitted works without first obtaining approval of the military commander. Private performances of a work (as well as all public lectures), which before the war were immune from censorship, could now be forbidden if local authorities considered it inappropriate or offensive given the "seriousness of the times." Spontaneous additions to or deviations from the officially approved script were more severely punished. Whereas before the war any drama that had once been approved by the local censor did not need to be resubmitted again if others wanted to perform it later, authorities now declared that any works approved before the outbreak of war had to be resubmitted for approval.[81] More significantly, bans issued under the commanders' authority could be appealed only to the minister of war, not through the administrative law courts. These new lines of authority and responsibility circumvented the civilian Interior Ministry; during the war the Prussian minister of the interior had to plead with his local police officials, who had gotten used to dealing directly with military headquarters on censorship matters, to please also keep him informed about their theater censorship decisions and policy recommendations.[82]

The military soon found it a "regrettable inconvenience" (*bedauerliche Mißstand*) that censorship of theaters and other popular entertainments was so uneven throughout the nation and that in some regions there was none at all. To facilitate "a more uniform execution of censorship," therefore, several district military commanders used their emergency powers to institute formal prior censorship of theaters in cities where it had not existed.[83]

Such arrangements were valid only for the duration of the war; a permanent, nationwide legal settlement of censorship and other issues affecting the theater industry was still sorely needed. In late March 1917, therefore, the Reichstag formally requested the chancellor to resubmit the theater law of 1914 for parliamentary approval. By then, however, the civil truce had long since broken down and serious political, social, and economic divisions plagued the war-weary nation. Since Chancellor Bethmann-Hollweg feared debate over the theater law would simply lead to "sharp differences of opinions and conflicting interests" that Germany could ill afford, he ignored the Reichstag's request.[84] In May 1917 various professional associations representing Germany's writers, playwrights, stage managers, and other theater professionals held a large public meeting in Berlin to voice concern about the further erosion of freedoms on the stage since 1914 (one participant bemoaned that "already during peacetime the German stage lived in a state of emergency under a spiritual state of siege"), but their proclamations fell on equally deaf ears.[85] Nothing further was done to alter Germany's complex system of theater censorship until the imperial order was overthrown and all forms of censorship were abolished on 12 November 1918.

Conclusion

Compared to other nations, even the most liberal, there was nothing peculiar about the laws restraining free literary expression in Germany. Like most of its neighbors, the empire exercised no prepublication censorship over books, journals, newspapers, and other publications, but authorities could (and did) prosecute authors or suppress certain publications that violated the nation's laws, especially those regarding blasphemy, obscenity, or lèse majesté. Moreover, like many other Western nations, Germany required privately owned commercial theaters to be licensed and required most of these to obtain prior state approval for any dramas they performed. In these ways, state oversight of literary life was no different in the German Empire than elsewhere.

Of course the devil is in the details, and what mattered in the end was how those laws were worded and interpreted, how often and impartially they were applied, and how severely offenders were punished. For example, while other nations also prohibited and punished expressions of blasphemy or lèse majesté, Germany generally defined these offenses more broadly or inflexibly and levied heavier punishments (see chapters 3 and 5). On the other hand the German legal definition of obscenity was narrower than that used in England and the US and less likely to be applied against genuine art and literature (see chapter 6). In any case the state's ability to intervene in German literary life was limited by strict, clearly defined legal guidelines and procedures. To suppress a published literary work, much less punish its author, required persuading a panel of judges—or in some states, a lay jury—that the criminal laws had been violated. This was by no means easy to do: as we shall see, German courts (and especially lay juries) frequently dismissed such charges or, if the case went to trial, acquitted the defendants, even during the repressive 1890s. Since they could never be sure whether a confiscation or criminal indictment would succeed, and since officials who overstepped their legal authority were often called to account by the independent and relatively impartial German courts (and by a vigorous free press), even the most conservative authorities were cautious about intervening against literary publications and when they did, were usually careful to observe all the proper legal procedures. [86]

Theater censorship, the most pervasive and intrusive form of state intervention into literary life and one that took place on a daily basis throughout much of the empire, was also circumscribed and mitigated by legal safeguards and court decisions. The practice itself was (unsuccessfully) challenged several times in state courts. While local police censors enjoyed much latitude in censoring dramatic performances, in Prussia, Saxony, and several other states (although not Bavaria) their decisions were frequently appealed to an administrative law court. The possibility of legal appeal distinguished most of the German Empire from Britain, where the London theater censor's decisions were final. The administrative law courts sought to articulate increasingly clear and stringent criteria for banning performances and regularly overruled censors' decisions. Although some of those verdicts infuriated the emperor, he could do little to curb these courts' independence.

Such legalism served to curb arbitrary, capricious, impulsive, or idiosyncratic actions by the censoring authorities. Yet Germany's decentralized federal structure and the resulting fragmentation of its legal and administrative systems created a certain confusion, unpredictability, and even arbitrariness concerning censorship decisions within the nation as a whole. Laws, legal procedures, censorship policies, and criteria for granting theater licenses differed from state to state and frequently from city to city; as a result, authorities in different places regularly made very different decisions about the same work. At the same time, however, the legal peculiarities of some regions and the absence of any uniform national approach to theater censorship created enclaves where censorship was negligible or even nonexistent and islands of tolerance or immunity where it was difficult to convict for a press offense. As shall become clearer in subsequent chapters, this diversity and disunity of censorship laws and practices, while certainly frustrating for German writers and theater operators, served also to protect their freedom of expression.

Although in the years before World War I theater censorship decisions were becoming more centralized within Prussia, Saxony, and Bavaria, and more coordinated between these states, several attempts to establish a more nationally unified censorship system were successfully resisted by various interests. The issue was part of the larger unresolved problem of Germany's national unity and as such was caught up in the empire's constitutional deadlocks, where the powers of the central state (the imperial government) stood against those of the local states (especially Prussia and Bavaria), and the powers of the monarchy, administration, and police contraposed those of the Reichstag and judiciary. Efforts to centralize and standardize censorship laws, particularly theater censorship, miscarried also because ultimately they contravened the legal basis for censorship: to protect public peace, security, and order. To justify banning the public performance of a drama and to have it upheld by the courts, authorities had to argue persuasively that the piece was likely to lead to a public disturbance or somehow cause harm to the audience. This in turn depended upon many contingencies: the nature of the audience; the nature of the surrounding community (or in more modern parlance, "community standards"); unique political, religious, social, or other conditions in that place at that particular time; and so on. Germany was extremely diverse: the populace of Berlin differed enormously from that of Iphofen, Bavaria, and conditions in Hamburg were not like those in Krotoszyn, Posen. The more censors could point to specific local situations as grounds for their actions, the easier it was to defend them; where the situation was different and the work posed little or no threat to public order, a different decision would be in order. However much some groups, whether on the Left or the Right, desired more consistency in censorship decisions, the great diversity of local situations made it difficult (if not impossible) to establish uniform national standards and have all decisions made from one central office. Faced with the difficult choice of local diversity and contradictory censorship decisions on the one hand or more uniformity, consistency, and national predictability on the other, the government usually preferred the former, while many on both the Right and the Left, having lost confidence in local decision making, preferred the latter. Substantial changes to the censorship system became possible only after the outbreak of the war, when the exigencies of national mobilization and the need for more administrative centralization and bureaucratic intervention allowed the military to sweep aside legal technicalities, long-standing constitutional balances, and deference to local considerations. Only then did the system become more uniform and centralized.

Since, in the end, so much about literary censorship in imperial Germany depended on the local censor, it is to these censors we now turn.

Notes

1. Reinhard Frank, ed., *Das Strafgesetzbuch für das Deutsche Reich, nebst dem Einführungsgesetze*, 8.–10. rev. Aufl. (Tübingen, 1912); Justus Olshausen, *Kommentar zum Strafgesetzbuch für das Deutsche Reich*, 8. Aufl. (Berlin, 1909); Franz Eduard von Liszt, *Lehrbuch des deutschen Strafrechts*, 9. Aufl. (Berlin, 1899).
2. Ewald Löwe, ed., *Die Strafprozeßordnung für das Deutsche Reich mit Kommentar*, 12. Aufl. (Berlin, 1907); Franz Eduard von Liszt, *Das deutsche Reichs-Preßrecht, unter Berücksichtigung der Literatur und der Rechtsprechung* (Berlin and Leipzig, 1880), 123–29, 142–44; Heinz-Dietrich

Fischer, ed., *Deutsche Kommunikationskontrolle des 15. bis 20. Jahrhunderts* (Munich, 1982), 132–35; Alex Hall, *Scandal, Sensation and Social Democracy: The SPD Press and Wilhelmine Germany 1890–1914* (Cambridge, 1977), 46ff., 64–72.

3. For negative assessments of the imperial legal system see Hans-Ulrich Wehler, *The German Empire 1871–1918,* trans. Kim Traynor (Dover, NH, 1985), 127–29; Wehler, *Deutsche Gesellschaftsgeschichte. Dritter Band: Von der 'Deutschen Doppelrevolution' bis zum Beginn des Ersten Weltkriegs 1849–1914* (Munich, 1995), 857, 1238–39; and Albrecht Funk, *Polizei und Rechtsstaat. Die Entwicklung des staatlichen Gewaltsmonopols in Preussen 1848–1914* (Frankfurt, 1986). More positive appraisals are offered by Thomas Nipperdey, *Deutsche Geschichte 1866–1918. Band I: Arbeitswelt und Bürgergeist* (Munich, 1990), 655–65, and *Band II: Machtstaat vor der Demokratie* (Munich, 1992), 118–34, 182–93; Retallack, *Germany in the Age of Kaiser Wilhelm II,* 34–42; and Kenneth F. Ledford, *From General Estate to Special Interest: German Lawyers 1878–1933* (Cambridge, 1996), 1–85. Nipperdey states unequivocally, "The German Empire of 1871 was a *Rechtsstaat.* That is a central part of its constitutional reality. … The rule of law—despite some breakdowns—was entirely beyond doubt; the German order remained a just, legally-determined one in which even the little man, far more than seventy years earlier, was able to claim his rights and be afforded after all a modicum of justice." (2: 182, 193).

4. For example Wehler, *Deutsche Gesellschaftsgeschichte,* 744.

5. Nipperdey, *Deutsche Geschichte,* 2: 133–34.

6. In the 1870s the overall acquittal rate in press cases was 18.5 percent, while for those heard by the Bavarian *Geschworengerichte* the rate was 30.3 percent. By the 1880s the acquittal rate of the nonjury courts in press cases was 30 percent. Fischer, *Deutsche Kommunikationskontrolle,* 141.

7. Ludwig Thoma, "Gegen die Staatsanwälte," in *Gesammelte Werke* (Munich, 1932), 7: 369–70; Robin J. V. Lenman, "Censorship and Society in Munich, 1890–1914, With Special Reference to *Simplicissimus* and the Plays of Frank Wedekind," (PhD diss., Oxford University, 1975), 7–8, 11–12.

8. Korfiz Holm to Albert Langen, 22 Mar. 1899, *Das Kopierbuch Korfiz Holms (1899–1903). Ein Beitrag zur Geschichte des Albert Langen Verlags und des "Simplicissimus,"* ed. Helga Abret and Aldo Keel (Berne, 1989), 58; Heine to Holm, 15 Jul. 1899, StBM, Nachlaß Thomas Theodor Heine.

9. The case involved Harden's article "König Otto" in *Die Zukunft* VI Jg., no. 29 (16 Apr. 1898): 97–102. See chapter 3.

10. StAM/PDM 1046. The case involved the May 1903 cartoon "Gesandtenerziehung." See chapter 6.

11. The Catholic *Bayerische Kurier,* for example, urged the Bavarian government to use §360 sect. 11 against *Simplicissimus* since §184 had proven so unsuccessful in the past. Lenman, "Censorship and Society," 94, n. 3.

12. Thoma quoted in Ann Taylor Allen, *Satire and Society in Wilhelmine Germany:* Kladderadatsch *and* Simplicissimus *1890–1914* (Lexington, KY, 1984), 184. For more on this case, see chapter 5. Thoma later crusaded relentlessly to have such questionable legal practices stopped. See his "Gegen die Staatsanwälte," 370–373.

13. Roger Chickering, *Imperial Germany and the Great War, 1914–1918* (Cambridge, 1998), 34. For an example of how independent-minded deputy commanding generals resisted implementing some censorship policies even when pressured by the War Ministry, see Karl Brunner's report to the PrIM, 29 July 1916, LAB A, Rep 30 Berlin C, Tit. 121, Bd. 16985.

14. Quoted in Wolfgang G. Natter, *Literature at War, 1914–1940: Representing the "Time of Greatness" in Germany* (New Haven, CT, 1999), 44.

15. PrIM to local police, 9 Feb. 1915, quoted in Kurt Koszyk, "Entwicklung der Kommunikationskontrolle zwischen 1914 und 1918," in *Pressekonzentration und Zensurpraxis im Ersten Weltkrieg. Text und Quellen,* ed. Heinz-Dietrich Fischer (Berlin, 1973), 164; and definition of *Burgfrieden* in Oberzensurstelle's 1917 *Zensurbuch,* reprinted ibid., 210.

16. Kurt Mühsam, quoted in Ernst Fischer, "Der 'Schutzverband deutscher Schriftsteller' (1909–1933)," *Archiv für Geschichte des Buchwesens* 21 (1980): 192. Indeed, in 1915 the military's chief censorship office admitted it was not possible "to sharply distinguish between political, military, and economic questions [so] it is left to the judgment of the authorities … to decide which writings they wish to view as political." Quoted in Natter, *Literature at War*, 225, n. 20.

17. PrWM memo of 1 Apr. 1916 to all *stellvertretende Generalkommandos* (a copy was also sent by the PrIM to all local police and RPs), and Saxon IM memo of 20 Jun. 1916, LAB A, Rep 30. Berlin C, Tit. 121, 16985.

18. Henry Vizetelly, *Berlin Under the New Empire: Its Institutions, Inhabitants, Industry, Monuments, Museums, Social Life, Manners* (London, 1879; reprint New York, 1968), 2: 236.

19. Schöndienst, *Geschichte des deutschen Bühnenvereins*, 229.

20. LAB A/74, Th 5; Gerdi Huber, *Die Klassische Schwabing: München als Zentrum der intellektuellen Zeit- und Gesellschaftskritik um 1900* (Munich, 1973), 240.

21. On state control of theater in nineteenth-century Europe see Robert J. Goldstein, ed., *The Frightful Stage: Political Censorship of the Theater in Nineteenth-Century Europe* (New York and Oxford, 2009).

22. Friedrich Schiller, "Die Schaubühne als eine moralische Anstalt betrachtet," in *Sämtliche Schriften*, 5 vols. (Munich, 1968), 5: 92–101. A translation, "The Stage Considered as a Moral Institution," has been published in Frederick Ungar, ed., *Friedrich Schiller: An Anthology for Our Time* (New York, 1959), 263–83.

23. Arthur Brehmer and Max Grube, "Der Kaiser und die Kunst," in *Am Hofe Kaiser Wilhelms II*, ed. A. Brehmer (Berlin, 1898), 360; Wilhelm II's "Rede zu Kunstpersonal der Königlichen Schauspiele, 16 Juni 1898," in *Reden Kaiser Wilhelm II*, 98–99.

24. *Die Theaterzensur. Fünf Vorträge, gehalten in der Versammlung des Berliner Goethebunds in der Philharmonie am 8. III. 1903* (Berlin, 1903), 33.

25. See Conrad Alberti [pseudonym of Konrad Sittenfeld], *Was erwartet die deutsche Kunst von Kaiser Wilhelm II? Zeitgemäßige Anregungen von **** (Leipzig, 1888), 70, and Franz Mehring, *Gesammelte Schriften. Bd. 12: Aufsätze zur ausländischen Literatur. Vermischte Schriften*, ed. Thomas Höhle, Hans Koch, Josef Schleifstein (Berlin, 1976), 268. On the importance of drama and theater to avant-garde modernists and Social Democrats, see Peter Jelavich, *Munich and Theatrical Modernism: Politics, Playwriting, and Performance, 1890–1914* (Cambridge, MA, 1985) and Vernon Lidtke, *The Alternative Culture: Socialist Labor in Imperial Germany* (New York, 1985), 136–58. Americans recognized that "in Germany the theater is taken most seriously and is looked upon as an educational factor, quite as important as the church, State or school." ("Owing to the Complex Rules as to Religious Subjects and the Deference Due to Royalty the Berlin Censor Has His Hands Full," *New York Times*, 27 Sept. 1908, SM8.)

26. PrIM memo, 5 Dec. 1899, LAB A/74, Th 25; remark by PrIM to Prussian parliament, 19 Feb. 1903, quoted by Wolfgang Schulze-Olden, "Die Theaterzensur in der Rheinprovinz (1819–1918)" (Inaug. diss., Cologne, 1965), 26; comment by MPD, 19 June 1907, quoted by Lenman, "Censorship and Society," 244.

27. Gustav Le Bon, *Psychologie der Massen*, trans. Rudolf Eisler (Stuttgart, 1982), 21. Le Bon's work was translated into German in 1908.

28. Ibid., 44.

29. See for example Dr. Leuthold, "Theaterpolizei," in *Wörterbuch des deutschen Verwaltungsrechts*, ed. Karl Freiherr von Stengel (Freiburg, 1890), 2: 625–26; Otto Opet, *Deutsches Theaterrecht* (Berlin, 1897), 149–50; Dr. von Bar, "Rechtmäßigkeit und Zweckmäßigkeit der Theaterzensur?" *Deutsche Juristenzeitung* 8 (1903): 205–6; Wilhelm von Polenz, "Über die Grenzen des Unanständigen in der Kunst," *Das Magazin für die Literatur des In- und Auslandes* 62, no. 24 (17 June 1893): 384–85.

30. When the Commercial Code was extended to Alsace-Lorraine in 1888, any prior state regulations relating to theaters remained in effect. Since an 1864 French law abolished all licensing

requirements for the theater, during the imperial era those who wished to operate a theater in Alsace-Lorraine needed no license.

31. Robert von Landmann and Gusta Rohmer, *Kommentar zur Gewerbeordnung für das Deutsche Reich,* 5. Aufl. (Munich, 1907) 1: 257.

32. Köln RP, 24 Mar. 1879, quoted in Schulze-Olden, "Theaterzensur in Rheinprovinz," 114. Kurt Heinzmann, *Deutsches Theaterrecht* (Munich, 1905), 25ff.; Leuthold, "Theaterpolizei," 625.

33. One authority claimed that in 1870 alone ninety new theaters were licensed in the North German Confederation and the number of theaters in Berlin increased from nine to sixteen. Whereas Germany had fewer than two hundred prior to 1869, by the mid-1890s it had six hundred. L'Arronge, *Deutsches Theater,* 24; G. Wahnrau, *Berlin, Stadt der Theater. Der Chronik. I. Teil* (Berlin, 1957), 457; Annemarie Lange, *Berlin zur Zeit Bebels und Bismarcks. Zwischen Reichsgründung und Jahrhundertwende* (Berlin, 1972), 95–97; *Verwaltungsbericht des Königlichen Polizei-Präsidiums zu Berlin für die Jahre 1871–1880* (Berlin, 1882), 62–63; *[Zweiter] Verwaltungsbericht des Königlichen Polizei-Präsidiums von Berlin für die Jahre 1881–1890* (Berlin, 1892), 67.

34. See especially L'Arronge, "Das Theater und die Gewerbefreiheit," *Nord und Süd* (Oct., 1881), and his *Deutsches Theater,* 21, 31; PrIM memo of 30 Mar. 1879, quoted in Schulze-Olden, "Theaterzensur in Rheinprovinz," 72; Alberti, *Was erwartet die deutsche Kunst?* 101–3. Similar charges can be found in Wahnrau, *Berlin,* 457, and Charlotte Engel-Reimers, *Die deutschen Bühnen und ihre Angehörigen. Eine Untersuchung über ihre wirtschaftliche Lage* (Leipzig, 1911), 20–22.

35. Landmann and Rohmer, *Kommentar,* 1: 257; Arthur Wolff, "Theaterrecht," in *Wörterbuch des Deutschen Staats- und Verwaltungsrechts,* 2. Aufl., ed. Karl von Stengel and Max Fleischmann (Tübingen, 1914), 3: 590–91; Leuthold, "Theaterpolizei," 625; Heinzmann, *Deutsches Theaterrecht,* 25–41; *Dritter Verwaltungsbericht des Königlich-Polizeipräsidiums von Berlin für die Jahre 1891–1900* (Berlin, 1902), 376; Hessische IM decree of 20 Mar. 1912, "Ausführungsverordnung zur Gewerbeordnung," *Hessische Regierungsblatt,* 1912.

36. *[Zweiter] Verwaltungsbericht,* 66–67; Berlin police report of 2 Mar. 1901, LAB A/74, Th 5; *Dritter Verwaltungsbericht,* 376–78.

37. Wolff, "Theaterrecht," 590–91; Landmann and Rohmer, *Kommentar,* 1: 262; Oscar Blumenthal, *Verbotene Stücke* (Berlin, 1900), 10; Heinzmann, *Deutsches Theaterrecht,* 29–41; Leuthold, "Theaterpolizei," 625. A PrIM circular of 5 Dec. 1899 urged local authorities to remove "ungeeignete Elemente von der Gewerbe als Theaterunternehmer" by revoking their licenses, and to ensure that such elements did not receive licenses in the future. LAB A/74, Th 25.

38. Wenzel Goldbaum, *Theaterrecht* (Berlin, 1914), 67–68; Dr. Schmid, "Theaterzensur," *Zeitschrift für die freiwillige Gerichtsbarkeit und die Gemeindeverwaltung in Württemberg* 51 (1909): 148–49; Amtmann Bazille, "Die Theaterzensur in Württemberg in rechtlicher und verwaltungspolitischer Hinsicht," *Württembergische Zeitschrift für Rechtspflege und Verwaltung* II, no. 4 (1 April 1909); Albert Hellwig, "Die Filmzensur in Württemberg. Ihre Notwendigkeit, ihre rechtliche Grundlagen, und ihre zweckmäßigste Gestaltung," *Zeitschrift für die freiwillige Gerichtsbarkeit und die Gemeindeverwaltung in Württemberg* 55 (Jan. 1913): 21; Hellwig, *Rechtsquellen des öffentlichen Kinematographenrechts. Systematische Zusammenstellung der wichtigsten deutschen und fremden Gesetze* (Mönchen-Gladbach, 1913); Hamburg police order of 21 Oct. 1898, StAH, Nr. 2170, Vol. 23; Michaela Giesing, "Theater, Polizei und Politik in Hamburg um 1900," *Makse und Kothurn* 42, no. 2–4 (1996): 122, 133–34.

39. Maria Sommer, "Die Einführung der Theaterzensur in Berlin," *Kleine Schriften der Gesellschaft für Theatergeschichte,* Heft 14 (Herbst 1955/Sommer 1956): 32–42 (quote from 41); Heinrich H. Houben, *Polizei und Zensur. Längs- und Querschnitt durch die Geschichte der Buch- und Theaterzensur* (Berlin, 1926; reprinted as *Der ewige Zensor,* Kronberg, 1978), 106ff.

40. PrIM to all OPs, 28 July 1884, cited in Schulze-Olden, "Theaterzensur in Rheinprovinz," 76, 78, 80; PrIM memo of 9 Apr. 1895, LAB A/74, Th 24.

41. Frankfurt PP to Regierungsreferent of Erfurt, 13 June 1893, HHStA/407, Nr. 25, Bd. 2. Also Frankfurt Polizeiverordnung of 25 Nov. 1889, in *Ewald's Polizei-Verordnungen für Frankfurt am Main* (1906), 1; Frankfurt PP to Intendant der Stadttheater, 5 Sept. and 14 Sept. 1891, HHStA/407, Nr. 25, Bd. 1; *Frankfurter Finanzherold*, 14 Nov. 1891 and *General Anzeiger*, 9 Dec. 1891; Frankfurt RP to PrIM, 17 Oct. 1904, GStA PK/1000, Nr. 7, Bd. 3; and HHStA/407, Nrs. 408, 409; Schulze-Olden, "Theaterzensur in Rheinprovinz," 67–81, 95–97; OP Hanover to PrIM, 2 July 1895, GStA PK/1000, Nr. 4, Bd. 2.
42. Dresden police instituted prior theater censorship on 24 Dec. 1876 and Leipzig on 10 Mar. 1894. Goldbaum, *Theaterrecht*, 67; G. Krais, "Über Theaterzensur," *Blätter für administrative Praxis* 51 (1901): 29 n. 2, and Schmid, "Theaterzensur," 148. Munich's censorship ordinance, which closely paralleled Berlin's, is quoted in Krais, "Über Theaterzensur," 31ff. and Lenman, "Censorship and Society," 214–15.
43. Court costs even at the first instance could run into thousands of marks; in Oct. 1895 the *Bezirksausschuß* ruled against the Neue Freie Volksbühne and assessed its costs totaling three thousand marks. (See chapter 4.)
44. District administrative councils in Prussia consisted of the district administrative president—a professional civil servant and a judicial officer appointed by the state—and four laymen elected by the provincial assembly. While on most councils these laymen generally came from a narrow elite of estate owners and upper-middle-class businessmen, Berlin's tended to be slightly more democratic: the Berlin District Administrative Council that ruled on Hauptmann's *Die Weber* in March 1893, for example, had as its four lay members a *Techniker*, a *Maurermeister*, a *Verlagsbuchhändler*, and a *Bankier*. (*VL*, 1: 342–44)
45. Kenneth F. Ledford, "Formalizing the Rule of Law in Prussia: The Supreme Administrative Law Court, 1876–1914," *Central European History* 37, no. 2 (2004): 203–24; Nipperdey, *Deutsche Geschichte*, 1:662ff; 2:118–19; Michael John, "Constitution, Administration, and the Law," in Chickering, *Imperial Germany*, 202–3; and even Wehler, *German Empire*, 128.
46. "Gesetz betreffend die Einrichtung eines Verwaltungsgerichthofes und das Verfahren im Verwaltungsgerichtssachen," *Gesetz- und Verordnungsblatt für den Freistaat Bayern*, 1878, 369ff; Lenman, "Censorship and Society," 95 n. 2, 216.
47. Maximilian Harden, *Berlin als Theaterhauptstadt* (Berlin, 1888), 14. To avoid embarrassment to his royal employer, von Hülsen went so far as to change words like *Serenissmus* to *Ein Großer* and *Monarch* to *die erhabene Regierung*. Charlotte Klinger, "Das Königliche Schauspielhaus unter Botho von Hülsen, 1869–1886" (Diss. phil., Berlin, 1954), 203–4.
48. Hans Schorer, *Das Theaterleben in Münster in der zweiten Hälfte des 19. Jahrhunderts* (Emsdetten, 1935), 146, 158; Wilhelm Herrmann, "Mannheimer Theaterzensur im 19. Jahrhundert," *Mannheimer Hefte*, no. 2 (1976): 74–78.
49. *Verwaltungsbericht*, 64; *[Zweiter] Verwaltungsbericht*, 294. Another 443 such groups came into existence between 1890 and 1896, when police ceased keeping records on them. (*Dritter Verwaltungsbericht*, 383.) On Munich see Nipperdey, *Deutsche Geschichte*, 1:793.
50. Julius Hart, "Die Entstehung der 'Freien Bühne': Persönliche Erinnerungen von Julius Hart," *Velhagen und Klasings Monatshefte* 24, Bd. 1 (1909/10): 291–92.
51. Berlin police Tagesbefehl of 17 July 1875, LAB A/74, Th. 3; BPP to PrIM 10 Oct. 1888, LAB A/74, Th 952; *[Zweiter] Verwaltungsbericht*, 64; Charlottenberg PP decree, 18 July 1896, LAB A/74, Th 3796; Lenman, "Censorship and Society," 233, 237; Michael Meyer, *Theaterzensur in München 1900–1918. Geschichte und Entwicklung der polizeilichen Zensur und des Theaterzensurbeirates unter besonderer Berücksichtigung Frank Wedekinds* (Munich, 1982), 58–59, 286–87; Schulze-Olden, "Theaterzensur in Rheinprovinz," 131. As an example of how dramatist Ferdinand Bonn tried to use bogus "private" performances to circumvent a police ban on his work, and how police continually thwarted him, see LAB A/74, Th 496.
52. See decisions of Pr OVG of 25 Aug. 1883, 4 Jan. 1895, and 5 Oct. 1906, and the discussion of the Freie Volksbühne and Neue Freie Volksbühne in chapter 4.
53. Verdicts of Berlin Schöffengericht, 29 May 1883, Berlin Landgericht, 30 Oct. 1883, Royal

Kammergericht, 31 Jan. 1884, and Pr OVG, 2 May 1892, 12 Jun. 1892, 1 Dec. 1892, 3 Jan. 1894. Also Pr OVG, 3 Jan. 1909, Bavarian Verwaltungsgerichthof, 19 Jan. 1896; Saxon OVG, 16 Mar. 1901; Württemberg ambassador in Bavaria to Württemberg Foreign Minister, 3 Jul. 1908, in HStA Stuttgart, E151cII, Nr. 270a.

54. Center delegate Rintelen, quoted in Peter Mast, *Künstlerische und wissenschaftliche Freiheit im Deutschen Reich 1890–1901* (Rheinfelden, 1980), 141–42.

55. Von Heller to Bavarian Justice Minister, 4 Mar. 1893 (Auszug von Bericht über Gerichtsverhandlungen), in BHStA, MA 76 781; Mast, *Künstlerische und wissenschaftliche Freiheit,* 141–42; Robin J. V. Lenman, "Art, Society, and the Law in Wilhelmine Germany: the Lex Heinze," *Oxford German Studies* 8 (1973): 94–95.

56. Remarks by von Heereman, 21 Feb. 1895 in Prussian Landtag, quoted in Manfred Brauneck, *Literatur und Öffentlichkeit im ausgehenden 19. Jahrhundert. Studien zur Rezeption des naturalistischen Theaters in Deutschland* (Stuttgart, 1974), 250.

57. Quoted in Mast, *Künstlerische und wissenschaftliche Freiheit,* 142.

58. Petition to Wilhelm II, "Gegen die Corruption der Bühne," Jan. 1898, GStA PK, Rep. 77, Tit. 435, Nr. 23, Bd. 2, Bl. 87ff.

59. Mast, *Künstlerische und wissenschaftliche Freiheit,* 152–54; Lenman, "Art, Society, and the Law," 96–97.

60. Max Halbe (founder of the Munich Goethebund) to Munich police, 15 Mar. 1900 and police report on the Munich Goethebund, StAM/PDM, 2401; press reports in *Vorwärts* 27 Mar. 1900 and *Börsenblatt für den deutschen Buchhandel,* 28 Mar. 1900. The charter of the Berlin Goethebund, founded by Hermann Sudermann, stated: "The purpose of [this] association is to resist all attacks on the free development of artistic and scholarly life, in particular by guaranteeing its legal protection." Satzungen des Berliner Goethebunds, undated [Mar. 1900] in Deutsches Literaturarchiv, Marbach, Cotta Archiv, Nachl. Sud. xxv4.

61. Andreas Pöllinger, *Der Zensurprozeß um Paul Heyses Drama "Maria von Magdala" (1901–1903)* (Frankfurt, 1989), 32–40, 118–49; Hermann Sudermann, *Drei Reden, gehalten von Hermann Sudermann* (Stuttgart, 1900); Huber, *Das klassische Schwabing,* 88–90; Lenman, "Art, Society, and the Law," 100–104, 107; Meyer, *Theaterzensur in München,* 15–27.

62. Gordon A. Craig, *Germany 1866–1945* (New York, 1978), 262.

63. Nipperdey, *Deutsche Geschichte,* 2:128.

64. Hermann Sudermann, in *Die Theaterzensur. Fünf Vorträge,* 3–14.

65. M. G. Conrad, "Goethebund," *Die Gesellschaft,* 16, Pt. 2 (1900): 69.

66. Petition of Verband der deutschen Goethebunds, 10/11 Nov. 1900, in Deutsches Literaturarchiv, Marbach, Cotta Archiv, Nachl. Sudermann, XXV3. See also *Dritter Verwaltungsbericht,* 335.

67. StenBer/RT, 10. Leg. Periode, II. Session, Drucksache 16 (Bd. 189, 281).

68. Remarks by Ernst Müller-Meiningen, Dr. H. Pachnicke, and A. Traeger, StenBer/RT, 10.Leg. Per., II.Session, Sitzung von 30. Jan., 6 Feb., and 20 Feb. 1901, Bd. 180, 1016–27, 1160–61, and 1459–65; quotations from 1022, 1019, 1026–27.

69. Remarks by A. Stadthagen, ibid., 6 Feb. 1901, Bd. 180, 1164–73.

70. Remarks by Dr. Stockmann, ibid., 30 Jan. 1901 and 20 Feb. 1901, and by Himburg, 6 Feb. 1901, Bd. 180, 1028–34, 1163–64, 1465–67.

71. Remarks by H. Roeren, ibid., 6 Feb. 1901, 1152–59 and his remarks in the Prussian Landtag, 15 Feb. 1901, StenBer/Pr, 27. Sitzung am 15.2.1901, Bd. 442, 1721–28.

72. Remarks by Bassermann, 6 Feb. 1901, StenBer/RT, Bd. 180, 1148–52.

73. Remarks by PrIM, 13. Feb. 1901, in StenBer/Pr, 19. Legislaturperiode, III. Session, 25. Sitzung am 13. Feb. 1901, Bd. 442, 1503–19.

74. Debate and votes on 20 Feb. 1901, StenBer/RT, Bd. 180, 1467–76.

75. *Protokoll der Delegierten Versammlung der Genossenschaft Dtr. Bühnenangehöriger zu Berlin am 11. Dec. 1902,* 19; Engel-Reimers, *Die deutschen Bühnen,* 740–72; Josef Urban, "Von der Notwendigkeit und dem Inhalt eines Reichstheatergesetzes. Die privatrechtlichen Probleme des

Bühnenrechts nach geltenden Rechte und den deutschen und österreichiscen Gesetezentwür-
fen" (Inaug. diss., Griefswald, 1915); Richard Treitel, *Bühnenprobleme der Jahrhundertwende in
Spiegel des Rechts. Theaterrechtlichen Aufsätze,* ed. Manfred Rehbinder (Berlin, 1990).

76. BHStA, M Inn 72 737, Nr. 643, 61. Bericht des Petitionskommission [Feb. 1905]; "Die Theaterzensur in der Reichstagkommission," *Vossische Zeitung,* 8 Mar. 1905; *Frankfurter Zeitung,* 28
Apr. 1903; Huber, *Das klassische Schwabing,* 91.

77. Remarks by Müller-Meiningen in *Der Tag,* 8 Mar. 1903, quoted in Schulze-Olden, "Theaterzensur in Rheinprovinz," 23, and in Reichstag, 19 Feb. 1903, StenBer/RT, X. Leg. Periode, II.
Session, 262. Sitzung 19 Feb. 1903, Bd. 187, 8024–30.

78. Remarks by Müller-Meiningen, StenBer/RT, 203 Sitzung 10 Feb. 1909, 6824, and 145. Sitzung, 11 Mar. 1911, 5360–61; Remarks by Barth in StenBer/Pr, 16. Sitzung, 7 Feb. 1903, Bd.
459, 1015–21 and by Hirsch (SPD), 25 Sitzung 13 Feb. 1911, Bd. 555, 1788–93; StenBer/
Bav, 156. Sitzung vom 20 June 1906, IV. Band, 842–95.

79. "Entwurf eines Gesetzes, betreffend Änderung der Pars. 33, 33a, 33b, 35, 40, 42a, 45, 49,
147, 148 der Gewerbordnung," StenBer/RT, 13. Leg. Periode, 1. Session, Bd. 304 (Anlagen
zu den Stenographischen Berichten; Berlin, 1914), Aktenstück 1431. See also GStA PK, Rep.
120 BB, IIb1, Nr. 37, Adh. 2, Bd. 1, Bl. 214–222, and Schöndienst, *Geschichte des deutschen
Bühnenvereins,* 226ff.

80. Schulze-Olden, "Theaterzensur in Rheinprovinz," 126.

81. See my "All Quiet on the Home Front: Popular Entertainments, Censorship and Civilian
Morale in Germany, 1914–1918," in *Authority, Identity and the Social History of the Great War:
Essays in Comparative History,* ed. Frans Coetzee and Marilyn Shevin-Coetzee (Providence, RI,
1995), 77, n.7.

82. Stengel and Fleischmann, *Wörterbuch des Verwaltungsrechts,* 1:398; OVG decisions of 7 Oct.
1915 and 21 May 1917; Schulze-Olden, "Theaterzensur in Rheinprovinz," 99–100; PrIM to
Prussian Polizeipräsidenten, 7 May 1917, LAB A/74, Th 134.

83. OK in den Marken to PrWM, 29 Dec. 1914, LAB A/74, Th 134; LAB, Rep. 2, Abt. I, 3446;
Schulze-Olden, "Theaterzensur in Rheinprovinz," 99–100.

84. StenBer/RT, 23 Mar. 1917, 2625.

85. The "Kartell freier Kunstverbände," consisting of the Protective Association of German Writers (Schutzverband deutscher Schriftsteller), Goethe League, Association of German Dramatists (Verband deutscher Bühnenschriftsteller), Union of Artistic State Managers (Vereinigung
künstlerischer Bühnenvorstände) and Society for Theater History. See Arthur Eloesser's comment in *Die Zukunft der deutschen Bühne. Fünf Vorträge und eine Umfrage,* ed. Reichsverband
deutscher Schriftsteller (Berlin, 1917), 78. Also Fischer, "Der 'Schutzverband'," 192–94.

86. See Lenman, "Censorship and Society," 314–17.

Chapter 2

THE CENSORS

The German censors _ _ _ _ _ _ _ _ _
_ _ _ _ _ _ _ _ _ _ _ _ _ _ _ _ _ _ _
_ _ _ _ _ _ _ _ _ _ idiots _ _ _ _ _ _
_ _ _ _ _ _ _ _ _ _ _ _ _ _ _ _ _ _ _.
—Heinrich Heine, *Reisebilder, Zweiter Teil. Ideen. Das Buch Le Grand,*
Chapter XII (1826)

A censor is a human pencil or a pencilized human, a living blue line scratched
across the products of human genius, a crocodile lying in wait along the bank
of the river of ideas and biting off the heads of the writers swimming there.
—Ultra, in Johann Nestroy, *Freiheit in Krähwinckel,* Act I, scene 14 (1849)

*F*ew occupations are as detested as that of the censor. Like the despised medieval
hangmen to whom some Germans frequently compared them,[1] modern censors
are "literary executioners" with a thankless job. In performing their duties censors
meet with near universal condemnation and have long been objects of ridicule
and vilification.

To most writers and liberal-minded citizens the very institution of censorship
is anathema and those who exercise it personify blind reaction and ignorance in
action. If one believed their most outspoken critics in imperial Germany, police
censors fell into one or more of the following categories: uncultured, inartistic
petty functionaries incapable of recognizing, much less understanding and appreciating, genuine art and learning; puritanical, self-righteous moralists who (as
was said of the English stage censor in the 1880s) were convinced the nation was

---

Notes for this section begin on page 80.

"rushing towards an abyss of national degradation in morals and manners, and only held back on the edge of the precipice by the grasp of a strong hand";[2] or benighted obscurants who tyrannically wielded their blue pencils to throttle any stirrings of enlightenment and progress. Yet moderates who reluctantly accepted the need for censorship and conservatives who enthusiastically demanded it were equally critical of the hapless censors who had to apply it: the former continually condemned censors for being too harsh and petty while the latter constantly faulted them for being too lax and tolerant. And everyone complained the decisions of the censors were arbitrary and inconsistent; why, their critics demanded, did censors permit X yet ban Y, or vice versa?

While some police censors, especially in isolated provincial areas, certainly deserved the contempt in which they were held, most, especially those in larger metropolitan areas, were conscientious, university-educated, pragmatic men put in a difficult position. Pulled among many opposing influences and interests—their bureaucratic superiors, the local populace, the nation's literary and artistic community, various political parties, private associations, and pressure groups—the office and work of the empire's censors was as demanding as it was unappreciated.

The Dilemma of Local Standards

Before the revolutions of 1848, when most European states had an extensive system of prior press censorship, the task of censoring publications was often assigned to a specially appointed collegium or commission. Decisions of these central bodies, which typically operated under the supervision of the minister of the interior, generally applied to the entire territory, yielding a single statewide standard for what was permissible. Moreover, within the German Confederation the 1819 Karlsbad Decrees established a nationwide commission on press censorship that coordinated and further standardized the work of the individual states' censorship commissions.

After 1848, however, responsibility for press censorship was increasingly transferred to local police officials. Although the Imperial Press Law abolished prior press censorship, it retained the right of police to oversee and regulate all publications not concerned with art or science and to exercise a punitive, postpublication censorship over them when necessary. Because local police were responsible for supervising theaters and other public amusements, they also handled theater censorship.

Germany's police forces were highly diverse. In a few of the more liberal states like Württemberg, all police were under local municipal control. In Bavaria and Saxony, police in the capital cities of Munich and Dresden were a branch of the state bureaucracy and thus directly under royal control, while in the remaining towns and cities police were controlled by local municipal authorities. In Prussia, by contrast, police in all major and several minor cities were commanded by royal officials appointed by the central state government. Thus, of the fifteen largest cities only police forces in Leipzig, Nuremberg, and Stuttgart were controlled by the city's residents; in the other twelve—and in many other sizeable German cities and towns—police were part of the state civil service.

Most crown-appointed urban police commissioners (who usually held the title of police president or police director) were independent higher civil servants. Usually of noble birth, they had experience in some branch of civil administration, held a rank within the bureaucracy roughly equivalent to other district administrative presidents, answered directly to the state's minister of the interior, and received the majority of their budget from the state, not the city government. This autonomy from the municipal governments of their respective cities had two important consequences. First, because liberal, democratic politics was stronger at the municipal than at the state level, police in most German cities remained strongholds of conservatism largely beyond the control of the urban, liberal, bourgeois elite. Second, although urban police were highly sensitive to local conditions, they were able to remain relatively aloof and insulated from local interests, pressure groups, and party politics.

Censorship duties were usually assigned to the so-called political police, one of many internal police branches concerned with broad questions of public welfare. Whereas English and American police have narrower, more clearly defined duties, in Germany police traditionally handled many aspects of everyday public administration (fire, water, sanitation, health, poor relief, etc.) that elsewhere are normally handled by municipal governments. The urban police governed all aspects of municipal public affairs, intervening continually in many aspects of everyday life. Political police oversaw the diverse forums of civic political life, from collecting information about potential subversives (especially socialists and anarchists), to monitoring public and private clubs and associations (especially those of a political nature) and all public meetings, to regulating public amusements such as theaters and music halls. It was the local political police who exercised prior press censorship before 1874 and punitive press censorship thereafter, and who were responsible for prior theater censorship where this existed. As the system of stage censorship was extended (and became increasingly centralized in the capital cities of the major states), and as the number of works to be examined grew each year, censorship bureaus within the political police division also grew in size, responsibility, and importance. In Berlin, for example, the police units handling theater, film, and other forms of censorship became so large they were eventually separated from the political police division and consolidated into an autonomous administrative division (Abteilung VIII); the division chief, a senior administrative councilor (*Oberregierungsrat*) stood directly under the police president in the hierarchy and by 1914 supervised ten other police officials. In Munich the press and theater censorship bureau similarly evolved into a separate office (Referat VI) employing two mid-level officials and a staff of six. In Hamburg, by contrast, which had no formal theater censorship, the political and the commercial police (who oversaw theater licensing) battled over which was responsible for watching over the content of performances. A truce was reached by which commercial police were authorized to raise objections to performances and entertainments that were of "moral, religious, or political concern," while political police were to be involved only if a performance violated some aspect of the Criminal Code such as libel or incitement to illegal acts.[3]

As the number of police officials engaged in censorship expanded and censorship divisions of the major police forces in turn developed their own internal subdivisions and administrative units, this branch of police work often became an important avenue of career advancement. The officials who headed the censorship units in Berlin (Kurt von Glasenapp) and Munich (Dr. Dietrich Bittinger) during much of the Wilhelmine era both served also as their city's assistant police commissioner; Bittinger used his post to become police director of Stuttgart in 1911.

Transfer of censorship decisions from unitary state- or nationwide censorship collegia to diverse local police forces produced in the late nineteenth century a decentralized, fragmented system fraught with inconsistencies and contradictory decisions. A work permitted by censors in one city was often banned by those in another, or vice versa. There was, however, a compelling rationale for this lack of uniformity in censorship decisions. Both the government and the courts consistently maintained censorship was justified only for pragmatic, utilitarian social reasons: to protect public peace, order, or security. It was not the content, "truth," or artistic value of a work that was the censor's concern, but rather its *Wirkung*, its probable effect upon the public. If an audience was likely to react to a work in a way that threatened public peace, order, or security, the state claimed the right and duty to ban it, regardless of its other intrinsic merits. Given the enormous diversity of the German population, it was obvious an audience in one locale (for example, an urban, heavily Protestant community) would respond to a work quite differently than patrons in another locale (for example, a rural, staunchly Catholic community). The probable *Wirkung* of any particular work—and therefore its potential to provoke a public disturbance or somehow cause harm to the audience or citizenry—would thus vary greatly from place to place and setting to setting. Any decision to permit or ban a work had to take into account many contingencies such as the type, repertoire, and general reputation of the particular theater, the nature of the audience and of the surrounding community, unique local conditions at the time, and community standards. Since these differed greatly across the empire, so too would censorship decisions about any given work. The more that censors could point to specific local situations as grounds for their decision, the easier it was to defend their action and have it upheld on appeal; where the situation was different, the work might pose no threat to public peace, security, or order and a different decision would be in order. Censorship judgments, the government regularly reiterated, had to be made at the local, not the state or national level. The Prussian minister of the interior, responding to parliamentary complaints about the contradictory decisions of local police censors, declared in 1901 that such disparity is unavoidable:

> The most defective arrangement of all would be if one tried to regulate all censorship from Berlin. Too many local conditions come into play, which only local police are in a position to evaluate properly. A work may be unobjectionable when performed on a first-class Berlin

stage by excellent actors in a serious manner before an audience with a literary education, but could, under other circumstances, at a second- or third-rate theater, before a less educated audience and performed in a provocative manner, be highly objectionable from the standpoint of morals or public order. The diversity of circumstances must be taken into consideration.[4]

Provincial officials, such as a longtime theater censor with the Munich police, similarly warned against attempts to centralize and standardize censorship decisions because that ignored the crucial role unique local conditions played in the decision-making process.[5]

Yet divergent local rather than uniform national rulings inevitably made theater censorship appear contradictory and arbitrary, which in turn exposed both censorship and censors to frequent ridicule. As we have seen, various governmental and nongovernmental forces tenaciously lobbied to coordinate, rationalize, standardize, and centralize censorship decisions in hopes of eliminating embarrassing contradictions and plugging annoying loopholes. Although efforts to standardize and centralize censorship laws made little headway against the political, legal, and institutional forces that sustained multiformity, pressures promoting more uniformity gradually gained the upper hand in the day-to-day administration of those laws. By World War I the political and bureaucratic advantages of centralization had overcome the logic and traditions of decentralization.

Prussia led in the drive to coordinate and centralize censorship decisions within its boundaries. In 1908 the Ministry of the Interior, embarrassed by a new round of public and parliamentary criticism after Berlin theater censors disagreed with those in other cities about several controversial plays, abandoned its earlier defense of local diversity and now declared it imperative for local authorities to avoid mutually inconsistent decisions. To bring greater conformity and coordination to censorship decisions, the interior minister instructed all royal police commissioners under his authority to have their theater censors, before deciding to permit or ban a particular piece about which they might have the slightest reservations, first inquire of the Berlin police president how the work had been handled there. If, because of unique local conditions, they were convinced a decision was justified that differed from that of the Berlin censor, then they must obtain the local police commissioner's express approval and the commissioner should in turn inform the interior minister before making the decision public. To simplify this process and reduce the voluminous correspondence it would generate, a few months later Berlin police were directed to inform all other royal police commissioners in Prussia whenever the Berlin theater censors banned a work; if that work was later submitted in another Prussian city, police there could then take Berlin's decision into account before making their own decision.[6] After 1912 the Interior Ministry had the Berlin theater censorship office regularly publish a list of works that had been approved, banned, or passed with significant alterations in the capital, and local police elsewhere in Prussia could approve only works that had been previously passed by the Berlin censor; any deviations generally required the interior minister's approval. These attempts to create more consistency yet accommodate local circumstances left many local Prussian officials perplexed and uneasy about when they could or should deviate from decisions reached in Berlin.[7]

Several other German states undertook similar efforts at centralization. In 1912 Saxony designated the Dresden theater censorship office as Saxony's central clearinghouse for theater censorship (*Landesstelle fur Theaterzensur*). As such, Dresden censors kept a master list of all works approved or banned throughout Saxony and encouraged local censors to consult it before making their own decisions. Likewise, Bavaria designated the Munich police as the state's central theater censors; after 1910 local police were urged to consult with Munich censors before deciding about a work.

The major states also began cooperating more closely on censorship. Police in various German cities (including Vienna) had long consulted on an informal, ad hoc basis and exchanged information concerning particularly important censorship cases. In 1912 the Berlin, Dresden, and Munich police agreed to systematically exchange their master lists of all works banned and approved in each state, with the aim of better coordinating their decisions.[8]

The perpetual tension between the need for local discretion and the desire for more national uniformity in censorship matters produced an unusual predicament in the final decade of the German Empire. On the one hand, as we have seen, the Prussian and imperial governments staunchly maintained theater censorship was a state and local, not an imperial matter and they thwarted any attempts to replace local jurisdiction with more uniform national legislation. On the other hand, the problems inherent in local decision making drove Prussia and other states to centralize and standardize the way they actually applied censorship. By 1914 the major states of the empire had gone a long way toward removing theater (and also film) censorship decisions from local hands and investing them instead in police censors in the state capital. At the same time, the other major states looked increasingly to Prussia to take the lead and were less likely to approve works not already passed in Berlin. The theater censors of the Berlin police force (and, over them, the Prussian Ministry of the Interior) thus came increasingly to function as a quasi-central censorship office for the entire empire. To the delight of some and dismay of others, in the empire's last years the delicate balance between a uniform national standard and diverse local standards tipped decidedly toward the former and (the interior minister's warning of 1901 notwithstanding) that standard was set primarily by the censors in Abtheilung VIII of the Berlin police.

Censorship as a Vocation

Who staffed these censorship bureaus? What training, qualifications, or experience did they have? How did these men come to be censors? How much independence did they exercise in their duties, and how did they view their unusual vocation?

Under the prior censorship systems of the early nineteenth century, censors had the formidable task of examining all books and periodicals before they went to print (and sometimes all dramas before they were performed) and of writing reports on those considered objectionable. They often oversaw imported printed matter and the offerings of local bookstores and lending libraries as well as watching the foreign press and book trade for dangerous works before they were introduced locally. From their superiors they often received only vague, general instructions for judging specific works and then were frequently rebuked or even punished when their decisions displeased those higher up. In Russia, for example, literary censors were sometimes imprisoned for approving works their superiors thought should have been banned, while in many German states they were commonly fined considerable sums for their misjudgments or held liable for any legal costs their decisions might later incur if challenged and reversed.[9]

Because in most states, especially smaller, poorer ones, they were overworked and underpaid (if indeed paid at all) and seldom given the financial resources and manpower necessary to carry out their assignments, it was often difficult to find men qualified to serve on the censorship collegia. Given the aggravations of the position it is hardly surprising few men chose the job of censor. Rather, they were generally assigned to their office by the monarch, and once pressed into service were often forbidden to resign. Traditionally, they were chosen from the small pool of educated men already in government service whose position involved some familiarity with books and perhaps foreign languages: university professors, royal librarians and archivists, and members of the church hierarchy. Often, they were expected to assume the censor's demanding tasks in addition to their other bureaucratic duties.

As with any institution of social control, if officials who are charged with enforcing rules are to be effective they must have the cooperation and respect, either voluntary or coerced, of those they deal with.[10] Writers, journalists, or artists subjected to censorship were presumably more likely to accept and cooperate with censors who enjoyed some standing in the intellectual and artistic community than with censors who were strangers to it. It was no accident, then, that many men appointed as censors were themselves writers, journalists, or booksellers or had close ties to the literary world. In pre-1848 Germany, for example, authors such as E. T. A. Hoffmann, Jakob Grimm, Joseph Freiherr von Eichendorff, and August Friedrich Ernst Langbein were all state censors at one time; Austria and Russia, too, appointed noted dramatists, poets, and journalists to their censorship commissions. Many of these writer-censors not only knew their fellow authors whom they were called upon to censor, but were often on good terms with them. In several cases relations between censor and censored were so close it was difficult to distinguish between them: in *Vormärz* Prussia, for example, the censor Langbein published his poems in one of the journals he was assigned to censor, while in Hesse, Bernhardi secretly edited a liberal newspaper he and his fellow censors were supposed to be censoring.[11] Indeed, far from being ruthless and petty-minded functionaries eager to silence the slightest hint of unorthodox expression, many early nineteenth-century censors were sympathetic toward the authors they had to censor and sabotaged the institution from within by exercising their powers as liberally and tolerantly as possible. "Enlightened" censors like Jakob Grimm and Christian Schubart in Germany or Fedor Tiutchev, A. V. Nikitenko, and Vasilii Odoevski in Russia were often critical of censorship and sought to be as lax as possible when applying it (which is precisely why their governments often found it necessary to hold censors personally or financially liable for their decisions).

Dismantling the system of prior press censorship after midcentury brought major changes to the task of the censor and the type of person recruited for the position. Like many other areas of nineteenth-century life, censorship and censors became increasingly bureaucratized. In contrast to the more broadly educated, skeptical, unwilling scholar- or writer-censors of the early century, those who served as censors in imperial Germany were full-time, midlevel career civil servants with a narrow legal training. Because they were primarily administrative bureaucrats, not intellectuals, these police officials were generally afforded little respect from those they censored. As the writer Karl Gutzkow remarked:

> Censorship might still be bearable if from the outset it did not, as a branch of administrative bureaucracy, bear the stamp of literary incompetence. An official who has perhaps studied all the commentaries on the laws of the land but has never studied a work of a different scholarly discipline, not to mention art, an official whose thoughts are all directed towards small spaces in administrative buildings, who has only one God, namely his superior, and only one heaven, namely promotion—such a man should pass judgment on your writing?[12]

Censorship officials on major urban police forces like Berlin or Munich normally held the prestigious rank of administrative or police councilor (*Regierungsrat, Polizeirat*) or assistant administrative councilor (*Regierungsassessor, Bezirksamtsassessor*), positions that at the turn of the century earned annual salaries of 4,200 to 7,000 marks and sometimes carried an additional housing subsidy. They generally had no particular interest in the world of literature, art, or ideas and few, if any, ties to those who populated that world. Their work as censors was highly routinized, following prescribed guidelines requiring them to judge a work from a narrowly legalistic perspective and leaving little room for considerations such as literary merit. As one fin-de-siècle critic of Central European censorship complained, works were now being judged simply from the "mentality of the bureaucrats, ... who in most cases evaluate the intellectual creations entrusted to them the same way that a blind man evaluates colors"; another German parliamentarian, himself a judge, declared that juristically trained civil servants knew as much about art and literature as an elephant about flute playing.[13] And as career bureaucrats whose advancement depended on conscientiously performing their duties, these censors were not inclined to question, much less subvert the institution of which they were a part. Even more than the judiciary, professional police administrators who functioned as censors in Germany were recruited from a small, upper-class elite and were, for the most part, staunchly conservative, uncritical supporters of the existing system and its policies. For example Dr. Christian Roth, who became chief of the Munich police department's Referat VI in 1911, was not merely a political conservative but an archreactionary. After the brutal suppression of the Bavarian revolution of 1918–1919, Roth served briefly as Bavarian minister of justice, during which time he acquired the nickname "Böse Christian" (The Evil Christian). He was active in Bavaria's early Nazi movement and a key participant in Hitler's 1923 Beer Hall Putsch.[14]

Even though the Prussian minister of the interior tried to ensure that "censorship be entrusted only to officials whose knowledge, experience, and mature judgment will guard against blunders,"[15] this was not usually the case. Although one young Bavarian law student with literary interests (Robert Heindl) apparently aspired to become a police censor and was briefly employed by the Munich police's censorship bureau, and although Dr. Hermann Possart, son of Ernst von Possart (a famous actor, Berlin theater director, and later intendant of the Bavarian royal theaters) worked from 1901 to 1910 as a respected theater censor with the Berlin police, in general no special qualifications were expected of a censor.[16] Police officials assigned those duties were given no particular training for their job, needed demonstrate no particular prior aptitude for it, and often had no particular interest in it. Their only training was the standard, narrowly focused legal training shared by all civil administrators: public and administrative law (*Staats- und Verwaltungsrecht*). Although some in police administration spent their entire careers there, more often they had been posted to the police after serving in one or more positions elsewhere within the state bureaucracy. For example, Administrative Councilor Dumrath, chosen to head the Berlin police's new Subdivision for Theater Affairs when it was created in 1900 (and thus in charge of theater censorship for the city) had until then served as local prefect (*Landrat*) in West Prussia. (His unfortunate name, which could mean something like "stupid advice," became the butt of many jokes, as did another censor named Klotz who was the second highest-ranking censor in the office before and during the war.) In Munich both Dr. Dietrich Bittinger (the city's chief press, theater, and cinema censor until 1911) and Dr. Christian Roth, his successor, had served for a number of years as lower-level officials with various Bavarian district courts and rural administrative districts before being transferred to the Munich police.[17]

While censors attached to large, urban, state-controlled police forces like Berlin or Munich may have been ill prepared for their tasks, those in some of Germany's smaller cities were often woefully unqualified for theirs. Police forces in Leipzig, Nuremberg, and Stuttgart (as well as those in the city-states of Hamburg, Bremen, and Lübeck) enjoyed less prestige and a far smaller budget than their counterparts in most other German cities because those forces were locally controlled and police officials there were not part of the state civil service. Many duties that elsewhere were handled by university-trained civil servants were handled in municipally controlled police forces by the uniformed constabulary—that is, by common patrolmen (*Schützmänner*). These patrolmen, who had to be army veterans with several years service and have attained the rank of corporal (*Unter-*

offizier), were drawn heavily from the peasantry and the petit-bourgeoisie ranks of artisans, small shopkeepers, and minor officials; few had any education beyond the elementary level and virtually none were gymnasium, much less university, graduates. The painfully obvious inadequacies of these patrolmen, who have been aptly described as "reactionaries by profession" were one important reason why censorship responsibilities became increasingly centralized in the hands of better-trained officials in the major metropolitan police forces.

Although German police censors were nearly always narrowly trained jurists who had not chosen to be censors, had (at least at the outset) little understanding of the media and materials they were assigned to censor, and whose relevant training and experience for their task was highly questionable, here and there a censor could be found, especially in major urban areas, who transcended these limitations and performed his difficult calling in a way that won him widespread respect, even from writers and artists. One such man was Kurt [Curt] Karl Gustav von Glasenapp (1856–1937), who headed the Berlin censorship office during the empire's last two decades. Glasenapp, scion of an old Pomeranian noble family,[18] studied law and entered the Prussian civil service. Around 1890 he was posted to the Berlin police's political division as an assistant administrative councilor, where his duties included theater censorship and licensing. After promotion to administrative councilor in 1896 he became head of the theater subdivision in 1901 and thereafter served as Berlin's chief theater censor. In 1907 Glasenapp was promoted to senior administrative councilor and in 1910 became director of Abtheilung VIII, which was responsible for all theater, film, and pornography censorship and for the control of other pubic amusements. When a national film censorship board was established for Germany in 1920, it too came under Glasenapp's supervision.

After 1901, when Glasenapp directed all theatrical (and later film) censorship for Berlin, he functioned more and more as Germany's de facto national censor. The growing centralization and standardization of censorship meant other Prussian cities increasingly followed the censorship decisions of the Berlin police and other German states increasingly followed the decisions of Prussia. Thus, Glasenapp gradually emerged as imperial Germany's most influential censor: although local police throughout the nation were theoretically free to reach their own decisions regarding a particular drama or film, by World War I they ordinarily deferred to the decisions made by Glasenapp's unit in Berlin. Since it was in the huge, lucrative Berlin market where most new dramas and films premiered (and thus, where they were first submitted for censorship), Glasenapp and his subordinates normally had the first, and last, word on whether a work would be banned.

Despite growing criticism of censorship, Glasenapp enjoyed much personal respect: his sensitivity, fairness, and prudence as a censor were recognized and valued across the political spectrum (as was that of his assistant, Dr. Hermann Possart).[19] Glasenapp, who had a genuine love for and extensive knowledge about the theater and visited other European capitals to learn about and consult on theater censorship abroad, took his responsibilities seriously yet appeared to be fairly broad-minded regarding theatrical censorship. Rather than banning a questionable script outright he often attended a dress rehearsal to see how it would be staged, and on occasion even discussed a work with its author, although this went against prevailing procedures. Directors and stage personnel in the theater industry praised Glasenapp's intelligence and artistic discernment and he appears to have been on friendly, even intimate, terms with some of the authors he censored, including avant-garde writers like Arthur Schnitzler and Frank Wedekind.[20] He served on the commission to draft a new theater law in 1912–1913, and when the first draft was released, the liberal theatrical journal *Die Schaubühne* greeted it as a "most gratifying sign of the great sympathy in official circles toward theater employees. ... I see in this draft the expert hand of Senior Administrative Councilor von Glasenapp, to whom all theater employees owe a great 'thank you.'"[21] Indeed, so strong were his relations with the literary and entertainment community that after he retired from the Berlin police force in the mid-1920s he became managing director of the Association of German Writers (*Verband deutscher Erzähler*), a lobby group for Germany's literati that sought to improve their working conditions and opposed the censorship of public entertainments.[22] Although he had moved from overseeing and controlling writers to representing their interests, in both roles Glasenapp functioned as an intermediary between the artistic community and the state.

If a sensitive, liberal-minded, highly respected censor like Glasenapp inspired confidence and trust within the artistic community and thereby helped legitimize censorship, some of his colleagues did exactly the opposite. Critics frequently charge that those who act as censors of others are blatant hypocrites acting out of questionable or even twisted psychological motives. "Show me a censor," said one writer, "and I will show you an individual suffering from frustrated desire"; another wit defined a censor as a man who gets paid for his dirty thoughts. The renowned psychoanalyst and Freud biographer Dr. Ernest Jones claimed, "it is the people with secret attractions to various temptations who busy themselves with removing these temptations from other people; really they are defending themselves, under the pretense of defending others, because at heart they fear their own weakness."[23] Given the often arbitrary way German police officials were assigned to censorship duties, it would be hard to argue such men became censors to satisfy their own dark, unconscious drives. Nevertheless, the issue of moral hypocrisy in censors fascinated many critics of censorship in the last years of the empire. As the cases of Traugott von Jagow and Dietrich Bittinger show, when a censor's embarrassing private moral behavior appeared to conflict with his public role as a defender of morality he quickly became a cause célèbre; when such censors became objects of widespread ridicule and disrespect, especially in the artistic community, they undercut the legitimacy of censorship itself.

Archconservative Traugott von Jagow was appointed police president of Berlin in 1909 and was Glasenapp's immediate superior. Although Glasenapp's division normally handled most questions of theater censorship, unique or difficult cases were sometimes passed up to the police president for final decision. When the censorship division was reluctant to pass Carl Sternheim's drama *Die Hose* (*Underpants*) in February 1911 on moral grounds, Max Reinhardt, director of the Deutsches Theater, appealed to von Jagow and invited him to attend a dress rehearsal to see for himself how inoffensive the performance would be. (On the *Die Hose* case, see chapter 6.) Leaving little to chance, Reinhardt also asked Tilla Durieux, one of his most attractive and popular actresses, to sit next to von Jagow during the performance and distract him with conversation whenever the language or action on stage became a little racy. The stratagem worked and von Jagow approved the play. He also sent this personal note to Ms. Durieux: "Dear Madam: Since I must exercise censorship over the theaters, I would like some personal contact with actors' circles. It would be a pleasure for me if we could continue our conversation of today. Would you mind if I paid you a visit? Perhaps Sunday at 4:30 PM? Respectfully, von Jagow. (Please address personally)."[24]

Von Jagow did not know Durieux was married to Paul Cassirer, publisher and coeditor of the radical, avant-garde journal *Pan*. A few weeks earlier von Jagow had ordered two issues of *Pan* confiscated and charged Cassirer and his colleagues with obscenity. (On the *Pan* affair, see chapter 6.) Cassirer and his coeditors Wilhelm Herzog and Alfred Kerr decided to exploit the incident, hoping von Jagow would drop the charges against them or perhaps even resign from office. Cassirer sent the police president a note accusing him of behaving boorishly toward his wife and challenging him to a duel.[25] The next day an imposing military officer in full uniform appeared in Cassirer's office with von Jagow's apology: "Herr Cassirer, my friend, His Excellence the police president of Berlin, Herr Traugott von Jagow, has instructed me to apologize to you in his name. On his word of honor, he did not know that Ms. Durieux was your wife. He assumes this embarrassing incident is now settled." Cassirer indicated he was satisfied, but could not guarantee that others (namely, the firebrand Alfred Kerr) wouldn't discuss it further in the press. Indeed, over the next weeks Kerr and others published several caustic articles, poems, and cartoons about the affair, castigating von Jagow for cynical moral hypocrisy and abusing his office and ridiculing the double standards in respectable Wilhelmine society. The scandal was quickly picked up by the Social Democratic press and even by papers in the US, Argentina, England, and Hungary.[26] Although he remained Berlin police president until 1916, the affair embarrassed von Jagow and added fuel to a growing anticensorship movement in Germany on the eve of the war.[27]

As the von Jagow affair was dying down in Berlin, another scandal involving a police theater censor and an actress flared up in Munich. In late 1911 an obscure Munich journalist published an article charging Dr. Dietrich Bittinger, head of the Munich Police Department's Referat VI, with making indecent advances on an actress who visited him in his office, supposedly to discuss a matter of theater censorship. Bittinger successfully sued for libel but the journalist appealed the decision and won a retrial. At this second trial (February 1912) another actress testified that at a ball three years earlier, Bittinger had grabbed her under her skirt—something Bittinger claimed he didn't remember and which at any rate, he said, happened all the time at a *bal paré*. Although upholding the journalist's original conviction for libel, the court reduced his fine from four hundred marks to fifty, implying Bittinger's reputation was less sterling than previously thought. Munich's liberal and socialist press quickly publicized the miniscandal, drawing attention to this guardian of morality's own lack of morality. Bittinger, meanwhile, had left Munich to assume the position of police director of Stuttgart.[28]

Although neither of these scandals found much resonance beyond the local left-wing press, both raised questions about the moral standards of censors who professed to uphold public morality by banning immoral materials. For those who already opposed censorship in principle as either ineffectual or unnecessary, these two incidents merely confirmed their worst opinions about arrogant censors and provided further proof the institution of censorship had to be abolished.

The Censor's Work

Like most work of public welfare divisions in the police forces in larger cities, that of the censors was highly routinized. After visiting the Berlin police in 1913–1914, one American observer commented on the "over-organization" he found:

> There are bureaus and sub-bureaus, specialties and sub-specialties, with an interminable line of reports and documents proceeding through official channels to the [Police] President's office. Every official method is carefully prescribed; every action, even to the smallest detail, is hedged about with minute rules and regulations. Police business is reduced to a methodical and, as far as possible, automatic routine. … [It is] a piece of machinery from which the human element has been completely eliminated, leaving no room for individual initiative or imagination. … [A]s one surveys the entire organization of the Berlin department, the impression becomes firmly fixed that it is a huge, ponderous machine, impeded by its own mechanical intricacy and clogged with work.[29]

While bureaucratic organization was less systematized and routines less rigid the further one got from Berlin and Prussia, censors everywhere operated within a highly structured setting that imposed significant institutional constraints on their work.

Since artistic and scholarly publications were exempted from censorship under the Press Law, officials in the press censorship bureau were rarely involved in literary censorship. In scrutinizing the extensive outpouring of the periodical press, however, press censors also clipped and filed articles and references to anything that might be of use to other police divisions. Thus, they often forwarded to the theater censor newspaper items about dramas in which the latter might have an interest—for example, reports about controversial plays banned in another cities, or reviews of dramas performed elsewhere that raised questions about those works' suitability for the public stage.

Where theater censorship existed, theater directors were usually required to submit to police two copies of the script (*Textbuch*) of any work to be performed publicly, and had to do so at least two weeks before it premiered. Pieces previously approved and publicly performed were routinely reapproved; all "new" works (that is, those never before submitted to police or approved for public performance in the city) had to be individually examined. In Berlin and other large cities each text was assigned to a lower-level official (the *Lektor,* or reader) who wrote a brief synopsis and analysis of the piece and marked (usually in blue pencil) any dialogue, stage action, or other aspect that might be objectionable or impermissible. (One of the more pedantic readers in Berlin also marked grammatical and spelling errors he found.[30]) This report then passed to a superior who decided whether to approve the piece, approve it provided certain alterations were made, or forbid its performance completely. In highly sensitive or particularly controversial cases the matter was sometimes referred to the police president for final judgment. A letter, under the police president's signature, informed the theater or music hall of the decision. One copy of the script was returned to the theater, containing the censor's blue markings of passages or scenes that had to be cut or altered; the second copy was kept in police files. (By 1901 the Berlin police had collected over eleven thousand *Textbücher.*[31]) For future reference the Berlin police also kept a huge card file of all works submitted for censorship there; a separate card for each drama indicated what action had been taken as well as other pertinent information (for example, whether the work was "Social Democratic"). Before reading a newly submitted drama, censors referred to this card file to see if it had been previously approved or banned in the city. They also frequently consulted whatever press clippings had been collected concerning the work to see if it had been banned elsewhere or what audience reaction had been when it was performed. After the move to centralize and coordinate theater censorship beginning in 1908, provincial police also began checking the master lists of bans and approvals distributed by the Berlin, Munich, or Dresden censors.

If unable or unwilling to decide from the script alone—for example, if they wanted to see exactly how a sensitive scene or action would be staged—censors sometimes insisted on attending the dress rehearsal, to which theaters were obligated to admit them.[32] Once a script was approved a police official or simple constable from the censorship bureau might also attend the opening and/or subsequent performances to ensure they corresponded exactly to the approved script; any deviations (for example, extemporaneous comments by the actors or inclusion of dialogue that had been ordered removed) were grounds for a fine or rescinding approval for the play. With particularly sensitive or controversial pieces a constable was often sent to the premier and wrote a report on audience reaction; if there were outbursts or disturbances, permission for the play might be withdrawn. Contemporaries report that at many theatrical performances a policeman was "often the most attentive listener in the hall, constantly comparing the spoken words with the manuscript in his hands."[33]

Although their work might appear to outsiders as highly routinized, German theater censors actually had relatively wide discretionary power to decide which works were suitable for public performance. They were not given a detailed checklist of forbidden topics, situations, language, or other items against which to evaluate a script. Rather, they were guided by a broad mandate to prevent the performance of any material that, because of its general tendency, the manner of its depiction, or its probable effect upon an audience, was likely to pose a danger to public peace, security, or order. In Prussia and most other states this included material that violated various provisions of the Criminal Code, attacked the existing state order or state religion, attacked the social order or the family, offended public morality by grossly violating the sense of shame and morality, depicted "notorious" situations from private life, or portrayed concrete events from the life of a person still living. Individual states sometimes imposed additional specific interdictions for public entertainments; in Prussia, for example, policemen and other public officials could not be portrayed in an "obscene or inappropriate manner" and neither deceased members of the Hohenzollern dynasty nor characters from the Bible could appear on stage without express government approval.[34] (See chapters 3 and 5.)

Different officials in different settings necessarily applied these general and specific taboos differently. For censors, like many other social-control agents, are "definition controllers" or "judges of normality" (Foucault) who decide (usually on the basis of subjective value judgments rather than objective criteria) what conforms to acceptable norms. Their power to name or label, their ability to determine what range of behavior is to be designated as obscene, blasphemous, inflammatory, or otherwise intolerable uniquely positions them not only to identify but also actually to "produce" what they claim to suppress. When the law regarding obscenity and morally offensive materials was broadened after 1900, for example (see chapter 6), one contemporary observer remarked: "The impossibility of concretely defining [obscenity] has the inevitable consequence that the judge's individual interpretation is given wide latitude, that subjective judgment occupies a large place in the evaluation, analysis, and investigation of inculpated works. The penalties imposed for [such] transgressions ... thus differ greatly, and no other legal regulations yield such divergent judicial verdicts as these."[35] (It was no coincidence that from 1902 until World War I, the annual number of prosecutions and convictions for obscenity was about 50 percent higher than during the 1890s.[36])

Once censors decided to permit or prohibit a drama's public performance, the theater director was informed in writing. Police were not required at this time to explain the reason for a ban or identify what they found unacceptable, beyond stating generally that it was proscribed on "moral," "religious," or "public-order" grounds; only if the decision were appealed did police explicate what was objectionable and why. In reaching a decision censors seldom discussed or negotiated scripts with the theater director, and almost never with the playwright. Like most bureaucrats, police resisted any external, unofficial interference in their area of jurisdiction (in this case, pending censorship matters) and much preferred to confine their interaction with the public to formal, prescribed legal procedures. More importantly, playwrights had no legal role or rights in the censorship process.

In nineteenth-century Germany, dramatists generally gave their new works to agents, who in turn sold the scripts to theaters after negotiating the royalties, advances, and other compensations due the author. Since, under the law, it was the theater director who submitted the work for censorship, police dealt only with him and only he had the right to appeal a ban. Some directors had a censored dramatist participate in the appeal process as a co-plaintiff or witness, or worked closely with an author in revising the banned work so it would pass censorship, but directors had no obligation to do so and they could (and frequently did) refuse to appeal a police ban despite the author's wishes. Directors were often less inclined than authors to appeal a ban because they knew they had to deal with the censors on numerous future submissions. They probably knew also that officials in agencies of social control tend to be easier on those who are respectful and cooperative and deal more harshly with those who are not. Although both the Prussian Ministry of the Interior and the German Stage Association (*Deutscher Bühnenverein*) after the turn of the century pushed to give authors a larger, more direct role in the censorship and appeals process, it was the theater directors with whom the police dealt almost exclusively.[37]

In exercising their professional judgment to approve a work or not, censors were subject to various overt and covert pressures, some from outside the official bureaucracy, others from within. First, a censor could be penalized for mistakes—for example, approving a work he should not have. Although they were not fined or imprisoned for "wrong" decisions as in Russia, a few did lose their positions after their too-lax or too-stringent rulings caused embarrassing controversy. The Stettin police official who foolishly banned Emil Augier's *Les Fourchambaults* in 1878, sparking outcries from liberals and a debate in the Prussian parliament, was quickly put on "leave for an undetermined time," and soon thereafter resigned. Conversely, at the turn of the century Administrative Councilor Dumrath, new head of the Berlin theater censorship office, was removed from his position after only nine months because his decision to approve Max Dreyer's *Volksaufklärung* (*Popular Enlightenment,* which dealt with sexual and reproductive topics) aroused the wrath of the conservative press and conservative delegates condemned his decision in the Reichstag.[38]

More significantly, German censors (like those everywhere) had an incentive to find something objectionable in what they scrutinized. For once censorship becomes institutionalized and censors are assigned to identify and suppress nonconformist expressions, they develop a vested interest in the existence of such material. If the raison d'être of an undertaking depends on finding and controlling a certain deviant behavior—when its power and authority, its budget, its employees' jobs, and its continued existence is contingent upon the pursuit of this behavior—then that behavior will indeed be found, especially when the seekers themselves can define what constitutes deviance. Thus an antivice society or morality league organized for the purpose of identifying and combating obscenity, if it is to be successful (and if it is to continue receiving contributions from supportive patrons), must find obscenity—and always does.[39] The same is true for other agencies, private or public, whose function it is to identify and combat other stigmatized behavior, be it witchcraft, "un-American activity," official corruption and waste, "secular humanism" in textbooks—or supposedly dangerous, nonconformist expressions that violate established norms and must therefore be censored. And the more of this it can find the more the agency's existence is legitimatized and the easier it becomes to demonstrate its effectiveness and justify expanding its power, activities, staff, and budget. As one contemporary critic bluntly put it, "The censor must, from time to time, promulgate a ban in order to justify the existence of his office."[40] This was not mere speculation: Ludwig Sendach, a fin de siècle theater censor in neighboring Austria, confided in his memoirs that no matter how lenient and tolerant he wished to be, in his office "from time to time something 'objectionable' had to be found in the submitted works, for otherwise censorship would soon have been suspected of being *unnecessary*! [emphasis in original]" The institutionalized pressure Sendach felt to "produce" was reinforced by the internal competition and rewards of the hierarchical bureaucracy in which he served: he soon realized the more passages he red-lined and the stricter a reputation he acquired, the more trust and respect he received from his superiors.[41] In Hamburg competition between political and commercial police over control of theater performances meant the former, to justify their involvement, frequently claimed a performance violated some aspect of the Criminal Code. (In such cases, however, the police director sided with the commercial police, who found nothing objectionable in the works that political police sought to incriminate.[42])

So Germany's censors always found much to do. As the number of theaters proliferated, so too did their work. Quantitative data in this area is sketchy and incomplete, but some does exist. (See tables 2.1–2.6.) In the later 1870s, for example, Berlin theaters submitted an average of over 530 dramas annually to police for censorship. By the 1890s this number had risen to about one thousand, although nearly three-fourths of these were works that had been previously approved there, leaving an average of about 275 "new" works needing the censors' scrutiny each year. Even in Frankfurt (whose population was about one-sixth that of Berlin), prior to World War I theaters were submitting about 240 dramas to the police each year.

Table 2.1 Dramas Submitted and Banned in Berlin, 1876–1880

	Total Works Submitted	Banned	% Of Submissions Banned
1876	231	7	3.03%
1877	210	8	3.81%
1878	218	11	5.05%
1879	1284	25	1.95%
1880	719	18	2.50%
Totals	2662	69	2.59%

Source: *Verwaltungsbericht des königlichen Polizei-Präsidiums zu Berlin für die Jahre 1871–1880* (Berlin, 1881), 63.

Table 2.2 Dramas Submitted and Banned in Berlin, 1891–1900

	Total Submitted	Previously Approved	New Dramas	New Dramas Approved	% of New Dramas Approved	New Dramas Banned	% of New Dramas Banned	New Dramas Approved with Cuts	% of New Dramas Approved with Cuts
1891	419	200	219	98	44.75%	10	4.57%	111	50.68%
1892	468	232	236	106	44.92%	9	3.81%	121	51.27%
1893	577	346	231	115	49.78%	12	5.19%	104	45.02%
1894	678	470	208	100	48.08%	15	7.21%	93	44.71%
1895	1208	965	243	119	48.97%	15	6.17%	109	44.86%
1896	1105	858	247	126	51.01%	17	6.88%	104	42.11%
1897	1486	1189	297	134	45.12%	27	9.09%	136	45.79%
1898	1969	1548	421	217	51.54%	22	5.23%	182	43.23%
1899	1100	764	336	174	51.79%	11	3.27%	151	44.94%
1900	1051	757	294	193	65.65%	19	6.46%	82	27.89%
Totals	10061	7329	2732	1382	50.59%	157	5.75%	1193	43.67%

Source: *Dritter Verwaltungsbericht des Königlich. Polizeipräsidiums von Berlin für die Jahre 1891–1900* (Berlin, 1902), 373–74.

Table 2.3 New Dramas Banned in Berlin, 1900–1917

	Total Submitted	New Dramas	New Dramas Banned	% of New Dramas Banned
Jan–Sept 1900 (a)	n.a.	216	16	7.41%
1 Aug 1914 – 15 June 1917 (b)	n.a.	n.a.	152	n.a.
1916 (c)	n.a.	n.a.	65	n.a.

Sources: (a) StenBer/Pr, 25. Sitzung von 13 Feb. 1901, Bd. 442, 1510.
(b) LAB A74, Th 135, questionnaire of 19 June 1917.
(c) StenBer/Pr, 57. Sitzung am 14. Feb. 1917, 3487.

Table 2.4 Dramas Banned or Withdrawn in Berlin, 1901–1903

	Total Submitted	Banned	Approved	With-drawn	Pending
1 May 1901 – 26 Jan. 1903	723	12	630	51	29
%		1.66%	87.14%	7.05%	4.01%

Source: StenBer/Pr, 16. Sitzung, 7. Feb. 1903, Bd 459, 1024.

Table 2.5 Dramas Submitted and Banned in Frankfurt, 1909–1914

	Total Submitted	New Bans	"Re-Bans"	Total Bans	Clearly banned for moral reasons
1909		14		14	at least 5
1910		17	2	19	at least 7
1911		18	1	19	at least 2
1912		14	2	16	at least 3
1913		5	2	7	
1914		3	1	4	
date unspecified		16		16	
Totals	1429	87	8	95	
%		6.09%	0.56%	6.65%	

Source: HstA Wiesbaden, Abt. 407, Nrs. 407, 408, 409

Table 2.6 Dramas Banned in Munich, 1908–1918

	Total Banned
1908–1914	50
1914–1918	28
Total	78

(of these, 58 banned for moral reasons)

Source: Michael Meyer, *Theaterzensur in München 1900–1918,* 154

How many of these were not approved? Police banned a relatively low percentage of the dramas they reviewed, although the rate rose slowly throughout the imperial era. In Berlin in the late 1870s, 2.6 percent of all dramas submitted for censorship were forbidden. In the 1890s, when censorship was most stringent, a mere 1.56 percent of all submitted dramas were banned outright, although this represented 5.75 percent of the "new," previously unperformed and uncensored works submitted. In the years between 1900 and 1914, police in Berlin and Frankfurt proscribed between 6 and 7 percent of the new dramas submitted.

Outright bans, however, were but one form of state intervention: far more frequently, censors exercised their power by approving works on the condition that deletions or alterations be made in the script. In the 1890s, for example, Berlin police demanded expurgations in about 44 percent of the new dramas they scrutinized. After the outbreak of war, censors prohibited works far more frequently: whereas Berlin police turned down an average of about fifteen dramas per year in the late 1870s and throughout the 1890s, during the war the city's civilian or military censors banned about fifty dramas a year, and sixty-five dramas in 1916 alone. (In Munich, curiously, the war did not seem to affect the number of works banned each year, which remained steady at approximately eight.)

German censors were far more likely to ban dramas from the public stage than their English counterparts. During the forty-two-year period between 1871 and 1912, the lord chamberlain refused to license (that is, banned) only eighty stage plays in all England—approximately two per year—while approving over 16,600. (See Table 2.7) In the German Empire, by contrast, police in larger cities often banned that many plays about every five years: the Frankfurt censors refused over ninety-five works in the six-year period between 1909 and 1914, and Berlin censors banned more than ninety-five dramas in the five-year period between 1896 and 1900. In two particularly active years near the turn of the century (1897 and 1898), more works (forty-nine) were banned in Berlin alone than the English stage censor proscribed during the *two decades* between 1890 and 1910.

The rising rate of proscriptions by German stage censors suggests that as censorship offices became larger and more formally organized, the more material they inevitably found (or "created") that had to be censored, and the more likely they were to find something objectionable in the materials they monitored. In short, the more censors there were, the more they found to censor—indeed, the very presence of the censors and size of their operations more or less guaranteed an endless supply of such material. At the same time, drawing public attention to the existence of such forbidden material helped censors justify their efforts. Theater critic Fritz Mauthner speculated, for example, that Berlin police actually used the private Freie Bühne and Freie Volksbühne (which were not subject to police censorship and so performed several avant-garde Naturalist dramas police had banned from the public theaters) to generate public support for theater censorship, for these uncensored private theaters made it clear just what the police were protecting the general citizenry from.[43] (See Figure 2.1)

Censorship, like other institutions of control, thus becomes self-fulfilling and self-perpetuating; the interests of the organization create a need to identify and recruit larger numbers of potential deviants. Much as the criminal justice establishment develops a vested interest in the existence of at least some criminality, or asylums a vested interest in insanity, or hospitals a vested interest in illness, censorship too develops a vested interest in the existence of at least some expressions that endanger or subvert the society's political, social, moral, or religious norms. Once censorship is institutionalized, if such expressions did not exist, the censors would be forced to invent them.

Table 2.7 Dramas Considered, Allowed (Licensed), and Banned (Refused)
by the English Lord Chamberlain, 1871–1912

	Plays Considered	Licenses Granted	Licenses Refused
1871	268	263	5
1872	207	206	1
1873	247	247	0
1874	179	178	1
1875	213	213	0
1876	344	344	0
1877	276	272	4
1878	204	204	0
1879	272	272	0
1880	252	252	0
1881	286	286	0
1882	302	302	0
1883	288	287	1
1884	320	320	0
1885	290	288	2
1886	297	294	3
1887	307	304	3
1888	348	348	0
1889	288	287	1
1890	297	297	0
1891	245	244	1
1892	397	396	1
1893	362	362	0
1894	433	433	0
1895	378	374	4
1896	463	461	2
1897	484	481	3
1898	442	440	2
1899	470	464	6
1900	469	466	3
1901	515	513	2
1902	521	519	2
1903	541	538	3
1904	469	468	1
1905	522	520	2
1906	581	579	2
1907	540	536	4
1908	564	560	4
1909	580	577	3
1910	606	604	2
1911	614	608	6
1912 (to Oct. 31)	1076	1070	6
Total	16757	16677	80
%		99.52%	0.48%

Source: Fowell and Palmer, *Censorship in England,* 353.

Figure 2.1 Freie Bühne

(Ernst Retemeyer Drawing, *Kladderadatsch* April 1890)

Upstanding citizens must hold their nose as they hurry past the repugnant offerings of the Freie Bühne

Citizens as Censors, I: Private Moral Entrepreneurs

The police functionaries who staffed the censorship agencies were not the only ones who sought to enforce rules and norms governing artistic expression. Efforts by official censors were both reinforced and impeded by what might be termed *private censors* or unofficial "moral entrepreneurs." The concept of moral entrepreneur was suggested by sociologist Howard Becker to characterize those enterprising individuals or groups, either public or private, who take upon themselves the task of censuring or punishing certain forms of social behavior. By helping discover and point out impermissible behavior and enforcing the rules designed to control it, these self-appointed, unofficial moral entrepreneurs are no less important in guarding social norms than are the official government agents charged with rule enforcement.[44]

As happened across the US and Europe in the mid- and late nineteenth century, a vigorous morality movement arose in Germany that expressed alarm over the moral degeneration of modern society. These righteous moral reformers were especially agitated about vices rampant among the urban masses: alcoholism; prostitution; homosexuality; rising rates of venereal disease, illegitimacy and crime; the spread of pornography and morally harmful pulp fiction; and the popularity of various "indecent" or religiously offensive entertainments. Fearing such immorality represented a breakdown of the traditional moral order that threatened their nation with moral chaos, a number of crusading zealots (most notably Anthony Comstock and Josiah Leeds in the US, William Coote and W.T. Stead in Britain, and Rènè Bérenger, Jules Simon, and Frederick Passy in France) founded a plethora of private, voluntary purity alliances, vigilance associations, antivice societies, morality leagues, and other pressure groups to combat modern evils. They sought to draw public attention to the problem of immorality, mobilize public opinion against it, impose informal sanctions (such as boycotts) against establishments that produced or made available immoral materials, and pressure authorities to more stringently enforce existing laws against immorality or, where they believed these to be inadequate, to create new, sterner laws to eradicate these evils.

Censorious private moralists became increasingly active in Germany in the late 1880s. They included prominent Catholic and Protestant politicians such as Hermann Roeren, Adolf Gröber, and Adolf Henning (Roeren and Gröber were both Reichstag delegates for the Catholic Center Party, Henning for the Conservative Party); journalists and writers such as Dr. Armin Kausen (a.k.a. "Dr. Otto von Erlbach"), Otto von Leixner, Franz Weigl, and Dr. Ernst Schulze; Protestant clergymen like Abraham Böhmländer and Ludwig Weber; and other dignitaries such as Princess Elise zu Salm-Horstmar (sister of imperial Chancellor Prince Chlodwig Hohenlohe-Schillingsfürst) and the wife of Count Udo von Stolberg-Wernigerode (a prominent Conservative and Pan-German politician). These activists organized a network of first local, then national morality leagues to combat perceived moral disorder and lobby for stronger social controls and general moral reform. Local chapters of such organizations as the Men's League for the Suppression of Public Immorality (Männerverein zur Bekämpfung der öffentlichen Unsittlichkeit), the League for the Elevation of Public Morality (Verein zur Hebung der öffentlichen Sittlichkeit), the People's Association for the Suppression of Smut in Print and Pictures (Volksbund zur Bekämpfung der Schmutzes in Wort und Bild), or the Morality Commission of the German-Evangelical Women's League (Sittlichkeitskommission des Deutsch-Evangelischen Frauenbundes) sprang up in nearly all major cities and attracted hundreds of thousands of members. Many groups also published regular periodicals and occasional pamphlets that were widely distributed. After the turn of the century several such associations joined forces to form a nationwide umbrella organization, the General Conference of German Morality Leagues (Allgemeine Konferenz der deutschen Sittlichkeitsvereine), which held annual, well-publicized conferences. In the years before the war German moral crusaders also allied with like-minded reformers in other nations: a German branch of the Swiss Association Against Immoral Literature (Association suisse contre la littérature immorale) was founded and the German morality movement regularly sent delegates to the meetings of the International Congress for the Suppression of Immoral Literature.

The moral entrepreneurs most active in the German morality campaign, which focused its attention increasingly on immoral literature, art, and popular entertainments, were usually Catholic and Protestant clergymen, teachers and pedagogues, and medical professionals. Their various morality leagues enjoyed the support of the Catholic and Protestant Churches and press. While formally independent of political parties, the membership and outlook of the morality associations were also closely linked to, and their efforts often abetted by, the Catholic Center Party, the Conservative Party, and various anti-Semitic parties like the German Social Reform Party. Through their meetings and other public activities, their flood of publications, and their countless petitions to local and national governments and parliaments (during the Lex Heinze campaign of the late 1890s, for example), these lay moral reform groups frequently and prominently complained about the growing problem of public immorality and what they regarded as the state's lax or selective censorship of entertainments and publications. Besides campaigning tirelessly for stiffer laws that would criminalize more types of public immorality and make it easier for police to oversee and prohibit objectionable materials and behavior, they also reported suspected transgressors to authorities and demanded official action be taken against them.[45]

Although one might expect Germany's official censors to have welcomed the activities of these unofficial moral entrepreneurs, in fact there was much tension between the two groups. As Becker explained in his study of the sociology of deviance, crusading moral reformers ("rule-creators") are typically driven by a moral fervor and righteous wrath that stands in sharp contrast to the generally detached, pragmatic, and professional approach of official "rule-enforcers." Self-righteous moral crusaders are dissatisfied with existing laws and want tougher ones to correct existing evils. Applying an absolutistic ethic, they are concerned primarily with ends, not means, and have little interest in legalistic details. By contrast, official agencies charged with enforcing the laws are staffed not by righteous moral crusaders but by trained bureaucrats who take a more disinterested, objective view of their function. Enforcement officials have little stake or interest in the actual content of the law or the abstract ends behind it; rather, their primary concern is how that law is to be applied in particular cases—the concrete details of its enforcement. Working with limited time and resources and realizing they cannot deal with everything at once, professional enforcement agents by necessity must adopt a pragmatic, discretionary, long-term approach that involves constant choices and priorities. They naturally choose to deal with what they consider the worst, most blatant violators first, overlooking or deferring lesser infractions. Decisions by officials about what and when to punish often have less to do with the deviant behavior itself than with other factors, such as where the offense ranks on that official's particular list of priorities, whether they feel a need at that particular time to justify their existence and demonstrate to external constituents they are doing their job, or whether the offender shows proper respect for and cooperation with the enforcement agents and their routines. This selective, pragmatic, routine approach to rule (law) enforcement naturally infuriates private moral entrepreneurs, who want the rules and laws to be used to stop all the evil all at once. Out of righteous indignation moral crusaders frequently denounce professional enforcement agents for taking the evil in question too lightly and for failing to "do their duty"—as when the Catholic champions of the Lex Heinze bill in 1898–1900 complained about the laxity of "hardened police officials." The result is often renewed calls by private moral reformers for additional laws and stricter enforcement. Imperial Germany's official censors thus had continually to contend with and react to pressure from unofficial moral censurers.

On one level the work of private morality leagues certainly reinforced that of the government censors. By defining, identifying, describing, and dramatizing the problem of immoral literature, art, and entertainments, crusading moralists helped justify the need for state censorship. Throughout this period the authorities, wide segments of the general populace, and even some within the intellectual-artistic community became increasingly convinced that a serious problem existed that could be solved only by enforcing certain limits on literary expression, and that the existence and work of police censors was necessary. Moreover, private moral crusaders could sometimes work closely with official censors and even enter their ranks, as the case of Dr. Karl Brunner illustrates. Brunner, a secondary-school history teacher and part-time university lecturer in Baden at the turn of the century, made a national name for himself in the crusade to stamp out smutty pulp fiction and sensationalistic penny novels (*Schmutz- und Schundliteratur*); he eventually became a full-time leader within the movement and, beginning in 1910, served as editor of the periodical *Die Hochwart* (*The High Guardian*). After Berlin police created a Central Police Office for the Suppression of Obscene Materials (Zentralpolizeistelle zur Bekämpfung unzüchtiger Schriften, Abbildungen, und Darstellungen) in 1911 to supervise national efforts against pornography, Brunner assisted it as a (unpaid) "literary advisor" and translator. Because of his expertise in the area of sensationalistic mass entertainments, he soon began advising the Berlin theater and film censors as well. By 1913 the Berlin police president found Brunner's contributions so indispensable he was appointed to a full-time, permanent position on the police force as an administrative councilor in Abtheilung VIII, which handled theater and film censorship, the control of pornography, and the colportage trade. During the war, when several of his colleagues were called to military service, Brunner rose to an important position of leadership within the Berlin police's censorship division; he remained a prominent literary and film censor in the capital until the early 1920s.[46]

Brunner's successful transition from private moral crusader to official rule enforcer was unusual, however. More often relations between unofficial censurers and the state censors were strained, even antagonistic. Like most governmental authorities, officials responsible for censorship jealously guarded their professional, bureaucratic independence and resisted external efforts to meddle in their area of responsibility. While the imperial, state, and local governments sought to maintain a polite distance from the private moral crusaders and pressure groups and resisted their attempts to shape censorship polices and laws, authorities could not afford simply to ignore them. When criticized for laxity or dereliction of duty by private moral entrepreneurs or by the churches, political parties, and conservative press, local police and the state interior ministers naturally responded by justifying official policies and activities. As complaints by conservatives and moral cru-saders over the government's alleged laxness in suppressing immoral materials and entertainments became increasingly frequent and strident after 1890, local and state censorship authorities began publishing more frequent official reports, issu-ing press releases, or testifying to parliament about their work and effectiveness. Censors lamented the alarming rise of indecent materials, pointed to the competi-tive commercial reasons for it, and cited the (steadily increasing) number of publica-tions they had recently confiscated and the number of dramas they had banned. By doing so they sought to demonstrate—to their superiors, to the morality move-ment, and to the public—they were, indeed, aware of the problem, deeply con-cerned about it, and dealing adequately with it. The censors' public relations cam-paign was sometimes directed even at carping individual moral reformers who, authorities felt, were simply misguided eccentrics. In October 1914, for example, Countess Udo zu Stolberg-Wernigerode and Countess von Schwering-Löwitz, two elderly but influential women from the German-Evangelical Women's League, com-plained to Berlin police about immoral plays being performed in three theaters and about how the theater in general had become merely "a breeding ground of crudeness, frivolity, and cynicism." The police president, mindful of their prestige and influence, arranged for the two countesses to attend the theaters in question, accompanied by a retinue of officials that included the chief of the theater censor-ship division, his first assistant, the intendant of the Prussian royal theaters, and (because of the wartime state of siege) the two highest military authorities in the Berlin military district. As the police president later superciliously reported the ex-perience to the minister of the interior, it turned out neither grand dame had ac-tually seen the particular plays they had complained about; at the theater one of the women, who was half deaf, had great difficulty actually following the action on stage, and when the performances were over both were forced to agree there was nothing objectionable in what they had seen. Upon further discussion with them the police president discovered neither of these self-appointed critics had attended the theater in several years and they harbored many misconceptions about it.[47]

Nothing better illustrates the conflicting mindsets and opposing roles of the unofficial moral reformer and the official police censor than the complete trans-formation of Karl Brunner from the former to the latter. Before entering police service in 1911 Brunner had crusaded ardently for stricter state controls over sen-sationalistic pulp fiction; seven years later, having risen to a high position within the Berlin police force from which he supervised state censorship of various popular entertainments, he now urged the government to resist the "chicaner-ies of irresponsible complainers and fanatics … [both anticensorship] aesthetes and [repressive] morality campaigners, who are intractable to the considerations and requirements of [we] level-headed, responsible officials who seek simply to observe the law." Although Brunner and other officials had initially used special wartime powers to restrict the circulation of popular reading material,[48] by Octo-ber 1918 he had come to realize that escapist pulp fiction satisfied important and legitimate needs of the modestly educated lower social strata. Warning against the "sometimes fanatically exaggerated demands" of certain righteous reformers who hoped to ban any trashy popular fiction they personally disliked, Brunner counseled tolerance and argued the broad populace was entitled to books, light theatrical pieces, films, and other entertainments that had little higher artistic value. "It cannot and must not be the primary aim of the authorities," he wrote,

> to wield their power in these questions of popular culture and popular taste except to insure that such popular offerings don't violate the interests of public order and morality. ... Even under the [wartime] state of siege, state authorities have neither the right nor even the interest in interfering in the inner questions of personal life—in this case, the question of what a man of the people reads, how he tries to satisfy his need for amusement and diversion, provided public order is not violated.

Brunner feared that if extremists pressured the government into overstepping traditional legal boundaries to suppress harmful popular entertainments, then the delicate balance between freedom and censorship the government had hitherto sought to maintain would be upset, and another bitter, polarizing dispute would be unleashed like that over the ill-fated Lex Heinze at the turn of the century. For the sake of public harmony and order, Brunner urged the government to turn a deaf ear to the moral crusaders so as to avoid provoking any new battles over freedom of expression.[49]

While some complaints and demands from crusading moralists could be refuted or easily deflected by official censors, many others could not. Once private moral entrepreneurs publicly "blew the whistle" on a rule violation and brought it to the attention of the official rule enforcers, the transgression could not be ignored. Because of the widely publicized nature of many of the morality movement's exhortations and because of the broader public accountability of the formal agencies of control, German authorities often felt compelled to intervene against a work or prosecute an author for an offense they would otherwise have preferred to overlook. This was especially true in Munich, where the morality movement was strong and the insecure moderate government sought to steer a delicate course between liberals and the Catholic Center party. It was also true in Hamburg, where despite (or because of) the absence of prior censorship, complaints in the conservative press sometimes forced police to take steps against specific performances, only to have those actions annulled by the city government or courts.[50] During the war, public protests often persuaded military commanders to rescind approvals recently granted by civilian censors (see chapter 6). On occasion, complaints from conservative moral reformers about the laxity of official censors might even cost a censor his position. Thus in 1901, shortly after the bitter controversy surrounding the Lex Heinze, vehement criticism in the conservative press of his tolerant policies probably played a role in the decision to remove Administrative Councilor Dumrath as chief of the Berlin theater censorship office. Regardless of how independent and insulated official censors sought to remain from unofficial morality crusaders, the existence and agitation of the latter inevitably influenced the work of the former.

Citizens as Censors, II: Censorship Advisory Boards

As censorship duties passed from the hands of (relatively) educated and humanistically trained civilians to (relatively) uneducated police bureaucrats unfamiliar with the literary arts, observers frequently complained about their incompetence and urged police to consult civilian literary experts before making important censorship decisions. Such experts, it was hoped, would mediate between growing conservative demands for police interference in literary life on the one hand and liberal demands for free artistic expression on the other.

Such a system existed in Austria, where in 1850 an advisory board (*Beirat*) of literary experts was established to advise theater censors. It fell into disuse in the 1870s and was abolished in 1881, but in 1903 the practice of obtaining external literary advice was reinstituted for Vienna. The Austrian interior minister degreed that officials assigned to theater censorship in the capital must be fully qualified and have some literary knowledge ("literarisch gebildet sein"); if they had reservations about the admissibility of a piece they were to submit it to a standing three-member advisory board consisting of one administrative and one judicial official with literary knowledge, and one layman experienced in the dramatic arts (for example, a playwright, theater critic, or theater director). Those experts each wrote an opinion about whether the work should be performed and under what conditions; they could also be called together for an oral discussion of the case. In an attempt to reform (and salvage) its system of stage censorship, in 1909 England also established an Advisory Board of five prominent citizens to advise the lord chamberlain on censorship issues, but it appears never to have been very active or influential.[51]

In the late 1870s a growing number of Germans, upset over controversial censorship decisions in Berlin or embarrassing gaffes by provincial officials, recommended German police also seek the advice of literary experts in problematic cases or when judging a work that may have artistic merit. Throughout the 1880s and 1890s liberal parliamentarians, dramatists, literary journalists, defense lawyers, and theater directors urged authorities to create an Austrian-style advisory board of civilian literary experts, or create new cultural bodies (such as an Imperial Office for Literature, Theater, Scholarship, and Art; a Ministry of Fine Arts; or an Academy of Writers) to handle all censorship duties as France had done. Proponents of such agencies, which were to be staffed by writers, artists, and state officials possessing some literary or artistic training, believed they would also help centralize and standardize censorship by issuing rulings that would be valid nationwide.[52] As one famous 1888 literary manifesto stated, bureaucratic police censors took things too literally and grasped only the words, missing the larger meaning of the work: "The general spirit of the work is what is decisive in art and only an artistically trained man is capable of judging that, not a bureaucrat. ... Only the spirit of a work of art should determine its admissibility, and only men schooled in literary matters are capable of discerning this."[53] The interior minister routinely rejected suggestions to consult literary experts, however, because it would be too time-consuming and likely to create endless disagreements.

There were indeed many potential problems with the concept of literary advisors. Consulting them on some occasions, for example, would be an implicit admission police lacked the competence to decide certain cases, and by implication, perhaps all cases. Moreover, imperial authorities continually insisted a decision to ban a work from the public stage had little to do with its literary merit but rather depended on its probable effect upon public order and security—something police, not literary experts, were best qualified to assess. Nor would involving external advisors in the censorship process necessarily be advantageous for writers and the theater industry. For if the experts' opinions were only advisory and police retained final authority, then little would actually change; but if the nongovernmental experts' decisions were binding and they agreed to ban a work, could that ban then be appealed to an administrative court? If no appeal were possible, the victims of censorship would now be robbed of any legal avenue of recourse; yet if legal appeal were possible, nonliterary jurists would be extremely unlikely to overturn a ban that had been sanctioned by a board of literary experts, thus making all such appeals pointless. Finally, it might be difficult to find members from the literary community who were both willing and temperamentally fit to serve on a board that would be passing judgment on their peers. Followers of a particular stylistic school, or someone with a professional or personal axe to grind could easily misuse their authority, while the very nature of that kind of authority would repel others from serving at all. As one Reichstag delegate succinctly observed: "What writer would ever be a party to serving as chief executioner vis á vis his rivals, and if one ever found someone who was of sufficient rank and reputation, what police president would bow to his [wishes]?"[54] Subsequent developments demonstrated these concerns were well founded.

Despite the potential problems, calls for the establishment of literary advisory boards continued until, at the turn of the century, some governing authorities seemed willing to consider it. In late 1899 a newly appointed conservative Prussian interior minister, Georg Freiherr von Rheinbaden, assumed office. Although determined to institute much stricter censorship over the theater, especially in Berlin, he admitted that besides issues of public order, security, and morality, censors should consider a work's literary merit. Since police officials usually lacked the knowledge and qualifications to do this, however, Rheinbaden urged them to consult appropriate literary experts before banning a work whose "basic tendency seems questionable or its artistic merit doubtful." He suggested Berlin police appoint a special consultant, perhaps a professor, to advise them on difficult cases.[55]

Berlin's police president adamantly opposed the idea, which he found not only unnecessary and impractical, but also eminently unwise. Literary experts, he argued, judge a work only from a narrow artistic perspective; they are not in a position to decide if and when other considerations, such as legal regulations or unique local situations, should override literary ones. Although police censors may lack formal literary training they are, he pointed out, well-educated ("wissenschaftlich gebildet") and almost always do take literary merit into consideration; when they ban a piece it is because they are convinced other factors outweigh its artistic value. Consulting civilian experts would prove unworkable: Were experts to advise police on every case, or only on "doubtful" ones? Who determines what is doubtful? Were advisers to advise only on theatrical performances, or on other media, such as the press or the cinema, as well? If so, regular police work would soon grind to a halt. Finally, the police president warned that, far from ending controversy, involving literary experts would surely lead to still greater discord. For once an "official" advisor or advisory board was created, various interest groups and factions within the literary, legal, and educational community would all demand representation. He also astutely observed that, given the then current bitter debate within the artistic community over modernism, even literary experts could not agree on what constitutes artistic merit. Avant-garde modernists and conservative, antimodern traditionalists disagreed vehemently on issues of immorality, good vs. bad art, and the like; any "expert" pronouncement on such matters is, by its very nature, highly personal and subjective and would hardly be accepted by those in the opposing camp. And when, for legal or technical reasons, police sometimes found it necessary to ban a work experts judged to be of artistic value, they would be subject to even more bitter public condemnation than if no experts had been consulted. For these reasons the interior minister's idea simply invited trouble. (For good measure, the police president also pointed out two possible academic experts the interior minister had suggested were too leftist or Jewish to be acceptable to him, while the third, a historian, lacked sufficient literary experience.)[56] After weakly defending the concept of literary experts and suggesting several alternative candidates (whose backgrounds and political affiliations the police president promptly investigated and each of whom he found less than satisfactory), the interior minister let the matter drop.[57]

Still, Rheinbaden did not abandon the idea. When a delegation from the theater industry visited him the following year with yet another request to establish a board of expert advisors he indicated he was perfectly willing to consult experts and asked them to suggest names. They returned later and, with some chagrin, informed him that despite their best efforts they could not find any professional literary experts willing to undertake such a task.[58]

Although none of these discussions resulted in a permanent advisory board, about this time both the Berlin police and the Prussian Ministry of the Interior began consulting individual experts on an ad hoc basis. The monarch's permission was needed to perform any drama dealing with his Hohenzollern forebears (see chapter 3); before making their recommendation to the emperor, these two agencies occasionally consulted external experts regarding the work's artistic merits.

The only German city to establish a formal literary advisory board for theater censorship was Munich. In 1902 a former police theater censor there suggested literary experts might occasionally be consulted as to the purely literary value of a questionable work, although he opposed the idea of establishing a commission of experts to handle censorship. In June 1906 Bavarian liberals, angered over a recent ban of Frank Wedekind's drama *Tod und Teufel,* attacked theater censorship in the state parliament and suggested a panel of experts be created to formulate general guidelines and advise the censor on appropriate cases. A year later, after yet another controversy over the Munich police's refusal to allow a public production of Wedekind's controversial *Frühlings Erwachen,* Munich Police Director von der Heydte began exploring ways to improve the censorship process and the public's attitudes toward it and received permission from the Bavarian minister of the interior to investigate the possibility of establishing a board of experts. Von der Heydte recognized the advantages of drawing upon civilian experts regarding artistic decisions, for prior to becoming police director he had served for seven years in the artistic division of the Ministry of Education, where he worked closely with an advisory board of artists and art connoisseurs that advised the government on art purchases and on an international art exhibit held in Munich in 1905.[59] After inquiries to Berlin and Vienna about their experiences in this area, in February 1908 the interior minister approved the Munich police director's detailed plan for a five-person standing Censorship Advisory Board (*Zensurbeirat*). It was to consist of distinguished civilian advisers who, "by the high level of their general education and/or their recognized expertise, can be relied on to give an objective, authoritative opinion" whenever the Munich theater censor or police elsewhere in Bavaria had reservations about approving a drama for public performance. The board's opinions would be advisory only; the final decision would still be made by police, whose ultimate concern had to be the work's likely effect on public order and morality, regardless of its literary merit. The Munich police director was aware of the risk involved: once such a board was established it would be difficult consistently to ignore its advice. On the other hand, he hoped relying on a board of prominent experts would lend credibility to police decisions, make them appear less arbitrary, and generate more public support for them. A decision backed by the authority of the board would be "in political terms a kind of absolution vis-à-vis the public, and would be seen as a welcome easing of the administration's responsibility towards the outside world."[60]

Advisory board members would have to meet exacting criteria. The police director wanted to include respected artists, writers, and people from the theater industry, but also prestigious experts from medicine and from elementary, secondary, and higher education. At the same time he wanted men who accepted the need for theater censorship, held views about art that would not be irreconcilable with those of the police, were not prominently involved in politics, and would be willing to endure the scorn and criticism their actions and decisions would inevitably arouse in the press. "Without overlooking the modernists, we must consider men of a conservative orientation whose entire previous activity and careers will guarantee that censorship will not be diverted from its legitimate function as a positive, state-supporting, national, and monarchist institution."[61]

A list of twenty-five prestigious experts was complied and invited to serve on the board; only one declined. The group included four writers (Dr. Max Halbe, Wilhelm Weigand, Karl Freiherr von Gleichen-Russwurm, and Josef Ruederer); two artists (Anton Stadler and Adolf Ritter von Hildebrand); four physicians or professors of medicine; four theater directors or actors; six university academics (representing literature, philology, history, and science); three Gymnasium teachers or rectors; and one librarian. All were male, with an average age about fifty; the group was evenly balanced between Protestants and Catholics (no Jews were included); all were well-educated, established, and prominent men of the Munich community; and their politics ranged from the staunchly conservative (two were members of a local morality league) to the moderately liberal. To give the board credibility with the intellectual community and liberal press, it included some mildly avant-garde dramatists and artists but no one known as a resolute modernist. With only a few personnel changes for resignations and deaths, this same blue-ribbon collegium of experts served for ten years until theater censorship was abolished in 1918.[62]

At its first meeting in late March 1908 the police director explained that in examining a work, they were to assess its artistic merit and ethical standpoint, while the police would consider any nonartistic (for example, political) dimensions. If members had concerns about how a text would be performed or interpreted on stage, they could attend a dress rehearsal before making a final recommendation. Several members suggested it might be desirable to recommend that some works be performed only before exclusively male or female audiences, although it was agreed this might create enormous logistic and financial difficulties for theaters. The police director closed by reiterating the merely advisory function of the Censorship Advisory Board: under current law, final authority had to rest with the police. However, he hoped the board, by sharing some responsibility for censorship, would reduce public pressure on the police; at the same time he believed the respect board members enjoyed in the community would help create wider public acceptance for theater censorship.[63]

To distribute the (unpaid) work evenly, the board was divided into four six-man commissions. Each new work submitted to police for censorship would be sent to a commission; the six members were each to write a brief opinion and make a recommendation about its acceptability for public performance. Particularly difficult cases might be considered by more than one commission or discussed at a general meeting of the entire board. Soliciting the opinions of advisory board members significantly prolonged the censorship process, however: instead of police reaching a decision on a work within a few days, routine cases could now take a month or two, and difficult ones sometimes took several months.

Public reaction to the creation of the Munich Censorship Advisory Board was mixed. The Left, both in Munich and Berlin, was skeptical. While acknowledging the board as a minor step forward, the Social Democratic press pointed out it lacked real decision-making authority and feared it would be a palliative that, by making theater censorship a little more palatable, would simply help preserve an institution that should be abolished. The liberal press was generally more enthusiastic and hopeful the board would moderate police interference in art and reduce the number of embarrassing missteps by police censors. Not surprisingly, Munich conservatives and clericals were suspicious of the board. The city's leading morality league, the Men's League for the Suppression of Public Immorality, had traditionally opposed involving *any* effete aesthetic "experts" in censorship cases and advocated relying instead on the "healthy moral sense of the [broad] populace." Others on the Right complained, both in the Munich press and Bavarian parliament, that board members were all moderates and liberals who, because they did not truly represent the views of Bavaria's Catholic citizens, would contribute to a further decline of public moral standards.[64] Munich theater directors, on the other hand, clearly hoped the board would be more liberal than the police, and in the first few months of its operation they resubmitted many works police censors had previously refused to approve. The police director was so pleased with the board's work that in subsequent years he and the state prosecutor also consulted it on other selected obscenity cases (for example, whether to confiscate certain novels or postcards under §184, or whether certain crime novels should be banned from sale in railway stations). In hopes of instituting a more uniform theater censorship throughout Bavaria, the police director also tried to persuade police in other cities to adopt the Munich board's recommendations on each drama; his provincial colleagues, however, generally ignored Munich's advice and continued to make their own decisions locally.[65]

Although complete data are lacking, it is clear Munich police did not consult the Censorship Advisory Board on every drama submitted for censorship and in the board's later years consulted it less and less often (see Table 2.8). Of the more

Table 2.8 The Work of the Munich Censorship Advisory Board (*Zensurbeirat*)

	Referred to the Zensurbeirat	Majority on Beirat favor a ban	Majority on Beirat favor allowing	Other, or no decision	Police decide to ban	Police decide to allow	Police allow with cuts	With-drawn or no decision
1908	13	6	5	2	6	7		
1909	5	1		4	1	1	2	1
1910	12	6		6	6	6		
1911	18	7	3	8	10	5		2
1912	17	1	2	14	3	4	2	
1913	12	1		11	1			7
1914	10			10	1			7
1915	1			1	1			
1916	8			8	2	3		3
1917	3			3	1	1		
1918	6			6	1	1		3
Total	105	22	10	73	33	28	4	23
%		20.95%	9.52%	69.52%	31.43%	26.67%	3.81%	21.90%

Source: Compiled from Michael Meyer, *Theaterzensur in München 1900–1918*, 322–337.

than one hundred difficult or "borderline" cases referred to the board between 1908 and 1918, about a third resulted in a more or less clear recommendation to police: a majority of board members favored allowing ten of the dramas in question, while in another twenty-two instances a majority favored banning the work or affirmed an earlier police ban. The Munich police always followed a board recommendation to ban, but they also banned many works the board had favored permitting: between 1908 and 1918 police approved outright twenty-eight works that had been considered by the board and they allowed another four works only with alterations; thirty-three works, however, were banned.[66] In any case the existence of the Censorship Advisory Board did not significantly reduce the number of theater bans issued by the Munich police. For one thing, the majority of these civilian literary experts were hardly champions of unlimited artistic freedom: they were about twice as likely to recommend a work be prohibited from public performance as to recommend it be permitted. And for another, police felt increasingly free to ignore the board's advice whenever it did recommend a work be allowed.

Berlin police took an interest in Munich's experiment with a civilian advisory board and asked for further information about it. They did so again in 1912 after the German Writers' Defense League (Schutzverband deutscher Schriftsteller), angered over several recent confiscations and bans in Berlin, demanded once again that Berlin create a board of literary experts to advise censors. However, because he was convinced censorship was essentially a legal rather than artistic decision and because he feared endless conflicts with civilian advisors over what posed a threat to public order, the Berlin police president decided not to follow Munich's (and Vienna's) example. Instead he hired for his theater censorship office the morality campaigner Karl Brunner, who was familiar with the literary and theatrical world.

In May 1908, shortly after Munich's Censorship Advisory Board was established, one of Germany's leading liberal newspapers commented: "We are anxious to see how long the complicated organism just created in Munich can hold together. There are posts which, if they must be filled, are tolerable only for a bureaucratic official but not for free men, and in which only an official will not have it held against him."[67] As some of Munich's leading writers—including the respected Max Halbe and Thomas Mann—soon learned, this was a prescient warning. For by the eve of the war, writers who agreed to serve on the board to mediate between art and the state found themselves in a most difficult position: distrusted and often ignored by the police, they were also scorned and attacked by many of their literary colleagues.

Service on the Censorship Advisory Board became a divisive issue within the Munich literary community in 1911 when Frank Wedekind, furious that during its first three years of operation the board had four times recommended banning various of his dramas from public performance (see chapter 6), launched a vehement public campaign against the board and the police to whom it reported. Convinced that board members were unable to comprehend and unqualified to judge his work, and incensed that members of the artistic community would collaborate with the state in persecuting another artist, Wedekind published several satirical and expository attacks on it. In these he criticized the board's lack of real authority vis-à-vis the police and these supposed experts' superficial, subjective, and sometimes contradictory evaluations of his works; he also denounced the scandalous behavior of "honorable gentlemen" who participated in the board's "tomfoolery" and thereby "helped German literature weave its own noose."[68]

Wedekind's criticisms, reinforced by a widely publicized April 1911 petition on his behalf signed by nearly forty leading writers, artists, musicians, and theater directors, eventually persuaded Max Halbe, the most prestigious playwright on the board, to resign. Halbe, a friend of Wedekind's and a signer of the April petition protesting the bans of his work, had consistently voted to pass every work submitted to him by the police. Frustrated that police regularly overruled his and other board members' recommendations and uncomfortable with the growing public criticism directed at the board, in early December 1911 Halbe informed the Munich police director (who, after 1909, bore the title of police president) that "in light of intensified differences of principle, my continued cooperation with [the Censorship Advisory Board] no longer seems advisable."[69] Halbe's resignation letter was reprinted widely in the German press and several liberal papers suggested other liberals on the board, such as the playwright Joseph Ruederer, should also resign in protest over the way it was being used by police as a "cover" for antiartistic policies. One Berlin daily declared, "It would be a welcome development if the entire Censorship Advisory Board were dissolved so that the police would be left to bear sole responsibility for all the inexplicable bans recently imposed."[70]

Although displeased with many "stupid things" the Munich police had done, Ruederer and other liberals on the board were persuaded that, for the time being, their presence was necessary to prevent the group from falling completely under conservative and clerical influence, which was on the dramatic rise in Bavaria during the winter of 1911–1912. (Because of pressure from the Right, the government of the conservative liberal Prime Minister Podewils collapsed and in early February 1912 was replaced by a far more conservative government headed by Georg von Hertling, head of the Catholic Center Party.) At a meeting hastily called by the Munich police president to discuss Halbe's resignation and the future of the board, the remaining members reaffirmed the board's importance and assured the police president they had no desire to follow Halbe's example. As Halbe's replacement on the board, Ruederer suggested the respected but generally apolitical writer Thomas Mann.[71]

To increase public pressure on the board, in late December Wedekind sent each member seven questions he claimed were "occasioned by the abusive, inhuman treatment I have had to put up with for the past three years from the Munich Censorship Advisory Board and which, according to statements by the police president, is a result of judgments the board has made about my literary work." These polemical, sarcastic questions, which Wedekind simultaneously published in several leading German newspapers, demanded to know what qualified them, and not him, to serve on the board, what right one colleague had to judge another in secret session, and why a writer who is judged by the board had no opportunity to defend himself. "What basic difference is there between the secret proceedings of an Inquisition and those of the Munich Censorship Advisory Board?" Wedekind asked. Although some board members suggested they compose a collective response to the provocative questions, the police president persuaded them any reply would simply incite Wedekind to further attacks, and it was best simply to ignore the questionnaire.[72]

Receiving no satisfaction from board members, in February 1912 Wedekind published a satirical poem ridiculing a recent censorship ruling by Police President von der Heydte, whom he accused of turning the "art city" Munich into a national laughing stock. The following month he published an essay in the Berlin press ("Torquemada. Zur Psychologie der Zensur") again comparing censorship of his and other author's works to the Inquisition and denouncing Germany's "fanatical muzzling of dramatic literature." Wedekind's latest salvo immediately prompted further reports in the liberal press about the "scandal" of the Munich Censorship Advisory Board and the resignation of "several" of its members.[73]

To counter the rising tide of negative publicity about the board and correct misinformation being spread about it (only one member, Halbe, had actually resigned), in late March the Munich police issued an eight-page press release patiently explaining the need for preventive theater censorship; the police's ultimate legal responsibility in this area; the fact that police officials, because of their general educational background, were quite competent to judge literary matters; the reasons why police censors nevertheless voluntarily seek the advice of literary experts on certain censorship issues; how board members were originally chosen and how it normally operated; and why board recommendations, although immensely helpful to the police, could not and should not be more than advisory. This official defense of the board ended by listing all twenty-four current members, including the newly appointed Thomas Mann.[74]

Such proclamations did little to pacify critics, however. In July, for example, Ernst Müller-Meiningen, one of Bavaria's leading liberal politicians, complained in the state parliament that Munich censors were "hunting [Wedekind] down like a wild animal" and he reproached the board and police for never informing the playwright of the reasons any of his works were banned. Müller-Meiningen also attacked the legal status and procedures of the Censorship Advisory Board, which, he demanded, must be transformed into a genuine "literary court" with open, trial-like hearings similar to those of the administrative courts: authors must have the opportunity to testify in their own behalf, there must be direct examination and cross-examination of the "accusers" and the "defendant," the board must issue public, written verdicts detailing the specific reasons for its decisions, and those decisions must be legally binding upon the police. Until this is done, he warned, the board would remain a worthless and irrelevant institution whose recommendations are consistently ignored by arbitrary police bureaucrats.[75]

Thomas Mann, who in mid-March agreed to join the board as Halbe's replacement and whose reputation, it was hoped, would restore some of its credibility, was no supporter of censorship. A few years earlier he had condemned preventive theater censorship as a "despicable tutelage of the public in matters of taste." For Mann, "censorship is a force that inhibits culture, for it substitutes suppression, a crude ban, for the education the public really needs. Only art itself, in combination with free and serious criticism, is qualified to educate the public, not the state."[76] Mann, a member of the executive committee of the Munich chapter of the German Writers' Defense League, also signed the April 1911 petition protesting the Munich police bans of Wedekind's dramas. Although before the creation of the advisory board he had proclaimed, "any compromise [between art and the state], such as the union of playwrights and officials in a censorship collegium, would be disgraceful," to the surprise of many he now agreed to join it because he was convinced he could mediate between artists and the police: "I consider it my task as a member of the board to warn the overseers of public order against interfering with works of literary status. Since we do have these censorship authorities, I value this opportunity of letting them know my opinion from case to case."[77]

Although Mann intended to use his board position to defend Wedekind's (and others') artistic freedom, Wedekind and his supporters nevertheless viewed Mann's collaboration with the authorities as an act of artistic betrayal. In February 1913, for example, the modernist playwright and anarchist journalist Erich Mühsam published a scathing article denouncing the Munich police president and his "literary lackeys," the Censorship Advisory Board. Singling out Mann and the other three writers on the board by name, Mühsam (who, like Halbe and Mann, was also a member of the local chapter of the German Writers' Defense League) accused them of helping police persecute their fellow authors and demanded they follow Halbe's example and resign.[78]

The mounting pressures on Mann finally made his position untenable in late April 1913, when the board recommended banning Wedekind's *Lulu*. (See chapter 6.) Although Mann and four other board members had voted to allow public performances of the drama in Munich, sixteen favored banning it, as did the police president.[79] The police agreed, however, to allow two private performances for invited guests, provided the theater observed all the conditions governing such closed performances, one of which was that they must not be publicly advertised. When notices appeared in the Munich press in late May announcing the two private performances, police threatened to prohibit the performances if there were any further publicity.

At this point the Munich chapter of the German Writers' Defense League, which previously had consistently supported the concept of civilian literary experts advising the censors, joined the controversy on Wedekind's behalf. At a meeting on 20 May it passed a resolution protesting the public ban of *Lulu;* the resolution, published widely in the Munich press the following day, declared: "The membership unanimously regards the work of Wedekind as one of the most outstanding monuments of modernist literature and the authorities' bans on their public performance as a regrettable blunder. The membership authorizes the executive committee to champion Frank Wedekind's interests in every regard."[80]

A deputation from the Writers' Defense League then visited the Munich police offices to discuss the *Lulu* ban with Dr. Roth, head of the censorship bureau, but after a long wait learned Roth could not meet with them because he was out of town. Angered over this perceived slight and alarmed to learn police were threatening to prohibit the two scheduled private performances of *Lulu* as well, the Defense League leadership published additional protests in the local press about heavy-handed police attempts to suppress the drama. They also scheduled another general Defense League meeting to discuss whether writers should serve on the Censorship Advisory Board. This put Thomas Mann in an intolerable situation: as a member of both the Censorship Advisory Board and the Defense League's executive committee, he would certainly be criticized at the meeting. On the eve of the Defense League meeting, therefore, Mann informed the Munich police president he was resigning from the board "because of collegial considerations"; at the same time, however, he testily informed Kurt Martens, chairman of the local Defense League, that he objected to the meeting to discuss his (Mann's) situation and that he was resigning from the Defense League as well. "I joined [the Censorship Advisory Board] as well as [the German Writers' Defense League]," Mann explained, to be socially and professionally active:

> But one is not thanked for that sort of thing, and the conduct of the league disturbs me. … As long as I belonged to the Censorship Advisory Board and the executive committee of the league simultaneously, as long as I thought it possible to hold both these positions, it was gross tactlessness on the part of the league to place on the agenda discussions and *resolutions* on the relationship of the league and the Censorship Advisory Board—assuming that the league even took notice of my presence on its executive committee. But that seems not to have been the case—to judge from the high-handedness with which the honorable membership meeting [of 20 May] passed over me with a "unanimous resolution." I would have been ready to back any action in favor of Wedekind's tragedy, but that did not suffice; my membership on the Censorship Advisory Board had to be elevated into "the most important question facing writers today." That is the limit. I will not have the Mühsams … or whoever the radical loudmouths are, telling me what I am to do or not do. I have had my fill of the German Writers' Defense League. … So let there be an end of my social activity and the petty fiction of solidarity among writers. … I am of course resigning from the Censorship Advisory Board because I do not wish to be exposed to the amiable imputation that I took the side of the police against freedom, collegial fellowship, and matters of the spirit. After all, I feel most comfortable affiliated with no organization and unburdened by any official position.[81]

The next day the general meeting of the Defense League passed a resolution protesting the police's bans and threats regarding *Lulu* and condemning the literary experts on the Censorship Advisory Board: "In light of recent experiences with the Censorship Advisory Board," the members agreed, "serving on the Munich Censorship Advisory Board is no longer compatible with the honor of a German writer." Cooperation with state censorship authorities, the league declared, undermines public respect for free creative writers; moreover, the board's secret deliberations and recommendations permit its "literary personalities" to camouflage their genuine, often nonartistic goals. This proclamation was widely reprinted in the Munich press, accompanied by an article by league chairman Kurt Martens attacking the police and board as "front men" for the reactionary Center Party and warning modern dramatists that they now had to defend themselves not only against petty police bureaucrats, but also against the antimodernist literary "dignitaries" who had been summoned to assist police.[82]

Thomas Mann, clearly the primary target of these Writers' Defense League attacks, chose not to respond publicly. But privately he felt both unjustly maligned and deeply saddened over the way the controversy was poisoning his relations with his fellow writers. As soon as the league's declaration appeared in the press, Mann wrote board member Joseph Ruederer and other colleagues to point out that he (Mann) had resigned not only from the board, but also from the German Writers' Defense League and that he "wishes to distance himself as much as possible from the league's condemnation of the Censorship Advisory Board that was published today." That same day, in a conciliatory letter to Wedekind, Mann lamented the "vexations" of the past few weeks and explained that:

> if a bourgeois element in my work … inspired the bourgeois authorities with a crude confidence in me, why should I not have utilized this confidence to mediate politically between genius and authority? This mode of making myself publicly useful amused me, and I imagined that now and then I could claim a victory. … No matter. Since my resigning as an "arm of the police" has reinstated me in your good will, I am delighted to have resigned. The suppression of your greatest work was in any case a prime reason for resigning. Aside from the odium of this particular public office, I feel most comfortable entirely without any official position whatever.[83]

Although Wedekind and Martens both wanted to continue the Defense League's fight against the Censorship Advisory Board, and although the league's national office publicized Mann's resignation from the board (without, however, mentioning he had also resigned from the Defense League), the literary community's campaign against the board quickly waned after the climactic events of late May 1913. Writers still serving on the board (including Sulger-Gebing, who like Mann also belonged to the Defense League) continued in their posts, and a mass meeting planned for June to protest theater censorship never took place. Erich Mühsam launched a press campaign that summer to have Munich Police President von der Heydte and Dr. Roth, head of the censorship division, indicted for misusing their public offices (on grounds their threats to prohibit the two private performances of *Lulu* in May were illegal and amounted to an attempt to blackmail the Defense League and liberal press), but the public prosecutor refused to act.[84] Opponents of the police president and his Censorship Advisory Board were surely heartened in late July 1913, however, when for reasons probably unrelated to the recent censorship controversies von der Heydte resigned as police president to become senate president of the Bavarian Supreme Administrative

Court—where, ironically, he would hear any appeals lodged against police censorship decisions. A senior official from the Ministry of the Interior, Baron von Grundherr zu Altenthan und Weyerhaus, replaced him as head of the Munich police. Neither von der Heydte nor his successor attempted to name a replacement for Thomas Mann on the Censorship Advisory Board; given the current atmosphere, asking a writer to serve on the board would be tantamount to asking him to commit professional suicide and become a reviled outcast from the literary community.

The controversy over writers serving on the Censorship Advisory Board flared up again in June 1914 after Munich police banned public performances of Wedekind's drama *Simson oder Scham und Eifersucht* (*Samson, or Shame and Jealousy*), even though most members of the board had voted to approve it. The Munich chapter of the Defense League—now chaired by Max Halbe, a board defector—vehemently protested this latest ban and petitioned the Bavarian parliament to investigate the whole issue of theater censorship in Munich. At a public banquet later that month in honor of Wedekind's fiftieth birthday, Halbe again condemned the police ban and the hostility of some board members toward Wedekind and called upon writers who still served on the board to resign; a public meeting of several hundred members of the Munich literary community two weeks later likewise demanded their resignations. These outcries appear to have created a crisis within the Censorship Advisory Board, and by early July one of the remaining writers on the board, Joseph Ruederer, reported it was about to disband. The outbreak of war three weeks later, however, immediately diverted public attention to more pressing matters. The remaining members of the steadily shrinking board (between 1915 and 1917 one member resigned and four died, none of whom were replaced) continued to perform their duties until, on 21 November 1918, the provisional government of the newly proclaimed Bavarian "free state" abolished the Censorship Advisory Board and all prior theater censorship.[85] (Despite the travails of the Munich board, late in the war several prominent members of the German theatrical community continued to call for a national board of civilian literary experts to advise on theater censorship decisions, but such appeals came to nothing.[86])

Germany's experience with a civilian board of literary experts who, by advising the official censors, were to mediate between *Geist* and *Macht* proved enormously disappointing for nearly everyone involved. The Munich Censorship Advisory Board did not, as many in the literary community had hoped, reduce the number and obtuseness of bureaucratic intrusions into theatrical life; nor, as the Munich police president had hoped, did it relieve public pressure on the police, create more uniform and centralized censorship policies in Munich, or generate broader public support for theater censorship. On the contrary: as the Berlin police president had warned at the turn of the century, creating an advisory board of literary experts eventually produced more, not less, public controversy and police isolation.

By granting the lay experts only advisory powers and then regularly overruling their recommendations, Munich police invited—and received—the enmity of the literary community and of liberal public opinion; pressure mounted on police to at least follow the recommendations of the Censorship Advisory Board or even to surrender completely to it all decision-making authority regarding censorship. As some had warned, service as an advisor to police censors itself became a highly contentious issue that deeply divided the literary community. Writers like Halbe, Mann, or Ruederer who accepted such an appointment soon found the post an odious and thankless one: denounced as submissive police lackeys, self-serving collaborators with the enemies of art, and unprincipled artistic traitors who had violated the honor of German writers, they found themselves isolated from and ostracized by their fellow writers. Writers who agreed to serve as censorship advisors were soon faced with a serious dilemma: if they remained on the board in hopes of doing what little they could to protect art from police interference, they found themselves increasingly taken advantage of by the authorities and reviled and discredited as a writer; but if, during a period of increasing conservatism in Bavarian politics, they resigned their position they relinquished all influence over the police censors and ran the risk of being replaced by more conservative appointees less committed than they to artistic freedom and literary modernism. If the exercise of "collegial" censorship in the early nineteenth century put literary men in a difficult position, by the turn of the twentieth century it put them in an impossible one. The example of the Munich Censorship Advisory Board suggests that by the end of the imperial era, the gulf between art and the state, between the intellectual community and the official censors, had become so deep and wide it could no longer be bridged by such schemes as civilian advisory boards or panels of literary experts. While a relatively liberal, artistically sensitive censor like Glasenapp might maintain good relations with the literary community, members of that community who collaborated with censorship authorities soon found themselves ostracized by many of their fellow writers.

Conclusion

Germany's police censors were rarely powerful petty tyrants or zealous anti-intellectual persecutors of hapless artists, as they were often portrayed by their victims and opponents. Assigned a central function within a complex system designed by others, censors occupied an unpopular, awkward, problematic position in which they were frequently presented with knotty predicaments. They had, for example, to reconcile the often-conflicting wishes and policies of their bureaucratic superiors with the specific dictates of the censorship laws. Their independence as professional civil servants was continually challenged (and gradually eroded) by pressures within the bureaucracy for centralization and by external pressures from private moral entrepreneurs, political parties, and other interest groups. And censors found it nearly impossible to win credibility with and cooperation from the prestigious artistic and literary community they had to monitor. Attempts to enlist literary experts from the intellectual community to assist with censorship exacerbated rather than reduced the censors'—and the experts'— isolation from and unpopularity within the literary world. Entangled within an intricate system and charged with performing an onerous, even impossible task, the lot of the imperial German censor was not an easy one.

Notes

1. Bruno Wille, "Die Justiz als Kunstrichterin. Gloßen zum Urteil des Oberverwaltungsgerichts über die 'Freie Volksbühne,'" *Allgemeine Theater-Revue für Bühne und Welt* 1, no. 3 (8 May 1892): 1–5; Paul Victor, "Execution an einem Buch," *Berliner Börsen-Courier,* 9 Jan. 1898.
2. Frank Fowell and Frank Palmer, *Censorship in England* (London: 1913; reprint New York, 1969), 185.
3. "Giesing, "Theater, Polizei, und Politik," 127.
4. PrIM von Rheinbaden, StenBer/Pr, 19 Leg. Periode, III. Session, 25. Sitzung, am 13 Feb. 1901, Bd. 442, 1503–19.
5. Gottlieb Krais, "Über Theaterzensur. Vom Standpunkte des Zensors," *Die Gesellschaft* 18, no. 1 (1902): 7–14.
6. PrIM to PPs, 10 Mar. 1908, and PrIM memo, 22 Aug. 1908, LAB A/74, Th 25. Smaller, municipally controlled police forces in Prussia were still requested to inquire of Berlin first before making a decision.
7. PrIM directives of 30 Oct. 1912, 13 Jun. 1916, 16 Feb. 1917, LAB A/74, Th 25 and 28. On local police confusion, see Kiel PP to Posen PP, 28 Aug. 1909, quoted in Hubert Orlowski, *Polnisches Schrifttum unter Zensur. Wilhelminische und nationalsozialistische Zensurpolitik im Vergleich* (Frankfurt, 1988), 7.
8. Dresden PP to BPP, 6 Apr. 1912, Munich PP to BPP, 11 Nov. 1912, LAB A/74, Th 27; Meyer, *Theaterzensur in München,* 104. Viennese police also inquired of their German counterparts whether a particular work was approved or banned there; see Vienna Police to Munich PD, 26 Oct. 1903, in StAM/PDM 4598.
9. Aleksandr Nikitenko, *The Diary of a Russian Censor,* abr., ed., and trans. by Helen Galtz Jacobsen (Amherst, MA, 1975); Frederik Ohles, *Germany's Rude Awakening: Censorship in the Land of the Brothers Grimm* (Kent, OH, 1992), especially 48–69; Wolfram Siemann, "Ideenschmuggel: Probleme der Meinungskontrolle und das Los deutscher Zensoren im 19. Jahrhundert," *Historische Zeitschrift* 245 (1987): 71–106.
10. Howard S. Becker, *Outsiders: Studies in the Sociology of Deviance* (New York, 1963), especially 158–63.
11. Ohles, *Germany's Rude Awakening,* 59; Mary Lee Townsend, *Forbidden Laughter and the Limits of Repression in Nineteenth-Century Prussia* (Ann Arbor, MI, 1992), 189–91.
12. Karl Gutzkow, *Säkularbilder* (1846), quoted in Marianna T. Choldin, *A Fence Around the Empire: Russian Censorship of Western Ideas under the Tsars* (Durham, NC, 1985), 172.
13. Ottokar Stauf von der March, *Zensur, Theater, und Kritik* (Dresden, 1905), 13; Ernst Müller-Meiningen's remarks, StenBer/RT, Bd. 169, (7 Feb. 1900), 3928.
14. BHStA MInn 84 753; on Roth's role in the Beer Hall Putsch, see Harold J. Gordon, *Hitler and the Beer Hall Putsch* (Princeton, NJ, 1972), 85, 94, 190–96, 204, 214, 422, 447, 501, 571.
15. PrIM memo to PrRPs, 5 Dec. 1899, LAB A/74, Th 25.
16. Around 1903 Heindl was a member of Munich's Akademisch-Dramatischer Verein. His 1907 University of Erlangen dissertation on the legality of theater censorship (Heindl, "Die Theaterzensur," [Diss. jur. U. Erlangen]) concluded local police censorship ordinances were legally

compatible with the Prussian constitution's guarantee of free speech. He joined the Munich police as a *Rechtspraktikant,* where one of his early duties was to take minutes of the meetings of the newly created Censorship Advisory Board. Heindl rose to the rank of *Polizeirat* (assistant police commissioner) and was later called to serve as the assistant police commissioner in Dresden. (Meyer, *Theaterzensur in München,* 54, n. 29, and Raymond Fosdick, *European Police Systems* [1915; reprint Montclair, NJ, 1972], 152.) Possart began as a *Gerichts-Assessor* in Division I's Subdivision for Theater Affairs and eventually rose to *Regierungsrat;* he read theater scripts, recommending whether they should be passed, banned, or approved with alterations. *Handbuch über den Königlichen Preußischen Hof und Staat* (Berlin, 1901–1910). I am indebted to Peter Jelavich for bringing the Possart family connection to my attention.

17. *VL,* 2: 50; BHStA, MInn 64 066, 84 753. In fin-de-siècle Austria, where conditions were similar to those in the German Reich, the official in charge of theatrical censorship in Vienna describes in his memoirs how he was one day suddenly transferred from the executive-administrative branch of the city police force to the press branch, where he took up the task of theater censorship; his superiors neither knew nor cared whether he had any interest in literature. Ludwig Sendach, "Erinnerungen und Gedanken eines ehemaligen k.u.k. Wiener Zensors," *Bühne und Welt* 4, pt. 1 (1902/03): 780.

18. The Glasenapps had a long history of distinguished military and government service to the Prussian state. Economic hardships forced Kurt's father Sigismund to enter a bourgeois profession, and he became a successful Potsdam pharmacist. Sigismund, reputed also to be a talented graphic artist, married Elisabeth Spener, a descendant of the seventeenth-century Pietist theologian Philipp Spener. The couple's three sons all entered government service: Otto became vice-president of the Reichsbank and Gerhard became a general-leutnant in the Prussian military. Ernst von Glasenapp (probably Kurt's cousin) served as police president of Cologne and Warsaw during World War I, while his nephew Helmuth was a noted religious scholar at the University of Tübingen. See Helmuth von Glasenapp, *Meine Lebensreise* (Wiesbaden, 1964), 7–9.

19. Hans A. Knudsen, *Deutsche Theatergeschichte,* 2. Aufl. (Stuttgart, 1970), 255. An admiring 1908 article in the *New York Times* about Possart ("Owing to the Complex Rules") claimed his "ability is unquestioned" and his "artistic and literary valuation … inspires confidence in the entire theatrical fraternity."

20. In 1906 Glasenapp was one of a small circle who attended Wedekind's wedding dinner. Wedekind felt Glasenapp understood his work and served as an advocate for it in Berlin. Günter Seehaus, *Frank Wedekind und das Theater* (Munich, 1974), 63; Ernst Stern, *Bühnenbildner bei Max Reinhardt* (Berlin, 1955), 45–48; Frank Wedekind to a Theaterdirektor, 4 Jun. 1907, and to Tilly Wedekind, 14 Apr. 1916, in Wedekind, *Gesammelte Briefe,* ed. Fritz Strich (Munich, 1924), 2: 174, 333; Artur Kutscher, *Frank Wedekind. Sein Leben und sein Werke* (Munich, 1922–31), 2: 203 and 3: 233; Arthur Schnitzler to Olga Schnitzler, 19 Nov. 1904, in: Schnitzler, *Briefe 1875–1912,* ed. Therese Nickl and Heinrich Schnitzler (Frankfurt, 1981), 495.

21. Richard Treitel, "Reichstheatergesetz," *Die Schaubühne* 9, no. 1 (1913): 11–13, 69–74 (reprinted in *Bühnenprobleme der Jahrhundertwende,* 30.) In a 1917 speech the Expressionist theater director Leopold Jessner praised Glasenapp for having raised the artistic reputation of German directors. *Zukunft der deutschen Bühne,* 61.

22. The Verband Deutscher Erzähler worked closely with the Verein Deutscher Bühnenschriftsteller und Bühnenkomponisten and the Verband Deutscher Filmarbeiter. Friedhelm Kron, *Schriftsteller und Schriftstellerverbände. Schriftstellerberuf und Interessenpolitik 1842–1973* (Stuttgart, 1976), 63–69, 308, 402 n.170.

23. Scott, *"Into Whose Hands,* 191; Jones, quoted by Henry Miller in *Obscenity and the Law of Reflection* (New York, 1945), 7.

24. For detailed but sometimes conflicting accounts see Tilla Durieux, *Meine ersten neunzig Jahre* (Berlin, 1971), 154–60; Wilhelm Herzog, *Menschen, denen ich begegnete* (Bern, 1959), 238–39, 399, 467–72; Paret, *Berlin Secession,* 225–26.

25. Herzog, *Menschen*, 471.

26. Durieux, *Ersten neunzig Jahre*, 157–60. See Alfred Kerr's "Vorletzter Brief an Jagow" and "Nachlese," *Pan* 1, nos. 9 and 10 (1 Mar. and 15 Mar. 1911): 287–90, 321–26; also "die Affäre Jagow-Durieux," *Vorwärts*, 3 Mar. 1911.

27. In 1920 von Jagow participated in the right-wing Kapp Putsch and was to be Kapp's interior minister. "Traugott von Jagow (1865–1941)," in *Biographisches Staatshandbuch*, Bd. I, ed. Wilhelm Kosch (Bern, 1963), 598.

28. See newspaper clippings from *Das kleine Journal*, 27 Nov. 1911; *Münchener Post*, 24 Feb. 1912; *Münchener Kritik*, 25 Feb. 1912; and *Münchener Neueste Nachrichten*, 25 Feb. 1912, in Bittinger's personnel file, BHStA, MInn 64 066.

29. Fosdick, *European Police Systems*, 141–42.

30. Dagmar Walach, "Das doppelte Drama oder die Polizei als Lektor. Über die Entstehung der preussischen Theaterzensurbibliothek," in Antonio Jammers et al., *Die besondere Bibliothek, oder, die Faszination von Büchersammlungen* (Munich, 2002), 272.

31. This Prussian Theater Censorship Library, now part of the Landesarchiv Berlin, contains sixteen thousand theater pieces submitted between 1851 and 1918.

32. Because judging the effect (*Wirkung*) of a work rather than its simple content necessarily required seeing a performance rather than merely reading the text, after 1900 censors were increasingly urged to attend rehearsals and performances. PrIM memo to RPs, 5 Dec. 1899, LAB A/74, Th 25; Krais, "Über Theaterzensur. Vom Standpunkte des Zensors," 13.

33. Lothar Hirschmann, "Das Berliner Residenz-Theater und das Neue Theater unter der Leitung von Sigmund Lautenberg, dargestellt aus der Publizistik der Zeit," (Diss. phil, F.U. Berlin, 1960), 74 (quoting Leopold Schönhoff, *Kritische Theaterbriefe* [Berlin, 1900], 214); Schulze-Olden, "Theaterzensur in Rheinprovinz," 93.

34. Heindl, "Theaterzensur," 24ff.; P. Lehmann, *Polizei-Handlexikon. Ein Auszug aus sämmtlichen in das Gebiet der polizeilichen Thätigkeit einschlagenden Gesetzen, Verordnungen, Bekanntmachungen, u.s.w. mit besonderer Berücksichtigung der für Berlin erlassenen Specialbestimmungen* (Berlin, 1896), 267–69.

35. Georg Kreyenberg, quoted in Georg Jäger, "Der Kampf gegen Schmutz und Schund. Die Reaktion der Gebildeten auf die Unterhaltungsindustrie," *Archiv für Geschichte des Buchwesens* 31 (1988): 179.

36. See my "Pornography, Society, and the Law in Imperial Germany," *Central European History* 14 (Sept. 1981): 215, 220.

37. Engel-Reimers, *Die deutschen Bühnen*, 83–96. After a long struggle, in the years before the war the Bühnenverein established a standard contract with theaters that obligated a theater director, if the dramatist so requested, to appeal bans of works rejected by censors, keep the dramatist well informed at each stage of the process, and bear the legal costs involved. In 1899 the PrIM urged local police, before banning a work, to initiate informal *oral* discussions with the theater director and playwright in hopes of an amicable resolution. Because such negotiations were not conducted in writing, it is difficult to determine whether the practice became widespread. See PrIM memo to Pr RPs, 5 Dec. 1899, LAB A/74, Th 25 and Krais, "Über Theaterzensur. Vom Standpunkte des Zensors," 13.

38. Adolf Gerstmann, "Zur Frage der Theater-Zensur," *Deutsche Schriftsteller Zeitung* 1, no. 23 (1 Dec. 1885): 541; *VL*, 2: 50–53. Glasenapp replaced Dumrath as chief theater censor.

39. On how the organizational characteristics of social control agencies help create deviance, see Richard Hawkins and Gary Tiedeman, *The Creation of Deviance: Interpersonal and Organizational Determinants* (Columbus, OH, 1975), 178–214; also Gary T. Marx, "Ironies of Social Control: Authorities as Contributors to Deviance Through Escalation, Nonenforcement and Covert Facilitation," *Social Problems* 28, no. 3 (Feb. 1981): 221–46.

40. Alfons Fedor Cohn, "Die Zensur," *Die Schaubühne* 7, no. 26/27 (6. Juli 1911): 3.

41. Sendach, "Erinnerungen," 782, 785.

42. Giesing, "Theater, Polizei, und Politik," 127–28.

43. Fritz Mauthner, "Die freien Bühnen und die Theaterzensur," *Das Magazin für die Literatur des In- und Auslandes* 60, no. 51 (19 Dec. 1891): 801–2.

44. Becker, *Outsiders*, 147–63.

45. On the German morality movement, see Andrew Lees, *Cities, Sin, and Social Reform in Germany, 1870–1914* (Ann Arbor, MI, 2002); Hermann Roeren, *Die öffentliche Unsittlichkeit und ihre Bekämpfung. Flugschrift des Kölner Männervereins zur Bekämpfung der öffentlichen Unsittlichkeit* (Cologne, 1904); Adolf Henning, *Die öffentliche Sittenlosigkeit und die Arbeit der Sittlichkeitsvereine: Eine Denkschrift* (Berlin, ca. 1898); Ludwig Weber, *25 Jahre der Sittlichkeitsbewegung* (1911); StAM/PDM 362, 1110, 4775; Schulze-Olden, "Theaterzensur in Rheinprovinz," 197; Lenman, "Censorship and Society," 51–53, 183–89; Meyer, *Theaterzensur in München,* 39–44, 309–16; and Jäger, "Der Kampf gegen Schmutz," 180–84. Kausen's Munich Männerbund, founded in 1906, after one year claimed four hundred members and an additional fifty thousand people affiliated with several institutional members; by 1910 it claimed 31 branches and affiliated groups throughout Bavaria. The Verband zur Förderung deutscher Theaterkultur, which opposed indecencies in the theater industry and grew to the largest of all the morality groups, had three hundred and fifty thousand members in 1916.

46. Dr. Karl Brunner, *Unser Volk in Gefahr! Ein Kampfruf gegen die Schundliteratur* (Pforzheim, 1909); BPP to PrIM, 25 Apr. 1912, LAB A/74, Th 125; BPP to PrIM, 3 Jun. 1912, GStA PK , Rep. 77, Tit. 380, Nr. 7, Adhib. 2, Bd. 1; PrIM to Pr Finance Minister, 24 Jul. 1913, GStA PK , Rep. 77, Tit. 380, Nr. 7, Bd. 10; Baden Ambassador in Berlin to Baden State Ministry, 28 Mar. 1914, General Landesarchiv Karlsruhe, Abt. 233/12655.

47. BPP to PrIM 13 Oct. 1914, LAB A/74, Th 28. For another example of police attempting to "enlighten" members of a morality league, see Munich PD to Sittlichkeitsverein, 13 Jun. 1907, quoted in Meyer, *Theaterzensur in München,* 43.

48. See my "All Quiet on the Home Front."

49. Brunner to PrIM, 28 Oct. 1918, GStA PK , Rep. 77, Tit. 380, Nr. 7, Adhib. zu Bd. 11.

50. At the turn of the century, to mollify the malcontented Bavarian Center Party whose growing political influence could not be ignored, Bavarian Interior Minister Max von Feilitzsch sometimes found it "advisable simply for political reasons" to institute legal proceedings against outspoken critics of the Catholic Church, even when the case was likely to result in exoneration or dismissal; for then, he noted, "the charge can no longer be made that the state has not done everything it could in order to ensure the punishment of an insult [to the Church]. (von Feilitzsch letter of 11 Jul. 1900, quoted in Jelavich, *Munich and Theatrical Modernism,* 40; also Lenman, "Censorship and Society," 28.)

51. Meyer, *Theaterzensur in München,* 76–79; Karl Glossy, *Vierzig Jahre Deutsches Volkstheater. Ein Beitrag zur deutschen Theatergeschichte* (Vienna, 1929), 33ff. Austrian observers were unhappy with this system: they complained these "experts" were often nothing more than pensioned officials or military officers with few or no literary qualifications; they had no real power to decide, only advise; and that they weren't even informed of the final decision. Sendach, "Erinnerungen," 781; Stauf von der March, *Zensur,* 41–50.

52. See comments by Schmidt and Johannes Miquel in the Prussian Landtag (StenBer/Pr, 13 Legislatur-Periode, III Session 1878–79, 20. Sitzung, 17 Dec. 1878, 405–8); suggestions by the brothers Hart, Oscar Blumenthal, Ernst von Wildenbruch, and Karl Bliebtreu, discussed in Schulz, "Naturalismus und Zensur," 115–16; Richard Grelling, "Die Theater-Zensur," *Das Magazin für die Literatur des In- und Auslandes* 59. Jg., no. 44 (1 Nov 1890): 681–83; discussion in the pages of *Deutsche Dichtung,* 1892; Leonhard Lier, "Künstlerische, nicht polizeiliche Zensur," *Der Kunstwart* 11, H.6 (2. Dec. Heft, 1897): 186–88; and J. Lewinsky, "Über Theaterzensur," *Deutsche Revue* 26, no. 4 (1901):166.

53. Alberti [Sittenfeld], *Was erwart die deutsche Kunst?,* 100.

54. Pöllinger, *Zensurprozeß,* 189, n. 39; StenBer/RT, 42. Sitzung vom 6. Feb. 1901, vol. 175, 1162B.

55. PrIM to PPs, 12 Nov. 1899, and to RPs, 5 Dec. 1899, LAB A/74, Th 25.

56. BPP to PrIM, 12 Feb. 1900, LAB A/74, Th 23. The three academics were Prof. Eugen Wolf, Prof. Richard Schmitt, and Dr. Max Hermann.

57. PrIM memo of 12 Mar. 1900 and BPP replies of 26 Sept. and 28 Sept. 1900, LAB A/74, Th 25.

58. Pöllinger, *Zensurprozeß*, 147.

59. BHStA M Inn 64 378; Lenman, "Censorship and Society," 247.

60. On origins of the Zensurbeirat, see Krais, "Über Theaterzensur. Vom Standpunkte des Zensors," 13–14; Lenman, "Censorship and Society," 247–51; Jelavich, *Munich and Theatrical Modernism*, 247–50; and Meyer, *Theaterzensur in München*, 66–74, 79–95 (quote from Munich PD to Bavarian IM, 19 June 1907, in StAM/PDM, 4342, vol. 1, and in Meyer, ibid., 73–4.) Meyer's is an exhaustive study of the board's workings and reports.

61. Munich PD to Bavarian IM, 19 Jun. 1907, quoted in Meyer, *Theaterzensur in München*, 74.

62. Meyer, *Theaterzensur in München*, 86–95; Lenman, "Censorship and Society," 251–61.

63. Protocol of meeting of 20 Mar. 1908; copy in LAB A/74, Th 125.

64. Lenman, "Censorship and Society," 264–65, 280–81; Meyer, *Theaterzensur in München*, 119–30; Jelavich, *Munich and Theatrical Modernism*, 250–51.

65. Meyer, *Theaterzensur in München*, 104.

66. These figures are deduced from information in Meyer, *Theaterzensur in München*, 154 and 322–37. Surviving records indicate that in many cases the board simply visited a rehearsal without making a recommendation; in many others, no decision is indicated.

67. *Berlin Nationalzeitung*, quoted in Meyer, *Theaterzensur in München*, 120.

68. Wedekind, "Zensurbeirat," *Der Komet* 1, no. 4 (22 Mar. 1911), also reprinted as "Münchener Zensurbeirat" in *Gesammelte Werke* (Munich, 1924), 1: 122–23; "Wer, Was, Warum," *Münchener Neueste Nachrichten*, 24 Nov. 1911; Kutscher, *Frank Wedekind*, 3: 56–57; Meyer, *Theaterzensur in München*, 218–24, 253–57, Lenman, "Censorship and Society," 286–90; Jelavich, *Munich and Theatrical Modernism*, 253–54.

69. Halbe to Munich PD, 1 Dec. 1911, StAM/PDM, 4342, vol. 2, also quoted in Meyer, *Theaterzensur in München*, 254. The April petition eventually appeared in several German newspapers and literary journals, for example "Aktion für Frank Wedekind," *Berliner Tageblatt*, 8 Jun. 1911, and "Für Frank Wedekind," *Die Aktion* I, no. 17 (12 Jun. 1911): 531–32. On the origins of the petition, see DLA Marbach, Cotta Archiv, Nach. Sud. V 30, Bl 90; Kutscher, *Frank Wedekind*, 3: 61; Wedekind, *Gesammelte Briefe*, 2: 255, 369; and Jelavich, *Munich and Theatrical Modernism*, 253–54.

70. *Berliner Tageblatt*, 2 Dec. 1911.

71. Lenman, "Censorship and Society," 289–90; Meyer, *Theaterzensur in München*, 254–57.

72. "Sieben Fragen," reprinted in Wedekind, *Werke in drei Bänden*, ed. Manfred Hahn (Berlin, 1969), 3: 246–46 and Meyer, *Theaterzensur in München*, 258–59; it appeared on 29 and 30 Dec. in newspapers in Munich, Berlin, Dresden, Düsseldorf, Frankfurt, Hamburg, Nuremberg, and other cities. See also Kutscher, *Frank Wedekind*, 3: 52–54 and Jelavich, *Munich and Theatrical Modernism*, 255–56.

73. Wedekind, "Herr von der Heydte," *Die Aktion*, 19 Feb. 1912 and in *Werke*, 2: 708–9, also reprinted in Meyer, *Theaterzensur in München*, 345; Wedekind, "Torquemada. Zur Psychologie der Zensur," *Gesammelte Werke*, 9: 391–95, first published in *Berliner Tageblatt*, 17 Mar. 1912; *Berlin Börsen-Courier*, 24 Mar. 1912; see also Kutscher, *Frank Wedekind*, 3: 48–51 and Meyer, *Theaterzensur in München*, 266–71.

74. Copy of Munich police Presserklärung, Mar. 1912, in StAM/PDM, 4342, vol. 2 and LAB A/74, Th 125.

75. Müller-Meiningen, StenBer/Bav, 77. Sitzung, 2 Jul. 1912, 481–82; Meyer, *Theaterzensur in München*, 263–66.

76. Mann's response to a questionnaire about theater censorship sent by Robert Heindl, reprinted in Heindl, "Die Theaterzensur," 65ff. Mann's 1902 short story "Gladius dei" may also have been a condemnation of Munich's turn-of-the century morality campaigners. Stephan Füssel,

"Thomas Mann's 'Glaudius dei' (1902) und die Zensurdebatte der Kaiserzeit," in *Zwischen den Wissenschaften: Beiträge zur deutschen Literaturgeschichte,* ed. Gerhard Hahn and Ernst Weber (Regensburg, 1994), 427–36.

77. Thomas Mann to F. Wedekind, 7 Dec. 1912, in *Briefe 1889–1936,* ed. Erika Mann (Frankfurt, 1961), 97–98; *Letters of Thomas Mann 1889–1955,* selected and translated by Richard and Clara Winston (New York, 1970), 60.

78. Erich Mühsam, "Polizeidiktatur," *Kain* II, no. 11 (Feb. 1913):161–64.

79. Meyer, *Theaterzensur in München,* 273–85, which also reprints the written opinions of each board member.

80. *Münchener Neueste Nachrichten,* 21 May 1913; Fischer, "Der 'Schutzverband," 114; Meyer, *Theaterzensur in München,* 285–89.

81. Lenman, "Censorship and Society," 303; Mann to Munich PD, 26 May 1913, StAM/PDM, 4342, vol. 2, also quoted in Meyer, *Theaterzensur in München,* 288. See also Jelavich, *Munich and Theatrical Modernism,* 258 and Mann to Kurt Martens, 26 May 1913, *Briefe,* 102–3.

82. SDS declaration, published in *Münchener Zeitung,* 28 May 1913 and *Münchener Neueste Nachrichten,* 29 May 1913; Kurt Martens, "Das neueste Zensurverbot," *Münchener Neueste Nachrichten,* 28 May 1913; Fischer, "Der Schutzverband," 114–15 and Herbert Lehnert and Wulf Segebrecht, "Thomas Mann im Münchener Zensurbeirat (1912/13). (Ein Beitrag zum Verhältnis Thomas Mann zu Frank Wedekind)," *Jahrbuch der deutschen Schillergesellschaft* 7 (1963): 191.

83. Mann to Ruederer and to unknown "Professor," 29 May 1913, quoted in Lehnert and Segebrecht, "Thomas Mann," 192–3; Mann to Wedekind, 29 May 1913, in Kutscher, *Frank Wedekind,* 3: 57.

84. Wedekind to Max Halbe, 31 May 1913, Wedekind, *Briefe,* 2: 281; Lenman, "Censorship and Society," 305–06; Mühsam, "Der Münchener Zensor. Offener Brief an den Herrn Kgl. Staatsanwalt beim Landgericht I zu München, Justizpalast" and "Der Zensurskandal," *Kain* 3, nos. 3 and 4 (June and July 1913): 40–44; 56–63; Meyer, *Theaterzensur in München,* 296–98.

85. Meyer, *Theaterzensur in München,* 298–99; Jelavich, *Munich and Theatrical Modernism,* 259.

86. See the comments of Franz Dülberg, Walter Harlan, Ludwig Klinebergerl, Prof. Julius Ferdinand Wolff, and Fedor von Zobelitz in *Zukunft der deutschen Bühne,* 77, 95–96, 113, 157, 162.

Chapter 3

DEFENDING THE POLITICAL ORDER

[S]overeigns and guardians of the state—if they knew how to do it—could use the stage to correct and enlighten popular opinion of government and the governing class. Legislative power might speak to its subjects in unfamiliar symbols, might defend its actions before they had time to utter a complaint, might silence their doubts without appearing to do so.
—Friedrich Schiller, *The Stage Considered as a Moral Institution*

*A*lthough the German Empire was born amidst military victory and booming economic growth, its ruling elites quickly came to regard the new order as precarious and insecure. The initial optimism at the empire's founding in 1871 soon gave way to pessimistic uncertainty as it became clear Bismarck's complex new polity contained many internal structural instabilities and tensions and as the economic crash of 1873 ushered in two decades of depression. By the end of the 1870s many imperial leaders had adopted a crisis mentality and were driven by profound fear of subversion and revolution. Believing the imperial order was threatened externally by the French and by liberal free trade, and internally by Catholic and socialist subversion and anti-German minorities, Germany's rulers abandoned the liberal policies and outlooks of the "founding years" and turned instead toward more conservative, authoritarian, and defensive economic, political, and social policies designed to protect the precarious status quo. Although the most serious internal crises had passed after 1895–1896 and the empire enjoyed a period of relative prosperity and stability until the outbreak of World War I, the doggedness with which literary censorship was used to defend the existing political and social order indicates that, to the very end, those in control of the nation never overcame their acute sense of the fragility of the imperial political and social system. Throughout the imperial era, but especially after 1890, censors regularly intervened against works they believed encouraged disrespect for the empire's monarchs and other key political institutions, that endorsed particularistic tendencies hostile to the empire, or that ran counter to its diplomatic policies, whether or not this had been the author's intent (and often it had not). In every area save one—defending the public dignity of the emperor and of other German monarchs—imperial authorities were fairly successful in intervening against literary works perceived as threatening Germany's internal political legitimacy and external diplomatic interests.

Lèse Majesté

Authorities defended the political order by suppressing works they believed might undermine public respect for and confidence in fundamental imperial institutions. At the apex of the empire sat the emperor, an office Bismarck intended as an agency to overcome particularistic interests and promote imperial unity and centralization. After 1871 the emperor came increasingly to be regarded as the visible symbol, and under Wilhelm II as the personification and actual sovereign, of the new German nation.

German law, like that of most other nations, considered an attack on the dignity and majesty of the head of state to be an attack on the dignity and majesty of the state itself. The emperor's prestige and honor (as well as that of his family and fellow princes who reigned in the various federal states) were protected under several paragraphs of the Criminal Code. The most important of these, §95, stated, "Whoever insults the emperor, the sovereign of his [own] federal state, or the sovereign of another federal state in which he finds himself, will be punished with not less than two months jail, or with fortress arrest from two months to five years."

The German law against *Majestätsbeleidigung,* or lèse majesté, was in many respects harsher and less flexible than elsewhere. Several nations, including Austria, France, Italy, and the Netherlands, distinguished between insults made directly to the head of state in his or her presence and those merely committed publicly—for example, in the press or through other public media; sentences for the latter were generally lower, involving either a fine or up to a year imprisonment. Germany's §95 made no such distinction and also punished, with equal severity, insults made privately (for example, in small gatherings, private conversations, or personal correspondence), which meant vengeful citizens could report their neighbors or enemies to the authorities for remarks made up to five years earlier. (Conrad Alberti, later a defendant in the Leipzig Realists' Trial discussed in chapter 6, wrote a novella in 1887 about an innocent man accused of lèse majesté under just such circumstances and the tragic consequences that resulted from his conviction.[1]) Moreover, until 1909 the German law on lèse majesté did not require the state to demonstrate malicious intent, nor did the remarks have to relate literally to the head of state: it punished words or actions, in public or in private, whether true or not, that others were likely to interpret as an intentional insult, and also punished merely oblique references to the sovereign if these were likely to be generally understood as relating to him.[2]

Because the concept of lèse majesté was ill defined (for example, were acts of omission, such as failing to stand for a cheer to the emperor, also punishable?), legal opinion concerning the application of §95 differed greatly and this statute was one of the Criminal Code's more controversial. The charge of lèse majesté was frequently used to punish such behavior as criticisms of the emperor in the press or at public meetings and insulting gestures (for example, sticking out one's tongue at an imperial procession), but was applied with unusual regularity and severity against socialists and the socialist press. Convictions under §95 reached a peak in 1878, just before enactment of the Anti-Socialist Law, remained fairly high in the 1880s, rose sharply again after the expiration of the Anti-Socialist Law in 1890, and reached a new high in 1894. (See figure 3.1)

Citing numerous examples of its abuse and widely conflicting legal opinions about what constituted lèse majesté, in May 1897 Social Democrats introduced a resolution in the Reichstag to abolish this "crime." It found little support: Left-Liberal delegates did not want §95 rescinded but agreed a major overhaul of the statute was needed and the punishment should be significantly reduced, while Conservatives wanted the punishment significantly increased. Spokesmen for the

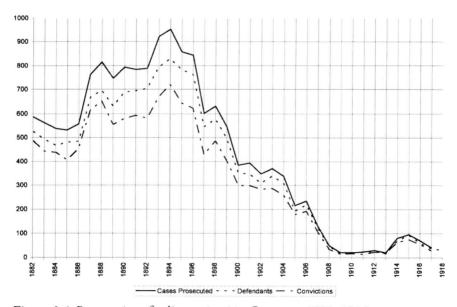

Figure 3.1 Prosecutions for lèse majesté in Germany, 1882–1918

1882–1896: Par. 94-97, Slandering a state monarch; 1897-1918: Par 95, Slandering emperor or state monarch

Source: Statistisches Reichsamt, *Statistisches Jahrbuch für das Deutsche Reich* (Berlin, 1880ff).

National Liberal, Progressive, and Center Parties admitted there were problems with the law but believed only minor reforms in its application were necessary. The SPD motion to abolish the crime of lèse majesté thus failed, as did the Left-Liberal's motion to establish a special commission to reform the statute, and §95 remained in force. After the Reichstag debate, however, both the conservative and liberal press began questioning the wisdom and effectiveness of Germany's lèse majesté statute.[3] After the turn of the century an academic commission that had studied criminal codes of other nations in preparation for a fundamental rewriting of the Imperial Criminal Code suggested a number of changes in §95, including punishing only insults committed publicly and allowing the libeled monarch discretion to decide whether an insult should be prosecuted.[4] In 1908 the statute against lèse majesté was amended to remove its worst features. Now an insult against the head of state could be punished only if it was premeditated and done with malicious intent; the statute of limitations was also reduced from five years to six months and if there were extenuating circumstances punishment could be reduced to a fine or up to a mere week incarceration.[5] After this reform, prosecutions under §95, which had been declining steadily since the mid-1890s, became increasingly rare—around twenty per year. While changes to the law were surely part of the reason lèse majesté was no longer pursued so vigorously, a precipitous decline in Wilhelm II's popularity was also responsible. Following the *Daily Telegraph* affair of late 1908, the most serious crisis of Wilhelm II's reign before 1914, his standing with his subjects collapsed and he was subjected to a barrage of public criticism that before 1908 would have been hard to imagine.

Although insulting the emperor or his fellow monarchs in print was less dangerous (and perhaps more tempting) during the final decade the imperial era, before the turn of the century it was one of the literary offenses that usually drew a quick and severe, if not always effectual, response from authorities. During the early reign of Wilhelm II, who cared intensely about his public image and paid close attention to how he was depicted in the press, §95 was invoked against a number of imaginative writers and satirists, especially in the 1890s when the emperor's attempts at a "personal regime" and his constant theatrics provided lampoonists with abundant grist for their satirical mills. As Thomas Kohut has noted, the government's harsh attempts to suppress such satire and punish its creators not only reveal Wilhelm II's personal vulnerability to criticism but also "reflect the susceptibility of the Kaiser's symbolic leadership to parody. The epics performed upon the imperial stage could survive opposition, but their symbolic effect was destroyed when the performer was made to seem ludicrous."[6]

In the early 1890s, however, convicting writers for lèse majesté was not always easy, especially in southern states where respect for Prussia and its monarch was often in short supply and where trial by a lay jury was often required. In 1891, for example, the young Munich Naturalist poet and novelist Hanns von Gumppenberg was charged with lèse majesté after he recited at a public meeting "*An die deutsche Nation*" ("To the German Nation"), a poem by the proletarian poet Karl Henckell critical of the imperial throne. After a conservative newspaper demanded he be prosecuted for attacking the emperor personally and monarchy in general, Gumppenberg was tried by a Munich court for lèse majesté but initially acquitted. The prosecution appealed that decision, however, and he was eventually convicted and sentenced to two months' fortress arrest, half the sentence the prosecutor had sought.[7]

Two years later even Prussian prosecutors were unable to convict Maximilian Harden, literary critic and editor of *Die Zukunft* (*The Future*). Harden was indicted in Berlin in 1893 for two satires of the emperor and his entourage published in *Die Zukunft* in late 1892: *König Phaeton,* about Wilhelm II's bombastic style and self-delusions, and *Monarchenerziehung* (*Monarch's Education*), which criticized his sycophantic entourage and urged him to educate himself about the true wishes of the German people. A sympathetic judge who found the articles to contain many "irrefutable truths" acquitted Harden, noting, "Respect for a prince is not manifested in Byzantine servility at his feet and [in] flattering him; true and genuine respect consists in courageously speaking the truth."[8]

The most famous satire of Wilhelm II, Ludwig Quidde's sensational essay *Caligula: Eine Studie über Cäsarenwahnsinn* (*Caligula: A Study of Emperor's Madness*), also initially escaped the law. Quidde's was a clever piece of lèse majesté that, in the words of one historian, "struck [imperial Germany] like a bomb."[9] On the surface merely a historical study of the depraved Roman emperor, this essay was actually a thinly veiled, devastating satire of Wilhelm II's bizarre personality and Byzantine megalomania. Published in late March 1894, it received little public notice until the ultraconservative press bitterly condemned it two months later and demanded Quidde be severely punished. The newspaper article, which quite explicitly stated many parallels between Caligula and Wilhelm II at which Quidde had only hinted, created an immediate national sensation and Quidde's satire was soon the talk not only of the German but also the international press. Everyone suddenly wanted to read *Caligula:* within a year it went into more than thirty printings, sold hundreds of thousands of copies, and was probably read by a million or more people, making it the most famous political pamphlet of the imperial era.[10]

Contrary to Quidde's—and everyone else's—expectations, however, Bavarian authorities did not prosecute him for *Caligula.* There are several possible reasons: officials may have been pessimistic about obtaining a conviction, not only because such trials there required persuading a lay jury but also in Quidde's case it would be difficult to prove the essay was an insult to Wilhelm II (whom Quidde was careful never to mention by name).[11] Furthermore, for the state to charge Quidde with lèse majesté would have been to admit that Caligula's deranged behavior did indeed bear some resemblance to Wilhelm II's.

Although he initially escaped prosecution for the *Caligula* essay, Quidde immediately became a marked man: "From then on the state prosecutor took an especially affectionate interest in my public activities, and two years later, I indirectly had to atone for the *Caligula* essay with three months' fortress arrest."[12]

The state was able to obtain its revenge against Quidde in January 1896, when at a public meeting sponsored by the Social Democratic Party he carelessly made a joke at the emperor's expense, was immediately charged with lèse majesté, and sentenced to three months incarceration. (Since this infraction was not committed in print, it did not require a jury trial.) Quidde knew that

> it was revenge for *Caligula*. The speech of the state prosecutor … made that quite clear. He began his remarks to the court by pointing out I had continually eluded punitive justice, first with *Caligula* and thereafter often with great impudence, but that fortunately I had now been caught and would not be allowed to escape again. The final verdict of the court also referred to the *Caligula* essay as a way of proving that [this time] I was guilty of intentional lèse majesté.[13]

Like Quidde, the Bavarian writer Oskar Panizza also evaded punishment for his sharp attacks on the emperor, but only temporarily. After serving a harsh sentence for blasphemy (see chapter 5) Panizza renounced his German citizenship in 1896 and emigrated first to Switzerland, then France. Safely abroad, he published two bitter literary attacks on the social climate and political culture of his German homeland: *Abschied von München: Ein Handschlag* (*Farewell to Munich: A Handshake*; 1897) and *Parisijana. Deutsche Verse aus Paris* (*Parisiana: German Verses from Paris*; 1899), a series of vitriolic poems attacking Germany's tyrannical rulers and denouncing Wilhelm II as a "mad dog" and "public enemy of mankind and culture."[14] Alerted to these publications by reviews and denunciations in the conservative press, Munich police confiscated both works and issued warrants for Panizza's arrest for slandering the emperor. To force Panizza's return from exile they also seized his financial assets in Germany, which he had been using to support himself. Financially destitute, Panizza returned to Bavaria in 1900, was placed under psychiatric observation, declared mentally incompetent, and committed permanently to an asylum.[15]

The state enjoyed some success in convicting writers and journalists of lèse majesté at the end of the 1890s, when Wilhelm II's neoabsolutistic program reached its zenith and criticism of his autocratic style and ineffectual policy initiatives became increasingly vocal. In 1898 Julius Trojan, editor of the popular satirical journal *Kladderadatsch,* was sentenced to two months' fortress arrest for publishing a cartoon, "*Aus dem Lager den himmlischen Heeerscharen*" ("From the Camp of the Heavenly Host"), lampooning the emperor's statement that no one could be a good soldier who was not also a good Christian.[16] That same year Maximilian Harden was again indicted for publishing *Pudel-Majestät* (*Poodle-Majesty*), a fable about a king who, to escape his entourage of sycophantic flatterers and learn what people really thought of him, changed himself into a poodle. Although like Quidde's essay Harden's never mentioned Wilhelm II by name, a Berlin court sentenced him to six months' fortress arrest for lèse majesté. In 1900 Harden suffered the same punishment yet again for his article *Der Kampf mit der Drachen* (*The Fight With the Dragon*), which criticized the emperor's so-called

"Hun Speech" that called upon German troops departing for China during the Boxer Rebellion to treat rebellious Chinese with ruthless terror.[17]

Perhaps the most famous convictions for insulting the emperor, however, involved the 1898 "Palestine Issue" of the satirical journal *Simplicissimus.* This sharp-edged Munich-based journal was Germany's foremost magazine of aggressive political satire and cultural criticism. Its colorful, controversial avant-garde cartoons and biting literary pieces attracted a mass, largely urban readership that included members of Germany's business and professional elite, middle-class youth, young officers, and many social democratic trade-unionists. Because Wilhelm II's megalomania, constant posturing, and lack of tact were favorite targets of this journal, imperial authorities watched it particularly closely. A cartoon in early 1898 satirizing the emperor's delusions of grandeur by depicting him ordering time to go backwards had led to the government temporarily banning sales of the journal at newsstands in railway stations, and two weeks before the "Palestine Issue" appeared, *Simplicissimus* publisher Albert Langen had received a warning the Prussian government was upset with the way his journal "mockingly persecuted" the emperor.[18] In late October 1898, during a well-publicized trip by Wilhelm II to the Holy Land (during which he compared himself to a modern Crusader and made reckless comments about a German protectorate over all Muslims, immediately antagonizing both France and Britain), *Simplicissimus* published an issue devoted to satirizing the Palestine trip. A cover-page cartoon by the artist Thomas Theodor Heine depicted the medieval crusaders Geoffroi de Bouillon and Friedrich Barbarossa snickering over the pointlessness of Wilhelm II's modern crusade, while the poem "*Im Heiligen Land*" ("In the Holy Land") by one "Hieronymous Jobs" (pseudonym of the young dramatist Frank Wedekind) presented an ancient King David's mocking reflections about the emperor's pompous and tactless behavior in the Holy Land.

Police in Leipzig (where *Simplicissimus* was printed) immediately confiscated the Palestine issue as well as the next issue, which was then in press and contained "*Meerfahrt*" ("Ocean Voyage"), another Hieronymous/Wedekind poem about the emperor's trip that concluded with a cryptic remark that "a screw is loose" somewhere on Wilhelm II's ship *Hohenzollern.* There are conflicting accounts about just how much Langen, the publisher, did to avoid running afoul of the law. Ludwig Thoma, a member of the *Simplicissimus* editorial staff who had a legal degree, later claimed Langen realized the first version of Wedekind's poem would virtually invite legal action so he made the author tone it down. When Thoma saw the final proofs of the Palestine issue, he said he warned the journal's editor the attack on the emperor was still too sharp and would lead to confiscation and prosecution, but was told it had already been examined and approved by the firm's lawyer, and besides had already gone to press. Wedekind, on the other hand, subsequently claimed that although Langen had assured him nothing would be printed unless the firm's lawyer first declared it legally unobjectionable, Langen nevertheless went ahead with the two poems in question even though the lawyer had examined them and warned they were "impossible" (*unmöglich*).[19]

A magistrate was sent from Leipzig to Munich to question Langen and Heine and discover who Hieronymous Jobs was. While searching the *Simplicissimus* editorial offices he confiscated a large number of files and discovered the incriminating handwritten manuscript of Wedekind's two poems, which would soon reveal the author's identity. Langen and Heine were summoned to appear in Leipzig, where it was clear they would be indicted for lèse majesté. Langen, expecting a prison sentence of two years and concerned about his wife's frail health and the survival of his publishing house during his absence, immediately fled to Switzerland on the advice of his attorney. Wedekind was tipped off by a friendly Munich police official that with the manuscript in their hands, Saxon authorities were on the verge of discovering his identity and arresting him. He remained in Munich just long enough to appear in the premier performance of his new play *Erdgeist* (*Earth Spirit*) on 29 October; while two Saxon officials waited in the theater lobby after the performance to apprehend him, he slipped out a back exit and also fled to Switzerland. Heine dutifully reported to Leipzig, where in December 1898 he was tried and sentenced to six months in jail, later commuted to six months' fortress arrest. In July 1899 Wedekind returned from exile and also surrendered to the Leipzig court; he was sentenced to seven months in jail, later commuted to six months' fortress arrest. Albert Langen, who eventually settled in Paris, spent the next four and a half years in exile directing his publishing house and exploring various schemes to return safely to Germany. After an influential conservative Saxon politician quietly negotiated an arrangement by which Langen was allowed to secretly "purchase" his amnesty from the Saxon government for 20,000 marks, he was allowed to return to Munich in May 1903.[20]

For a decade following the Palestine Issue, *Simplicissimus'* critical satires of Wilhelm II continued to infuriate conservatives and imperial officials. After its confrontation with Saxon authorities in 1898, the journal kept its editorial offices in Munich but wisely moved its printing operations from Leipzig (where press offenses were not tried by juries and convictions were relatively easy to obtain) to Stuttgart (where such offenses did require a jury trial and convictions were less likely). For several years Württemberg and Bavarian authorities wrangled over which state had jurisdiction over the journal, each preferring the other take responsibility and bear the expenses of prosecution and court trials, the outcome of which were unpredictable. Not until 1908 was an arrangement worked out under which Stuttgart authorities reluctantly agreed to accept primary jurisdiction and initiate prosecutions if necessary. This jurisdictional confusion and increasing reluctance by both states to indict the journal when a jury trial was likely to end in acquittal allowed *Simplicissimus* enormous independence and quasi-immunity from prosecution. Delegates in the Bavarian parliament and voices in the conservative press regularly stormed that the journal's "poisonous malice against Throne and Altar" was destroying "the respect for authority upon which we rely for the preservation of our political institutions," while Prussian authorities frequently chided the Bavarian government for being too tolerant of *Simplicissimus'* disrespect of the Prussian king and German emperor. Nevertheless, after the notorious Palestine Issue of 1898, neither Bavarian nor Württemberg prosecutors were willing to invoke §95 against *Simplicissimus* for its increasingly frequent satires of the emperor, and prosecutors in other states could not do so.[21]

Laws against lèse majesté also protected sovereigns of the various federal states like Bavaria and Saxony. If those punished for satirizing the emperor before 1908 learned that the truth of their charges was no defense, the same was true for discussions of the hapless Bavarian monarchs of the Wittelsbach house, two of whom in the imperial era (Ludwig II and Otto I) were obviously demented or insane. After Ludwig II's tragic death in 1886 authorities in Bavaria and elsewhere tried to suppress embarrassing material about him, even when this simply reported the facts. Thus Prussian courts in 1887 banned one popular pamphlet about *Der Romantiker auf dem Throne* (*The Romantic on the Throne*) from colportage sales because, even though its depiction was accurate, it portrayed Ludwig II in a way that could discredit and disparage him in public opinion. (In contrast to the established German book trade, restrictions on the colportage trade allowed authorities to forbid the sale of specific titles or types of material on public streets and places such as railway stations.) And in 1907 the Bavarian government succeeded in persuading several other German states, including liberal Hamburg, to ban from their stages Ferdinand Bonn's *Ludwig II von Bayern* because it "display[ed] a great lack of piety for the unfortunate king," would perpetuate the "idiotic myth" that Ludwig was poisoned by one of his advisors, and "harm[ed] the good name of [the reigning] Prince Regent [Luitpold]."[22]

Realizing, however, that sensational jury trials for lèse majesté would only draw unwelcome attention to the embarrassing mental state of these kings, Bavarian authorities often overlooked all but the most glaring references to their sovereigns' psychic conditions. One it could not ignore was Maximilian Harden's frank discussion of Otto I's insanity in an 1898 issue of *Die Zukunft*, for which the author was convicted of the lesser crime of "criminal nuisance" (*grober Unfug*) rather than lèse majesté and jailed for two weeks.[23] The Bavarian government was even reluctant to prosecute satires of the relatively competent Ludwig III (regent 1912–1913, king 1913–1918). When *Simplicissimus* published a cartoon in May 1914 satirizing a meeting between the king and a delegation of teachers seeking raises, royal advisors decided not to prosecute because a trial would not only generate favorable publicity for (and incite additional attacks from) *Simplicissimus*, but also involve embarrassing public testimony from the teachers about their meeting with the king. Shortly thereafter, the journal published two more cartoons lampooning Ludwig III's lack of support for the grand artistic projects of his predecessors. This time the three journalists responsible for the cartoons were indicted for lèse majesté, but because of the outbreak of war in August the trial was postponed. Some months later, after *Simplicissimus* adopted a nationalistic, progovernment position regarding the war, the Bavarian monarch dropped the charges in this and all other pending cases of lèse majesté.[24]

Saxony's royal family also tried to prosecute *Simplicissimus* for lèse majesté, but with an equal lack of success. After Crown Princess Luise of Tuscany abandoned

Crown Prince Friedrich August (her husband of twelve years) in 1902, eloped to Geneva with the one-time French language tutor of her children, and was granted a divorce the following year, the embarrassing scandal found its way into the pages of *Simplicissimus,* which in late 1903 charged the crown prince with having mistreated his wife. King Georg of Saxony (who had just agreed to pardon the journal's publisher Albert Langen for the Palestine issue) demanded the Württemberg government prosecute. Although a good deal of time and money was spent on the case, prosecutors were unable to convince a Stuttgart jury to convict the defendants.[25]

Despite the empire's relatively harsh law against lèse majesté, the state thus found it increasingly difficult to punish printed attacks, especially satirical ones, on the emperor and other monarchs. While §95 was frequently and successfully applied before the turn of the century to intimidate socialist critics of Germany's sovereigns, against bourgeois writers and intellectuals it was markedly less effective. Individual journalists or satirists were sometimes successfully punished in the 1890s, but in the first decade of the new century it became ever more difficult to defend the emperor and his fellow monarchs against mockery in mass circulation journals like *Simplicissimus.* The successful movement to mitigate §95, the jurisdictional and legal complexities existing in southern Germany, the reluctance of many local authorities there to initiate legal proceedings whose outcome might prove embarrassing, and the declining popularity of Wilhelm II himself all combined to shield lampoonists from the provisions of the criminal code.

Monarchs Offstage

Censors only had the power to punish ex post facto those who ridiculed the emperor or other German monarchs in print, but in theaters they were able to prevent any portrayal of these sovereigns. Although the legal basis was dubious, in Germany as in other monarchies reigning monarchs by longstanding tradition could not be depicted on stage without their express consent. As the Berlin theater censor explained, to protect "the unique position a reigning sovereign occupies in the life of a state, it cannot be permitted for just anyone to bring the personality of the monarch onto the stage. ... It is totally impermissible that the actions of a reigning ruler who appears in a dramatic presentation should be subjected to the critical evaluation either of a playwright or an audience, much less to an audience's applause or hisses (*Bei- oder Mißfall*)."[26] Actors or entertainers were not permitted to publicly portray the emperor either in serious dramas or in lighthearted vaudeville skits.

As Ludwig Quidde discovered, however, the penalties and proscriptions surrounding any direct treatment of the emperor could be circumvented with a *text à clef*, in which a fictional or historical character substituted for the monarch. When Oscar Blumenthal wished in 1904 to treat dramatically the conflict between Bismarck and the new young emperor Wilhelm II, which resulted finally in

Bismarck's dismissal in 1890, he set his work *Die tote Löwen* (*The Dead Lions*) in fourteenth-century Castille, with King Marco and Duke von Oliveto representing Wilhelm II and Bismarck, respectively. Although the drama had been allowed in Hamburg, Lübeck, Leipzig, Erfurt, and Breslau, Berlin police banned it in the capital, where "the memory of these events from contemporary history, which were experienced here first-hand, is still quite immediate." According to the censor the work was obviously about the conflict between Wilhelm II and Bismarck and thus fell under the spirit, if not the letter, of the prohibition against portraying a reigning monarch on stage. Such prohibitions were necessary because

> in a monarchical state it must be considered a disruption of public order when a living ruler's governmental decisions of such world-historical significance are brought upon stage in this way and subjected to the criticism and judgment of the theatergoing public. Some segments of the populace—specifically those who, at the time, were passionately moved in their innermost being by the change of events—will be profoundly disturbed by such proceedings, particularly since the events were played out here, where the monarch also now resides.[27]

However, in an opinion very narrowly drawn so as to apply only to this instance, the Supreme Administrative Law Court to which the ban was ultimately appealed (an initial appeal to the provincial governor had upheld the police) ruled that neither the actual content of *Die tote Löwen* nor its probable effect on the public justified its prohibition. In the view of the judges the play did not actually put the emperor (that is, a character portraying him) on stage for the audience's judgment, nor was it necessarily illegal—contrary to the police's contention—to put contemporary governmental decisions and controversies surrounding them on stage for an audience's critical evaluation. Even if the actions of King Marco in many ways reminded the audience of those of a living ruler, this *in and of itself* posed no threat to public order, for one must also have reason to believe the audience would react negatively. Since the play had already been performed peacefully in other Prussian cities, the court saw little ground for assuming it would cause unruly outbursts from Berlin audiences.[28]

It was also forbidden to depict the emperor's Hohenzollern forebears on stage. In 1844 King Friedrich Wilhelm IV, upset by Karl Gutzkow's portrayal of Friedrich Wilhelm I in *Zopf und Schwert* (*Pigtail and Sword*), decreed that henceforth "dramas in which deceased members of my royal house appear on stage may be performed only if my express approval is granted." The order was amended in the 1880s: no permission would be granted unless at least one hundred years had passed since the figure's death; once a piece had been performed in a royal theater or been approved for a public theater it could also be performed elsewhere; and (after 1900), dramas submitted for royal approval were to be accompanied by a summary of the contents and the written opinions of two or three literary experts testifying to their literary value.[29] The purpose of this careful screening was quite simple: as the Berlin police president explained, it was important nothing be permitted that might undermine loyalty to the ruling dynasty by arousing false

impressions about the personalities, deeds, and character of its members, especially among society's lower and semieducated strata.[30]

These restrictions on portraying royal ancestors encompassed many figures and
events crucial to European history. Since historical drama was a popular nineteenth-century genre with both playwrights and audiences, the desire of Friedrich
Wilhelm IV and his successors to control their family's theatrical image inhibited
an important aspect of the German theater. Between 1878 and 1918, for example, the royal Civil Cabinet rejected about 80 percent of the more than fifty works
submitted for approval; less than 10 percent were approved outright, while another 10 percent were approved only after revisions were made. Wilhelm II often
took a detailed interest in the works submitted for his approval, frequently wanting to know, for example, which actor was going to play the role of the Hohenzollern in question.[31] Although some works submitted (for example, J. Baltz's *Hohenzollern zur See* [*Hohenzollerns at Sea*] or *Bitte, recht freundlich!* [*Smile, Please!*])
were rejected because they were frivolous, undignified farces with which the dynasty wanted no association, most were light comedies, serious dramas, or historical tragedies by noted authors such as Otto Ludwig, Fritz von Unruh, Paul Ernst,
Emil Ludwig, or Herbert Eulenberg, and were by no means critical or disparaging
of the Hohenzollerns. Indeed, a good many were highly patriotic and historically
accurate and contained idealized, even fawning portrayals of some of the dynasty's
most popular and beloved figures, such as Friedrich the Great or Queen Luise.

Why then were so many refused permission? Sometimes, as with Otto Ludwig's *Die Torgauer Heide* (*The Torgau Heath*), the issue was a single word. To show
the camaraderie between Friedrich the Great and his soldiers, in the play the
latter address him affectionately as "Fritz." Wilhelm II considered this disrespect-
ful, and, beginning in 1889, rejected the work several times before the theater
agreed in 1908 to change "Fritz" to "Sire."[32] Others were rejected because they
dealt with embarrassing aspects of the dynasty's history, for example, illegitimate
scions or (as with E. Mügge's *Barbarina*) Friedrich the Great's fascination with
and kidnapping of the Italian dancer Barbera ("La Barberina") Campanini.[33]

Dramas about Friedrich the Great posed a particularly difficult problem. On
the one hand he was the most famous, historically significant, and beloved Hohenzollern king and thus a favorite of playwrights, audiences, and theater managers.
On the other hand, those aspects of his life that were often the most compelling
and dramatically rich, such as his painful, humiliating treatment by his brutal
father Friedrich Wilhelm I, reflected badly on the royal house. In the 1870s, for
example, Heinrich Laube's *Prinz Friedrich* was not permitted because character-
izing Friedrich Wilhelm I as an inhuman, tyrannical father might also imply he
was an inhuman, tyrannical monarch.[34] Since Wilhelm II disapproved of how
dramas like G. Weck's *Haus Hohenzollern* treated this bitter father-son conflict,
after 1901 the emperor began approving such works only if literary experts would
attest to their high artistic value. Then, peeved by Ferdinand Bonn's *Der junge
Fritz* (*Young Fritz*) and *Friedrich der Große,* in December 1909 Wilhelm II issued
a cabinet order stating he no longer wanted this tragic episode from the history of

his ancestors portrayed on the stage in any form and dramas containing such material would be automatically rejected.[35] (Bonn, until then a "fervent patriot" and admirer of Wilhelm II and the Hohenzollerns, was planning a dramatic trilogy about Friedrich. When his attempts to change the emperor's mind about these bans brought him only "grief and shame," Bonn became embittered and allegedly burned the unfinished manuscript of *Der alte Fritz,* the last in the trilogy.)

For reasons now unclear the emperor imposed a similar blanket prohibition against any works in which Queen Luise, spouse of Friedrich Wilhelm III (reigned 1797–1840) appeared on stage. The beautiful and charming Luise had quickly won the hearts of her Prussian subjects and became a symbol of German beauty and purity. The privations she suffered after fleeing the invading Napoleonic army in 1806–1807 led to her death in 1810, and this "martyrdom" quickly transformed her in the popular mind into a kind of Hohenzollern Joan of Arc, a symbol of German resistance and vengeance during the 1813 War of Liberation against Napoleon. Wilhelm II's original 1895 refusal to approve any works about Luise was, curiously, reiterated in June 1913 and was, even more curiously, apparently enforced throughout World War I.

In the end, the house of Hohenzollern's hypersensitivity to its historic image and the heavy-handed controls it used to keep so many of its forebears off the public stages of Germany was sadly short-sighted. By prohibiting the performance of numerous highly patriotic plays dealing with some of the emperor's most popular ancestors, the monarchy lost numerous opportunities to establish closer emotional ties with the populace and heighten nationalist feeling. But more seriously, such policies created a kind of Gresham's law in this field, for bad Hohenzollern dramas drove out good ones, virtually guaranteeing that little of lasting artistic merit would be written about the dynasty. As the literary critic Heinrich Stümcke noted at the turn of the century, to allow only one-sided, completely laudatory depictions of characters produces only one-dimensional, dehumanized, wooden stereotypes. The best artists, however, are interested in exploring all dimensions of a character, the shadowy and negative as well as the light and positive; they want to examine a great ruler not only at the peak of his success, but also at his times of conflict, doubt, and failure, for it is often precisely those experiences that made someone like Friedrich the Great heroic, "great," and fascinating. "From the standpoint of art, it must therefore be considered a serious mistake when police and censors prevent the performance of a work on the grounds that members of the ruling dynasty are depicted as human beings with human weaknesses. ... In doing so, they confine the playwright to the narrow and, in poetic terms, unfruitful realm of patriotic festivals, which even under the hand of a talented author can never meet the highest demands of art." When only light, superficial works can be performed, Stümcke warned, talented writers quickly turn to other, more promising areas and he pointed to a number of basically pro-Hohenzollern dramatists (Gustav von Putlitz, Karl Gutzkow, Ernst Wichert, Ernst von Wildenbruch) who, out of frustration, abandoned their plans for inspiring works based on historical themes and turned instead to other topics. "In the end, there can be no doubt that a dramatic author's inclination and desire to work up material from our national history for the stage is frequently killed off in advance by the sense that his precious little craft [*Glückschifflein*], if it somehow manages to survive the Charybdis of literary criticism, will, with deadly certainty, fall victim to the Scylla of a royal ban."[36]

Even the outbreak of the war did not significantly alter the monarchy's short-sighted policies. On the one hand, the emperor did try to stir up patriotic sentiment by encouraging performances of older works like Ludwig's *Die Torgauer Heide* (although still with "Sire" rather than "Fritz") and he approved a slightly larger number of new Hohenzollern dramas than before the war. On the other hand, the crown explicitly reiterated its long-standing prohibition on any works dealing with Queen Luise or the conflict between Friedrich the Great and his father; it continued to refuse approval to the works of such popular writers as Paul Ernst (*Preußengeist* [*Spirit of Prussia*]), Herbert Eulenberg (*Der Morgen Nach Kunersdorf* [*The Morning After Kunersdorf*]), and Emil Ludwig (*Friedrich, König von Preußen*); and it generally discouraged for the duration of the war the submission of any Hohenzollern dramas for royal approval.[37]

The perceived perils of portraying Hohenzollern dynastic history on stage during wartime are perhaps best illustrated by the September 1917 ban of Hans Bötticher's *Friedrich der Große*. Not only did this drama contain the taboo subject of young Friedrich's conflict with his father, but Berlin police also feared its portrayal of a harshly militaristic ruler (Friedrich Wilhelm I), of war-mongering generals, and of Friedrich the Great's unleashing an aggressive war to satisfy his ego and lust for conquest would all cause political and morale problems on the home front. Moreover, they feared Friedrich the Great's preemptive attack on Saxony in 1756 might remind Germans of the empire's attack on Belgium in 1914![38]

Only the collapse of the monarchy in 1918 ended the stifling censorship of Hohenzollern characters on stage, resulting in the final irony that it was much easier to stage a drama about the Hohenzollerns in the Weimar republic, after the dynasty was deposed, than in the imperial era, when it reigned.

Pillars of the Imperial Order

Next to the monarchy the military (more precisely, the Prussian army) was the central institution of the German Empire. A "state within the state" immune from civilian control, its function was as much to defend the monarchy and ruling elite against internal revolution as to defend the nation from external threats. As a reliable praetorian guard of the monarchy and a formidable opponent of any political change, the military was an institution Germany's rulers defended tenaciously.

Civilian esteem for the military was extraordinarily high after the Franco-Prussian war and nowhere was this more apparent than in theaters: between 1870 and 1914 dramas about the military and military life flooded the German stage and proved enormously popular. (One study has counted well over eight hundred theatrical works written and/or performed in the imperial era simply about the *contemporary* German military.[39]) This profusion of military plays and of uniforms on stage—the military's "massive objectification in the theater"—did much to increase its popularity and make it "an object of patriotic adoration."[40]

By stressing the more harmless, even comic aspects of military life and avoiding its sinister features, much of this promilitary literature propagated and reinforced a popular image that military service was an elevating and uplifting experience for young recruits. Maintaining public confidence in the ennobling quality of military service and in the officer corps that trained new soldiers was especially important because of universal compulsory military service: when every German male had to serve at least a year in the military, every family was likely to worry about what kind of men would be commanding their sons and what impact military service would have upon these youths. For this reason authorities were quick to react to literary works, especially dramas, that depicted how officers and military service might brutalize and morally corrupt young recruits.

Mistreatment and harassment of conscripts by ruthless, sadistic officers and a harsh system of military justice that left victims with little legal redress and stripped defendants of most of the rights civilians enjoyed was a serious problem, especially before 1900, when modest reforms were made to the military penal code. These conditions were the subject of Elsa von Schabelski's 1893 drama *Notwehr* (*Self Defense*), in which a young recruit is so mercilessly persecuted by a brutal officer (who desires the recruit's fiancée) that in a moment of desperate self defense he is forced to kill the officer, for which he is sentenced to death but at the last minute pardoned by the emperor. Berlin police banned this drama because in their view it misrepresented actual conditions in the military and might encourage uninformed members of the public to believe common soldiers were entirely defenseless against their superiors' cruelest whims. Both the District Administrative Council and Supreme Administrative Law Court, to which this decision was appealed, upheld the ban on the grounds that even if isolated cases of abuse do occur, a sensationalistic play like this, which (falsely) portrays such abuses as widespread, was "likely to cause among common soldiers dissatisfaction with their condition and insubordination toward their superiors." In the opinion of the courts, a public performance of *Notwehr* would threaten public order and security both directly and indirectly: directly, because it might provoke disturbances and violent outbursts among the many soldiers and officers likely to attend; and indirectly, because it would "undermine [soldiers'] confidence in the wisdom of military institutions and respect for their superiors, thereby attacking the moral foundations essential for discipline and order in the army." Any threat to army discipline endangers public peace, order, and security because, on the one hand, the discipline and order of the army forms a part of public order, and on the other hand, the maintenance of public peace, security, and order outside the army is predicated on discipline within it. A public performance of *Notwehr* would undoubtedly provoke in audiences not only sympathy for the victim and loathing for his tormentor, but [this] would direct itself against the state itself [for not only allowing, but even encouraging such abuses to take place]. ... The passionate bitterness that would be aroused against the state and its institutions and the resulting antipathy toward military service, which is based on universal conscription, presents a danger to the common good against which the police must justifiably intervene.[41]

Two decades later the same arguments were revived when Berlin censors considered Leo Jungman's *Die letzten sechs Wochen* (*The Last Six Weeks*) whose plot mirrored that of *Notwehr*: six weeks before his discharge, a young soldier is pitilessly persecuted by his commanding officer, who holds a personal grudge against him; provoked into striking the officer, through false testimony he is court-martialed and sentenced to three years' imprisonment. Although the work was already being performed in Bremen, Saarbrücken, and a few other small cities, the Berlin police president banned it there in March 1910 and wrote these other cities strongly urging they do the same. Convinced that many of the events depicted in the drama simply could not occur under Germany's (recently revised) military penal code, he considered Jungman's play "an unjustified and embittered attack against state order. ... The piece *unjustly* attacks military law and judicial procedures, *unjustly* accuses these of harshness, and thereby *unjustly* arouses rage and bitterness toward the essential institution of the military and against military service itself." After an unsuccessful appeal to overturn the ban, the author tried three times to rewrite the play to satisfy the censor's objections, but each revision was rejected.[42]

Officers' brutality against civilians, also a persistent problem, was another topic censors preferred not be depicted in the theater. As Gordon Craig noted, much of the officer corps viewed civilian society "with a mixture of contempt and hostility and regarded themselves as forming a castle guard to watch over their master's unruly subjects and see to it that they did their duty."[43] After the minister of war refused to investigate or condemn an 1896 incident in which an army lieutenant drew a sword in a restaurant and killed a civilian, Hermann Sudermann wrote *Morituri* (*We, Who Are About to Die, Salute You*), which mildly satirized the cruelty and arrogance often displayed by the military. Although approved for performance in Berlin in February 1897, some provincial governments, such as Baden's, refused to allow the piece to be performed in their theaters.[44] Less fatal, more amusing confrontations between officers and civilians were likewise taboo, such as the famous "Captain of Köpenick" incident of October 1906 in which the unemployed shoemaker and ex-convict Voigt, dressed in a secondhand captain's uniform, played upon civilian deference to military authority to arrest the obedient mayor of Köpenick and confiscate the city's treasury. The incident led immediately to a wave of theatrical satires in 1906–1907 (at least eight of which were entitled *Der Hauptmann von Köpenick*); while some were allowed in liberal Hamburg or smaller Bavarian cities such as Amberg, Passau, and Ulm, none were permitted in Berlin until 1911, when a comedy about *Schuster Voigt vor Gericht* (*Shoemaker Voigt on Trial*), dealing with the "captain's" subsequent trial, was approved.[45]

Besides jealously guarding the military against charges of petty brutality, imperial censors also vigilantly protected it from accusations of moral corruption. For example, when a disillusioned young lieutenant stationed in a small garrison town in Alsace-Lorraine published a roman à clef in late 1903 exposing the dissipated lifestyles and base sexual debauchery of the officers he served with (Lt. Oswald F. Bilse, *Aus einer kleinen Garnison* [*Life in a Garrison Town*], 1903), he was immediately court-martialed and imprisoned for six months, ostensibly for failing to obtain prior permission from his superiors and for insulting his fellow officers, but in fact for revealing conditions the military found embarrassing. The emperor considered the military judge's sentence too lenient and reportedly had him immediately pensioned "for not knowing better how to protect the interests of your class."[46] Similarly, Cologne police required that some sexually suggestive lines spoken by a general be removed from a 1905 comedy there, and when a popular Berlin theater asked permission in 1909 to perform *Herzelied* (*Sorrow*), a play about an officer's romantic involvements, the censor refused on the grounds the lieutenant was presented in too negative a light and the uncritical petty-bourgeois audiences and social democratic workers who frequented that theater were likely to take him as typical of the entire officer corps.[47]

Against *Simplicissimus'* many biting satires of the arrogant, brutal officer corps in the years preceding the war, the authorities had only limited legal recourse. When a 1908 cartoon made fun of the virtual illiteracy of aristocratic officers in a certain regiment, the regiment successfully sued the *Simplicissimus* editorial board for libel, receiving a monetary award that even some segments of the liberal press considered too modest.[48] Yet when another cartoon in September 1909 about "*Reichs-Manöver*" ("Imperial Maneuvers") portrayed intellectually and morally decrepit Bavarian generals and showed Bavarian soldiers cheerfully raping a peasant girl, the Bavarian government banned that issue from sale in the state's railway stations but saw little chance of a more general confiscation or prosecution.[49]

Ironically, the German government was not terribly concerned with broader literary attacks on war and militarism in general, such as Bertha von Suttner's polemical *Die Waffen nieder!* (*Lay Down Your Arms!*) Lauded as the "*Uncle Tom's Cabin* of the peace movement" in Germany and as "one of the most successful and effective pieces of antiwar literature ever written," this 1889 antiwar novel was enormously popular and by 1905 had gone through thirty-seven editions.[50] While authorities were contemptuous of the peace movement, they took little action against it since the Press Law protected pacifist literary works. A dramatized version of von Suttner's novel was banned in Berlin in December 1910, however, even though the play had been performed in Frankfurt and Nuremberg.[51]

Once the war began, censors paid still closer attention to the public image of the officer corps. O. E. Hartleben's *Rosenmontag. Eine Offiziers-Tragödie* (*Monday Before Lent: An Officer's Tragedy*), the story of a young officer driven to suicide because his colleagues did not consider the girl he loved *standesgemäß* (socially acceptable for an officer), had been a huge success after Berlin and Munich censors passed a slightly cut version in 1900; but when a Breslau theater asked to perform it in 1917, the play was banned because it implied the despicable behavior of a few was representative of many. "Permitting this piece at the present time," the censor said, "just when the officer corps is so heroically bleeding and proving itself, and when we must avoid anything that might arouse ill-will against the army, is out of the question."[52] During the war, district military commanders in Stettin, Berlin, and Munich ordered Hans Brennert's *Blau und Rot* (*Blue and Red*) banned because it allegedly caricatured the German officer corps and "might occasion an unfavorable view of the life and activities within military circles"; the farce *Nachtmanöver* (*Night Maneuvers*), about the amorous adventures of officers, was banned in Berlin 1916, as was the more serious, but disturbing, drama *Die Verwundeten* (*The Wounded*).[53]

Authorities, especially in Prussia, were also keen to prevent theatrical performances that tarnished the public's image of the legal and judicial system. Thus in November 1895 the Prussian ministers of the interior and justice intervened against Hermann Haas' drama *Das Recht* (*The Law*), a thinly veiled fictionalized account of a notorious 1888 Prussian murder case in which a man was sentenced to life imprisonment despite some evidence for, and a near universal popular belief in, his innocence. The piece had already been performed in over one hundred theaters in Bavaria, Baden, Hamburg, and elsewhere when it was banned throughout Prussia. Because it sensationalized and (in the government's opinion) misrepresented a grievous miscarriage of justice, its public performance in Prussia would threaten public order by unnecessarily "agitating and alarming the populace." The District Administrative Council, to which this decision was appealed, overturned the ban but the Supreme Administrative Law Court later upheld the government's proscription because the work was "likely to fundamentally undermine [the audience's] trust in the criminal justice system."[54] That court also upheld a 1907 Breslau ban of Hermann Armer's courtroom drama *Vor dem Schoffengericht* (*Before the Jury*) because it made light of perjury and "portrayed a state institution in a laughable and derogatory manner," while another drama, *Der Causa Kaiser* (*The Lawsuit Emperor*), was banned in Munich in 1917 as "a crass defamation of the judiciary and the bar [*Richter- und Anwaltstandes*]."[55]

Censors also tried to ban several works that reflected unfavorably on police officials, a group to which the censors themselves belonged. Hans Hyan's *Schlossermaxe* (*Locksmith Max*), a light suspense-comedy about safecrackers, was banned in Berlin in 1912 because it portrayed two Berlin policemen as stupid, crude incompetents. Police argued—and both the provincial governor and Supreme Administrative Law Court, to which the ban was appealed, later agreed—the play "mocked and ridiculed police officials in an especially crude way; ... public order and security is endangered when police are made laughable in public. Such an offense is likely not only to undermine public respect for police officers, but also public trust in them." The fact that the theater in question was frequented by many workers who "will greet with *Schadenfreude* any efforts to make police officials look ridiculous and repulsive on stage" was also a consideration. At a German Writers' Defense League protest meeting on the eve of the court's verdict, one speaker quipped that the three things not allowed on Berlin stages are God (see chapter 5), the Hohenzollerns, and policemen. Why? Because German police are more holy than the monarch, and the nation's rulers fear public confidence in them might sink even lower than it is.[56]

At times, however, courts felt censors were oversensitive in this regard. After the police president of Königsberg took offense at a 1904 satirical piece in *Simplicissimus* suggesting Prussian police collaborated with and sometimes did the bidding of Russian police, the Stuttgart prosecutor reluctantly pressed libel charges against Ludwig Thoma (author of the article) and Julius Linnenkogel (editor at the time), but a Württemberg jury acquitted both men.[57] When Berlin police wanted to prohibit Lothar Schmidt's *Fiat Justicia* in 1911 for ridiculing police, the District Administrative Council overturned the ban, apparently unconvinced by the argument that although the play was set in Serbia, the police characters had the same titles and ranks as Berlin's police force![58] The council also thwarted Berlin Police President von Jagow's attempt to strike a particular line from Gerhart Hauptmann's *Die Ratten (The Rats)*, in which a vaudeville theater director remarks offhandedly he knows the former Berlin Police President von Maidai well; considering that character's occupation and character, to von Jagow such an implied acquaintance amounted to a defamation of the former police president. The District Administrative Council reversed the decision, noting wryly that "public order will not be threatened if director Hassenreuther claims the generally well-known and even very popular former police president as one of his acquaintances."[59]

Although constitutionally the national Reichstag and state parliaments (*Landtage*) were also key imperial institutions, the public image of parliament and parliamentarians received far less of the censors' attention. Whether this was because parliaments were more highly regarded and needed less protection, or because authorities were less willing to intervene on their behalf, is difficult to say. While it is true that in turn-of-the-century Munich police would not allow even the feeblest jokes about the Bavarian parliament to be told on stage, it was also true that in Dresden, censors in 1903 required a theater to change the line "Uncle Peter is without doubt the dumbest fellow in the family, and they made him a chamberlain [*Kammerherr*]" to read instead "they made him a parliamentary delegate [*Abgeordnete*]."[60] Theater censors were, in any case, uneasy about direct references or indirect allusions to specific parliamentarians. Thus Friedrich Pastor's *Die Moralisten (The Moralists)*, a drama á clef about conservative party politics, was approved for Berlin in 1896 on the following conditions: (1) a character's name be changed from Hammerstein and the actor playing that role not look like Baron von Hammerstein, head of the Conservative Party; (2) the actor playing a court chaplain not look like Court Chaplain Stöcker, head of the Christian-Social Party; and (3) the character named Herzog Heinrich II not look like Wilhelm II.[61] Likewise, when O. Blumenthal and E. Radelburg's *Die strengen Herren (The Stern Masters)*, which ruthlessly satirized the puritanical moral crusaders in the Reichstag who were trying to push through the Lex Heinze, was submitted for

review in 1900, the Berlin censor believed it ridiculed and libeled certain prominent Reichstag delegates and would not pass it until it was toned down.[62] Such
hypersensitivity marked a real change from the 1870s, when an English visitor to
Berlin commented that politics and satire on the stage "are rather the rule than
the exception … and great statesmen not only do not mind being mentioned by
name, but are to be seen laughing at the impersonations of themselves."[63]

Imperial censors, then, could claim much success defending the images of the
army and judicial system (even though the latter often undercut much of the
censors' work in other areas); efforts to protect the less prestigious police were less
effectual. Guarding the honor of the nation's elected legislators was, for whatever
reason, a lower priority.

Suspect Minorities

Among the new empire's many internal political problems, one of the most
troublesome was the assimilation of resentful minorities. The heterogeneous,
multiethnic nation that emerged from the wars of unification contained several
conquered regions and foreign nationality groups that had been forcibly annexed
to Prussia or the empire and whose identification with and loyalty to the German nation-state was questionable. These dissident groups—the Poles of eastern
Prussia, the Danes of northern Schleswig, the French of Alsace-Lorraine, and, in
a different way, the "Guelph" party of Hanoverian patriots—were often regarded
by Bismarck and his successors as enemies of the empire (*Reichsfeinde*) whose
particularism threatened national unity. Accordingly, censors consistently suppressed works they feared might promote separatism or nationalist consciousness
in these regions.

During unification Prussia's eastern Polish provinces (Posen, West Prussia,
Upper Silesia) opposed being included in a German national state. In both the
Prussian parliament and national Reichstag after 1871 these regions consistently
returned a faction of between twelve and twenty delegates who championed the
rights of the 2.5 million Polish citizens there and resisted increasingly harsh efforts to Germanize this area. Prussian authorities, pressured by radical German
nationalist groups in the area, carried on a long, bitter struggle to make German
the required language in schools and for all government business and public meetings. When, in 1894, local police began requiring that private as well as public
theatrical performances receive prior approval and that Polish-language scripts
submitted for censorship be accompanied by an officially notarized German translation, Polish spokesmen condemned the new policy as one designed to prevent
all Polish-language performances by making the approval process too costly and
cumbersome.[64]

Fearing the Polish minority represented a "counter-nation" that sought to res-
urrect a Polish nation state, Prussian authorities were apprehensive of any expressions of Polish patriotism, nationalism, or solidarity. Since Polish nationalists

often used folktales and other forms of popular literature to make allegorical allusions to Polish history and contemporary situations, authorities were continually on the lookout for tendentious, agitational works of popular literature that could "enliven in the Polish population the longing for a reestablishment of Poland and incite them to participate actively [in that effort]."[65] When a Polish language journal in Posen, on the fifty-third anniversary of the Polish uprising of 1830, published a literary paraphrase of Seweryna Duchińa's famous poem "Jeszcze Polska nie zginela" ("Poland has not yet perished," which became the Polish national anthem after World War I), the editor was sentenced to two months' jail for inciting social classes to violence against each other. The court ruled the poem contained "revolutionary ideas" that, given the dangerous situation in Posen, were a "more or less veiled summons to violence." For there Germans live side by side with Poles, who are well aware

> that in the not too distant past their home was part of the Polish state and [they] have still not come to terms with the historically, politically, and legally sanctioned facts by which the province of Posen has become an integral part of the Prussian monarchy. The frequently mentioned [Polish] revolutionary uprisings [of 1830–1831, 1846, 1848, and 1863–1864], the last of which was only twenty years ago, occurred partly in the province of Posen and affected Posen most profoundly, so the memory of those is still very much alive in the Polish population.

Poles lived in "more or less silent opposition to the existing situation," the court acknowledged, and considered Germans "intruders, enemies, and oppressors." For Polish readers, therefore, this poem could be provocative and inflammatory and could endanger the public peace by inciting Poles to violence against Germans.[66]

Control of Polish-language material tightened after the turn of the century, when Polish societies, associations, and cultural institutions proliferated and became centers of Polish nationalist consciousness and agitation. Authorities confiscated and banned numerous publications, including novels, songbooks, dramas, histories, pictures, and even certain prayer books and hymnals because they might threaten public order by arousing the Polish minority to violence against the German majority.[67]

Censors paid particularly close attention to Polish-language theatrical performances, which they regarded less as cultural events than as political statements against the German populace and Prussian monarchy.[68] The government declared performances in Polish to be public assemblies, which, under a provision of the 1908 imperial law governing associations (*Reichsvereinsgesetz*), could be held only in areas where 60 percent or more of the population was Polish. (Besides eastern Prussia, some western cities like Bochum had large numbers of Polish settlers and immigrant workers.) Police observers were sent to every performance, even after the work had been approved, to report on the size and nature of the audience and its reaction to the performance, and those reports were shared with other provincial governors. Entrepreneurs or directors seeking a license to operate a new Polish-language theater were routinely turned down, ostensibly for lacking sufficient financial resources or because there was "not sufficient demand for such a theater," but in fact for political reasons. As the Posen police president explained privately to the provincial governor, he rejected one such application because "experience shows that [popular and so-called national Polish plays] often tend to preach the conflict between [German and Polish] nationalities in a covert or even overt manner. It cannot be denied that the way such allusions are expressed, staged, and contextualized can greatly affect the public and that is why Poles regard Polish theatrical performances as a very popular opportunity for national solidarity and political agitation."[69]

Although police allowed some dramas to be performed publicly in Polish, these were carefully screened; besides the usual moral, religious, or political reasons, a number were banned or had to be revised because of their supposed anti-German or overly Polish-nationalist tendencies. The historical drama *Eva Miaskowska,* set during the Poles' heroic seventeenth-century defeat of the Turks, is a case in point: After an initial performance in Posen it was banned by police in Gembitz in 1909, since it was "likely to awaken and reinforce Polish nationalist consciousness to a dangerous degree." Both the District Administrative Council and the Supreme Administrative Law Court upheld the ban because its constant focus on the Polish fatherland and flagrant nationalist feeling strengthened Polish nationalist consciousness, and

> given the psychological situation that agitation for a Greater Poland has created among a great many Poles, would lead to a revival of hopes for a future Polish-national commonwealth. Perceptions would thereby be awakened that would lead to behavior that endangers the state order, namely, the existence and the constitution of the Prussian state. Under these circumstances a performance would lead not to a state-preserving [*staatserhaltende*] sense of Prussian and German patriotism, but rather to a yearning for a future Polish fatherland.[70]

The drama *Stary-Mundur,* about the 1863 Polish insurrection against Russia, was of course banned by police in Stettin in 1916 because it "glorified revolutionary ideas" and Polish national liberation.[71] Besides prohibiting public performances, authorities could—and did—ban and confiscate the printed text of many Polish dramas, as well as songs, poems, and novels (including some by Henryk Sienkiewicz, author of *Quo vadis* and winner of the 1905 Nobel Prize for literature.)

Equally troubling to Prussian authorities were expressions of regional anti-Prussian patriotism in the province of Hanover, which had been forcibly annexed by Prussia in 1866 following the Kingdom of Hanover's defeat in the Austro-Prussian war. Throughout the imperial era the deposed Guelph dynasty of Hanover and its supporters remained "a small but persistent thorn in the empire's flesh."[72] From exile in Austria, King Georg V (and later his son Ernst August) never accepted Hanover's annexation and continued to insist on and work for the restoration of their kingdom. Their efforts had the support of an irreconcilable Guelph party in Hanover that consistently garnered about 30 percent of the votes cast in the region and after 1871 was represented by between four and eleven delegates in the Reichstag. It was in this context that in October 1911 police in the small Hanoverian town of Lüchow banned G. H. Ayrer's *Schlacht bei Langensalza* (*Battle at Langensalza*), which dealt with the defeat of Hanoverian troops in 1866 and ended with a stirring patriotic speech by the deposed King Georg V. Although this work had already been performed over 150 times throughout the province of Hanover, a recent electoral victory by a Guelph candidate and increasing propagandistic activity by the Guelph party now convinced both police and the courts that Ayrer's drama might "inflame German-Hanoverian-minded spectators on the one hand and insult and provoke national-minded patriotic spectators on the other," causing political outbursts that could endanger public peace, security, and order. The ban was appealed to, and upheld by, both the district administrative president and the Supreme Administrative Law Court.[73]

While the loyalty of native Hanoverians to the empire and the German national cause was never in doubt once war broke out with France in 1914, that of the population in Alsace-Lorraine was. After France was forced to cede the department of Alsace-Lorraine to the new German Empire in 1871, anti-German movements and parties were strong in the region (which until 1911 remained a specially administered *Reichsland* within the empire). Although anti-German political sentiments subsided after 1890 and Alsace-Lorraine became more of a normal federal state and more integrated into the imperial system after 1911, French revanchism and the problem of divided nationalist loyalties there posed a serious problem again once Germany and France were at war. Civilian censors and military commanders did not always agree, however, on just how serious this problem was for German public morale.

Soon after the outbreak of the war, the provincial governor of Alsace-Lorraine (which now was under virtual military dictatorship) secretly asked the help of all local police throughout the empire in suppressing public discussion about the physical impact of the war upon Alsace-Lorraine or about the general stance of this area's population toward the war.[74] This latter issue was precisely what interested the young Alsatian writer René Schickele, whose 1914 drama *Hans im Schnakenloch* explored, in a balanced and sensitive way, some of the dilemmas the war presented to French families in Alsace, where one son might fight on the German side and another on the French. After police in Frankfurt and Nuremberg permitted the play there, in December 1916 Berlin censors also approved an extensively revised script from which all politically sensitive passages had been removed. It was an immediate box office success and received widespread praise in the capital, including from the conservative press. In April 1917, however, General Ludendorff reported he had received complaints from German patriots that the work "glorifies anti-German Alsatianism" and he asked the local military commander to find out why it passed the censors.[75] Berlin police defended their decision, pointing out this was a very popular work of high literary quality that, on the whole, left a basically pro-German impression. Moreover, to ban it now, after the fact, would be a serious political mistake: the public uproar that would surely ensue would do more to disrupt public peace and order than the play ever would. To appease the military, however, the police and theater in question struck from the script several additional passages to which ardent German patriots might object.

But Ludendorff was not appeased. After Leipzig authorities, too, approved the play, the general insisted Schickele's drama did *not* make a German-national impression on its audience; in fact, Ludendorff argued, the author's even-handed treatment of both French and German viewpoints and his depiction of the horrible effects of the war on one family created in spectators "an inner estrangement [*innerlichen Abkehr*] from the war," which was reason enough to ban it. "If we forbid anything to be published in the press and so forth that can unfavorably affect the public's attitude toward the war, it shouldn't be permitted to spread such ideas to the populace through the far more impressionable form of a theatrical piece," he wrote. After Berlin police once again disputed the unpatriotic effect of the play, reiterated the political dangers of an outright ban, and excised still more potentially questionable passages, in June they were informed that General Headquarters considered any works about the German-French conflict in Alsace-Lorraine to be inappropriate, and when the theater season ended in two weeks, *Hans im Schnakenloch* must no longer be performed. So after ninety-nine well-attended performances in Berlin and several elsewhere, the play was closed. A request by a Berlin theater in September 1918 to perform Schickele's piece now that the political situation had changed (it was fairly clear by now the region would returned to French control) was curtly refused.

Foreign Considerations

German officials also felt compelled to intervene in literary life in the interests of the empire's foreign policy (something I have discussed extensively elsewhere)[76] and were rarely questioned when they did so. Plays, operettas, films, caricatures, or other popular entertainments that might prove diplomatically embarrassing or harmful—especially those dealing with Russia, Austria-Hungary, France, or Turkey—were regularly banned or had to be excised, often at the express request of the chancellor, the Foreign Office, or foreign ambassadors. Imperial authorities seem to have realized, however, that censoring works in order to avoid offending other nations is an ensnaring undertaking. Once a government has assumed the role of censor, no matter how liberal its policies or how infrequently it uses that power, it necessarily assumes responsibility for (and can legitimately be held responsible for) what it allows and does not allow in public. Censoring authorities relinquish any position of neutrality or indifference: if they choose not to prohibit a potentially offensive work, it will be perceived by observers as actually condoning or endorsing that piece; the very decision *not* to intervene to prevent a possible insult could, and probably would, itself be interpreted as an intentional insult by the foreign power in question. Thus, the empire felt it had little alternative but to respond to virtually every foreign complaint and intervene even where there was but the slightest chance of offending a foreign power.

While state interventions into literary life for other reasons (social, moral, religious) frequently met with resistance in the press or from the courts, it is striking how censorship in the interest of imperial foreign policy generated so little public controversy and how government bans in this area were rarely rescinded. Whether because of a supposed German tradition of the primacy of foreign policy (*Primat der Außenpolitik*), or concern about Germany's increasingly precarious international situation after Bismarck's departure in 1890, or because foreign policy was still regarded as the exclusive domain of the elite aristocratic circles that staffed the German Foreign Office, few Germans questioned the censors' decisions when they acted because of diplomatic concerns.

Notes

1. Conrad Alberti, "Eine Majestätsbeleidigung," in *Plebs. Novellen aus dem Volke* (Leipzig, 1887), 79–180.
2. Frank, *Strafgesetzbuch,* 201–3; Karl von Birkmeyer, et. al., *Vergleichende Darstellung des deutschen und ausländische Strafrechts. Besonderer Teil, I. Band* (Berlin, 1906), 91–112; Alex Hall, "The Kaiser, the Wilhelmine State and Lèse-Majesté," *German Life and Letters* 27 (1973–74): 101–15. English law considered expressing contempt for the king a misdemeanor punishable with jail, but by the end of the nineteenth century the law was rarely invoked. Similarly in France, defamation of the president of the republic was a punishable offense but in practice rarely prosecuted. Nevertheless, one comparative study of political crime in Europe maintains Germany's punishment of crimes like lèse majesté was relatively lenient compared to France and England. Barton L. Ingraham, *Political Crime in Europe: A Comparative Study of France, Germany, and England* (Berkeley, CA, 1979), 187–90.
3. Helga Abret and Aldo Keel, ed., *Die Majestätsbeleidigungsaffäre des 'Simplicissimus'-Verlegers Albert Langen* (Frankfurt, 1985), 4–13; *Münchener Neueste Nachrichten* 8 Nov. 1898; Ludwig Fuld, "Majestätsbeleidigung," *Neue Deutsche Rundschau* 4, no. 1 (1898): 224; Leo Berg, "Über die Zufälligkeit und die Grenzen der Majestätsbeleidigung als Strafbegriff im modernen Staatsleben," *Die Gegenwart* 27, Bd. 33 (1 Jan. 1898): 6–8; also *Die Gesellschaft* 5 (1898): 297–98.
4. Birkmeyer, *Vergleichende Darstellung,* 108–12. On whether Germany should follow England in abolishing lèse majesté as a legal offense and rely merely on informal social sanctions for its punishment, the commission stated, "The development of opinion [in Germany] regarding the state is not yet developed enough to appear to justify such a step." (ibid., 112).
5. Law of 17 Feb. 1908, Frank, *Strafgesetzbuch,* 201.
6. Thomas A. Kohut, *Wilhelm II and the Germans: A Study in Leadership* (New York, 1991), 148.
7. Hanns von Gumppenberg, *Lebenserinnerungen. Aus dem Nachlaß des Dichters* (Berlin and Zurich, 1929), 172–80; Lenman, "Censorship and Society," 18; Jelavich, *Munich and Theatrical Modernism,* 36–37.
8. Harden later claimed that judge (Alexander Schmidt) was removed from office seven months later, presumably for that acquittal, and forced into retirement. Bruce Uwe Weller, *Maximilian Harden und die 'Zukunft'* (Bremen, 1970), 109; Harry Young, *Maximilian Harden, Censor Germaniae: The Critic in Opposition from Bismarck to the Rise of Nazism* (The Hague, 1959), 60; Harden, "Landesgerichtsdirektor Schmidt," *Die Zukunft* 7, no. 37 (16 June 1894): 486–89,

"Auf der Anklagebank," *Die Zukunft* 25 (12 Nov. 1898): 273–83, and "Prozeßbericht," *Die Zukunft* 9, no. 3 (20 Oct. 1900): 100–101. In fact, the PrJM tried to transfer him to a less politically sensitive civil court but the senior judges supervising the courts twice refused the minister's demand. Schmidt eventually transferred voluntarily, and later resigned for other reasons. Benjamin Carter Hett, "The 'Captain of Köpenick' and the Transformation of German Criminal Justice, 1891–1914," *Central European History* 36, no. 1 (2003): 13.

9. Hans-Ulrich Wehler, introduction to Ludwig Quidde, *Caligula. Schriften über Militarismus und Pazifismus,* ed. H-U. Wehler (Frankfurt, 1977), 12–13.

10. See Quidde's account in his "Erinnerungen. Im Kampf gegen Cäsarismus und Byzantinismus im Kaiserlichen Deutschland," in Wehler, ed., *Caligula,* 19–32.

11. After the conservative press called for Quidde's prosecution, he issued a clever statement seeming to deny he had Wilhelm II in mind when he wrote about Caligula, without, however, actually doing so. See his 23 May 1894 statement in the *Vossische Zeitung* and in the *Frankfurter Zeitung,* reprinted in "Erinnerungen," 30–31.

12. Quidde, "Erinnerungen," 32.

13. Ibid., 47.

14. Michael Bauer, *Oskar Panizza. Ein literarisches Porträt* (Munich, 1984), 196, 220; Peter D. G. Brown, *Oskar Panizza: His Life and Works* (New York, 1983), 57–59, 97–105.

15. Munich police order of 30 Jan. 1900 and warrant of 10 Feb. 1900, StA München, St.Anws. 7122; Bauer, *Panizza,* 36–7, 208–16; Brown, *Panizza,* 58.

16. Jane Clapp, *Art Censorship: A Chronology of Proscribed and Prescribed Art* (Metuchen, NJ, 1972), 173–74; Allen, *Satire and Society,* 111–12; and Johannes Trojan, *Zwei Monate Festung,* 3. Aufl. (Berlin, 1899).

17. Young, *Harden,* 60; Weller, *Harden,* 112–14; Harden, "Prozeßbericht," 101.

18. See editorial comment, *Simplicissimus* II, no. 41 (1897/98): 320; and Bjørnstjerne Bjørnson to Albert Langen, 8 Oct. 1898, as quoted in Helga Abret and Aldo Keel, ed., *Im Zeichen des Simplicissimus. Briefwechsel Albert Langen Dagny Bjørnson 1895–1908* (Munich, 1987), 60. Langen later claimed that Th. Th. Heine's father had warned his son "a great *coup* is being prepared against [*Simplicissimus*]." (Langen to Dagny Bjørnson, 5 Nov. 1898, *Im Zeichen,* 188–90.)

19. Ludwig Thoma, *Erinnerungen. Gesammelte Werke, Band 1* (Munich, 1956), 158–61; Wedekind to B. Bjørnson, 28 Sept. 1899, in Wedekind, *Gesammelte Briefe,* 2: 16. Korfiz Holm, also on the editorial staff, blamed the firm's lawyer, who reportedly suggested a few changes in the original version but assured the staff there was no danger involved in publishing the revised version. Holm, *ich, kleingeschrieben. Heitere Erlebnisse eines Verlegers* (Munich, 1932), 81–109.

20. See the detailed accounts and correspondence in Abret and Keel, *Im Zeichen,* 55–102, 182–242; Abret and Keel, *Die Majestätsbeleidigungsaffäre;* Holm, *ich kleingeschrieben,* 81–109 and his *Farbiger Abglanz. Erinnerungen an Ludwig Thoma, Max Dauthenden, und Albert Langen* (Munich, 1940), 61–66; T. Heine correspondence in StBM, Nachlaß Heine; Kutscher, *Wedekind,* 2: 17–26, and Wedekind, *Gesammelte Briefe,* 1: 314–40; Allen, *Satire and Society,* 40–41, 121–25; and Lenman, "Censorship and Society," 84–86.

21. Lenman, "Censorship and Society," 96; StenBer/Bav, xii (14 Jan. 1904), 428–32; complaints in *Die Gartenlaube,* 1908, 641.

22. Landmann and Rohmer, *Kommentar,* 513; Hanseatic Gesandter to Bremen Bürgermeister, 26 Mar. 1907, StA Bremen, 4, 14/1–VI.D.1, and Bremen Senat to Stadttheater, 27 Mar. 1907, StA Bremen, 3-S.23.a. Nr. 44; *Frankfurter Zeitung,* 28 Mar. 1907; BPP memo of 24 Mar. 1907, GStA PK/1000, Nr. 5, Bd. 4, Bl. 27; Hamburg police memo of 28 Mar. 1907, StA Hamburg, Pol. Nr. 2170, Vol. 23; Hessian IM to Kreisämter, 10 May 1907, StA Darmstadt, G15 Friedberg, XIX. Abt., III Abschnitt, Bd. 1.

23. Harden, "Das Urtheil im Fall Harden," *Die Zukunft* 6, no. 33 (14 May 1898): 312–17; Young, *Harden,* 60 n. 3; Weller, *Harden,* 403, n. 39.

24. Allen, *Satire and Society,* 170–71, 60–61; Lenman, "Censorship and Society," 148, 151–54.

25. Lenman, "Censorship and Society," 113.

26. Memo of Glasenapp, 27 Sept. 1904, LAB A/74, Th 495. See also GStA PK/1000, Nr. 4, Bd. 1, Bl. 67–70 and Nr. 5, Bd. 7, Bl. 88; and Lenman, "Censorship and Society," 245.

27. Glasenapp's report of 27 Sept. 1904, BPP order of 3 Oct. 1904, and BOP decision of 31 Oct. 1904, LAB A/74, Th 495. Text of the play, with extensive marks by the censor, is in LAB C/A.

28. OVG decision of 19 June 1905, LAB A/74, Th 495.

29. Pr Ministry of the Royal House and IM Decrees of 27 April 1844, 3 May 1883, 28 July 1884, 20 Oct. 1884, 27 Dec. 1900, GStA PK/1000, Nr. 5; GStA PK/ZK, Nrs. 21008–21011; and LAB A/74, Th 60–62. Also *VL*, 2: 599; Houben, *Polizei und Zensur*, 123–30; and Heinrich Meissner, "Monarchisches Prinzip und Theaterzensur. Eine Skizze nach den Akten," *Preußische Jahrbücher* 206 (Dec. 1926): 316–36. The Berlin police president could submit proposed dramas directly to the monarch's Civil Cabinet, while all other local censors were to work through the Interior Ministry.

30. GStA PK/1000, Nr. 5, Bd. 4, Bl. 293ff.

31. GStA PK/ZK, Nr. 21013, Bl. 102–12.

32. *VL*, 2: 361–63.

33. GStA PK/1000, Nr. 5, Bd. 2, Bl. 137–42.

34. Walach, "Das doppelte Drama," 270.

35. Civil Cabinet to PrIM, 13 Dec. 1909, GStA PK/1000, Nr. 5, Bd. 7, Bl. 247; also GStA PK/ZK, Nr. 21011, Bl. 61; LAB A/74, Th 496 and 134; Ferdinand Bonn, *Zwei Jahre Theaterdirektor in Berlin. Ein Beitrag zur deutschen Kulturgeschichte* (Berlin, 1908) and *Mein Künstlerleben. Was ich mit dem Kaiser erlebte und andere Erinnerungen* (Munich, 1920), 71–141.

36. Heinrich Stümcke, *Hohenzollernfürsten im Drama* (Leipzig, 1903), 245–49. He reiterates these criticisms again during the war: see his *Theater und Krieg* (Oldenburg and Leipzig, 1915), 37–38. The left-liberal Reichstag delegate Ernst Müller-Meiningen voiced similar conclusions before Stümke. In his 1900 speech to the Goethebund, he asserted that the House of Hohenzollern, with princes like the Great Elector or Friedrich the Great, had more members than any other royal house "who would be well-suited, if brought to the stage, to inflame the truest and best patriotism." *Die Theaterzensur. Fünf Vorträge*, 32.

37. PrIM to district police presidents, 19 Sept. 1914, LAB A/74, Th 134; *VL*, 2: 361–63; Schulze-Olden, "Theaterzensur in Rheinprovinz," 100.

38. Berlin police memo to PrIM 15 Sept. 1917, LAB A/74, Th 36.

39. Roswitha Flatz, *Krieg im Frieden. Das aktuelle Militärstück auf dem Theater des deutschen Kaiserreichs* (Frankfurt, 1976), "Stückenverzeichnis," 289–344.

40. Ibid., 4–18.

41. BPP ban of 18 Jan. 1893, BZA decision of 11 Jul. 1893, and OVG decision of 9 Aug. 1893, LAB A, Rep. 30, Berlin C, Tit. 75, Th 560. A copy of the play, with censor's markings, is in LAB C/A.

42. BPP to Bremen police 27 Jun. 1910, StA Bremen, 4, 14/1–VI.D.1, and BrOP decision of 8 Sept. 1910, LAB A/74, Th 434. Revised scripts are in LAB C/A. The Bremen police chief replied to Berlin he had read the work, "and found nothing that caused any serious misgivings. There is no question of any derision of military institutions, only a strong criticism of the existing military penal code. The performances held here were well attended and the public showed a lively interest in the course of the action. For the military stationed here the work was of course forbidden by the garrison commander." (Letter to Berlin PP, 25 Mar. 1910, StA Bremen, 4, 14/1–VI. D. 1.)

43. Gordon A. Craig, *The Politics of the Prussian Army 1640–1945* (New York, 1964), 252.

44. Flatz, *Krieg im Frieden*, 323; *Hamburger Echo*, 28 Jan. 1897, and Hall, *Scandal*, 128.

45. Flack, *Krieg im Frieden*, 102–3, 307.

46. Schulz, "Naturalismus und Zensur," 119, n.40; Hall, *Scandal*, 129. The book was translated into English as *Life in a Garrison Town*, trans. Arnold White (New York, 1914) and contains

an informative introduction about the background of Bilse's trial. Bilse was a pseudonym for Fritz von der Kyrburg.

47. Schulze-Olden, "Theaterzensur in Rheinprovinz," 92; Heinz-Dieter Heinrichs, "Das Rose-Theater. Ein volkstümliches Familientheater in Berlin von 1906 bis 1944" (Diss., F.U. Berlin, 1965), 129, n. 42.
48. The *Hamburger Nachrichten* actually considered the fine levied too lenient and complained about humor like *Simplicissimus*'s that encouraged citizens to hold the officer corps in contempt. Allen, *Satire and Society,* 109–10.
49. Lenman, "Censorship and Society," 138–39.
50. Roger Chickering, *Imperial Germany and a World Without War: The Peace Movement and German Society, 1892–1914* (Princeton, NJ, 1975), 12, 89.
51. Flack, *Krieg im Frieden,* 340.
52. *VL,* 2: 268. On the earlier cuts, see Dr. Müller's comments in StenBer/RT, 10. Leg. Per., 2. Sess, 37. Sitzung vom 30 Jun. 1901, Bd. 180, 1023.
53. LAB A/74, Th 36; Flack, *Krieg im Frieden,* 324, 338.
54. PrIM memo to BPP, 10 Nov. 1895 and 26 May 1898; BZA decision of 19 Apr. 1898, and OVG decision of 18 Jan. 1899, LAB A/74, Th 431. See also Hamburg police report 3 Nov. 1895, StA Hamburg, Pol. S. Nr. 2170, Vol. 23.
55. OVG decision of 16 Dec. 1907; LAB A/74, Th 36.
56. Censor's report, 7 Oct. 1912; BPP reply to OP, 3 Feb. 1913; OP decision 27 Feb. 1913; police report on Schutzverband meeting 21 Jan. 1913; and OVG decision 22 Jan. 1914, LAB A/74, Th 769.
57. Lenman, "Censorship and Society," 108–9.
58. BZA decision of 25 Jan. 1912, LAB A/74, Th 3827.
59. Werner Buth, "Das Lessing-Theater unter der Direktion von Otto Brahm 1904–1912," (Phil. diss., F.U. Berlin, 1964), 111–12.
60. Lenman, "Censorship and Society," 245; remarks of Dr. Barth in StenBer/Pr, 16. Sitzung, 7 Feb. 1903, Bd. 459, 1015. (The play in question was Erich Schlaikjer's *Pastor Rieke.*)
61. BPP to PrIM, 20 Mar. 1896, GStA PK/1000, Nr. 4, Bd. 2, Bl 136–38. Edited version of the script is in LAB C/A.
62. Censor's reports, 21 Jul. 1900 and BPP letter 28 Aug. 1900, LAB A/74, Th 494. The text of the play, with extensive markings by the censor, is in LAB C/A.
63. Vizetelly, *Berlin Under the New Empire,* 2: 236–37.
64. Remarks by Dr. Rzepnikowski, StenBer/PR, 25. Sitzung am 21. Feb. 1895, Bd. 391, 787.
65. Marek Rajch, *Preußische Zensurpolitik und Zensurpraxis in der Provinz Posen 1848/49 bis 1918* (Frankfurt, 2002), 14, 29, 32.
66. Judgment of Posen Landgericht, 7 Mar. 1884, quoted in ibid., 62–63.
67. Beginning in 1903 Posen political police compiled an annual catalog of forbidden Polish publications and images; by 1911 it was 112 pages long and contained hundreds of titles. For each entry an annotation indicated when, where, and why the piece was banned and the court cases upholding the bans. See Orlowski, *Polnisches Schrifttum unter Zensur,* 9–19 and Rajch, *Preußische Zensurpolitik,* 49–52.
68. Rajch, *Preußische Zensurpolitik,* 48.
69. Posen PP to RP, 19 May 1918, as quoted in ibid.
70. Gembitz police ban of 21 Jan. 1909; BZA decision of 3 Dec. 1909; and OVG decision of 7 Jul. 1911, LAB A/74, Th 130. For examples of other works banned or cut, see Posen police to Danzig PP, 13 Sept. 1911, 3 Sept. 1912, 13 Sept. 1913, Sept. 1914, and Sept. 1918, GStA PK Berlin, Rep. A 209, Nr. 3; and Bochum police to Posen police, 13 Dec. 1912, as quoted in Orlowski, *Polnisches Schrifttum,* 8–9.
71. LAB A/74, Th 36.
72. Otto Pflanze, *Bismarck and the Development of Germany. Volume II: The Period of Consolidation 1871-1880* (Princeton, NJ, 1990), 106.

73. OVG decision of 7 Jan. 1913, LAB A/74, Th 112.
74. Confidential memo of PrIM to local police directors, 4 Nov. 1914, LAB A/74, Th 134.
75. The account that follows is taken from *VL,* 2: 508–18, which reprints in full most of the documents without, however, indicating the source.
76. See my "Diplomacy By Other Means: Entertainment, Censorship, and German Foreign Policy, 1871–1918," in *Zensur und Kultur/Censorship and Culture. Zwischen Weimarer Klassik und Weimarer Republik mit einem Ausblick bis heute/From Weimar Classicism to Weimar Republic and Beyond,* ed. John McCarthy and Werner von der Ohe (Tübingen, 1995), 123–33, and my essay in Goldstein, *The Frightful Stage,* 22–69.

Chapter 4

Defending the Social Order

The minister of justice is supposed to prevent this nonsense!
—Wilhlem II, upon learning the Supreme Administrative Law Court
had overturned the Berlin police ban of "Die Weber," 1894

While conservative elites worried about securing the political order, many Germans were more apprehensive about the threat posed by the "social question." The social question—by which was meant a nexus of social problems related to the polarization of modern society into two antagonistic social classes, the miserable working and living conditions endured by workers, and increasing alienation of the working classes from both traditional values and bourgeois life—predated the empire. But it became more acute after 1871 when the economic crash of 1873 and rise of the socialist movement threatened bourgeois society with imminent social revolution, or so it was widely feared. Nervous observers pointed to several ominous developments as evidence of intensifying class struggle and the possibility of a revolutionary overthrow of the social order: the dramatic growth of socialist trade unions; the socialists' adamant opposition to the creation of the new empire and their support for the Paris Commune in 1871; their joining together into a single Social Democratic political party (SPD) in 1875 behind a Marxist platform demanding the political and economic emancipation of the working class and a democratic, egalitarian state; and the socialists' growing success in parliamentary elections.

The Campaign against Socialist Literature, 1870–1895

Believing Social Democracy was "an enemy against whom the state and society are bound to defend themselves,"[1] throughout the 1870s Bismarck waged an energetic political and legal war against it. Although the Reichstag thwarted his efforts to amend the Press Law and the Criminal Code to repress socialist agitation, following two assassination attempts against the emperor in 1878 (which the government immediately attributed to socialists), Bismarck persuaded parliament to approve a comprehensive new "Law against the Publicly Dangerous Endeavors of Social Democracy" authorizing the government to prohibit all political organizations, trade unions, clubs, societies, publications, and other activities "in which social-democratic, socialistic, or communistic endeavors aiming at the overthrow of the existing political or social order are manifested in a manner dangerous to the public peace, and particularly to harmony among the classes of the population."[2] While this "Anti-Socialist Law" was in force (1878 to 1890), the imperial government used it to conduct a ruthless campaign against Social Democratic activity of every kind, including socialist literary works and literary activities, both of which played a crucial role within the movement.

Before the emergence of the Naturalist literary movement in the mid-1880s, works of social realism and social criticism were rare in German literature. Even during the first decade of the new empire, amid rising social distress and political tensions spawned by rapid industrialization and proletarianization of the lower classes, the nation's most prominent writers and artists largely avoided social and political themes, choosing instead remote historical and mythological subjects, celebrating the cult of the genius-hero, or exploring the development of the individual personality. Middle-class writers of the 1870s and early 1880s, even those who adopted the Realist style, rejected German factory workers as both an aesthetic subject and as a legitimate political force in national life.

Until the mid-1880s literature with a genuine critical or radical social content could be found only within the "alternative culture" of the socialist labor movement. From its beginnings in the 1860s, the organized German labor movement recognized how valuable poetry, prose, and drama were, both as entertainment and to disseminate ideas. A number of socialist political leaders, journalists, and freelance writers (especially those associated with the early wing of the socialist movement led by Ferdinand Lassalle) produced a substantial body of socialist prose, poetry, and dramas, although nearly all were highly tendentious and of low artistic quality. Amateur working-class dramatic societies (*Arbeiter-Theatervereine*) also played an important role in the huge network of voluntary recreational, educational, cultural, and service associations affiliated with the SPD and socialist trade unions. After 1890 these were supplemented by a number of Free People's Stage Associations (*Freie Volksbühne Vereine*) that provided working-class subscribers with inexpensive tickets to special members-only performances commissioned from professional theaters. Poetry recitations, declamatory prose readings, amateur theatrical performances, and tableaux vivants (*Lebende Bilder:* posed pictures with persons) also figured prominently at most labor movement festivals, celebrations, and meetings.

These socialist literary works, dramatic societies, and other literary activities became an integral part of the social-cultural milieu of the German labor movement. Socialists and trade unionists, Vernon Lidtke has demonstrated, "made intensive use of various forms of literature, poetry, and drama especially, to broadcast their criticism of contemporary German society and to promote their views of an alternative."[3] Along with its other educational, recreational, and cultural institutions and activities, the socialist movement's literary activities posed a real subversive threat to the imperial order. For the social-cultural milieu of socialism stood in dramatic opposition to the basic norms and existing social arrangements of imperial Germany and posited a radical and credible alternative to these. The shared beliefs and values expressed through the Social Democratic movement and in its small but growing body of literary works represented the vision of a radically different kind of society, an alternative culture in the midst of the empire. Defenders of the imperial order fully recognized that socialist singing clubs, gymnastic associations, amateur dramatic societies, novels, poetry recitations, and the like profoundly endangered the existing social order and their own way of life; they regarded such activities as "a highly dangerous agitational medium of the [Social Democratic] party" that inculcated workers and their families "with the feelings of the 'outcast' working class and inoculated them with the poison of socialism."[4] For that reason socialist literary life became a special target of censorship.

Under the Anti-Socialist Law, between 1878 and 1888 German police outlawed over one hundred socialist cultural or recreational associations, including many workers' dramatic societies like the Theaterverein Germania of Dortmund and the Offenbacher Theaterklub; in Bremen, the Dramatische Lesezirkel was banned because the police president considered it "a cover for socialist agitation."[5] A large number of socialist songbooks, poetry anthologies, and satirical works were also confiscated and banned; these included J. Vahlteich's *Der Deklamator. Gedichtsammlung* (*The Declaimer: Poetry Anthology*; 1878) and *Elend und Erlösung. Ein soziales Zeitgedicht* (*Misery and Salvation: A Social Poem for the Times;* 1879), and the poetry of two writers from the Lassallean wing of the movement, F. W. Dornbusch's [pseudonym for Friedrich Wilhelm Fritzsche] *Blut-Rosen. Sozialpolitische Gedichte* (*Blood-Roses: Social-political Poems;* published 1876, banned 1880) and Karl Frohme's *Ein Immortellenkranz. Sozialdemokratische Dichtungen* (*An Everlasting Crown: Social Democratic Poems;* banned 1879). The same fate befell a volume of poetry by Georg Herwegh, a radical poet and early collaborator with Marx who had been active in the revolution of 1848 and later associated with the Lassallean socialists; his *Neue Gedichte* (*New Poems*), published in 1877, was banned the following year. Although the anarchosocialist and early Naturalist John Henry Mackay and the left-wing writer Karl Henckell published many of their dramas and poetry collections anonymously in Switzerland in the 1880s, several were confiscated and banned in Germany.[6]

Among the many socialist literary works proscribed were those of August Otto-Walster, a Social Democratic journalist and party speaker who composed a number of novels, stories, dramas, and poems with socialist content. In 1878 authorities banned both his drama *Ein verunglückte Agitator, oder die Grund und Bodenfrage. Lustspiel in 2 Akten* (*An Ill-Fated Agitator, or the Fundamental Land Question. A Comedy in 2 Acts;* 1877) and his major novel *Am Webstuhl der Zeit. Sozialpolitisches Roman in 3 Bänden* (*At the Loom of Time: A Social-political Novel in 3 Volumes;* 1873). In the opinion of police and the special semijudicial body to which police bans under the Anti-Socialist Law could be appealed, the obvious intent of Otto-Walster's widely read novel was "to disseminate the most essential doctrines and allegations of the Social Democrats and Communists to the widest possible circle in an easy and accessible—and therefore doubly effective—form. The heroes of the novel, in their speeches and in their conversations, translate the doctrines of socialist theoreticians into everyday language, and there is hardly a current slogan of the most extreme Social Democrats the novel lacks." Its plot and characterization, authorities charged, was designed "to cultivate in a most penetrating manner the hatred of the poor against the propertied classes [and] to subvert the existing state and social order"; the third volume, especially, "becomes a primer for suborning the military into disobedience, breach of oath, and rebellion."[7]

After a stunning electoral victory by the SPD in February 1890, Bismarck's dismissal in March (in large part over disagreements with Wilhelm II concerning how best to handle the social question), and the expiration of the Anti-Socialist Law in October 1890 (which allowed the Social Democrats to resume a full range of political and cultural activities), Bismarck's successors continued their relentless campaign to repress socialist literary expression. In a Reichstag speech a year after he replaced Bismarck, Chancellor Caprivi declared, "the struggle against Social Democracy is the most serious question of our time. ... I consider it currently the greatest danger to the Reich, and so I believe the means of fighting against it must be fully utilized with each new opportunity."[8] However, having now lost their extraordinary powers to confiscate and ban socialist literary works and dissolve socialist dramatic clubs and literary associations, state and local officials resorted to a variety of other more circumscribed legal methods to restrict socialist literary activities and harass socialist literary organizations.

One such weapon was the Criminal Code. Although imperial authorities invoked its paragraphs frequently against socialist journalists and political agitators for such offenses as inciting class hatred or libeling state officials, nothing in the code gave the state legal recourse against socialist writers' imaginative or fictional assaults on the status quo. So rather than suppressing printed socialist literary texts after 1890, censors targeted instead the amateur literary and dramatic activities of socialist voluntary associations. Although legally powerless to halt the spectacular increase of socialist recreational, educational, entertainment, and service associations after the expiration of the Anti-Socialist Law, imperial authorities were always anxious—and usually able—to prevent these organizations from utilizing tendentious socialist poetry, prose, and drama to entertain members and disseminate socialist ideas.

What enabled the state to do this were the laws regulating associations and assemblies (*Vereinsgesetze*). These local statutes, which remained in force until superseded in 1908 by a uniform, more liberal national law, restricted the right of citizens to form associations and organize public meetings. Although provisions varied slightly from state to state, these laws generally divided associations into three types: First, harmless private associations like choral or bicycle clubs that required no police supervision. Second, associations that sought to influence public affairs (*Einwirkung auf öffentliche Angelegenheiten*), a sphere authorities defined very broadly. Associations of this type often could not be formed without prior official approval, were required to report their meetings and activities (and sometimes even membership lists) to the police, and were subject to other forms of oversight. Finally, there were outright political associations, which were subject to the severest limitations and the greatest police supervision.

Throughout the 1890s aggressive officials in Prussia, Saxony, Bavaria, and other states attempted to use the associations laws to harass and impede socialist associations in general and prohibit or restrict their literary and dramatic activities in particular. The state was fairly successful in preventing Social Democratic associations and festivals from staging performances of notoriously tendentious socialist dramas. In Saxony, for example, police in Leipzig, Chemnitz, and Zwickau frequently invoked provisions of the associations laws throughout the 1890s to forbid SPD gatherings from performing such works as Paul Gent's *An die Scholle gefesselt* (*Bound to the Land*), Max Kegel's popular 1876 farce *Preß-Prozeß oder Die Tochter des Staatsanwaltes* (*Preß-Prozeß or the Public Prosecutor's Daughter,* which satirized the persecution and imprisonment of a dissident newspaper editor), and various agitational dramas and declamatory poems by Friedrich Bosse.[9] A performance of Richard Lipinski's *Friede auf Erden! oder Der Ausweisung am Weihnachtsabend* (*Peace on Earth! Or the Expulsion on Christmas Eve*) and of a declamation entitled *Weihnacht* were banned from a 1894 SPD Christmas festival in Chemnitz on the grounds that "the sole intent, and likely result, of these works is to use Christian festivals and the dramatic arts to serve hateful political passions; to degrade religious behavior in a most gripping manner; to cast aspersions on royal personages; to arouse class hatred, envy, dissatisfaction, and enmity within members of the audience; and to thereby encourage them to immoral and illegal behavior."[10] In Berlin police summarily forbade Social Democratic associations from performing dramas like A. Witz's *Bilder aus der großen Revolution* (*Scenes from the Great Revolution,* an epic poem about the French Revolution), Franz Stahl's *Die Erstürmung des Schloßes bei Schorndorf* (*The Storming of the Castle at Schorndorf,* set during the Peasant's War of 1525), or Julius Türk's *Weltwende* (*Turning Point in History,* an allegorical work about the historic struggle between capital and labor). To the authorities these pieces "[were] animated by a revolutionary spirit," "blatantly express hatred against the existing state," "openly preach revolution from beginning to end," and their revolutionary slogans and action would exert a strong influence on a working-class audience.[11]

Authorities were decidedly less effective, however, in thwarting the socialist Freie Volksbühne Vereine that sprang up suddenly after 1890. These societies sought to bring workers into direct contact with the new, socially conscious drama of the bourgeois Naturalist movement—works which, in the opinion of many Social Democratic leaders, seemed perfectly tailored to fit the needs and aspirations of the socialist movement.

The Freie Volksbühne Movement, 1890–1914

On 23 March 1890, within a month of the SPD's dramatic electoral victory and three days after Bismarck's resignation, the young Naturalist writer and prominent Social Democrat Bruno Wille issued a proclamation in a socialist newspaper calling for the creation of a Freie Volksbühne (Free People's Stage). The private theatrical association he proposed was modeled on Otto Brahm's year-old Freie Bühne. Only a private theater, Wille believed, could bring modern, socially conscious drama to a broad audience, because "public performances of plays in which the revolutionary spirit lives are frustrated either by capitalism, for which [such plays] don't prove very successful at the box office, or by the police censor. These obstacles do not exist for a private association." By using dues from subscribing members to stage special private, members-only performances, the Freie Volksbühne, like the Freie Bühne, could sidestep police censorship and provide a new outlet for modern plays that were either banned from public theaters or considered too financially risky for the regular commercial stage. Unlike the middle-class Freie Bühne however, Wille foresaw the primary audience for his Freie Volksbühne to be the socialist working class of Berlin: for a nominal membership fee the new organization would make theatrical performances accessible to workers who could not afford to attend commercial theaters, while also introducing them to works by Naturalists and other modernists. The Freie Volksbühne would use the artistic and literary arena to promote the struggle for proletarian emancipation by supporting and bringing to the working class "the new art … of truth and reality, the art of emancipation and of social regeneration."[12]

Though not officially associated with the SPD, Wille's project had the informal backing of several prominent party leaders and its early proclamations and meetings were widely publicized in SPD newspapers. As noted above, the party had long used private clubs and cultural associations to further its aims; indeed, the severe curtailment of SPD political activities under the Anti-Socialist Law had forced much socialist activism into the channels of cultural and educational organizations. As the authorities well knew, these ostensibly harmless literary and debating societies, chess and bicycling clubs, and the like were frequently only covers used by the SPD to circumvent the law against socialist agitation.

Wille's call for a socialist theatrical society and the subsequent organizational meeting in late July (which attracted two thousand participants) thus aroused immediate official concern. When Emperor Wilhelm II first read of the creation of the Freie Volksbühne, he declared "this business must by all means be stopped" and demanded his officials investigate the organization and find some means of preventing it from performing its proposed repertoire.[13] After considering the legal means at their disposal, Berlin police reluctantly informed him that as long as the association sponsored plays only for its members and not for profit, the Freie Volksbühne could neither be required to obtain an operating license nor subjected to police censorship. However, they indicated the law governing associations might be applied if the organization was discovered to have subversive tendencies.[14]

The Berlin Freie Volksbühne began its performances of socially conscious dramas in October 1890 to an audience of several hundred workers, SPD party members, and intellectuals. (The first performance was Ibsen's *Die Stützen der Gesellschaft*.) An educational lecture on social and political issues raised by the drama preceded each performance and a discussion session followed the performance. Police kept the organization under close surveillance, diligently noting how many known Social Democratic activists (and Jews) attended the meetings and performances and what was discussed at each. They also harassed the organization in petty ways, requiring it, for example, to meet narrow technicalities of the associations law and of city safety codes that were rarely enforced for other meetings.

After monitoring its activities for several months, on 20 April 1891 the Berlin police president invoked Prussia's Associations Law against the Freie Volksbühne. However, rather than classifying the group as a political organization—a move that would have drastically curtailed its activities and in all likelihood destroyed it[15]—police simply decreed the Freie Volksbühne was an association that sought to influence public affairs. It was ordered to submit all members' names, addresses, and occupations to the police; notify police of the date and agenda of each meeting and provide detailed information about any scheduled speakers; report immediately all changes in its bylaws and membership rolls; and permit police to monitor all meetings and performances to insure that the audience was not incited to illegal behavior. (Police could dissolve any meeting at which "propositions or motions were debated that constituted an invitation or incitement to illegal activity.") Leaders of the Freie Volksbühne interpreted the police's action as merely the first step toward having the organization ultimately declared a political association, which would have subjected it to unacceptable restrictions. To preserve the organization's freedom of action, and perhaps its very existence, they appealed the police decree through the administrative law courts.

In the hearings that followed, police argued the Freie Volksbüne was no mere theatrical society, but an overtly political organization whose ultimate purpose was "to make propaganda for the aspirations and ideals of Social Democracy."

Citing statements by Wille and other founders boldly proclaiming their goal of using socially conscious art to help liberate the working classes, police charged the association with using "clearly tendentious literary works to indoctrinate the people—that is, the working population—with a certain view of the existing social order and to convince them of the necessity of changing it." Each drama was carefully chosen to make existing political, economic, and social conditions appear intolerable, and the lectures and discussions bracketing performances encouraged the working-class audience to interpret the works in terms of the contemporary class struggle.[16] As further evidence of the Freie Volksbühne's political nature, police pointed out its founders and officers were all prominent SPD activists, the rank-and-file membership was also overwhelmingly Social Democratic, collections for striking workers and other SPD causes were often taken up and tickets to other SPD functions often distributed at the meetings, and so on. Social Democratic organizations like the Freie Volksbühne were particularly dangerous, police concluded, because they enticed many unsuspecting, hitherto-uncommitted people, especially women and young people, into the party and subtly indoctrinated them to socialism. For these reasons the organization must be more closely supervised.[17]

The District Administrative Council, to nearly everyone's surprise, decided in June 1891 against the police and in the Freie Volksbühne's favor, but its decision unleashed a storm of bitter criticism in the conservative press and was soon overturned. The Supreme Administrative Law Court ruled in January 1892 that the Freie Volksbühne was indeed an association that sought to influence public affairs and that its real purpose (*Tendenz*) was political, not artistic. Literary works, the court noted, were a subtle, but highly effective vehicle for promoting Social Democratic ideas:

> Because works that poetically portray workers' unjust treatment, exploitation, or oppression at the hands of the bourgeoisie or civil service directly evoke fantasy and passion, the reading, discussion, or mere theatrical performance of such works must, without a doubt, be considered far more capable of disseminating and strengthening the social-democratic outlook among the working population—and, consequently, of gaining adherents for the [Social Democratic] party—than theoretical or sober factual treatments of the ... political and social position of the fourth estate ever could.

Whatever the original or stated artistic aims of the Freie Volksbühne, the court declared, in practice it "performs, reads, or discusses exclusively (or nearly exclusively) those literary works that are especially well suited for spreading the ideas of the Social Democratic Party"; each work chosen for the repertoire was calculated to

> expose the "hollowness and untenability" of the social relations and state institutions it portrays, to arouse the passions of workers who see them, to increase as much as possible workers' dissatisfaction with existing conditions, and to most effectively awaken and fortify in workers a desire to change [these conditions] and join with the goals of the Social Democratic Party. ... [The Freie Volksbühne] exists not simply to satisfy cultural needs and

cultivate artistic tastes, but rather it consciously and actively utilizes dramatic art to arouse the emotions, prejudices, and passions of wide segments of the population in the interests of party agitation and for the purpose of bringing about a change in the existing social order. Its goal of influencing public affairs is thus obvious.[18]

Accordingly, the court ruled, the Freie Volksbühne must obey the police order of 20 April 1891 and furnish authorities with detailed information about its members and activities. At the same time, however, the Supreme Administrative Law Court decision added that, while the evidence clearly indicated the Freie Volksbühne sought to influence public affairs, it did not indicate the association qualified as a political organization under the Associations Law. The Freie Volksbühne thus suffered only a partial legal setback for its legal status as a *nonpolitical* association was now officially recognized and police were prevented, at least for the time being, from imposing the Associations Law's most restrictive provisions.

Following this ruling the Freie Volksbühne submitted information about its membership, bylaws, and meetings to police. It also voluntarily discontinued the lectures and discussion sessions accompanying each dramatic performance, since lawyers for the organization warned these might be seen as political discussions and provide police with an excuse to intervene again. The organization also took care to ensure its public proclamations, advertisements, and meetings never advocated any illegal activity or specifically called for political action.[19]

In the final analysis the police's legal victory over the association in 1891–1892 was a hollow one. Not only had the state refrained from applying the most stringent clause of the Associations Law, but once police had won new supervisory powers over the Freie Volksbühne they hesitated to make full use of them. For example, police monitors at Freie Volksbühne meetings and performances could have interpreted the law in such a way as to justify dissolving any gathering where social or political issues were discussed, or halting performances in which any type of crime was portrayed onstage.[20] This police never did. In fact, authorities soon lost interest even in the membership lists and other information the Freie Volksbühne was now required to submit; within a few months police no longer bothered to double-check the membership rolls for accuracy, much less use them to harass members.

Indeed, in some respects the outcome proved more advantageous to the Freie Volksbühne than to the authorities. For although the organization now had to report its activities to police, with the exception of the educational lectures those activities were not curtailed in any significant way, much less proscribed. Moreover, since the Supreme Administrative Law Court specifically declared the Freie Volksbühne could not be classified as a political association, police were powerless to impose further restrictions on it. A stalemate had thus been reached, analogous to the larger stalemate between the SPD and the empire that existed after 1890, in which the existence of the Freie Volksbühne was assured and its rights now legally recognized and protected. As the Berlin police were themselves later forced to admit, use of the Associations Law against the Freie Volksbühne in 1891 proved to be "not altogether unproblematic [*nicht ganz unbedenklich*]";[21]

despite having to open its activities to police scrutiny, the Freie Volksbühne after 1892 was able to continue its dramatic performances and other activities unhindered. Being classified as an association that sought to influence public affairs proved perhaps an inconvenience, but hardly an obstacle to the group's further development.

Since applying the Associations Law against the Freie Volksbühne proved unfruitful, after 1892 authorities adopted a different legal tactic: revoking its status as a private association and having its performances declared "public" and thus subject to the same prior censorship as other commercial theaters. Heightened police efforts against the Freie Volksbühne after 1892 were also partially a response to significant new developments within the organization.

The early Freie Volksbühne rested on an uneasy alliance of two distinct groups: an artistic faction, composed of bourgeois intellectuals and writers like Wille who had vague socialist sympathies but whose primary concern was promoting the new Naturalist art; and a socialist faction, composed of SPD party leaders who gave their tacit approval to the Freie Volksbühne and of the masses of rank-and-file workers who joined it, all of them less interested in Naturalism or other forms of art than in the struggle for socialism. The artistic faction, with the support of a few maverick socialist militants and journalists, founded the Freie Volksbühne, held all its key leadership positions, and exercised tight control over its activities; the proletarian socialist faction, on the other hand, came to resent the often-condescending aesthetic elitism of the association's bourgeois leadership and their refusal to place the Freie Volksbühne squarely behind the goals of the SPD. Tensions between these two factions peaked in the summer and fall of 1892. In a stormy meeting in October the mainstream SPD faction, led by Julius Türk, rebelled against Wille and the other bourgeois Naturalist officials of the Freie Volksbühne and managed to gain control of the executive council. Wille and his supporters complained the organization was being politicized—something they feared would give authorities an opportunity to crack down further under the Associations Law and severely curb Freie Volksbühne activities. To protect art from politicization, Wille's artistic faction seceded to form a separate entity, the Neue Freie Volksbühne. By the end of 1892, therefore, there were two independent organizations: the old Freie Volksbühne, now firmly under the control of the orthodox Social Democrats who wanted it to serve the larger goals of socialism; and the new Neue Freie Volksbühne, controlled by Wille and his clique of bourgeois Naturalist authors and maverick anarchosocialists, who were more interested in art, artistic freedom, and independence from politics.

To replace Wille, members of the Freie Volksbühne elected as their chairman Franz Mehring, the socialist academician who edited the SPD organ *Die Neue Zeit* (*New Times*) and served as the party's leading literary expert and critic; Türk and other SPD activists were also elected to positions of leadership. Mehring immediately denied the Freie Volksbühne had become a mere instrument of the SPD and assured members the new officers sought neither "a literary nor a political domination" over the association.[22] Although still not formally associated, the actual as well as perceived relationship between the SPD and the Freie Volksbühne was now closer than ever and after 1892 the latter operated as if it were carrying out the cultural policy of the former. Mehring promised, for example, the association would be "an effective tool for political emancipation," an "auxiliary arm of the great emancipatory struggle of the working class," and "a proletarian association that promotes and enjoys art from the class standpoint of the proletariat. … The goal of the Freie Volksbühne is simple: to promote, in the artistic and literary arena, the proletarian struggle for emancipation." To accomplish this goal the group would seek "to open the way for talented young writers who seek to comprehend the social conflicts and problems of our time in their fundamental depth, and who therefore are coolly brushed off by everyone else."[23]

Between 1892 and 1895 membership in the Freie Volksbühne grew from twenty-four hundred to nearly eight thousand (most of whom were skilled workers), partly because the enrollment fee and membership dues were cut in half (to 50 pfennig) and partly because Mehring broadened the repertoire of dramatic offerings. In contrast to Wille, Mehring regarded modern Naturalism not as socialist art, but as the expression of bourgeois cultural decadence and pessimism. In the absence of genuinely class-conscious new works, the proletariat was better served, Mehring believed, by the works of Goethe, Schiller, Lessing, and others who wrote about the revolutionary struggle of the bourgeoisie at the end of the eighteenth and beginning of the nineteenth century. Fewer dramas by unknown new Naturalist authors and more works by classical dramatists were thus offered. The repertoire began also to contain more contemporary works of light entertainment after the association reached an agreement with Berlin's Lessing Theater, whereby Freie Volksbühne members could attend a certain number of performances each season from that theater's offerings. Ironically then, although the Freie Volksbühne was firmly under the control of orthodox Social Democrats after 1892, its dramatic repertoire actually became less socialist and more like that of commercial theaters. This was due in part to Mehring's own theories of art, in part to the fact the Freie Volksbühne relied heavily on the Lessing Theater to provide dramatic performances rather than staging its own, and in part to the diversified, rather individual tastes of the association's expanding membership, which tended to prefer diversion and entertainment to a steady fare of preachy, ideological social dramas. Indeed, Mehring and Türk grew increasingly defensive about the less-ideological direction the repertoire was taking and were concerned the Freie Volksbühne was losing its class consciousness and that its performances were catering merely to a "Sunday afternoon public" seeking not edification but simply low-cost amusement.[24]

Paradoxically then, while the leadership, membership, and stated orientation of the Freie Volksbühne became more socialist after October 1892, its actual literary activities became less so. This may explain why Berlin police paid relatively little attention to it in late 1892 and 1893. Indeed, the police's primary concern now seemed to be that the general public could easily obtain access to these "private" performances and the Freie Volksbühne was really becoming a public commercial theater in disguise. Throughout 1893, police periodically checked to see whether the statutes of the association were being violated by allowing non-members to attend the member-only performances. Authorities found not only that the Freie Volksbühne was fairly strict about excluding nonmembers from performances and did not actively recruit new members, but also that many who joined after 1892 were not Social Democrats at all, merely people interested in obtaining inexpensive theater tickets.[25]

After the Neue Freie Volksbühne staged a private performance of Gerhart Hauptmann's *Die Weber* (*The Weavers*) (the police ban of which had just been overturned by the court; see below) in October 1893, followed by seven private performances of the work at the Freie Volksbühne in December—all of which drew enthusiastic, overflow crowds—imperial authorities took a sudden new interest in these two theatrical societies. The highly publicized performances brought a sudden, although temporary, increase in the membership of both associations as hundreds of new subscribers enrolled simply to see Hauptmann's notorious drama, then promptly dropped out. Police were also concerned both organizations had stressed to their members the contemporary relevance of Hauptmann's revolutionary drama.[26] Performances of *Die Weber* by the Freie Volksbühne and Neue Freie Volksbühne had also unleashed a flood of alarmist articles and reviews in the conservative press warning these dangerous socialist or anarchist associations were preaching revolution from the stage and had to be stopped.

The first cities to take strong action against socialist "free people's stage" societies (which proliferated after 1890) were Hamburg, Kiel, and Hanover. In Hamburg a nonsocialist, Naturalist Freie Volksbühne attracted eighteen hundred members and in October 1893 rented a theater to perform Hauptmann's *Vor Sonnenaufgang* (*Before Sunrise*). After the first performance the police director summoned the theater owner and demanded he cancel his agreement with the association. When the Freie Volksbühne contracted with another Hamburg theater for a second performance, the police director wrote to that owner: "In the interest of policing order and morality, I would like to humbly suggest, to the extent it is still possible, not to lend your theater to this stated purpose." Although it cost the theater nine hundred marks to break the contract, it did so. Unable to gain access to any Hamburg theaters, the association then turned to neighboring Altona (under Prussian jurisdiction), where it found a theater to stage *Die Weber* in early 1894.[27] When a small Freie Volksbühne was founded in Kiel in 1894, authorities there attempted first to dissolve it but finally succeeded in forcing it to submit its performances to prior police censorship. In Hanover, police followed the tactics of the Berlin police, declaring the Freie Volksbühne to be an association that seeks to influence public opinion; when it refused to submit its membership lists to police scrutiny, however, police initiated criminal proceedings against the organization's leaders and eventually had it dissolved.[28]

In Berlin, following the public premiere of Hauptmann's *Die Weber* in September 1894 and pressure from the minister of the interior to "exercise appropriate vigilance and severity" to ensure other subversive dramas were not performed in public,[29] the police president decided to intervene against private theatrical associations, such as the Freie Volksbühne, whose performances were not subject to prior police censorship. On 18 April 1895 he sent the following notice to both the Freie Volksbühne and the Neue Freie Volksbühne:

> On the basis of observations made by this office, and according to the current statutes of the Freie Volksbühne and Neue Freie Volksbühne, we must consider the performances these associations sponsor to be public ones, and therefore subject to [the censorship provisions] of 10 July 1851. I hereby inform the officers [of both organizations] that according to §5 of the aforementioned decree, the text of every play to be performed must be submitted to us for censorship at least fourteen days in advance. The further performance of plays without prior approval of the censor will be prohibited.[30]

As the police president later explained to the interior minister, it was less the easy access to private performances that prompted his actions than the political orientation of the societies. He viewed Mehring's Freie Volksbühne as a "Jewish-progressive organ" based on Social Democratic principles; while political subjects were not expressly discussed at the meetings, he noted, "most of the members belong to the Social Democrats and stand on the ground of the modern workers movement." He also labeled Bruno Wille of the Neue Freie Volksbühne an extreme socialist agitator who, under the cover of these so-called private performances, had been performing more and more plays that were banned from the public stages. His crackdown on the two groups, the Berlin police president hoped, would be supported by his superiors and the courts and would encourage police in other cities to take similar actions. (Indeed, police in Frankfurt, Altona, Nuremberg, and other cities soon contacted Berlin to inquire about the decree and whether it might also be applied to private theater societies in their cities.[31]) "If I succeed in carrying this plan through," he concluded, "I will be in a position to prevent or partially prevent the social-democratic plague from spreading its propaganda to the broad masses through the performance of socialistic theatrical works."[32]

In January 1896 Berlin police persuaded the Supreme Administrative Law Court, to which the ruling was appealed, that the two free people's theaters were not closed, private associations but mere façades created to evade the censorship that applied to all public commercial theaters. That ploy enabled them to offer plays to the general public the police had otherwise banned (or would ban, if these were submitted for censorship). The large membership of the societies (together, they had close to ten thousand members); their extremely loose structure and membership requirements; the ease with which virtually anyone (including five plainclothes policemen using fictitious names) could obtain membership cards and pass them on to others; the fact all performances were widely advertised and reviewed in the press—these and many other factors convinced the court the Freie Volksbühne and Neue Freie Volksbühne were in fact public organizations sponsoring public theatrical performances, for which they must obtain the censor's prior permission.[33]

The ruling forced both associations to make some difficult choices. Wille's Neue Freie Volksbühne chose to do whatever necessary to preserve its existence as a private, uncensored theatrical society. After negotiations with police and extensive revisions of its bylaws, in November 1896 the organization approved a new charter significantly tightening membership requirements. Having eliminated the laxness to which authorities had objected, the Neue Freie Volksbühne once again regained its status as a private theater society immune from police censorship.

The Freie Volksbühne, by contrast, chose extinction rather than compromise. At a general meeting in March 1896, Mehring reported on the organization's plight. Although the court had indicated reorganizing and tightening the association might allow it to regain its censor-free status, Mehring expressed doubt his association could ever satisfy police and courts without sacrificing its very essence and purpose. The alternative of submitting to police censorship like all other commercial theaters was also unacceptable to him; he believed the Freie Volksbühne "must never sink to the level of an ordinary theatrical undertaking. … An organ like the Freie Volksbühne, which has set the highest possible artistic standards for itself, cannot function with its plays being chosen for it by police headquarters." At his recommendation the membership voted unanimously to dissolve the Freie Volksbühne; its small treasury of one thousand marks was divided equally between the SPD, striking workers in Cottbus, and the Berlin Worker's School.[34]

While it might appear the Freie Volksbühne's dissolution represented a decisive victory for police, this was not the case. First, there was more to Mehring's decision to disband than met the eye. During his tenure as chairman the highly principled and ideologically orthodox Mehring had become disillusioned with the Freie Volksbühne. He believed it had drifted away from its original mission of creating and promoting a new proletarian art and he was frustrated that, in accordance with the wishes of its rapidly expanding membership, the association's repertoire was being filled with more and more older, standard works and fewer truly socialist or class-conscious new dramas. In his eyes the Freie Volksbühne was no longer an agent of social emancipation but had evolved into either a "bourgeois theatrical enterprise" or a "dramatic soup-kitchen"—a simple consumer's cooperative for obtaining inexpensive theater tickets. The unfavorable outcome of the long legal battle with police presented Mehring with a convenient excuse to end what he had come to regard as a failed experiment that had outlived its usefulness. As he said later, "when the Freie Volksbühne received its coup de grâce from [Interior Minister] Köller, as chairman at the time this end did not seem to me too terrible. I had long wondered whether the game was really worth it, and now when an honorable death on the field of battle cut short all pangs of doubt, so much the better! The literary organization of the proletariat is a nice frill, but is not absolutely necessary for their class struggle."[35]

Second, the dissolution was short lived. Social Democratic leaders had second thoughts about the value of a theatrical society, for a year after the decision to dissolve the Freie Volksbühne they decided to refound it on terms that would satisfy the police and courts. Under the new charter—which, like that of the Neue Freie Volksbühne, was expressly approved by police—membership regulations were tightened enough to again qualify the association's performances as private, closed gatherings immune from censorship or other police controls. To provide and strengthen the "bonds of internal solidarity" and "personal contact" among members that authorities insisted must exist in any private association and were lacking in the old Freie Volksbühne, the new reformed society deliberately sponsored more festivals and social events in addition to its artistic meetings.[36]

In contrast to the original Freie Volksbühne, which had (under Wille) been supported first by a maverick radical faction within the SPD, then (under Mehring) was controlled by mainstream, orthodox party members, the new, reorganized organization under Conrad Schmidt was controlled by conservative reformists within the party, and increasingly became identified with the party's revisionist wing.[37] The new charter reflected this by proclaiming a more conservative mission: instead of serving as a forum for "revolutionary" or socially critical works, or even as an outlet for "timely, realistic art," after 1897 the stated purpose of the Freie Volksbühne was merely to offer its members "important literature."

Thus, by 1897 the socialist Freie Volksbühne (as well as its bourgeois cousin, the Neue Freie Volksbühne) was back in operation holding private, uncensored theatrical performances. In this regard efforts by imperial authorities to control or silence this socialist literary forum had been unsuccessful. But by 1897 the socialist Freie Volksbühne (as well as the Neue Freie Volksbühne) had largely forsaken its original function of offering workers socially critical, even revolutionary dramas and offered instead merely "important" literature. In this regard efforts by authorities to control or silence it had succeeded.

While the Berlin Freie Volksbühne survived its running battle with Prussian authorities in the 1890s, its Munich counterpart did not. After the expiration of the Anti-Socialist Law, Munich Social Democrats founded a number of workers' reading clubs and amateur dramatic societies, but several efforts to establish a Freie Volksbühne there never succeeded. The theatrical society most closely resembling Berlin's Freie Volksbühne was Concordia, founded in late 1895 by a small circle of Munich workers. Although the Munich SPD did not directly support it, this society subordinated artistic objectives to political agitation, tendentious sloganeering, and mobilization of the working class. Its membership remained extremely small (there were seldom more than a dozen members) but Munich police subjected it to strict police oversight and regulation "because of its *Tendenz*" and because the organization was comprised of "well-known Social Democrats of an independent (anarchistic) orientation."[38] The Concordia was required to submit its statutes, executive committee minutes, and the text of all dramas it wished to perform to the Munich police, who noted with great concern that the group held "subversive" discussions after each rehearsal. Scheduled performances were frequently prohibited by police: in 1896, for example, the group was forbidden to hold a public May Day performance of *Der Völkerfrühling: Weltenmai* (*Springtime of the People: World-Wide May Day*); the following year police allowed a May Day performance of Gent's *An die Scholle gefesselt* only after passages calling for the social emancipation of workers were excised; and in December 1897 a planned performance of Hauptmann's *Die Weber* had to be cancelled after the police censor refused to permit it. Munich police applied other forms of pressure on the organization as well, for example, forbidding anyone in the military service from joining. The Concordia was finally dissolved in 1899.[39]

Hamburg's Freie Volksbüuhne succumbed to similar police pressure. When the sympathetic director of the Carl-Schurze Theater agreed to lend his theater and acting ensemble to the group in 1898, Hamburg police contacted the military commander of the nearby Prussian garrison in Altona, who then forbade any noncommissioned officers and troops from frequenting that theater, regardless of what it performed. When the director capitulated and withdrew from the arrangement, the boycott was lifted. The same thing happened the following year with a second Hamburg theater. Thwarted by this ironic alliance between the Hamburg authorities and Prussian military, in March 1900 the Hamburg Freie Volksbühne voted to dissolve.[40]

Besides stepping in between socialist audiences and socialist dramas, German police tried also to keep works by socialist dramatists away from the general audiences in the commercial theaters, although here their success was mixed. In Spring 1894, for example, Berlin police initially approved Franz Held's *Ein Fest auf der Bastille* (*A Festival at the Bastille*), which depicted a young hero caught up in the storming of the Bastille and the revolutionary events that follow, and it was performed some twenty times on the commercial stage without incident. However, after a Social Democratic reading club asked to hold a special performance for its members, the Berlin police president not only refused but also forbade any further performances in the public theaters. The work, he said he now realized, was written by a longtime social-revolutionary agitator, it distorted history, amounted to a provocative apology for and inflammatory glorification of violent insurrection, and would "suggest to dissatisfied and revolutionary dispositions the possibility of a repetition [of the revolutionary events it depicts]."[41] The Supreme Administrative Law Court overturned the ban; pointing to the works' many previous public performances, the judges found it unlikely an audience would draw parallels between the French Revolution and the present or that the drama would "agitate the audience against our state and its institutions, or will occasion similar [revolutionary] behavior here in the present." While the court agreed police might have been justified in prohibiting the special performance before an audience of socialists, it saw no grounds for banning all future public performances for general audiences.[42]

In 1897 and again in 1901 Berlin censors banned the public performance of *Ausgewiesen* (*Expelled*), a drama by the Social Democrat Carl Böttcher that depicted how the repressive Anti-Socialist Law, which allowed the government to expel suspected subversives from their places of residence, frequently ruined the careers, families, and lives of many innocent people. Police objected to the drama's socialist content and its portrayal of authorities as cold-hearted, ruthless tormenters of the workers; because memories of the Anti-Socialist Law were still fresh and the passions it had aroused still intense, they feared the play might provoke violent outbursts from the "uncritical and highly excitable working-class audiences" that attended the two theaters where it was to be performed. (A public performance at a third theater was permitted in 1907, however, because that playhouse was frequented by a more educated and respectable clientele.)[43] And in liberal Hamburg, which had no formal system of theater censorship, the political police "urgently advised" in late 1896 that Böttcher's drama *Streik!* be kept off the public stage there. The piece had been publicly performed in Berlin in March 1891, but in the midst of Hamburg's bitter 1896–1897 dock strike, a theater director there decided it would be wise voluntarily to submit it for police approval first. Although Böttcher claimed his piece was a "conciliatory work ... that is more inclined to unite than to divide agitated parties," Hamburg police feared a public performance would "make crass propaganda for the striking masses and exaggerate the misery they are suffering." The theater waited until the strike collapsed in February 1897 to perform it (a performance it advertised as having "the permission of the highest authorities"), but quickly dropped it from the repertoire when it proved a box office flop.[44]

After 1900 the government's relentless war against Social Democracy eased considerably. Efforts between 1897 and 1899 to enact repressive new antisocialist legislation, revise the associations laws, and drastically increase punishments for engaging in strike activity were all defeated by parliament; at the same time an economic upturn, significant reforms in the labor laws, and improved working conditions for miners and iron and steel workers did much to reduce class tensions and fear of social revolution. The SPD, too, embraced a more moderate, reformist stance: after emerging from the repression of the Anti-Socialist Law, the party became less and less inclined to engage in actions that might provoke authorities, much less attempt to overturn the imperial order. And as long as socialists refrained from active revolutionary activity, the state saw little need to resort to force. The growing moderation and revisionism of the Social Democratic movement on the one hand, and the resulting stalemate between the movement and the state on the other, served to integrate socialists into the prevailing system. By 1914, the existence and activities of the Social Democrats served more to stabilize than to upset the imperial order.

This softening of attitudes is also reflected in censorship policies. After the turn of the century imperial authorities were less obsessed with repressing overtly socialist literary activity: workers' cultural groups were no longer systematically harassed and fewer dramas were banned for threatening the social order. Still, as the Berlin censor's dealings with the Freie Volksbühne illustrates, authorities continued to worry about socialist literary activity and fictional treatments of the "social question" from a socialist perspective right up to World War I.

After its refounding in 1897, Berlin police paid little attention to the Freie Volksbühne. Over the next twelve years the association grew to over eighteen thousand members and expanded its repertoire from ten to twenty dramas each season. Few pieces chosen were avant-garde dramas or works with a social or political message, however; standard classics and works of light entertainment and diversion dominated the season. When the Freie Volksbühne and Neue Freie Volksbühne (which, with thirty-eight thousand members, was twice as large as the Freie Volksbühne) laid plans to build their own theaters, form their own permanent ensembles, and begin offering concerts, operas, and other forms of entertainment to their rapidly expanding membership, Berlin police once again claimed these organizations were abusing their privileged status as private associations.[45] In July 1910, therefore, police again declared the Freie Volksbühne and Neue Freie Volksbühne to be public enterprises whose activities must be subject to the same ordinances that applied to public commercial theaters. This time (in contrast to 1895) prior censorship of Freie Volksbühne performances was not really the issue, since by 1910 it tended to perform all the same works that had been approved for the regular, censored theaters. Indeed, police argued, precisely because the Freie Volksbühne's repertoire and other features no longer differed significantly from that of commercial bourgeois theaters, there was no longer any reason it should be exempt from the fire, safety, tax, and censorship regulations that applied to all public theaters. (Privately, however, the Berlin police president admitted the Freie Volksbühne's "social-democratic orientation" played a role in his decision to curb its independence.[46])

The Freie Volksbühne immediately appealed the police decree to the courts and simultaneously organized several mass rallies to protest the action and collect funds for the legal battle. During the summer and fall of 1910 the state's attempt to bring the Freie Volksbühne under tighter control also unleashed a wave of criticism in the nonsocialist press and literary community, demonstrating just how much socialists had overcome their earlier isolation and been integrated into national life. The liberal Goethe League, many prominent bourgeois intellectuals and writers, and several literary journals and liberal or moderate newspapers signed petitions or printed editorials praising the Freie Volksbühne for bringing cultural education and edification to the working classes and condemning the police president's "arbitrary" efforts to "ride his armed officers onto the proscenium and station a constable next to every writer."[47] Despite this widespread public support, in September 1911 the Supreme Administrative Law Court ruled for the police: as "nothing more than an institution for providing artistic enjoyment at an inexpensive price," the Freie Volksbühne (and Neue Freie Volksbühne) no longer qualified as private theatrical societies, and so, like regular commercial theaters, must obtain prior police approval for all performances.[48]

Having obtained censorship authority over the Freie Volksbühne, seven months later police prohibited it from performing Emil Rosenow's *Die in Schatten Leben* (*Those Who Live in the Shadows*). Rosenow, an SPD journalist and Reichstag delegate and the most successful of all socialist dramatists, modeled his drama on Zola's *Germinal;* it depicted an impoverished family of miners being ruthlessly exploited by a corrupt and powerful family of mine owners who were supported by the Church. The Berlin censor, noting Rosenow's Social Democratic activism, found the work "provocative" and "tendentiously one-sided" because it deliberately and grossly misrepresented miners' legal rights and status while stereotyping mine owners and managers as ruthless, exploitive tyrants. The Supreme Administrative Law Court, to which this case was appealed, upheld the ban. In a January 1914 decision the court ruled that, if shown to the overwhelmingly working-class audiences of the Freie Volksbühne, the play was likely to "agitate," "inflame," and "provoke" them by "filling them with a deep embitterment and hatred [not only] against the entrepreneurial class, [but also against the Church,] state, and society that allows such [exploitive] conditions to exist."[49] Although police in Hanover also banned this work, between 1912 and 1914 it was performed publicly in Stuttgart, Frankfurt, Hildesheim and Mannheim, without (as one liberal paper dryly noted), revolution breaking out in any of those cities.[50]

Socially Critical Literary Naturalism, 1880–1914

The fear—not altogether unjustified—of imperial authorities that the Social Democratic movement was using literature to subvert or overthrow the existing social order colored also their reading of socially conscious literature by nonsocialist authors. When the social question finally began attracting the interest of middle-class writers in the mid-1880s, censors suspected many of the resulting texts were either disguised Social Democratic propaganda or works that might, perhaps unwittingly, encourage social revolution. Censors reacted accordingly.

Anxious defenders of the social order were deeply suspicious of two types of nonsocialist literature. The first concerned works set during historical instances of violent social insurrection, regardless of the author's political orientation or social philosophy: any dramatic performance on the public stage that might favorably depict, glorify, or condone violent revolution or social insurrection made censors apprehensive. Plays set during the French Revolution always posed a potential threat because they were likely to contain inflammatory revolutionary rhetoric and action that might inspire an audience, especially one containing workers, to rebellion or social insurrection. In late 1879, for example, when painful memories of the Paris Commune were still fresh and shortly after the enactment of the Anti-Socialist Law, Berlin police forbade performance of Paolo Giacometti's *Maria Antonietta,* a historical drama set during the Revolution. Members of the city's lower classes, it was feared, might be incited by some of the stirring revolutionary scenes and speeches and might regard the revolutionary events on stage as something to be imitated in real life—despite the fact the work was to be performed in Italian! The ban sparked a brief but ineffectual complaint from a Progressive delegate in the Prussian parliament.[51] Similarly, in 1898–1899 Berlin police (and those in Vienna) refused to allow a public performance of Arthur Schnitzler's *Der grüne Kakadu* (*The Green Cockatoo*), an examination of the moral degeneracy of French society set on the eve of the storming of the Bastille, until several lines of revolutionary rhetoric were cut. Munich banned it altogether; once war began in 1914, Berlin completely proscribed it as well.[52] In 1917, after the outbreak of the Russian Revolution, Munich authorities also forbade performances of another work set during the height of the French reign of terror, Ferdinand Bonn's *Eine deutsche Kaisertöchter* (*A German Emperor's Daughter*).[53]

The second category of works to deeply trouble authorities were those of the early Naturalist literary movement, which they equated—not unreasonably—with socialism. Following Zola in France, the young, mostly middle-class German Naturalist authors active from the mid-1880s to mid-1890s were "bourgeois with a bad conscience," impelled by a passionate social consciousness. The social question and plight of the proletariat became the central theme of early German Naturalism. Most Naturalist writers felt an emotional solidarity and strong identification with the destitute, downtrodden working classes; they produced socially engaged art exposing and condemning the exploitation and injustices of modern bourgeois-capitalist society and demanding social justice for the fourth estate. Although only a few early Naturalists joined the Social Democratic Party, many embraced a vaguely romantic, utopian, humanistic socialism and felt a close emotional affinity for the Social Democratic movement; they were allies, sympathizers, or fellow travelers of the Social Democrats, and some, like Bruno Wille, established a fruitful collaboration with them.

The similarities and parallels between literary Naturalism and socialism were evident to many contemporary observers, both sympathetic and hostile, on both the Left and the Right. The two movements were referred to as "intellectual twins" and Naturalism was called "the muse of the fourth estate," "the poetic counterpart of socialism," "the artistic expression of socialism," "the literary manifesto of the Commune," and "a kind of bourgeois socialism in the artistic arena."[54] Imperial authorities from the emperor down naturally saw no difference between standard Social Democratic agitational propaganda and the passionately proproletarian dramas of the young Naturalists, which were doubly dangerous because most Naturalist social dramas were also set during times of violent social conflict or insurrection.

Although the German public and the courts generally tolerated the state's suppression of explicitly Social Democratic literature and even of otherwise innocuous historical works with revolutionary settings, they were less tolerant of attempts to suppress the socially conscious, "proletarian" dramas of the Naturalists. Indeed, heavy-handed police treatment of these works sometimes generated great public outcry and court reversals of the bans. Ludwig Fulda's Naturalistic social drama *Das verlorene Paradies* (*Lost Paradise*), for example, which treated a bitter wage dispute between striking factory workers and a ruthless employer who wanted to use force against them, was approved for public performance in Berlin in November 1890 but subsequently banned in several smaller Prussian cities as a threat to the social order and an incitement to illegal behavior. These provincial bans remained in force throughout the 1890s, but following the mitigation of class tensions after 1900 they were challenged in the courts and eventually overturned in 1903.[55] A more direct setback for censors came after Berlin police in March 1892 banned *Hanna Jagert*. This play, ostensibly by "August Winter," was in fact the work of Otto Erich Hartleben, a Naturalist sympathizer of the Social Democratic Party and active participant in Bruno Wille's Freie Volksbühne. Because one of his earlier plays had aroused both public and police disapproval when performed privately by the uncensored Freie Bühne, Hartleben submitted *Hanna Jagert* under a pseudonym in hopes it would more easily pass police censorship.[56] Set during the Anti-Socialist Law, it was based on the real-life story of a sexually emancipated, politically active feminist who was briefly married to a prominent SPD agitator. Police considered the play morally offensive because it represented a bold apology for "free love, as preached by Social Democracy," but they objected also to a scene in which Hanna's Social Democratic husband receives a tumultuous homecoming after his release from prison.[57] The theater appealed the ban first to the provincial governor (who upheld the police), then to the Supreme Administrative Law Court, but in the meantime requested permission to stage a revised version of the play from which a prosocialist prostitute and the triumphal homecoming scene were removed. Police rejected this request because the revisions did not address their central objection: the play attempted to win over audience sympathy to the strong, independent socialist heroine. In December 1892 the court overturned the police ban because it found nothing in the play, including the triumphal Social Democratic homecoming, that presented a danger to either public order or morality.[58] After the theater and author agreed to remove a few minor political references to SPD leader August Bebel and Emperor Wilhelm II, the drama finally premiered in April 1893.[59]

The censors' setback in the *Hanna Jagert* case was soon overshadowed by a far more significant defeat. In what has been called "the most spectacular political censorship trial in the history of German literature,"[60] courts thwarted several tenacious, at times desperate efforts by federal, state, and local officials to ban Gerhart Hauptmann's *Die Weber*, the most famous Naturalist social drama of the 1890s and to many the zenith of the Naturalist literary movement.

Hauptmann's piece depicts with great historical accuracy and compassion the spontaneous, bloody uprising of Silesian weavers in 1844 and the underlying social and economic misery responsible for it. The drama was written in 1890–1891 amid a bitter press controversy concerning the current misery and exploitation of Silesian weavers, socialist activity in the region, and fears of another uprising. This highly charged atmosphere—as well as the fact that Hauptmann had obtained much of his information about Silesian conditions from the socialist press and had toured the area with a socialist journalist—virtually guaranteed his drama (first composed in a dialect version, *De Waber*) would be interpreted by authorities as a piece of crass Social Democratic propaganda.[61]

Silesia's district administrative president expressed concern about *De Waber*, of which he had heard rumors, as early as October 1891; after reading laudatory reviews of the play upon its publication in January 1892, he immediately warned local authorities about it.[62] When the Deutsches Theater in Berlin requested permission to perform *De Waber* in February 1892, police refused. According to the Berlin police president, much of the work's action and dialogue were "blatantly [calculated] to provoke class hatred," and its "one-sided, tendentious characterizations" would make "outstanding propaganda for [the Social Democrats'] teachings and for their complaints about the oppression and exploitation of workers." The play posed a serious threat to public order because "the powerful portrayals in the drama, which will doubtless have immensely more impact when portrayed [live] on the stage, and which are already enthusiastically discussed in the daily press, will serve as a focal point for those social-democratic elements of the Berlin population that are inclined to demonstrations."[63] A request by a Breslau theater to perform the play was turned down by Breslau police on the same date for the same reasons.[64]

After Hauptmann completed a High German version of the play, Berlin's Deutsches Theater submitted it to the censor in December 1892. Since this version was virtually identical to *De Waber,* the Berlin censor prohibited *Die Weber* as well. (Soon thereafter, Breslau police also banned this version.) This time the Deutsches Theater immediately appealed the Berlin ban to the District Administrative Council.

Police argued to the council that in Berlin, "at a time when the social-revolutionary movement is still experiencing a steady growth," a tendentious work like *Die Weber* would have a "highly inflammatory effect" upon a large segment of the populace. It promoted class hatred, depicted the entire existing social order as unjust and unworthy of continued existence, and both justified and glorified revolution by implying the weavers' revolt was a logical and necessary result of their misery and those who participated in the rebellion were heroes. Although police were confident more mature elements of the Berlin public could recognize that the miserable conditions depicted in Hauptmann's drama were exaggerated, unrepresentative, and in no way comparable with the lot of manual workers today, they feared "certain audiences from the lower social classes, who have been conditioned by constant Social Democratic slogans about the eternal oppression of the proletariat and about the latter's approaching day of victory" would be inclined to "regard current conditions as similar to those the play portrays as justifying revolution." After seeing the play such people "might let themselves be swept up into open outbursts of party passion." Police felt compelled to ban the work because they were convinced that, under current conditions, a public performance of *Die Weber* would "either directly incite this segment of the population to disturb the public order, or would strengthen their tendency toward violent rebellion against the existing order."[65]

Before the District Administrative Council reached a decision, however, the respectable, middle-class Freie Bühne announced it would hold a private (and thus uncensored) performance of *Die Weber* for its members, perhaps in hopes an uneventful private performance would persuade authorities to permit public performances. This private premier in late February attracted much public interest and was widely discussed in the Berlin press. The performance probably did more to harm than to help chances of a public performance, however, for it merely confirmed authorities' worst suspicions about the play's political message. Although Hauptmann, the Deutsches Theater, and other opponents of the ban had argued *Die Weber* was simply a historical drama and had little to do with contemporary issues, some press reviews, especially from the Left, praised the work as one of great contemporary significance. Sympathetic liberals, Naturalists, and Social Democrats hailed its "revolutionary spirit," its "powerful inflammatory effect," its great topicality, and called it "the most dangerous and provocative drama ever composed in the German language."[66] Such comments simply played into the hands of police, who argued (not implausibly) the public was likely to interpret *Die Weber* not as an historical but as a contemporary drama with a strong political message relevant to the present times.

It came as no surprise, therefore, that in early March 1893 the District Administrative Council upheld the police ban of *Die Weber*. Although ostensibly historical in nature, to these officials the piece

clearly suggests violent rebellion is a solution to life's distress, a suggestion that is also pertinent to our own times. ... Since here in Berlin the number of unemployed grows each year, and especially since there are numerous notorious Social Democrats and down-and-out men here who blame their misery solely on the rich and the propertied, there is a legitimate concern that if *Die Weber* were performed here in a public theater, it would arouse the passions of dissatisfied elements in the audience in a way that would endanger public order.[67]

This decision was immediately appealed to the Supreme Administrative Law Court. In hearings before that body Berlin police reasserted their belief that, "given current conditions, ... a public performance of *Die Weber* will either directly evoke disturbances of the public order, or will strengthen the inclinations of a portion of the population to rebel against the public order." Pointing to the Social Democratic press' high praise of the work and statements about its contemporary relevance and revolutionary effect, police argued the SPD could and would use a public performance to inflame party passion and draw parallels between 1844 and current social conditions. While there was perhaps little danger middle-class audiences attending the Deutsches Theater would themselves be provoked to violent demonstrations, police feared that were the drama performed publicly in one Berlin theater, then they would be forced to allow it in other, less socially exclusive venues. Finally, sweeping aside their usual defense of local discretion in censorship issues, police also argued that once *Die Weber* was widely performed in Berlin, provincial authorities, who followed the capital's lead, would feel compelled to permit the play as well.[68]

In early October 1893 the Supreme Administrative Law Court freed *Die Weber* but only for the Deutsches Theater in Berlin, where the high price of tickets and limited amount of inexpensive standing room (*Stehplätze*) guaranteed that audiences would be drawn mostly from the well-heeled higher social strata least inclined to rebellion or disruptions of public order. While it found the original police ban of January 1892 unjustified, the court also pointed out that repealing it affects only the Deutsches Theater and "does not absolve police from their duty of independently assessing whether performances [of *Die Weber*] may also be allowed in other Berlin theaters, nor does it rob police of their right to censor [those other performances]; still less should it prejudice police authorities in other locales."[69]

It did not. Within days of this decision the theater in Breslau again requested permission for a public performance of a slightly expurgated version of *Die Weber*. In line with the reasoning of the court, the theater promised Breslau police it would raise ticket prices for the performance to screen out workers and would immediately cancel all further performances if the first provoked public disturbances. However, the county prefect for the district secretly directed Breslau police to ignore the recent court decision —which applied only to Berlin—and to continue banning *Die Weber* from Breslau. So Breslau police reaffirmed their earlier ban on the grounds that since the city was located in the immediate vicinity of the events depicted in the play and since there were numerous geographic and personal points of contact between the 1844 weaver uprising and the present time, completely different conditions existed in Breslau than in Berlin. They dismissed the notion that raising ticket prices would effectively exclude "those elements of the population that should be excluded" from the public performance and noted such a tactic was incompatible with the nature and purpose of a public theater; moreover, police feared such a move "would undoubtedly lead to such hateful remarks and provocations in the press and in public meetings, that one must fear gross disturbances at the box office."[70]

This ban of *Die Weber* was appealed to the district administrative president, who upheld it. After proposing to raise admission prices still higher, the theater again requested permission for a public performance; this request was similarly denied, appealed, and upheld, whereupon the Breslau theater appealed to the Supreme Administrative Law Court. In July 1894 that court for a second time overturned a police ban of the play and freed *Die Weber* for public performance in Breslau, where, judges believed, neither the anticipated audience nor the political situation posed any greater danger than in Berlin.[71]

The way was now clear for public performances of *Die Weber* in both Berlin and Breslau. Before these could be staged, however, during the fall and winter of 1893–1894 both Berlin Freie Volksbühne societies sponsored several private performances. (Hauptmann had refused to allow these associations to perform his play until it had been cleared for public performance.) On 15 October 1893, shortly after the final court decision lifting the Berlin ban, Wille's Neue Freie Volksbühne held the first of four closed, private performances for its members, and on 3 December 1893 Mehring's Freie Volksbühne began a series of eight private performances for its members (and for the police observers who of course attended and carefully noted each time the audience cheered or applauded the action on stage).[72]

The long-awaited public premier of *Die Weber* finally took place in Berlin months later, on 25 September 1894; its premier in Breslau occurred the following week. Since the court had agreed to lift the ban only if members of the lower social classes were essentially excluded from the audience, both the Deutsches Theater and the Breslau theater raised the prices of their least expensive tickets from 30 or 50 pfennig to 1 mark or more (the equivalent of one-third or more of a day's wages for the average worker in 1894). Only an elite audience, therefore, attended the first public performances of *Die Weber*—although a delegation of SPD party functionaries did attend opening night, and the private performances staged by the Freie Volksbühne had made the play accessible to Berlin's working classes.[73]

After *Die Weber's* public premiers, the emperor himself leapt into the bitter controversy. According to his intimate friend Philipp zu Eulenburg, when Wilhelm II first learned the Supreme Administrative Law Court had freed the play, the monarch vented his anger against that body "in a very lively and energetic manner" and snapped, "The minister of justice is supposed to prevent this nonsense!"[74] Alarmist reviews in the conservative press after *Die Weber's* public premiere calling the work "fuel for revolution" and "the drama of the Revolution" further agitated him. Upon reading one press report comparing the bourgeois audience that applauded *Die Weber* to the upper-class intellectuals who helped undermine French society on the eve of the French Revolution, the emperor commented, "Quite right!" and telegraphed Dr. Persius, president of the Supreme Administrative Law Court, demanding to know why his court had permitted the performance.[75] The judge's immediate (and secret) reply respectfully explained the legal basis for the court's verdict (a copy of which he enclosed) and assured the monarch the court was convinced a public performance of *Die Weber* at the Deutsches Theater posed no real threat to public order. Although he admitted the administrative law courts may sometimes err in individual cases—and may in fact have underestimated the potential danger of Hauptmann's play—Persius reassured the emperor "that the 3d. Senate of the Supreme Administrative Law Court ... ardently seeks in its verdicts to strengthen and reinforce the authority and the actions of the police and to preserve, with full power and energy, the inalienable rights of the state against the subversive forces of our day."[76]

The volatile emperor was not placated. In the margins of the court's written verdict he scribbled a number of angry comments about its reasoning, including: "intellectual nonsense"; "thoroughly wrongheaded and faulty"; and "unbelievably foolish and artificial."[77] He then wrote the Prussian ministers of the interior and justice asking why they hadn't intervened to prevent the Supreme Administrative Law Court's scandalous decision and asking whether or not there was some action that could now be taken to counter what he termed the Deutsches Theater's "provocation against the government and the existing social order." The interior minister replied that once the administrative law court had lifted the police ban of *Die Weber,* public performances of the play could not be stopped unless the audience engaged in serious outbursts or disturbances. Press reports about the debut, the minister continued, had been greatly exaggerated, for the Berlin police president's report on the performances indicated audiences had been well behaved. Should the need arise, however, the interior minister assured his sovereign he and the police president stood ready to intervene immediately and halt any further performances.[78]

Powerless to stop *Die Weber* and unable to openly criticize, much less discipline the Supreme Administrative Law Court (however much he disapproved of that body's decision, he could hardly publicly disavow the verdict of a tribunal that dispensed justice in the sovereign's name), the frustrated emperor could vent his anger only through indirect and symbolic actions. To protest the Deutsches Theater's performance, for example, he quietly cancelled the royal box there and the four thousand mark annual subsidy it entailed.[79] He also took advantage of the next chance to rid himself of his hapless minister of justice and strike a blow against the recalcitrant judicial system. Because of their longstanding political disagreements, in late October 1894 both Reich Chancellor Caprivi and Prussian Interior Minister zu Eulenburg (who served also as the Prussian chancellor) resigned their posts. Declaring he wanted a minister of justice who would reform "the totally deplorable condition of the Prussian judiciary with the necessary ruthlessness and determination," the emperor used this personnel change as an opportunity to personally demand (and obtain) the Prussian minister of justice's resignation as well; as his replacement, Wilhelm II suggested a notorious arch-conservative who could "regain control over the law courts of Prussia and cleanse the Augean stables."[80] (There were also reports, probably untrue, that the monarch encountered Supreme Administrative Law Court President Dr. Persius at a court reception a few months later and treated him so rudely Persius resigned his judicial post.[81])

The new interior minister, Ernst von Köller, quickly made known his displeasure with the Supreme Administrative Law Court. After reportedly reprimanding the unfortunate judge who had written the verdict, he criticized the court in a February 1895 Prussian parliamentary debate. In response to conservative complaints about lax theater censorship, the interior minister defended the police censors but pointed out that "*for the time being,* [emphasis added] above the police's decisions stand the decisions of the Supreme Administrative Law Court." Although the court had recently overturned the *Die Weber* bans in Berlin and Breslau, von Köller reminded parliament the rulings applied only to these two specific instances; the court did not—and indeed, could not—order that a work like *Die Weber* must be generally permitted. "I therefore hope," he added, "our police officials continually reexamine each case anew and, if need be, ban such works again so the whole question can be brought up again and decided anew; and I hope that in the near future, the decisions of the Supreme Administrative Law Court will turn out differently." Von Köller then pointedly praised police in Halle and other cities that had recently prohibited *Die Weber.*[82] Liberal delegates responded to the minister's remarks by praising the Supreme Administrative Law Court as "one of the most valuable advances of the last decade" and chided him for questioning the court's judgments; they also accused him of wanting to undermine the independence and widespread public respect the administrative law courts enjoyed. The interior minister and his conservative supporters denied these charges but emphasized that "in these difficult times" police must be allowed a certain amount of freedom to act against public threats; while the administrative law courts should be independent, they should not be permitted to exercise broader powers than they deserved.[83] Throughout the spring and summer of 1895 conservative complaints about the Supreme Administrative Law Court's rulings on *Die Weber* continued to be aired in the Reichstag and the press.

As authorities hoped, the Prussian court decisions to free *Die Weber* in Berlin and Breslau did not deter police in other German cities from banning it. After its public premiere in the fall of 1894, theaters across the empire asked permission to perform the now famous work; following the practice of the Deutsches Theater, most theaters also promised to limit lower-class attendance by raising their minimum price of admission. Only Frankfurt and a handful of smaller towns in southern Germany, however, agreed to permit public performances.[84] During late 1894 and throughout 1895 police in numerous Prussian cities banned *Die Weber* from the public stage. Authorities in Halle, for example, had no objections to a drama like this in peaceful times, "but at the present time of ferment and discontent, of social-revolutionary agitation and economic tension, the performance of such a work is likely to strengthen the tendency toward violent rebellion against the existing order [that is to be found] among the lower social strata of the population, which is most affected by misery and which is especially stirred by the social-revolutionary movement; under certain conditions, [a performance of *Die Weber*] could lead to public outbursts of party passions."[85] Königsberg, Tilsit, Stettin, Görlitz, Bielefeld, and Minden also banned the play (in some cases for several years), while in Aachen, Halle, and Wiesbaden, even public recitations of it were prohibited.[86] The decision by Hanover police in August 1895 to ban the work there, however, was overturned by the Prussian Supreme Administrative Law Court in October 1896; in its third ruling on *Die Weber,* the court once more declared the play presented no immediate danger to public order and must be allowed on the public stage.[87]

In most other federal states, too, Hauptmann's controversial drama encountered staunch official resistance. While the bans in Munich (August 1895) and Leipzig (October 1895) were perhaps predictable, those in more liberal cities like Hamburg (October 1894), Bremen (April 1895), and Stuttgart (January 1896) are more surprising. (Indeed, *Die Weber* appears to be the only drama ever banned in Württemberg in the imperial era.) The Hamburg prohibition was lifted by 1896, however, and in November 1901 the Saxon Supreme Administrative Law Court overturned the Leipzig ban.[88]

Despite authorities' best attempts to ban *Die Weber* from the German stage, regular "private" performances by Berlin's free stages were held already in 1893; thanks to the Supreme Administrative Law Court, by 1896 public performances were permitted not only in Berlin, but in other major cities like Hamburg, Frankfurt, Breslau, and Hanover. Other European nations, surprisingly, succeeded in banning the work much longer. Public performances of *Die Weber* were prohibited in Paris until 1898, and even then only an extensively expurgated version was allowed. In Austria, censors banned it for more than a decade: the work, again in expurgated form, was first performed publicly in Graz in 1903 and in Vienna in May 1904. Russia banned the play until late 1904; even publication of the text was permitted only under stringent conditions, and during the revolution of 1905 was prohibited completely.[89]

The extensive publicity and sensationalistic press coverage generated during the extended legal battle over *Die Weber* created enormous public interest in the work. As one contemporary critic noted a few years later, "If the authors of the clumsy ban had intended to stir up a feverish excitement for this piece across all of Germany and create massive sales for the printed edition, they could not have found a better way." Hauptmann and his play became an international sensation; book sales rocketed, a flood of new members temporarily joined Berlin's two Freie Volksbühne to see the private performances, the work was performed by the Deutsches Theater over two hundred times within two years, and it quickly became a box-office hit in other cities as soon as the bans there were struck down. Contrary to the intentions of imperial authorities, the entire controversy also heightened public awareness of Germany's "social question" and further polarized attitudes about it.[90]

Although its efforts to censor Hauptmann's socially critical drama were largely thwarted, the state continued for more than a decade to intervene against other Naturalist works seen as endorsing social rebellion. Here censors were more successful. After a German translation of Bjørnstjerne Bjørnson's *Über unsere Kraft II* (*Beyond our Power II*) appeared in 1896, for example, Berlin police refused for several years to permit its public performance. This work revolved around a desperate confrontation between oppressed factory workers and their brutal employer, ending with an anarchists' attempt to kill the industrialist and spark a worker's revolution by dynamiting a workers meeting. It was first performed publicly in Stuttgart in November 1900; the following year it was allowed also in Berlin and Munich.[91]

Likewise, Franz Adamas' Naturalistic *Familie Wawroch,* which strongly resembled Zola's *Germinal* and Hauptmann's *Die Weber* and dealt with a bloody confrontation between oppressed miners and their heartless employer, was banned in Berlin in 1900 because police feared the socialistic speeches and revolutionary slogans might provoke a lower-class audience to outbursts and disruptive disturbances. After an expurgated version was publicly premiered in Vienna, the Berlin theater in question asked permission to perform the Viennese version, but police refused again, citing reports that tumult and demonstrations had followed the Vienna performance.[92] A third, still further expurgated version of *Familie Wawroch* was submitted to Berlin police in October 1900, from which most militant political utterances had been eliminated. This version was approved. However, when the play finally premiered in September 1901 and a scene in which the miners riot provoked outbursts from the audience, Berlin police immediately threatened to ban it if any more such disturbances occurred. The controversial riot scene was promptly dropped and other revisions made for all future performances, but by now the work was so eviscerated and tame the theater lost interest in it and, after a few more performances, dropped it from the repertoire.[93]

One of the last nonsocialist, pseudo-Naturalist dramas dealing with social rebellion to fall victim to state censorship before the war was Leopold Kampf's *Am Vorabend* (*On the Eve*), a very sympathetic account of the Russian Revolution of 1905. Between 1905 and 1907 numerous cities (including Essen, Frankfurt, Dresden, Düsseldorf, Berlin-Charlottenberg, and Hamburg, where theater censorship did not legally exist) banned public and/or private performances—and in some cases even public readings—of the work because in their eyes it glorified revolutionaries and assassins.[94]

Conclusion

For much of the imperial era, government anxiety about socialism and socialist literature overshadowed concern about literature that transgressed other norms. Socialist literary activities and works were widely regarded as part of general socialist agitation and propaganda, and after 1878 both were severely suppressed under the Anti-Socialist Law. When those exceptional legal measures expired in 1890, authorities tried by other legal means to prevent socialist organizations, especially the socialist-backed Free People's Stage movement, from using socially tendentious literature to inspire and inflame working class audiences. Police censors sought also to keep such literature out of public theaters, where middle-class audiences might prove susceptible to its influence.

What is most striking about the empire's fierce use of literary censorship to combat the perceived threat of social revolution is not what divided the conservative defenders and the radical assailants of the established social order, but rather what united them. Both sides shared the same assumptions, ingrained in Germany since the late eighteenth century, about the enormous power of dramatic art and the theater's extraordinary importance within national public life. These shared assumptions, as deeply rooted in Wilhelm II, his officials, and the middle-class public as they were in Naturalist writers, SPD officials, and the rank-and-file membership of the socialist dramatic associations, rested on the (not unreasonable) conviction that seeing a work of literature performed live on stage was a far more powerful and emotional experience than merely reading it, and on the (rather more questionable) belief that watching a certain kind of dramatic action, for example a social insurrection, soon leads, directly or indirectly, to its reenactment. Just as many modern observers are convinced viewing violence on television or in films makes certain kinds of people (but not, of course, themselves) more prone to such behavior, defenders of the established social order in imperial Germany feared—and many of its most socially radical opponents hoped—that viewing social protest or working-class revolt on stage would inspire workers (if not the "better" social classes) to imitate it in real life. Common also to all participants in these censorship battles was an awareness that the German theater, a traditionally middle-class institution that had been central to the rise and sociocultural triumph of the German bourgeoisie, was now being appropriated by the fourth estate and transformed into a weapon against the bourgeois order. For these reasons, socialist dramatic performances, socialist dramatic societies, and prosocialist Naturalist dramas became a crucial battleground, especially between 1892 and 1897, where attackers and guardians of the social order warred tenaciously and where much ink, if little blood, was shed.

During the 1880s and 1890s German courts and public opinion supported, or at least tolerated, these state efforts to dissolve, regulate, or hamper socialist literary associations. They acquiesced too in government attempts to hinder working-class audiences' access to blatantly socialist literature as well as to socially critical Naturalist works that could promote the socialist agenda. Courts and liberal public opinion began to object, however, when authorities tried to exercise this same tutelage over nonsocialist middle-class audiences by banning socially critical dramas from the legitimate, respectable commercial theaters. (Similarly, as we shall see in the next chapter, when antimodernist Catholics tried to transform the government's 1894 Anti-Revolution Bill from an antisocialist measure into a potential weapon against academic and artistic freedom in general, liberal and even conservative circles united to defeat it.) Socialists had long opposed censorship because they had long been its primary target; but to the extent the government's antisocialist censorship measures in the early 1890s began to impinge also on nonsocialist middle-class literary life, censorship issues became an increasingly important concern of members of the middle-class cultural elite as well.

Had it not been for the tactical error of trying to proscribe socially conscious Naturalist dramas not only for "impressionable" socialist audiences, but also for the "better," more respectable social classes—a move that produced a small mutiny in the conservative and bourgeois ranks—perhaps imperial censors would have been more successful in their war against socialist literature and literary socialism. As it was, each side won its share of skirmishes, but neither decisively triumphed over the other.

Notes

1. Quoted in Theodore S. Hamerow, ed., *The Age of Bismarck: Documents and Interpretations* (New York, 1973), 246.
2. Quoted in Vernon L. Lidtke, *The Outlawed Party: Social Democracy in Germany, 1878–1890* (Princeton, NJ, 1966), 339.
3. Lidtke, *Alternative Culture*, especially 21–49, 75–101, 136–58 (quote from 158.)
4. Ibid., 7–9 and 201, and Peter von Rüden, *Sozialdemokratisches Arbeitertheater (1848–1914). Ein Beitrag zur Geschichte des politischen Theaters* (Frankfurt, 1973), 57–60.

5. PP report, 30 Jul. 1883, quoted in Rüden, *Sozialdemokratische Arbeitertheater*, 60. For statistics on socialist publications and associations banned under the Anti-Socialist law, see Otto Atzrott, ed., *Sozialdemokratische Druckschriften und Vereine verboten auf Grund des Reichsgesetzes gegen die gemeingefährlichen Bestrebungen der Sozialdemokratie von 21. Okt. 1878* (Berlin, 1886; Nachtrag, 1888), v–vi. A more recent compilation, *Verbotene Druckschriften in Deutschland. Band 1: Die Sozialistengesetze 1878–1918*, ed. Herbert Birett (Ruggell, Liechtenstein, 1987), lists over seventeen hundred social democratic publications banned between 1878 and 1890.

6. Thomas A. Riley, *Germany's Poet-Anarchist John Henry Mackay: A Contribution to the History of German Literature at the Turn of the Century, 1880–1920* (New York, 1972), 130.

7. Atzrott, *Sozialdemokratische Druckschriften;* Ursula Münchow, ed., *Aus den Anfängen der sozialistischen Dramatik, I.* (Berlin, 1964), 197–98; Decision of Reichskommission, quoted in Bodo Rollka, *Die Belletristik in der Berliner Presse des 19. Jahrhunderts. Untersuchungen zur Sozialisationsfunktion unterhaltender Beiträge in der Nachrichtenpresse* (Berlin, 1985), 409.

8. Caprivi speech of late Feb. 1891, quoted in J. Alden Nichols, *Germany After Bismarck: The Caprivi Era, 1890–1894* (Cambridge, 1958), 75–76.

9. August Bebel, *Die Handhabung des Vereins- und Versammlungsrechts im Königreich Sachsen* (Berlin, 1897); Rüden, *Sozialdemokratische Arbeitertheater*, 95–96; Lidtke, *Alternative Culture*, 82, 156.

10. Chemnitz police order of 7 Dec. 1894, cited in Rüden, *Sozialdemokratische Arbeitertheater*, 95.

11. Police ban of 4 Feb. 1893, LAB A/74, Th 54; BPP ban of 5 Aug. 1895, and BPP to BOP, 9 Aug 1895, in LAB A/74, Th 55.

12. Wille, "Aufruf," *Berliner Volksblatt* 23 Mar. 1890, and Wille as quoted in Vernon L. Lidtke, "Naturalism and Socialism in Germany," *American Historical Review* 79 (Feb. 1979): 23 n. 28.

13. Wilhelm II's marginalia on clipping from *Allgemeine Zeitung* 12 Aug. 1890, and Wilhelm II to PrIM, 16 Sept. 1890, GStA PK/ZK, Nr. 21012, Bl. 154, 163. At its founding meeting on 29 July 1890 the Freie Volksbühne announced its intention to hold private performances of such works as Ibsen's *Nora, Gespenster, Die Stützen der Gesellschaft* and *Ein Volksfeind;* Tolstoy's *Die Macht der Finsternis;* Büchner's *Dantons Tod;* Griepenkerl's *Robespierre;* Hart's *Der Sumpf* and *Die Familie Selicke;* Alberti's *Brot;* Zola's *Thérèse Raquin;* and Hauptmann's *Vor Sonnenaufgang.* (*Neue Preußische Zeitung,* 30 Jul. 1891.)

14. PrIM report of 30 Aug. 1890, GStA PK/ZK, Nr. 21012, Bl. 158–60; and RR report, quoted in Siegfried Nestriepke, *Geschichte der Volksbühne Berlin. I. Teil: 1890–1914* (Berlin, 1930), 49.

15. Political associations, for example, were forbidden from having female members; this would have devastated the Freie Volksbühne, nearly half of whose membership was female. Membership data in Nestriepke, *Geschichte der Volksbühne*, 89.

16. See summary of arguments in Wille, "Die Freie Volksbühne und der Polizei-Präsident," *Freie Bühne* 2, no. 2 (1891): 673–75; *Vorwärts*, no. 150 (1 Jul. 1891); and *Neue Preußische Zeitung*, no. 11 (8 Jan. 1892).

17. Wille, "Volksbühne und Polizei-Präsident"; *Vorwärts* no. 150 (1 Jul. 1891); *Neue Preußische Zeitung* no. 11 (8 Jan. 1892); Nestriepke, *Geschichte der Volksbühne*, 50–52; Brauneck, *Literatur und Öffentlichkeit*, 36; Inge Reiner, "Die Stellung der deutschen Sozialdemokratie zur Volksbühnenbewegung (1890–1896)" (Magisterarbeit mss., F.U. Berlin, Mar. 1976), 69–70.

18. OVG decision of 6 Jan. 1892, reprinted in *Die Freie Volksbühne. Eine Schrift für den Verein 'Freie Volksbühne,'* Heft 1 (1891); portions also quoted in Nestriepke, *Geschichte der Volksbühne*, 55–56, and Brauneck, *Literatur und Öffentlichkeit*, 38.

19. *Vorwärts*, 17 Jan. 1892, reporting on Freie Volksbühne meeting of 15 Jan.; *Freie Bühne* 3 Jg. (1892): 1, 560, cited by Herbert Scherer, *Bürgerliche-oppositionelle Literaten und sozialdemokratische Arbeiterbewegung nach 1890. Die "Friedrichshagener" und ihr Einfluß auf die sozialdemokratische Kulturpolitik* (Stuttgart, 1974), 95; Nestriepke, *Geschichte der Volksbühne*, 56ff.

20. Richard Grelling, "Die Maßregelung der Freien Volksbühne," *Das Magazin für die Literatur des In- und Auslandes* 61 (6 Feb. and 13 Feb. 1891): 92–93, 108–10. Grelling was the lawyer who argued the appeal.

21. Berlin police official Böttger to Kiel PP, 1894, quoted in Nestriepke, *Geschichte der Volksbühne*, 131.
22. In his open letter Mehring declared: "The newly elected executive council of the Freie Volks-bühne affirms that no organ of the SPD, either official or semiofficial, played any role, either direct or indirect, in our election. … The Freie Volksbühne [under its new officers] will remain what it has been: a haven of noble relaxation and pure artistic appreciation for the working class after their hard days of work and struggle." See *Vorwärts*, 16 Oct. 1892; also Mehring, *Gesammelte Schriften*, 12: 248–55.
23. Mehring, *Gesammelte Schriften*, 12: 272–74; "Proletaräische Ästhetik," *Die Volksbühne* 2. Jg. 1893/94, H.2 (Oct. 1893): 8–9; and Mehring in *Volkstribühne*, 1 Nov. 1892, as quoted in Heinrich Braulich, *Die Volksbühne. Theater und Politik in der deutschen Volksbühnenbewegung* (Berlin, 1976), 52.
24. Mehring, *Gesammelte Schriften*, 12: 266–74, 285–99; and J. Türk, "Die Tätigkeit der Freie Volksbuhne," *Volksbühne* 2, no. 8 (Apr. 1894): 10–13.
25. Police observer's report of 1 Jun. 1893, cited in Cecil Davies, *Theater for the People: The Story of the Volksbühne* (Austin, TX, 1977), 45, and Braulich, *Die Volksbühne*, 54.
26. Police observers at the Oct. 1893 premiere in the Neue Freie Volksbühne took a copy of the program note for *Die Weber* written by Wille and placed it in the police files, after marking passages that stressed the contemporary relevance of the weavers' revolt and reminded the audience the "great fight for freedom still continues." See Brauneck, *Literatur und Öffentlichkeit*, 67–68.
27. Giesing, "Theater, Polizei, und Politik," 129–31, quote from 131.
28. Nestriepke, *Geschichte der Volksbühne*, 152.
29. PrIM to all local police departments, 9 Apr. 1895, LAB A/74, Th 24.
30. BPP decree, 18 Apr. 1894, copy in LAB A/74, Th 1104.
31. Altona police to BPP 8 May, Nuremberg police to BPP 9 May, LAB A/74, Th 24; Frankfurt police to BPP 23 Jul. and Berlin police response, 29 Jul., ibid., Th 1100.
32. BPP to PrIM, undated, 1895, in LAB A/74, Th 24; Berlin police report on Freie Volksbühne of 6 Jun. 1895, in ibid., Th 1100.
33. BPP to OVG, 29 Jul. 1895; report of Politische Polizei, 16 Jul. 1985; Berlin police brief to OP, 20 May 1895; and OVG decision of 24 Jan. 1896, in LAB A/74, Th 1100.
34. *Vorwärts* no. 60 (11 Mar. 1896); Mehring, *Gesammelte Schriften*, 12: 285–89.
35. Mehring, *Gesammelte Schriften*, 12: 285–99; also the perceptive analysis in Reiner, "Stellung der Sozialdemokratie," 65, 74–80.
36. *Vorwärts* no. 62 (14 Mar. 1897); Nestriepke, *Geschichte der Volksbühne*, 148–50.
37. Mehring was originally offered the chairmanship but declined it; he served briefly on the new executive committee but soon withdrew completely from Freie Volksbühne activities. Mehring, *Gesammelte Schriften*, 12: 300–305.
38. Rainer Hartl, *Aufbruch zur Moderne. Naturalistisches Theater in München, Teil I* (Munich, 1976), 126, 127, 128 n. 4.
39. Ibid., 130–32; Rüden, *Sozialdemokratisches Arbeitertheater*, 97.
40. Giesing, "Theater, Polizei, und Politik," 131–32.
41. Berlin Political Police to BPP 5 Oct. 1894, BPP memo 11 Oct. 1894, BPP to BOP 12 Feb. 1895, LAB A/74, Th 594. Text of drama is in LAB C/A.
42. OVG decision, 9 Jan. 1896, LAB A/74, Th 594.
43. Ban of 20 Dec. 1897, LAB A/74, Th 65; BPP to PrIM, 29 Jul. 1903, GStA PK/1000, Nr. 7, Bd. 3, Bl. 191ff; text of play in LAB C/A, Nr. 188 and LAB A/74, Th 65. Before 1897 Böttcher's piece had been performed publicly in Hamburg and at the Meiningen Court Theater. For a partial list of Social Democratic plays banned from Berlin stages in the late 1890s and early 1900s, see LAB A/74, Th 56.
44. Report of Abt. II of Hamburg police, 22 Dec. 1896, StAH, Nr. 2170, Vol. 23; and Giesing, "Theater, Polizei, und Politik," 126–27.

45. Mehring, *Gesammelte Schriften,* 12: 306–10; June 1910 internal police memo, and BPP directive of 23 Jul. 1910, LAB A/74, Th 1101; Nestriepke, *Geschichte der Volksbühne,* 361–62.

46. See BPP public statement to the press, cited in *Vorwärts* no. 186 (11 Aug. 1910) and his private memo to PrIM 9 Sept. 1910, LAB A/74, Th 1101.

47. Nestriepke, *Geschichte der Volksbühne,* 363–68, 413–16.

48. OVG decision of 22 Sept. 1911, LAB A/74, Th 1101.

49. Berlin censor's report; BPP ban of 1 May 1912, BPP to OP, 29 May 1912; OP decision of 14 Aug. 1912, and OVG decision of 26 Jan. 1914, LAB A/74, Th 799.

50. Hildesheim police to BPP, 23 Nov. 1912, LAB A/74, Th 799; *Bühne und Welt* 16, Pt. 1 (1913/14): 189; *Berliner Tageblatt,* 4 May 1912.

51. Remarks by Dr. Hänel and PrIM in Prussian Landtag, StenBer/Pr, 16. Sitzung am 2 Dec. 1879, Vol. 278, 345–47.

52. Berlin police ban of 24 Nov. 1898, BPP to BZA 8 Jan. 1899, censor's report of 10 Mar. 1899, LAB A/74, Th 308; text, with censor's markings, in LAB C/A; and O. P. Schinnerer, "The Suppression of Schnitzler's *Grüne Kakadu* by the Burgtheater: Unpublished Correspondence," *Germanic Review* 6 (1931): 183–92.

53. *Frankfurter Zeitung,* 16 Feb. 1918; LAB A/74, Th 36.

54. Literature on the relation between Naturalism and socialism in Germany is extensive. One of the best places to begin is Lidtke, "Naturalism and Socialism," especially 14–22. For some of the contemporary characterizations cited, see Viktor Zmegac, ed., *Geschichte der deutschen Literatur vom 18. Jahrhundert bis zur Gegenwart, Band II* (Königstein, 1985), 156, 173; Brauneck, *Literatur und Öffentlichkeit,* 101; and Walter Ackermann, "Die zeitgenössische Kritik an den deutschen naturalistischen Drama" (Diss. phil., U. Munich, 1965), 30.

55. *VL,* 1: 203; and OVG decision of 29 May 1903, as quoted in *KK,* 128.

56. Joachim Wilcke,"Das Lessingtheater in Berlin unter Oscar Blumenthal (1888–1893). Eine Untersuchung mit besonderer Berücksichtigung der zeitgenössischen Theaterkritik" (Diss. phil., F.U. Berlin, 1958), 63.

57. BPP to OP, Apr. 1892, as quoted by *VL,* 2: 257; Wilcke, "Das Lessingtheater," 63–68.

58. OVG decision of 1 Dec. 1892, quoted in Blumenthal, *Verbotene Stücke,* 42. The verdict is reprinted in Richard Grelling, *Streifzüge. Gesammelte Aufsätze* (Berlin, 1894), 242–52.

59. LAB C/A, *Hanna Jagert;* see also *KK,* 117–18.

60. Brauneck, *Literatur und Öffentlichkeit,* 51.

61. Authorities regarded Hauptmann with suspicion since 1887, when he had to appear in court to answer questions about his relationship with two prominent socialists. Wolfgang Leppmann, *Gerhart Hauptmann. Leben, Werk und Zeit* (Bern, 1986), 114.

62. Breslau RP to BPP, 9 Oct. 1891 and 15 Feb. 1892, LAB A/74, Th 304, and as cited in *VL,* 1: 338 and Helmut Praschek, ed., *Gerhart Hauptmanns "Weber." Eine Dokumentation* (Berlin, 1981), 248, 368.

63. BPP, 3 Mar. 1892, LAB A/74, Th 304, reprinted in Praschek, *Hauptmanns "Weber,"* 254–55.

64. *VL,* 1: 355. Plans to hold a private performance for Theaterfreunde in Hamburg in June 1892 were soon abandoned as too risky. Praschek, *Hauptmanns "Weber,"* 369.

65. BPP to BZA, 4 Feb. 1893, published in *Berliner Börsencourier,* Morgen Ausgabe, 8 Mar. 1893, 1–2, and extensively reprinted in Brauneck, *Literatur und Öffentlichkeit,* 54–55.

66. See Julius Hart's review in *Tägliche Rundschau,* 28 Feb. 1893; Fritz Stahl's review in *Deutschen Warte,* 28 Feb. 1893; Franz Mehring's review in *Die Neue Zeit* Jg. 1892/93, Heft 24, 769ff; the review in the liberal *Gegenwart* (11 Mar. 1893); and the highly laudatory reviews in *Der Sozialist,* 3, 10, and 17 Dec. 1892. Modern scholars, too, agree that regarding the content and public effect of the work, the revolutionary character of the piece is undeniable; see for example Karin Gafert, *Die soziale Frage in Literatur und Kunst des 19. Jahrhundets. Ästhetische politisierung des Weberstoffes* (Kronberg, 1973), 1: 250.

67. Decision of BZA 7 Mar. 1893, LAB A/74, Th 304, also quoted in *VL,* 1: 342–44.

68. BPP to OVG, 10 May 1893, as cited in *VL,* 1: 345 and Grelling, *Streifzüge,* 261–63.

69. OVG decision 2 Oct. 1893, fully reprinted in Hans Schwab-Felisch, *Gerhart Hauptmann. Die Weber. Vollständiger Text des Schauspiels. Dokumentation* (Frankfurt, 1963), 243–48.
70. Director Fritz Witte-Wild of Lobetheater to Breslau police, 9 Oct. 1893, Landrat von Goldfuß circular of 10 Oct. 1893 (in which he told Breslau police not to let it be known their ban was instigated by a higher administrative level), and Breslau police ban of 12 Oct. 1893, cited in *VL*, 1: 355–6 and Praschek, *Hauptmanns "Weber,"* 370.
71. OVG decision of 2 Jul. 1894, reprinted in Schwab-Felisch, *Hauptmann. Die Weber,* 248–254; see also *VL*, 1: 356.
72. Davies, *Theater for the People,* 47–48; Braulich, *Die Volksbühne,* 50; report to Berlin Political Police, 16 Oct. 1893, LAB A/74, Th 304, also reprinted in Praschek, *Hauptmanns "Weber,"* 279–80.
73. *VL*, 1: 352, 358; Brauneck, *Literatur und Öffentlichkeit,* 58; report of RA Rötgen to Berlin PP, 2 Oct 1894, LAB A/74, Th 304, also reprinted in Praschek, *Hauptmanns "Weber,"* 288–89. According to reports in the conservative, liberal, and socialist press, naval and army officers were ordered not to attend the public performances in Berlin or Breslau, even in civilian dress. A few officers did attend opening night in Berlin; the police observer present dutifully noted their names. See BPP to PrIM, 4 Oct. 1894 concerning the 25. Sept. 1894 performance, in GStA PK/ZK, Nr. 21013, Bl. 91–94; also *VL*, 1: 354, 358; Brauneck, *Literatur und Öffentlichkeit,* 72, 231 n. 29, and Praschek, *Hauptmanns "Weber,"* 289–91.
74. Memo of P. Eulenburg, 30 Sept. 1894, GStA PK/ZK, 2.2.1, Nr. 21013, Bl. 74.
75. See reviews in *Deutsche Warte,* as cited in *VL*, 1: 353 and in *Hamburger Nachrichten,* 1 Oct. 1894 and *Der Reichsbote,* nos. 226, 227 (27, 28 Sept. 1894), as cited in Brauneck, *Literatur und Öffentlichkeit,* 68, 226. Wilhelm II's marginalia on *Berliner Politischer Nachrichten* article, 26 Sept. 1894, in GStA PK/ZK, No. 21013, Bl. 73. Also Brauneck, *Literatur und Öffentlichkeit,* 71.
76. Confidential letter of Dr. Persius to Wilhelm II, 1 Oct. 1894, in GStA PK/ZK, Nr. 21013, Bl. 77–79, also reprinted in Praschek, *Hauptmanns "Weber,"* 286–87.
77. Wilhelm II's marginalia on OVG decision of 2 Oct. 1893, GStA PK/ZK, Nr. 21013, Bl. 84; also Brauneck, *Literatur und Öffentlichkeit,* 72.
78. Wilhelm II to PrIM and PrJM, 5 Oct. 1894, and PrIM to Wilhelm II, 7 Oct. 1894, in GStA PK/ZK, Nr. 21013, Bl. 75, 90. See also Brauneck, *Literatur und Öffentlichkeit,* 71–72.
79. Shortly after *Die Weber* premiered, the Berlin press reported the emperor, out of anger at the theater, had decided to cancel the royal box there and end the crown's annual subsidy; upon the demand of the Deutsches Theater, however, the press soon printed a retraction of this story. After several days of confusion over just what action the emperor had taken, a source close to the monarchy reported that while he had not cancelled the royal box, he had decided not to attend any future performances in the Deutsches Theater. (Brauneck, *Literatur und Öffentlichkeit,* 72, and Praschek, *Hauptmanns "Weber,"* 253, 296) Five months later in Apr. 1895, after controversy over *Die Weber* had subsided, Wilhelm II did quietly cancel the royal box at the Deutsches Theater "as a result of the performance of *Die Weber.*" Marginalia note, 17 Apr. 1895, in GStA PK/ZK, Nr. 21013, Bl. 90.
80. John C. G. Röhl, *Germany Without Bismarck: The Crisis of Government in the Second Reich 1890–1900* (Berkeley, CA, 1967), 124–25.
81. Schwab-Felisch, *Hauptmann. Die Weber,* 103, 264, and Praschek, *Hauptmanns "Weber,"* 252, 359 n. 54. Schwab-Felisch checked the personnel records of Persius (and of Richter, the judge who actually wrote the Oct. 1893 decision) and found no reference to this alleged incident, or to their resignations after the Weber decision.
82. PrIM Köller's remarks in Prussian Landtag, 21 Feb. 1895, quoted in Schwab-Felisch, *Hauptmann. Die Weber,* 227.
83. For a full account of these debates, see Schwab-Felisch, *Hauptmann. Die Weber,* 225–41.
84. On 23 July 1894, shortly after the OVG had lifted the Breslau ban, Frankfurt police gave the Stadttheater permission to perform *Die Weber* on condition ticket prices not be lowered

and no Sunday or holiday performances be held. (Since weekday performances began too early in the evening for most workers to attend, banning weekend and holiday performances was another way of insuring workers did not attend.) As late as 1900 the play was still being performed in Frankfurt under these restrictions. See Frankfurt Police to Stadttheater, 23 Jul. 1894, HHStA/407, Nr. 25, Bd. 2; also *VL*, 1: 360, and Brauneck, *Literatur und Öffentlichkeit*, 59. During 1894–1895 public performances of *Die Weber* were also permitted in Heilbronn, Darmstadt, Göppingen, Eßlingen, Weimar, and Gotha.

85. Decision of OP of Provinz Sachsen, upholding Halle police ban of 13 Feb. 1895, quoted in *VL*, 1: 358–59, and Brauneck, *Literatur und Öffentlichkeit*, 220.

86. See *VL*, 1: 358–64; Praschek, *Hauptmanns "Weber,"* 251, 359 n. 51, 374; and Schulze-Olden, "Theaterzensur in Rheinprovinz," 79–80.

87. Decision of OVG, 15 Oct. 1896, Nr. III. 1276; see also *VL*, 1: 361–64. The tone of the verdict clearly displays impatience and irritation with Prussian police for ignoring prior court rulings on the play and continually attempting to ban it.

88. See *VL*, 1: 360, 364–66, and for the long controversy over *Die Weber* in Stuttgart, HStA Stuttgart, E151c/II, Nr. 291. Also Müller-Meiningen's comments in the Reichstag, 30 Jan. 1901. (StenBer/RT, 10 Leg. Periode, 2. Session, 37. Sitzung von 30 Jan. 1901; Bd. 180, 1016ff.) The first public performance of *Die Weber* in Saxony was held on 13 April 1902. Police in Hamburg visited private *Weber* performances and wrote reports on audience reactions but did not intervene to halt the play; Giesing, "Theater, Polizei, Politik," 125–26.

89. Praschek, *Hauptmanns "Weber,"* 369–71, 374; Glossy, *Vierzig Jahre Deutsches Volkstheater*, 46–51; Franz Hadamansky, "Der Kampf um *Die Weber* in Wien," *Phaidros* 2 (1947/48): 80ff; Ackermann, "Die zeitgenössische Kritik," 45–46. Hungarian authorities permitted a public performance in Buda in August 1895, but after socialist demonstrations the interior minister intervened and in September 1895 it was banned from all Hungarian stages; the ban continued until July 1900. E. Mandel, "Gerhart Hauptmanns "Weber" in Rußland," *Zeitschrift für Slawistik* 12 (1967): 5–19; and Praschek, *Hauptmanns "Weber,"* 376. Initially, it was banned also in cities like New York (Oct. 1894) and Milan (Feb. 1895) where volatile labor tensions existed.

90. Adalbert von Hanstein, quoted in Gafert, *Die Soziale Frage*, 249; Eberhard Hilscher, *Gerhart Hauptmann: Leben und Werk. Mit bisher unpublizierten Materialien aus dem Manuscriptnachlaß des Dichters* (Frankfurt, 1988), 152–53; and Breuer, *Geschichte der literarischen Zensur*, 192.

91. *Bühne und Welt* 3, Pt. 1 (1900–1901): 214–15; Abret and Keel, *Im Zeichen des Simplicissimus*, 215–16.

92. Police ban of 18 Apr. 1900, LAB A/74, Th 672; also *VL*, 2: 7–8. In July the play was performed in Prague, where it also led to public demonstrations and disturbances, all of which Berlin police duly followed and noted.

93. See text in LAB C/A. Mentions of Social Democracy, May Day demonstrations, and antistate and antiemployer striker shouts were removed. LAB A/74, Th 672, and *VL*, 2: 8–9.

94. Political Police to PD, 27 Nov. 1905, PD order of 1 Dec. 1905, and various newspaper clippings in StAH, Nr. 2170 and Giesing, "Theater, Polizei und Politik," 134–35; Censor's report, 22 Mar. 1906, LAB A/74, Th 3796. In Hamburg commercial police saw no reason to ban it, but political police did. A private performance was allowed but public performances were cancelled, although the reason was not specified. The liberal Hamburg press quickly suspected police were behind the cancellation and complained that art in Hamburg was being measured by a "Prussian police baton." Hamburg police wished also to ban public readings of the work but were overruled by the Hamburg City Senate. Although banned in several German cities, Kampf's play was performed in New York and Paris.

Chapter 5

DEFENDING THE RELIGIOUS ORDER

> The Holy Scriptures should remain holy; literary license should not
> twist and turn that which we have absorbed since childhood …
> for this could shake and undermine belief in the old traditions.
> —Berlin police president, May 1904

Religion and Social Order

Since religion was not only vitally important for many Germans but also functioned as an "ideology of legitimation"[1] in the German Empire, authorities were keenly interested in literature dealing with religious subjects. The alliance between throne and altar grew close in Germany during the nineteenth century; in return for the state's promotion of its interests, orthodox Christianity became a pillar of traditional secular authority and social hierarchy. Church and state were most closely identified in Protestant territories like Prussia, where the ruling princes served as head of a state church staffed and governed by state-appointed officials and financed by state-levied church taxes. After the king of Prussia (and head of the Prussian Evangelical State Church) became German emperor in 1871, the interests of Protestantism, the monarchy, and the new nation-state became more intimately entwined; Protestant churches could be counted upon by the imperial government for enthusiastic and unswerving support. The Catholic Church was less closely identified with state authority, and stood in hostile opposition to it during the anti-Catholic *Kulturkampf* of the 1870s. Nevertheless, after 1860 its reactionary emphasis on tradition, loyalty, and obedience also supported hierarchic authoritarianism and the status quo in political and social life. Once the *Kulturkampf* ended, the Catholic Church aligned itself more enthusiastically behind imperial authority and the German nation-state. Traditional Christianity, then, provided crucial ideological and institutional support for the empire's conservative social and political order.

Yet throughout the nineteenth century the intellectual authority of Christianity was steadily eroded across Europe as its doctrines and values were attacked by liberal skepticism, materialist philosophy, Darwinism and modern science, and Nietzschean and Marxist criticism. Nowhere were the decline of religious faith in general, and the rejection of orthodox Christianity in particular, as pronounced as in the new German Empire. Already in the 1870s observers bemoaned a "crisis of religion," especially among the nation's educated youth. Although declining church membership was due primarily to spiritual alienation and profound religious indifference among urban masses uprooted from their traditional religious life by industrialization and urbanization, many believers blamed the religious crisis on a steady stream of scholarly and popular works that brazenly challenged everything from Christian doctrine to the very existence of a deity. Several of these anti-Christian attacks (for example, those by D. F. Strauß, August Bebel, Max Nordau, Ernst Haeckel, and Paul de Lagarde) proved immensely popular. These works were censored only during the Anti-Socialist Law (1878–1890), when authorities used their extraordinary powers to suppress any publications considered subversive of the existing political or social order.[2]

No less damaging to orthodox faith was "higher" criticism, the rigorous application of historical and philological methodology to the study of biblical texts that was pioneered by German Protestant scholars and reached its culmination in Wilhelmine Germany. This higher biblical criticism questioned the authorship and historical reliability of key biblical texts, revealed many Judeo-Christian doctrines as myths or psychological projections, and ultimately doubted not only the physical resurrection of Jesus but even his historical existence. By the turn of the century higher criticism had produced three distinct camps among German Protestants: radical debunkers who doubted Jesus' divinity or denied his historical existence; conservatives who objected to any "modern" interpretation of Christ and who accepted the literal and historical accuracy of the Bible; and, between these two poles, liberal modernists who struggled to disentangle the mythology surrounding Jesus from the basic message and teachings behind his life. From the 1890s on, battles among these opposing camps intensified; over the objections of thousands of lay parishioners, for example, ecclesiastical courts sometimes removed from their posts popular pastors who questioned Jesus' divinity or refused to assent to the literal truth of the Apostles' Creed. These controversies over Jesus were confined largely to German Protestantism; neither higher criticism nor theological modernism affected the Catholic Church, which held firmly to traditional dogma.

Germany's imaginative writers contributed to the nation's religious crisis; as Roy Pascal observed in his study of the empire's literary life, "Nothing in the literature of the period is more striking than the frequency of disbelief, even of provocative rejection of Christian tenets and the Christian Church."[3] Modern writers, especially Naturalists, railed against organized and dogmatic religion, while others condemned the social and political reactionism of the Christian churches and the moral hypocrisy of its clergy. In much of the literature of imperial Germany, "Christianity was suddenly considered as something antiquated, as some dust-covered relic from the day before yesterday that one had best banish from the world in one blow. ... Everywhere voices were heard proclaiming the uselessness of the Christian religion and its absurdity in the modern world."[4]

Although such sweeping philosophical, theological, or literary assaults on Christian belief attacked a crucial pillar of the imperial order, these were, surprisingly, not the works that most concerned the censors. Rather than seeking to defend Christianity from its many critics—something which, in the late nineteenth century, was no longer feasible—the empire intervened against religious expressions for a less ambitious purpose: to prevent the flagrant violation of believers' religious sensibilities, for such violations could breach the civic peace. The literature most likely to be censored on religious grounds was, consequently, that which authorities believed might endanger public order because it ridiculed the faith of others, aroused confessional enmity, or treated profanely those things Christians held most sacred.

This concern with social and confessional harmony arose from severe interconfessional divisions. As Thomas Nipperdey has observed, for most late nineteenth-century Germans the antagonism between Protestantism and Catholicism "was incomparably more important than that more basic antagonism between Christians and non-Christians. ... [C]onfessional division and tension was a fundamental, everyday, and vital fact of German life."[5] The mutual contempt of many Protestants and Catholics, and the malicious expression of this sectarian animosity, especially anti-Catholicism, were further complicated by the fact that Catholics were also politically active and increasingly powerful. It was against this backdrop of bitter interconfessional conflict that imperial censors scrutinized literature that touched upon religion.

Blasphemy and Sectarian Conflict

Since ancient times societies have severely punished blasphemers, often with death. By dealing harshly with those who spoke impiously of the gods, a community sought to avoid a worse, collective punishment from the angered deity. As secularism spread and attempts to regulate man's relation with God abated, blasphemy came to be regarded less as a religious than as a social crime. Blasphemers were now punished not for offending God, but for offending the religious sensibilities of their fellow citizens and thus threatening the community's political and social cohesion. For where religion was still regarded as the moral basis of the state, and especially where sovereigns claimed authority by the grace of God, an attack on religion became an attack on political authority and thus a form of treason. But even where political authority was more secularly grounded, violating the deeply held religious sensibilities of one's compatriots not only embittered some citizens against others, but could lead to public disturbances. Those whose religious sensibilities were outraged might resort to (illegal) violence against the blasphemers, and perhaps even against the authorities who tolerated such outrages.[6]

For these reasons, during the nineteenth century all European nations treated blasphemy as a breach of the peace; in Germany, the Imperial Supreme Court defined it as "an offense that indirectly endangers the public order of the state."[7] Paragraph 166 of the Imperial Criminal Code stated:

> Whoever publicly causes a scandal by blaspheming God through irreverent, insulting remarks [*beschimpfende Äußerungen*], or who publicly reviles one of the Christian Churches or another of the legally incorporated and officially recognized religious associations within the federal domain or reviles their institutions or rituals, as well as anyone who commits an irreverent, insulting act in a church or in another designated place of religious assembly, shall be punished with up to three years' imprisonment.[8]

Since most other nations allowed a fine as an alternative to imprisonment, and also set the maximum prison sentence far lower (generally three or six months), imperial Germany's blasphemy law was comparatively harsh; only Russia and Finland treated blasphemers as severely. The German law was unusual in another respect: it required no demonstration of malicious intent. In contrast to British common law, for example, which stipulated that only offenders who intentionally insulted, offended, or ridiculed religious believers were guilty of blasphemous libel, §166 made no such distinction. Whether a person accused of blasphemy had intended to shock the religious sensibilities of others was irrelevant; the fact that others had been grossly offended was sufficient cause for legal action.

Germany's blasphemy law did not punish critiques of religion or church doctrine that were "fitting and decent" (*sachliche Kritik*); authorities intervened only against those who, in a coarse or gross manner, expressed their disrespect or contempt (*Mißachtung*) for an officially recognized religious confession. Only those institutions and rituals were protected that were sanctioned by churchly authority and considered essential to the church's internal governance, its relations with the external world, the fulfillment of its mission, and the practice of its beliefs.[9] Although a church's teachings and dogma were not specifically protected under §166, courts generally ruled that to revile a church's doctrine (such as the Catholic doctrine of papal infallibility, or the Protestant doctrine that the Bible was the basis of all Christian belief) was indirectly to revile the church itself and was thus a punishable offense.[10]

As with lèse majesté, the willingness of authorities to invoke criminal sanctions against blasphemy varied over time. While annual statistics on cases related to §166 exist only after 1897,[11] it is clear prosecutions for blasphemy gradually declined during the 1880s, rose steeply after 1890, and reached a dramatic peak in 1894, when twice as many people were prosecuted as in 1889. (See figure 5.1.)

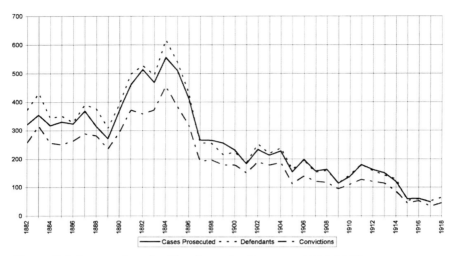

Figure 5.1 Prosecutions for Blasphemy in Germany, 1882-1918
1882–96: all religious crimes, Par. 166-168; 1897-1901: Par. 166 only; 1902-18:
Blasphemy, Insulting a religious denomination, and insulting mischief in a Church.
Source: Statistisches Reichsamt, *Statistisches Jahrbuch für das Deutsche Reich* (Berlin,
1880ff).

After the mid-1890s §166 was invoked less frequently, although there were an
unusually large number of cases in 1902–1904 and again in 1911. By the end
of World War I only about fifty cases of blasphemy were prosecuted in Germany
each year and nearly a third of those ended in acquittal. The dramatic decline in
blasphemy cases after the mid-1890s surely reflects a more selective enforcement
of the law rather than any sharp decline in the incidence of blasphemous expressions. German jurists, anticipating a reform of §166 after 1909 (see below), may
have prosecuted only those cases where blatant malicious intent could be demonstrated. In any case, official concern over blasphemous literature was most acute
in the 1890s.

During much of the imperial era the legal protections provided religious confessions under §166, as well as local censors' power to ban religiously offensive
dramas, were most often invoked against writers who maligned Catholics, the
nation's most important religious minority. (Catholics comprised about 36 percent of the population both in Prussia and the nation.) Just as the empire was being founded, the uneasy coexistence between German Protestants and Catholics
was seriously strained by an upsurge of sectarian animosity that had many causes:
the reactionary, dogmatic, ultramontane policies of Pope Pius IX during the two
decades preceding German unification; Protestant Prussia's defeat of Catholic
Austria and France and the creation of a Protestant, Prusso-German empire in
which Catholics were a permanently threatened minority; and the founding by
Catholics in 1870 of a Vatican-supported Center Party that opposed the cen-
tralizing powers of the new empire and joined with Poles, Alsatians, and other

embittered, anti-Prussian opponents of the empire to champion the church's autonomy and the rights of the German Catholic minority. Such developments encouraged Bismarck and his liberal, nationalist supporters to brand Catholics as unpatriotic enemies of the new Germany and to see the church under Pius IX as a bigoted, irrational enemy of enlightenment and culture. Anti-Catholic animosity climaxed in the famous *Kulturkampf* of 1871–1878, when Bismarck and the National Liberals sought to consolidate the new empire with a relentless political and legal crusade against the Roman Catholic Church.

Not surprisingly, during the *Kulturkampf* the antiblasphemy law was rarely invoked against literary works. Prominent German authors (including Ludwig Anzengruber, Conrad F. Meyer, Eduard Griesbach, Paul Heyse, and Wilhelm Busch) published strident, bellicose anti-Catholic novels, dramas, and satires, but as long as open conflict between the secular state and the traditionalist church remained official policy, none of these works were censored. Although Prussia banned several Catholic books attacking the state's *Kulturkampf* (and ruthlessly used the press laws to censor and convict Catholic journalists),[12] popular expressions of anti-Catholicism were tolerated because they were politically advantageous: they rallied a majority of Germans loyal to the empire against a common foe—Germany's Catholic minority—that was vilified as an enemy of the nation.

But by 1878 it had become clear to Bismarck that the *Kulturkampf* was an embarrassing and increasingly counterproductive stalemate. Like Bismarck, Pope Leo XIII (who succeeded the intransigent Pius IX in February 1878) was anxious to end the church's struggle with the German state. Breaking with the anti-Catholic liberals, Bismarck ended the *Kulturkampf* and throughout the 1880s relations between the empire and church improved steadily. The Catholic Center Party gradually emerged as a political force, especially after it won significant national and Prussian electoral victories in 1884 and 1888. While still generally an opposition party, during the 1880s Center support proved increasingly important to the imperial government.

As they reconciled with the Catholic Church in the late 1870s, Prussian authorities displayed a new willingness to halt the circulation or performance of anti-Catholic works. In May 1878, for example, police in the Prussian (and heavily Catholic) province of Posen confiscated the eighth edition of Wilhelm Busch's *Der heilige Antonius von Padua* (*St. Anthony of Padua*). This humorous illustrated fairy tale about how an ascetic holy man and his pet pig earn the Virgin Mary's favor had been confiscated in Baden before the *Kulturkampf* as an intentional affront to Catholics (the publisher was indicted for blasphemy but not convicted and Busch, a resident of Prussia, was beyond Baden's jurisdiction) but became popular with Prussian readers during the *Kulturkampf*.[13] It was now banned in Polish areas of Prussia (and in Austria was banned until 1902.) The desire to improve relations with the church may also have prompted confiscation of two combatively anticlerical books by Michael Georg Conrad in Breslau, capital of the religiously mixed province of Silesia. Conrad's *Spanisches und Römisches* (*Spanish and Roman;* 1877) and *Die letzte Päpste* (*The Last Popes;*

1878) scornfully condemned the ruthlessness and corruption of papal politics and contrasted the scandalous luxury of the higher clergy with the poverty of the Catholic masses. Both books were confiscated in 1878 by the Breslau prosecutor, who also indicted Conrad's publisher for blasphemy. (Conrad, living in Paris at the time, was not prosecuted.) [14]

To dampen anti-Catholic animosity, after 1878 Berlin authorities also began banning dramas considered potentially offensive to the Roman Church. Thus the director of the Prussian royal theaters banned Heinrich Bulthaupt's *Eine neue Welt* (*A New World*) because he feared the theme (Columbus's return to Spain at the height of the Inquisition and the church's ruthless repression of spiritual freedom) might antagonize Prussia's Catholic citizens.[15] Similarly, in June 1888, when Berlin university students and faculty scheduled a benefit performance of August Trümpelmann's musical spectacle *Luther und seine Zeit* (*Luther and His Times*) to raise funds for a Luther monument in Berlin, the Prussian ministers of the interior and religion forbade the performance. The reason: several scenes contained "crass language and tactless polemics against rituals and doctrines of the Catholic Church" that would grossly offend Berlin's one hundred thousand Catholic residents, endanger the confessional peace, and possibly lead to public disturbances. Following protests in the press and an appeal to the emperor, the government agreed to allow a public performance if the entire fifth scene and several references to the religious hypocrisy and greed of the pre-Reformation Catholic Church were excised.[16]

Throughout the 1890s Prussian censors continued to block anti-Catholic dramas. After a controversial trial in Aachen in 1895 in which several Alexian friars were convicted of torturing inmates in a mental asylum run by that order, playwright A. Winter composed *Der Irre von Marienburg; oder Im Kloster der Alexianer* (*The Lunatic of Marienburg, or In the Alexian Cloister*), a sensationalistic piece about the sadistic abuse of inmates and novice friars within the Marienburg asylum. After the drama played in Hamburg, Hanover, and several smaller, predominantly Protestant Prussian towns, the Catholic press condemned it as a malicious defamation that encouraged confessional hatred and called for its ban. In December 1895 the Prussian interior minister took the unusual step of directing all provincial governors in Prussia to ban the play, which was "directed against the institutions of the Catholic Church as such, and in particular, against church discipline and monasteries themselves."[17] Berlin censors also excised several passages from Gerhart Hauptmann's *Florian Geyer,* a drama about the sixteenth-century German peasants' war, for they feared the peasants' derogatory references to the priesthood (*Pfaffen; Pfaffenknecht*) might offend Catholics. And in 1900, before a Berlin theater could perform *Die Dame von Maxim* (*The Woman from Maxim*), the interior minister ordered the character of a lecherous abbé be replaced by that of a lecherous schoolteacher.[18]

While they might confiscate books or ban dramas considered anti-Catholic, Prussian authorities seldom initiated legal proceedings against the authors. After 1890, however, as the political power of the Catholic Church rose dramatically, particularly in Bavaria (whose population was 71 percent Catholic), authorities there began prosecuting anti-Catholic imaginative writers under §166.

Beginning with the 1890 election, the Catholic Center Party assumed a pivotal parliamentary position in both the Reichstag and Prussian parliament. Anxious to demonstrate its patriotism, the party became one of the government's most reliable backers and within a decade its support had become indispensable in governing the nation. In Bavaria too, a significant rapprochement occurred: as the liberals' political influence declined steadily after the mid-1880s, that of the Bavarian Center Party rose significantly, and it wrested a number of significant concessions from the governing liberals. After the Center won an absolute majority in the Bavarian parliament in 1899, the Bavarian government became increasingly dependent on the party, which itself was moving more to the Right.

One of the Bavarian Center Party's frequent complaints during the 1890s was that the Catholic Church was not receiving "adequate protection against insults" from Bavaria's liberal government.[19] While the government had little desire to alienate its liberal supporters by imposing tighter restrictions on the press and free speech, neither could it afford to ignore the growing pressure of the politically influential Catholics. To mollify the Center Party, the Bavarian ministry of the interior sometimes instituted legal proceedings against outspoken critics of the church "simply for political reasons," even when the case was likely to result in exoneration or dismissal; for then, as the interior minister noted, "the charge can no longer be made that the state has not done everything it could in order to ensure punishment for of an insult [to the church]."[20]

Given the church's political power in the 1890s, it is hardly surprising that it was in Bavaria that §166 was most frequently, and most successfully, invoked. In 1891, for example, the Bavarian government indicted the agnostic Naturalist Hanns von Gumppenberg for blasphemy after the Catholic press in Munich complained bitterly about his play *Messias,* which depicted Jesus as a human rather than divine figure who for noble purposes knowingly deceives believers, and about a public talk Gumppenberg held to defend his aesthetic treatment of Christ. Charges were dropped when the Catholic reporter could not attest that Gumppenberg had actually used some of the disparaging references to Christ that his newspaper had reported.[21] Although Gumppenberg escaped punishment for blasphemy (he was soon convicted of lèse majesté, however; see chapter 3), another Munich Naturalist, Oscar Panizza, was not so fortunate.

Panizza, whose profound hatred of the Catholic Church permeated much of his work, wrote several vitriolic parodies of Christian mythology and Catholic rituals and dogmas. While his early, rather oblique anti-Catholic works passed largely unnoticed, his later, more direct ones did not. Whether or not he deliberately provoked a confrontation with the church and Bavarian authorities, as some observers believed (see chapter 7), given the political climate in Bavaria his anti-Catholic crusade was destined to incite a harsh official reaction.

The first major battle in Panizza's escalating polemical war with the church came with the appearance in 1893 of *Die unbefleckte Empfängnis der Päpste (The Immacu-*

late Conception of the Popes), a clever hoax supposedly written by a Spanish friar and "translated" by Panizza. It parodied the doctrine of the Immaculate Conception by providing elaborately documented doctrinal and canonical "proofs" that, like the Virgin Mary, all the popes had also been immaculately conceived. The Catholic press immediately condemned the book as anti-Catholic blasphemy. In May, Stuttgart authorities confiscated all unsold copies of the work they could locate there and, through an *objektives Verfahren,* got it permanently banned throughout the empire. (No charges were brought against Panizza, either because it was not clear he was the author or because the work had been published abroad.) The same fate befell Panizza's 1894 *Der teutsche Michel und der römische Papst. Altes und Neues aus dem Kampf des Teutschtumes gegen römisch-wälsche Überlistung und Bevormundung in 666 Thesen und Zitaten* (*The German Michel and the Roman Popes: Old and New from the Struggle of Germandom Against Roman-Franco Fraud and Tutelage, in 666 Theses and Quotations*), a polemical discourse on the eternal and irreconcilable conflict between Germany and the Vatican that bitterly attacked the dogmas, history, and political policies of the Catholic Church. This work too was confiscated under §166 and its distribution in Germany outlawed.[22]

Although Panizza escaped prosecution for both these polemics, for his 1894 published drama *Das Liebeskonzil. Eine Himmels-Tragödie in fünf Aufzügen* (*The Council of Love: A Heavenly Tragedy in 5 Acts*) he received a year in prison—the harshest sentence imposed on any writer in imperial Germany. This hilarious, scathing satire ridiculed the church's increasingly anthropomorphized presentation of the "Holy Family" (God, Jesus, and the Virgin Mary) by carrying the notion to absurdity (Mary is oversexed, vain, foul-mouthed, and jealous; Jesus a passive, masochistic, emaciated asthmatic; God a senile, embittered cripple). Moreover, it also suggested God and Mary were directly, and the sexually depraved renaissance popes and Catholic clergy indirectly, responsible for unleashing syphilis upon humanity.

After learning of the book from a favorable review in the local Social Democratic newspaper, in December 1894 the Munich prosecutor notified police. After a preliminary interview in which Panizza imprudently agreed certain passages of the work clearly blasphemed God and the Holy Trinity, disparaged the cult of Mary, and would probably scandalize a pious Christian reader, police ordered all unsold copies of *Das Liebeskonzil* confiscated.[23] In March 1895 Panizza was charged with over ninety counts of publicly blaspheming God and reviling the institutions and rituals of the Christian Church, in particular the Catholic Church. Obtaining the indictment, however, required some questionable behavior by police. A successful prosecution depended on the state's proving a reader had been offended by the contents of *Das Liebeskonzil.* After finding that only a score of copies had been sold in Munich and that the purchasers were all either noted anticlericals who would clearly not find *Das Liebeskonzil* offensive, or urbane Catholics who would brush it off as something no one could take seriously, Munich police contacted their counterparts in other cities to inquire whether anyone there had complained about Panizza's drama. Obligingly, the Leipzig police president reported that indeed, a police sergeant had purchased the book and that he and another police official had read the play and their religious sensibilities had been deeply offended. The next day, Panizza was formally indicted.[24]

Panizza's trial took place in the Munich Superior Court before an all-peasant jury on 30 April 1895. Although several of his literary friends attended, the trial was closed to the general public because authorities feared the subject matter posed a danger to public morality.[25] Panizza presented his own defense but the jury found him guilty of "a crime against religion, committed through the press." He was sentenced to a year in prison (the prosecutor had requested eighteen months), ordered to pay all costs of the trial, and all remaining copies of *Das Liebeskonzil* were to be destroyed. In justifying its harsh sentence the jury commented that Panizza's drama was "inclined to offend the religious and moral sensibilities of others in the deepest way possible, and that the excesses of this work cannot be excused under artistic freedom; rather, it improperly abuses such freedom." On the other hand, the jurors also noted as a mitigating factor the fact that the publication was so offensive "it has been soundly rejected by all upstanding people and has found very limited distribution." While Panizza and his friends were shocked by the severity of his punishment, some considered it too lenient: one juror is reported to have commented, "If that dog had been tried in Lower Bavaria, he wouldn't have escaped alive."[26]

While Panizza's conviction was appealed he was released on bond, set by the court at the exorbitant sum of eighty thousand marks. In July 1895 the Imperial Supreme Court rejected Panizza's appeal and he was ordered to report to prison. Despite continued efforts by his attorney and physicians to have his sentence reduced or commuted because of mental illness, Panizza was forced to serve the full year. When he complained that other prisoners convicted for fraud and even rape served lesser sentences, he was told by one of his warders: "If you had committed anything else, you would have been out long ago."[27] When released in August 1896 Panizza was a broken man, both physically and spiritually. He soon renounced his Bavarian citizenship and from abroad published attacks that later led to his arrest for lèse majesté (see chapter 3).

During this time Prussian authorities, too, began successfully invoking the blasphemy law against anti-Catholic satirists. In 1899, after Captain Dreyfus was retried by a French court and sentenced to ten years in prison, Siegmar Mehring published a satirical poem in *Ulk* suggesting Dreyfus's sentence was the result of popular hysteria orchestrated by France's Jesuits. The Berlin prosecutor confiscated the issue and indicted Mehring and the periodical's publisher and editor (Rudolf Mosse and Arthur Levysohn) for blaspheming the Catholic Church. (All three defendants, like Dreyfus, were Jewish.) While his codefendants were acquitted, the court found Mehring guilty of gross mockery and defamation of the Roman Catholic priesthood. Mehring was sentenced to six months' imprisonment, later commuted to three months.[28]

But for a technicality, Prussian authorities also would have imprisoned the renowned Impressionist poet Richard Dehmel, whose *Weib und Welt. Gedichte mit einen Sinnbild* (*Woman and World: Poems with a Symbol;* 1896) so offended the conservative aristocratic writer Börries von Münchhausen that he filed a complaint with the Prussian state prosecutor.[29] Münchhausen took particular offense at "Venus consolatrix," in which Dehmel described a Lucifer-induced vision of a beautiful woman who appears before him, slowly disrobes her sensuous body, then seems to dissolve into the Virgin Mary and Mary Magdalene. Berlin police confiscated the book in July 1897 for both obscenity and blasphemy but because more than six months had transpired since the book's publication, Dehmel himself could not be indicted. In August 1897 a Berlin court found that "Venus consolatrix" contained not only obscene descriptions of nudity, but was also blasphemous under §166, for by describing the Virgin Mary as baring her body and genitals, Dehmel profaned a central institution of the Catholic Church. "Venus consolatrix" had to be removed from all future editions of *Weib und Welt,* and the judges noted that only the statute of limitations prevented Dehmel's receiving three months' imprisonment.[30] In 1900 another Dehmel poem, "Die Magd" (The Maid), did earn a socialist newspaper editor who printed it one month in prison because a Magdeburg court considered it a "blasphemous attack on the Christian doctrine that God became man."[31]

The courts did not, however, sanction all state attempts to censor anti-Catholic dramas or prosecute anti-Catholic authors, even in Bavaria. In September 1891, after the Catholic and conservative press in Munich denounced Naturalist M. G. Conrad and his circle as atheists who sought to "overthrow the entire Christian Weltanschauung,"[32] police there seized 545 copies of *Modernes Leben: Ein Sammelbuch der Münchener Moderne* (*Modern Life: A Scrapbook of the Munich Moderns;* 1891), an anthology of works by Conrad's circle of writers. Besides containing several obscene contributions, police charged that Conrad's "Jenseits. Novellistische Seelenstudie" (The Hereafter: Novelistic Studies of the Soul) was blasphemous and violated §166. In December, however, the Munich court dropped indictments against Conrad and the other contributors and released the anthology for distribution.[33] Richard Dehmel had a similar experience concerning a collection of his early poems, *Aber die Liebe, ein Ehemanns- und Menschenbuch* (*But Love: A Husband's and Human's Book;* 1893). Given the prevailing political climate in Bavaria at the time, Dehmel's publisher, after having the manuscript examined by a lawyer, agreed to publish it only after Dehmel deleted several lines from "Venus domestica." Dehmel complied, but on the condition he be allowed to insert a note protesting that he had agreed to the deletion only "out of consideration for the law against blasphemy," and that he could not understand how anyone could find his poem religiously offensive. Shortly after their publication a clerical newspaper predictably denounced Dehmel's poems, especially "Venus Madonna" (which spoke of the Madonna as "alluring" and "stimulating"), as blaspheming the Catholic Church's veneration of Mary. The Munich police confiscated *Aber die Liebe* in December 1893 and charged Dehmel, his publisher, and a local Munich bookseller with distributing blasphemous materials. Once again, however, the Munich court dismissed the charges and in May 1894 released the book for circulation.[34]

The most important acquittal during this period involved Ludwig Thoma, a popular Bavarian satirist and playwright whose biting wit was frequently directed against the Philistine mentality of the powerful Bavarian Center Party. In a January 1904 "Center Party" issue of *Simplicissimus* devoted entirely to the Catholic clergy and the clerical deputies in the Bavarian parliament, Thoma wrote a mock Lenten sermon ("Fastenpredigt der Sankt Abraham a Santa Clara" [Lenten Sermon of Saint Abraham of Santa Clara]) zealously attacking the church's and Center Party's stifling social, economic, and intellectual influence and its inquisitorial campaigns against all modern ideas. Having recently been rebuked by political Catholics for not acting against a *Simplicissimus* cartoon ridiculing a Centrist leader, the Bavarian government could not ignore Thoma's attack, even if the chances of conviction seemed slim. The Munich prosecutor had Stuttgart police raid the firm where *Simplicissimus* was printed, seize all copies of the special issue they could find, and prohibit any further printing. To intercept the copies already distributed, police in Bavaria also sealed off all railway cars arriving from Stuttgart and stood guard outside local bookstores and newsstands.[35] Thoma and *Simplicissimus* editor Julius Linnenkogel were charged with "offenses against religion" under §166. At the preliminary court hearing, however, the judge dropped all charges. Moreover, the court later ruled Thoma's "Fastenpredigt" did not legally defame either the institutions or the practices of the Catholic Church, so the "Center issue" could not be banned under an *objektives Verfahren* and was released for circulation.[36]

Nor was the Catholic Church always successful in persuading police to ban ostensibly anti-Catholic plays. In 1899, for example, the Archbishop of Freiburg demanded the Baden government halt a Mannheim performance of Max Halbe's *Jugend* (*Youth*). To the archbishop the play, which contained a fanatic young Polish priest whose hateful and unforgiving moralism nearly ruins the life of the young, joyful heroine, was a cunning but serious defamation of the Catholic clergy. Since no system of censorship existed for Baden theaters, however, the request was ignored.[37] Likewise, Prussian authorities were not pressured into banning the anticlerical Karl Schönherr's *Glaube und Heimat* (*Faith and Home*), which concerned the brutal forced expulsion of Protestants from Salzburg during the Austrian Counter-Reformation. Despite strong protests in the Catholic press, during the 1910–1911 season the work was performed uncut in a dozen German cities.[38] When performed again in Berlin shortly after the outbreak of the war, Catholics appealed directly to the district military commander for its ban. Both military authorities and local police insisted, however, that the work was an attack upon religious fanaticism of all kinds; indeed, because they believed the drama preached commitment to high ideals, love of homeland, and willingness to sacrifice, Berlin authorities considered the play particularly appropriate for Germany's "difficult times" and performances were allowed to continue.[39]

The declining ability of Catholics in the decade before World War I to obtain bans or convictions reflects a waning of Catholic political influence after 1905 in both Prussia and the nation and a resurgence of anti-Catholic antagonisms throughout the empire. The precarious confessional truce between Protestants and Catholics deteriorated significantly, as did the close political cooperation between the government and the Center Party that had been established after the *Kulturkampf.* In 1906 Chancellor von Bülow and the Center Party broke their political alliance; the imperial government's anti-Catholic electoral campaign in 1907 revived a wave of anti-Catholic hysteria. Although Catholics and the imperial government reconciled again in 1909, the Center's strength in the Reichstag receded after the 1912 election.

During the decade before the war Pope Pius X (1903–1914) exacerbated Protestant antagonism, for, like his mid-century predecessor Pius IX, he adamantly opposed any movement to modernize the church. Pius's placing of many progressive books on the proscribed Index, his antimodernist encyclical of 1907, and the antimodernist oath he imposed on all Catholic theologians and professors in 1910 seriously alienated liberals and moderates of all faiths; his militantly anti-Protestant encyclical of 1910 denouncing the Reformation enraged German Protestants and provoked formal protests from the Prussian, Saxon, and even Bavarian governments. It is surely not coincidental that after 1905–1906, no German writers of note were prosecuted under §166 for insulting the Catholic Church, no serious literary works were confiscated for anti-Catholic content, and there were few bans of allegedly anti-Catholic dramas.

In sharp contrast to the frequent intervention against anti-Catholic literary works between 1878 and 1905, only a handful of anti-Protestant works were censored. All such cases occurred in predominantly Protestant areas between 1905 and World War I as censorship of anti-Catholic works was declining, and all involved slandering the Protestant clergy. As the German Protestant Church increasingly identified itself with the propertied and the powerful and, after 1895, officially reprimanded the "social parsons" who attempted to advocate for the disadvantaged, writers frequently portrayed Protestant pastors as aloof, uncaring social conformists who were "indifferent or hostile to the poor, the young, to change and new ideas."[40] Because of the Protestant clergy's crucial political function, authorities could not ignore church complaints about works that portrayed Protestant parsons unfavorably.

The most celebrated of such cases again involved Ludwig Thoma and the satirical journal *Simplicissimus.* After a meeting of the General Conference of German Morality Leagues in October 1904, where clergymen from across Germany denounced obscenity and the sexual laxity of the lower classes, Thoma published a satirical poem in *Simplicissimus* ridiculing the moral hypocrisy and sham prudery of Protestant pastors, who preached sexual restraint for others but were noted for producing large families of their own.[41] The High Consistory of the Prussian Evangelical Church demanded Thoma be prosecuted for libeling a clergyman (§196 of the Criminal Code). Police confiscated that issue of *Simplicissimus* and in June 1905 a Stuttgart court sentenced Thoma to six weeks' imprisonment and fined *Simplicissimus* editor Julius Linnenkogel two hundred marks, although the prosecutor had asked for heavier punishment. *Simplicissimus* was also required to print a copy of the court's verdict.[42]

Censors also screened dramas for anti-Protestant content. In 1913 A. Paul's *Drohnen* (*Drones*) was banned in Berlin because the behavior and comments of Krank (a Protestant pastor) during a bizarre burial scene, in which a drunken man falls unconscious into the open grave, ridiculed the ministry. The provincial governor eventually permitted the drama on the condition the pastor's offending comments be excised.[43] In 1917 the Protestant Church was also successful in suppressing Hermann Essig's *Pastor Rindfleisch* (*Pastor Beef*), a comedy about a new pastor in a rural parish who tries to persuade his skeptical congregation it is their traditional obligation to provide their pastor with a cow. The Berlin censor objected to the petty, greedy, and duplicitous way the pastor was portrayed; he found the play inappropriate because it degraded pastors, for whom the public had deep respect. The Evangelical Church Council, whose opinion the police solicited, was outraged at this "*Simplicissimus*-style" caricature of a pastor and denounced Essig's play as a deliberate defamation of the clergy in general, and of the Protestant parsonage in particular, one that should "not under any circumstances" be permitted.[44] It was approved for the Berlin stage only after the author agreed to rename his play *Kuhhandel* (*Shady Business*) and (once again) replace the pastor with a schoolteacher.

Unfortunately the religious confession that benefited least from §166 or from theater censorship was the one that surely needed it the most: Germany's Jews. Comprising approximately 1 percent of the population, Jews were the most maligned and vulnerable religious group in the empire. The imperial era was marked by periodic waves of popular anti-Semitism, which reached special intensity in 1879–1881 and again in 1887–1893, and by an outpouring of anti-Semitic literature. Despite the Jewish community's frequent and tenacious appeals to German authorities to suppress anti-Semitic publications and indict those who vilified Judaism, few anti-Semitic works were confiscated or banned, and still fewer anti-Semitic publicists were prosecuted. Although several subtle and not-so-subtle anti-Semitic literary works circulated during the imperial era, none were ever censored.

There were four major reasons why the law was seldom invoked against anti-Semitic literature. First, although Jews made up a high percentage of Germany's lawyers, Jews who did not convert to Christianity were excluded from the state judiciary; they had access only to the lowest rank of the judicial bureaucracy. As late as 1910, not a single one of Prussia's 373 public prosecutors was Jewish.

Second, before crimes like blasphemy could be prosecuted, a plaintiff first had to file a complaint and convince the public prosecutor a crime had been committed. With anti-Catholic or anti-Protestant literary works, prosecutors often took a general complaint—or even an unfavorable review in the local press—as sufficient grounds for ordering a confiscation, but they never did so regarding anti-

Semitic works. Prosecutors turned a deaf ear to Jewish complainants and refused to prosecute when Jewish organizations attempted to initiate legal proceedings against specific works and authors.[45] Although plaintiffs could themselves bring charges in certain kinds of criminal cases if prosecutors failed to act, the effort and expense of doing so, and the minimal prospects for success, usually discouraged such direct appeals to the courts.

Third, in most anti-Semitic tracts Jews were attacked not as a religious community but as a race or ethnic group. Many anti-Semites circumvented the provisions of §166 by tailoring their language to avoid defaming Jews as a religious community or attacking their religious practices, for example by accusing Jews of "blood murder" (*Blutmord*) rather than ritual murder (*Ritualmord*). Since few anti-Semitic publications thus qualified as religious defamation under §166, prosecutors often declined to prosecute, and courts declined to convict.

Fourth, even when anti-Semites maligned aspects of Jewish faith like Talmudic law, it was difficult to convince Germany's non-Jewish judiciary to consider these as institutions or rituals central to the Jewish religion, and thus protected under §166.

Many imperial, state, and local authorities thus remained "impartial" on the "Jewish question," ignoring both Jewish requests for protection as well as radical anti-Semites' demands for stronger state action against "Jewish excesses."[46] Public prosecutors' reluctance to bring anti-Semites to court and the judiciary's exceedingly narrow interpretation of §166 as it pertained to Judaism were major obstacles in obtaining legal protection for Jews against even the most scurrilous journalistic and literary attacks. Indeed, during the 1870s and 1880s many Jewish leaders and defense organizations came to view legal appeals as futile. This frustration was evident in a May 1892 article in the Orthodox *Jüdische Presse*, which asked: "Are we Jews outside the law? Can our personal, our civil, our religious honor really be dragged in the filth, be ridiculed and derided in this way without hindrance or penalty? Has some law removed us Jews from the protection of those paragraphs that bring the disrupters of civil peace and the despoilers of religious sanctities to punishment?"[47]

Only in the mid-1890s, when political anti-Semitism climaxed in Germany, did authorities start intervening against literary works that might exacerbate Christian-Jewish tensions. This was especially true in Berlin, which contained the nation's largest concentration of Jews (4 percent of the city's inhabitants, constituting about one-fifth of all German Jews) and which was the scene of several disruptive anti-Semitic demonstrations. After various Jewish defense organizations launched a bold effort in 1893 to prosecute anti-Semitic expressions in the courts, prosecutors became more responsive to Jewish complaints, and courts began interpreting §166 more liberally. After 1896, for example, references to ritual murder, or allegations that reciting the Kol Nidre prayer allowed Jews to break their sworn oaths and commit perjury, were considered a defamation of the Jewish religion and thus punishable under §166; previously, such comments were considered as references to Jews as a race.

The state's new (albeit selective) sensitivity in the late 1890s to works that might exacerbate Christian-Jewish hatred meant police attempted to suppress not only anti- but also philo-Semitic works such as L. Jean-Christ's *Eleazar*. This drama about the church's persecution of Jews in fifteenth-century Mecklenburg was (according to the author) a plea for Christian-Jewish reconciliation; its title character is an elderly Jew who becomes embittered after a corrupt, intolerant church burns both of his (converted) children at the stake. The Berlin police president, however, believed the "brutal" portrayal of religious hatred in *Eleazar* was inflammatory, its "fanatic" and "bigoted" hatred toward Christians would deeply offend Christian spectators, and it might incite violent outbursts, especially since the two theaters proposing to perform the work were "in the hands of [a] Jewish director ... and numerous members of the Jewish faith are in the cast." The play was thus banned in July 1894 in the interests of interconfessional harmony and public order. After a lengthy appeal, however, the Supreme Administrative Law Court lifted the ban in June 1896.[48]

Carl Weiser's philo-Semitic drama *Rabbi David*, about a fifteenth-century rabbi unjustly convicted of ritual murder, encountered the same official reaction, although it condemned religious bigotry and pleaded for Christian-Jewish reconciliation. (Ever since Jewish butcher Wolf Buschoff had been acquitted for "ritual murder" in Xanten in 1891–1892—the first such case in Germany since Jewish emancipation—this controversial issue had been at the forefront of anti-Semitic propaganda.) When a Berlin theater asked to perform *Rabbi David* in July 1899, the police president refused, fearing the pro-Jewish work might provoke disruptive, even violent demonstrations from Berlin's rabid anti-Semites. Such demonstrations had occurred in 1893 after the performance of von Valis' *Moderne Teutonen*, a philo-Semitic drama critical of German attitudes toward Jews, and the memory of France's nationwide anti-Semitic riots of 1898 were, no doubt, also fresh in his mind. He also argued that this theater's Jewish patrons might be so offended by the play's crass treatment of Jews that they too might disrupt the peace.[49] The District Administrative Council overturned the ban in January 1900, but the tenacious police president appealed to the Supreme Administrative Law Court, arguing that in the intervening months Christian-Jewish tensions had become more volatile in Berlin (since September 1899 there had been two violent street clashes in the capital between anti-Semites and their opponents, and anti-Semites were charging that another "ritual murder" had been committed in Konitz). He was sure anti-Semitic riots could be expected if *Rabbi David* were performed. Although this police appeal was also refused,[50] the theater by now decided not to perform *Rabbi David*, perhaps because of the highly charged atmosphere of which the police president had warned. Cases such as *Eleazar* and *Rabbi David* reinforce the argument that when authorities in imperial Germany occasionally intervened on behalf of Jewish interests, their primary concern was to preserve public order from the anti-Semitic rioting that sporadically flared up over particularly controversial works.[51]

One final example, drawn from visual art, illustrates how difficult it was for imperial authorities, especially in Catholic regions, to protect the religious sensibilities of both Jews and Christians. In 1903 complaints by the Munich rabbi prompted the prosecutor there to invoke §166 and order the confiscation of postcard-sized reproductions of a seventeenth-century etching depicting the supposed ritual murder by Jews of the two-year-old St. Simon of Trent. The confiscation (upheld in the Munich courts) aroused fervent criticism in the Bavarian press: liberals condemned it because the postcards reproduced a legitimate work of art that was on display in the Munich Royal Kupferstichkabinett, while representatives of the Bavarian Catholic Church criticized the government for ignoring insults to Catholicism while going to absurd lengths to appease Jews.[52]

Once again, censors found themselves in an unpopular and perhaps impossible situation. Given the deep anti-Semitic currents in Wilhelmine society, the few efforts to suppress anti-Semitic works that were not thwarted by prosecutors or courts could easily lead to further alienating both the local religious and local artistic communities. Is it any wonder German censors showed less inclination to defend the religious sensibilities of the (politically feeble) Jews than those of the (politically powerful) Catholics and Protestants?

Blasphemy Law between Reaction and Reform

Using §166 and theater censorship to uphold interconfessional harmony had two ironic consequences. First, the censors' actions often exacerbated political and confessional differences, especially those separating Germany's Catholics from their liberal and Protestant opponents. Second, Jews, Catholics, and Protestants were all critical of the blasphemy law and its enforcement and placed little faith in its ability to protect their religious sensibilities. Indeed, many Catholics and Protestants sought, with equal lack of success, to have the blasphemy law fundamentally rewritten: Catholics found §166 too narrowly drawn and its judicial interpretation prejudicial to Catholic interests, so hoped to strengthen it; militant Protestants found the law too confining and harmful to the Protestant cause, so hoped to abolish it.

Catholics clearly benefited most from the protections of §166 and from police censorship of religiously offensive dramas. This fact was only too clear to Germany's liberals and more militant Protestants, many of whom had supported the *Kulturkampf* and opposed the rapprochement with Rome after 1878. These elements resented how censorship favored Catholics, and they regularly protested the ban of anti-Catholic works and the prosecution of anti-Catholic critics.

The Naturalist critic Conrad Alberti, for example, condemned the 1886 ban of Bulthaupt's *Eine neue Welt* as "one of the worst injustices ever committed by the bureaucracy against the Holy Spirit of art"[53] (an assessment he no doubt revised when he was convicted in the 1891 Leipzig Realists' trial; see chapter 6). Two years later, when authorities banned Trümpelmann's *Luther und seine Zeit,* a liberal Berlin newspaper protested the suppression of this "pious and patriotic work" and wondered what the authorities could possibly have found offensive about it.

Even Emperor Friedrich III, days before his death, demanded Bismarck explain the ban.[54]

The founding of the militantly anti-Catholic Protestant League (Evangelischer Bund) in 1886 provided Protestants with an organized means of agitating against the censorship laws. In August 1887, for example, a Protestant synod and presbytery in the Rhineland complained to the imperial minister of justice that the blasphemy law was frequently used to punish Protestants who criticized Catholicism, but was seldom invoked against Catholics who criticized Protestantism.[55] During the controversy over Trümpelmann's *Luther und seine Zeit* in 1888, two thousand Protestant leaders from the Rhineland and Westphalia (where the population was two-thirds Catholic) petitioned the Reichstag to change §166 because the current statute prevented Protestants from replying to Catholic attacks. The petitioners complained that the Catholic press and clergy could denounce the Protestant marriage sacrament as "concubinage" or call Martin Luther an advocate of "free love" with impunity, for example, while Protestant clergy who attacked doctrines of the Catholic Church were charged with blasphemy. The petition (later signed by thirty-three thousand people) expressed grave concern over the increasing power of Catholics and concluded: "It is now therefore our holy duty, especially for our clergymen, to affirm the Evangelical truth against false Roman doctrines in the most decisive manner, and on all sides. The [present] wording of §166 completely disregards the essential differences that exist between the different religious confessions, and the way [§166] is currently applied causes us to fear that our Evangelical pastors could be reduced to complete silence vis à vis the Roman Catholic Church." Because they had little hope §166 would ever be invoked on the same scale against Catholics as against Protestants, they asked the Reichstag to delete from §166 the clause that made it illegal to publicly revile the institutions or customs of one of the Christian Churches, leaving it a crime only to blaspheme God.[56]

In subsequent years Rhineland and Westphalian Protestants submitted additional petitions to the Reichstag complaining the interpretation of §166 depended too much upon the subjective religious beliefs of the judges involved. On this point they were in agreement with Catholics and Jews, who were equally displeased that secular courts, rather than the religious confessions themselves, determined which institutions, rituals, or dogmas were essential to a church. Because of their minority status in the Reich and their gross underrepresentation within the ranks of the bureaucracy and judiciary, even in Catholic states like Bavaria, Catholics objected to secular officials (almost invariably Protestants) making such determinations for the Catholic Church. An 1892 editorial in the Center Party's organ *Germania* proclaimed:

> When church authorities declare something to be dogma or a[n essential] church institution, the secular court should simply accept this as a given, then reach a judgment accordingly. … In deciding whether a confession has been insulted, its legitimate representatives must be heard [from], who should pronounce an opinion based on their feelings. Concerning the application of §166—that is, whether something has or has not been reviled—an

ecclesiastical court should decide; at the very least, the secular courts should consult with clerical assessors.[57]

This was an approach with which Germany's long-suffering Jews, whose religion was neither understood nor recognized by the Gentile judiciary, heartily agreed.[58]

Catholics also resented that §166 was so narrowly drawn. Frightened by a wave of anarchist violence that swept Europe in the summer of 1894, in December the imperial government introduced an Anti-Revolution Bill (*Umsturzvorlage*) to the Reichstag. The Center Party took this opportunity to try to expand §166 so it could be used not only against those who ridiculed the religion of others, but also against those more subdued or scholarly critiques and denials of Christian doctrine that were not hitherto illegal.

The Anti-Revolution Bill proposed not only to defend the state against subversive and revolutionary forces by severely punishing those who sought to incite others to illegal actions, but also to protect "the legal and moral bases of state and society" by punishing anyone who openly denounced or attacked religion, the monarchy, marriage, the family, or property in a way that endangered public peace. In initial Reichstag debates over the bill, Center Party delegates argued that anarchism and political subversion were but symptoms of Germany's deeper moral and religious crisis; their concern was not anarchist literature, but the erosion of Christian belief, especially by "respectable" scholarly works that challenged traditional doctrines and spread heresy and religious doubt. Center delegate Peter Spahn declared that while Catholics generally supported academic and scholarly freedom, "what we want is that professors, whose salary we pay with our taxes, not use their scholarly works to violate our feelings in such fashion. ... And we further demand they not use their professorial chairs to rob our children of their beliefs and their morals."[59] Another prominent Center parliamentarian added that his party would not support a bill that punished common people for attacking religious dogmas but not a professor with his "load of citations and his hay wagon full of notes."[60]

After being referred to a parliamentary commission dominated by the Center and chaired by Spahn, the Anti-Revolution Bill was transformed by the Catholics from a bill intended to defend the state against revolution into a weapon that could be used to attack their secular critics.[61] In this "clericalized" version of the bill (first read in April 1895) §166 protected not only the institutions and rituals of recognized religions, but their specific doctrines as well; moreover, the new bill would make it a crime to publicly attack Christianity or belief in God.[62]

Center delegates were adamant that if the government wished to defend religious feeling, then the law must also apply to those novels, philosophical addresses, university lectures, and other intellectual works that were the root of the religious crisis because they "poison our national soul in 'polite, decent' form, arouse doubt and unbelief in the hearts of our youth, and thereby undermine the foundations of our entire cultural life."[63] At the second reading of the Anti-Revolution Bill in May, a party spokesman made it clear one of their primary concerns were the religious "transgressions" to be found "in the ostensibly scientific works of the royal professors in Berlin and elsewhere."[64] Clearly, the higher biblical critics were among the primary targets of such complaints. The Center's determination to invoke the Criminal Code against this movement was evidence both of the depth of antimodernist sentiment within the church and of the tremendous impact such criticism and other forms of theological modernism had exerted upon Germans by the end of the century.

Although some on the extreme Catholic Right believed the proposed revisions did not go far enough, the bill elicited vehement protests from Protestants, even among conservative clergymen who also were disturbed about the decline of religious belief in Germany. Halle theologian (and Protestant League founder) Willibald Beyschlag, for example—no friend of liberalism or religious modernism—used the archconservative *Deutsch-Evangelische Blätter* to remind his readers of the Catholic Church's long tradition of resorting to force when confronted with doctrinal deviance. Beyschlag urged Germans to oppose Rome's latest attempt to dupe state authorities into pulling the church's chestnuts out of the fire for it: "Once the existence of God and the immortality of the soul have to be defended in Germany with a six-hundred-mark fine, as [the Center] wants," Beyschlag proclaimed, "then it means an end to German Christendom!"[65] Others in the Protestant League opposed the Center's bill for the same reasons the Rhineland and Westphalian petitioners had objected to the existing §166: they feared it would hinder rather than help their efforts to combat "satanic powers."[66]

Liberals, of course, were equally alarmed over the clericalized §166 that emerged from the Reichstag commission. The moderate-liberal *Kölnische Zeitung* denounced it as an attempt by Ultramontanes to return "to the brutal style of persecution" of the Inquisition, while the Naturalist writer Karl Bleibtreu characterized it as "a kind of military state of siege against all free expression." Maximilian Harden saw the bill as a "Counter-Reformation" designed "to enchain free scholarly research and the intellectual life of the educated classes and subject it to the censorship of the judiciary."[67] (See Figure 5.2)

Fears the Roman Church would use a tougher §166 to stifle art and crush even its scholarly critics seemed all the more legitimate when, at the height of the debate over the Anti-Revolution Bill (30 April 1895), Oskar Panizza was sentenced to a year in prison for *Das Liebeskonzil*. All the leading liberal papers in Berlin, the Social Democratic press, some conservative papers, and even some media in Catholic regions, although usually careful to distance themselves from Panizza's crude ideas, immediately denounced the author's harsh sentence in Catholic Bavaria as "fanatical." A hastily written tract by Theodor Lessing about Panizza's case warned that if the state continued to use force against literature and art to protect abstract concepts like God or Christianity, then "after all thinking and spiritually agile men have emigrated, one can set up a thoroughgoing police state." The *Kölnische Zeitung* hoped Panizza's conviction might help strengthen those who opposed harsher blasphemy laws or wanted §166 repealed altogether.[68]

The Anti-Revolution Bill was indeed headed for defeat. Chancellor Hohenlohe, who had originally submitted the bill to the Reichstag, found the commission's

Verbrecher, die erdichtete Thatsachen, von denen sie wußten, daß sie erdichtet sind, öffentlich behauptet haben, um dadurch Staatseinrichtungen verächtlich zu machen. (§ 131.)

Figure 5.2 The Anti-Revolution Bill
(Ludwig Stutz Drawing, *Kladderadatsch* December 1894)
German writers (Hauptmann, Ibsen, Wildenbruch, Suderman) being arrested and led away because their works undermine the established order.

draft (and the proposed changes to §166 in particular) unacceptable. He and the Prussian ministry of justice did not want to see particular religious doctrines protected by the law, for the state might then have to defend doctrines it regarded as questionable, perhaps even as objectionable; besides, Hohenlohe wondered, how were secular judges to decide what constituted a church doctrine? The government also feared the Center's radical amendments to the Anti-Revolution Bill were arousing so much opposition that its passage was becoming impossible; there were also reports that popular concern over the vagueness of the proposed law and over the arbitrary way it might be applied was undermining public faith in the whole judicial system.[69]

When the Anti-Revolution Bill came up for its second reading in May 1895, it was opposed, though for different reasons, by the Social Democrats, Progressives, National Liberals, and even Conservatives and Free Conservatives. The government attempted to persuade the Center to sacrifice some its most objectionable amendments, especially the proposed changes to §166, so the rest of the bill could pass. When the Center adamantly refused, Hohenlohe saw no alternative but to withdraw his government's support, and on 11 May the Reichstag soundly defeated the Anti-Revolution Bill.

The fate of the Anti-Revolution Bill reveals much about the bitter confessional divisions of the time. As Peter Mast points out,[70] the Center's futile attempts to revise the blasphemy law revived the passionate interconfessional animosities of the *Kulturkampf*. The more Catholics insisted on using their newfound political influence to transform the bill into a weapon against religious dissent, the more liberals, Protestants, and the government united in opposition to them. Liberal intellectuals and cultural nationalists repeated their earlier charges that Catholicism was a reactionary force trying to stifle German culture. Conservative Protestants became more convinced that broadening the blasphemy law would only benefit Catholics. Even the imperial government, for which Christian principles and belief served as a crucial ideology of legitimation, resisted Catholic attempts to give censors greater power to halt the spread of religious unbelief. On this issue, Germany's political Catholics were clearly out of step with the rest of their countrymen, who, in the last analysis, supported the cultural and religious pluralism that Germany enjoyed.

Although, as we have seen, the use of §166 to punish anti-Catholic authors declined steadily after 1900, the liberal and Protestant backlash generated by such cases did not. In early 1903 the liberal artists and intellectuals of the Munich Goethe League held a mass meeting at which they condemned the way §166 was unfairly used in Munich to stifle criticism of the church and demanded changes in the law.[71] The following year editorials in the liberal press of Munich and Frankfurt condemned the prosecution of Ludwig Thoma for his anti-Catholic "Fastenpredigt," the confiscation of the *Simplicissimus* "Center Party" issue, and the underhanded tactics of the clerical "black troops." The Center had grown so powerful in Bavaria, these papers complained, that it dictated policy to state law-enforcement agencies; if the Bavarian government did not begin standing up to the Catholics on censorship, "Bavaria's reputation as a center of artistic life will be forever destroyed."[72] When it became known that Stuttgart police had alerted Munich authorities in advance about the contents of the "Center Party" issue, left-wing papers in Protestant Württemberg strongly condemned such enthusiastic collaboration with pro-Catholic Bavarian authorities. A vehement debate over the affair ensued in the Bavarian parliament when Socialist and liberal delegates accused the Center of misusing §166 to punish not only its religious but also its political opponents.[73]

Like their predecessors in the late 1880s and 1890s, militant Protestants believed the blasphemy law unfairly shielded Catholicism from Protestant criticism and refutation. In 1907–1908, as Catholic political influence waned and anti-Catholic sentiment again rose, the Protestant League, the German Protestant Congress, and the German Pastors' Congress all passed resolutions advocating either the abolition of §166 or the elimination of those clauses that punished criticism of religious institutions and rituals. Liberal Protestant circles were coming to regard laws against blasphemy as unnecessary and an obstacle to free religious inquiry. Thus a meeting of the Württemberg Evangelical Pastors' Association resolved in May 1908, "The majority of this assembly declares itself opposed to the legal punishment of blasphemy, since it is incompatible with the essence of the Evangelical faith and the modern state, it is ineffective against the worst offenses, and it is a sign of mistrust of the power of truth."[74]

Widespread public dissatisfaction with §166 and the abuses to which it could lead—especially because of its silence on the crucial matter of intent—could no longer be ignored by German lawmakers. In 1909 a commission established for the purpose of revising the Criminal Code recommended that the broad provisions of §166 be replaced by more carefully worded statutes that would require the demonstration of malicious intent on the part of the offender, and thus greatly limit application of the law. The maximum sentence was to be reduced from three to two years' imprisonment and the possibility of a fine rather than incarceration was introduced.[75] The outbreak of war in 1914 forestalled the enactment of these reforms, however, so the original provisions of §166 remained in force throughout the imperial era.

The Sacred and the Profane

Some pious writers, far from being hostile to the Christian faith or the institutions of the church, chose sacred Christian legends and biblical characters as their subject matter and were surprised when their devout, pro-Christian, works were censored too. For German authorities frequently invoked sanctions when they believed artists, directors, or actors violated social taboos surrounding the holy and the sacred.

Before World War I philosophers like Rudolf Otto were increasingly interested in humans' fascination with the mysterious terror and impelling power of "the holy." People, places, and objects associated with the apprehended presence of the holy become consecrated and take on an aura of its mystic terror or danger. In art, Otto argued, the impelling power of the numinous and the spiritual is represented and expressed through the sublime—by that which inspires the viewer with awe, veneration, and a sense of power and grandeur.[76] At the same time, anthropologists, sociologists, and psychologists were exploring the "taboos" that operated in primitive societies to preserve the distinct "otherness" of the holy by strictly separating it from the secular or profane. A community's myths and traditions, they discovered, "possess a sacred character; they must not be spoken of lightly, or be told on ordinary occasions, or be represented in an unbecoming way."[77]

A number of controversial censorship decisions related to religion involved what censors considered "unbecoming" representations of the holy, portrayals of the sacred in an unsacred— that is, profane—manner. Such cases were most common in states like Prussia or Thuringia, where the predominantly Protestant population had rejected papal authority and grounded their faith instead on scripture. Police and civil courts sometimes intervened in the artistic—particularly the dramatic—interpretation of biblical material, for they feared dramatic works with biblical themes or characters might so offend the Christian populace as to disrupt the public peace. There were several plausible grounds for such fears. First, dramatists who chose biblical themes were likely to incorporate scriptural passages directly into the dialogue in ways that could be problematic. Second, and more importantly, serious creative writers must inevitably exercise some degree of literary license, using their imaginative powers to embellish the Bible's often-meager accounts of characters and actions. Such artists will explore the behavior of the characters they write about, perhaps speculating on their motives; to make their work worthwhile and dramatic they must flesh out and "humanize" these historical biblical figures and interpret scriptural events. To do this, however, they run the serious risk either of trivializing the subject matter (that is, of viewing biblical events or characters as commonplace, and thus divesting them of their sacred "otherness"), or of challenging traditional interpretations. Third, no matter how skillfully a work was written or how pious the playwright's intentions, the actors who portrayed biblical characters might not lend them the respect and dignity they deserved, and might even degrade them. This was a danger not only with inexperienced amateurs, but also with skilled professional actors. For the acting profession did not enjoy high public esteem in nineteenth-century Germany; actors, and particularly actresses, were often seen as immoral, promiscuous bohemians. There was also concern some actors might be so identified in the public mind with their prior roles, such as scoundrels or villains, that to cast them as pious biblical figures might appear as sacrilegious. Even the talent that enabled professional actors to play different personae credibly could be a disadvantage. In the opinion of the Thuringian Supreme Administrative Law Court, for example:

> The demand that one's religious utterances be in accord with one's inner religious beliefs—something that is particularly important in religiously sensitive circles—cannot be expected of professional actors, whose artistic careers consist precisely in their being able [convincingly] to utter many diverse beliefs. It is therefore neither a contradiction nor a medieval-minded slander of the acting profession to claim that the portrayal of events considered sacred is sometimes more offensive when done by professional actors than when done by dilettantes.[78]

Finally, there was widespread suspicion that whenever a commercial theater included a biblically based drama alongside less-edifying secular works (especially frivolous comedies), sacred material was being exploited for profane commercial motives. In the eyes of the Prussian ministers of the interior and religion, *"any* inventively embellished dramatic treatment of material derived from the Holy Scriptures, relating to the holy truths of the Christian faith, and performed on stage by professional actors may be offensive to Christian religious sensibilities and, under certain circumstances, seem like a profanation."[79] Works dealing specifically with Jesus Christ were the most problematic of all. For as Otto demonstrated, the person of Christ is "the object of divination par excellence;" in his person and life, Christians get "a real divination—a direct, first-hand apprehension of holiness manifested."[80]

German authorities were thus extremely reluctant to have biblical material, especially portrayals from the life of Christ, treated on the public stage, for such performances could directly or indirectly demean events and figures sacred to Christians, and thus have an unpredictable, perhaps dangerous effect on a Christian audience familiar with the biblical stories depicted. As the imperial authorities repeatedly emphasized, in a Christian society like Germany, anything that might violate people's religious sensibilities was also a violation of public morality and public order. Prussian officials were convinced "the portrayal on stage of events from scriptural history, in particular from the life of Jesus Christ, seems likely to violate the religious sensibilities of spectators and listeners [in the audience], as well as those of the general public, and thus to provoke disturbances among wide groups of people and to disrupt public order, which it is the duty of the police to uphold."[81] (Modern readers inclined to dismiss such concerns might recall that the 1988 film *The Last Temptation of Christ* sparked mass protests in the US and a firebombing in Paris, while the controversial 1985 French film *Hail Mary*, in which Mary is depicted as a teenager who pumps gas and Joseph as a taxi driver, caused mass protests, bomb threats, and at least one arrest when it was shown at a midwestern university. Mel Gibson's controversial *The Passion of the Christ* [2004] has sparked heated debates, although no disruptions of the peace.)

To guard against offenses to religious sensibilities, several German states prohibited any public performance of biblical subject matter, including passion plays and other portrayals from the life of Christ. Exemptions could be granted when a work and its manner of performance were completely inoffensive and the overall effect evoked "the seriousness and solemnity appropriate to the subject matter." Exemptions usually required the express consent of the highest levels of state government. In Bavaria, only the state ministry (that is, the cabinet) could grant exemptions; in Prussia, exemptions required the approval of the monarch himself or (after 1897) the joint approval of the ministers of the interior and religion.[82]

Exemptions were frequently granted for major dramatic works like Grillparzer's *Esther* or Hebbel's *Judith* and for lesser-known pieces like E. N. Méhul's opera *Joseph und seine Brüder in Egypten* (*Joseph and His Brothers in Egypt*) and M. F. Arnd's *Simson* (*Sampson*) because these treated Old Testament subjects that were, as one Prussian official explained, "more distant from [contemporary] religious sensibilities" and thus less likely to cause offense.[83] By the turn of the century the Prussian government had become surprisingly liberal in permitting public performances of dramas based on Old Testament themes. In July 1904, for example, the interior and religion ministers approved Adolf Paul's satirical comedy *David und Goliath*, even though the Berlin police president wished it banned because its lighthearted approach might undermine public faith in religious traditions.[84] And in January 1908, neither Berlin police nor the interior or religion ministers objected to Otto Borngräber's *Die ersten Menschen* (*The First Humans*), a Naturalistic-Monist drama based on the Cain and Abel legend that (according to the police censor who reviewed it) sought to demonstrate man's evolution from the animal world. The cabinet ministers apparently agreed with the censor that "from a religious standpoint, this work is unlikely to cause any particular offense, since the biblical account of Creation and the lives of the first humans is today no longer widely regarded as necessarily a component of Christian doctrine, but rather is largely relegated to the realm of Jewish mythology."[85]

That German civic authorities, and even police censors, at the turn of the century could adopt such a casual attitude toward Old Testament legends is striking confirmation of the pervasive influence of higher biblical criticism, which (in the words of Franklin Baumer) "taught people to think of religions as historical phenomena, appropriate to a particular time and place, but as outgrowing their original context, as ever-changing both in form and content, their 'mythology' perhaps at last becoming outmoded."[86] Indeed, during the imperial era concern in Prussia over the potential dangers posed by dramas based on the Old Testament declined considerably. Whereas originally only the monarch could approve Old Testament–based works, by 1914 local police were authorized to exempt these from the general ban on biblical materials. On the eve of the war even Frank Wedekind's *Simson oder Scham und Eifersuch* (*Samson, or Shame and Jealousy*), which reworked the Samson and Delilah story, was approved in Prussia (although banned in Munich). It was one of the few works by that controversial playwright not widely banned during the imperial era (see chapter 6). To forbid it, Prussian authorities were convinced, would simply create publicity for Wedekind and lead to a court appeal the censors would probably lose.[87]

Protestant authorities were more cautious, however, about dramas based on the New Testament. Requests to stage such works were routinely rejected, a policy the general public found increasingly difficult to understand and which, beginning in the late 1890s, generated significant public controversy. Much of this attention centered on a series of turn-of-the-century plays by well-known authors in which John the Baptist or Mary Magdalene figured prominently.

In 1897 a respected Berlin theater asked permission for Hermann Sudermann's *Johannes,* a reverential portrayal of John the Baptist's conflict with Herod Antipas and of the prophet's death due to the scheming of Herod's vengeful wife. Although the Berlin police president found nothing objectionable about the work, he refused to approve it "because of existing general regulations" against dramas with biblical content.[88] The theater appealed the ban, first to the provincial governor (who upheld it), then to the Supreme Administrative Law Court.

During this appeal the ban was roundly criticized in both the liberal and conservative press. Since critics saw nothing in this work by one of Germany's most popular dramatists that in any way degraded its biblical characters, they believed authorities were acting out of unnecessarily narrow piety and suggested the rigid prohibition against any work based on the New Testament needed to be reexamined. Some felt prohibiting a wholesome, inoffensive piece like *Johannes* did more to harm than to promote religion.[89] When the Württemberg cabinet permitted *Johannes* in the Stuttgart Royal Theater, conferred a special royal medal on Sudermann, and then publicized its decision in a way that implied criticism of the Prussian ban, the Prussian interior minister intervened before the Supreme Administrative Law Court could issue its ruling.[90]

At the minister's request, in November 1897 Wilhelm II established new guidelines for the performance of dramas with biblical content. To provide a firmer legal basis for prohibiting such works (and avoid potentially embarrassing situations where the Supreme Administrative Law Court might have to pass judgment on the monarch's exemption of a work from the general ban), the emperor authorized the interior and religion ministers to decide which biblical dramas could be performed publicly. He also indicated that even works based on the New Testament might be permitted provided there was nothing offensive about them and Christ was not portrayed on stage.[91] The two ministers instructed the Berlin police president to rescind his ban of *Johannes* on condition that minor revisions be made, and they informed all local Prussian officials that while the general proscription against biblical material on stage was still in force, "exemptions to this rule can be granted [by the interior and religion ministers] under special circumstances."[92] *Johannes* premiered in Berlin in January 1898; soon thereafter, permission was also granted for performances in several other Prussian cities. (Although *Johannes* was also permitted in Austrian theaters, the English censor did not approve it.)

John the Baptist and the unusual circumstances surrounding his death also figured in another controversial case a few years later involving Oscar Wilde's *Salome*. This notorious drama combined two subjects about which German censors were particularly sensitive: biblical figures and perverse, even pathological sexuality. Salome's relation with her lecherous stepfather Herod is clearly incestuous, and her sensual passion for the ascetic prophet is quenched only when she holds his bloody, severed head, whose dead lips she then kisses passionately. When this drama was submitted to the shocked English censor in 1892, he at first assumed it was a pornographic joke; after realizing it was intended as a serious dramatic work, he immediately banned it, both for its immoral and its biblical content.[93]

In Germany, however, *Salome* had been performed privately in Munich, had its public premier in Lübeck in October 1901, and had also been staged publicly in Breslau by the time the famous director Max Reinhardt asked Berlin police to approve it in March 1902. The Berlin police president and the ministers of the interior and religion all agreed it should not be permitted because it would grossly offend both the moral and religious sensibilities of Christians and thus posed a threat to public order. Suggesting that the death of John the Baptist (a figure who is close to Christ and central to Christianity) is the result of Salome's jealousy and sexual frustration was bad enough, but in addition "the entire atmosphere of the piece reeks of sensuality, and under these conditions, it arouses all the more offense when passages from the Holy Scriptures are continually quoted word-for-word [in the dialog]."[94]

After Reinhardt's theater submitted a revised version—which police rejected—and held a private, invitation-only performance to demonstrate the audience would not riot, the ban was appealed first to the District Administrative Council, then directly to the interior minister, and finally to the Supreme Administrative Law Court.[95] Meanwhile, public interest in *Salome* grew and public performances were held in Hamburg and Stuttgart in January 1903; the following month, there was another private performance in Berlin.

The Supreme Administrative Law Court repealed the police ban in June 1903 and freed *Salome* for public performance in Prussia. Analyzing carefully how the characters were presented, the court found John the Baptist was portrayed quite admirably, refusing to succumb to Salome's seductions even though it cost him his life. Nor was the link between John's death and Salome's sensuality problematic, since her behavior in no way affected his biblical mission and role.[96]

After Reinhardt's innovative and highly acclaimed Berlin production in 1904, Wilde's *Salome* became a popular piece in other cities as well; the Vienna censor (somewhat reluctantly) approved it in December 1903, and by 1908 the Munich Schauspielhaus had performed the work 138 times, indicating censors in Catholic areas seemed less concerned over dramatic portrayals from the New Testament. (Richard Strauß's 1905 opera of the same name, which had been directly inspired by Reinhardt's Berlin production, encountered more difficulty however. It was banned from the Vienna Royal Opera in 1905 and not permitted in that city until August 1918. When the opera was performed outdoors in Bremen in 1915, citizens protested to the city Senate, which prohibited any further open-air performances but did allow it indoors.[97])

While Prussia ultimately permitted dramas about John the Baptist on the public stage, it adamantly refused to allow two works about Mary Magdalene by the well-known authors Paul Heyse and Maurice Maeterlinck. Because Mary Magdalene's story was more closely related to Christ than was John the Baptist's, police and courts viewed these dramas more critically, even though it was the intention of both authors to treat their heroine sympathetically, even heroically.

Heyse's *Maria von Magdala,* a fictionalized account of Christ's crucifixion, suggested Judas's betrayal of Jesus stemmed partly from his jealousy over the one-time harlot Mary Magdalene, to whom he was attracted. The Roman judge Flavius (a nephew of Pilate who is also attracted to Mary) offers to allow Jesus to escape in return for sexual favors from her, a proposition she ultimately refuses because it would betray Jesus' teachings. Jesus does not appear on stage, but when a mob is about to stone Mary, his voice is heard offstage. After the Munich Royal Theater was dissuaded by local clergy from staging it, in September 1901 a Berlin theater requested permission for a public performance of *Maria von Magdala.* The Berlin police president waited until after its well-received public premier in Bremen in October, then recommended to the interior minister it be permitted in Berlin as well, for it was no more likely to offend religious sensibilities than the recently approved *Johannes.*[98] Although an external literary expert they consulted also saw no reason to prohibit the play, the ministers of the interior and religion nevertheless ordered it banned in January 1902 because "the manner in which passages from the Holy Scriptures are used is offensive, as is the way the person and final passions of Christ are placed in dramatic juxtaposition to a wanton woman's (*bühlerische Weibes*) decision as to whether she should prostitute herself to the sensual passions of [Flavius]."[99]

Because the theater missed the deadline for appealing the ban, Heyse revised his drama to remove scriptural passages. But in May 1902 the Berlin police president refused to approve this new version because the changes did not alter the basic problem:

> Precisely the fact that the viewer is placed in the position of asking himself whether Christ would have accepted the aid Flavius was willing to offer, and the fact that neither Flavius nor Mary doubted for a minute Christ would escape through the unlocked prison door, is religiously offensive. In other words, [Heyse creates] a situation in which the captured Lord, in complete disregard of His deeply religious significance, might, given the circumstances, have behaved just like any other man who wished to cling to life.[100]

The District Administrative Council revoked this ban in October 1902, however. The tribunal found that, given the sophisticated audiences likely to attend the performances, it was extremely unlikely any religious spectators would be offended by the motives or actions of Heyse's characters. On the contrary: "In the end the work appears to be far more an exaltation of the Passion story, which is central to Christian consciousness and which is [here], in a somewhat different form, brought much closer to modern man."[101]

That decision was unacceptable to the interior and religion ministers, who, more than the Berlin police, were convinced Heyse's drama would undermine the "attitude of solemnity and consecration surrounding the venerated life and death of Christ." At their insistence, in November 1902 the Berlin police president appealed the District Administrative Council's ruling to the Supreme Administrative Law Court. In January 1903 that court reinstated the ban of *Maria von Magdala* because in the drama, Christ's suffering and death—the very basis of Christianity—

> is completely encrusted (*überwuchernd umgeben*) not only with many freely invented literary embellishments, but is also closely linked to the basest, most reprehensible human drives. [Because of the behavior of various characters] the idea is suggested to the spectator that [Christ's crucifixion and] the work of salvation depends on the decisions of others, namely, that of the one-time great sinner Mary. Any work whose performance can leave such an impression with the audience is an attack on the Christian religion, which in Prussia, because of our state's historical and constitutional formation, forms part of the public order.[102]

Within two weeks left-liberal delegates in the Prussian parliament forced the interior minister to defend his ban; soon thereafter Progressives in the Reichstag condemned the ban as a "disgraceful joke" (*schmählicher Streich*) and used the case as another opportunity to push for the abolition of all theater censorship (see chapter 2).[103] Some conservatives considered the play pro-Christian and expressed puzzlement over the ban, while a liberal journal commented that "a respectable urban or rural citizen can only shake his head and wonder why something that is safe and permitted in Stuttgart and Hamburg, in Berlin and the surrounding villages is banned and despised." Across Germany, local branches of the Goethe League held mass meetings to express solidarity with Heyse.[104]

Once the Berlin ban of *Maria von Magdala* was upheld, police in other Prussian cities also forbade it. (In many cities where performances were banned, public readings of the play were held.) In Bavaria, Munich police forbade the work but public performances were allowed in Nuremberg. A Hamburg theater began public performances in February, Stuttgart soon followed, and in Oldenburg the grand duke himself sponsored it at the royal theater.[105] After initial police resistance, the Goethe Leagues in Berlin, Munich, and Kiel staged private performances in the spring of 1903. (During 1902–1903 Heyse's play was widely performed in the US as well, where it met with a favorable response from many clergymen; after May 1903 is was also permitted in Austria.[106])

A few years later Heyse's controversial drama inspired a similar case, with a similar outcome. After being deeply moved by Heyse's work, in 1908 the Belgian writer Maurice Maeterlinck composed his own version of Mary Magdalene's story, *Marie-Magdeleine* (German translation: *Maria Magdalena*). Maeterlinck's play was both artistically inferior to Heyse's and religiously tamer. He places Mary's actions at a greater distance from Jesus' betrayal, trial, and crucifixion and suggests no romantic-sexual relationship between Judas and Mary; however, like Heyse, he presents Mary with an opportunity to use her sexuality to help win Jesus' release—which she immediately rejects—and his Jesus, too, utters biblical passages offstage.

In November 1909, after its public premier in Leipzig, a respected Berlin theater asked to perform the work. The Berlin police president, as he had with Heyse's piece, recommended to the interior and religion ministers that it be exempted from the general ban. He felt Maeterlinck's drama avoided many of the religious problems that made Heyse's piece objectionable and that the theater would give an "artistically accomplished and worthy performance." But the police president pointed out another, more pragmatic reason for permitting the drama: Banning Heyse's play had generated large public protests against censorship, he said; "if public sympathy for [Heyse] played a not inconsiderable role then, then in this case one must consider a repetition of these protests and attacks against the censorship ban ... all the more likely, since Maeterlinck, too, enjoys great respect in numerous literary circles."[107]

While the interior minister favored allowing the piece, the religion minister was opposed because Maeterlinck still left the impression Christ's crucifixion depended on Mary's decision to refuse Flavius, and he objected also to Christ's offstage appearance. The work was banned. After an unsuccessful appeal in September 1910, the following year the theater submitted a revised script. Although the Berlin police president urged its approval, the ministers of the interior and religion adamantly refused to permit public performances of *Maria Magdalena* anywhere in Prussia.[108] Because of the Supreme Administrative Law Court's earlier decision upholding the ban of Heyse's drama, it was clear further appeal was pointless. (In England, the theater censor likewise refused to permit public performances because of the play's biblical content.)

The reason public performances of *Johannes* and even the scandalous *Salome* were ultimately allowed in Prussia, while Heyse's and Maeterlinck's treatments of Mary Magdalene were not, is simple: the latter two works touched too closely upon the life of Jesus Christ, whose divinity and even historical existence had become a topic of heated controversy within the German Protestant Church. The church insisted dramatic portrayals of Jesus' life were permissible only under the most sacred conditions—when the physical location, participants, and material itself were all religiously consecrated ("religiöse Weihe des Orts, der Personen und des Stoffes"). Since the church considered neither commercial theaters nor professional actors sufficiently consecrated, it opposed virtually any portrayal of Christ on the public stage.[109] While German officials and jurists defined "sacred" more liberally than the church (not automatically excluding commercial theaters and professional actors) and insisted each case must be judged individually, in practice they always found grounds for forbidding performances in which Christ appeared on stage.

In 1897, for example, Berlin censors prohibited A. von Wilbrandt's *Hairan*, about an ancient religious prophet who is unjustly accused, tried for his teachings, and killed by a mob. Although recognizing the many parallels between Hairan and Christ, the police president initially approved the work because it was not, strictly speaking, a work treating biblical material. However, press reports and complaints from conservatives prompted the interior minister to close the play after two performances because, in his judgment, it did indeed treat the life of Christ and was thus inappropriate for commercial theaters.[110]

A more controversial case involved *Jesus,* a cycle of plays by the anonymous author "W." In 1910 the small town of Eisenach in (Protestant) Thuringia planned a "Protestant Passion play" to rival the popular appeal of the famous Oberammergau spectacular in neighboring Bavaria—and, it was hoped, attract just as many free-spending tourists.[111] The Eisenach City Theater proposed to hold annual performances of the *Jesus* cycle, a fictionalized account of people and events from biblical history written to appeal to modern interests. Besides focusing on the decadence and sexual immorality of the times, W. speculated freely on aspects of Jesus' life (Jesus' temporal father Joseph becomes an illegitimate son of Herod the Great, Jesus travels to India during his youth, and the adult Jesus becomes a physician rather than carpenter). In February 1911, however, local authorities banned *Jesus* on the grounds its performance would violate the religious sensibilities of the Thuringian State Church and of wide segments of the populace. This decision polarized public opinion: while representatives of the church and some middle-class parties in the Thuringian parliament supported the ban, much of the Eisenach business community and local citizenry did not. A meeting attended by some two thousand people passed a resolution complaining that the ban not only would cause serious economic harm to Eisenach, but was also "a totally unjustified act of oppressive coercion and an attack on self-government."[112]

After the Thuringian state ministry refused to overturn the ban, it was appealed to the Thuringian Supreme Administrative Law Court. In January 1913 that body reaffirmed police's proscription of *Jesus* because it divested Christ of any religious sacredness. In the life and person of Jesus, the court declared, "countless Christians, including those who have no feeling whatever for the official church, find religious inspiration. The still overwhelming majority of religiously minded Christians can find religious inspiration only in this ideal figure of Jesus." But the Jesus in W.'s work, afflicted with human weakness and forced to confront the sexual stimuli of the decadent society around him, falls far short of the chaste, idealistic image most Christians have of him. Because Jesus' life was stripped of its idealized holiness, and because of the commercial rather than religious motives behind the planned annual performances, the court believed the undertaking would seriously offend the religious sensibilities of the majority of the population and create a public scandal.[113]

In contrast to Eisenach's commercially oriented Passion play cycle, nonprofessional Passion plays, especially in Catholic areas, were frequently exempted from the general prohibitions against biblically based works. Each case was scrutinized individually, however, as authorities considered the actors, audience, setting, and whether the play was performed in a dignified manner. In June 1875, for example, Berlin police refused to permit a touring company of the Oberammergau Passion Play to perform in a respected Berlin theater until Emperor Wilhelm I intervened and granted permission.[114] Similarly, a professional theater ensemble was refused permission to perform Fidelius Müller's *Passion unseres Herrn Jesu Christi* (*Passion of Our Lord Jesus Christ*) in Eschweiler in 1901 because "edification is not served when actors who perform in other theatrical pieces play also in Passion plays."[115]

Permission to perform Passion plays was, however, usually granted to amateur lay Christian associations, provided the performance was a private one for association members only and staged "in enclosed premises, ... under clerical direction, and without the participation of professional actors."[116] Yet even the most pious lay associations sometimes had trouble obtaining permission if they lacked proper social credentials. In February 1903 the Prussian religion minister thus rejected a request by the Aachen Christian Union for Dramatic Art "Polyhymnia" to perform J. Beberich's *Das Leben und Auferstehung Jesu Christi* (*Life and Resurrection of Jesus Christ*) because the group consisted of members from the artisanry and petite bourgeoisie who were "not in a position to stage theatrical plays in a dignified manner."[117] Three years later the Association "Lätita" of Weisweiler was also denied permission to perform this same piece because "the actors are miners and factory workers, and women from the same circles. However great their good will, they lack the necessary cultivation and schooling, as well as the requisite costumes, to produce this play in the worthy manner required."[118]

Protestant authorities also found musical treatments of Christ unsuitable for the public stage. In spring 1896 the Berlin Philharmonic asked permission to perform Heinrich Bulthaupt's innocuous and pious opera *Christus,* in which Christ appeared briefly on stage. Although the piece had been performed publicly in Bremen, Berlin censors refused until 1903 to allow it, and then only if performed in a music academy.[119] Heinz Ewers and Eugen d'Albert's opera *Die toten Augen* (*Dead Eyes*), about the blind man whose sight Christ miraculously restored, met a similar fate. The Berlin police president and interior minister proscribed it in 1912 because Christ appeared briefly on stage, an appearance considered peripheral to the plot. Ewers replaced Christ's onstage presence with an offstage voice; this version was performed in Dresden in March 1913. Three years later a Berlin opera house asked permission to perform it. After checking with Dresden police about how the opera was received there (reviews were critical), Berlin police and the interior minister still refused to permit it because the Christ's offstage comments were out of context and made "too harsh an impression" and they objected to the fact the once-blind man later commits a murder, leaving the impression that Christ's miracle was indirectly responsible for the death of an innocent man. Ewers revised the work yet again, removing the murder and adding some contextual background to Christ's remarks. The opera finally premiered in Berlin in October 1916.[120]

Conclusion

The punctilious way imperial authorities sought to keep dramatic portrayals of Christianity's most sacred figures off public (and sometimes private) stages was as shortsighted as their policies regarding Hohenzollern dramas. Those latter policies discouraged the writing and public performance of artistically notable works that might have helped Germany's theater-going populace identify more closely with the Prussian dynasty and its history (see chapter 3). In the same way, the censors' general opposition to dramatic portrayals of Christ's life and teachings could hardly have encouraged playwrights, theaters, or performers who hoped through drama to introduce or reintroduce people to the holiest elements of the Christian faith. From the standpoint of the state there were legitimate reasons for denying audiences the opportunity to see the pro-Christian works of Heyse, Maeterlinck, von Wilbrandt, Bulthaupt, or Ewers, and even highly devotional Passion plays. Yet this kind of censorship likely helped erode, rather than preserve, religious faith. Certainly such attempts to defend the religious order met with much less public understanding and support, and generated more public controversy, than did the censors' policies in any other area. Even conservative Christians often found it hard to comprehend why pious, reverential works like Heyse's were banned. Censorship of literature on religious grounds also revealed a troubling lack of consensus among imperial authorities: not only did the Berlin theater censor, the police president, the Prussian interior minister, the Prussian religion minister, the Brandenburg District Administrative Council, and the Prussian Supreme Administrative Law Court frequently disagree about particular works, but authorities elsewhere (for example in Württemberg and Oldenburg) disagreed sharply with the Prussians. These differences reflected the deep religious divisions within the empire and the increasingly politicized nature of that discord. Using literary censorship to defend the religious order, protect religious sensibilities, and preserve interconfessional harmony in an age of declining religious belief and increasing religious tension was a most problematic undertaking indeed.

Notes

1. Wehler, *German Empire*, 113.
2. After 1878 several supposedly anti-Christian socialist books and journals were banned, including Lassalle's *Die religiöse Frage und das arbeitende Volk*, Bakunin's *Gott und der Staat*, J. Most's *Die Gottespest und die Religionsseuche*, and the journals *Freidenker* and *Der Freimaurer*. Some banned works turned out not to be socialist: a ban of George Lommel's *Jesus von Nazareth. Historische Studie* (1883), for example, was lifted four months later after legal appeals.
3. Pascal, *From Naturalism to Expressionism*, 161.
4. Richard Hamann and Jost Hermand, *Naturalismus* (Munich, 1972), 86.
5. Nipperdey, *Deutsche Geschichte*, 1: 528–29.
6. For a recent example of how quickly outraged religious sensibilities can lead to violence against "blasphemers" and the authorities who allegedly tolerate the outrage, consider the wave of riots throughout the Muslim world in early 2006 over the Danish "Mohammed cartoons."
7. Decision of Reichsgerichtshof, 3 Mar. 1882, cited in Ansgar Skriver, *Gotteslästerung?* (Hamburg, 1962), 43.
8. Quoted in Olshausen, *Kommentar zum Strafgesetzbuch*, 1: 634 and Skriver, *Gotteslästerung?* 31.
9. According to German court rulings, for the Christian churches these included such things as the veneration of Christ, the priesthood, and clerical garb and ordination rites. For the Catholic Church these included the papacy, the celebration of mass, the celibacy of the priesthood, the veneration of relics, the cult of the Virgin Mary, and monastic orders as an established institution of the Church. Individual personages (e.g., individual popes or Martin Luther), events (e.g., the Vatican Council), specific monastic orders (e.g., the Jesuits), or individual objects of veneration (e.g., a relic such as the holy cloak of Trier) were not protected unless attacks on these "passed over" into an attack on the general institution or custom. See Frank, *Strafgesetzbuch*, 293–95, and Skriver, *Gotteslästerung?* 41–52.
10. Frank, *Strafgesetzbuch*, 294–95. A November 1880 Reichsgericht decision ruled that "protected" Catholic institutions and practices included the veneration of Christ, the Catholic priesthood, crossing oneself, confession, the veneration of relics, celibacy, the cult of the Virgin Mary, and the belief in Mary's immaculate conception. Siegfried Leutenbauer, *Das Delikt der Gotteslästerung in der Bayerischen Gesetzgebung* (Cologne, 1984), 270–71.
11. Criminal statistics are unavailable before 1882, and from 1882 to 1896 statistics concerning §166 were combined with those for other religious crimes (§167, which punished the prevention or disruption of church services, and §168, which punished the looting of corpses or the desecration of cemeteries).
12. See F. Hermann Meyer, "Bücherverbote im Königreich Preußen von 1834 bis 1882," *Archiv für Geschichte des deutschen Buchhandels* 14 (1891): 317–49, especially listings for 1870–1876.
13. *VL*, 1: 90–92; Skriver, *Gotteslästerung?* 63–64; Dieter P. Lotze, *Wilhelm Busch* (Boston, 1979), 53–58; and Harald Just, "Wilhelm Busch und die Katholiken: Kulturkampfstimmung im Bismarck-Reich," *Geschichte in Wissenschaft und Unterricht* 25 (Feb. 1974): 68–71.

14. M. G. Conrad, *Von Emile Zola bis Gerhart Hauptmann. Erinnerungen zur Geschichte der Moderne* (Leipzig, 1902), 68; Maximilian Schlesinger, "Das jüngste Deutschland vor Gericht," *Monatsblätter. Organ des Vereins Breslauer Dichterschule* 16, no. 10 (Oct. 1890); 156; Hedwig Reisinger, "Michael Georg Conrad. Ein Lebensbild mit besonderer Berücksichtigung seiner Tätigkeit als Kritiker" (Inaug. diss; U. Munich, 1939), 21, 62.

15. *VL,* 2: 43–45. In November 1890 a new director permitted the play at the Berlin Hoftheater, but only after the entire fifth act was removed.

16. Gutschrift of Berlin Police, 29 May 1888, BPP to PrIM, 31 May 1888, PrIM to BPP, 1 Jun. 1888, in LAB A/74, Th 69. Also Eberhard Dellé, "Das Victoria-Theater in Berlin (1859–1891)" (Phil. diss. F.U. Berlin, 1954), 216–17. Police also demanded the character named "Bebel" be changed to "Lange" (August Bebel was the leader of the Social Democratic party, which was outlawed at the time). Police suspected the author was attempting some pro–Social Democratic political statement with this character, or that the audience might interpret it as such.

17. *Germania,* 8 Nov. 1895; PrIM to all Pr OPs, 2 Dec. 1895, GStA PK/1000, Nr. 7, Bd. 2, Bl. 147. It is not clear whether "A. Winter" was "August Winter," the pseudonym used by Otto Erich Hartleben for *Hanna Jagert.*

18. Blumenthal, *Verbotene Stücke,* 60–61; Ernst Müller-Meiningen's remarks in StenBer/RT, 10. Leg. Periode, 2. Session, 37. Sitzung am 30 Jan. 1901, Bd. 180, 1020; Hirschmann, "Berliner Residenz-Theater," 74; and comments of Hirsch in StenBer/Pr, 25. Sitzung 13. Feb. 1911, Bd. 555, 1788.

19. IM letter of 11 Jul. 1900, quoted in Jelavich, *Munich and Theatrical Modernism,* 40.

20. Ibid.

21. Ibid., 35–36.

22. Panizza, "Selbstbiographie [17. Nov. 1904]," *Tintenfisch* 13 (1978): 15; Friedrich Lippert and Horst Stobbe, *Im memoriam Oskar Panizza* (Munich, 1926), 13–15; Brown, *Oskar Panizza,* 31–32.

23. Transcript of the police's interview with Panizza, 8/12 Jan. 1895, StA München, St.Anw. 7120.

24. Police interrogations of 12 Feb. 1895; Munich Untersuchungsrichter to Munich PP, 16 Feb. 1895; Leipzig PP to Staatsanwalt Munich, 27 Feb. 1895; and Anklageschrift 1 Mar. 1895, in StA München, St.Anw. 7120. Also report in *Kölnische Zeitung,* 2 May 1895; Bauer, *Oskar Panizza,* 154; Brown, *Oskar Panizza,* 38; Jelavich, *Munich and Theatrical Modernism,* 57; and Hans Prescher, "Hinweise auf Leben und Werk Oscar Panizza," in Oskar Panizza, *Das Liebeskonzil und andere Schriften,* ed. and intro. by Hans Prescher (Neuwied, 1964), 253.

25. StA München, St.Anw. 7119.

26. Panizza, *Meine Verteidigung in Sachen "Das Liebeskonzil"* (Zurich, 1895) 36–37; StA München, St.Anw. 7119; Brown, *Oskar Panizza,* 43–45; Walter Rößler, "Ein Bißchen Gefängnis und ein Bißchen Irrenhaus. Der Fall Oskar Panizza," *Sinn und Form* 32 H.4 (Jul./Aug. 1980): 840; and Bauer, *Oskar Panizza,* 153.

27. Panizza to Max Halbe, 25 Apr. 1896, StBM, Halbe Archive.

28. *KK,* 158–61. The court noted that while the Jesuit order itself was not a central institution of the Catholic Church—and indeed was no longer even legal in Germany—Mehring's derision of the Jesuit order was nevertheless an indirect derision of the spiritual orders as such, which were central to the church. Mehring appealed unsuccessfully to the Reichsgericht in March 1900.

29. See Dehmel to his lawyer Rocholl, 21 Jul. 1897, Stadt- und Universitätsbibliothek Hamburg, Dehmel Archiv, and copy of lawsuit filed against Dehmel by Münchhausen, Mar. 1898, ibid. For more on the complexities of the Dehmel-Münchhausen affair, see chapter 6.

30. Decision of Berlin Landgericht, 30 Aug. 1897, in Dehmel Archiv (also partially reprinted in *KK,* 134 and *VL,* 1: 116); Dehmel to Rocholl, 21 Jul. 1898, Dehmel Archiv; and Dehmel to Isi Dehmel, 31. Aug. 1897, in Dehmel, *Ausgewählte Briefe aus den Jahren 1883–1902* (Berlin, 1922), 268–69. In subsequent editions of his poetry the offending lines of "Venus consolatrix"

were omitted and in their place appeared: "The middle passages of this fantasy, which indicate the union of the fabulous virtues of the Magdalenean and of the Nazarenian Mary in the feminine essence described here, had been declared immoral by a verdict of the Berlin Landgericht of 30 Aug. 1897, and can therefore not be communicated publicly." (See Dehmel, *Gesammelte Werke* [Berlin, 1916], 1: 344.)

31. See accounts in *Vorwärts*, 26 Jan. 1900 and *Münchener Neueste Nachrichten*, 10 Apr. 1900; also Dehmel to Carl Dehmel, 9 Jun. 1900, in Dehmel, *Ausgewählte Briefe*, 352.

32. *Augsburger Abendzeitung*, 4 Feb. 1891 and *Münchener Fremdenblatt*, 2 Feb. 1891, as quoted in Jelavich, *Munich and Theatrical Modernism*, 41–42.

33. Bauer, *Oskar Panizza*, 129; Brown, *Oskar Panizza*, 26, and Jelavich, *Munich and Theatrical Modernism*, 37.

34. *VL*, 1: 111–12; *Augsburger Postzeitung*, 20 Nov. 1893; IM to Pol. Dir., 2 Dec. 1893, StAM/ PDM 3740; *KK*, 131.

35. Lenman, "Censorship and Society," 95–100; Allen, *Satire and Society*, 182ff.

36. Allen, *Satire and Society*, 185; Lenman, "Censorship and Society,"100ff.

37. *Bühne und Welt* 1, pt. 2 (1898/99): 952–53.

38. The Berlin theater censor was initially reluctant to approve the work. After checking with higher authorities and police in other cities where the play had been performed without incident, he approved it. Since the author was attacking the church's actions of two hundred years ago, not the contemporary church, it was felt the play would not offend Catholics. *VL*, 2: 518ff.

39. *VL*, 2: 527ff.

40. Pascal, *From Naturalism to Expressionism*, 187.

41. Allen, *Satire and Society*, 163.

42. Lenman, "Censorship and Society," 114–15; Otto Gritschneder, ed., *Angeklagter Ludwig Thoma. Unveröffentlichte Akten* (Rosenheim, 1978); and Allen, *Satire and Society*, 162–64, 185–87.

43. LAB A/74, Th 816.

44. *VL*, 2: 72–76.

45. See for example Maximilian Parmod [Max Apt], *Antisemitismus und Strafrechtspflege*, 3. Aufl. (Berlin, 1894).

46. See Barnet Harston, "Reluctant Justice: Government Legal Intervention on Behalf of Jews in Imperial Germany," *German Studies Review* 27, no. 1 (Feb. 2004): 81–102.

47. Translated and quoted in Sanford Ragins, *Jewish Responses to Anti-Semitism in Germany, 1870–1914: A Study in the History of Ideas* (Cincinnati, 1980), 38.

48. BPP ban, 3 Jul. 1894, 11 Jun. 1895; BPP to BZA 31 Jan. 1895 and 29 Jun. 1895; BPP to OVG 9 Mar. 1895; and OVG decision 15 Jun. 1896, LAB A/74, Th 592.

49. BPP memo, 26. Jul. 1899, and BPP to BZA 31 Aug. 1899, LAB A/74, Th 438.

50. OVG decision 22 Sept. 1900, LAB A/74, Th 438.

51. Hartson, "Reluctant Justice," 98–99.

52. *KK*, 174–75; Lenman, "Censorship and Society," 99.

53. Sittenfeld [Alberti], *Was erwartet die deutsche Kunst*, 99.

54. *Berlin Börsen-Courier*, 6 Jun. 1888; Friedrich III to Bismarck, 2 Jun. 1888, Bismarck to Friedrich III, undated, and PrIM to Friedrich III, 4 Jun. 1888, in GStA PK/1000, Nr. 6, Bd. 1, Bl. 180, 187, 189ff.

55. Skriver, *Gotteslästerung?* 58.

56. Ibid., 58–59.

57. Berlin *Germania*, 10 Feb. 1892, quoted in Skriver, *Gotteslästerung?* 57.

58. See Parmod, *Antisemitismus und Strafrechtspflege*, especially 44ff.

59. Spahn speech, quoted in Mast, *Künstlerische und wissenschaftliche Freiheit*, 75–76.

60. Gröber speech, quoted by Robert W. Lougee, "The Anti-Revolution Bill of 1894 in Wilhelmine Germany." *Central European History* 15 (Sept. 1982): 231.

61. Ibid., 232.

62. The new §166 was to read: "Whoever publicly uses irreverent, insulting remarks to attack belief in God or Christianity, or who blasphemes God, or who publicly reviles one of the Christian churches or another of the legally recognized religious associations within the federal domain or reviles their doctrines, institutions, or rituals, as well as anyone who commits an irreverent, insulting act in a church or in another designated place of religious assembly, shall be punished with up to three years imprisonment." See Mast, *Künstlerische und wissenschaftliche Freiheit*, 79.

63. Quoted in Mast, *Künstlerische und wissenschaftliche Freiheit*, 78.

64. Quoted in Lougee, "Anti-Revolution Bill," 233.

65. Beyschlag, quoted in Mast, *Künstlerische und wissenschaftliche Freiheit*, 82–83.

66. Lougee, "Anti-Revolution Bill," 236.

67. *Kölnische Zeitung*, quoted in Lougee, "Anti-Revolution Bill," 234; K. Bleibtreu, "Staat und Litteratur," *Das Magazin für die Literatur des In- und Auslandes* 64, no. 12 (23 Mar. 1895): 362; and Harden, quoted in Mast, *Künstlerische und wissenschaftliche Freiheit*, 81.

68. Theodor Lessing, *Der Fall Panizza. Eine kritische Betrachtung über 'Gotteslästerung' und künstlerische Dinge vor Schwurgericht* (Munich, 1895); *Kölnische Zeitung*, 2 May 1895; see also *Vossische Zeitung*, 2 May 1895, *Badischer Landesbote*, 11 May 1895, and other press comments as quoted in Prescher, ed., *Das Liebeskonzil und andere Schriften*, 163–65.

69. Mast, *Künstlerische und wissenschaftliche Freiheit*, 84–86.

70. Mast, *Künstlerische und wissenschaftliche Freiheit*, 83, 98–99.

71. *Berliner Tageblatt*, 24 Mar. 1903.

72. *Münchener Neueste Nachrichten*, 13 Jan. 1904, and *Frankfurter Zeitung*, 15 Jan. 1904, quoted in Allen, *Satire and Society*, 183.

73. Allen, *Satire and Society*, 183; Lenman, "Censorship and Society," 100ff.

74. Quoted in Skriver, *Gotteslästerung?* 60.

75. §166 was to be replaced by two new statutes: §222 ("Whoever publicly blasphemes God in a malicious, scornful, and derisive manner will be punished with imprisonment of up to two years.") and §223 ("Whoever maliciously and publicly reviles one of the Christian churches or other legally recognized religious corporations within the federal domain will be punished with imprisonment of up to two years or with a fine.") Skriver, *Gotteslästerung?* 36.

76. Rudolf Otto, *The Idea of the Holy: An Inquiry into the Non-Rational Factor of the Idea of the Divine and its Relation to the Rational*, trans. John W. Harvey (London, 1923), 5–41, 62–73, 116–58, 179–82.

77. Huston Webster, *Taboo: A Sociological Study* (Stanford, CA, 1942), 299.

78. Thuringinan OVG, 5 Jan. 1913, cited in *KK*, 226.

79. PrIM memo to BPP, 6. Dec. 1902, GStA PK/1000, Nr. 6., Fasz. 3, Bl. 25ff.

80. Otto, *Idea of the Holy*, 147–48, 159.

81. Brandenburg OP decision of 12 Oct. 1897 concerning Hermann Sudermann's "Johannes," quoted in *VL*, 1: 593. This passage is a standard legal formulation used frequently by authorities to justify a ban.

82. Bavarian ministry decision Nr. 284, 7 Oct. 1854, and order of 3 Jul. 1868, quoted in Krais, "Über Theaterzensur," 40; PrIM to all RP, 8 Oct. 1875, in GStA PK/1000, Nr. 6, Bd. 1, Bl. 48, and PrIM decree of 30 Nov. 1895; Baden IM decree of 27 Aug. 1888. Quote is from PrIM decree of 6 Dec. 1902, cited in *VL*, 1: 440.

83. PrIM to Wilhelm II, 23 Sept. 1897, GStA PK/ZK, Nr. 21013, Bl. 166ff; BPP to PrIM 31 Aug. 1905, LAB A/74, Th. 66, Bl. 116.

84. BPP to PrIM 26 May 1904, and PrIM and PrRM to BPP, 25 Jul. 1904, in GStA PK/1000, Nr. 6, Bd. 4, Bl. 177ff., 180.

85. BPP to PrIM, 10 Jun. 1908, GStA PK/1000, Nr. 6, Bd. 5, Bl. 53. Also Borngräber's comments in W. Zils-München, ed. *Geistiges und künstlerisches München in Selbstbiographien* (Munich, 1913), 31–32. This work was banned in Munich from 1908 to 1912. The reason, however, was moral, not religious: this "erotic mysterium," as the author called it, saw Cain and Abel's

oedipal desire for and rivalry over their mother Eve as the cause of Cain's fratricide. See Meyer, *Theaterzensur in München,* 102–3. As indicated above, Catholic states seemed less concerned than Protestant ones in protecting the sacredness of the scriptures. When a Stuttgart theater, concerned about the Munich ban, voluntarily submitted the work to the city government for approval (there was no prior theater censorship in Württemberg), authorities approved the piece on condition certain cuts be made. Since this was the first case of theater "censorship" in that state, the Goethebund and others raised immediate protests about the legality of the act. See Bazille, "Theaterzensur in Württemberg."

86. Franklin L. Baumer, *Modern European Thought: Continuity and Change in Ideas, 1600–1950* (New York, 1977), 356.

87. BPP to PrIM, 11 Sept. 1913, GStA PK/1000, Nr. 6, Bd. 6. After successful public performances in Berlin and Vienna, the same piece was banned by the Munich police in July 1914, although since the relevant file has disappeared the reasons for the ban are unclear. See Meyer, *Theaterzensur in München,* 298–99; Lenman, "Censorship and Society," 308; and Kutscher, *Wedekind,* 3: 146. Despite protests from various Munich intellectuals, the work was not performed in Munich until a private performance in May 1918.

88. BPP ban of 9 Jul. 1897, in *VL,* 1: 589; and BPP to PrIM, 17 Aug. 1897, GStA PK/1000, Nr. 6, Bd. 2, Bl. 101.

89. *VL,* 1: 589–90. Even the conservative press, which supported banning New Testament themes and characters from commercial theaters, found nothing objectionable in the way Sudermann depicted his biblical characters. The Catholic Church's *Germania* thought the "ban" might even be a cheap publicity stunt by the Deutsches Theater.

90. *Staatsanzeiger für Württemberg,* 24 Aug. 1897, quoted in *VL,* 1: 591.

91. PrIM to Wilhelm II, 23 Sept. 1897, GStA PK/ZK., Nr. 21013, Bl. 166ff., also in PK/1000, Nr. 6, Bd. 2, Bl. 122–24; Civil Cabinet Chief Lucanus to PrIM, 2 Nov. 1897, and PrRM to PrIM, 10 Nov. 1897, GStA PK/1000, Nr. 6, Bd. 2, Bl. 133ff.

92. PrIM and PrRM to all RPs, 30 Nov. 1897, GStA PK/1000, Nr. 6, Bd. 2, Bl. 138.

93. John Russell Stephens, *The Censorship of English Drama 1824–1901* (New York, 1980), 112. It remained banned until 1931.

94. BPP to PrIM, 7 May 1902, PrIM to BPP, 11 Jun. 1902, and BPP to Direktion, Schall und Rauch, 14 Jul. 1902, BPP to BZA, undated, LAB A/74, Th 815.

95. Schall und Rauch brief to BZA, 8 Sept. 1902, oral arguments, 9 Dec. 1902, BZA decision of 9 Dec. 1902, Reinhardt to PrIM, 27 Dec. 1902, and PrIM to Reinhardt, 31 Jan. 1903, LAB A/74, Th 815.

96. OVG decision of 15 Jun. 1903, LAB A/74, Th 815.

97. *KK,* 184–85, and StA Bremen, 3-S.23a., Nr. 61.

98. BPP to PrIM, 2 Dec. 1901, GStA PK/1000, Nr. 6, Fasc. 3, Bl. 2f., also reprinted in Pöllinger, *Zensurprozeß,* 193–94. Von Possart, the censor who read the work, saw nothing in it that "would offend the piety of a religious audience." (Pöllinger, *Zensurprozeß,* 48–49.)

99. Gutachten von Prof. Seeburg, 26 Dec. 1901, PrRM to PrIM, 11 Jan. 1902, and PrIM to PrRM 17. Jan. 1902, PrIM to BPP, 17 Jan. 1902, and BPP memo 17 Jan. 1910, GStA PK/1000, Nr. 6, Fasc. 3, Bl. 6, 1, 8, 12; BPP to Lessing Theater, 5 Feb. 1902, in Bayerisches Staatsbibliothek, Heyse Archiv. See also *VL,* 1: 432–33 and Pöllinger, *Zensurprozeß,* 50–53.

100. BPP written and oral arguments to BZA, summarized in BZA decision of 7 Oct. 1902, in: GStA PK/1000, Nr. 6, Fasc. 3.

101. Decision of BZA 7 Oct. 1902, GStA PK/1000, Nr. 6, Fasc. 3, 17ff.; also reprinted in Pöllinger, *Zensurprozeß,* 196–205.

102. Pöllinger, *Zensurprozeß,* 63–66; Decision of OVG, 19 Jan. 1903, GStA PK/1000, Nr. 6, Fasc. 3, also reprinted in Pöllinger, *Zensurprozeß,* 205–8.

103. Theodore Barth's comments, and IM Hammerstein's reply, in StenBer/Pr, 19. Legislativperiode, V. Session, 16. Sitzung am 7. 2. 1903, 1021, 1025–26; Müller-Meiningen comments, StenBer/RT, 262. Sitzung vom 19. 2. 1903, 8024Bff.

104. *Bühne und Welt* 5, pt. 2 (1902/03): 653–55. At the Goethe League's Berlin meeting, the ban and theater censorship in general were condemned by writers Hermann Sudermann and Ludwig Fulda, Reichstag delegate Ernst Müller-Meiningen, and legal scholars Wolfgang Heine and Prof. Franz von Liszt. See *Die Theaterzensur. Fünf Vorträge.*
105. Frankfurt PP ban of 3 Apr. 1903, HHStA Wiesbaden, Abt. 407, Nr. 25, Bd. 4; newspaper clipping about Kiel Goethebund meeting in Heyse's "Tagebuch," following entry for 10 Feb. 1903, and about Aachen ban following entry for 13 Apr. 1903, in StBM, Heyse-Archiv; GStA PK/1000, Nr. 6, Fasc. 3; *VL,* 1: 444–49.
106. Pöllinger, *Zensurprozeß,* 66–67, 122–34, 141–45.
107. BPP to PrIM, 30 Nov. 1909, GStA PK/1000, Nr. 6, Fasc. 3.
108. PrIM to PrRM, 11 Dec. 1909, PrRM to PrIM 7 Jan. 1910, PrIM to BPP 18 Feb. 1910; Deutsches Theater to BPP and PrIM, 12 Sept. 1910, PrIM to Deutsches Theater, 29 Sept. 1910, BPP to PrIM, 3 May 1911, and PrIM to BPP, 24 Jun. 1911, GStA PK/1000, Nr. 6, Fasc. 3.
109. Gutachten des Landeskirchenrats Thüringen to Thuringian OVG, discussed in Thuringian OVG decision of 5 Jan. 1913, cited in *KK,* 226.
110. PrIM to BPP, 2 Mar. and 22 Apr. 1897, and BPP to PrIM, 3 Mar. and 29 Apr. 1897, GStA PK/1000, Nr. 6, Bd. 2, Bl. 40, 46, 74.
111. Annual performances of this spectacle, which was enthusiastically supported by the Eisenach tourist association (Fremdenverkehrsverein), had so much touristic potential the British travel firm of Thomas Cook offered to help underwrite the scheme financially by purchasing fifty thousand marks worth of admittance tickets each year. See *KK,* 228–29.
112. *KK,* 228.
113. OVG decision of 5 Jan. 1913, reprinted in *KK,* 225–31.
114. GStA PK/1000, Nr. 6, Bd. 1, Bl. 110; Georg Bochnik, "Das Belle-Alliance-Theater in Berlin, 1869–1913," (Phil. diss., F.U. Berlin, 1957), 81.
115. HStA Düsseldorf, Reg. Düsseldorf, 7991 cited in Schulze-Olden, "Theaterzensur in Rheinprovinz," 85.
116. Schulze-Olden, "Theaterzensur in Rheinprovinz," 83; PrIM and PrRM memo of 27 Oct. 1898, GStA PK/1000, Nr. 6, Bd. 3, Bl. 29.
117. Aachen PP to RP, 24 Jan. 1903, and decision of PrRM, 7 Feb. 1903, cited in Schulze-Olden, "Theaterzensur in Rheinprovinz," 85.
118. Landrat to Reg. Aachen, Dec. 1905, and decision of PrRM, 7 Feb. 1906, cited in Schulze-Olden, "Theaterzensur in Rheinprovinz," 86.
119. *VL,* 1: 45–46. A private performance was permitted in Berlin; in 1903 the Königliche Hochschule für Musik was allowed to stage a public performance with an admission charge.
120. BPP to PrIM, 16 Dec. 1911, PrIM to BPP, 5 Jan. 1912, BPP to Dresden PP, 5 Apr. 1916, Regierungsrat Klotz of Berlin police to PrIM, 10 Apr. 1916, and PrIM to BPP, 8 Jun. 1916, LAB A/74, Th 67.

Chapter 6

DEFENDING THE MORAL ORDER

There are two kinds of morality: the one we have, and the one we appear
to have. The latter must not be attacked under any circumstances.
—'Der Polizeipräsident', in Ludwig Thoma, *Plauderstünchen* (quoted in
Sehsucht nach Unterdrückung. Zensur und Presserecht bei Ludwig Thoma.)

In every age, from Schiller to Wedekind, the state has believed it must protect
the public from the demoralising influences of theatrical art. In every age
this practice turned out, a few decades later, to be in error. Should
this error … continue to be the practice for all future ages?
—Otto Falkenberg, *Zukunft der deutschen Bühne.*

Literature and the Sexual Revolution

Besides combating literary subversion of the political, social, and religious orders,
after 1880 German censors had to confront a radically new threat: the Sexual
Revolution. During the last quarter of the nineteenth century, across Europe
and North America one finds a new, obsessive interest in sexual behavior and an
unprecedented debate over the medical, sociological, political, psychological, and
moral dimensions of human sexuality. Fascinated with and yet fearful of sexuality
as a controlling force in life, thinkers from diverse disciplines focused increasing
attention on such issues as the dramatic increase of "private vices" (prostitution,
pornography), venereal disease, sex-related crimes, and "deviant" sexual behavior.
Their investigations often threw into question the institutional constraints of
marriage, adulthood, and the family, within which sexual activity had traditionally operated. This, in turn, helped feed a broad reaction against the prevailing

Victorian orthodoxy that sexual activity and gratification were sinful, physically debilitating, or both. Questions about the existence and power of female and childhood sexuality, women's sexual parity with men, the acceptable limits of sexual behavior, and the consequences of repressing sexual impulses were intensely debated. A great revolution in sexual attitudes and behavior had begun.

In imperial Germany, as elsewhere, sexual motifs permeated art and literature from the mid-1880s on, and it was here the "sexual question" was perhaps most sharply debated. Modernist literature in Germany acknowledged the power of sensual drives and discussed sexual matters with an unprecedented frankness shocking to a society imbued with an idealistic literary tradition that demurely avoided such topics. In the Naturalist (or "Realist") literature of the late 1880s and early 1890s, many previously taboo subjects, such as adolescent sexuality, prostitution and venereal disease, pregnancy and childbirth, unwed mothers and abortion, incest, the horrors of defloration, and homosexuality were treated in frank, sometimes coarse language. At the same time Naturalists ruthlessly attacked what they considered the bourgeois moral hypocrisy of loveless conventional marriages and their predictable consequences: masturbation, adultery, prostitution, kept mistresses. Above all they preached freeing sexual fulfillment from repressive religious, moral, and social taboos and perhaps even from legal regulations. "What was new," notes literary historian Roy Pascal, "was the acknowledgement of sexuality without love, i.e., without profound attachment to a person, and the contention that sexual intimacy blessed by neither marriage nor love is not necessarily a sin or a crime, even for a woman."[1]

Many of the literary movements that followed Naturalism (including Neo-Romanticism, Impressionism, Symbolism, Jugendstil, Young Vienna, and Expressionism) expressed this preoccupation with the sexual and erotic in ever more radical ways. In much of fin-de-siècle German literature (and visual art), one can find what one scholar calls a "demonization of Eros":[2] a growing interest in decadent eroticism and "perverse" sexuality (sadism, masochism, necrophilia, exhibitionism, nymphomania); an emphasis upon the darker, destructive powers of sexuality (domination, self-destructive submission and self-abasement, rape); a new stress on hedonistic, libertine sensuality (the quest for ever-more-intense sensual stimuli and the attainment of ecstasy); a frivolous "raciness" (*Pikanterie*) that delights in what is spicy or erotic because of its simple entertainment value; or ambivalent, antifeminist male anxieties about sexually emancipated women (Woman as temptress, enchantress, femme fatal, castrator; Woman as Sin, Medusa, Delilah, Salome). Whether or not it was true (as aesthetician Konrad von Lange suggested in 1901) that "art *has* to depict the erotic that our culture represses, because it is one of man's deepest inner needs and fulfills his longing to complete his fragmentary existence," few would dispute Pascal's observation that in the literature of imperial Germany "there is an unprecedented preoccupation with sex, associated usually with a direct or indirect plea for the liberation of sexuality from the religious and ethical stigma. ... Through the visual arts and literature (and the musical drama) sex became, more insistently than through any other media, a publicly recognized fact, demanding public acknowledgement and discussion, hauled out of the conspiracy of secrecy." [3]

Defenders of the traditional moral order could not ignore the fact that in the Sexual Revolution, those storming the palace were usually the imaginative writers of the modernist movement. In 1907 the Imperial Supreme Court noted that the "nonchalant" way certain modern writers dealt with every possible aspect of sexual life created notoriety for them, but that notoriety was simply proof the average man regarded their literary and psychological treatments of sex "not with nonchalance, but with other feelings, such as shame and revulsion."[4]

Obscenity and the Law

For many, a revolution in sexual attitudes threatened the existing social and political order. German legal scholars writing in the 1890s reflect not only attitudes and concerns prevalent among conservative elites of fin-de-siècle Europe, but sentiments still shared by wide segments of modern society. One jurist, justifying antiobscenity laws, explained: "Morality is the main pillar on which the social edifice rests. It is the foundation of family life, which requires a moral community, and thus also the most important factor in preserving public order. For the family and its moral, civilizing power is the indispensable basis of all morals, and therefore also of all legal order. So the state ... has a very important interest in [seeing] that public morality is not violated." Another called public morality "a legal commodity that enjoys state protection."[5]

Although scattered attempts to suppress "licentious publications" in Western Europe date from the 1750s, legal proscriptions against obscene material became prevalent in Europe and North America only a century later. Beginning in the 1850s, Austria, Britain, Belgium, Germany, the US, Hungary, and France passed laws prohibiting the sale, distribution, or public display of obscene materials. In imperial Germany concern over pornography and obscene materials was reflected in §184 of the Criminal Code, which superseded the scattered state ordinances under which the problem had previously been treated. Paragraph 184 stated: "Whoever sells, distributes, or otherwise disseminates obscene (*unzüchtige*) publications, illustrations, or representations, or who exhibits or displays these in public places, shall be punished with a fine of up to three hundred marks or imprisonment for up to six months."

To convict under this law, prosecutors had to prove the offender was not only familiar with the contents of the materials in question, but was also aware of their obscene nature.[6] Such knowledge, we will see, was usually easier to prove than one might think, but if it could not be proven, courts could acquit a defendant yet still rule the materials he had written were obscene and must be destroyed—a fate that befell several German authors.

It is far easier to outlaw obscenity than to define it. Identifying the line separating obscene works from legitimate works of art and scholarship is akin to a fool's errand; definitions of obscenity that seem satisfactory in theory often prove unworkable in practice. As one German legal scholar of this period recognized, "Obscenity is anything that violates the recognized order of sexual life. But just what is allowed, what is recognized in sexual life, is so extraordinarily diverse and varies so greatly with time, place, and social standing, that one can find no general, universally applicable concept for it other than a purely formal one." The state desires, through its laws, to uphold some minimum standard of morality that can apply to all social classes and in all circumstances; yet, as this writer acknowledged, that standard can be identified only imperfectly, and—given the constant evolution of values and behavior—only for short periods of time.[7]

The judicial system in imperial Germany eventually defined obscenity as "anything that causes public annoyance by grossly offending the [public's] sense of modesty and morality (*Scham- und Sittlichkeitsgefühl*) in a sexual sense."[8] (This definition, broad as it was, was still narrower than the so-called Hicklin rule widely used in Anglo-Saxon nations during the latter half of the nineteenth century.[9]) Moreover, the courts ruled that allegedly obscene words, passages, or parts in a work must be judged not in isolation, but in their relation to the work as a whole: "It is not sufficient [grounds for declaring a work obscene] that individual passages or sentences, in themselves and taken out of content, offend the sense of morality. Rather, it is far more a matter of the character of the work as a whole. Scholarly works, reports, and debates often contain things that, in the context of the larger whole, are permissible, indeed even necessary."[10]

Police and courts in the German Empire—as well as the intellectual community and general public—recognized that exploring human sexuality was a legitimate pursuit of scholars and artists. Judges and legal scholars consistently held that true works of art and scholarship were never obscene per se, for the artist or scholar who dealt with sexuality did so not with a prurient intent, but with a higher, more ethical purpose in mind. Works that served a legitimate artistic or scholarly purpose and were written with a serious tone for an appropriate audience, even if they might contain some explicit language or frank discussion of sexual topics, were unlikely to grossly violate their readers' senses of shame and morality in a sexual sense—and were therefore not punishable under §184.[11] Only those works created or consumed solely for their sexual content were obscene. No such clear distinction between art and pornography existed in English law, and after the turn of the century there was growing concern in England that the law against obscenity was too often applied against genuine art and literature.

At first glance this would seem to give artists (as well as pornographers) free rein: one need only claim one's erotic novel or photograph was intended as an artistic or medical study and one would presumably be immune from §184. However, using the concept of "relative obscenity," imperial courts consistently held that obscenity was neither absolute nor necessarily inherent in a work. Rather, external circumstances—for example, the use to which it was put or the audience for which it was intended—often determined whether that work was obscene.[12] In short, any given work might be legally obscene in one context but not in another.

When applied to works of art and literature, this doctrine of relative obscenity revealed strong class prejudices and social fears, for it meant, as one German legal scholar admitted, the potential danger of an artistic or scholarly work must be judged in terms of the social standing of its viewers or readers; what was permissible before a "serious audience" could well endanger the morality of a "lower audience" (*unterer Leserkreis*).[13] A work was not obscene if it were confined to an audience capable of appreciating it for its higher artistic or scholarly value. But that same work could be ruled obscene under §184 if it were intended for a broader audience that would be less inclined to appreciate its artistic or scholarly value and where many would be interested in the work only for its sexual content (or, conversely, where some would be offended because of their conventional sense of morality and modesty).[14] For literary works this meant that if it could be shown a text was no longer intended for a select audience capable of appreciating its higher artistic purposes but was being offered instead to the general public, then that particular text was no longer immune from §184. It was legal to sell certain of Zola's works in the original French, for example, but not in German translation. In September 1882 Berlin police successfully confiscated and banned "lewd" German translations of his notorious *Nana* and *Pot Bouille,* and later that decade Munich police did the same with a translation of his coarse novel of peasant life, *La Terre.* But judges in both cities overturned police attempts to ban the French-language versions; since these circulated only within a narrow, better-educated circle of readers, they posed no threat to the general public.[15] A police attempt in 1886 to prosecute Berlin book dealers for displaying French-language copies of *Nana* was also blocked by the court on the grounds the dealers had not actually made the contents of the book accessible to the general public and had therefore not violated §184.[16] As late as 1899 police in some cities were still confiscating sensationalistic translations of *L'Argent, Debacle,* and *Le Docteur Pascal,* although the French originals and tamer German translations circulated freely.[17] In this regard Germany was significantly more liberal than England, where in the late 1880s Henry Vizetelly, the respectable publisher of Zola's novels, was heavily fined and imprisoned for three months. Similarly, German authorities had no objection to a limited, highly priced printing of the works of the Italian anthropologist and ethnologist Paolo Mantegazza. But a low-priced popular edition of the same work with drawings on the cover hinting at its erotic content was banned on the grounds the publisher clearly intended to attract readers who would read the work solely for its sexual content.[18]

Whether a literary work was in German or a foreign language, its price, the number of copies printed, the type of illustrations or dust jacket it had, the way it was advertised, whether it was sold by reputable bookstores or peddled by colporteurs, even the general reputation of the publishing house—all were scrutinized by authorities to determine if a work was a legitimate artistic or scholarly creation intended for serious readers, or a thinly disguised attempt to capitalize on the prurient interests of a broader public. If found to be the latter, a work could be ruled obscene. Whether the author intended for his work to be distributed to a general audience was irrelevant; it was the effect or probable effect of the work on public morals that most concerned authorities.[19] In the parlance of modern literary theory, imperial authorities cared less about the author's intended "meaning" than about the "significances" readers assigned to the work. Although they knew nothing of modern reader response or reception theory, censors and the courts focused on how readers or audiences "constructed" their own meanings from a work, a process determined by such factors as the social standing, degree of sophistication, and purposes of those readers' "interpretive communities."

The legal immunity from §184 granted to German artists and scholars was thus a dubious one. While they were free to explore all sexual matters in their works, these works could be legally distributed to a relatively small elite. The artistic and scholarly community was allowed complete freedom *within its realm*—but the boundaries of that realm were drawn narrowly indeed, and it was effectively separated from broader German society.

Paragraph 184, then, was used primarily to combat the underground trade of pornography and other sexually explicit material, the production and popular consumption of which flourished after the 1860s as never before.[20] The number of prosecutions for obscenity rose in the late 1880s, declined slightly after 1891, then in the late 1890s rose dramatically again, reaching an all-time high at the turn of the century. Except for another brief peak in 1911 (after the establishment of a Central Police Office for the Suppression of Obscene Materials), prosecutions gradually declined during the last years of the empire. (See figure 6.1.) The increase in obscenity trials in the 1890s, when many Germans felt increasingly overwhelmed by a rising tide of sexual immorality, was accompanied

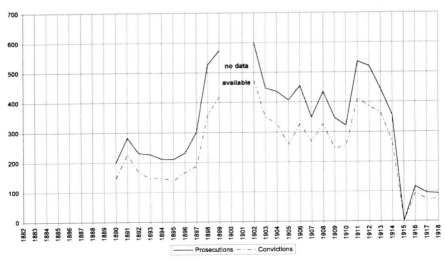

Figure 6.1 Prosecutions for Obscenity in Germany, 1890–1918

Source: Statistisches Reichsamt, *Statistisches Jahrbuch für das Deutsche Reich* (Berlin, 1880ff).

by a concerted effort to rewrite §184. Conservative forces such as the emperor, the Catholic Center Party and anti-Semitic parties, police in major cities, and various morality leagues (such as the Munich-based League for the Elevation of Public Morality) demanded a significant tightening of the law to make it easier to prosecute material they considered morally offensive but that might not meet the strict legal definition of obscene. After a Munich court refused in 1891 to prosecute the author of a poem the local police considered obscene and then released the confiscated journal, the Munich police director complained bitterly to the Bavarian Ministry of the Interior "this case once again demonstrates the necessity of expanding §184 of the Criminal Code; it shows how—against the concurring view of the police, a prosecutor, and a judge—the concept of 'obscene' can be interpreted so narrowly at a higher level that the greatest offenses against public decency … go unpunished."[21]

An opportunity to pass a tougher antiobscenity law arose in 1892 when the Prussian government drafted the "Lex Heinze." This law (discussed in chapter 1) proposed to toughen the law against pimps and prostitutes and broaden the provisions of §184 concerning obscene publications and materials, which were considered a cause of prostitution. The revised law would punish not only those who sold, distributed, or publicly exhibited obscene materials, but also anyone who "manufactured, stocked for the purpose of selling, advertised, or recommended" such materials. Moreover, the punishment for violating §184 would be doubled (from a maximum of three months' incarceration or a three-hundred-mark fine to six months or six hundred marks), and those who engaged in such activities for a living would be sentenced to not less than three years or a fine of fifteen hundred marks. The Catholic Center Party subsequently inserted more extreme clauses that could be used to suppress visual art and theatrical performances that, although not legally obscene, were "capable of causing offense by grossly violating the sense of shame and morality."[22]

Although the proposed amendments to §184 were defeated in 1893–1894, courts nevertheless began implementing some of them informally. After 1893 the courts declared that an author who gave an obscene manuscript to a printer for mass distribution was also liable, as were illustrators, printers, and publishers.[23] After the Lex Heinze was reintroduced in 1897, creating another bruising, three-year-long battle, §184 was eventually altered slightly in 1900. The final compromise version made it illegal not only to distribute or display, but also to compose, manufacture, store, advertise, or publicly extol any obscene works or to give these to any person under sixteen years of age. The punishment was made more severe as well: a fine of up to one thousand marks or up to one year of imprisonment, or both. The definition of obscene was not altered, however, nor was the law extended to include material that was merely offensive rather than legally obscene, as the morality reformers had desired. On the other hand, police could now intervene if obscene material was merely publicly announced—for example, if the title of an obscene book appeared in an advertisement. And whereas previously a work was considered obscene only if it could be shown to be offensive to the average adult, now authorities could consider its effect on the "public at large," which included children as well as the emotionally unstable.

Authors on Trial

German authorities invoked §184 only sporadically against authors, publishers, or editors of serious literature, and when they did were seldom able to obtain the verdicts they sought. In southern Germany, where jury trials were required, it was virtually impossible to convict authors of obscenity. In the few north German trials where defendants were convicted, their punishment was often a nominal fine, rather than the imprisonment suffered by several writers and artists convicted of blasphemy or lèse majesté.

Not surprisingly, it was at the height of the Naturalist movement, 1889–1892, that authorities most often invoked §184 to confiscate modernist literary works and prosecute those responsible. The offending authors' frank discussions of sexual behavior, hitherto considered off-limits for respectable art, was seen, often correctly, as a deliberate and calculated affront to complacent middle-class sensibilities. Many contemporary literary critics and journalists (not to mention conservative Philistines) reacted to the Naturalists' works with horror and indignation; they labeled it not only pornographic, but also (to cite only a few colorful examples) "evil pus," "the breeding grounds of beastly depravity," "cesspool-fodder," "prostitution-literature," "pimpish art"—and worse.[24] Broad segments of German society, unaccustomed to such sexual motifs in "fine literature," had a hard time distinguishing between the work of the early modernists and that of traditional pornographers. Police often had the same difficulty: as late as 1895 Munich police boasted of the "especially severe actions" they had taken "against the outrages of *modern* and *pornographic literature*"—by which they meant their confiscations of works by Oskar Panizza and Richard Dehmel (see chapter 5).[25]

The most famous literary trial for obscenity was the so-called "Leipzig Realists' trial" of 1890. This three-day trial was one of the first confrontations in Germany between literary modernism and the state, and was paradigmatic in that both the state and the defendants raised issues and adopted strategies that would reappear in nearly all subsequent obscenity trials. For these reasons, the case of the Leipzig Realists warrants close examination.

In early 1889 the Wilhelm Friedrich Verlag of Leipzig, Germany's leading publisher of early Naturalist literature, issued Wilhelm Walloth's novel *Dämon des Neides* (*Demon of Envy*) and Hermann Conradi's *Adam Mensch*. The former dealt with the amoral, self-destructive lifestyles of Berlin's bohemian artists and students, paying particular attention to a decadent young artist's relationship with a "fallen" girl from a "good" Berlin family; the latter was a psychological study of a cynical, decadent young Berlin intellectual whose unconventional Nietzschean morality led him into a life of dehumanized sexual licentiousness. In June 1889 the Leipzig public prosecutor, citing the obscene and sometimes blasphemous language and subject matter of the novels, ordered police to confiscate all remaining copies of the two books. Searching for incriminating evidence needed to prove obscene intent under §184, Leipzig police raided Friedrich's publishing firm as well as the lodgings of Walloth and Conradi and seized files and private correspondence.[26] Soon thereafter the Wilhelm Friedrich Verlag published Conrad Alberti's *Die Alten und die Jungen* (*The Old and the Young*), which explored the corruption and moral bankruptcy of Berlin society, especially prostitution. Acting on anonymous readers' complaints the prosecutor ordered this work seized as well and confiscated correspondence between Alberti and his publisher.[27] These searches and preliminary interrogations were carried out with thoroughness and brutality: the police raid on his quarters so upset the highly strung young Walloth that he suffered a nervous breakdown.[28]

Walloth, Conradi, Alberti, and Friedrich were indicted in February 1890, accused of knowingly producing and distributing materials containing numerous obscene passages. Conradi's indictment for *Adam Mensch,* for example, charged that "seduction scenes, extramarital sexual relations, unnatural acts of gratification, and obscene activities are not only found throughout, but are handled, emphasized, and portrayed with evident deliberateness; the author takes pleasure in depicting—or, what is no less titillating—in intimating at such things." The state asked that Walloth, Alberti, and Friedrich be fined for distributing obscene material and Conradi be imprisoned for obscenity and blasphemy.[29]

The sickly Conradi died in March 1890 and so was not present for the June trial, although a lawyer representing his estate argued his case. The defendants all adopted a common strategy and aggressively defended not only their Naturalistic (at the time termed "Realist") style, but also their right as artists to create without interference from the law. Conrad Alberti served as primary spokesman for the group.

At Emperor Wilhelm II's accession to the throne in 1888, Alberti (a pseudonym for Konrad Sittenfeld) had anonymously published an influential manifesto entitled *Was erwartet die deutsche Kunst von Kaiser Wilhelm II?* (*What Does German Art Expect from Emperor Wilhelm II?*). Claiming to speak for the modernist movement, Alberti called upon the state and the new monarch to suppress the frivolous and immoral entertainments and French farces he said were systematically debasing the spirit, morality, and family life of the German people and to promote serious art, which has a spiritually and morally ennobling function.[30] At his trial Alberti developed this theme by arguing that the supposedly obscene passages in his work were no more immoral or offensive than any contained in great classical works. If the state wished to outlaw works like his novel, Alberti claimed, it should also ban works by Goethe, Schiller, Lessing, Shakespeare, Plato, or Ovid. (Here Alberti snidely commented that some prosecutors might be unfamiliar with or unable to understand Ovid, at which his prosecutor leapt to his feet and vigorously objected to Alberti's aspersions. The presiding judge reprimanded Alberti for his rude remark and fined him forty marks.[31])

Alberti and his codefendants also argued that, according to established judicial practice, a few isolated passages were not sufficient to make an entire work obscene; to be punished under §184, the overall thrust (*Tendenz*) and intent of a work must be obscene. Considered in their entirety, they argued, the novels were clearly not obscene. Indeed, each author insisted a deeply moral purpose stood behind his work: the immorality of modern urban life was graphically portrayed to make evident its inevitable consequences and convince readers such evils needed changing. "It was my intent, in any case, to compose a highly moral and ethical work," Alberti told the court, "and I maintain that in writing it I have performed, if not a poetic service, then an ethical one."[32]

Walloth and Conradi's lawyer likewise affirmed the intent and overall effect of *Dämon des Neides* and *Adam Mensch* were idealistic and ultimately moral, for to combat immorality, writers must portray and analyze it. "The passages which have been singled out [in my book] as obscene," Walloth argued, "are there to prove the protagonist faced an unhealthy, abnormal stimulus." Writers must deal with shocking or unpleasant subjects in their work because these are part of reality, Walloth continued. "Not only the perfect, but also the corrupt and imperfect must be portrayed. ... Gentlemen, sexual relations cannot be ignored. Not every mention of sexual life is obscene, not even every mention of grossly offensive sexual relations. No, rather it all depends—and this is the way the Imperial Supreme Court views the matter—on what purpose or goal is being served."[33]

Alberti argued that the more art wished to elucidate the complex workings of the human soul, the more it became the duty of art to grapple with sexual problems. "In depicting general humanity," he said, "[the portrayal] of sexuality is absolutely necessary, and it follows from the very nature of art." Conradi's lawyer pointed out that "a novelist is not responsible for the corruption of the times in which he lives; rather, the times are responsible for the corruption of his portrayal."[34] One may regret that a talented author adopts Realism and concerns himself with unpleasant subjects, but if he does so objectively and accurately, and speaks with an inner sincerity, then one can hardly fault him. Indeed, when a writer or artist loves truth enough to portray accurately the world he sees, then his work should be considered something valuable and worthwhile.[35]

Walloth and Conradi's representative emphasized the novels were intended for, and would be intelligible to, only a limited circle of well-educated readers. Although the allegedly offensive passages might conceivably prove harmful to some within the general public, the novels were "intended only for serious, learned men" who could appreciate them for their literary merit, and should be judged accordingly. The defendants introduced testimony from several prominent literary experts, all of whom agreed the three novels had an overall moral intent and possessed literary merit, and that artists like Alberti, Conradi, and Walloth must be free to explore subjects and themes some might find offensive. Under no circumstances must the obscenity law be applied against genuine works of art. Alberti summarized the Realists' case by asserting that the ultimate issue was the sovereignty of art and the freedom of the artist. "A modern artist must be allowed, as long as he is pursuing moral goals in his work as a whole, to go, in individual cases, to the limits ... allowed even the most exemplary artist."[36]

None of these arguments swayed the prosecutor, who saw dangerous social implications in the Realists' claims to complete artistic freedom. He agreed with his adversaries that the ultimate issue was not merely the three novels under indictment, but rather the whole artistic theory of literary Realism. Nor did he deny art must sometimes deal with base or crude subject matter; but true art, he told the court, must always seek to elevate and ennoble such material. None of the three novels did that; in each, "the concept of striving for beauty, which is inherent in art, is lacking."[37]

Although the authors claimed a noble and idealistic rather than commercial reason for writing what they did, the prosecutor cited confiscated correspondence that proved they had deliberately included sexually offensive material to shock readers, attract wider attention to their books, and ultimately increase sales. In a letter to Friedrich, for example, Alberti suggested the publisher rent a large display window on Berlin's busy Friedrichstraße and display all the books recently published by the firm, each "opened to the raciest passages." In another letter, Walloth asked Friedrich whether including indecent material (*Unanständigkeit*) in his novel was more likely to help or hurt the book's success.[38] Ultimately, the prosecutor pointed out, an artist's motives or intent are largely irrelevant—it was, rather, the effect of the material that mattered most. Whether or not the authors so intended, each of the works on trial had caused a public offense by grossly violating the sense of modesty and morality.

The prosecutor took special aim at Alberti's contention there should be no limits on the freedom of the creative artist. The presiding judge had expressed his uneasiness over what he called "literary license," and had wondered aloud what the ultimate consequences would be if artists were allowed unlimited freedom to portray anything obscene or crude simply because it existed or had been experienced by the artist.[39] In his summary the prosecutor insisted writers and publishers did not stand above or apart from the rest of society. If Alberti, Walloth, Friedrich, and others like them went unpunished, the prosecutor pleaded, "then it must be feared the limits of literary portrayal will be pushed even further in the future. We must show these gentlemen that the Criminal Code does indeed draw a limit. The dignity of humanity is in your hands," he told the court; "protect it."[40]

The Leipzig court found Alberti and Walloth guilty of violating §184 and fined them 300 and 150 marks, respectively (in addition to Alberti's forty mark fine for contempt), although it was later rumored that the publisher Friedrich paid their fines. It is surely ironic that Alberti, who had called for more government suppression of immoral entertainment, received the most severe sentence levied against a writer under §184. Had he not died before the trial, Hermann Conradi would also certainly have been found guilty of obscenity and blasphemy and would most likely have been imprisoned. The publisher Wilhelm Friedrich was acquitted, however, because he convinced the court he had sent the final manuscripts to the printer without actually reading them; legally speaking, therefore, he was not guilty of intentionally publishing anything blasphemous or obscene. (He later admitted that even had he been aware of the passages, he would have published the works anyway. The sentence may have had a "chilling effect" on other publishers, however, for at least one now began refusing certain manuscripts he feared might invite similar legal action.[41]) Although the court ordered all remaining copies of the three novels destroyed, three-quarters of them had already been snatched up by readers, so the decision had limited impact.

Imperial authorities never again won as decisive a victory against "obscene" modernist writers as in the Leipzig Realists' trial. Nevertheless, many features of that trial are typical of subsequent cases where §184 was invoked against printed literature or where police banned "immoral" dramas. One finds private moral entrepreneurs whose complaints prod officials to action. One finds defendants who claim their work is intended only for an elite audience but who are also interested in broad commercial success. One finds modernists who largely reject the ideology of traditional artistic idealism but still claim for their art (at least in court) some higher idealistic purpose. One finds defendants who argue their works are no more immoral than certain respected literary classics or than many popular entertainments tolerated by the police. And one finds artists who proclaim the absolute independence of "true" artists from legal restraints and preach the primacy of artistic considerations over other values but who, in other contexts, demand the state more energetically suppress pornographic or immoral entertainments that lack a higher artistic purpose.

The Leipzig Realists' trial also raised a set of interlocking questions in which technical/legal issues were entangled with artistic/stylistic ones. For example, does the overall (moral) tone or effect of an entire text outweigh any (immoral) tone or effect of its individual parts, and are the objectionable parts really integral or necessary to the whole? Does an author's (subjective and moral) intent outweigh his text's (objective and immoral) effect upon readers or spectators? May an artist choose a subject that is offensive or shocking to most people, and if so, may he adopt an ethically neutral stance toward it, or should he treat it from some "higher" moral or ethical perspective? Because each literary trial or prohibition of a drama in the empire involved different authorities in different contexts examining different texts and reaching different answers to these questions, it is all but impossible to discern any larger patterns in the outcomes of German censorship cases involving obscenity and/or immorality. Seemingly similar cases have quite different outcomes, and judicial decisions about whether a particular text was obscene or a particular drama morally impermissible end up looking quite arbitrary indeed.

In the two years following the Leipzig Realists' trial, Prussian and Saxon authorities successfully prosecuted two other modernist authors. In January 1891, Naturalist author Paul Ernst's *Zum ersten Mal* (*The First Time*), a short story about the corrupting influence of big city life upon a naive young theology student and his encounter with a prostitute, was published in the socialist *Berlin Volkstribüne*. Berlin police confiscated the publication and charged Ernst with violating §184. Ernst's lawyer argued the intent of the story had been a moral one: to expose and condemn the corruption of modern urban life. The judge admitted that, had the story appeared in a different kind of publication, it might indeed have had a moral effect; but its publication in a sensationalistic Social Democratic newspaper with a mass readership was evidence Ernst wished to arouse the base instincts of the masses rather than pursue higher artistic purposes. Ernst was pronounced guilty and fined one hundred marks.[42]

That same year §184 was successfully invoked twice against the young Impressionist and prosocialist author Hermann Bahr. When the second edition of his *Fin de Siècle* (a collection of political parables and erotic vignettes) appeared in 1891, Berlin police considered six of the stories obscene and confiscated the book. The Berlin criminal court overturned the confiscation but the state prosecutor successfully appealed the case to the Prussian Superior Court, which in July 1892 fined Bahr 150 marks. Bahr's appeal to the Imperial Supreme Court was unsuccessful: it agreed that in the six stories "sexual relations between man and woman, as well as abnormal and aberrant gratification of the sexual drive, are portrayed in a cynical manner that grossly violates the sense of shame and morality in a sexual sense"; in those stories "the sexual material is deliberately emphasized and [Bahr's] intent is to arouse the reader sexually."[43]

Bahr also became the target of Saxon censors. In November 1891 Dresden police seized his *Russische Reise,* a fictional account of his travels to Russia that included descriptions of a St. Petersburg bordello, and the local publisher, E. Pierson, was indicted for obscenity. In late 1892 a Dresden court ruled the bordello passages exuded "an impure sensuality" and other passages contained obscene implications that served to heighten the overall effect of the bordello scene. While acknowledging the artistic value of portions of the book, *taken as a whole* the court did not view it as a legitimate work of art that justified the obscene effect of the individual passages. Here the formless, episodic style of writing Bahr helped pioneer, and that later became characteristic of Impressionist literature and art, clearly worked to his disadvantage. Citing Bahr's own declaration that his goal was simply "to botanize [*sic*] for new sensations, to grasp them with sharpened senses, to savor them … and record them with … the first word from everyday usage that sprang to mind," the court found that *Russische Reise* "has no unity at all. The objectionable parts are not mitigated by an artistic or a scholarly purpose; they have no inner relation to the rest of the book's contents and are completely dispensable. … But because of the 'sexual aftertaste' of these passages, the book as a whole is obscene and therefore undermines certain values of the civil order, namely, its accepted morality."[44] Because the obscene passages were not integrally related to the rest of the book, the court ordered them simply excised from all remaining unsold copies, rather than prohibiting and destroying the entire volume. (From the total printing of fifteen hundred copies, however, only 355 actually remained in stock.) The publisher Pierson was acquitted. His defense was nearly identical to Friedrich's at the Leipzig Realists' trial: he had published the work without full knowledge of its contents and was thus not guilty of knowingly publishing obscene material. Although skeptical of his claims, the court was unable to prove his culpability.[45]

These initial convictions of Naturalist authors and publishers (some of whom were no doubt already suspect because of their socialist sympathies) proved to be singular, however, for the courts thwarted most other efforts to punish literary modernists under §184. In January 1891, for example, Berlin police confiscated an issue of the Naturalist journal *Freie Bühne* because it contained a short review, using fairly explicit language, of the drama *Die Dirne Elisa* (*The Prostitute Elisa*), which dealt with a young prostitute who falls in love with one of her clients but eventually kills herself when he continues to mistreat her and expect sexual favors from her. Police wished to prosecute the journal's editors for obscenity, but in February a Berlin court quashed the charges and released the issue: in light of the review's serious nature and overall artistic intent, the isolated passages referring to sexual relations were not legally obscene.[46] Shortly thereafter the court ruled Heinz Tovote's Naturalistic novella *Der Erbe* (*The Heir*) was also a legitimate artistic effort and ordered it released after Berlin police had it confiscated.[47]

Police in Munich suffered similar setbacks. As part of their campaign against the Naturalist and modernist writers around Michael Georg Conrad and his Modern Life Society (Gesellschaft für modernes Leben), in September 1891 they seized an issue of *Moderne Blätter. Wochenschrift der Gesellschaft für modernes Leben zu München* (*Modern Journal: The Munich Modern Life Society Weekly*) because it contained a short story by the avant-garde Naturalist Anna Croissant-Rust describing a young bride's fear of defloration on her wedding night. They also confiscated *Modernes Leben: Ein Sammelbuch der Münchener Moderne* (*Modern Life: A Scrapbook of the Munich Moderns*), co-edited by Croissant-Rust, because they considered five of the contributions either obscene or blasphemous. (See chapter 5.) Although the state prosecutor wanted to prosecute the writers under §184 for their obscene contributions to these two publications, the Munich superior court refused: it released *Moderne Blätter* a few days after its confiscation, and in December 1891 also released *Modernes Leben*.[48]

For the rest of the Wilhelmine era the judicial system regularly blocked German authorities, especially in Bavaria, from using §184 to punish writers and artists—which is precisely why Bavarian conservatives so ardently campaigned for the Lex Heinze in the 1890s. The Munich police's running battle with *Simplicissimus* is a case in point. Ever since its founding in 1896, the journal was often the target of state action because it delighted in using risqué poems, jokes, and cartoons to explore and satirize the fin-de-siècle sexual revolution. Conservatives, shocked as much by the cynicism as the frankness of many of the journal's humorous pieces, regarded *Simplicissimus* as simple pornography. (Indeed, police files lump *Simplicissimus* into the same category as notoriously indecent "gentlemen's" magazines like *Satyr* and *Auster*.) Although police in Munich confiscated several early issues of *Simplicissimus* for obscenity, most were promptly released by the courts. Thereafter, police routinely sent "indecent" issues to the prosecutor's office with the recommendation they be confiscated and those responsible indicted, but the prosecutor just as routinely declined to take action, probably because he knew how difficult it would be to obtain a jury conviction.[49] When, under growing political pressure from the Catholic Right, the Bavarian government in 1904–1905 indicted members of the *Simplicissimus* staff for obscenity, the prosecutor was unable to persuade the jury to convict the defendants.

The only courtroom victory Bavarian censors scored against *Simplicissimus* came when they abandoned §184 and invoked instead the crime of "public nuisance." To protest the servile behavior of German foreign ambassadors, in 1903 the journal published a now-famous cartoon, "Gesandtenerziehung" (Ambassador Training): it showed would-be ambassadors being trained on gymnastics equipment shaped like a human buttocks, with the diplomatic candidates being shown how to crawl into the anus-like opening. Because authorities found the cartoon "uncommonly coarse and grossly offensive" but were pessimistic about obtaining a conviction under §184, they charged the cartoonist and editor with creating a public nuisance. The defendants were convicted and fined thirty marks each for depicting something that was "unseemly and dirty" (*ungehörig und unflätig*) and "inclined to deeply and grossly offend the general public's legitimate sense of propriety and morality, as well as [its] nationalist feelings."[50]

Because they found the Criminal Code so ineffective against *Simplicissimus*' risqué content, police used other legal weapons to limit its circulation. For example, the Commercial Code gave local authorities power to ban from the colportage trade any printed or pictorial work they considered morally or religiously offensive, even if it was not legally obscene or blasphemous under the Criminal Code. Beginning with the third issue of *Simplicissimus* in April 1896, which contained a one-act skit by Arthur Schnitzler about an adulterous woman impregnated by her lover and the latter's cynical advice to her, Munich police frequently banned individual issues from the colportage trade there. (The journal's staff knew there was little they could do to get such bans overturned, but they nevertheless complained to the authorities "just to show [them] we won't take this kind of thing lying down."[51]) Authorities in Bavaria, Prussia, Saxony, and Baden also banned *Simplicissimus* from state-operated railway station newsstands.

Efforts after 1892 to convict modernists of obscenity in Prussia fared little better than in Bavaria; north German censors could claim only rare and limited success. At the turn of the century, for example, five books were put on trial in a case that might be termed the Impressionist and Jugendstil equivalent of the Leipzig Realists' trial a decade earlier. Between 1896 and 1899, Berlin's reputable Schuster & Löffler Verlag issued Paul Remer's *Unter fremder Sonne* (*Under a Foreign Sun,* an account of the author's travels in South America containing illustrated descriptions of sexual practices there), Ernst Schur's *Geht, es sind Schmerzen an denen wir Leiden* (*Go, It is Aches We Suffer From,* a collection of lyric poetry), Theodore Kabelitz's *Gründe und Abgründe. X-Strahlen in das Frauenleben* (*Reasons and Abysses: X-Rays into the Life of Woman*), Pierre d'Aubecq's *Die Barrisons, ein Kunstroman* (an illustrated novel about the notorious Barrison sisters, scantily clad vaudeville dancers who scandalized Europe in the mid-1890s), and an illustrated third edition of Richard Dehmel's *Aber die Liebe, ein Ehemanns- und Menschenbuch* (a collection of poetry that had been charged with blasphemy and obscenity in 1893 but acquitted by a Munich court; see chapter 5). These five books came to the attention of Prussian authorities because of Börries von Münchhausen, an archconservative poet who in 1897 had denounced Dehmel to the state prosecutor and initiated a trial against Dehmel's *Weib und Welt* for blasphemy and obscenity (see chapter 5); since then Dehmel and Münchhausen had feuded bitterly. In a caustic June 1898 review of Schur's poetry collection, Münchhausen now denounced Schur and other Schuster & Löffler authors as "spiritual children of the head pornographer of Pankow, Richard Dehmel." Books published by Schuster & Löffler, Münchhausen charged, are sensationalistic trash "that corrupts the taste of the public or scares them away from purchasing new poetry books." He cited several other critics' strong condemnations of Dehmel's works and asked rhetorically why the state prosecutor allowed such products to be sold.[52]

Over the next year police confiscated the five Schuster & Löffler books named above on grounds of obscenity. Whether Münchhausen filed a formal legal complaint as he had earlier with *Weib und Welt* is unknown, but according to the publishing house, most of the confiscations occurred because of anonymous denunciations to the authorities.[53] Citing negative reviews of the works, the prosecutor justified the seizures on grounds the books "caused public offense."[54] Schur, Dehmel, Remer, and Kabelitz were indicted for obscenity; d'Aubecq, who resided in Austria, was not. The indictment charged that several passages in Dehmel's book dealt exclusively with "extramarital sexual relations or perverse sexual inclinations"; it condemned d'Aubecq's novel as "lascivious" and noted that while Remer's travelogue was, on the whole, unobjectionable, it did contain lewd illustrations of nude women. The prosecutor also indicted illustrators Herman Freiling and Thomas Theodor Heine and publishers Richard Schuster and Ludwig Löffler.[55]

In September 1899 the court dismissed all charges against Remer, Freiling, and Heine because the sexual descriptions and illustrations in Remer's travelogue and the illustrations in d'Aubecq's novel were not intended to stimulate readers sexually. Charges against the other defendants were sustained, however; the court especially noted that although the first edition of Dehmel's *Aber die Liebe* had been acquitted of obscenity in 1893–1894, that was irrelevant in this case and did not make the work immune from further prosecution.[56]

The trial took place in March 1900, just as the national debate over the Lex Heinze and amendments to §184 were reaching a fever pitch. The court would not allow Dehmel to call literary experts to testify about the literary quality and overall moral purpose of his work, insisting such experts were superfluous "since [the court itself] is capable of forming a judgment."[57] Applying the standard legal criteria (the character of the work as a whole, the author's subjective purpose and intention, the intended readers' objective understandings and sensibilities, etc.), the tribunal decided Schur's volume of poetry was obscene. His poems contained numerous passages where "sensuality as such, often in the most offensive form possible ... was foremost, without any serious artistic purpose being discernible."

The same was true of Kabelitz's book. Both works were ordered destroyed, and Schur and Kabelitz were each fined thirty marks. Schuster and Löffler were found guilty of disseminating obscene works and fined fifteen marks each. In justifying these surprisingly light fines, the court cited as extenuating circumstances Schur's naiveté, the fact that Kabelitz probably had no evil intentions, and Schuster & Löffler's general integrity and good name, as well as the fact that the author, not the publisher, was primarily responsible for a book's contents. The court acquitted the other two works. It declared d'Aubecq's novel to be a "difficult-to-understand satire suited only for a very narrow circle of readers," but not obscene. Likewise Dehmel's volume, although containing sensual and questionable passages, was "a thoroughly philosophical and allegorical collection of poems [that is] very heavy fare and suitable only for literary connoisseurs; the type of reader for whom the book is intended will be fully aware of the author's intent regarding the question-able passages and is not likely to interpret or perceive them as obscene."[58]

After this modest victory Berlin authorities could occasionally prohibit cir-culation of an obscene work but could rarely convict its author. In 1904, for example, they invoked §184 against one of Germany's most noted fin-de-siècle dramatists, Frank Wedekind. His play *Die Büchse von Pandora* (*Pandora's Box*), the second half of the "Lulu" cycle tracing the fate of a sexually emancipated young woman who progresses from seductress to adulteress to prostitute, met with no trouble when it was first printed in a literary journal in 1902. When published as a separate text in 1904, however, Berlin police confiscated it and indicted Wedekind and publisher Bruno Cassirer for obscenity. In May 1905 the Berlin Superior Court found the drama to be a serious literary work and acquit-ted the defendants, but this verdict was overturned by the Imperial Supreme Court. The case was retried in Berlin in January 1906, where judges decided the text would indeed have an obscene effect upon a normal reader and ordered all remaining copies destroyed; however, they again acquitted Wedekind and his publisher on the grounds they were unaware of the work's obscene effect.[59] (After the trial Wedekind claimed he knew that publishing *Pandora's Box* could get him indicted for obscenity; when he was, it simply confirmed his belief the drama met the highest demands of human, if perhaps not bourgeois, morality.[60]) Bavar-ian authorities had even less success. A few months after Wedekind's acquittal in Berlin, the Munich prosecutor wanted to indict him and publisher Albert Langen for obscenity because of *Totentanz* (*Dance of Death*), a one-act play set in a brothel dealing with such issues as white slavery, masochism, and nymphoma-nia. However, after considering the challenged passages within the context of the entire text, a Munich court dismissed the charges. And when police there wanted to confiscate Wedekind's *Schloß Wetterstein* (*Wetterstein Castle*) in late 1910, they dropped the idea when a member of the Munich Censorship Advisory Board warned that doing so would only lead to a controversial trial that would make Wedekind a martyr and publicize his book more widely.[61]

The outcome again fell short of expectations when Berlin authorities seized writings by Arthur Schniztler and Felix Salten, two prominent Austrian authors of the decadent "Young Vienna" movement (apparently because their works had been published by the Wiener Verlag of Austria, one of Europe's largest producers of pornography and erotic pulp fiction). Schnitzler's daring Impressionist *Reigen* (*Roundelay*), a cycle of ten dialogues between sexual partners before and after intercourse, had first been submitted to the respected German publisher S. Fischer in 1897. After the firm's legal advisor warned Fischer that printing the work would result in "a legal prosecution and conviction," the publisher advised Schnitzler to have the text published in Austria. Since German authorities would not be able to press charges against an Austrian author and publisher, at worst they would confiscate it.[62] The Wiener Verlag issued a public edition of the work in 1903 and aggressively marketed it in Germany; by the end of the year eleven thousand copies had been sold in both Austria and Germany. Following bitter complaints from conservatives about efforts to perform the play in Munich and Vienna (see below), in March 1904 Berlin police confiscated *Reigen* and persuaded the court to ban the work from sale in the empire. This did not, however, stop the book's circulation; by 1914, nearly seventy thousand copies had been printed in Vienna, most which were sold (illegally) in Germany. Nor did it prevent public readings of the play in Breslau (1903) and Berlin (1905 and 1909).[63] Efforts to ban Salten's 1905 novella *Der Schrei der Liebe* (*The Cry of Love*), about an eighteenth-century Italian custom concerning the consummation of marriages on the wedding night, failed when a Berlin court acquitted him of obscenity in February 1907 and ordered his confiscated book released; the prosecutor's appeal to the Imperial Supreme Court was unsuccessful.[64]

Two of the hardest-fought legal battles between state authorities and (allegedly) obscene modernist writers erupted on the eve of the war. Both cases involved young Expressionists whose works had appeared in politically radical literary journals; both were ultimately appealed to the Imperial Supreme Court in April 1914; and both involved frustrating, embarrassing setbacks for the prosecution without, however, entirely exonerating the defendants.

The Bavarian case began when Expressionist poet Hugo Ball published his poem "Der Henker" (The Executioner) anonymously in the premier issue (October 1913) of *Die Revolution*, a wildly visionary, avant-garde Munich journal that combined a vaguely anarchistic political orientation with Expressionist and futurist art. "Der Henker" is a bizarre and baffling recounting of an executioner's anguished, depraved thoughts as he prepares to execute a beautiful woman; it combines brazen erotic language and images with vague religious references but is so difficult to decipher one scholar has said it "reads like the code of a secret cult."[65] After a Bavarian Center Party delegate to the Reichstag complained about the poem to the Bavarian Ministry of Justice and demanded the prosecution of those responsible, Munich police confiscated the fifty-two unsold copies of that issue of *Die Revolution* and indicted the publisher, editor and, after they learned his identity, Hugo Ball.[66] In mid-November, however, the Munich court dismissed charges against all three defendants because it was impossible to prove they—or anyone else—were aware the poem was obscene. For the court, the meaning and content of the poem as a whole is so obscure and incomprehensible it leaves room for all possible interpretations. ... The defendants, who seriously make themselves out as representatives of a new artistic movement, as experts of a literary 'futurism,' have revealed in their testimony such an eccentricity and confusion of moral perceptions that it must seriously be doubted whether they were even conscious of the immoral manner of their thinking and speaking that manifests itself in such an *objectively* tangible way in the poem.

The court concluded it was futile to prosecute.[67]

The prosecutor, however, insisted on an "impersonal process" to declare the poem itself obscene so it could be destroyed and banned. At the December hearing, where publisher Heinrich Bachmaier tried again to explain the poem's meaning, intent, and high artistic value, the Munich Superior Court concluded "Der Henker" was not obscene under §184 because "the entire wording and context of the poem is completely incomprehensible, even with the commentary of the publisher." "The reader's fantasies will not be aroused in a morally depraved manner; the cited words and depictions of lasciviousness and debauched lust [*Geilheit und Wollust*] become so submerged among the other incomprehensible words that the normal reader will feel aversion and disgust—not because his sense of shame and morality is violated, but rather because of the impenetrability of [the poem's] contents."

The court further noted that although *Die Revolution* sells for only ten pfennig and thus falls into the hands of the lower social strata, they will not be offended by it, merely angered at having spent good money on what they will consider trash. Because "the journal and the poem are intended only for a circle of readers that can no longer be considered part of the large majority of normal-thinking people whom the Criminal Code seeks to protect," the court lifted the ban of *Die Revolution*.[68] The frustrated prosecutor appealed the verdict but in April 1914 the Imperial Supreme Court upheld the lower court's decision, reiterating the established precedent that a "shameless" or offensive word or phrase is not ipso facto obscene; much depends on the context within which it is used. In the case of Ball's poem, the court agreed, the complete unintelligibility of the larger context robbed isolated words and phrases of any ability to violate the reader's sense of shame and morality.[69] In short, the poem could not be obscene if no one could understand it. Although the strange outcome of this lengthy obscenity trial represented another in a long series of legal defeats for Bavarian censors, given the humbling grounds for the court's decision, it was also something less than a victory for the literary defendants.

The second case was more complex and more politically charged. In the last years before World War I, prosecutions for obscenity assumed a central role in a bitter, escalating legal war and personal feud between Berlin Police President von Jagow and the publishers and editors of the radical, avant-garde literary and political journal *Pan* (whose contributors included noted leftists such as Kurt Eisner, Heinrich Mann, and Kurt Tucholsky). In January and February 1911, shortly after *Pan*'s editors had criticized the Berlin police's brutal suppression of striking workers in Moabit, the journal published the first German translation of Flaubert's Egyptian diary, which contained descriptions of Egyptian prostitutes and erotic native dances. Citing public complaints about the offensive nature of the diary, police confiscated those two issues and charged publisher Paul Cassirer and editor Wilhelm Herzog with producing, selling, and distributing obscene printed matter in a public place. In response, *Pan* carried a series of taunting, vitriolic personal attacks on von Jagow criticizing not only his ban of the Flaubert journal and his callous behavior in the Moabit affair, but also publicizing the embarrassing scandal over his proposition to Cassirer's wife, actress Tilla Durieux (see chapter 2) and hinting von Jagow had once been jailed for striking a judge.[70] In an apparent act of retaliation, although again citing public complaints, in April 1911 police confiscated another *Pan* issue containing Herbert Eulenberg's "Brief eines Vaters unserer Zeit" (Letter from a Father of Our Times), in which that controversial Expressionist playwright offered advice to university students about sex, venereal disease, and how to treat prostitutes when visiting a brothel. Cassirer and Herzog were again indicted for obscenity, as was Eulenberg. Shortly thereafter, the cabaretist Hans Hyan's erotic novel *Die Verführten* (*The Seduced*), published by Cassirer's Pan Verlag, was confiscated under §184. These latter two confiscations, in turn, produced a new round of protests not only in *Pan* and other avant-garde literary journals, but also from the recently founded German Writers' Defense League, which, through declarations published in the liberal press, condemned the "arbitrary, unjustified confiscations" as "a serious attack on the rights of free authors."[71]

When all these cases were brought to court, the results were highly disappointing for the state. Hyan's novel was quickly ordered released for sale. A Berlin court issued the curious verdict that the portion of the Flaubert diary printed in the January issue was not obscene because passages describing sexual events were essential to the whole text and would neither shock nor arouse learned readers who were knowledgeable of other cultures; however, the diary entries in the February issue were obscene because they might offend or arouse lust in certain younger, less-educated readers. Cassirer and Herzog were fined fifty marks each—half the fine the prosecution had sought. At the second trial in September 1911 the court ruled Eulenberg's essay was not obscene, released that issue of *Pan,* and acquitted Eulenberg, Cassirer, and Herzog.[72]

A brief truce ensued, but within eighteen months *Pan* was the target of still another police action. The February 1913 issue published two anonymous Expressionist poems: "Sie hat an ihrem Liebesmunde" (She Has at Her Love Mouth), concerning a genital sore and possible syphilis, and "Betrachtung," (Contemplation), dealing with a man's cynical, postcoitus reflections about prophylactics, accidental pregnancy, and future sexual conquests. Berlin police immediately confiscated the issue and indicted its editor, Alfred Kerr, who had penned the most vitriolic attacks on von Jagow's behavior during the 1911 confrontation. After authorities discovered the identity of the poems' author (Alfred Henschke, better known as Klabund), he too was indicted for violating §184, but his trial was postponed due to illness. At Kerr's trial a Berlin court ruled that, while the two poems were indeed obscene, Kerr was not guilty of deliberately publishing obscene material because he had, like any true artist, considered the poems merely from an artistic, not a moral or legal standpoint. In the opinion of the court, "to the extent that the artist's efforts are directed solely toward perfectly expressing his artistically applicable ideas in the suitable art medium, [his efforts] are of a purely technical kind and are not immoral."[73]

The prosecutor appealed Kerr's acquittal and in April 1914 the Imperial Supreme Court overturned the lower court verdict and ordered Kerr retried. According to the higher court, "it is not a question of whether the author of the poem, in his authorial activity, acted immorally, much less of whether he was pursuing obscene purposes, but rather of whether the poems composed by him are obscene. ... The nature (*Beschaffenheit*) of the work, not the motives and intent (*Willensrichtung*) of he who created it, determines its obscenity." The court soundly rejected the argument that anything with even minimal artistic value was ipso facto immune from §184; even though a work has artistic value, it might still be obscene.[74]

The lower court retried the case and in August 1914 ruled that Klabund's "poetically botched work" (*dichterische Machwerk*) was clearly obscene and that a man of Kerr's education should have been aware the poems would have a grossly obscene effect upon readers. Kerr was fined one hundred marks and all remaining copies of that issue of *Pan* were ordered destroyed. When Klabund was well enough to stand trial in January 1915, the court also found him guilty and imposed a fine of fifty marks (although the prosecutor, curiously, had requested a fine of only twenty marks).[75] While Berlin Police President von Jagow had finally wrung out a minor legal victory against *Pan* and his nemesis Kerr, the fact that it took four years and six separate trials to do so underscored how difficult it was for the state to convict German writers of obscenity. In such cases the courts drew some surprisingly nuanced (if not always consistent) distinctions between which literary works were legally obscene and which were not.

Morality Plays

Although often frustrated in attempts to prosecute authors and distributors of morally offensive literature, German authorities were more successful in keeping immoral dramas off the public stage, at least temporarily. Far more dramas were banned on moral grounds than for any other reason. In Munich, for example, 74.3 percent of all dramas banned between 1908 and 1918 were forbidden for moral reasons.[76] Although police records elsewhere do not always indicate why a work was proscribed (police did not need to specify a reason unless the ban was appealed), a review of surviving scripts submitted to censors in Berlin and other cities and of these censors' recommendations leaves little doubt that there, too, a large majority of all theatrical bans were because of moral objections.

Of these several hundred bans, most were French or German farces (*Schwänke, Posse*), light comedies (*Lustspiele*), or low boudoir burlesques with suggestive titles like *Eine Badereise—Endlich zu zweien* (*A Trip to the Baths—Finally Just the Two of Us*, banned in Berlin 1897); *Die Liebesschule* (*School of Love*), *Die Brautnacht* (*The Bridal Night*), *Das Hührenbett* (*The Whore's Bed*), *Der Erotische Zirkus* (*The Erotic Circus*), all banned in Frankfurt between 1909 and 1912; or *Die Schöne Ehebrecherin* (*The Beautiful Adulteress,* banned in Munich, 1914). However, about two dozen of the dramas prohibited in the imperial era were serious literary efforts by noted German and foreign writers (especially Naturalists) such as Emil Augier, Henrik Ibsen, Gerhart Hauptmann, O. E. Hartleben, Arthur Schnitzler, Karl Schönherr, Carl Sternheim, Hermann Sudermann, Leo Tolstoy, and Frank Wedekind.[77]

One of the most interesting and controversial of such incidents involved Hermann Sudermann's drama *Sodoms Ende* (*Sodom's End*). This case, which occurred a few months after the Leipzig criminal court had wrestled with issues of morality and Realist art, and which quickly drew in the Prussian cabinet and emperor, reflects many of the broader artistic and legal issues evident in the Leipzig Realists' trial. However, it also reveals the censors' special concerns and procedures when dealing with morally questionable dramatic art, including the dynamics of negotiation and compromise; the traditional function of the German theater as a "moral institution"; the crucial role of the intended audience and of the work's actual staging; the frequent influence, and at times intrusive meddling, of external authorities and moral entrepreneurs; and the local limitations of theater censorship, as compared to the more standardized, national jurisdiction of the criminal law.

In October 1890 Berlin's Lessing Theater requested permission to stage a public performance of *Sodoms Ende,* a detailed portrayal of the moral depravity and sexual hedonism rampant among the cynical, amoral upper-class elite in elegant Berlin-West. Seduction, refined forms of prostitution, borderline incest, and other forms of upper-class decadence figured prominently in the piece. The first police reader considered the work "hyperrealistic" and believed "this naturalistic direction is, in my humble opinion, hardly appropriate for a public stage;" the second reader expressed reservations about the subject matter and Sudermann's "continual, most pronounced naturalistic treatment" of it but saw no legal reason to ban the play.[78] Nevertheless, Police President von Richthofen prohibited the play because "its entire content is not appropriate for a public performance." When Oscar Blumenthal, director of the Lessing Theater, went to von Richthofen to inquire about the reason for the ban, he received a curious answer that soon became widely known as the establishment's reaction to the whole Naturalist movement:

BLUMENTHAL: But why this ban? Why?

V. RICHTHOFEN: Because it suits us!

BLUMENTHAL: I understand completely, Herr President, that you wish to remind me, through this laconicism, that under the police ordinance of 10 July 1851 the authorities are not obligated to give a reason for the ban of a piece.

V. RICHTHOFEN: Well, so you are aware of that then!

BLUMENTHAL: I only mean, Herr President, that the possibility does exist of removing, through prudent revisions, the objections that have led to this ban. Perhaps it is a matter of only a few daring passages?

V. RICHTHOFEN: Oh, no!

BLUMENTHAL: Or particular scenes?

V. RICHTHOFEN: No again!

BLUMENTHAL: But what, then?

V. RICHTHOFEN: The whole direction does not suit us! (*Die janze Richtung paßt uns nich!*)[79]

Because the scheduled public premiere was only three days off,[80] Blumenthal appealed the ban directly to Minister of the Interior Herrfurth, complain-

Der Dichter Sudermann wird nachdrücklich darauf aufmerksam gemacht, daß sein neues Stück mit dem polizeilichen Sittenkodex im Widerspruch steht.

Figure 6.2 Sodoms Ende
(Gustav Brandt Drawing, *Kladderadatsch* October 1890)
It is vigorously pointed out to the playright Sudermann that his new play is incompatible with the police's moral code.

ing police had no business passing such sweeping judgments on whole artistic movements. He expressed his willingness to make some alterations, but told the minister "it must also be remembered the work will not be performed before a popular [*volkstümlich*] audience but rather an audience well educated in literature and accustomed to apprehending all the details of a work in relation to its basic premises, and from which, therefore, we need not fear embarrassments or misunderstandings."[81]

After reading the drama Herrfurth asked Blumenthal to resubmit it after cutting a few minor passages. (This would allow von Richthofen to save face; he could claim he was approving the play not because of external pressure but because the revised script was different from the one he rejected.) Despite the cuts suggested by Herrfurth, von Richthofen refused to lift his ban "because the entire design and execution of the work appears likely to violate the moral sense."[82] In desperation Blumenthal approached the interior minister again. They agreed that the way the piece was actually performed would be a crucial consideration; before deciding to uphold or overturn von Richthofen's ban, Herrfurth would attend a dress rehearsal to see that the production would be discreet and inoffensive. So on 30 October three observers from the interior ministry, the playwright Sudermann, and a few others attended a special private performance.[83] At the interior minister's request the Berlin police president gave his permission for the public performance of a slightly expurgated version of *Sodoms Ende*.

The story did not end there, for the young emperor, who fancied himself an artistic connoisseur, became involved. A month after the play's premiere Wilhelm II was increasingly concerned *Sodoms Ende* "was causing offense, indeed was scandalizing the serious and better [*wohlgesinden*] circles of the populace." He demanded a copy of the script and an explanation of why the interior minister approved its public performance.[84] The minister responded that he had passed the work only after reading it carefully himself and hearing a report it was being staged in such a way that he would not be ashamed to attend it with his wife. He gently pointed out the play's message was basically a moral one and that many classical works dealing with sex, such as *Faust*, were regularly performed in the royal theaters. Unless some clear danger to public morals or public order existed (and with *Sodoms Ende* it did not), police could not and should not exercise tutelage over the theater-going public.[85]

Unsatisfied, the emperor responded that however noble the author's motives, experience shows the performance of plays with immoral content, "especially when the portrayal is coarsely realistic, has a sensually stimulating and demoralizing effect on the large majority of the audience. But at a time when it is the foremost task of my reign to protect and strengthen the moral bases of our state and social life, I must attach especially great importance to the public theater not being misused to impugn and poison the moral principles of our nation." Wilhelm urged exercising "appropriate caution and strictness" when approving dramas and pointed out that a "suitable influence" (*geschickten Einwirkung*) upon theater directors could make them more mindful of their duty to perform "good" dramas that will promote patriotism and make the theater an "abode of the nation's elevation and cultivation" (*Stätte der Hebung und Veredelung der Nation*).[86] Herrfurth dutifully sought to pressure Blumenthal by summoning him after *Sodoms Ende* had played for several weeks and politely suggesting the Lessing Theater might quietly let *Sodoms Ende* "fade away (*versickern*)." Blumenthal politely refused.[87]

Far from fading away, the controversy generated in Berlin over *Sodoms Ende* followed it to other cities. When submitted for approval in Vienna, the police president there said the work presented "the most repulsive and, from a moral standpoint, most reprehensible situations," but he reluctantly approved it because everyone knew it had been approved in Berlin and a ban in Vienna would only give it undeserved publicity.[88] While Vienna followed Berlin's example, police in Kassel and Munich did not. Braunschweig allowed several public performances but suddenly forbade *Sodoms Ende* in July 1892, while the first performances in Halle and Bielefeld were greeted with demonstrations by conservative Christian circles determined to stop them.[89]

In late 1892 the emperor again sought to use "suitable influence" to prevent a second run of *Sodoms Ende* in Berlin. Blumenthal had arranged for the Wallner Theater, a *Volkstheater* catering to a broader, petit-bourgeois clientele, to produce the play. These performances sparked protests by anti-Semites who condemned the work as a *Jüdenstück* (Jewish piece). What had been merely irksome for Wilhlem II at the more exclusive Lessing Theater now proved intolerable at the more popular Wallner Theater. In November 1892, in protest over the Wallner Theater's performance of *Sodoms Ende,* he cancelled his royal box there. (He took the same action with the Berlin Theater two years later when Blumenthal became director there, and, more famously, as described in chapter 4, with the Deutsches Theater in 1895 to protest *Die Weber.*)[90]

As with *Sodoms Ende,* many dramas were approved on condition that the dress rehearsal was not offensive or indecent (*anstößig*) or that specific changes be made in the script. Some changes were minor, such as changing the name of a character or a line or two of dialogue, or removing an offensive word. Thus *Die Schlange* (*The Snake*) was passed in Berlin in 1895 after a brief reference to a woman "giving herself" was removed; the farce *Geteilte Leibe* (*Divided Love*) was approved in Berlin in 1907 only if two characters did not call each other "*Ehebrecherin*" (adulteress) and "*Bigamist*"; and in *Wem Gehört Helene?* (*To Whom Does Helene Belong?*), Helene must lie on a sofa rather than a bed when two men enter, and she cannot refer to a man's "*Bedürfnisse*" (needs or desires) or say that a "cold" man "*kann eben 'ne Frau nicht glücklich machen*" (can't satisfy a woman).[91]

In many cases, however, censors demanded substantial changes. To get permission for Gerhart Hauptmann's path-breaking social drama *Vor Sonnenaufgang* (*Before Sunrise*) in 1889, for example, the theater director submitted to the Berlin censor a completely sanitized version of the original script. Set in a Silesian coal mining community, the play graphically portrayed and critiqued the environment in which miners lived and worked and their treatment by the decadent, lazy landowning family. When he wrote it Hauptmann himself believed the piece—which contained coarse peasant language and treated several "unsuitable" topics like hereditary alcoholism, adultery, and a father's drunken sexual assault on his daughter—was much too naturalistic and shocking ever to be performed publicly. Although the theater claimed the bowdlerized version merely "freed [the drama] of materialistic excesses," in fact it did serious violence to both the plot and naturalistic tenor of the play.[92] Still, the police censor recommended against the work because of its realistic tendency and coarse expressions, but the police president approved it on condition the words *Titte* (teat) and *Scheißkerle* (sack of shit) be changed. The conservative Men's League for the Suppression of Public Immorality vehemently protested this decision and demanded all performances, public or private, of "this dirty and at the same time tendentious social-democratic play," be prohibited, but the police president rejected their complaint and allowed the expurgated *Vor Sonnenaufgang* to premier on 30 November 1889.[93]

Lighter fare such as Hans Schwarz's *Moderne Menschen* (*Modern Men,* approved 1892), Leon Gaudillot's *Associés* (*Associates,* banned 1894 and 1895, approved 1895 and 1897), and *Die Dame von Maxim* (approved 1900) all required extensive revisions or cuts, sometimes of entire scenes, before the Berlin censor would approve them. When the Prussian minister of the interior attended the premier of *Die Dame von Maxim,* he demanded six additional changes in its wording and staging.[94]

Among serious dramatists, however, the oft-censored Frank Wedekind probably suffered the most tampering with his scripts. This is hardly surprising since Wedekind's primary aim (in the words of one leading literary scholar) was "to violently shake the structure of an ossified, intellectually degenerate, morally confused, instinctually unsure world from the ground up," and his works focused intensively on the psychology and physiology of love; the cause, course, and cure of sexual diseases; and sexual hysteria.[95] Berlin was the first city to permit a public performance of his shockingly frank *Frühlings Erwachen* (*Spring Awakening,* published 1891), a "childhood tragedy" about confused, frustrated adolescents who become tragic victims of oppressive bourgeois morality. Desperately in need of enlightenment about the "facts of life," they meet with a conspiracy of silence about sexual matters from their families, school, and the church, all of which seek to suppress their nascent sexuality. Their sexual ignorance has tragic results: severe emotional disturbances, a bungled abortion resulting in the death of a young girl, interest in illicit underground sexual guides, reform school, and suicide. Berlin police passed the work in 1906 on condition that several characters' names and various terms (such as "*Beischlaf*" [coition] and "*Abortivmittel*" [aborticide]) be changed, several descriptions altered, parts of some scenes cut, and three scenes eliminated entirely. Wedekind considered these "censors' whims" as "idiotic" (*blödsinnig*), but they allowed the work to be performed in Berlin, and two years later in Munich (where the public performances generated intense criticism from morality groups and parliamentary petitions to stop the performance, petitions the Bavarian government ignored).[96]

If a work were proscribed the theater director could sometimes compromise, making sufficient alterations to gain the censors' approval, as Blumenthal did with *Sodoms Ende*. Such negotiations eventually rescued Tolstoy's *Macht der Finsternis* (*Power of Darkness*), a brutally naturalistic treatment of a decadent peasant family plagued by the wife's adultery; her murder of her husband; her new husband's alcoholism, wife abuse, and incest with his stepdaughter; and the murder of the child born of this incest. The work premiered privately at Berlin's Freie Bühne in January 1890, but police rejected requests by two commercial theaters to perform it publicly.[97] When director Otto Brahm asked again in 1900, police again refused on the grounds it would endanger public morals and public order. The censor acknowledged the play's overall moral *Tendenz*, but complained its atmosphere was "as if saturated with brandy" and that Tolstoy groveled in the dirt of human existence.[98] The case was appealed to the provincial governor, who acknowledged that while the work dealt with repulsive behavior in a crassly realistic manner, it was a deeply serious and ultimately moral work that neither excused nor exalted the family's immoral and illegal behavior. He overturned the police's outright ban of the play, although privately expressed his dislike of the piece and explained that he overruled the police because he was convinced the Supreme Administrative Law Court would not uphold the ban.[99] Police approved a greatly expurgated version of *Macht der Finsternis* in which extensive dialogue was cut from acts 1–5, much of which dealt with the poisoning of the first husband and infanticide of the illegitimate child.

The famous director Max Reinhardt reached a similar compromise with Berlin police a decade later over Carl Sternheim's *Die Hose* (*Underpants*). The play opens just after an attractive young woman's sudden loss of her underpants during a royal parade. Her petit- bourgeois, social-climbing husband, fearing the incident will ruin his social and career aspirations, takes in two boarders to cover his anticipated financial difficulties. Both boarders seek (but fail) to cuckold the snobbish, calculating husband. In the end he finds the boarding business so lucrative he decides—after seducing a neighbor—it is time he and his wife have a son.

A few days before the scheduled premier of *Die Hose* in February 1911, police refused the production on moral grounds. In a lengthy letter to Police President von Jagow, Reinhardt defended the play's moral intent and expressed a willingness to accommodate any police concerns. He insisted the piece was a purely artistic comedy, took offense at the police's erotic interpretation of it, and in a tortured explanation argued that Sternheim intended the woman's underpants as "a symbol of the petty-bourgeois philistinism that clings to real, material things and thus obstructs the path for minds that aspire to the spiritual. At exactly the moment [the husband] regains his full superiority through an exchange of ideas [with his boarders], to some extent the pants drop (symbolically)—i.e., the philistinism is overcome." Sternheim, Reinhardt continued, was willing to change the possibly misleading title to *Der Riese* (*The Ogre*, its original title) and make any other reasonable changes authorities might suggest. Reinhardt also guaranteed the police president the work would be performed in a decent, discreet way that would reflect the author's "purely intellectual interpretation." Von Jagow agreed to attend the dress rehearsal to see how inoffensive the performance would be; his encounter there with the actress Tilla Durieux soon led to a public scandal (see chapter 2). Nevertheless, he consented to a public performance, provided it was called *Der Riese*.[100] When *Die Hose* was banned in Munich the following year, Sternheim was again willing to make extensive changes to the play so it would be acceptable to the censor.[101]

However, if censors decided the problem lay not in specific lines or scenes but the work as a whole, then they could not be swayed by mere revisions. For example, Maurice Donnay's *Die Verliebten* (*les Amants; The Beloved*), about a love triangle between a married count, his mistress, and a theater director, was first banned by Berlin police in October 1896 because it depicted *wilde Ehe* (unmarried cohabitation) as something normal and unremarkable. A revised script was also rejected. After unsuccessful appeals to the provincial governor and the Supreme Administrative Law Court, in November 1898 the theater revised the script again; police refused permission for it as well. Ironically, this drama's artistic unity and refined style apparently worked against it: the court decided the play would have a "harmful effect on moral perceptions precisely because it [directly subverts existing moral views in Germany regarding marriage] not through coarse, crude, sexually offensive language, but rather in a refined way; in pleasant, repeated, poetically tinged treatments and not in attention-getting dialogue."[102]

Many of Wedekind's works met a similar fate. When his *Totentanz* (for which authorities tried to indict him) was banned by Munich police in June 1906 on grounds of "public morality and decency," he and the theater director revised the piece and resubmitted it in December 1909, but that version was also barred. It was reworked again as *Tod und Teufel* (*Death and the Devil*) and was rejected a third time (May 1910), as was a fourth attempt in January 1911. (When police forbade even a public reading in April 1911, Wedekind unleashed his angry public attack on the Censorship Advisory Board, discussed in chapter 2.) Wedekind later rewrote some scenes in iambic pentameter to demonstrate his subject could be treated in classical form, but public readings of this version, not to mention public performances, were prohibited as well (September 1916).[103]

His *Die Büchse der Pandora* (which was confiscated in Berlin and for which he was indicted but acquitted; see above) met the same stiff-necked resistance. When writing it Wedekind "never dreamed it would be performed [publicly]," and indeed it never was during his lifetime (although a private performance was held in Nuremberg in 1904.) Still, he implored theaters not to refer to it as a comedy, for he thought that would reduce its chances of passing the censor.[104] After *Büchse* was prohibited from public performance in Munich in November 1908, Wedekind created another version "in which there is hardly a word left at which the censor could take offense."[105] In May 1910 it too was rejected, this time with a police statement that "there is no prospect for approval of another reworked stage treatment."[106] Using portions of his earlier *Erdgeist* (*Earth Spirit*) and of *Büchse*, Wedekind completely reworked the Lulu story and in 1913 created a "new" play, *Lulu, Tragödie in fünf Aufzügen mit Prolog* (*Lulu: A Tragedy in Five Acts with Prologue*). A Munich theater submitted it for police censorship, assuring authorities Wedekind had omitted the parts that had caused *Büchse* to be banned before: "If individual passages still cause concern, of course we are ready, with the author's consent, to work toward removing any causes for objections."[107] After consulting with the Censorship Advisory Board, in May 1913 police banned this "new" version too. The theater next invited police officials and the advisory board to a special closed performance of the play, one where "we have tried above all to make further cuts in the text, which primarily seek to clarify the criminal and sexual-pathological character of the last act so that it will create only a symbolic effect. The heroine's 'death of atonement' and all elements that were decisive for the censorship authorities' ban of a public performance have been repressed."[108]

Police officials and the advisory board declined the invitation. The theater submitted still another revised text, again inviting police to a dress rehearsal; police reiterated their ban and declined again to attend a rehearsal. At this point the Munich chapter of the German Writers' Defense League publicly protested the police's intransigent attitude and announced it would hold a private performance of *Lulu*. As described above (chapter 2), the Defense League also passed a resolution stating service on the Censorship Advisory Board was unworthy of a German writer, causing Thomas Mann to resign both from the board and the Defense League. Although the private performance was held in May 1913, *Lulu* was not performed publicly in Munich until 1928.[109]

Censors were equally adamant about Wedekind's *Schloß Wetterstein*, which examined prostitution, rape, and sadism. After being banned in Munich in 1911, it was also forbidden in Berlin in January 1913, "since it must be considered contrary to public order and morality to put sexual perversities on stage." (In his preface to the text Wedekind wrote, "I will not be surprised if this play is forbidden by the censors, as it is only a logical accompaniment of the notorious indifference and obtuseness that characterize our entire public life." The Berlin censor underlined this sentence in red.) In fact, Berlin authorities were so shocked at the piece that the public prosecutor considered confiscating it (just as Munich police considered doing three years earlier), and police collected opinions on its contents from medical, criminal, literary, and pornography experts before deciding to ban it. The theater submitted a revised script, which supposedly removed all objectionable parts and which would make it "absolutely clear" that one scene to which police had objected "deals merely with an intellectual rape in the sense of a struggle between intellectual factors." After consulting experts again (one of whom argued that regardless of the revisions, the play's sadistic content would perhaps push over the edge the "many" who teetered on the border between normal and abnormal sexual feelings), police also rejected this version (May 1913). An ill-timed third revision was submitted in late June, just when the city was abuzz about the sadistic murder of a young girl and the outbreak of war; not surprisingly, police banned it as well on 31 July 1914.[110] While other writers and directors could sometimes appease censors with expedient changes, the issues

Wedekind explored were so scandalous that no changes he was willing to make would soften the censors' resolve.

As Wedekind's experience illustrates, censors frequently argued that certain immoral behavior simply should not be portrayed in public theaters. For example, in 1892 police in Breslau prohibited the performance of Richard Nordmann's *Gefallene Engel (Fallen Angel)*, which dealt with an illegitimate child who, as a young woman in Vienna, is betrayed by her immoral grandparents, falls under the influence of cynical procuresses and pimps, and is seduced first by a young military cadet, then (unknowingly) by her own grandfather. The censor objected to the play's immoral content, especially its focus on pimping (*Kuppelei*), procuring (*Verkuppelung*), and adultery, and its "coarse, naturalistic" depiction of "the filthy abuses and manifestations of life and goings-on in a large city." The ban was upheld by the district administrative president but nullified by the Supreme Administrative Law Court, which in doing so articulated a legal principle that later appellants frequently cited. In this case, the court stated, it is irrelevant whether the drama is morally ennobling and furthers the theater's primary function as a place of moral education (*Bildungsanstalt*); and it is equally irrelevant if and how the work meets any aesthetic expectations and standards. Police may only consider whether a ban is necessary in order to uphold public order, peace, and morality, or to meet an imminent threat. The ban of *Gefallene Engel* meets none of those criteria. Acknowledging the play does treat immoral actions and views, the court also pointed out that "portraying immorality does not in itself endanger public order or morality; this depends far more on *how* the portrayal is handled." Despite its sensationalist title and grounding in modern, Naturalist views about art, the judges decided nothing in Nordmann's play violated the sense of shame or provoked viewers to immoral thoughts or deeds.[111]

After this important decision Prussian and Saxon courts frequently affirmed that drama bans must be based not on whether immoral subjects were depicted, but only on how those subjects were handled and the probable effect on the audience. Thus, when Berlin police in 1900 prohibited Richard Jaffe's *Der Außenseiter (The Outsider)*, a play depicting a young nobleman's reactions to the lax morals of the upper classes, the Supreme Administrative Law Court overturned that ban: "Not every portrayal of immoral conditions in a drama justifies its prohibition, otherwise depicting moral abuses on the stage would never be possible. Whether a ban is permissible depends far more on the *Tendenz* of the piece, the manner of the portrayal, and the consequent effect of the performance on the audience."[112]

The Supreme Administrative Law Court reiterated this principle in 1912 in striking down Königsberg's effort to ban the expurgated version of Wedekind's *Frühlings Erwachen* performed in Berlin. The court ruled the subject matter of the play (the problems of puberty) is widely discussed and therefore not likely in itself to offend the public's sense of shame. Nor was Wedekind's handling of this subject likely to offend the public and arouse disturbances, as Königsberg police maintained; he does not portray immoral behavior as something worthy of imitation, and the serious content and effect of the whole work eclipse any offensive parts.[113]

Just as the minister of the interior had found a basic moral message in *Sodoms Ende* that the police and emperor had not, German judges occasionally overruled police when they derived a different meaning from a work than had the censors. Such was the case with Eugen Löwen's *Sünder und Gerechte* (*The Sinners and the Righteous*), forbidden in Berlin in 1895. To police, the sensationalized, offensive subject matter (a scheming ex-prostitute who arranges for the seduction of her sister) and the ending (a double murder—the seducer by the sister, and the ex-prostitute by a scorned former lover) pandered to base instincts and "presents to a [lower-class] audience objectively immoral actions and ideas within the milieu of bourgeois life in a way that could confuse moral concepts, and perhaps cause imitation." But the Supreme Administrative Law Court revoked the ban in 1896, arguing the actions and fate of the play's characters arouses the audience's revulsion and condemnation: "It is hard to imagine how the performance of a work with such subject matter and with such an ending—a work in which everything that is unjust and immoral ... finds its punishment—could be inclined to confuse moral concepts [or] degrade moral thinking."[114] Similarly, the Saxon Supreme Administrative Law Court disagreed with censors over the moral effect of *Macht der Finsternis:* after Leipzig police sought to prohibit the expurgated version that had been passed in Berlin, in 1901 the court reversed the ban. In the court's reading, Tolstoy makes it clear to even the most immature and uneducated spectator that the immorality he depicts is reprehensible and not to be imitated. The court concluded that an audience may leave the performance "deeply shaken, full of horror and disgust, but not confused about what is good and moral, or inclined to opinions or behavior that endangers public order and morality."[115]

Although courts (and less frequently, a higher administrative authority) sometimes revoked police prohibitions of supposedly immoral dramas, more often they concurred with the censors. The Prussian Supreme Administrative Law Court affirmed "police are justified and obligated to prevent any debasement (*Verschlechterung*) of morality that touches upon the public interest, whether that consists of a debasement of moral behavior, or simply a debasement of moral thought and feeling that, as an effect of the performance, is likely to cause a deterioration of moral behavior."[116] On at least seven occasions, appeals courts ultimately upheld local police bans of immoral dramas, and in one case even reinstated a ban that had earlier been overturned by the District Administrative Council.[117] Censorship decisions appealed through the administrative rather than judicial route were still less likely to be successful: the Prussian interior minister upheld Berlin police bans of A. F. Hennequin's *Niniche* (1879) and Ibsen's *Ghosts* (1889), for example, and the Bavarian interior minister upheld decisions by Munich police to ban Wedekind's *Schloß Wetterstein* (1911) and Sternheim's *Die Hose* (1912).

The level of an audience's sophistication and social standing were often a determining factor in the censors' decisions, especially during the heightened social tensions and class conflict of the late 1880s and early 1890s. Thus Blumenthal hoped to persuade police to allow *Sodoms Ende* by assuring them the audience at his theater was well educated, familiar with fine literature, and unlikely to be offended by or to misinterpret the piece. Berlin's most respected theaters frequently pointed out to censors that their audiences were "entirely respectable and peaceful" or, because of their higher prices, drew their public "from the most exclusive social circles."[118]

Less well-bred audiences, however, elicited concerns. For example, Ibsen's *Gespenster* (*Ghosts*), which ruthlessly exposed the hypocritical lies on which seemingly respectable bourgeois marriages were based, was banned in Berlin in 1889 even though it had been performed in other cities. The Berlin police president argued the social and political situation there was far different from the cities where *Gespenster* had been allowed: "Seeing that the democratic and socialist press [here] continually implies to the unpropertied classes that the moral degeneracy of the so-called higher classes is an established fact, the effect of such a theater piece ... upon a large urban public composed of the most diverse social strata must arouse all the more serious concerns from a moral and social standpoint."[119] To justify banning M. Halperin's *Die Kindermörderin* (*The Child Murderer*) and *Sünder und Gerechte* in 1895, Berlin authorities pointed out the two theaters seeking to perform the pieces (National and Alexanderplatz) were widely known for their low admission prices and for pandering to lower-class audiences seeking simple entertainment and sheer sensual stimulation rather than literary edification. Indeed, within the last year police had to ban a dozen questionable, sensationalist works in those establishments. "Considering such an audience and such theater management," police considered it self-evident that there was "an especially great danger that the performance of immoral theater pieces there would undermine morals."[120]

Although authorities usually argued it was the less-refined, lower-class audiences needing paternalistic protection, they sometimes maintained that more-refined, upper-class audiences must be shielded from crude works. For example, in 1893 Berlin police prohibited the Lessing Theater from performing Francesco Garze's *Herr d'Albert*, about a young man who (unwittingly) falls in love with his father's mistress, because the subject matter would violate the moral sensibilities of the theater's upper-class audiences.[121] When a ban of Hans von Reinfels' *Die Sitte* (*Morality*) was appealed to the Supreme Administrative Law Court in 1892, the court acknowledged the work may not be morally harmful for much of the clientele that frequents popular theaters, since "portions of that audience are already so depraved [*verderbt*] their morality cannot be worsened any further." Because it could offend a mixed audience, however, police were justified in banning it.[122]

To some, the censors' confusing double standards toward elite and popular audiences had the paradoxical effect of sanctioning poor art while proscribing good. When playwright Lothar Schmidt's comedy *Nur ein Traum* (*Only a Dream*) was banned shortly before the war, he asked why his piece was prohibited but far more immoral works were permitted in cabarets, lower-class theaters, and music halls. "I'll gladly explain it to you," the Berlin censor said, "You see, Herr Doktor, your comedy realistically portrays the milieu [of elite Berlin society] in Grünewald. The farces playing in [a more popular] theater ... are in their premises and form so silly and inane that no audience would think about existing reality, while with you, every spectator must instinctively say to himself: 'Yes, such things must happen just as you portray them!' That's why the farces go on uncensored, but not your racy stories."[123]

In sum, local control of theater censorship produced numerous inconsistent decisions about morally suspect works. It is not surprising some dramas were allowed in cosmopolitan Berlin but not in smaller towns or in more conservative and Catholic Munich;[124] more surprising was that some works were acceptable in smaller towns, but not in Berlin. Ibsen's *Gespenster,* for example, had already been permitted in Frankfurt, Danzig, and Königsberg before Berlin censors forbade it. In a more puzzling set of decisions, Dreyer's *Tal des Lebens* (*Valley of Life*) had been banned in Berlin (1902), Munich (1903), and a few other Prussian cities but was performed publicly in a variety of North German, Saxon, Bavarian, and South German cities.

Given the local and diverse ways Germany censored moral topics in the theater, it is difficult to compare German censorship with that of other nations—to decide, in other words, whether German censors were more or less "prudish" than their counterparts elsewhere. One of the few ways to determine this is to compare how a particular drama was handled in different nations, especially in more cosmopolitan European metropolises. In those rare cases where direct comparisons are possible, the evidence is ambiguous.

In some cases, the empire appears more conservative than its neighbors, especially with more popular entertainment pieces. Hennequin's musical comedy *Niniche* was banned both in England (1878) and Berlin (1879), but the English ban was lifted in 1883 while the work was not performed in Berlin until 1899. (However, this may be because no Berlin theater sought permission until then.) Garze's *Herr d'Albert* was banned in Berlin (1893) even though it had been performed in several Italian, Spanish, and South American cities, while Donnay's *Die Verliebten,* banned in Berlin from 1896 to 1898, was permitted in Vienna. Regarding more serious literature, Tolstoy's *Macht der Finsternis* was allowed in Vienna after 1899 but banned briefly in Berlin and some other German cities until 1901. (Performances were not permitted in Russian until 1905). Schnitzler's *Reigen* was never performed publicly in Germany or Austria before 1918 but was permitted in Hungary in 1912 and Russia in 1917, while Walter Hasenclever's *Der Sohn* (*The Son*) was permitted in Vienna in January 1917, a full year before it could be performed publicly in Germany.

On the other hand, with some important literary works Germany proved more tolerant than its neighbors. Vienna censors approved Sudermann's *Sodoms Ende* in 1891 only because it had already been allowed in Berlin; although Halbe's

Jugend (*Youth*) was being performed in Berlin and Hamburg after 1893, it was banned in Vienna until 1901; and Berlin censors approved Sternheim's *Die Hose* two years earlier than censors in Vienna (1911 vs. 1913) and Schnitzler's *Professor Bernhardi* six years earlier (forbidden in Vienna from October 1912 to December 1918, but performed in Berlin in November 1912). Perhaps more significantly, Ibsen's *Gespenster* was approved in Berlin in 1894 (even earlier in some German cities), but was not performed publicly in England until 1914. Likewise, Berlin, Hamburg, and a few other cities allowed public performances of Wedekind's *Frühlings Erwachen* after 1906 (and Munich after 1908); no public performances took place in England until 1913. Similarly, Wilde's notorious *Salome* was performed in Germany in 1901 and Maeterlinck's *Monna Vanna* played on German stages (except Munich), but both were forbidden by the English censor. Based on such fragmentary and conflicting data, prewar Berlin authorities appear neither significantly more nor less puritanical than those in other European capitals. While the empire initially mounted much resistance against some of the more controversial dramas of the time, thanks largely to the courts that resistance often yielded earlier in Germany than it did elsewhere.

Comparing German to English theater censorship around the turn of the century, one German observer warned against assuming the English censor was more liberal and tolerant. "Theater censorship in England operates essentially on the same principles as in Prussia," Konstantin von Zedlitz noted; "however, it is considerably more arbitrary, for its decisions cannot be appealed." Citing several recent examples, he argued much of the repertoire of Berlin's leading theaters would be unthinkable on the prudish, conservative London stage and English directors wouldn't dare submit them for licensing:

> If the Berlin and London censors were to exchange places for a year, the former would, on the whole, scarcely reject a single one of the pieces submitted to him [in London], while the latter, in Berlin, would surely disallow two or three times as many as happens now. As much as theater censorship on the continent may be in need of reform, to copy the English situation would be, in this and many other cases, a *reformatio in pejus* [change for the worse].[125]

That was also the view of the *New York Times*, which reported in 1908, "The moral aspects of any work of art are apt to be judged much more leniently in Germany than in England and America." Certain topics that would offend good taste on the English-speaking stage are taken in Germany as a matter of course, the sanguine correspondent claimed. "'The play's the thing'—its outline, rather than its content, is the chief consideration and if it satisfies as a work of art, the crassest exposition of moral situations is quite calmly accepted."[126] While Frank Wedekind would have found this last assertion laughable, in the years before the war German courts had obliged censors to focus more on a drama's gist than on its offensive content or passages, and police there were more willing than in England to negotiate compromises.

Morals, Morale, and the Military

This all changed dramatically in 1914. As soon as military authorities assumed control of theater censorship, "the seriousness of the times" meant censors would no longer approve performances that lacked a sufficiently demure or sedate tone. Local authorities quickly banned numerous operettas, musical comedies, farces, and similar works that had been routinely permitted before the war but were now considered too "burlesque," "bawdy," or simply "not serious enough." For example *Angele*, O. E. Hartleben's popular erotic comedy about a fickle woman's selfish pursuit of love, had been approved by Berlin censors in 1905, yet when another theater sought permission for it in 1915, police refused because it was considered too risqué for wartime.[127] Similarly, although Carl Sternheim's *Die Hose* (under the title *Der Riese*) had been allowed in Berlin since February 1911, military authorities forbade it in November 1915. The percentage of new dramas approved fell sharply. Before 1914 Berlin police banned about fifteen new dramas each year; during the war this rose to over fifty per year, with sixty-five being rejected in 1916 alone.

District military commanders, mindful of First General Quartermaster Erich Ludendorff's concern that theaters must be closely watched because they can have an even greater effect than the press upon the public's attitude toward the war,[128] often banned works civilian censors were inclined to permit. Berlin police, for example, approved Sternheim's comedy *Zwischen den Schlachten* (*Between Battles*; also known as *Der Scharmante* [*The Charmer*]) in February 1915 with only minimal changes, but after the first few performances military authorities suddenly banned it.[129] When Hermann Essig's *Ihr stilles Glück* (*Her Quiet Happiness*) came before the chief Berlin police censor, Glasenapp, in 1917, he had reservations about this "dismal, at times sordid love story" set among poor workers, but saw its literary value. He persuaded the theater to drop the more offensive scenes and recommended it for public performance, but the district military commander nevertheless banned it because its objectionable content would offend public tastes.[130]

As Karl Schönherr's *Die Weibsteufel* (*The Devil Woman*) illustrates, during the war private moral entrepreneurs exerted strong pressure on military commanders to intervene against lax civilian censors. While some commanders readily yielded, others stood behind the local censor's decisions. Schönherr's drama, about a mountain couple who make their living from smuggling, explores the destructive resentments unsatisfied passions can create. The husband compels his wife to befriend a new border guard in order to spy on him, while the guard tries to seduce the wife to extract information about her husband. She ruthlessly plays the two men off against each other, persuading the guard to murder the husband and then abandoning him to face the consequences alone. This drama was performed in both Vienna and Berlin in early 1915 without difficulties. In late 1915, public performances of the popular piece were planned across the country, but strong public outcries from religious groups and morality leagues put enormous pressure on civilian and military authorities to prevent the performances. The Catholic newspaper in Mainz persuaded the area's military commander to ban the work "in order to preserve the civil peace" (October 1915). Because of pressure by the Bishopric of Munich on the government, in November Munich's police director ruled, "From the standpoint of public order and morality, there would be no objection to the public performance [of *Weibsteufel*]. However, since the work has encountered significant opposition from many circles and a performance in our city would generate such unease (*Beunruhigung*) and annoyance (*Ärgernis*) among wide circles of the populace that the civil peace would be endangered, police permission for the piece must be postponed until after the end of the current war."[131]

Although the play was approved in Nuremberg, after the first performance protests by local Catholic clergy convinced the city theater to drop it (December 1915); in Leipzig, complaints by the Bonn Morality League caused the theater to cancel its approved performance too. Although banned in Essen, Saarbrücken, Aschaffensburg, Cologne, and Dortmund, *Die Weibsteufel* was performed in over a dozen other towns and cities, although not without local protests. Complaints by the League for the Suppression of Public Immorality in Cologne persuaded the military commander to ban it there, but when authorities in Hamburg and Bremen forbade the play because of protests by the Catholic Society, counterprotests by the Berlin Goethe League persuaded the district military commander to reverse the ban—provided the content of the play was not discussed in the press (December 1915 and January 1916). Amidst this swirling controversy and after concerns voiced by the Prussian General Synod, the military commander for the Berlin district asked the chief Berlin theater censor, Glasenapp, to explain why he had originally approved the play. He responded that no concerns had been raised about *Weibsteufel* when it was submitted in Berlin, and in his opinion the uproar was a personal vendetta against Schönherr by Catholics offended by his earlier piece *Glaube und Heimat* (see chapter 5). The controversy would soon pass, Glasenapp believed, but in the meantime it simply increased public interest in the play and boosted attendance. The commander accepted his assessment and permitted performances to continue in Berlin; by January 1916, it had been performed 150 times there. Whenever other cities inquired about how Berlin was handling this controversial play, they were told neither the police nor military authorities there had the slightest reservations about it.[132]

The playwright most frequently censored during the war was the controversial Expressionist Carl Sternheim, whose "From the Heroic Life of the Bourgeoisie" cycle satirized and critiqued Wilhelmine society. These plays followed three generations of the brutally egotistical, social-climbing Maske family as it clawed its way up from the petite bourgeoisie to the capitalistic upper bourgeoisie, and finally into the nobility. During the war Sternheim saw seven of his dramas forbidden by censors, mostly by the military authorities. Sometimes moral concerns were cited, sometime no reason was given, but it is clear the real basis for the bans was his unflattering portrayal of leading sectors of German society. To make matters worse, because of a controversial 1910 essay in which he complained about the "aesthetic crudeness" of Germany and expressed his "sincere loathing of all Germanness," followed by his decision to live in Belgium and contribute to the left-wing journal *Die Aktion,* Sternheim had a reputation as being unpatriotic and un-German; before the war and during its early months he was the subject of several hostile press attacks.

In December 1914, at the recommendation of police, the district military commander for Berlin banned Sternheim's *Das leidende Weib* (*The Suffering Wife*), "because [at this time] it is likely to violate the legitimate feelings of the public and thereby endanger public order." It dealt with a love triangle between a young military officer, an ambassador's wife, and a jealous count, and ends with her suicide and his seeking death in battle. Police noted it was probably the first time an eminent author had chosen the current war as a subject, but they were unhappy that author was Sternheim, "whose un-German attitude has been sufficiently documented." The censor disliked the crude portrayal of German peasants, the officer's request not to be sent to the front (because of his love for a woman), and the way the scheming count was portrayed as being able to influence military assignments. At a time "when the unity of the nation in thought and will should be stressed," he feared the play would be divisive and argued "the literary work one wants to see onstage in our great times requires other characters than Sternheim draws, and other ideas than he expresses."[133]

Der Snob (*The Snob*), the second work in the "Heroic Life" cycle, had passed Berlin censors in February 1914, and his *Zwischen den Schlachten* was approved shortly after the war began. The district military commander, aware of criticism of the plays in the conservative press, asked the Berlin police censor whether these works were fit for wartime. Police pointed out one could not ban Sternheim's works because of his personality or political reputation and argued that *Zwischen den Schlachten* was fundamentally a moral, antiadultery work that had been distorted in the press. At the same time, they agreed Sternheim's "untrue, distorted image of leading circles of the German people, whom he considers 'snobs,' has been offensive ever since [*Der Snob*] opened."[134] Although the theater performing *Der Snob* dropped it from the 1915 season (how voluntarily is not clear), in February 1915 the commander formally banned it from the Berlin military district and the next month did the same with *Zwischen den Schlachten*.[135] In November 1915 *Die Hose*—approved for Berlin in 1911—was also banned by the military commander.

Sternheim's *1913,* the third play in the "Heroic Life" cycle, was submitted for censorship in 1915. Set on the eve of the war, it painted an unflattering picture of the nobility, heavy industry, and arms trade and depicted a sexually emancipated daughter and shallow playboy son of the Maske family. The Berlin censor worried that Sternheim's scorn for the social circles he depicts would have the destructive effect of sharpening social conflicts: "In a piece that tries to depict Germany right before the war, just now it should be totally unacceptable to portray certain sectors of the populace—who have all done their duty in the war—as unscrupulous and egotistical, and thus as antinational (*volksfeindlich*), or as decadent. That would be an attack upon members of our nation that must absolutely be avoided during this time of civil peace."[136] This was enough to persuade the district military commander to ban the work because its "performance at the present time is likely to disturb the inner peace."[137] Soon thereafter the Berlin censor also banned Sternheim's *Der Kandidat* (*The Candidate*), which dealt with an ambitious candidate for the Reichstag who is courted by three different political party leaders for their own selfish personal reasons and who is ultimately willing to give up his wife to one of them in order to win the election.

Of the eight Sternheim plays submitted for censorship in Berlin after the outbreak of the war, by early 1916 six had been banned (five after consultation with the military commander, one on the Berlin censor's authority alone), while a seventh had been "voluntarily" dropped by the theater. Only his *Bürger Schippel* (*Citizen Schippel*) was permitted in public theaters. Yet that was not the end of Sternheim's problems. When his story *Ulricke. Eine Erzählung* (*Ulricke: A Story*) was published in April 1918, police confiscated it and charged Sternheim with obscenity, making him the last prominent German author to run afoul of the obscenity laws of the empire. Not until early 1919, after the empire had ceased to exist, was the book released and charges against Sternheim dropped.[138]

Notes

1. Pascal, *Naturalism to Expressionism,* 229.
2. Horst Fritz, "Die Dämonisierung des Erotischen in der Literatur des Fin de siècle," in *Fin-de-siècle. Zur Literatur und Kunst der Jahrhundertwende,* ed. Roger Bauer et al. (Frankfurt, 1977), 442–64.
3. Lange, *Das Wesen der Kunst* (1901), quoted in Iwan Bloch, *Das Sexualleben unserer Zeit in seinen Beziehungen zur modernen Kultur,* 2. Aufl. (Berlin, 1907), 804; Pascal, *Naturalism to Expressionism,* 251, 253.
4. *KK,* 189, 190.
5. Nicolaus Hatzipetros, *Begriff der unzüchtigen Schrift und ihrer Verbreitung (Str. G. B. §184)* (Diss. U. Göttingen, 1896), 5.
6. RG decisions of 15 Dec. 1879, 14 Feb. 1893, and 22 Mar. 1895; Olshausen, *Kommentar zum Strafgesetzbuch,* 1: 723.
7. Olshausen, *Kommentar zum Strafgesetzbuch,* 1: 723.
8. This definition was established by a RG decision of 15 Dec. 1879 and upheld in decisions of 16 Feb. 1881 and 19 Feb. 1893. (ibid., 1:719.)
9. After 1868 the "Hicklin rule" became the standard legal test for obscenity in Britain and the US. It declared: "The test of obscenity is … whether the tendency of the matter charged as obscenity is to deprave and corrupt those whose minds are open to such immoral influences, and into whose hands a publication of this sort may fall." Norman St.-John Stevas, *Obscenity and the Law* (London, 1956), 66–70.

10. RG decision of 22 Mar. 1895; also 19 Feb. 1883.

11. Frank, *Strafgesetzbuch*, 321; Rudolf Schauer, *Zum Begriff der unzüchtigen Schrift. Ein Beitrag zur Erläuterung des §184 R.St.G.B.* (Leipzig, 1893), 39–41; Hatzipetros, *Begriff der unzüchtigen*, 26.

12. RG decisions of 15 Jan. 1891, 6 Nov. 1893, and 10 Dec. 1897.

13. Hatzipetros, *Begriff der unzüchtigen*, 29.

14. RG decision of 22 Mar. 1895; Schauer, *Zum Begriff der unzüchtigen*, 36–37.

15. BPP to PrIM 1 Sept. 1882, GStA PK, Rep. 77, Tit. 380, Nr. 7, Bd. 3, Bl. 75ff; StAM/PDM, 3703 and 3733.

16. RG decision of 12/18. Oct. 1886, *Entscheidungen des Reichsgerichts in Strafsachen*, Bd. 14, 397.

17. StAM/PDM, 3703; BPP to PrIM, 22 Jul. 1899, GStA PK, Rep. 77, Tit. 380, Nr. 7, Bd. 5, Bl. 116ff.; and *Nationale Zeitung*, 6 Jul. 1899.

18. Schauer, *Zum Begriff der unzüchtigen*, 47–48.

19. Schauer, *Zum Begriff der unzüchtigen*, 38, 44–49; Olshausen, *Kommentar zum Strafgesetzbuch*, 1: 719–20.

20. See my "Pornography, Society, and the Law."

21. Munich PD to Bavarian IM, 16 Sept. 1891, quoted in Jelavich, *Munich and Theatrical Modernism*, 142.

22. Mast, *Künstleriche und wissenschaftlich Freiheit*, 140.

23. RG decision of 13 Jan. 1893; also 7/8 Dec. 1899.

24. See the characterizations of Naturalist/Realist literature in Max Nordau, *Entartung* (Berlin, 1892), passim; H. von Pilgrim, "Die Bühne und ihre Zukunft," *Das Magazin für die Literatur des In- und Auslandes* 3 (1887): 329, 340; Friedrich Kirchner, *Gründeutschland, ein Streifzug durch die jüngste deutsche Dichtung* (Vienna, 1893), 57ff; and comments in the Munich Catholic and anti-Semitic press quoted by Lenman, "Censorship and Society," 47.

25. Munich police report of 9 Oct. 1895, StAM/PDM 1110.

26. Paul Ssymank, "Leben Hermann Conradis," in: *Hermann Conradis Gesammelte Schriften*, ed. Paul Ssymank and G. W. Peters (Munich, 1911–1912), 1: ccx; and E. Wendelberger, "Das epische Werk Wilhelm Walloths. Ein Beitrag zur Geschichte des Frühnaturalismus" (Diss. typescript, U. Munich, 1953), 11.

27. Conrad Alberti [pseud. for Konrad Sittenfeld], ed., "Der Realismus vor Gericht. Nach dem stenographischen Bericht über die Verhandlungen am 23., 26., und 27. Juni 1890 vor der Strafkammer I des Königlichen Landgerichts zu Leipzig gegen Conrad Alberti, Hermann Conradi, Willi Walloth, und deren Verleger (§184 und §166 des Reichsstrafgesetzbuches)," *Die Gesellschaft* 6 (Aug. 1890): 1167.

28. W. Friedrich to M. G. Conrad, 17 Nov. 1889, cited in Manfred Hellge, *Der Verleger Wilhelm Friedrich und das "Magazin für die Literatur des In- und Auslandes." Ein Beitrag zur Literatur- und Verlagsgeschichte des frühen Naturalismus in Deutschland* (Sonderausgabe aus dem *Archiv für Geschichte des Buchwesens*, Bd. 16, Lieferung 4; Frankfurt, 1976), 1153–54; and Wendelberger, "Epische Werke," 11.

29. *VL*, 1: 12, 106–7; Alberti, "Realismus vor Gericht," 1143–47.

30. Alberti, *Was erwartet die deutsche Kunst?* especially 9–10. This manifesto was published by Wilhelm Friedrich.

31. Alberti, "Realismus vor Gericht," 1151–52, 1220–21, 1229; *VL*, 1: 11; Alberti, "Die vernagelte Litteratur," *Die Gesellschaft* 6 (Aug. 1890): 1137. (The prosecutor's name was Nagel.)

32. Alberti, "Realismus vor Gericht," 1153; also 1151, 1197–200; *VL*, 1: 13.

33. Alberti, "Realismus vor Gericht," 1167, 1180–81, 1156, 1193.

34. Ibid., 1220, 1181; Schulz, "Naturalismus und Zensur," 100.

35. Alberti, "Realismus vor Gericht," 1181–82.

36. Ibid., 1151–52, 1180–83, 1197–200; *VL*, 1: 13.

37. *VL*, 1: 13.

38. Schlesinger, "Das jüngste Deutschland vor Gericht," 157.

39. Alberti, "Realismus vor Gericht," 1181–82.

40. Ibid., 1181–82, 1190.

41. Ibid., especially 1141ff., 1156ff., 1201ff.; *VL*, 1: 10–13, 106; Schulz, "Naturalismus und Zensur," 96–102; Ssymank, "Leben Conradis," cxxi; Wolfgang Heine, "Das Leipziger Autodafé. Unjuristische Gloßen eines Juristen," *Moderne Dichtung* 1 (1890): 565; and Peter de Mendelssohn, *S. Fischer und Sein Verlag* (Frankfurt, 1970), 61. J. Schabelitz of Zurich, who had issued several daring avantgarde works for Munich writers in the past, refused to publish Frank Wedekind's *Frühlings Erwachen* in 1891 because his legal advisor feared that "in Germany, one could get at least two years prison for it." Quoted in Kutscher, *Wedekind*, 1: 234.

42. Paul Ernst, *Jünglingsjahre* (Munich, 1931), 225–26; Karl A. Kutzbach, "Paul Ernst, Frühste dichterischen Arbeiten," *Der Wille zur Form* 7 (Oct. 1961), citing *Berliner Volks-Tribüne* 5 (1891), no. 17, 268–70; Scherer, *Bürgerliche-oppositionelle Literaten*, 84.

43. *VL*, 1: 42; RG decision of 13 Jan. 1893, in *KK*, 129.

44. *KK*, 129–30; also *VL*, 1: 43ff.

45. *VL*, 1: 43ff.

46. Siegmund Feldman, "Die Dirne Elisa," *Freie Bühne* 2, Heft 3 (1891): 68–70; "Beschluß in der Strafsache wider den Schriftsteller Otto Brahm und den Redakteur Wilhelm Bölsche wegen Vergehens gegen Par. 184 des Strafgesetzbuches," *Freie Bühne* 2 (1891): 129–30.

47. "Kunst und Polizei," *Das Magazin für die Literatur des In- und Auslandes* 61, no. 50 (10 Dec. 1892): 817; Paul Schettler, "Heinz Tovote," *Die Gesellschaft* (Mar. 1893): 293.

48. *Moderne Blätter* 1, no. 23 (5 Sept. 1891): 7–8; Jelavich, *Munich and Theatrical Modernism*, 37; Lenman, "Censorship and Society," 43; Bauer, *Oskar Panizza*, 129; Brown, *Panizza*, 26. The five contributors were Croissant-Rust, Otto Julius Bierbaum, Ludwig Scharf, Julius Schaumberger, Oskar Panizza, and Michal Georg Conrad.

49. *KK*, 150–51; StAM/PDM, 1110. Between December 1901 and January 1904, for example, police referred fifteen different issues of *Simplicissimus* to the prosecutor, who acted on only two.

50. Verdict of Munich Schwurgericht, June 1903, *KK*, 167–70.

51. *KK*, 142–50; Allen, *Satire and Society*, 159; StAM/PDM, 1100; L. Thoma to A. Langen, 16 Dec. 1900, Ludwig Thoma, *Ausgewählte Briefe*, ed. Josef Hofmiller and Michael Hochgesang (Munich, 1927), 15.

52. Börries von Münchhausen, "Dalldorfer Lyric," *Die Gegenwart* 25 (18 Jun. 1898): 393–94.

53. *Berliner Tageblatt*, 11 Jul. 1899.

54. Anklageschrift des Staatsanwalts, Landgericht Berlin, 27 Jul. 1899, in Staats- und Universitätsbibliothek Hamburg, Dehmel Archiv; *VL*, 1: 123ff.

55. Heine, serving his sentence for lèse majesté for the "Palestine Issue," was released temporarily to travel to a nearby city court so he could file an affidavit in this case. He wondered if his indictment in the Schuster & Löffler trial was concocted by the Berlin prosecutor simply to sabotage any possibility of a pardon and parole. See Heine to K. Holm, 13 Jul 1899, in StBM, Heine Nachlaß.

56. Beschluß des Landgericht I Berlin, 7 Sept. 1899, Staats- und Universitätsbibliothek Hamburg, Dehmel Archiv.

57. *Münchener Neueste Nachrichten*, 22 Mar. 1900; *VL*, 1: 123–27.

58. Landgericht I Berlin verdict of 22 Mar. 1900, Staats- und Universitätsbibliothek Hamburg, Dehmel Archiv; partially reprinted in *VL*, 1: 128, and "Kunstpolizei," *Die Gesellschaft* 16, Bd. 1, Heft 2 (1900): 129.

59. Kutscher, *Wedekind*, 1: 391–92; Wedekind, *Gesammelte Briefe*, 2: 362 n. 104; *KK*, 267. A full account of the first court verdict was published in *Die Fackel* 7 (9 Jun. 1905).

60. Wedekind's foreword to 1906 edition of *Büchse der Pandora*, quoted in Breuer, *Geschichte der literarischen Zensur*, 202.

61. Staatsanwalt to Munich PD 29 Apr. 1906 and court decision of 15 Feb. 1906, StAM/PDM 4590; Meyer, *Theaterzensur in München*, 227–28.

62. de Mendelssohn, *S. Fischer,* 437–38 and "Zur Geschichte des *Reigen.* Aus dem Briefwechsel zwischen Arthur Schnitzler und S. Fischer," *Almanach. Das sechsundsiebzigste Jahr* (Frankfurt, 1967): 18–35. While he dared not issue a public edition of *Reigen,* Fischer, as a favor to Schnitzler, printed two hundred copies of a private edition in 1899 that were designated as "Printed as a Manuscript, Not for Sale" and which Schnitzler distributed privately to friends.

63. StAM/PDM 4598; Kurt Riess, *Erotica! Erotica! Das Buch der verbotenen Bücher* (Hamburg, 1967), 422; Breuer, *Geschichte der literarischen Zensur,* 221. Gerd K. Schneider, *Die Rezeption von Arthur Schnitzlers Reigen 1897–1994* (Riverside, CA, 1995), 39–40 gives a different figure of thirty-five thousand copies printed. The Wiener Verlag's appeal of the ban to the Imperial Supreme Court was rejected.

64. *KK,* 189–90.

65. For an intelligent discussion of the poem see Gerhardt E. Steinke, *The Life and Work of Hugo Ball: Founder of Dadaism* (The Hague, 1967), 74–82.

66. Staatsanwalt to Bavarian JM, 28 Oct. 1913, BHStA, MJu 17 402; *Die Revolution,* no. 3 (15 Nov. 1913).

67. Report of Staatsanwalt, 3 Dec. 1913, in BHStA, MJu 17 402; also partially reprinted in Lenman, "Censorship and Society," 201.

68. Urteil of I. Strafkammer, 17 Dec. 1913, StAM/SA 1735; partially reprinted in *KK,* 234.

69. RG decision of 6 Apr. 1914, in BHStA, MJu 17 402; StAM/SA 1735; reprinted in *KK,* 235; report of Munich PD to Bavarian IM, 24 Apr. 1914, BHStA, MA 92 811.

70. "Tagebuch des jungen Flaubert," *Pan* 1, nos. 6 and 7 (16 Jan. and 1 Feb. 1911); Alfred Kerr, "Jagow, Flaubert, *Pan,*" *Pan* 1, no. 7 (1 Feb. 1911): 217–223; Kerr, "Ballade von Alexanderplatz," *Pan* 1, no. 8 (16 Feb. 1911): 255–56; Kerr, "Vorletzter Brief an Jagow" and "Nachlese."

71. Eulenberg, "Brief eines Vaters unserer Zeit," *Pan* 1, no. 11 (1 Apr. 1911): 358–63; Eulenberg, "Ein Protest" and Herzog, "Der denunzierte Dichter," *Pan* 1, no. 12 (16 Apr. 1911): 393–95, 396–98; *Die Aktion,* 10 Apr. 1911; Fischer, "Der `Schutzverband'," 111–12.

72. Wilhelm Herzog, "Die unzüchtige No. 7," *Pan* 1, no. 18 (15 Jul. 1911): 587–90; letters and affidavits by Richard Dehmel, Gerhart Hauptmann, and Hugo von Hofmannsthal, ibid., 591–93; Kerr, "Freisprechung," *Pan* 2, no. 1 (1 Oct. 1911): 34.

73. Landgericht decision of 27 Nov. 1913, discussed in RG decision of 15 Apr. 1914, partially reprinted in *KK,* 237–38; and *Berliner Tageblatt,* 27 Nov. 1913, reprinted in Klabund, *Briefe an einen Freund,* ed. Ernst Heinrich (Cologne, 1963), 146ff. For Kerr's statement to the court, see Kerr, "Den Richtern," *Pan* 3, no. 31 (23. Dec. 1913): 715–25.

74. RG decision of 15 Apr. 1914, in *KK,* 238, *Berliner Tageblatt,* 15 May 1914, and Klabund, *Briefe,* 147ff.

75. *Berliner Tageblatt,* 20 Aug. 1914 and 14 Jan. 1915; Klabund, *Briefe,* 148–49.

76. Meyer, *Theaterzensur in München,* 154.

77. Augier's *Les Fourchambaults* was banned in Stettin 1878; Ibsen's *Gespenster* was banned in Berlin, Breslau, and Stettin, 1887–1894; Hauptmann's *Vor Sonnenaufgang* was approved in Berlin with cuts, 1889; Hartleben's *Angele* was banned in Berlin 1915; Schnitzler's *Reigen* was banned in Munich 1903; Schönherr's *Der Weibsteufel* was banned in Munich 1915–1918; Sternheim's *Die Hose* was banned in Berlin and Munich, 1911–1912, and six other of his works were banned during the war; Tolstoy's *Macht der Finsternis* was banned in several cities 1892–1901; and Wedekind's *Frühlings Erwachen* and six other plays of his were banned in numerous cities at various times.

78. Quoted in *VL,* 1: 582–83 and Wilcke, *Das Lessingtheater,* 59–60.

79. Blumenthal, *Verbotene Stücke,* 16–17.

80. The Lessing Theater had been rehearsing the piece for two weeks, arranged for a guest appearance by the famous actor Joseph Kainz, already sold out the first three performances, and had no replacement for the work. Contrary to normal procedures the theater neglected to submit the script to police the customary two weeks in advance and supposedly discovered the over-

sight shortly before opening night. See Blumenthal, *Verbotene Stücke,* 16, and Wilcke, *Das Lessingtheater,* 60–61.

81. Blumenthal, *Verbotene Stücke,* 22, also quoted in Wilcke, *Das Lessingtheater,* 62.
82. PP to Blumenthal 27 Oct. 1890, in Blumenthal, *Verbotene Stücke,* 31.
83. Ibid., 31–33; Wilcke, *Das Lessingtheater,* 63.
84. Civil Cabinet to IM, 1 Dec. 1890, GStA PK/1000, Nr. 4, Bd. 1, Bl 263ff.
85. IM to Kaiser, 6 Dec. 1890, Ibid., Bl 268ff. Also Margaret Mieruch, "Die Stellung der Berliner Theaterzensur zu den deutschen Naturalisten" (Maschineschriftliche Hausarbeit zur Magisterprüfung, F.U. Berlin, c. 1975), 78.
86. Kaiser to IM 10 Dec. 1890, GStA PK/1000, Nr. 4, Bd. 1, Bl 274.
87. Blumenthal, *Verbotene Stücke,* 35.
88. Memo of Vienna PP, 27 Dec. 1890 and comments of Stadthalter, quoted in Glossy, *Vierzig Jahre Deutsches Volkstheater,* 80–81.
89. *VL,* 1: 587ff.
90. Wedel (Minister of Royal House) to Kaiser, 30 Jun. 1894, GStA PK/ZK, 2.2.1. Civil Cabinett, Nr. 21013, Bl. 54–55; Wilhlem II to Wedel, 19 Jul. 1894, Bl. 56.
91. LAB C/A, "Die Schlange," "Geteilte Liebe," "Wem Gehört Helene?"; *VL,* 1: 204.
92. Hauptmann, *Annalen von Jahr 1889,* quoted in Hans von Brescius, *Gerhart Hauptmann. Zeitgescheheen und Bewußtsein in unbekannten Selbstzeugnissen. Eine politisch-biographische Studie,* 2. Aufl. (Bonn, 1977), 25.
93. LAB C/A, Nr. V.309; Bochnik, "Das Belle-Alliance-Theater," 170–71; and Ackermann, *Die Zeitgenössische Kritik,* 20.
94. "Kunst und Polizei," 817; LAB C/A. "Associés;" Hirschmann, *Berliner Residenztheater,* 74. The IM's changes included dropping an obscene song, removing certain gestures by actors, and removing a bed from one of the scenes.
95. Albert Soergel and Curt Hohoff, *Dichtung und Dichter der Zeit. Vom Naturalismus bis zur Gegenwart* (Düsseldorf, 1961), 1: 656, 665.
96. LAB C/A, Nr. 3708; Wedekind to F. Basil, 21 Jan. 1907, in Wedekind, *Gesammelte Briefe,* 2: 171; Kutscher, *Wedekind,* 1: 258; and Lenman, "Censorship and Society," 271–76. Wedekind claimed later he published *Frühlings Erwachen* in Switzerland because lawyers told him publishing it in Germany would bring two years' imprisonment for the author, publisher, and printer (*Werke,* 3: 351).
97. A private performance was allowed in Munich in 1898, and that year Berlin police also approved a special one-time public performance of the fifth act as part of a Tolstoy Festival. LAB C/A, and E. Pechstedt, "L. N. Tolstojs Drama 'Macht der Finsternis' und die deutsche Theaterzensur," *Zeitschrift für Slawistik* 13, no. 4 (1968): 560; and Meyer, *Theaterzensur in München,* 13.
98. Pechstedt, "Macht der Finsternis," 560, citing from LAB A/74, Nr. 3867.
99. Brandenburg OP to IM, 24 Sept. 1900, GStA PK/1000, Nr. 7, Bd. 2, Bl 249; and Pechstedt, "Macht der Finsternis," 562–63.
100. Reinhardt to PP 13 Feb. 1911, quoted in Karl Deiritz, *Geschichtsbewußtsein, Satire, Zensur. Eine Studie zur Carl Sternheim* (Königstein, 1979), 169.
101. Sternheim wrote to the PD on 7 Mar. 1912 he was submitting a revised text in which "above all, and with the greatest care, every word and gesture that might somehow offend the public's delicate feelings have been rooted out, often to the point of endangering that the sense of the piece will still be understandable." Quoted in Manfred Linke, *Carl Sternheim in Selbstzeugnissen und Bilddokumenten* (Reinbeck bei Hamburg, 1979), 69 and Deiritz, *Geschichtsbewußtsein, Satire, Zensur,* 167. Linke believes the letter was meant ironically. In any case, it did not persuade Munich police to remove the ban.
102. LAB C/A; LAB A/74, Th 668; Wilcke, *Das Lessingtheater,* 71; Blumenthal, *Verbotene Stücke,* 52–57. Quote from OVG decision of 13 Jan. 1897.
103. StAM/PDM 4590; Lenman, "Censorship and Society," 284; Meyer, *Theaterzensur in München,*

212–23; and Kutscher, *Wedekind*, 3: 55, 238. Although banned from public performance, a private performance was held in Nuremberg in 1905.

104. Preface to third edition, 1906, in Wedekind, *Werke*, 3: 346; Kutscher, *Wedekind*, 1: 395; Wedekind to director of Deutsches Theater, 17 Jun. 1907, *Gesammelte Briefe*, 2: 180.
105. Wedekind to Leopold Jeßner, 30 Sept. 1910, *Gesammelte Briefe*, 2: 248.
106. Meyer, *Theaterzensur in München*, 188–90.
107. Meyer, *Theaterzensur in München*, 273, citing Munich police memo 25 May 1913.
108. Letter to PD, 17 May 1913, quoted in Meyer, *Theaterzensur in München*, 286; Lenman, "Censorship and Society," 301–3.
109. Meyer, *Theaterzensur in München*, 271–98.
110. LAB A/74 Th 317, which contains reports from the Munich PD, Medizin Rat Schlegtendahl, criminal inspector Behr and Karl Brunner of the Zentralpolizeistelle, and Prof. Roethe. On the Munich bans see Lenman, "Censorship and Society," 285–86 and Meyer, *Theaterzensur in München*, 224–50.
111. OVG decision of 8 May 1893, GStA PK, Rep. 184, Pl. Nr. 1622.
112. OVG decision of 29 Sept. 1900, LAB A/74, Th 671.
113. OVG decision of 28 Feb. 1912, found in LAB A/74, Th 112; also Meyer, *Theaterzensur in München*, 187, 341; and Kutscher, *Wedekind*, 1: 258.
114. Berlin PP to OP, 6 Aug. 1895, and OVG decision of 27 Feb. 1896, LAB A/74, Th 595.
115. Saxon OVG decision of 16 Mar. 1901, in LAB A/74, Th 112. The RP of Schleswig-Holstein lifted a Kiel police ban of the work for the same reason. Pechstedt, "Tolstojs Drama," 563; *Vossische Zeitung*, 19 Apr. 1901.
116. OVG decision of 3 Mar. 1913 regarding *Peter Fehrs' Modelle*, GStA PK, Rep. 184 Pl. Nr. 1622.
117. 1891 Berlin ban of Hans von Reinfels' *Die Sitte* (*Morality*); 1894 Berlin ban of H. L. Wagner and M. Halperin's *Die Kindermörderin* (*The Child Murderer*); 1895 Berlin ban of M. Braun, *Die Puppengräfin* (*The Puppet Countess*); 1896 Berlin ban of Maurice Donnay's *Die Verliebten* (*The Beloved*); 1900 Berlin ban of Julius Gans-Ludassy's *Der Letzte Kopf* (*The Last Head*); 1902 Berlin ban of Max Dreyer's *Das Tal des Lebens* (*Valley of Life*), which was also banned by Munich in 1903, also appealed, and also upheld by the Bavarian IM; and Danzig's 1911 ban of Johannes Tralow's *Peter Fehr's Modelle*. The ban reinstated was of Franz Dülber's *Die Korallenkettlin* (*The Coral Necklace*).
118. OVG decision 11 Jan. 1901 regarding *Ausflug ins Sittliche*, LAB A/74, Th 112; and Max Reinhardt, quoted in Robert J. Goldstein, *The War for Public Mind: Political Censorship in Nineteenth-Century Europe* (Westport, CT, 2000), 11.
119. BPP to PrIM 11 Dec. 1889, cited in Hirschmann, *Berliner Residenztheater*, 72.
120. BZA decision 5 Mar. 1895, and BPP to BZA 11 Jan. 1895, LAB A/74, Th 593; BPP to OP, 6 Aug. 1895, ibid., Th 595.
121. LAB C/A, Nr. H.467; BPP to IM, 22 Apr. 1893, GStA PK/1000, Nr. 4, Bd. 2, Bl 8ff.
122. OVG decision of 2 May 1892; also *Neue Preußische Zeitung*, no. 11, 8 Jan. 1892.
123. Lothar Schmidt [Lothar Goldschmidt], "Polizei und Bühne," *Die Aktion* (Berlin) 1. Jg., no. 38 (6 Nov. 1911): 1187–90.
124. For example, although Berlin permitted these works, the following cities chose to ban them: *Les Fourchambaults*, banned in Stettin, 1878; *Sodoms Ende*, banned in Kassel and Braunschweig, 1891–92; *Frühlings Erwachen*, banned in Königsberg, 1910; *Die Schiffbrüchigen* (*The Shipwrecked*), banned in Wiesbaden, 1913. And although Berlin had passed them, Munich nevertheless banned *Sodoms Ende*, *Frühlings Erwachen* (1907), and *Die Hose* (1911).
125. Konstantin von Zedlitz, "Die Theaterzensur in England," *Die Zeit. Wiener Wochenschrift für Politik, Volkswirtschaft, Wissenschaft, und Kunst* 34, no. 443 (28 Mar. 1903): 153–54.
126. "Owing to the Complex Rules."
127. *VL*, 2: 269–70.
128. Ludendorff to Berlin police, 19 May 1917, quoted in *VL*, 2: 514–15.

129. LAB C/A, Nr. 6140.

130. Glasenapp to OK 22 Aug. 1917, and OK to BPP 2 Oct. 1917, quoted in *VL*, 2: 76–78.

131. Munich PP letter of 15 Nov. 1915, StAM/PDM 4597; *VL*, 2: 530–33; Meyer, *Theaterzensur in München*, 140–52.

132. Glasenapp to OK in den Marken, 18 Nov. 1915, quoted in *VL*, 2: 532; Meyer, *Theaterzensur in München*, 140–52.

133. Quoted in Deiritz, *Geschichtsbewußtsein, Satire, Zensur*, 174–75.

134. LAB C/A, Nr. 5821; Deiritz, *Geschichtsbewußtsein, Satire, Zensur*, 170–71.

135. LAB C/A, Nr. 6140; OK to Berlin PP 5 Mar. 1915 and Glasenapp to OK 16 Mar. 1916, LAB A/74, Th 136.

136. Klotz to OK, 13 Dec. 1915, LAB A/74, Th 319, quoted in Deiritz, *Geschichtsbewußtsein, Satire, Zensur*, 172.

137. Glasenapp to OK 16 Feb. 1916, LAB A/74, Th 134.

138. Linke, *Sternheim in Selbstzeugnissen*, 158. Richard Dehmel on 12 Aug. 1918 wrote an expert opinion on Sternheim's behalf testifying to the nonobscene, literary nature of the work. (Staats- und Universitätsbibliothek Hamburg, Dehmel Nachlass.) Even later in the war—June 1918— police, on orders of the military commander, confiscated five hundred copies of Karl Otten's poetry anthology *Thronerhebung des Herzens* (*Coronation of the Heart*) and three hundred copies of his anthology *Scherz, Satire, Ironie und tiefe Bedeutung* (*Jokes, Satire, Ironie, and Deep Meaning*). No explanation was given, and the books were returned after the end of the war. (Breuer, *Geschichte der literarischen Zensur*, 217–18).

Chapter 7

THE CENSORED
Authors' Responses to Censorship

If the censor will not relent toward the spirit, then the spirit must seek to elude the censor.
—Karl Heinzen, *Mehr als Zwanzig Bogen* (1845). Quoted in Edda Ziegler,
Literarische Zensur in Deutschland 1819–1848. Materialien, Kommentare

*I*n Thomas Mann's short story of 1903 about the artist's problematic relation to bourgeois society, the aspiring young writer Tonio Kröger, after an absence of thirteen years, returns to his hometown for a brief visit. There he is confronted by a policeman who, suspecting Kröger to be a swindler wanted by the law, questions him about his identity and occupation. Kröger, although recognizing this guardian of civic order is acting within his rights, is nevertheless reluctant to reveal who he is. Unable to provide the requisite identity papers, he finally shows the policeman proof sheets of a story of his that is about to be published. The officer is not entirely convinced the young writer is not a wanted criminal, but in the end lets the matter drop and allows Kröger to leave the country. This unsettling confrontation with a representative of the German state drives home to Kröger his social isolation, his uneasy existence between two seemingly incompatible worlds: that of his bohemian artist friends, who regard him as a bourgeois, and that of the bourgeois, who try to arrest him. It also reinforces his longstanding aversion to his hometown and his eagerness to return to his self-imposed exile in the more hospitable south.

Tonio Kröger's situation is symbolic of that of many fin-de-siècle German writers. Many late nineteenth and early twentieth-century German literati shared three distinct but interrelated characteristics: an acute self-consciousness, a sense of alienation from bourgeois society, and an "unpolitical" withdrawal from the pressing social and political problems of the day. During the nineteenth century, but especially since Nietzsche, German writers became increasingly conscious of their existence as a distinct, semi-independent social group and were increasingly preoccupied with questions about the role of art in the modern world, the unique nature of the artistic calling, the artist's position and function in bourgeois society, and the artist's responsibilities to *Geist*. At the same time their intense concern with (and at times glorification of) the artist's special calling created in many writers a growing sense of separateness from the rest of society. Authors, particularly in the fin-de-siècle era, frequently were isolated and alienated from "normal" life; because of their artistic temperaments and special calling, many felt like outsiders who did not belong to bourgeois society. This sense of social isolation often resulted also in a conscious withdrawal from the real world, especially the world of power and politics. Perceiving the inner world of *Geist* rather than the external world as the authentic one, and regarding active involvement in social or political issues as incompatible with or even harmful to their "higher" artistic calling, German writers generally scorned political engagement. Many escaped from what they perceived as oppressive social or political conditions by retreating into the "unpolitical" realm of the spirit. But this unpolitical disdain for issues of power and politics had serious political consequences. Their "inner emigration" led many into resignation about the existence of social evil and political injustice; the result was widespread political fatalism concerning the possibility of sociopolitical change or silent acceptance of the status quo.

As the story of Tonio Kröger illustrates, external challenges, especially from authority, can play a significant role in the process by which individuals or groups clarify their self-image, define their social role, and choose their political responses, for such challenges often stimulate self-reflection. Mann's contemporary Hermann Hesse reached much the same conclusion: reflecting on the writer's calling shortly before World War I, Hesse observed that "the literati, exactly like every physician or judge or civil servant, are instructed and enlightened (*aufgeklärt*) about the essence and character of their vocation through the kinds of demands others make on them."[1]

Among the many external challenges faced by fin-de-siècle German writers, censorship was one of the most pervasive and potentially serious to their careers. Many who experienced it, especially those for whom it meant only the banning of one of their dramas from public performance, left little or no indication of how they responded or how that encounter affected them. But for others, especially the few whose works were confiscated and/or who were criminally prosecuted, the experience was a significant one they discussed in print or privately. Some authors responded to their censorship in simple and often predictable ways; others' reactions were more surprising and complex. We will look first at the more immediate, short-term, observable behavior of several authors who had to contend with the censor, then at how the experience of being challenged by censors affected a number of authors' more general views concerning their calling as writers, their relation to the imperial authorities, and their connection to German society.

Coping with the Censor

Censored authors coped with the experience of censorship by using many of the same recognizable strategies people generally adopt when they must contend with or respond to power. *Avoidance* of the censors was obviously one common—yet extremely hard to document—response. Many German authors, publishers, or theater directors may have chosen, either consciously or unconsciously, to exercise *self-censorship* by simply not writing about or publishing material or seeking to perform dramas that might arouse a censor's concern.

It is difficult, indeed impossible, to assess to what extent censorship had a "chilling effect" on the literary community in imperial Germany, since we cannot know what would have happened, what might have been written, had there been no censors. We know publishers were sometimes deterred from publishing a work because of fear of possible prosecution: at the Leipzig Realists' trial, for example, it was revealed that the Wilhelm Friedrich Verlag had refused to publish Hermann Conradi's earlier novel *Phrasen* (*Phrases*) until the author removed certain offensive material, and that Friedrich had also rejected the first draft of *Adam Mensch* after his firm's lawyer altered him to potential legal problems with the work, while in 1897 S. Fischer declined to publish Schnitzler's *Reigen* for the same reason.[2] Some authors (Wildenbruch, Bonn) whose historical dramas about the Hohenzollerns had been censored turned to other subjects instead, while the minor dramatist Jakob Scherek alleged that writers shied away from the topic of Jesus because of the blanket ban on depicting biblical figures.[3] Other writers, too, probably chose to avoid writing works they thought might bring them into conflict with authorities. Except for a statement by Carl Sternheim, however,[4] I have encountered no public or private remarks by writers in this period admitting or claiming they consciously made such choices, and if the choice was unconscious, we can know nothing about it. Since self-censorship leaves behind no evidence, we can only conjecture about its importance. On the other hand, there are several examples of German authors who, far from being deterred by censorship, were emboldened by it: after an initial encounter with the censor, Wilhelm Busch, Maximilian Harden, Ludwig Thoma, Alfred Kerr, Frank Wedekind, and most dramatically Oskar Panizza (see below) became more radically outspoken, even provocative, with their work.[5] In short, it is impossible to say to what extent authors of this period exercised self-censorship and one can easily overestimate the significance of any chilling effect on literary life. Certainly one scholar's claim that "self-censorship was not enough for the police of Wilhelmine Germany; they expected [authors'] self mutilation"[6] is pure hyperbole.

A few cautious men of letters chose *evasion*: anticipating or fearing a work might be censored, they published it anonymously, or under a pseudonym (O. E.

Hartleben and *Hanna Jagert;* Lt. Bilse), or abroad (Wedekind), or as a "private" manuscript (Schnitzler), or moved their editorial offices to where they were less legally vulnerable (*Simplicissimus*). Some had their dramas performed in private settings exempt from censorship, such as the Freie Bühne and Freie Volksbühne, while others cleverly coded, disguised, or distorted a work to make it more difficult to censor (Quidde's *Caligula;* Blumenthal's *Die tote Löwen;* Harden's *Pudel-Majestät*). Walter Hasenclever, in order to, as he admitted, "mislead the censor" about the pacifist message of his *Antigone* in 1917, consciously chose a classical Greek setting and cloaked it in Sophoclean style.[7] Writing in an indirect, subtle, heavily coded, allegorical, obscure, or equivocal style may well require, and yield, more imagination and literary and poetic skill than if it were done in a more direct, straightforward manner and may even involve inventing a new language. (Hugo Ball's strange language certainly baffled his prosecutor and the court.) Writing "between the lines" also requires readers to read between the lines.

Some authors and directors audaciously tried to hoodwink the censor. When Max Halperin's *Verkommen. Sittendrama in einem Aufzug* (*Depraved: Moral Drama in One Act*) was banned on moral grounds in October 1894, it was resubmitted two weeks later, with only minor changes, as *Kameraden* (*Comrades*), by "Norbert Hofmeister" (and banned again, for the same reason.)[8]

When censors did intervene to ban a work, especially a dramatic performance, the great majority of authors reacted with *submission* or *acquiescence,* simply accepting the prohibition or agreeing to changes or cuts the censor demanded. (Since the playwright actually played no formal legal role in the theater censorship process, it was normally the theater director who made such choices, although usually in consultation with the author of the banned work.) In one extreme case, the censored publisher Albert Langen professed *deference* and *repentance.* Desperate to return to Germany after four years self-imposed exile, Langen wrote a groveling amnesty petition to the Saxon government in which he: (1) denied any moral responsibility for the fateful "Palestine Issue" and placed the blame on others; (2) repudiated much of *Simplicissimus*'s biting political satire; (3) promised to be on his best behavior if allowed to return to Germany; and (4) promised to keep secret the circumstances of his pending amnesty and return.[9] In some cases authors and directors chose *accommodation,* working with the censor to revise or alter a script so it would be acceptable to authorities. Doing so, however, implied—certainly to the censors—an admission that the censor's initial assessment of the piece was justified, that the objectionable material to be removed was extraneous or gratuitous rather than essential to the piece. As a member of the Munich Censorship Advisory Board noted, "if, after the suppression of these passages, the piece [in this case, Sternheim's *Die Hose*] can still be performed, it will be proof the Royal Police Direction was completely right to eliminate them, since they are not an integral component of the [play's overall] effect."[10]

Rather than submitting to the censor's action, some authors, directors, and publishers chose *resistance,* which could take various forms. Many who were censored (as well as many other members of the literary community) publicly *protested,* in speech or writing, that particular censorship decision and/or the institution of censorship. Some (such as Sudermann, Halbe, Blumenthal, Dreyer, Hartleben, Hauptmann, Wildenbruch, Quidde, Schuster & Löffler, and J. Trojan) signed petitions or actively participated in organizations like the Goethe League or German Writers' Defense League to change or abolish censorship laws and procedures. Those under indictment often mounted a vigorous *legal defense,* sometimes using their public trials to draw attention to their situation and rally supporters and public opinion on their behalf. In the case of a prohibited drama, a confiscation, or a criminal conviction, many who were censored formally *appealed* the action through the administrative hierarchy or appropriate legal court. Such appeals, as we have seen, were often successful, especially in having theater bans reversed. One of the most radical (or desperate) forms of evasion or resistance chosen by a few who faced criminal charges was *flight* or *exit:* Panizza, Wedekind, and Langen all fled abroad to avoid arrest and punishment, although for each this provided but a temporary reprieve and probably resulted in heavier sentences for them later. Even Gerhart Hauptmann, fearing that passage of the reactionary Anti-Revolution Bill in the mid-1890s might lead to confiscation of his publications and his arrest, planned to escape to Switzerland if necessary.[11]

In addition to these fairly standard responses, many authors also *appropriated* censorship for their own uses. From the early Naturalists in the late 1880s to the Expressionists before and during World War I, many censored writers, as well as their publishers, recognized, appreciated, and capitalized on the notoriety and commercial benefits a ban of their works could bring, and a few even deliberately sought it.

The Leipzig Realists' trial, for example, revealed that both Alberti and Walloth were well aware that including titillating material in their novels could help market them to larger audiences. Walloth later noted in his memoirs that "scandals make the best advertisements" and that "nowadays authors can penetrate (*durchdringen*) [the market] only when they become involved in some scandalous political or sexual affair."[12] After the trial, Fritz Mauthner, an author and critic who was by no means unfavorably disposed toward Naturalism, accused both authors of using obscenity to cover up their lack of talent and of actually rejoicing when their works provoked a police ban, seeing this (mistakenly, in Mauthner's view) as a confirmation they were at the forefront of the literary vanguard.[13]

When the Munich Naturalists' journal *Moderne Blätter* and their anthology *Modernes Leben* were confiscated (but later released) in 1891 because of "obscene" pieces by Anna Croissant-Rust and others, at least two other authors commended her for the police's action; one wrote, "On what should I congratulate you now: on the police ban (*Verbot*), or on its being lifted (*Freigabe*)?" A gratified Julius Schaumberger, another *Modernes Leben* author whom police hoped to indict, wrote to a fellow anthology contributor: "With united effort we have brought it to the point where the police and courts are actively concerned with us."[14] They also knew how to capitalize on this situation. After the confiscation of *Moderne Blätter* was overturned in court, the journal attached large eye-catching orange stickers to front covers of that issue proclaiming *"Moderne Blätter* No. 22: Was confiscated but just released." When *Modernes Leben* was similarly freed two months later, its publisher subsequently increased sales by advertising the volume as having been the subject of a police action.[15]

Hermann Sudermann boasted of the sudden fame and commercial benefits the short-lived Berlin ban of *Sodoms Ende* brought him in 1890. When he first learned of it, he wrote his mother that "if anything were still lacking regarding my popularity, it is this brutal police decree." People had been coming up to him in the theater and on the street to congratulate him and express their envy; every day he received dozens of requests from theaters across Germany wanting to perform the banned work. "You can hardly imagine the excitement this ban has created in the theatrical world," he bragged; "in Vienna, Rome, and London they are writing newspaper editorials about it, American journalists come to interview me, and artists come to sketch my portrait." If the ban were not overturned, Sudermann believed he stood to make a tidy profit on the sale of the play's printed text.[16] Likewise, Hermann Bahr later recalled how his fame as an author grew after police confiscated *Fin de Siècle,* a book he admitted was rather cheeky and audaciously marketed (*"dreiste Erzählungen, frech boulevardierend"*).[17]

The renowned S. Fischer Verlag turned to its advantage the Berlin police's decision to ban Hartleben's *Hanna Jagert:* after the court later released it for the public stage, Fischer, in conjunction with the premier performance, issued a special printed edition (*Buchausgabe*) of the play, containing both the text of the original police ban and the court decision lifting it. The firm also published the texts of all the dramas performed by the uncensored Freie Bühne, covered them in bright red dust jackets with the prominent inscription "Accepted by the Freie Bühne," and placed them in every Berlin bookstore.[18] Similarly, after Richard Dehmel's *Aber die Liebe* was confiscated in June 1899, the book's publisher, the Schuster & Löffler Verlag, sent an advertising circular to German bookstores pointing out the volume in question stood under indictment and, depending on the outcome of the court trial, might soon be removed from circulation permanently; it urged bookdealers to immediately buy up all the publisher's remaining stock of the book while they still could, and to let their customers know these copies will be their last chance to procure the book.[19] Even foreign publishers sometimes used German censorship cases to market their wares: the New York publisher of an English translation of Bilse's *Aus einen kleinen Garnison* included on the title page the statement: "The Military Novel Suppressed by the German Government."[20]

The staff of *Simplicissimus* was especially adept at turning censorship to good account. After its first serious conflict with authorities over the "Palestine issue," the journal's editor noted the harsh sentences imposed on Wedekind, Langen, and Heine "resulted in our circulation rising within four or five weeks from fifteen thousand to, I think, eighty-five thousand. We were happy about this."[21] It was because of the "Palestine issue" that Wedekind first became widely known among the general public. After four issues of the journal were banned from the colportage trade in Bavaria, red stickers announcing "Banned from Colportage" were attached to these issues wherever they were still legally sold, and sales of those issues increased significantly. After the "Center Party" issue was confiscated, Conrad Haussmann, legal counsel for the journal, suggested to editor Ludwig Thoma that if the issue were not released soon, they should delete its offending passages, either by blacking them out or simply leaving empty white space instead: "That would heighten the moral impact of the confiscation to the advantage of the journal. ... But don't wait, if you act while the issue is still hot, you can print *twice* as many copies." He added that he would try to arouse as much interest in the upcoming trial as possible, in both Munich and Stuttgart. Indeed, on several occasions the journal's editors and lawyers used the their trials to generate maximum publicity—for example, reading the entire confiscated issue or offending parts into the court record so these could be published the next day in the courtroom reports of the city's newspapers.[22]

When Ludwig Fulda (whose own drama *Das Verlorene Paradies* was banned throughout the 1890s) learned Paul Heyse's *Maria von Magdala* had just been forbidden by the Berlin censor, he immediately told Heyse: "I can promise you now that as soon as this news becomes public, you will become enormously popular."[23] Theaters in Hamburg (where there was no censorship) regularly profited from such bans: in 1902–1903, they staged a number of controversial works (including Heyse's) that were forbidden in Berlin.[24] Even Tilla Durieux, the Berlin actress who was the cause of the "von Jagow scandal" arising from the ban of *Die Hose* in 1910, noted that although the whole controversy was embarrassing for her, it did help her career, for many more people now came to her performances simply out of curiosity.[25]

Expressionists were as adroit as Naturalists in finding silver linings when censored. When police in 1913 confiscated issues of the literary journals *Die Revolution* and *Pan* for allegedly obscene poems by Hugo Ball and Klabund, both poets saw the incident as an opportunity for self-promotion and a way to gain greater public recognition for their work. Klabund tried to have some of his other poems published quickly, arguing "It could be good business, especially if the poems were to come out right at the time of the trial." Although the trial of *Pan* editor Alfred Kerr was separate from his own, Klabund considered appearing there anyway because "the publicity alone would make my presence advantageous."[26] Ball, upon hearing his poem "Der Henker" was the reason why *Die Revolution* had been seized, was overjoyed at the poem's impact; he and the journal's publishers intended to act quickly to "publicize the case in an enterprising way." Ball expected he would be fined because of his poem, but saw it as something that will "attract attention (*eine große aufsehenerregnde Sache*)" and show the court "has taken notice of me," just as he knew Klabund and Kerr had become more widely known because of their trials. Indeed, Ball's widow later claimed the trial, not the poem, first aroused public interest in Ball.[27]

As Ball and Klabund were being tried they planned to coauthor an anthology, entitled *Die Konfiszierten* (*The Confiscated*), of about thirty writers whose works had also been confiscated; it was to be published by the Georg Müller Verlag, which had shown a "very gratifying interest" in the project.[28] Ball and the editors of *Die Revolution* placed a bold headline in issue #2 proudly announcing the confiscation of issue #1 and in subsequent issues discussed at length the police action and ensuing trial. When the court finally released issue #1, *Die Revolution* widely publicized the fact and at the same time announced the price of issue #1 was being raised from 10 to 50 pfennig.

Clearly, many censored authors and publishers realized that, whatever else it might entail, being censored could also be good business for them. As the literary journal *Der Dramatiker* (*The Dramatist*) half-jokingly told its readers, "Yes, who can blame an author whose morals might be a little elastic if he sets out to write works that must be banned? At first, huge publicity for his piece, then later the culpable passages are cut out—at least that way one gains a little ground. ... [T]here are people who have themselves denounced to the state prosecutor, simply to add a spicy sauce to their name."[29] The impoverished dramatist Heinrich Lautensack didn't go that far, but he tried something similar: After waiting over a year to learn whether the Berlin censor planned to ban one or both of his controversial but popular comedies *Hahenkampf* (*Cockfight*) and *Die Pfarrhauskömodie* (*The Parsonage Comedy*), Lautensack published a (presumably satiric) open letter to the censor asking him, "Finally ban at least one of them!!" (thereby making the other more popular).[30]

In fact Oskar Panizza, whose *Das Liebeskonzil* earned him a year's imprisonment, not only willfully exploited the notoriety his incarceration brought, but in fact actively *courted* a confrontation with the authorities as a way of achieving literary fame and success. Many of his friends and contemporaries, as well as his recent biographers Peter Brown and Michael Bauer, have commented on Panizza's martyr complex, his craving for literary fame, his often-stated intention to provoke authorities into taking action against him, and the numerous ways he sought to turn clashes with censors into advertisements for his work. Max Halbe, for example, who was close to him in the early 1890s, was struck by Panizza's craving for publicity: according to Halbe, he "thirsted for praise, for applause and fame as one who longs for a redeeming drink." Even before the publication of *Das Liebeskonzil*, Halbe came to believe "Panizza was prepared to pay any price to fulfill his ambitious literary dreams, even if it meant taking on the martyr's crown." If Panizza could not achieve literary fame the usual way, Halbe observed, perhaps he could do it by audaciously confronting, challenging, and "fatally wounding" prevailing religious beliefs, then "succumb[ing] to the counterattack of superior enemy power: if the poet became a martyr to his convictions, would not the latter receive the crown of life which was perhaps denied to the former? The poet as martyr. The martyr as poet. Was there any difference left?"[31]

Panizza and other young Naturalist writers in Munich were well aware that artists needed to make a "name" for themselves and that scandal can help. Like his colleague Schaumberger, he boasted in the early 1890s how everyone in Munich was interested in them: "They revile us as swine, wallowers in shit, fin-de-siècle men, literary Social Democrats, and I don't know what else, but they read us, discuss us, come to our readings, buy our books and pamphlets, etc.—in short, we are the focus of their interest." After authorities confiscated, then released the anthology *Modernes Leben* because of contributions by Panizza, Anna Croissant-Rust, and others, he inquired about what she was working on next, adding that he intends to stick with "something confiscatory" and would let the prosecutor lock him up if he wants. To another colleague Panizza wrote how he might approach the authorities on bended knee and ask, "Please expel me, or let some big blow-up occur over me, so that my book sales pick up."[32] He is alleged to have sent his just-published book *Aus dem Tagebuch eines Hundes* (*From the Diary of a Dog*) to police in 1892 in hopes its temporary confiscation would cause the book to be more widely noticed, and shortly before the controversy over *Das Liebeskonzil* erupted, he wrote that "suffering a jail term for defending an idealistic cause is almost a guarantee of popularity among the masses." His fellow writer O. J. Bierbaum had an inkling of what was to come when he predicted in 1893 that Panizza would soon be "among the most discussed modernist authors in Germany, and also the most notorious."[33]

Panizza apparently expected *Das Liebeskonzil* to be confiscated as soon as it appeared; when it was, Karl Kraus called him a "pugnacious fighting cock who seems to want to go right to being confiscated (*geradeaus auf das Confisciertwerden auszugehen scheint*)."[34] Although friends urged him to flee after he was indicted, Panizza insisted on staying in Munich so he could make a brilliant speech to the jury and enjoy the publicity his trial would stir up. After he had served his sentence he spoke of his and other literary martyrs' desire to "force their way into jail."[35] In 1901, after Panizza was indicted again (this time for lèse majesté) and faced a court hearing to determine his mental competence, his attorney asked him if an insanity verdict might not hurt the sale of his books. Panizza claims he "laughed at him. 'On the contrary,' I shouted, 'an official declaration like that, and being sent to a mental institution, would be the strongest possible advertisement. Look at *Nietzsche*!'"[36] While some censored authors recognized how the experience might ultimately benefit their careers or income, it is clear that early on Oscar Panizza consciously sought to provoke the censor's intervention in order to satisfy certain of his psychic needs, especially his hunger for notoriety.

Although they hardly equal Panizza's efforts to force the censors' hand, there were persistent rumors and suspicions that Albert Langen, publisher of *Simplicissimus,* had also deliberately orchestrated censorship incidents as publicity for his journal. Frank Wedekind, for example, who served six months' fortress arrest for the "Palestine issue," maintained that Langen had continually pushed him to write increasingly biting political poems and had assured him the journal would never publish anything that left him legally vulnerable. Yet—according to Wedekind—when told by the journal's lawyer that the Palestine issue would lead to immediate confiscation, Langen decided to publish it anyway and when police were searching his office, Langen "inadvertently" let police see Wedekind's manuscript, which allowed them to identify and prosecute him as author of the poem.

(Langen of course denied Wedekind's account of the incident.) Wedekind never forgave Langen for this presumed betrayal and several of Wedekind's subsequent dramas rehash the incident with plots and thinly veiled characters that present Langen in a most unfavorable light.[37] Thomas Theodor Heine, also sentenced to six months' fortress confinement in the Palestine affair, came to resent Langen for similar reasons: he blamed the severity of his own sentence on the fact that police had found letters in which Langen hoped Heine's imprisonment would prove advantageous to the journal; he was annoyed that Langen did nothing to help him with his defense costs; and he was angered at Langen for suggesting that he (Heine) was using the whole affair as a clever stratagem to become famous![38] These mutual suspicions and accusations surfaced again a few years later during the "Fastenpredigt" controversy, when it was rumored the current incident was another of Langen's ploys to generate publicity for *Simplicissimus*.[39] Similar accusations were raised against Cassirer and Kerr, who were accused of setting up the von Jagow/Tilla Durieux scandal in 1911 to increase circulation of their journal *Pan*.[40] Given the attention and possible marketing advantages being censored could bring an author, it is not easy to distinguish between those who merely recognized, appreciated, or exploited such a situation and those who knowingly instigated it.

There was certainly more to Panizza's (and possibly also Langen's and Kerr's) provocative flirtations with censorship than a desire to generate publicity and sell more copies, something that can perhaps best be explained by the sociology of deviant behavior. Those who analyze deviant behavior and institutions of social control have often noted that some deviant activity seems to derive support and nourishment, albeit unintentional, from the very agencies designed to suppress it. Kai Erickson, for example, suggests some social forces and institutions operate so as to actually promote deviant behavior, to "recruit" offenders, and to commit them to long-term service in the deviant ranks, while Michael Foucault insisted that modern disciplinary institutions like the prison actually produce and perpetuate the very delinquency they are supposed to control. Other institutions created to control and inhibit deviant behavior, such as mental hospitals, also frequently operate in such a way as to perpetuate this behavior.[41]

Indeed, in institutions and situations designed to control normatively deviant behavior, a mutually reinforcing dependency frequently arises between the controllers and the controlled, an unusual symbiotic relationship in which the activities of the one support and reinforce those of the other. For the relationship between deviants who violate norms and the conformists who define and enforce them is more complementary than antithetical. As Erickson notes, when a society feels particularly threatened by a certain type of behavior, be it religious heresy, theft, or witchcraft, it will impose more severe sanctions against that behavior and make a greater effort to combat it; yet the very fact the community emphasizes the importance of a particular set of values often seems to encourage deviant responses from some group members. Indeed, some people are probably attracted to a deviant act (for example, blasphemy) precisely because it is likely to offend, challenge, or test certain values the group holds dear. [42] The novelist Italo Calvino points out that

> repression must also allow an occasional breathing space, must close an eye now and then, alternate indulgence with abuse, with a certain unpredictability in its caprices; otherwise, if nothing more remains to be repressed, the whole system rusts and wears down. Let's be frank: every regime, even the most authoritarian, survives in a situation of unstable equilibrium, whereby it needs to justify constantly the existence of its repressive apparatus, therefore of something to repress. The wish to write things that irk the established authorities is one of the elements necessary to maintain this equilibrium. [43]

Foucault, too, has discussed these reciprocal relationships; he termed them "perpetual spirals of power and pleasure" in which authoritarian repression and clandestine evasion become mutually reinforcing. The exercise of power, he argues, involves a certain pleasure. The censor, for example, finds it personally satisfying (and in the case of pornography, perhaps even sexually exciting) to investigate, monitor, spy on, ferret out, control, and punish illicit materials (and unorthodox sexual activities). But there is also a certain pleasure involved in outwitting, deceiving, taunting, and mocking the censor, violating his taboos, and evading, circumventing or resisting his power. A dialectic arises between "the power that lets itself be invaded by the pleasure it is pursuing; and opposite it, power asserting itself in the pleasure of showing off, scandalizing, or resisting." [44] (Or as another scholar said of art and obscenity, "there is only as much pleasure possible as there are taboos to violate, and all pleasure ceases when one strips it of its wrongfulness." [45]) A cat-and-mouse game of circular incitements may exist between the censor and the controlled (censored) delinquent, a perpetual spiral of power and pleasure where each, through his actions, gratifies and encourages the other. "Pleasure and power do not cancel or turn back against one another," Foucault argues; "they seek out, overlap, and reinforce one another. They are linked by complex mechanisms and devices of excitation and excitement." [46] Surely there is no better example of this unusual dialectic of contention between censored and censor than the case of Oskar Panizza and the Munich police (although Alfred Kerr's running battle with Berlin Police President von Jagow probably qualifies as well.) What literary scholar Siegbert Klee said of Carl Sternheim is true of other Wilhelmine authors as well: to cultivate his own self-representation as a writer and to produce works that would provoke and challenge, he needed "clashes with the public, as well as with censors and critics." [47]

Censorship and Alienation

These different coping strategies tell us little, however, about the more important inner responses, the longer term affective and psychological impact such an experience had upon an author. For most, we can safely assume, running afoul of the censors naturally produced disappointment, frustration, and anger. For a few, it was a truly traumatic experience. The tragic case of Oskar Panizza, whose deepening insanity and escalating conflicts with censors in the 1890s were inseparably linked, will be examined more fully below, but there were other examples as well. Wilhelm Walloth, one of the three Leipzig Realists convicted and fined in 1890, reportedly suffered a nervous breakdown because of his indictment. The police raid on his home exacerbated his existing neuroses and he briefly entered a sanatorium where he was diagnosed with nervous exhaustion manifested as "rapid mood changes, insomnia, panic attacks, eccentric behavior, lack of essential self-control, and pathological mistrust." He improved enough to attend his trial, where his physician testified that Walloth was under psychiatric care and asked the court to treat his highly excitable, unstable patient leniently. Convicted nevertheless, Walloth felt he had been the victim of a gross miscarriage of justice and he withdrew from the world around him; as his psychic condition continued to deteriorate, he lost most of his creative energy.[48] The Munich Naturalist Hanns von Gumppenberg, sentenced to two months' fortress arrest in 1891 for lèse majesté, was nearly as traumatized as Walloth by his experience but was able to sublimate his neuroses through a cathartic semiautobiographical novel, *Der fünfte Prophet* (*The Fifth Prophet*, published 1895). "Heinrich Steinbach," the spiritualist hero, bore many unmistakable parallels to von Gumppenberg's own life: both were mystical, sensitive, aspiring writers, both were sons of minor administrative officials, both joined a circle of cultural dilettantes and modernist writers (M. G. Conrad's Modern Life Society), and both were indicted for blasphemy. (Although von Gumppenberg was convicted for lèse majesté, he had also once been indicted for blasphemy but the charges were later dropped). As a result of his conflict with authorities, "Steinbach" suffers a severe identity crisis (as did von Gumppenberg), sinks into madness, imagines he is the fifth prophet of God, and finally commits suicide.[49] Finally, Carl Sternheim, who suffered from depression much of his life and was institutionalized several times for nervous breakdowns, developed such a persecution mania after being indicted for obscenity in 1918 that his friends insisted he consult a noted brain specialist.[50]

While very few censored authors suffered such profound psychological consequences, there is evidence that for many others the experience significantly affected their self-image, their vocational identity, their perception of their place within society, and their level of political consciousness and engagement. While it comes as no surprise that contending with the state's censoring authorities generally aggravated these authors' sense of estrangement from German society, the extent of their alienation, the form it took, and the conclusions they drew from it varied greatly. We can identify three distinct types of alienation exhibited by censored authors in imperial Germany: *radical alienation, ambivalent alienation,* and what, for lack of a better term, might be called *internalized alienation.*[51] Radically alienated authors, because of the antipathy they perceived in Germany toward their own work and toward writers in general, completely severed their ties with German society to preserve their artistic integrity. Authors who internalized their alienation, despite certain resentments they may have harbored toward the imperial order, never abandoned their hope of becoming reconciled with their society, even if this meant sacrificing some artistic autonomy or even renouncing their own work. The ambivalently alienated seemed torn between these two poles.

The best example of an author impelled into radical alienation by censorship was Oskar Panizza, the subject of six different police confiscations and recipient of the harshest sentence given any censored writer. Panizza believed adamantly in the inner-directed artist's absolute autonomy from external constraints. His experience with censorship and his incarceration helped transform him from a critic to a hostile enemy of German society.

Before his confrontation with the state, Panizza had argued that artistic talent and genius bordered closely on what society labeled "abnormal" or "insane." To Panizza, all creative thought was the result of an individual's unique, mysterious demonic illusions. Artists must follow their own inner demons, regardless of the consequences; they must never compromise their convictions, even when these appeared to conflict with external "reality." Even though they might be labeled abnormal or even regarded as insane by others, artists must always place their deepest inner convictions—their "holy spirit"— above society's arbitrary and relative norms. To Panizza, true artists were thus martyrs; they were inevitably condemned and persecuted by society, which insisted on imposing on them its own meaningless standards.[52]

After his 1895 trial and conviction Panizza proclaimed even more passionately the eternal irreconcilability of artists and society. He spoke satirically—although with profound earnestness—of the "poet's divine right" (*Gottesgnadentum des Dichters*).[53] Poets were endowed with a special inspiration and ability to express their insights, he believed; this gift was bestowed only on artists, and it both enabled and compelled them to follow their inspirations and convictions regardless of all social considerations or legal constraints. According to Panizza, the burden artists bore was a heavy one and their special calling entailed suffering and constant struggle; they were answerable only to a higher authority and could not be absolved from their duties by any man, state, prosecutor, parliament, or nation. Society, however, refused to recognize the poet's calling; and because poets, in turn, refused to accept society's arbitrary norms, society tried to stifle poets and prevent them from expressing their inner, divinely inspired convictions. If poets insisted on following their convictions, society imprisoned them, forced them into exile, or declared them insane. But those whom society regards as insane are tolerated and left alone. To Panizza, then, the insane asylum was perhaps the only feasible alternative open to the artist within society. Although being declared insane meant social isolation, it meant also complete spiritual freedom. Panizza satirically suggested that until society was ready to recognize their right of self-expression and to heed their truths, artists should petition parliament for the freedom and protection offered by legal insanity. In another work, he advised the guardians of the state to declare all freethinkers criminal psychotics and to confine them to a huge asylum (he suggested the Pfalz); this, he reasoned, would both protect them from future social persecution and at the same time permit society to preserve its precious norms.[54]

Panizza's imprisonment irrevocably estranged him from the German social and political order and radicalized his political outlook. He emerged from prison a deeply embittered enemy of his native land and immediately repudiated it in the most decisive and vehement manner possible.

While in prison Panizza reflected on German society's brutal treatment of writers and voiced his anger in caustic satirical works. In *Ein Jahr Gefängnis* (*A Year in Jail*), his jailhouse diary, he spoke of a "land of the nonpromulgation of thoughts" (*Gedankennichtverlautbarung*) in Northern Europe where the climate was so frigid that most inhabitants had learned to breathe only through their noses. For those who exhaled through their mouth found that their breath immediately froze into a solid icicle protruding from their lips. Police would then quickly appear, grab hold of the frozen objects, and drag the unfortunates before a court, where they were sentenced to up to eight years in prison, depending on the length of the icy evidence. Thus the natives were extremely careful not to breathe their thoughts out through their mouths, where these could be heard, seen, and seized by the police—indeed, they had learned that even talking about breathing was dangerous.[55] In another of his prison works Panizza referred to the "burying alive" (*Lebendigbegraben*) of poets, writers, journalists, and artists in late nineteenth-century Germany and lamented that no voices cried out in protest.[56]

During his incarceration Panizza also reflected more deeply about Germany's social and political system and drew radical conclusions. In the early 1890s he had briefly tried to help form an alliance between Munich's avant-garde Naturalist writers and the city's Social Democratic working class. In prison Panizza came into closer contact with members of the proletariat and criminal underclass and his feelings toward them became more ambivalent. One the one hand, he developed a grudging admiration of the Social Democratic movement for its idealism, but on the other he was repelled by what he saw of this uneducated *Lumpenproletariat*. In his prison writings he leveled a strong critique against the entire Bavarian criminal justice system and radically reinterpreted the relation between the individual and the state. Panizza became convinced the great questions of the future would be the status of workers, the problem of individual liberation, and the destruction of old authorities, especially the monarchy. He embraced a vague anarchism and developed a deep interest in and admiration for earlier political martyrs like Karl Sand.[57]

As a result of the punishment imposed on him by society, it became clear to Panizza that life for him as a writer in Germany was impossible. At his trial he had already explained to the court why he published his *Das Liebeskonzil* in Switzerland: "Every German author, at one time or another, has something on his heart that he can't have printed in Germany, and then he goes abroad."[58] While in jail he wrote that flight abroad was one of the three fates open to a freethinker who wanted to express himself in Germany (the other two being imprisonment and insanity).[59] Fearing the social isolation he would encounter upon his release from prison—society would scorn him as a criminal, and even his embarrassed friends would avoid contact with him—he decided he must "leave the land of asphalt before it burns the soles of my shoes."[60] "I always saw," he later noted, "that those who expressed new ideas had to flee, and later, even if only through their writings, they were brought back. That suits me perfectly."[61] So upon his release from prison in 1896, Panizza renounced his Bavarian citizenship and resettled first in Zurich, then in Paris.

Once safely beyond the German border, Panizza poured out his hatred for the social climate and political system of his homeland. In his anti-German poems *Parisjana,* composed during his Paris exile, he denounced Germans as a backward, arrogant, smug, and hopelessly servile people while praising France as Germany's free, rational, enlightened antithesis.[62] Germans' *spießbürgerliche* intolerance and their hostility to artists and other intellectuals came under particular attack. In Panizza's eyes Germany was "a land of barbarians" populated by "a pack of horses" interested only in their potato sacks and who sought at every turn to "strangle the muses." In Germany, he charged, "one's Best, what one calls Soul," is treated *en canaille.* "Don't throw pearls to these sows, / no verses to these barbarians," he warned.[63] The antimonarchical, anarchist leanings Panizza had developed in prison now emerged with full revolutionary force in these poems. He denounced all bailiffs, police, executioners, and other guardians of public order and called upon the German people to rise up against their tyrannical rulers—especially Wilhelm II, a "public enemy of mankind and culture."[64]

When German authorities seized his financial assets and issued a warrant for his arrest, his family repudiated him as an embarrassment and sought to have him declared mentally incompetent. This final alienation from his family so psychically shattered Panizza he considered suicide; thereafter he bitterly blamed the Munich police and Bavarian government for splitting apart his family and destroying his ties with them. Broken and financially destitute, he returned to Bavaria in 1900, was immediately placed under psychiatric observation, and at the strong urgings of his family, was declared mentally incompetent.[65] A few years later he was committed permanently to an asylum, where he spent the final sixteen years of his life totally insulated from the society he despised. Of the three fates he once said were open to a writer in Germany—imprisonment, exile, insanity—Panizza had experienced them all.

No other censored author became so totally isolated and radically alienated from German society as Panizza. Only Hermann Conradi, indicted for obscenity and blasphemy in the Leipzig Realists' trial, merits comparison. Like Panizza, Conradi believed the artist and bourgeois society were natural enemies. Before his clash with the censor Conradi preached that if the creative impulse was not to be thwarted and weakened, artists must be allowed to follow the spontaneous impulses of their souls, even if these conflicted with the rules and norms society had laid down for the preservation of social order. Any potential social harm that might result from the artist's complete freedom would be more than offset, Conradi believed, by the rich artistic creations that would ensue. Conradi believed that to produce pure, natural, and original art, creative artists must insulate themselves from the influences of bourgeois society, avoiding normal bourgeois occupations so as not to fall under the influence of those social institutions and traditions that were products of "the herd instincts of the masses."[66] After he was indicted Conradi's disdainful scorn toward the guardians of the bourgeois order only deepened. He regarded the authorities' actions as "silly and childish" and he adopted a standpoint "rooted firmly in the a priori sovereignty of art."[67] The young writer considered his novel *Adam Mensch* "a first-rate psychological-artistic-cultural document, even if ten thousand old or 'young' embalmed herrings … bite out their moral teeth on it."[68] Even though he faced up to three years in prison if convicted, Conradi professed not the slightest concern over what "old fogeys" like the state prosecutor thought of him or his work and he refused "to dance to the whims of those gentlemen." At his preliminary court hearing, he later boasted, he had behaved with "unbelievable self-assurance, superiority, and casual sovereignty."[69]

Conradi died in the midst of his obscenity trial, thus cutting short any further development of his nascent radical alienation. Had he lived he would almost certainly have been convicted and sentenced to several months in prison. There seems every reason to believe that such a fate would have only deepened his hostility to bourgeois society and alienated him further from it.

A second group of authors experienced an ambivalent alienation after undergoing censorship. Like Panizza they saw in the very institution of censorship proof of German society's lack of respect for the value of literature and its disdain for writers and they were tempted to emigrate, like he had, to less-hostile settings abroad. Yet in the end, the forces binding these writers to their native society proved stronger than the forces repelling them from it.

More importantly, ambivalently alienated authors exhibited an unusually defensive reaction to the experience of censorship. Their clash with the authorities shook their self-confidence or produced in them a crisis of identity, which in turn led to a critical new self-awareness. Of course they never admitted the censor's charges against their work were justified. But while publicly proclaiming their innocence and defending their work, privately they expressed misgivings about their previous assumptions and values, they reproached themselves for their literary excesses, and they resolved to redirect their literary efforts. The two best examples of ambivalent alienation among censored authors are Frank Wedekind and Richard Dehmel.

After Wedekind had served six months under fortress arrest for lèse majesté in 1899, been twice indicted but acquitted for obscenity in 1904–1906, and seen several of his dramas confiscated or banned from the public stage, he published two essays on censorship in which he asserted that literary censorship in Germany was a product of that society's lack of respect for the arts and of the German bureaucracy's disdain for authors. Indeed, Wedekind claimed not to know which was worse: bourgeois society's general disinterest in literary life and its blind acquiescence to police harassment of writers, or the fact that only the police took art seriously in Germany, in the sense that they vastly overestimated its power to corrupt society.[70] "After all is said and done," Wedekind complained, "to the German authorities a German writer is merely a dumb child."[71] The banning of works like his *Die Büchse der Pandora* and *Totentanz,* while comparable works by English or Russian authors were passed, had made Wedekind realize "what a singularly thankless honor it is to be a German [writer] in Germany." By passing questionable foreign works but not German ones, he said, German theater censors eagerly ratify the "indescribable disdain" with which others, especially Russians, view Germans.[72]

In the midst of his first serious encounter with the censor Wedekind emigrated briefly, but ultimately found it an unsatisfactory solution. Facing up to a year's imprisonment for lèse majesté in 1898, Wedekind first fled to Zurich, then Paris, where he spent time with his exiled friend Oskar Panizza. But after eight months in exile Wedekind decided to "make my peace with the German Reich" and returned to face his punishment.[73] "I have almost learned to love Germany," he wrote a friend shortly before he repatriated from Paris.[74] Indeed, by World War I Wedekind had become so reconciled to his homeland he was delivering patriotic speeches in Munich theaters and was one of the original members of General von Moltke's political club, the German Society 1914 (Deutsche Gesellschaft 1914), which brought together a wide spectrum of political, military, industrial, academic, and cultural figures to discuss contemporary issues, including German war aims and possible territorial annexations.

Besides leading him to work through his ambivalent feelings toward Germany, Wedekind's brushes with censorship also prompted a series of critical self-reassessments. After he was indicted for lèse majesté Wedekind found it painful to admit that he had written the satirical poem in question not out of political conviction, but for simple material gain. One reason he fled to Switzerland after his indictment, he told a friend, was to avoid having to testify that in composing the poem he had ignored his own convictions and moral beliefs. To have admitted that in a public forum, he confessed, "would have been a disgraceful humiliation for me."[75] A few years later, when a Berlin court ruled the first edition of his *Die Büchse der Pandora* obscene and ordered it destroyed, Wedekind rewrote portions of the drama and published a new edition. In the new preface he acknowledged that the trial over the earlier version had caused him to more closely assess the play's ethical and artistic qualities. Removing all those passages to which the court had objected, Wedekind confessed, had actually improved the drama both ethically and artistically.[76]

But even the revised version of *Die Büchse der Pandora* was banned from the public stage. To answer those who condemned his work for its supposed lack of "ethical sincerity," Wedekind composed an autobiographical one-act play entitled *Die Zensur* (*Censorship*). Through the character of Buridan (a transparent self-portrait of himself), Wedekind justified his art and appealed for the release of *Die Büchse der Pandora*. At the same time, however, there is in *Die Zensur* a rather sympathetic portrayal of the censor's viewpoint, represented by the churchman

Prantl. Through Prantl, Wedekind appears in *Die Zensur* to be reproaching himself for three serious artistic and ethical shortcomings: First, that his art contains
an element of emotional exhibitionism; like other modern artists, he displays to
the entire world (and in return for money!) all his darkest personal secrets and
those inner emotional struggles best worked through in privacy. Second, that he
lacks concern for the ethical consequences of his art and its effect upon people's
lives. Third, that in his portrayals of human pain, misfortune, and despair, he
displays a certain schadenfreude and encourages it in others. Buridan/Wedekind,
the censor in the play charges, lacks empathy and any sense of brotherly love for
his destitute characters. After the writer Buridan has proclaimed his basic human
goodness, the censor Prantl tells him:

> Your 'human goodness' would never stop your Reason from writing a theater piece about
> some unfortunate creature you have just trampled into the ground. That is the most gro-
> tesque aspect of your performances: everything is the most living reality. Instead of plays,
> you create casualties. If a man dies by you, then it's just a human life gone; no trace of
> any spiritual participation. And whenever possible, you even boast of these abominations.
> Annihilated human lives are the milestones of your life's path. ... One sits before your art
> like imperial Rome sat before the gladiator's battles and the persecution of the Christians.
> Baiting wild beasts of prey are the summits of what you call art.[77]

Since Buridan/Wedekind makes no effort to refute Prantl's charges, readers are
left with the impression Wedekind implicitly recognized at least some validity in
the accusations of his critics and censors.

Richard Dehmel, another ambivalently alienated author, was twice indicted
for obscenity and blasphemy but acquitted both times. Because of a legal technicality he narrowly missed being indicted a third time (and would have almost
certainly been convicted), although on that occasion the court did rule his *Weib
und Welt* obscene and blasphemous, and ordered it destroyed. After his second
censorship trial in 1900, Dehmel complained bitterly that the writer's path in
Germany was strewn with more thorns than roses and he too toyed with the idea
of leaving. Yet after a brief trip abroad he admitted his "stupid German heart"
got the better of his "clever, cosmopolitan head" and he returned eagerly to his
homeland. Although still complaining about having to live with unpleasant state
prosecutors as fellow citizens, he rationalized that the situation elsewhere was
probably no better.[78] By World War I he had become an ardent supporter of the
war and was one of ninety-three distinguished intellectuals, scientists, and artists swept up in the "spirit of 1914" who signed a manifesto denying Germany's
guilt in starting the war, justifying Germany's violation of Belgian neutrality, and
expressing their wholehearted support of the German army.

As a result of his indictment Dehmel too searched his soul and admitted his
legal problems might be partly deserved. While quickly brushing aside the prosecutor's charges of obscene intent, in his journal and in private correspondence
Dehmel admitted that as an artist, he had let the uncreative "spirit of *mere opposition* (*bloßen Widerspruches*) against our times" speak too often and too loudly in

his work and he reproached himself for "partially disfiguring" his art with a faddish "truth-braggadocio" (*Wahrheitsrenommage*) that was actually less concerned with the truth than with boasting about one's interesting experiences. "So now it seems to me a half-deserved punishment of fate that last week the Munich prosecutor confiscated my second book [*Aber die Liebe*]," he wrote a friend; "I feel, through this indictment, … pushed onto the same bench with people who are alien and repulsive to my entire being. That is my penance."[79]

The third and most curious form of estrangement displayed by censored German authors is internalized alienation. Unlike the radically alienated writers who accepted or even embraced their social alienation as the only path by which they could remain faithful to their calling, authors who internalized their alienation were so profoundly distressed by their isolation from society that they longed for reconciliation with the censor and reintegration into society. To overcome their alienation these authors internalized the censor's values. Like the ambivalently alienated, they were willing to acknowledge some culpability when confronted by the censor, although their self-criticisms were even more sweeping. Moreover, just as Tonio Kröger had agreed—up to a point—with the policeman's right to carry out his civic duty by interrogating him, the authors who internalized their alienation agreed—up to a point—with the censor's right to censor art. Although they might vehemently object to the censor's judgment of their own work, they acknowledged society's ultimate right to define the boundaries for artistic life. The three authors who best exemplify internalized alienation are Ernst von Wildenbruch, Paul Ernst, and Hermann Sudermann.

Wildenbruch's keen patriotic admiration, almost worship, of Emperor Wilhelm I and the Hohenzollerns had twice been blunted in the early 1880s: once when the emperor had banned Wildenbruch's comic piece *Mein Onkel aus Pommern* (*My Pomeranian Uncle*) from all royal theaters, and again when the royal theater rejected his *Das neue Gebot* (*The New Commandment*) because it raised unwelcome political issues related to the Catholic Church. Angered at both decisions, he complained about "how patriotic poetry and poets are treated in our nation," and bemoaned that "in Germany the author has no rights."[80] When Bismarck convinced Emperor Wilhelm II to ban Wildenbruch's *Der Generalfeldoberst* (*The General Field Commander*) in 1889 for sensitive diplomatic reasons, the dramatist was outraged. Wildenbruch called Wilhelm's decision "a terrible blow" that "interrupted my life's work and condemned it to death." His personal relation with the emperor and Bismarck soured considerably after this episode and he freely expressed his resentments toward the monarch and his royal cabinet. Wildenbruch soon abandoned his plans for the rest of his Hohenzollern dramatic cycle and turned his hand instead to naturalistic social dramas.[81]

Despite his own unhappy experience with it, however, Wildenbruch continued to accept artistic censorship as a legitimate social institution. In 1900, after another drama of his was censored (Munich police ordered cuts and revisions in his *Die Tochter des Erasmus* [1899] before they would allow it to be performed publicly, on the grounds that the play contained historical inaccuracies) he explicitly reaffirmed the need for some form of state censorship over "immoral" or otherwise harmful art—as long as writers and other literary experts were consulted before the decisions were made. "Is theater censorship even necessary and advisable in the present circumstances?" Wildenbruch asked. "This question I answer loudly and decisively with 'Yes.' I do so, although I myself have experienced the bitter sorrow that results when a work is banned—when in one blow the hard work of a year or more is destroyed. Drama, and through it, the theater, is a power, and it lies in the nature of things that the state cannot leave uncontrolled any power that operates within the state's sphere."[82]

Paul Ernst was another censored author whose experience left him estranged from the imperial order, at least initially. After being indicted and fined for his story *Zum ersten Mal* (*The First Time*), this young, left-leaning Naturalist journalist became enraged over the hypocrisy of a society that prevented artists from portraying the scandalous social problems everyone knew existed. He also interpreted the judgment against him as proof of Germany's blatant system of class justice, for the presiding judge had told him that if his story had appeared in a middle-class rather than a working-class publication, it would not have been considered objectionable. But Ernst quickly internalized the censor's reprimand, to a far greater extent than the ambivalently alienated Wedekind or Dehmel had done. He claims in his memoir that partly as a result of his obscenity conviction, he was overcome by such a powerful feeling of social loneliness (*Einsamkeit*) that he completely reappraised his moral and political beliefs, which had always run counter to prevailing values. Did he alone, he wondered, really see the truth while everyone else wallowed in error? Was he alone moral and correct, and the rest of society immoral and misguided? Perhaps, Ernst concluded, it was he who was mistaken. He reproached himself for his youthful intellectual arrogance, abandoned both his Naturalist literary efforts and his left-wing political journalism, and returned home to his parents. In subsequent years, his politics and his art became increasingly conservative.[83]

Similarly, the Naturalist Hermann Sudermann, after his dramas *Sodoms Ende* and *Morituri* had been banned from public performance in the 1890s, voiced his resentments over the indignities writers must suffer in German society. In 1900 Sudermann helped found and lead the Goethe League to defend intellectual freedom against the Lex Heinze and other efforts by conservatives and authorities to crack down on obscene materials and immoral art. In his first speech to the organization, Sudermann complained that German writers and intellectuals were tired of being treated like unruly "stepchildren of the nation" who were arbitrarily disciplined and shoved hither and yon by the nation's political leadership. Considering their cultural importance, Sudermann continued, German society had not granted writers, artists, and academics the respect and influence they deserved.[84]

But like Ernst, Sudermann also engaged in a novel form of self-reproach. In his Goethe League speech he told the assembled artists and writers that they themselves were largely responsible for their lamentable position vis-à-vis the conservative political forces seeking to censor and silence them. Their own dis-agreements and lack of unity had hitherto condemned German intellectuals to political impotence, he charged. Worse, too many artists had been caught up in a hyperaesthetic, insular (*weltfremde*) arrogance; they had turned their backs on the great issues of the times and cut themselves off from the wider populace. As a result, the artistic and intellectual community had not only underestimated the power and irreconcilable hatred of its reactionary opponents, but some members had flirted and even cooperated with literature's most bitter enemies.[85] (This last charge, as we shall see, was soon leveled against Sudermann himself.) Was Sud-ermann in this speech perhaps projecting or transferring onto writers in general some of the self-criticism and vague sense of culpability that individual authors like Wedekind, Dehmel, and Ernst experienced after being challenged by the censor? And rather than blaming a writer's social isolation on external hostile forces such as the censor, as the radically and ambivalently alienated authors had done, was not Sudermann implying that some of the hostility directed toward German writers was the result of their own self-imposed isolation? This was the same conclusion that Paul Ernst had reached on a more personal level.

In addition, like Wildenbruch, Sudermann too was eager for a censorship in which writers and artists were actively involved. After the public controversy over the proposed Lex Heinze had abated, Sudermann wrote directly to the Berlin police president to offer the Goethe League's assistance in helping police with their difficult duty of removing raw, offensive pictures and printed material from the display windows of book and art stores without offending the sensibilities of the aesthetically educated citizenry. It was in the interest both of the authorities and of those sensitive to good art, Sudermann argued, to insulate the public from contact with all excesses and nuisances. In light of the difficulty of deciding what should be allowed and what was objectionable, Sudermann, on behalf of the Goethe League, offered to assist and advise police on difficult borderline cases. In the long term Sudermann suggested the establishment of a board of artists, literary experts, and book and art dealers that would advise police on questions of censorship.[86] When news of Sudermann's offer became public, critics denounced him and the Goethe League. Sudermann and his followers did not really oppose the state drawing up a blacklist of banned, unacceptable art, his critics charged—they merely wanted to help decide which works should be on the list.[87]

Conclusion

In his famous 1910 essay "Geist and Tat" ("Spirit and Deed"), Thomas Mann's older brother Heinrich compared the political consciousness and engagement of French men of letters to that of German writers. Whereas French literati from Rousseau to Zola have traditionally been bitter enemies of the powers-that-be, he argued, German intellectuals have generally meekly accepted oppressive au-thority and have frequently openly embraced it. "In Germany, ... the abolition of unjust power has found no support. [Here] one thinks more extensively than anywhere else, one thinks to the very end of pure reason, one thinks to Nothingness: meanwhile, it is God's grace and the fist that rules the country." Although a writer, by his very nature, should be a bitter enemy of dumb, blind power, "it is precisely the literary man [in Germany] who has worked for the prettification of the unspiritual, for the sophistical exoneration of the unjust, for his enemy-to-the death: power." What might account for this strange perversion of the author's calling, the elder Mann asked? Germany's errant literati have many excuses, he answered, but "above all they have one in the enormous distance that has arisen and that now separates ... German intellectuals from the people." Mann chastised the German intelligentsia for doing nothing to reduce their social isolation: "The time has come, and honor demands, that now, finally, finally, they fulfill the demands of the *Geist* in this country, too, that they become agitators and ally themselves with the people against power. ... He who exercises might and authority must be our enemy. An intellectual who sides with the ruling caste commits treason against the *Geist*."[88]

The cases of Panizza, Conradi, Wedekind, Dehmel, Wildenbruch, Ernst, and Sudermann discussed above illustrate just how close and enormously complex was the relationship, pointed out by both Thomas and Heinrich Mann, between German writers' social isolation, their sense of the artist's calling, and their strange, even perverse response to oppressive power. And they make clear as well just how unwilling or unable prewar German authors, even those who had personally been affected by oppressive state power, were to heed Heinrich Mann's call for a socially integrated and politically engaged German intelligentsia.

As a result of their encounters with censorship, these authors all experienced some degree of estrangement from imperial Germany, and all had to confront the problem of the writer's social isolation. The radically alienated authors blamed their isolation on a hostile society and/or state that forced artists into the role of outcast or outlaw. Because they were convinced it ostracized and victimized artists like themselves, these authors decisively repudiated German society. The ambivalently alienated authors also rebuked their nation for its belittlement and maltreatment of artists; at the same time, however, they believed their conflicts with the censor could be partly traced to their own shortcomings as writers, to the maladroit way they sometimes exercised their craft. The social or political criticism they voiced was thus tempered and supplemented by a *Selbstkritik*. Authors who internalized their alienation were more self-critical still, going so far as to imply that writers' isolation in Germany might be as much self-imposed as it was a result of some national antipathy toward art.

Far from lamenting their social and political isolation, radically alienated authors seemed almost to exult in it. For they concluded that modern writers could fulfill their mission only by withdrawing from bourgeois society and its norms, by remaining absolutely free from the dictates and constraints it continually sought to impose. To them, artistic integrity was possible only outside society. Ambivalently alienated authors, although feeling that the society and/or the state of imperial Germany thwarted artists from freely and fully exercising their craft, were at the same time unwilling either to sever completely their social ties or to sacrifice their artistic independence to society's dictates. They were thus torn between the seemingly irreconcilable demands of artistic integrity and social integration. Like Tonio Kröger, they accepted with resignation their isolation as the fate of the writer in the modern world. Authors who internalized their alienation wished to overcome their social isolation and believed it was possible to reconcile the artist's calling with society's norms. If artists were integrated into the structures of power, if artists became "insiders" who helped the state define and enforce the socially acceptable limits of artistic activity—that is, if they assisted the authorities in censorship—then the artificial conflict between art and society would be resolved. For these authors, then, artistic integrity was possible within German society.

If we examine how these alienated authors chose to respond to oppressive social or political conditions, we discover that none translated their sense of alienation into the kind of effective political action Heinrich Mann advocated. The radically alienated chose either complete withdrawal (Panizza first opted for actual emigration abroad, but eventually returned to what must be called an extreme form of "inner emigration," insanity) or, in Conradi's case, what can perhaps be characterized as a form of passive resistance. The ambivalently alienated Wedekind and Dehmel, by contrast, flirted with emigration but then lapsed into a resigned acceptance of their situation in Germany; moreover, the self-doubts aroused in them by the censors undercut their self-confidence and caused them grudgingly to admit the authorities might have been partially right. Finally, in internalizing their alienation, Wildenbruch, Ernst, and Sudermann ultimately submitted or acquiesced to the censor's power, and two of them even believed that artists should collaborate with the censoring authorities (which Thomas Mann himself did by serving briefly on the Munich police's Censorship Advisory Board). Collectively, then, these censored authors chose a wide range of responses to power, from willing collaboration to outright exit, but none chose anything like active rebellion against authority; none became, as Heinrich Mann urged, "agitators allied with the people against power" (although Panizza came the closest). Indeed, except for Sudermann, whose involvement with the Goethe League was short lived, none of these authors became politically active as a result of their censorship experience, and those, like Panizza or Conradi, who were driven to the most radical judgments about the powers-that-be, did little or nothing to translate their words into concrete actions.

Heinrich Mann's hope was that German writers would abandon their social isolation and become politically engaged. The experiences of the censored authors reveal just how few prewar writers were able or willing to do so. For those censored authors who were most eager to overcome their alienation (Wildenbruch, Ernst, Sudermann) were also the ones most willing to side with the "enemy" and commit treason against the *Geist,* while those who were the most bitter, uncompromising enemies of unjust power (Panizza and Conradi) were the ones who seemed almost to revel in their social isolation and who regarded the masses with a certain elitist disdain. Only after the war and the collapse of the imperial order did a new generation of writers begin to heed Mann's call to throw off their alienation and become actively and responsibly involved in social and political issues.

This is not to suggest, of course, that only authors who actually experienced censorship in prewar Germany wrestled with problems of alienation or drew these conclusions about society and power. Other individual experiences and psychological factors clearly played a role in these authors' alienation, and one can point to many other German authors who were *not* censored but who also exhibited the same kinds of alienation as the censored authors discussed above. But even with some of the noncensored authors, censorship played a significant role in their alienation. For example, the best-selling novelist and left-liberal journalist Bernhard Kellermann, addressing his fellow artists in 1919 only weeks after the collapse of the empire, reminded them that one of the reasons writers like him had withheld their support (*Zuneigung*) from the imperial system was because it had denied writers and poets one of their most fundamental rights, freedom. "The capitalistic, imperialistic Germany that just collapsed, with its officials and its police, was unable to awaken any love in the heart of the writer," Kellermann declared.

> Unspiritual, sterile, reactionary, intolerant, arrogant, and 'infallible,' it contradicted, in all its features, the essential nature of the writer. ... Increasingly, and ever more fatefully, the writer became alienated from [that] state. ... In no country was literature and everything spiritual more disdained than in the just-collapsed German authoritarian state. ...
>
> For literature and writers, this old state did nothing! Less than nothing! Far from fulfilling their demands for freedom, ... it offered unfreedom. ...
>
> The writer wrote with a shackled hand. Brochures, novellas, novels, were abruptly banned, the performance of dramas forbidden. Whoever overstepped the 'permissible degree' of criticism went to prison. ... [The old order] drove any writer who did not share its Weltanschauung out of the public forum.[89]

Free now after centuries of being beaten down, Kellermann called upon his fellow writers to support the new German republic as long as it granted writers complete freedom of expression; henceforth "our conscience and self-criticism shall be our only censors."

Imperial Germany's pervasive censorship system may thus help explain why questions about the writer's calling and his or her troubled relationship with bourgeois society and with the powers-that-be loomed so large there before 1918—and after. Writers who personally ran afoul of the censors were often forced to confront these questions more personally, more directly, and perhaps earlier than noncensored writers. Yet some noncensored authors, like Kellermann (and Thomas Mann?), also came to recognize that conflicts with state authority, especially in the form of censorship, created a huge distance between many writers and the German Empire. Because of that distance, few German literati mourned the sudden collapse and disappearance of the imperial order in 1918.

Notes

Portions of this chapter appeared earlier as "Trials and Tribulations: Author's Responses to Censorship in Imperial Germany, 1885–1914," *German Studies Review* 12, no. 3 (October 1989): 447–68. Used here with permission.

1. Hermann Hesse, "Der Beruf des Schriftstellers," *Wissen and Leben* (1910): 48.
2. Ssymank, "Leben Hermann Conradis," clxxi–cxcx, cxlvi.
3. Scherek, in *Zukunft der deutschen Bühne,* 139.
4. After all his dramas were banned in Prussia after 1914, Sternheim said, "The reworking of classical authors ... has been the only possibility for me to work with the stage." Ibid., 146–47.
5. When the publisher of Busch's *Der heilige Antonius* was indicted (and acquitted) for disparaging Catholicism and causing a public nuisance with an indecent publication, Busch decided to write more anti-Catholic pieces (*Die fromme Helene* and *Peter Filicus*). Harden responded to his first indictment for lèse majesté by becoming still more critical of Wilhelm II and his "personal rule." When Thoma was tried in 1905 for ridiculing Protestant clergymen, he wrote his lawyer, "The authorities won't find me defenseless. If I come out of this with a jail term, I'll launch an offensive against the hypocrites." When sentenced to six weeks' jail, he used the time to write his biting satire *Die Moral.* Just, "Wilhelm Busch und die Katholiken," 68–70; Weller, *Maximilian Harden,* 12–13; Thoma to C. Haussmann, 17 Apr. 1905, quoted in Gritschneder, *Angeklagter Ludwig Thoma,* 34.
6. Linke, *Sternheim in Selbstzeugnissen,* 69.
7. Michael Patterson, *The Revolution in German Theatre 1900–1933* (Boston, 1981), 28.
8. Walach, "Das doppelte Drama," 272.
9. Account by Paul Mehnert, 7 Nov. 1902, in Abret and Keel, *Die Majestätsbeleidigungsaffäre,* 75–82.
10. Undated opinion of Dr. Joseph Hofmiller, quoted in Deiritz, *Geschichtsbewußtsein, Satire, Zensur,* 165.
11. Hauptmann to Marie Hauptmann, undated letter (early 1890s), Deutsches Literaturarchiv Marbach, Hauptmann Archiv.
12. Heft 6 of Walloth's unpublished autobiography, "Lebensrätsel eines Wiedergeborener," Handschriftabteilung der Stadtbibliothek München, Nachlaß Wilhelm Walloth, L1538.
13. F[ritz] M[authner], "Das Obscöne vor Gericht," *Deutschland* 1, no. 41 (12 Jul. 1890): 683.
14. Anita Auspurg to Croissant-Rust, 12 Sept. 1891, and Leo Berg to Croissant-Rust, 27 Sept. 1891, in Croissant-Rust Nachlaß, Staatsarchiv Ludwigshafen; Schaumburg to Max Halbe, 30 Sept. 1891, quoted in Jelavich, *Munich and Theatrical Modernism,* 37.
15. See copies of *Moderne Blätter* in Staatsarchiv Ludwigshafen, Anna Croissant-Rust Nachlaß; Bauer, *Oskar Panizza,* 129.
16. Sudermann to Dorothea Sudermann, 28 Oct. 1890, in Deutsches Literaturarchiv Marbach, Cotta Archiv, Nachlaß Sudermann, XVI 139, Bl. 10.
17. Hermann Bahr, *Selbstbildnis* (Berlin, 1923), 257.
18. *VL,* 2: 255–60; Young, *Harden,* 18.
19. Rundschreiben of Schuster & Löffler Verlag, 19 Sept. 1900, in Staat- und Universitätsbibliothek Hamburg, Dehmel Archiv, Varia 14,5, no. 35.
20. Bilse, *Life in a Garrison Town.* A foreword by Theodor Dreiser and introduction by Arnold White discussed the author's trial and punishment at some length.
21. Holm, *Farbiger Abglanz,* 75
22. Meyer, *Theaterzensur in München,* 36; C. Haussmann to Thoma, 15 Jan. 1904 and 25 Apr. 1904, Thoma Nachlaß; Allen, *Satire and Society,* 184–85.
23. Fulda to Paul Heyse, 16 Feb. 1902, quoted in Pöllinger, *Zensurprozeß,* 53.
24. *Bühne und Welt* 5, pt. 1 (1902/03): 534.
25. Durieux, *Meine ersten neunzig Jahre,* 160.

26. Klabund to Herr Heinrich, 11 Feb. 1913, and 11 Aug. 1913, in Klabund, *Briefe,* 64–65, 69–70.

27. Emmy Ball-Hennings, *Hugo Ball. Sein Leben in Briefen und Gedichten* (Frankfurt, 1991), 248.

28. Steinke, *Life and Work of Hugo Ball,* 82; and Ball to his sister, 4 Nov. 1913 and 10 Nov. 1913, and letter of 27 May 1914, in Hugo Ball, *Briefe 1911–1927* (Zurich, 1957), 22–24, 29.

29. *Der Dramatiker* 2, no. 10 (1903): 157, quoted in Pöllinger, *Zensurprozeß,* 149–50.

30. Heinrich Lautensack, "Offener Brief an Herrn Regierungsrat Klotz von der Abtheilung für Theatersachen des Königlichen Polizeipräsidiums zu Berlin," *Die Schaubühne* 6, Bd. 2 (1910): 1103–5.

31. Max Halbe, *Jahrhundertwende. Geschichte meines Lebens 1893–1914* (Danzig, 1935), 72, 75ff.

32. Panizza to Cäsar Flaischen, 30 Aug. 1891, to Croissant-Rust, 21 May 1892, and to O. J. Bierbaum, 11 May 189[9?] quoted in Bauer, *Oskar Panizza,* 123, 19, 124.

33. Ernst Kreowski writing in 1904, Panizza writing in *Die Gesellschaft* in 1894, and Bierbaum writing in *Die Gesellschaft,* 1893, quoted in ibid., 254 n. 112, 20, 115.

34. Panizza to his publisher Schabelitz, 18 Nov. 1894, and Kraus writing in *Die Zeit,* Dec. 1894, quoted in ibid., 260 n. 3, 16.

35. Panizza to Halbe, 25 Apr. 1896, in StBM, Halbe Archiv; and quoted in Jelavich, *Munich and Theatrical Modernism,* 65. Numerous other examples can be found in Brown, *Panizza,* 24, 35–41, 177–179; Bauer, *Oskar Panizza,* 16–20, 123–24, 225 n. 17, 254 n. 112, 260 n. 3; and Jelavich, *Munich and Theatrical Modernism,* 57–65.

36. Panizza's Notizbuch, quoted in Bauer, *Oskar Panizza,* 124.

37. Kutscher, *Wedekind,* 2: 17–20; Wedekind to Bjørnson, 28 Sept. 1899 and 12 Mar. 1900, Wedekind, *Gesammelte Briefe,* 2: 13–16, 42; Ward B. Lewis, *The Ironic Dissident: Frank Wedekind in the View of His Critics* (Columbia, SC, 1997), 3, 85–6; Wedekind's *Oaha, die Satire der Satire* (1908), *König Nicolo* (1902), *Karl Hetmann, der Zwerg-Riese (Hidalla)* (1904) all are thinly veiled treatments of his experiences with *Simplicissimus* and Langen. Ironically, *Oaha* was banned briefly in Munich because it allegedly libeled a living person (Langen).

38. Heine to Korfiz Holm, undated (but shortly after Heine was sentenced), Heine to Holm 14 Nov. 1898, and Heine to Holm, 15 Jul. 1899, Heine Nachlaß, StBM. Heine also seriously considered the possibility that Wedekind was an agent provocateur working for the police. Heine to Holm, 21 Jun. 1899, ibid.

39. Allen, *Satire and Society,* 184.

40. Durieux, *Ersten neunzig Jahren,* 156–60.

41. Kai Erickson, *Wayward Puritans: A Study in the Sociology of Deviance* (New York, 1966), 14–15, 19, and "Notes on the Sociology of Deviance," *Social Problems* 9, no. 4 (Spring 1962): 311; "For the observation that prison fails to eliminate crime, one should perhaps substitute the hypothesis that prison has succeeded extremely well in producing delinquency. … Although it is true the prison punishes delinquency, delinquency is for the most part produced in and by an incarceration which, ultimately, prison perpetuates in turn." Foucault, *Discipline and Punish,* 277, 301.

42. Erickson, *Wayward Puritans,* 19–20.

43. Calvino, *If on a winter's night,* 236.

44. Michael Foucault, *The History of Sexuality. Volume I: An Introduction,* trans. Robert Hurley (New York, 1978), 45.

45. P. Gorsen, *Das Prinzip Obszön. Kunst, Pornographie, und Gesellschaft* (Reinbeck, 1969), 9.

46. Foucault, *History of Sexuality,* 48, 45.

47. Siegbert Klee, "Macht und Ohnmacht des Zensurspielers Carl Sternheim," in McCarthy and von der Ohe, *Zensur und Kultur,* 140.

48. Wendelberger, "Das epische Werk," 11; Alberti, "Realismus vor Gericht," 1141ff; and Schulz, "Naturalismus und Zensur," 96–97.

49. Eva Wolf, *Der Schriftsteller im Querschnitt: Außenseiter der Gesellschaft um 1900? Eine systematischer Vergleich von Prosatexten* (Munich, 1978), 116–19.

50. Deiritz, *Geschichtsbewußtsein, Satire, Zensur,* 142.

51. I use the term *alienation* primarily in its traditional, pre-Marxian sense to mean "a withdrawal of support," "a turning away from," "the process of becoming indifferent or hostile to," and "a separation that results in indifference or hostility." Since publication of Marx's early "Economic and Philosophical Manuscripts" around 1930, the term *alienation* has acquired powerful new connotations. This more recent, Marxian concept of alienation is not applicable to most authors discussed here, and I do not mean to imply they were alienated in a Marxian sense. Still, some of the authors who experience what I call "ambivalent alienation" and "internalized alienation" do exhibit some of the features of alienation as Marx conceived it: for example, their own work becomes something of an alien object to them.

52. Oskar Panizza, *Genie and Wahnsinn* (Munich, 1891); and Oskar Panizza, *Der Illusionismus und die Rettung der Persönlichkeit: Skizze einer Weltanschauung* (Leipzig, 1895). See also the discussions in Brown, *Panizza,* 23, 39–41; and Bauer, *Oskar Panizza,* 10, 39–51, 132, 168, 193–94.

53. "Vorrede" to *Das Liebeskonzil,* 3. Aufl. (Zurich, 1897), quoted in *KK,* 139.

54. *Dialog im Geiste Huttens* (written during Panizza's imprisonment, 1895–96; published in 1897), quoted in Panizza, *Das Liebeskonzil und andere Schriften,* 196; and Oskar Panizza, *Psichopatia Criminalis* (Zurich, 1898).

55. Panizza, *Ein Jahr Gefängnis. Mein Tagebuch aus Amberg,* quoted in *Das Liebeskonzil and andere Schriften,* 172–73. This diary, composed 1895–1896, was never published during Panizza's lifetime.

56. *Dialog im Geiste Huttens,* in *Das Liebeskonzil and andere Schriften,* 197.

57. Brown, *Panizza,* 47–51; Bauer, *Oskar Panizza,* 189–90. Sand was a young, nationalistic, and liberal student executed in 1819 for assassinating a reactionary writer.

58. Panizza, *Meine Verteidigung,* 26.

59. *Dialog im Geiste Huttens,* in *Liebeskonzil and andere Schriften,* 196.

60. Panizza to Max Halbe, 15 Jul. 1896, in StBM, Halbe Archiv; see also Brown, *Panizza,* 50–51 and *Das Liebeskonzil and andere Schriften,* 166–67.

61. Entry in Panizza's notebook, quoted in Bauer, *Oskar Panizza,* 194.

62. Oskar Panizza, *Parisjana. Deutsche Verse aus Paris* (Zurich, 1899). See also Brown, *Panizza,* 100–101.

63. Panizza, *Parisjana,* no. 1; and Brown, *Panizza,* 57–59, 97–105.

64. Bauer, *Oskar Panizza,* 196, 220; Brown, *Panizza,* 97–105.

65. Bauer, *Oskar Panizza,* 211–16, and Brown, *Panizza,* 58.

66. Hermann Conradi, "Gedanken über Kunst, Künstler, Künstlertum," sections iv–vi, in Ssymank and Peters, *Conradis Gesammelte Schriften,* 1: 240–41.

67. Ssymank, "Leben Hermann Conradis," 1: ccx, ccxvii.

68. Letter of 3 Dec. 1889, quoted in ibid., 1: ccxvii.

69. Ibid., 1: ccxvi–ccxvii.

70. Wedekind, "Torquemada," 9: 393; and "Vorrede zu 'Oaha'," *Gesammelte Werke,* 9: 449–451.

71. Wedekind, "Vorrede zu 'Oaha'," 9: 451.

72. Ibid., 9: 450, and *Werke,* 3: 365–67.

73. Wedekind to B. Heine, 12 Mar. 1899, *Gesammelte Briefe,* 1: 338.

74. Wedekind to R. Weinhoppel, 22 Mar. 1899, *Gesammelte Briefe,* 1: 342.

75. Wedekind to B. Heine, 12 Nov. 1899, *Gesammelte Briefe,* 1: 316.

76. Wedekind, "Vorwort" to *Die Büchse der Pandora, Gesammelte Werke,* 3: 101; Wedekind's comments on the third edition of *Die Büchse der Pandora,* as quoted in Kutscher, *Wedekind,* 1: 392; and Wedekind to L. Jessner, 30 Sept. 1910, *Gesammelte Briefe,* 2: 248.

77. Wedekind, *Die Zensur. Theodiziee in drei Szenen* (1907), in *Werke,* 1: 59–89. (Quotation is from scene 2.) See also Alan Best, "The Censor Censored: An Approach to Frank Wedekind's 'Die Zensur'," *German Life & Letters* 26, no. 4 (July 1973): 278–87.

78. Dehmel to C. Dehmel, 9 Jun. 1900, and Dehmel to D. von Liliencron, 9 Jul. 1900, Dehmel, *Ausgewählte Briefe,* 352, 354.

79. Gustav Kirstein, Walter Tiemann, C. R. Weiss, eds., *Richard Dehmels Tagebuch 1893–1894* (Leipzig, 1921), 78; Dehmel to H. Thoma, 17 Dec. 1893, *Ausgewählte Briefe*, 142.
80. Kathy Harms, "Writer by Imperial Decree: Ernst von Wildenbruch," in *Imperial Germany*, ed. Volker Dürr, Kathy Harms, and Peter Hayes (Madison, WI, 1985), 141, 143.
81. Berthold Litzmann, *Ernst von Wildenbruch. Zweiter Band: 1885–1909* (Berlin, 1916), 70–80, 105; and Helene Bettelheim-Gabillon,"Wildenbruch und Grillparzer im Spiegel der Zensur," *Österreichische Rundschau* 53, no. 5 (1917): 229–30.
82. "Theater and Zensur. Ein Mahnwort" (1900), in Ernst von Wildenbruch, *Gesammelte Werke,* ed. Berthold Litzmann (Berlin, 1924), 16:183.
83. Ernst, *Jünglingsjahre,* 227–28.
84. Sudermann, *Drei Reden,* 29.
85. Ibid., speech of 25 Mar. 1900.
86. Undated letter [mid-summer, 1900] to Berlin PP, in: Deutsches Literaturarchiv, Marbach am Neckar, Cotta Archiv, Nachl. Sud., V 30 BI. 74; also Lenman, "Art, Society, and the Law," 110 and *Münchener Post,* 5 July 1900.
87. See for example Leo Berg, *Gefesselte Kunst* (Berlin, 1901), 11–12. Dr. Ernst Leopold Stahl was another who staunchly opposed theater censorship yet advocated stronger censorship of "lower entertainments" and controls of those who operated theaters devoted "purely to entertainment." See his comments in *Zukunft der deutschen Bühne,* 78.
88. Heinrich Mann, "Geist and Tat" (written 1910, published in *Pan* January 1911), in *Essays* (Hamburg, 1960), 7–14.
89. Kellermann, "Der Schriftsteller und die deutsche Republik," 30–31.

CONCLUSION
Imperial Censorship: An Appraisal

> Everyone needs an adroit censor who is loyal and who understands
> how to convince us of our errors or our wrong-headedness.
> —attributed to Frederick the Great

> Police meddling with art are like bulls in a china shop.
> —Reichstag delegate Träger (Progressive), 1901

Censorship and Literary Life in Imperial Germany

*D*espite complaints by some that the German Empire was dismissive of writers and literature, the vehement debates about censorship chronicled above indicate that literature was highly esteemed, received much state and public attention, and that imaginative writers and their works were taken very seriously indeed. Cultural reactionaries and avant-garde artists, conservative government officials and radical socialists, traditionalist Catholics and liberal-minded Protestants, the marginalized and vulnerable Jewish community, the emperor, aristocrats, military commanders, and broad segments of the educated and propertied middle classes—all assumed reading literature and performing dramas had enormous power to transform people and social institutions. Those who feared such transformations wanted literature censored; those who welcomed change wanted it freed from censorship.

Censorship, especially of theaters, thus became a highly politicized, increasingly divisive issue throughout the Wilhelmine era. A steady stream of controversial police decisions and the well-publicized trials that often followed kept literary censorship continually before the public eye. So too did proposals in the late 1880s to change the blasphemy law and to involve literary experts in censorship decisions, pitched parliamentary battles throughout the 1890s over the

262 | *Banned in Berlin*

proposed Lex Heinze and Anti-Revolution Bill, political initiatives after 1900 to abolish all theater censorship or to establish external boards of literary experts, the decade-long attempt before and during the war to win approval for a new national Theater Law, and various efforts throughout the imperial era to standardize theater censorship policies yet preserve local discretion. If (as the Berlin theater censor said) "the best censorship is the one least talked about,"[1] then this continual attention was most unwelcome, for censors and their superiors had continually to defend censorship, explain its legal basis, and justify their actions to the monarch, press, parliament, courts, and public. Imperial authorities must sometimes have regretted they could censor expressions challenging the political, social, religious, or moral order, but not those challenging the legitimacy and operations of censorship itself.

In the Bismarck years, when the empire's ruling elite regarded socialists as the most dangerous *Reichsfeinde,* literary censorship was employed primarily against socialist writers and literary organizations. Although anxiety over the socialist threat and the severity of antisocialist censorship policies fluctuated, socialist literature remained the censors' the most consistent target from the 1870s through World War I. Because the socialist literary community remained isolated from the nonsocialist literary community, and from the rest of German society, these interventions aroused relatively little public controversy.

The wider the circle of authors (and readers) affected by state censorship, however, the more its legitimacy was questioned. Some of the first nonsocialist opposition arose when the young empire made peace in the late 1870s with another perceived enemy, the Catholic Church. Paragraph 166, the antiblasphemy law, was seldom applied against anticlerical literature during Bismarck's *Kulturkampf* but once imperial and church authorities came to terms after 1878, it was invoked against several anti-Catholic works. Some Protestant authors who had loyally supported the imperial order now found themselves at odds with its censors.

The end of the Bismarck era, the expiration of the Anti-Socialist Law, and the emperor's New Course in 1890 began a decade of domestic and foreign problems that left ruling elites feeling increasingly vulnerable. Deteriorating relations with Russia and Great Britain abroad were overshadowed at home by rising socialist and trade union militancy, declining Reichstag support for the government, the radicalization of disaffected agrarian landowners and of many lower-middle-class groups, rivalries and infighting within the ruling elites, and embarrassing attacks by the venerable Bismarck on his successors' domestic and foreign policies. Hysterically fearful of the "parties of revolution," Wilhelm II and his governing elite desperately sought to halt the Reichstag from further eroding the monarchy's power. Embarking on a policy of overt repression after 1894, they sought (largely unsuccessfully) to enact harsher legislation against socialists and other subversives and flirted with the idea of a coup d'état that would allow the monarchy to rule without the Reichstag. Their more aggressive and sweeping use of literary censorship now affected significantly more members of the German literary community.

For nonsocialist writers, state censorship posed a greater danger in the 1890s than at any other time before the war. A larger proportion of dramas was banned in the 1890s, for example, than in the years before or after (at least in Berlin, where data is most complete). More importantly, the number of Germans prosecuted for lèse majesté, blasphemy, and obscenity rose dramatically after 1890, reaching an all-time high around 1894–1895. Over thirty prominent writers and satirists were charged in the 1890s, and those convicted received heavier fines or longer jail terms than did later transgressors. At first prosecutors had only limited success winning convictions against writers indicted for obscenity and lèse majesté, and none with charges of blasphemy. From 1894 to 1900, however, while seeking to strengthen criminal laws (the Anti-Revolution Bill and the Lex Heinze) against obscene, blasphemous, and otherwise offensive expression, authorities were more successful in prosecuting several writers for blasphemy and lèse majesté. (Curiously, in the later 1890s the government was less inclined to indict writers and publishers for obscenity, and the few who were convicted received minimal fines.)

As a liberals and moderates were coming to realize, however, the most serious threat to intellectual freedom was posed not by the government, but by conservative public opinion, the growing parliamentary power of the Catholic Center Party, and private morality associations pressuring the government to criminalize vice.[2] The increasing electoral strength of the Center Party gave it a pivotal role in national, Prussian, and especially Bavarian politics throughout the 1890s. Backed by the powerful Catholic press, by conservative journalists and Protestant clergy, by a broad and growing network of local and national moral purity associations, and by temporary political allies like the anti-Semitic and Conservative parties, the Center spearheaded efforts in the 1890s to defend "traditional Christian values" against those liberal cultural developments (especially modernist literature) that profoundly offended their moral and religious sensibilities.

Much like the empire's "national opposition" (radical nationalist groups like the Pan-German League that berated the government for not vigorously defending the nation's interests), during the 1890s this popular movement of cultural reactionaries mobilized broad segments of the middle and lower-middle classes and pressured national and local governments to exercise more repressive censorship over art and literature. These private moral entrepreneurs sought to use the government's proposed Anti-Revolution Bill and the Lex Heinze to criminalize offensive literature and cultural activities that until then had been permitted. However, this legal warfare against liberal culture and modernist art met with widespread protest and vehement opposition not only from the intellectual community and liberal press, but from many cultural moderates as well. Broad sectors of German public opinion would not tolerate any further restrictions on free expression; liberals, progressives, and Social Democrats mobilized and worked together to defeat the Lex Heinze in 1900.

The "clericalized" versions of the Anti-Revolution Bill and Lex Heinze went further than even the conservative government wished; preferring the existing legal tools to the sweeping new ones proposed by the cultural Right, the government ultimately opposed both bills. The government was unwilling to forgo censorship as liberals demanded, but also unwilling to impose the more restrictive controls demanded by the reactionary Right. As Peter Paret noted regarding state policy toward modernist painters, the Prussian bureaucracy (and the Bavarian as well, at least until 1912) was conservative, but not reactionary: the "official" censors took a middle ground between freedom and control and were willing to tolerate avant-garde elements even though the emperor and many popular forces were not. From 1890 on, popular pressure from below, in the form of a broadly based grass-roots movement on the cultural Right posed a greater threat to artistic and literary freedom than did state censorship from above.[3] To counter this threat cultural liberals, who had organized into Goethe Leagues in 1900 to defeat the Lex Heinze and defend liberal culture, continued during the next decade to mobilize middle- and working-class political support for greater intellectual and artistic freedom.

As in other areas of imperial society and politics, 1900 also marks a turning point in literary censorship. Following the government's failure in the late 1890s to pass more repressive laws against socialism, after 1900 one sees a "civilizing of power relationships": reformist and modernizing forces gain strength, bolstered by increasing cooperation between Social Democrats and other liberal and progressive parties. Recent studies have noted a decline in the number of overtly political prosecutions, a "silent parliamentarization" of political life, an increasingly pluralistic society, a softening of state opposition to modernist culture, a strengthening of civil liberties, and an expansion of the liberal public sphere.[4]

There was a general liberalization of many censorship practices as well. Before 1900 the ascendant forces of the cultural Right had pressured authorities to vigorously prosecute writers and ban objectionable dramas, and there existed a real threat that more repressive legislation would further curtail offensive art and literature. After the Left thwarted the Lex Heinze in 1900 and a strong liberal movement emerged pressing for the reform or abolition of censorship, however, revisions to the Criminal Code (such as eliminating *fliegender Gerichtsstand* and reforming the lèse majesté law) in fact provided greater protections for authors. More importantly, government authorities began using the Criminal Code more cautiously. The few times authorities prosecuted satirists for lèse majesté after 1900, they had little success. Prosecutions for blasphemy and obscenity also declined. No prominent writers or satirists were convicted of blasphemy after 1900; when writers were occasionally indicted for obscenity, it was nearly impossible to win convictions from juries in South German states and the few who were convicted in North Germany received modest fines. State efforts in the early 1900s to punish some of Germany's most sexually explicit modernist writers, such as Frank Wedekind, Felix Salten, and Arthur Schnitzler, all came to naught.

In several aspects, theater censorship also eased after 1900. The Goethe League's initiative to abolish, or at least regularize it with a new national Theater Law drew strong support from the liberal public. As theater censorship came under intense discussion in parliament and the press, governing authorities proceeded more cautiously. To mollify critics, police in Berlin and Munich began to rely on external literary experts or civilian censorship advisory boards. In Prussia, decisions about permitting works with New Testament material were transferred from the (archconservative) monarch to the interior and religion ministers, who allowed more exemptions to the blanket ban; local authorities, who could now decide about Old Testament material, displayed more liberality and even approved works like *Die Erste Menschen* that questioned basic premises of scripture. A Naturalist drama like Fulda's *Das verlorene Paradies,* banned in the 1890s because of its treatment of labor disputes, was now permitted. Berlin authorities also eased their suppression of socialist literature and tolerated the activities of the private (uncensored) Freie Volksbühne and Neue Freie Volksbühne. By 1910 police in Berlin and other cities (and even sometimes in Munich) were approving, sometimes on court order, provocative avant-garde works such as Wedekind's *Frühlings Erwachen,* Wilde's *Salome,* Maeterlinck's *Monna Vanna,* Sternheim's *Die Hose,* and parts of Schnitzler's *Anatol* cycle, all of which would have been unthinkable before 1900. The move to centralize censorship decisions in Prussia and other states meant authorities in the hinterlands now tended to defer to the decisions of the more cosmopolitan capital cities. As one Berlin theater censor told the press in 1907, "for years now, it [has] been the goal of the censorship office to act with the greatest possible leniency"; the city's theater censors, he claimed, had established a good working relationship with theater directors by pointing out potential problems early in the production process to avoid wasting time and money later.[5]

This period of relative liberalization was short lived. Beginning in 1910 prosecutions for obscenity began to rise as part of a national effort to combat obscene publications and a few writers (Eulenberg, Hyan, Ball, Kerr, Klabund) were included. After the conservative Traugott von Jagow became police president of Berlin in 1909, he harassed the journal *Pan* and sought to rein in the Freie Volksbühne and Neue Freie Volksbühne by subjecting them to the same censorship as public theaters. Despite opposition from wide sectors of the liberal middle class (demonstrating that the liberal-progressive-socialist anticensorship front that emerged from the struggle over the Lex Heinze was still intact), von Jagow's action was upheld by the Supreme Administrative Law Court in 1911, as was his decision to ban Rosenow's socialist drama *Die in Schatten Leben* from these two theaters.

Censorship in Bavaria, too, began to tighten as the liberal government there fell increasingly under the control of the Christian Right. Since 1903 a conservative government under Clemens von Podewils had acquiesced to pressure from the Center Party to act more forcefully against modernist art. When the clerical Right finally gained a majority in the Bavarian parliament in 1912, it installed an even more conservative government under Georg von Hertling that was beholden to the Center Party and rightist morality associations and determined to take sterner actions against Munich's avant-garde artists and writers. The city's experimental Censorship Advisory Board had already begun to unravel by 1911 and over the next three years became increasingly dysfunctional, controversial, and irrelevant.

The outbreak of war in 1914, the declaration of a domestic "state of siege," and the administrative centralization needed for mobilization not only resurrected most of the press controls, including prior press censorship, that had died out after 1848, but also created a national system of censorship that was more centralized and geographically uniform than ever before. Most local military authorities moved quickly to close the loopholes that had frustrated prewar censors: prior theater censorship was now introduced in many areas that had not had it, previously approved dramas had to be resubmitted, many works passed by civilian censors before the war were forbidden for vague or spurious reasons and bans could not be appealed to the courts, censors could ban private as well as public performances, and criticism of censorship was forbidden. It goes without saying that after August 1914 a higher percentage of the plays submitted for censorship were banned. This radical tightening of theater censorship implemented many changes the cultural Right had campaigned for since the 1890s, encouraging morality leagues and other private moral entrepreneurs to believe the sterner military censors would be more sympathetic to their complaints than civilian censors had been. But local military commanders did not necessarily acquiesce to the cultural Right; as civilian authorities had before the war, the increasingly autonomous deputy commanding generals considered their district's local conditions and so frequently reached different decisions about the same drama. Even under a virtual military dictatorship, Germany did not achieve a completely centralized, uniform system of theater censorship.

Given the legal constraints, porousness, and irregularity of censorship in imperial Germany, one must ask how effective were efforts to control literature, especially those avant-garde, modernist literary currents that most challenged traditional moral and social norms? Were modernist writers "bridled," "isolated," and "restrained," and did the law succeed in keeping serious discussions of the social order off the public stage, as some have suggested?[6] Or was censorship "ineffectual" and unable to influence modern literature and the theater repertoire, as others contend?[7]

In fact, literary censorship as practiced in imperial Germany was reasonably effective in some areas but surprisingly ineffectual in others; in many respects, the efforts of the censors fell far short of their aims. German authorities were powerless, of course, to prevent the actual creation of unwanted literature. By the late nineteenth century, the time had long passed—or had not yet returned— when the state could prevent writers from practicing their craft by execution, imprisonment, or a blanket *Schreibverbot* or *Berufsverbot* (ban on writing or practicing a profession). Only self-censorship could prevent the actual production of literature but, as discussed above, it is impossible to document what role conscious or unconscious self-censorship played in imperial literary life. With the end of prior press censorship, the government was also powerless, at least in peacetime, to prevent the publication of literary works; it could only attempt to halt their physical distribution or circulation. Because they could never retrieve all (and seldom even a majority) of the copies, authorities could rarely prevent some interested readers from acquiring and reading a work. The only area in which German authorities were able to exert significant control was in the performance of dramatic literature: besides determining who could operate public theaters, police in many localities could usually prevent or halt the public (but seldom the private) performance of a drama or set very specific conditions for its performance.

Under these conditions, literary censorship was most successful and met least public opposition when used against plays and published satires that were perceived as threatening basic imperial political institutions (such as the emperor, the Hohenzollern dynasty, the military, and the legal system), the territorial unity of the empire (especially expressions of Polish nationalism) or the empire's diplomatic interests. Censorship actions in these areas affected popular entertainment and "trivial" literature almost exclusively, as few writers of "serious" literature treated such subjects. Authorities were also relatively successful in limiting the use of literature and drama in socialist gatherings, preventing or restricting the access of socialist audiences to propagandistic socialist literature, and preventing the performance of dramas that depicted social insurrection. They were also frequently able to keep off the public stage (or force suitable changes in) popular, trivial dramas and farces they judged to be immoral. Authorities were generally successful, too, in prohibiting most dramas with biblical themes and characters, especially from the New Testament, although this policy met with growing criticism because the public found it baffling and more apt to undermine than to strengthen religious piety.

However, after early successes with the Leipzig Realists and Oskar Panizza, censors frequently failed to obtain blasphemy or obscenity convictions of serious writers (even the most explicitly sexual modernists), to keep middle-class audiences from seeing tendentious socialist dramas on the commercial stage, or (after the *Kulturkampf* ended) to quash dramatic performances that might enflame Catholic-Protestant tensions. Moreover, authorities were generally unable to prevent legitimate theaters from performing serious, socially critical (but nonsocialist) Naturalist dramas like *Die Weber,* and they found it increasingly difficult to keep audiences from seeing "immoral" dramas by serious authors. In short, literary censorship was most effective when used to defend the political order, especially from the threat of socialism; it was far less effective in defending prevailing religious, social, and moral (sexual) norms, areas where modernists and other serious writers had much greater interest.

In the end, the state infringed more on the public's freedom of access to literature than on writers' freedom to express "facts or opinions that demanded expression" (Pascal). Authorities were often able to limit or restrict a literary work's diffusion, whether in print or on stage, to particular audiences of a certain nature or size. By interposing themselves between a literary work or dramatic performance and the broader audience for which it was intended (especially if that audience was considered to be socialist), censors could manipulate—but not completely control— who had access to the piece, when, and where, and in this way they could influence how the public read, received, or understood the work. Censorship was thus an important element in the *Wirkungsgeschichte* or *Rezeptionsgeschichte* of those facts and opinions writers chose to express.

Like many contemporary literary theorists, imperial authorities were concerned less with the work (text) itself or the intentions of its author than with the (anticipated) responses of its readers or audiences. This turns on its head what some have seen as the fundamental relation between literature and the law. Achim Barsch and others, for example, have argued that conflicts between the "literature system" and the "justice system" arise because jurists and administrators incorrectly assume the meaning of a text is fixed in the text itself and that certain textual meanings lead readers to certain responses. Recent literary theory and the "literature system," however, recognize that meaning is not fixed, but rather readers (or members of a theater audience) play an active role in "cognitively constructing" a work's meaning. How recipients "decode" a text depends on factors such as the recipient's personality; prior knowledge and experiences; familiarity with linguistic rules, interests, motivations; and his/her social relations; so a text will have different meanings—and different effects—for different recipients. Moreover (Barsch et al. argue), just as meaning is not inherent in a text, neither is "literariness," the quality of being a (reputable) work of literature; "a reader's decision to consider a text as literary, and to receive it accordingly, is indeed a subjective, individual decision." Accordingly, the effects of a work of art cannot be deduced from the text, but rather are grounded in "how a recipient, on the basis of his previous experiences, deals with the work in [different] social and situational contexts." Because of these two dissimilar, in principle incompatible constructions of reality, conflicts between the literature system and the justice system are all but inevitable. [8]

But in imperial Germany (and perhaps in most censorship systems) these two perspectives are in fact reversed. It was the censoring authorities—the "justice system"—who implicitly recognized the recipient's crucial role in the construction of literary meaning and who were preoccupied with the (anticipated) responses of readers or members of a theater audience. Conversely, it was writers and their defenders—the "literature system"—who usually argued that a censored work did not really "mean" what authorities alleged it did; that an author's intended meaning (which was, of course, purely innocent, artistic, apolitical) should be accepted as the correct one; that certain works were inherently good "art" and so must be judged by different standards than works of little artistic merit; and that one need not worry that certain (for example, working-class) audiences were likely to find more politically or morally questionable meanings in a work, or respond to it differently, than other (for example, middle-class) audiences. Ironically, too, censors and members of the nonliterary public frequently ascribed more power to literature—that is, its ability to affect people—than did members of the literary community, who, for expediency, often downplayed or dismissed a work's potential impact or effect on the public.

It is clear that literary censorship could do little to suppress avant-garde, modernist literature (and art) from developing and flourishing. Despite efforts by the state to impede their dissemination, the works of all major domestic and foreign fin-de-siècle writers—from Realists, Naturalists, Neo-romantics, and Young Vienna, to Jugendstil, Symbolists, Impressionists, Neoclassicists, and Expressionists—were published, circulated freely, and were (relatively) widely read in Germany. Police intervention might delay briefly the circulation of a newly published work, cutting into sales, but as often as not this actually served to advertise it and bring commercial benefits.

With dramatic art the picture was more complicated, for dramas are not simply texts intended for individual readers, but collaborative events involving live interaction between characters (actors) as well as between actors and audience. To translate its potential into actuality, to prevent its being "stillborn," a dramatic work must be enacted on stage before a live audience. Since the audience is an essential part of a play, the value, quality, and artistic success of a drama—its "stageworthiness"—become evident only when it is performed. A play's power depends also on the actors' ability to "make a speaker's words more expressive than can the reader's unaided imagination."[9] It was for these reasons, of course, that authorities often forbade the performance of an objectionable work, but not the text itself. Thus, while playwrights could publish their works and usually hold public readings, they faced more difficulty in having their works performed before a broad, public audience. Throughout much of Germany, especially in leading theater cities like Berlin and Munich, police often forbade public performances of certain works, or compelled changes in the script or the staging that differed from the playwright's, or director's, original vision. Official approval for a play also tended to "freeze" the script: instead of making revisions right up to opening night, or adjustments and experiments during its run, playwrights and directors were expected to follow the script that had been approved weeks earlier.

Since theater censorship was not geographically uniform, however, a play banned in one place was frequently performed elsewhere, allowing a dramatist (and the public) to assess it as a piece of theater, not merely as literature. Moreover, since private theaters were exempt from censorship, many censored plays (especially the most avant-garde), were nevertheless enacted for more limited, selective audiences. These "private" audiences were sometimes open to nearly anyone: when Wedekind's *Die Büchse der Pandora* was "privately" performed by Munich's Neuer Verein theatrical association in 1910, it seemed to have been accessible to almost anybody, and the association regularly sought to attract a wide segment of the population.[10] Thus, even heavily censored dramatists like Wedekind could often see how their works "played" to small—and sometimes to broad—audiences. In Hamburg, for instance, the Thalia-Theater was recognized as a leading showcase for Wedekind's drama. Similarly, Hasenclever's *Der Sohn*, while banned in Germany until January 1918, enjoyed private performances in Prague and Dresden in 1916 and public performances in Vienna and Zurich the following year.[11]

Although censorship may not have hindered the development of avant-garde literature and theater in Germany, it nonetheless estranged many writers from the empire. By seeking to control universal public access to certain works (through geographic, educational, social, or political restrictions on the audience), the censoring authorities often widened the distance between writers and society and heightened the sense of social and political alienation many writers felt. As Bernhard Kellermann observed, by trying to keep certain literary works out of the broad, universally accessible public forum, the imperial state drove many writers out of it as well.

The Ironies of Censorship

Thus, literary censors frequently produced outcomes directly contrary to those they intended. Bureaucratic organizations and professional experts who intervene in social life to eliminate misery or foster social harmony frequently fall victim to the Law of Unintended Consequences. Indeed, a subfield of "the sociology of irony" has arisen that, by distinguishing between intended ("manifest") and unintended ("latent") functions of organizations and systems, illuminates the unexpected consequences, paradoxes, contradictions, and even deceptions that frequently follow from agents' conscious motivations and professed goals.[12] Imperial Germany—where, by contemporary standards, both bureaucratic organization and efforts at social control were relatively advanced—offers abundant examples of policies or institutions that yielded ironic consequences, from Bismarck's counterproductive efforts to crush the political power of Catholicism in the 1870s, to the diplomatic and military policies that resulted in war in July 1914. Ironic results are especially striking, however, in the state's censorship of literature and the public stage; although it was their function to suppress expressions that violated established norms, imperial authorities often unwittingly promoted the very expressions they sought to silence.[13]

We have seen how censorship, like other methods of controlling deviant behavior, could become self-perpetuating. Censors developed a vested interest in the existence of at least some norm-violating expressions and a mutually reinforcing dependency frequently arose between censor and censored. The interests of the organization impelled it to identify and recruit larger numbers of potential deviants because the more censors there were, the more they had to find to censor. Organizational demands for efficiency and maximal processing of cases means pressures to enforce the rules remain constant, even though the actual number of violations may not: censors not only tend to find what they need to find, but they seem to find it at a fairly consistent rate.[14] Thus German authorities sometimes helped create deviance through "covert facilitation": using hidden or secret means, they generated opportunities for rule-breaking by potential deviants, as when obliging police officials in Leipzig took offense at Panizza's *Das Liebeskonzil* so the Munich prosecutor could have a reason to indict him. Similarly, the Central Police Office for the Suppression of Obscene Materials (Zentralpolizeistelle zur Bekämpfung unzüchtiger Schriften, Abbildungen, und Darstellungen), which employed more than a dozen individuals and had an annual budget of nearly twenty thousand marks, facilitated and encouraged norm violation. With the aim of prosecuting pornographic suppliers, that office subscribed to numerous domestic and foreign risqué publications and each year ordered hundreds of pornographic books, pictures, and paraphernalia—thereby making the office one of the major consumers of pornography in imperial Germany.[15]

Censors, who are charged with judging normality, are able to "construct" deviance by enlarging its definition and create more deviance to censor by broadening their activities. By subsuming more forms of behavior under their control, they were able to generate more rules to enforce and find more activities on which to focus their attention; this in turn greatly expanded their ability to identify and enlist more potential deviants. Throughout the imperial era, the censors' surveillance was steadily extended. Changes in the Commercial Code in the 1880s allowed local police to monitor sensationalistic pulp fiction (so-called *Schmutz- und Schundliteratur*) which, although not legally obscene, was considered morally deleterious. Police could now ban from the colportage trade any printed or pictorial works they considered religiously or morally offensive, and thousands of such titles were.[16] In 1900 the law regarding obscenity and morally offensive materials was broadened; it now became a criminal offense for colporteurs to sell or distribute to minors any printed or visual material "which, although not obscene, grossly offends the sense of modesty," and catalogs listing thousands of items meeting this criterion were soon compiled.[17] Similarly, the censor's reach was extended ever further into other public entertainments: the licensing of variety shows (so-called *Tingeltangel*) was tightened, and police tried to extend censorship to certain private theaters. Beginning in 1906 cinema performances were censored, and even the posters advertising them required police approval.[18] The outbreak of war in 1914, of course, extended prior censorship to the press and most other publications.

As the functional scope of the censors expanded, so too did their geographic reach. There was a constant tendency to centralize and standardize whatever censorship measures were introduced. To reduce the loopholes and inconsistencies that are inevitable in any patchwork system of federal states and local options, German authorities (and after 1914, local military commanders) were always eager to extend the theater censorship practices of Berlin (where they were usually introduced and were most efficiently administered) to other Prussian cities, then to other federal states, and finally to the entire empire. Likewise, when Berlin established a system of prior cinema censorship, it was soon adopted by several other Prussian and non-Prussian cities and federal states: by the war, the central film censor's office in Prussia functioned as the de facto film censor for all Germany. The same tendency toward national centralization and standardization is evident in the Central Police Office for Suppression of Obscene Materials, established in 1911 to coordinate the nation's fight against imported pornography, and the central military censorship office (Oberzensurstelle) established after 1914 to oversee and coordinate the work of local press censors.

One other source of deviance creation deserves mention: the private, unofficial moral entrepreneurs (see chapter 2). These self-appointed guardians of the norms also helped recruit potential targets for the censors; through complaints to prosecutors and petitions to lawmakers, they sought both to prod official agencies into more strictly enforcing existing rules and to persuade authorities to create new, tougher rules to combat the vices and deviance they perceived around them. As Peter Jelavich observes, it is paradoxical not only that these "democratic" popular institutions often were more eager for censorship than the supposedly authoritarian German state, but also that such organizations (especially after 1918) sometimes pressed authorities to act even when the groups thought the chances for a successful ban or prosecution were slim. Rather, they hoped to manufacture scandals that would discredit the government and mobilize their members and potential supporters. In this way they too developed a vested interest in the existence of objectionable material, the availability of which benefited them. "What was paradoxical here was the fact that censorship was demanded, not really in order to suppress offensive art, but to highlight its presence."[19]

Censorship was also counterproductive when it served to popularize works that transgressed established norms. A century earlier a 1775 German brochure on censorship noted, "One can be sure no book or publication will entice more readers than when the press announces it has been banned, and that those who purchase it will be heavily fined; for one immediately suspects that it must speak the truth, otherwise they wouldn't confiscate it."[20] As we have seen with *Simplicissimus, Die Weber, Salome, Maria von Magdala,* and numerous other cases, literary censorship frequently advertised and promoted the very materials it sought to suppress. For because of the free press, attempts to ban a work inevitably generated much passionate discussion in the newspapers and often stimulated public interest in the censored work. The prominent cultural critic Ferdinand Avenarius, commenting on German theater censorship, observed in 1903 that "If one is not able to see [a banned drama] on the stage, then one at least wants to read it or hear it read aloud, and so playwrights and publishers end up doing a good business anyway, even if the highest court upholds, rather than overturns, the police's decision. In this way, works that are initially ignored completely may sometimes gain a great glory and reputation."[21]

The extensive publicity that often surrounded acts of police censorship, especially bans that were eventually overturned by the courts, always had the potential of turning an unknown censored author into a celebrity and creating more publicity, a wider audience, and greater sales for the work. In this way the stern censors unwittingly helped create a number of bestsellers and box office hits. Commenting on this irony, the writer Ernst Wichert confided to Paul Heyse: "Works that come into conflict with the censor gain, for that very reason, a certain prospect of success. And it is amazing to see how the press immediately sides with [the banned work], before they can have the slightest idea of its content, which is often downright dirty [*recht unsauberen Inhalt*]. ... What a role: guaranteeing that the dirty birds are well-fed [*den Schmutzfinken das Futter zu sichern*]."[22]

The publicity generated by a successful ban can benefit the censors, but when a ban fails, the censors can be seriously undermined. Agencies of control enforce certain social norms by defining and punishing deviant behavior; each time the community or its agents censure deviance, it reaffirms the authority of the violated norm and reasserts the dividing line between permissible and impermissible behavior. The more widely publicized the punishment of deviant behavior is, the more the norm in question is reinforced.[23] Thus, when victims of censorship receive wide attention, it may ultimately work to the advantage of the censors—who, after all, want the public to be aware of which norms cannot be violated with impunity. But in cases where censorship fails—for example, where a censor's decision is later reversed by the courts or a superior, as often happened in imperial Germany—widespread publicity has the opposite effect: Here it helps erode traditional norms more rapidly because it publicizes the fact the norm is no longer enforceable.

Even Germany's official censors and nonofficial moral entrepreneurs came to recognize the counterproductivity of many censorship decisions. Beginning in the 1890s the conservative press frequently expressed anger and frustration at how attempts to ban works like *Die Weber* or *Das Liebeskonzil* had merely made the authors famous and boosted public interest in the banned works.[24] When the Munich Men's League for the Suppression of Public Immorality was founded in 1906 to fight obscenity, it decried how the censors' efforts produced unwelcome results:

> Because of the timid application of legal regulations, the poison ... spreads under cover of a "modernist" direction in art. The responsible authorities in Munich—and this cannot be emphasized enough—have not lacked for zeal and vigor in their fight against filth. But up to now the judges have handed the police and the public prosecutor defeat after defeat, so that finally the opposite of the desired goal is achieved: *pornography triumphs,* using shameless judicial acquittals and court releases [of confiscated material] for additional publicity, thus piquing public interest and increasing sales.[25]

By this time Berlin's chief theater censor and the police president had confided to the Prussian minister of the interior that when their bans of dramas were reversed by the courts, a curious public then flocked to the performances. Bans and their reversals, these two officials stated, only create greater publicity for such works and play into the hands of unscrupulous, greedy directors and authors who hope to provoke a ban and create a sensation as a way of overcoming their financial difficulties. In the future the censor and his supervisor planned to be far more cautious about banning works outright.[26] Indeed, from the turn of the century to World War I, both Prussian and Bavarian authorities often hesitated to prosecute *Simplicissimus* or to ban certain works by Wedekind or others because they feared the action might backfire and turn the authors into public martyrs.

Attempts at suppression not only increased the popularity and distribution of certain works, but may also have magnified their effect and social significance.

Intentionally crossing something out unintentionally underlines it; to signify a work, an action, or a person as deviant or socially harmful invests that object with a new meaning and enhanced significance. Psychologists have found that when information is restricted or censored it is empowered in unintended ways, becoming more desirable, more highly valued, and more persuasive than before it became scarce.[27] And Pareto and other sociologists have noted that repression of certain instincts or expressions can intensify people's sensitivity toward all references to what has been repressed; pent-up energies of expression concerning the forbidden may erupt at the slightest opportunity, and in extreme cases people develop an obsession with a taboo topic or type of behavior.[28]

Where criticism of something (such as a religion, a symbol, or a political issue) is commonplace, people become to some extent immunized to such criticisms and pay them less attention than where such remarks are strictly prohibited and where, consequently, the slightest critical expression about a taboo object makes a deeper impression. As noted playwright and theater director Heinrich Laube recalled of the pre-1848 era, when no open discussion of a topic is possible, the result is "a secretive silence, in which a spirited author's barest whisper is heard, understood, and interpreted to excess (*überreich gedeutet*)."[29] Lèse majesté, for example, was frequently and severely punished. But precisely because criticisms of the monarch were so heavily sanctioned, they were eagerly devoured by the public and made a deeper impression than in nations such as Belgium or Britain, where lèse majesté was more tolerated and where, as a result, people took much less notice of it. This point is well illustrated by Ludwig Quidde's famous *Caligula,* the clever, devastating satire of Wilhelm II's megalomania that immediately became a best-selling national sensation. Although Quidde escaped legal action at the time, many of his fellow citizens did not. During the *Caligula* craze of 1894–1895 (which coincided with a larger anarchist scare sparked by the assassination of French President Carnot in June 1894), German authorities zealously pursued alleged insults against the monarchy: more people were convicted of lèse majesté in Germany in 1894 and 1895 than at any other time. While verbal attacks on the monarch, like Quidde's, probably fanned fear of further attacks (whether verbal or physical), it may be that the fear also helped to inspire the attacks. Deviance usually appears precisely at those points where it is most feared, and in precisely the shape and form suspected: those terrified of witches or Communist subversives, for example, will soon find them everywhere. While it is true the deviance creates the fear, it is also true the fear creates the deviance.[30]

There are other ways that censoring a work alters its meaning: the targeted work or stigmatized passage comes to be read (or viewed) differently and thus understood differently. Literary scholars—especially since the rise of reception aesthetics, reception theory, and reader-response theory, which focus on the crucial role the reader plays in construing textual meaning—frequently point out, for example, how attempts to censor Hauptmann's *Die Weber* in the mid-1890s, Heyse's *Maria von Magdala* in 1901–1903, or Sternheim's *Die Hose* after 1911 profoundly altered these works' subsequent reception (*Rezeptionsgeschichte*), which is to say, how these works were interpreted by contemporary and subsequent readers.[31] Similarly, when a censor takes exception to—and thus draws attention to—a specific scene, passage, or image, it magnifies that particular element's role in determining the meaning of the work as a whole. Nothing illustrates this better than wartime press censorship in neighboring Austria-Hungary. For reasons of time and cost, newspaper publishers were allowed to leave a blank (white) space where government censors had deleted something from the final proof copy. The growing number of white spaces during the war was increasingly noticeable and embarrassing, and served to stimulate wild rumors among the general public. One group of editors pointed out to police that "the reader *must* gradually come to the conclusion that there, where the white space is, the dangerous truth once stood."[32] In Germany, such blank spaces were prohibited—just for this reason, no doubt; editors had to reset the type of that issue to mask what was excised.

Finally, as photography critic Andy Grundberg has pointed out,[33] once a work is censored or comes under attack from moral entrepreneurs, the notoriety it often brings the artist makes it harder for society to evaluate the artistic quality of the work. For opponents of censorship and defenders of the censored artist, the artistic quality of the banned work borders on the taboo, and few of its defenders dare to say the work is no good artistically. (Theodor Lessing, who wrote an impassioned defense of Oskar Panizza and *Das Liebeskonzil* upon hearing of Panizza's conviction, later admitted he composed his furious essay "without knowing anything about the condemned work," and never did read it.[34]) The notoriety that censorship confers can thus sometimes undermine others' ability to judge a work on its artistic merits; political, rather than aesthetic judgments come to dominate the discourse of both censors and censored. After the controversy over *Die Weber*, for example, many Germans knew Hauptmann simply as the piece's author, which aroused public literary, moral, and political expectations about him that he was often unable, and unwilling, to fulfill.[35] Similarly, once Heyse's *Maria von Magdala* came under attack from conservative authorities in 1902–1903, the sudden fame Heyse and his artistically mediocre drama enjoyed made it harder for critics, especially in the liberal press, to evaluate the artistic quality of his work. (As we saw above, Ernst Wichert was amused at how journalists often supported a banned work without knowing anything about it.) For months after the initial ban, antiestablishment Naturalist and modernist literary critics generally praised *Maria von Magdala* in glowing terms. Only after the Berlin Goethe League held a closed, private performance of the piece in May 1903 did these same circles begin to mercilessly dissect its artistic weaknesses.[36] When official interventions encourage artists and critics to abandon (even temporarily) aesthetic judgments for political ones, it illustrates again the curious reciprocity that can develop between the censors and the censored.

Still another way censors created deviance was to substantiate deviant behavior by labeling it: the deviant then became the thing he or she was described as being. Since, as Becker has argued, deviance is not an inherent quality but rather an attribute bestowed on a person by others, "the deviant is one to whom that label has been successfully applied."[37] Agents of social control develop a labeling process that convinces both the conformists and often the rule-breakers as well that they are, in fact, deviants or outsiders. Such labels are often self-fulfilling, for they set up expectations in both labeler and labeled that are easily fulfilled and that help push the deviant into further deviant behavior. A person labeled as a deviant or offender is stigmatized and disaffiliated from social conventions and routines. In response he or she must develop nonconventional behavior, and thereby is frequently pushed into a deviant subculture, membership in which may, in turn, raise his feelings of self-worth through acceptance of a new deviant identity. But whether or not she joins a deviant subculture, an accused deviant develops a new self-image: she is forced to think differently about herself and her place within her world, and so comes to adopt the perspective of the deviant or outsider. A labeled deviant may even embrace that label, perhaps developing (or adopting from his new subculture) a self-justifying rationale or "ideology" that provides reasons for continuing his deviant behavior. Once labeling occurs, it becomes almost irreversible, and a person can break out of his deviant status only with the greatest of difficulty. In sum: "The process of making the criminal is a process of tagging, defining, identifying, segregating, describing, emphasizing, making conscious and self-conscious: it becomes a way of stimulating, suggesting, emphasizing, and evoking the very traits that are complained of. The person becomes the thing he is described as being."[38]

As we have seen, being officially censored—labeled as deviant—or even having unofficial moral entrepreneurs request official intervention against them frequently produced in German writers and artists feelings of alienation, injustice, and defiance, which in turn pushed them toward further antisocial behavior and more social sanction. After his conviction for lèse majesté in connection with the "Palestine issue" of *Simplicissimus,* for example, the illustrator Thomas Theodor Heine quickly adopted his new label as *Majestätsbeleidiger* (someone who has committed lèse majesté) and his criminal status. On the cover of the next issue of *Simplicissimus* after he was sentenced, he published a humorous caricature entitled "This is how I'll draw my next picture," which depicted himself drawing in a jail cell, chained hand and foot, while a jurist and several guards look over his shoulder, watching every pen-stroke. (See Figure C.1) In "Traum des Majestäts- beleidigers" (Dream of A Person Convicted of Lèse Majesté) he presents a fantasy of being led, blindfolded and with a sign reading *Laesae Majestatis* around his neck, to the guillotine. (See Figure C.2) While the monarch, flanked by members of the nobility, clergy, and military, watched approvingly, the common people weep, wail, and wave good-bye to him. Clearly, for Heine his new criminal status was more a badge of honor than a disgrace. Nor did it deter him from further rule-breaking: a few years later his cartoon satirizing the German diplomatic corps earned him a conviction for *grober Unfug* and a thirty-mark fine.[39]

Ludwig Thoma was another who, once stigmatized by the censor, did his best to live up to his new label. After being unsuccessfully prosecuted for blasphemy

Figure C.1 Thomas Theodor Heine, "This is how I'll draw my next picture"*
"Life is earnest; art is serene."
* Herr Th. Th. Heine was imprisoned on 2 November for alleged lèse majesté, where he still languishes.
Thomas Theodore Heine, *Simplicissimus,* 1898

Figure C.2 Traum des Majestätsbeleidigers

Thomas Theodore Heine, "Dream of A Person Convicted of *Lèse Majesté*"

in 1904 for his satirical attacks on the Catholic Center Party, the following year Thoma was indicted for ridiculing the moral hypocrisy of Protestant clergymen. He wrote to his lawyer, "The authorities won't find me defenseless. If I come out of this with a jail term, I'll launch an offensive against these hypocrites." Thoma was sentenced to six weeks in jail, which he later used to write his biting satirical drama *Morality*.[40] Two weeks before beginning his sentence, he appeared at still another hearing because he had insulted a Württemberg judge in print. To a friend, Thoma wrote: "When [that hearing] is over, I'll prepare another little treat for that judge: namely, an article each line of which will contain two un-prosecutable libels (*zwei nicht zu fassende Beleidigungen*). So you see, my path to prison is paved with the best of intentions [*Vorsätze*—which can also mean 'premeditations']."[41]

Other writers, too, once suspected or labeled as deviant, were "recruited" by the state or by moral entrepreneurs into long-term service in the deviant ranks. For example, although Ludwig Quidde's biting *Caligula* brought no immediate legal consequences, the reaction of the conservative historical profession quickly ended his scholarly career. The ostracized Quidde was forced to resign from an important editorial position and excluded from any further activity as a professional historian. In the words of one biographer, "Within a few weeks and months, Quidde had to exchange the role of respected and influential scholar and scholarly organizer for that of proscribed outsider. This process was accelerated by the fact that he reacted to the [historical] guild's behavior by turning his activities almost entirely to politics, and thereby also sealing the break from his side."[42] Whereas previously Quidde had been minimally active in progressive-democratic politics, after the *Caligula* affair he became a prominent political journalist and organizer for Germany's democratic, pacifist, and antimilitarist forces. *Caligula* made him a marked man, watched closely by the state prosecutor.[43]

But there is no better example of how censorship created a permanent deviant than Oskar Panizza. As a result of his imprisonment for blasphemy and obscenity, Panizza progressively adopted the status and outlook of a deviant outsider and developed a comprehensive ideology justifying his norm-violating behavior. While incarcerated, for example, he used special stationery whose letterhead proudly identified him as "Oskar Panizza, presently in the Penal Institution Amberg in Bavaria" and he increasingly identified himself with other marginalized outsiders like the criminally insane, the despised Social Democrats, and early political martyrs. His prison writings express his conviction that the interests of artists are eternally irreconcilable with those of society and that artists must follow their inner convictions regardless of the social or legal consequences. Society always marginalizes artists, whether by imprisoning them as criminals, forcing them into exile, or declaring them insane. Identifying himself and other artists with another classic outsider group, he argued that society could preserve its norms and still permit the artists' rights of free expression only by declaring them to be criminal psychotics and confining them to a huge asylum. There they could be allowed to do as they pleased without disrupting society. Fearing that upon his release from prison, society would scorn him as a criminal and even his embarrassed friends would avoid him, Panizza renounced his Bavarian citizenship and left Germany. The vitriolic anti-German tracts he published from exile led to new confiscations, indictments, arrest, a forced return to Germany, and finally commitment to a mental asylum for the remainder of his life.

* * *

No one familiar with earlier and later periods of German history—or with other regimes in other places and times—would argue that all censorship is ineffectual, that neither governments nor private associations can effectively suppress opinions and restrict freedom of expression (at least in the short run), or that censorship cannot have dire consequences for the lives of the censored. In imperial Germany, however, a constellation of factors—a decentralized federal structure with widely varying state and local laws; institutionalized civil liberties, well-established legal safeguards of free expression, and a relatively free press; an independent judiciary that generally made an earnest effort to protect defendant's rights; and a healthy "public sphere" where public opinion served as a powerful deterrent—restrained the censors, thwarted the efficient exercise of censorship, and made it highly unpredictable. The German Empire exercised a prerogative to intervene in literary life in the name of public peace, order, and security that was perhaps broader than that of its Western neighbors, but still not broad enough to prevent the literary community from challenging and subverting many of the social norms the state was most determined to defend.

Notes

1. Regierungsrat Dr. Possart, *Berliner Tageblatt*, 13 Sept. 1907, quoted in Marven H. Krug, "Civil Liberties in Imperial Germany" (Ph.D. diss., University of Toronto, 1995), 171.
2. Lenman ("Censorship and Society," 42ff, 53, 313–317) examines this phenomenon in Munich, while Mast (*Künstlerische und wissenschaftliche Freiheit*, 221–30) and Jelavich, ("Paradoxes of Censorship," 272–73) see the same trend beyond Bavaria.
3. Peter Paret, "The Artist as Staatsbürger: Aspects of the Fine Arts and the Prussian State Before and During the First World War," *German Studies Review* 6 (Oct. 1983): 421–37.
4. For example Retallack, *Germany in the Age of Kaiser Wilhelm II* and Nipperdey, *Deutsche Geschichte*.
5. Possart in *Berliner Tageblatt*, 13 Sept. 1907, quoted in Krug, "Civil Liberties," 171.
6. For example Mayer, *The Persistence of the Old Regime*, 190, and Pascal, *From Naturalism to Expressionism*, 256, 261, 266.
7. For example Mommsen, *Bürgerliche Kultur und künstlerische Avantgarde*, 45–46.
8. Achim Barsch, "Literatur und Recht aus literaturhistorischer Sicht," in *Literatur vor dem Richter. Beiträge zur Literaturfreiheit und Zensur*, ed. Birgit Dankert and Lothar Zechlin (Baden-Baden, 1988), 63–90, quotes from 73, 85–86.
9. Laurence Perrine and Thomas R. Arp, *Literature. Structure, Sound, and Sense*, 6th ed. (Ft. Worth, TX, 1993), 865.
10. Lenman, "Censorship and Society," 237.
11. Giesing, "Theater, Polizei, und Politik," 137; Christa Spreizer, *From Expressionism to Exile: The Works of Walter Hasenclever (1890–1940)* (Rochester, NY, 1999), 61–62.
12. Robert K. Merton, "The Unanticipated Consequences of Purposive Social Action," *American Sociological Review* 1 (1936): 894–904 and *Social Theory and Social Structure*, 1968 enlarged edition (New York, 1968), 73–138; David Matza, *Becoming Deviant* (Englewood Cliffs, NJ, 1969), 69–85; Louis Schneider, "Ironic Perspective and Sociological Thought," in *The Idea of Social Structure: Papers in Honor of Robert K. Merton*, ed. Lewis A. Coser (New York, 1975), 323–37; Marx, "Ironies of Social Control," 242; Edward Tenner, *Why Things Bite Back: Technology and the Revenge of Unintended Consequences* (New York, 1997); and Steven M. Gillon, *That's Not What We Meant To Do: Reform and its Unintended Consequences in the 20th Century* (New York, 2000).

13. After completing this study I discovered additional recent analyses pointing out the "paradoxical" or ironic consequences of censorship, for example Kuhn, *Cinema, Censorship and Sexuality, 1909–1925,* Holmquist, "Corrupt Originals," and Jelavich, "Paradoxes of Censorship."

14. Hawkins and Tiedeman, *Creation of Deviance,* 341. Erikson notes, "The amount of men, money, and material assigned by society to 'do something' about deviant behavior does not vary appreciably over time, and the implicit logic … seems to be that there is a fairly stable quota of trouble that should be anticipated." *Wayward Puritans,* 24.

15. Stark, "Pornography, Society, and the Law," 218–19.

16. *Dritter Verwaltungsbericht,* 388. A comprehensive list of all titles banned by Prussian authorities was compiled in 1897 (*Verzeichnis der im Gebiete des Preußischen Staates auf Grund des §56 Nr. 10 der Reichs-Gewerbeordnung vom Feilbieten im Umherziehen ausgeschlossenen Druckschriften, andere Schriften und Bildwerke, herausgegeben im Ministeriums des Inneren zu Berlin* [Berlin, 1897]); annual supplements published in 1897 and 1898.

17. The Prussian *Verzeichnis derjenigen Druckschriften und anderen Schriften und Bildwerke welche von preußischen Behörden (der einzelnen Bezirksausschüßen, in Berlin von dem Polizeipräsidenten) zum Feilbieten im Umherziehen nicht zugelassen worden sind, herausgegeben im Ministeriums des Inneren zu Berlin* (Berlin, 1908) was 239 pages long and listed over 4,100 items; annual supplements from 1909 to 1914 added thousands more. Devising yet another form of control, Hamburg even reportedly passed an ordinance allowing street peddlers to display and sell *only* those titles listed in an official catalog compiled by the police. Prussian IM memo 1 Apr. 1910, in GStA PK, Rep. 77, Tit. 380, Nr. 7, Adh. 2, Bd. 1, Bl. 40ff.

18. See my "Cinema, Society, and the State: Policing the Film Industry in Imperial Germany," in *Essays on Culture and Society in Modern Germany,* ed. Gary D. Stark and Bede K. Lackner (College Station, TX, 1982), 122–86.

19. Jelavich, "Paradoxes of Censorship," 271–73.

20. Quoted in Theo Mechtenberg, "Vom poetischen Gewinn der Zensur," *Deutschland Archiv* 9 (Sept. 1985): 977.

21. Ferdinand Avenarius, "Theaterzensur," *Der Kunstwart* 16, no. 2, Heft 14 (Apr. 1903): 55.

22. Ernst Wichert to Paul Heyse, 22 Sept. 1901, quoted in Pöllinger, *Zensurprozeß,* 149.

23. Erikson, "Notes on the Sociology of Deviance," 310; *Wayward Puritans,* 10ff.

24. See for example *Die Nationalzeitung,* 26 Sept. 1894, which admitted the police ban of *Die Weber* and its later reversal by the courts "hatten sich als wirksamstes Agitationsmittel erwiesen"; the comments of the anti-Semitic *Deutschen Volksblatt,* 17 May 1896, lamenting how Panizza and "the moderns" used his trial and imprisonment as a "Reklametrommel" and as a clever, deliberate "Reklameschwindel"; and the complaint by the *Münchener Neueste Nachrichten,* 7 Feb. 1903, that the bungled police attempt to ban *Das Tal des Leben* made it a "sensation."

25. "Aufruf zum Anschluß an den Münchener Männerverein zur Bekämpfung der öffentlichen Unsittlichkeit," [1906], reprinted in Meyer, *Theaterzensur in München,* 309–10.

26. Kurt von Glasenapp and BPP to Prussian IM, 15 May 1902, LAB A/74, Th 804, and GStA PK/1000, Nr. 7, Bd. 3, Bl. 112–14.

27. Stephen Worchel and S. E. Arnold, "The effects of censorship and the attractiveness of the censor on attitude change," *Journal of Experimental Social Psychology* 9 (1973): 265–77; Stephen Worchel, S. E. Arnold, and M. Baker, "The effect of censorship on attitude change: the influence of censor and communicator characteristics," *Journal of Applied Social Psychology* 5 (1975): 222–39.

28. Vilfred Pareto, *The Mind and Society: A Treatise on General Sociology,* trans. Andrew Bongiorno and Arthur Livingston (New York, 1935), 3: 7211ff; J. M. van Ussel, *Sexualunterdrückung. Geschichte der Sexualfeindschaft* (Reinbeck, 1970), 34–55.

29. Laube, *Erinnerungen,* quoted in Susanne Ghirardini-Kurzweill, "Das Theater im den politischen Strömungen der Revolution von 1848" (Inaug. Diss., Ludwig-Maximilians-Universität zu München, 1960), 69.

30. Erikson, *Wayward Puritans,* 22–23.

31. See the exemplary studies of Brauneck, *Literatur und Öffentlichkeit*, Pöllinger, *Zensurprozeß*, and Michael Meyer, "Zur Rezeptionsgeschichte von Sternheims Komödie 'Die Hose' (1911–1926)," in *Carl Sternheims Dramen. Zur Textanalyse, Ideologiekritik und Rezeptionsgeschichte*, ed. Jörg Schönert (Heidelberg, 1975), 191–206. Also Siegbert Klee's unpublished paper "Hose 'runter: Sternheim und die bürgerliche Selbstentblößung," presented at the 1991 German Studies Association meeting, Los Angeles, October 1991.

32. John D. Halliday, "Censorship in Berlin and Vienna During the First World War: A Comparative View," *The Modern Language Review* 83, no. 3 (July 1988): 618.

33. "Art Under Attack: Who Dares Say That It's No Good?" *New York Times*, Sunday, November 25, 1990, Section 2, 1, 39.

34. Theodor Lessing, *Einmal und nie wieder. Lebenserinnerungen*, in *Gesammelte Schriften in Zehn Bänden* (Prague, 1935), 1: 234.

35. Leppmann, *Gerhart Hauptmann*, 161.

36. Pöllinger, *Zensurprozeß*, 44–70, 149–58.

37. Becker, *Outsiders*, 9; Hawkins and Tiedeman, *Creation of Deviance*, 42–59, 240–53, 342; Matza, *Becoming Deviant*, 143–57; Walter R. Gove, "The Labeling Perspective: An Overview," in *The Labeling of Deviance: Evaluating a Perspective*, 2nd ed., ed. Walter R. Gove (Beverly Hills, CA, 1980), 9–26.

38. Frank Tannenbaum, *Crime and the Community* (Boston, 1938), 19.

39. Allen, *Satire and Society*, 128; Lenman, "Censorship and Society," 91–92.

40. See Lenman, "Censorship and Society," 114–15; Thoma to C. Haussmann, 17 Apr. 1905, quoted in Gritschneder, *Angeklagter Ludwig Thoma*, 34; Allen, *Satire and Society*, 162–64, 185–87.

41. Thoma to Ludwig Ganghofer, 22 Aug. 1906, in Thoma, *Ausgewählte Briefe*, 76–77.

42. Reinhard Rürup, "Ludwig Quidde," in *Deutsche Historiker*, Band III, ed. Hans-Ulrich Wehler (Göttingen, 1972), 140.

43. Quidde, "Erinnerungen," 32.

ARCHIVES CONSULTED

Badisches Generallandesarchiv, Karlsruhe
Abt. 233: Staatsministerium
Abt. 234: Justizministerium
Abt. 356: Bezirksamt Heidelberg
Abt. 357: Bezirksamt Karlsruhe
Abt. 362: Bezirksamt Schwetzingen/Mannheim

Bayerisches Hauptstaatsarchiv, Munich
MInn: Ministerium des Inneren
MJu: Ministerium des Justiz
MA: Ministerium des Äusseren

Bayerisches Staatsbibliothek, Munich
Handschriftenabteilung
Paul-Heyse-Archiv

Bundesarchiv—Militärarchiv, Freiburg im Breisgau
RM 3: Reichsmarineamt
RM 5: Admiralstab der Marine

Deutsches Literaturarchiv, Marbach am Neckar
Cotta-Archiv, Nachlaß Sudermann
Gerhart Hauptmann Archiv

Freies Deutsches Hochstift/Frankfurter Goethe Museum, Frankfurt am Main
Handschriften-Abteilung
Bahr, Hermann

Geheimes Staatsarchiv Preußischer Kulturbesitz, Berlin-Dahlem
Rep. 77: Ministerium des Inneren
Rep. 84a: Justizministerium

Rep. 90
Rep. 184: Oberverwaltungsgericht
Rep. 209: Polizeipräsidium Danzig
Holdings formerly in Geheimes Staatsarchiv Preußischer Kulturbesitz Merseburg/Zentrales Staatsarchiv Merseburg:
Rep. 77: Ministerium des Inneren
Rep. 120: Ministerium für Handel und Gewerbe
2.2.1. Königliches Geheimes Zivilkabinett

Hauptstaatsarchiv Württemberg, Stuttgart
E 130a: Staatsministerium
E 150: Innenministerium
E 151c/III: Innenministerium
M 1/3: Kriegsministerium, Zentralabteilung
M 77/1: Stellvertretendes Generalkommando XIII. A.K.
M 77/2: Stellvertretendes Generalkommando, XIII. A.K.,
Denkschriften-Sammlung

Hessisches Hauptstaatsarchiv, Wiesbaden
Abt. 407: Polizeipräsidium Frankfurt
Abt. 405: Preußische Regierung Wiesbaden

Hessisches Staatsarchiv Darmstadt

Landesarchiv Berlin, Berlin
Pr. Br. Rep. 30
Pr. Br. Rep. 30 C/a: Theater-Zensur
Holdings formerly in Brandenburgisches Landeshauptarchiv, Potsdam/Staatsarchiv Potsdam:
Pr. Br. Rep. 2A: Regierungsbezirk Potsdam
Pr. Br. Rep. 3B: Regierungsbezirk Frankfurt/Oder
Pr. Br. Rep. 30 Berlin C: Polizeipräsidium Berlin
Pr. Br. Rep. 31A: Bezirksausschuß Potsdam

Staatsarchiv Bremen, Bremen
3. Senatsregistraturen
4,14/1. Polizeidirektion
4,20. Bremisches Amt Bremerhaven
4,89/1.

Staatsarchiv Hamburg, Hamburg
Pol.S.: Polizeibehörde—Politische Polizei

Staatsarchiv Ludwigsburg, Ludwigsburg
F 201: Stadtdirektion Stuttgart

Staatsarchiv München, Munich
Pol. Dir. München
St.Anw.

Staats- und Universitätsbibliothek Hamburg, Hamburg
Richard Dehmel Archiv

Stadtarchiv Ludwigshafen
Nachlaß Anna Croissant-Rust

Stadtbiblothek München, Munich
Literaturarchiv
Nachlaß Korfiz Holm
Nachlaß Thomas Theodor Heine
Nachlaß Ludwig Thoma
Nachlaß Wilhelm Walloth
Nachlaß Georg Kerschensteiner
Max-Halbe-Archiv

WORKS CITED

Abret, Helga, and Aldo Keel, eds. *Das Kopierbuch Korfiz Holms (1899–1903). Ein Beitrag zur Geschichte des Albert Langen Verlags und des 'Simplicissimus'.* Bern, 1989.
———. *Die Majestätsbeleidigungsaffäre des 'Simplicissimus'-Verlegers Albert Langen.* Frankfurt, 1985.
———. *Im Zeichen des Simplicissimus. Briefwechsel Albert Langen Dagny Bjørnson 1895–1908.* Munich, 1987.
Ackermann, Walter. "Die zeitgenössische Kritik an den deutschen naturalistischen Drama." Diss. phil., U. Munich, 1965.
"Die Affäre Jagow-Durieux," *Vorwärts,* 3 Mar. 1911.
Alberti, Conrad. See: Sittenfeld, Konrad.
Allen, Ann J. *Satire and Society in Wilhelmine Germany:* Kladderadatsch *&* Simplicissimus *1890–1914.* Lexington, KY, 1984.
Atzrott, Otto, ed. *Sozialdemokratische Druckschriften und Vereine verboten auf Grund des Reichsgesetz gegen die gemeingefährlichen Bestrebungen der Sozialdemokraten von 21. Okt. 1878.* Berlin, 1886; Nachtrag 1888.
Aulich, Reinhard. "Elemente einer funktionalen Differenzierung der literarischen Zensur. Überlegungen zur Form und Wirksamkeit von Zensur als einer intentional adäquaten Reaktion gegnüber literarischer Kommunikation." In *"Unmoralisch an sich ... " Zensur im 18. und 19. Jahrhundert,* Herbert G. Göpfert and Erdmann Weyrauch, eds. Wiesbaden, 1988: 177–230.
Avenarius, Ferdinand. "Theaterzensur." *Der Kunstwart* 16, no. 2, Heft 14 (Apr. 1903): 49–57.
Bahr, Hermann. *Selbstbildnis.* Berlin, 1923.
Ball, Hugo. *Briefe 1911–1927.* Zurich, 1957.
Ball-Hemmings, Emmy. *Hugo Ball. Sein Leben in Briefen und Gedichten.* Frankfurt, 1991.
Bar, Dr. von. "Rechtmäßigkeit und Zweckmäßigkeit der Theaterzensur?" *Deutsche Juristen Zeitung* 8 (1903): 205–8.
Barsch, Achim. "Literatur und Recht aus literaturtheoretischer Sicht." In *Literatur vor dem Richter. Beiträge zur Literaturfreiheit und Zensur,* Birgit Dankert and Lothar Zechlin, eds. Baden-Baden, 1988: 63–90.

Bauer, Michael. *Oskar Panizza. Ein literarisches Porträt.* Munich, 1984.

Baumer, Franklin L. *Modern European Thought. Continuity and Change in Ideas, 1600–1950.* New York, 1977.

Bazille, Amtmann. "Die Theaterzensur in Württemberg in rechtlicher und verwaltungspolitischer Hinsicht." *Württembergische Zeitschrift für Rechtspflege und Verwaltung* 2, no. 4 (1 April 1909): 113–28.

Bebel, August. *Die Handhabung des Vereins- und Versammlungsrechts im Königreich Sachsen.* Berlin, 1897.

Becker, Howard J. *Outsiders: Studies in the Sociology of Deviance.* New York, 1963.

Berg, Leo. *Gefesselte Kunst.* Berlin, 1901.

———. "Über die Zufälligkeit und die Grenzen der Majestätsbeleidigung als Straffbegriff im modernen Staatsleben." *Die Gegenwart* 27, Bd. 33 (1 Jan. 1898): 6–8.

Berger, Melvin. *Censorship.* New York, 1982.

Berghahn, Volker R. *Imperial Germany, 1871–1914: Economy, Society, Culture and Politics.* Providence, RI and Oxford, 1994.

"Beschluß in der Strafsache wider den Schriftsteller Otto Brahm und den Redakteur Wilhelm Bölsche wegen Vergehen gegen Par. 184 des Strafgesetzbuches." *Freie Bühne* 2 (1891): 129–30.

Best, Alan. "The Censor Censored: An Approach to Frank Wedekind's 'Die Zensur'." *German Life and Letters* 27, no. 4 (July 1973): 278–87.

Bettelheim-Gabillon, Helene. "Wildenbruch und Grillparzer im Spiegel der Zensur." *Österreichische Rundschau* 53, no. 5 (1917): 228–31.

Bilse, Lt. [Fritz von der Kyrburg], *Life in a Garrison Town,* Arnold White, trans. New York, 1914.

Birett, Herbert, ed. *Verbotene Druckschriften in Deutschland. Band 1: Die Sozialistengesetze 1878–1918. Band 2: Schmutz und Schund.* Ruggel, Lichtenstein, 1987, 1995.

Birkmeyer, Karl von, et al. *Vergleichende Darstellung des deutschen und ausländischen Strafrechts. Besonderer Teil.* Berlin, 1905–1908.

Bleibtreu, Karl. "Staat und Litteratur." *Das Magazin für die Literatur des In- und Auslandes* 64, no. 12 (23 Mar. 1895): 362–65.

Bloch, Iwan. *Das Sexualleben unserer Zeit in seinen Beziehungen zur modernen Kultur.* 2 Aufl. Berlin, 1907.

Blumenthal, Oscar. *Verbotene Stücke.* Berlin, 1900.

Bochnik, Georg. "Das Belle-Alliance-Theater in Berlin, 1869–1913." Phil. Diss., F. U. Berlin, 1957.

Bonn, Ferdinand. *Mein Künstlerleben. Was ich mit dem Kaiser erlebte und andere Erinnerungen.* Munich, 1920.

———. *Zwei Jahre Theaterdirektor in Berlin. Ein Beitrag zur deutschen Kulturgeschichte.* Berlin, 1908.

Brahm, Otto. *Theater. Dramatiker. Schauspieler.* Hugo Fetting, ed. Berlin, 1961.

Braulich, Heinrich. *Die Volksbühne. Theater und Politik in der deutschen Volksbühnebewegung.* Berlin, 1976.

Brauneck, Manfred. *Literatur und Öffentlichkeit im ausgehenden 19. Jahrhundert. Studien zur Rezeption des naturalistischen Theaters in Deutschland.* Stuttgart, 1974.

Brehm, Friedl. *Sehnsucht nach Unterdrückung. Zensur und Presserecht bei Ludwig Thoma.* Feldafing, 1957.

Brehmer, Arthur and Max Grube. "Der Kaiser und die Kunst." In *Am Hofe Kaiser Wilhelms II,* Arthur Brehmer, ed. Berlin, 1898: 313–84.

Brescius, Hans von. *Gerhart Hauptmann. Zeitgeschehen und Bewußtsein in unbekannten Selbstzeugnissen. Eine politisch-biographische Studie.* 2 Aufl. Bonn, 1977.

Breuer, Dieter. *Geschichte der literarischen Zensur in Deutschland.* Heidelberg, 1982.

———. "Stand und Aufgagen der Zensurforschung." In *"Unmoralisch an sich…" Zensur im 18. ud 19. Jahrhundert,* Herbert G. Göpfert and Erdmann Weyrauch, eds. Wiesbaden, 1988: 37–60.

Broder, Henryk M., ed. *Die Schere im Kopf. Über Zensur und Selbstzensur.* Cologne, 1976.

Brooks, Robert C. "Lese Majeste in Germany." *Bookman* 40 (1914): 68–82 [reprinted from June 1904].

Brown, Peter D. G. *Oskar Panizza: His Life and Works.* New York, 1983.

Brunner, Dr. Karl. *Unser Volk in Gefahr! Ein Kampfruf gegen die Schundliteratur.* Pforzheim, 1909.

Bückmann, Walter, ed. *Kunst vor dem Richter.* Frankfurt, 1964.

Burt, Richard, ed. *The Administration of Aesthetics: Censorship, Political Criticism, and the Public Sphere.* Minneapolis, 1994.

Buth, Werner. "Das Lessing-Theater unter der Direktion von Otto Brahm 1904–1912." Phil. Diss., F. U. Berlin, 1964.

Calvino, Italo. *If on a winter's night a traveler.* William Weaver, trans. San Diego and New York, 1981.

Chickering, Roger. *Imperial Germany and the Great War 1914–1918.* Cambridge, 1998.

———. *Imperial Germany and a World Without War: The Peace Movement and German Society, 1892–1914.* Princeton, NJ 1975.

———. ed. *Imperial Germany: A Historiographical Companion.* Westport, CT, 1996.

———. "The Quest for a Usable German Empire." In *Imperial Germany: A Historiographical Companion,* Roger Chickering, ed. Westport, CT: 1996: 1–12.

Cholodin, Marianna. *A Fence Around the Empire: Russian Censorship of Western Ideas under the Tsars.* Durham, NC, 1985.

Clapp, Jane. *Art Censorship: A Chronology of Proscribed and Prescribed Art.* Metuchen, NJ, 1972.

Cohn, Alfons Fedor. "Die Zensur." *Die Schaubühne* 7, no. 26/27 (6 Juli 1911): 1–6.

Conrad, Michael Georg. "Goethebund." *Die Gesellschaft* 16, pt. 2 (1900): 69–72.

———. *Von Emile Zola bis Gerhart Hauptmann. Erinnerungen zur Geschichte der Moderne.* Leipzig, 1902.

Conradi, Hermann. "Gedanken über Kunst, Künstler, Künstlertum." In *Hermann Conradis Gesammelte Schriften,* Paul Ssymank and G. W. Peters, ed. Munich, 1912: 1: 238–41.

Craig, Gordon A. *Germany 1866–1945.* New York, 1978.

———. *The Politics of the Prussian Army 1640–1945.* New York, 1964.

Davies, Cecil. W. *Theater for the People: The Story of the Volksbühne.* Austin, TX, 1977.

De Mendelssohn, Peter. *S. Fischer und Sein Verlag.* Frankfurt, 1970.

———. "Zur Geschichte des *Reigen.* Aus dem Briefwechsel zwischen Arthur Schnitzler und S. Fischer." *Almanach. Das sechsundsiebzigste Jahr.* Frankfurt, 1967: 18–35.

Dehmel, Richard. *Ausgewählte Briefe aus den Jahren 1883–1902.* Berlin, 1922.

———. *Gesammelte Werke.* Berlin, 1916.

Deiritz, Karl. *Geschichtsbewußtsein, Satire, Zensur. Eine Studie zur Carl Sternheim.* Königstein, 1979.

Dellé, Eberhard. "Das Victoria-Theater in Berlin (1859–1891)." Phil. Diss., F. U. Berlin, 1954.

Dittmar, Peter. *Lob der Zensur. Verwirrung der Begriffe, Verwirrung der Geister.* Cologne, 1987.

Dritter Verwaltungsbericht des Königlich-Polizeipräsidiums von Berlin für die Jahre 1891–1900. Berlin, 1902.

Dukes, Jack R. and Joachim Remak, eds. *Another Germany: A Reconsideration of the Imperial Era.* Boulder, CO, 1988.

Durieux, Tilla. *Meine ersten neunzig Jahre.* Berlin, 1971.

Engel-Reimers, Charlotte. *Die deutschen Bühnen und ihre Angehörigen. Eine Untersuchung über ihre wirtschaftliche Lage.* Leipzig, 1911.

Entscheidungen des Reichsgerichts in Strafsachen. Berlin, 1880–1944.

Erikson, Kai. "Notes on the Sociology of Deviance." *Social Problems* 9, no. 4 (Spring 1962): 307–14.

———. *Wayward Puritans: A Study in the Sociology of Deviance.* New York, 1966.

Ernst, Paul. *Jünglingsjahre.* Munich, 1931.

Eulenberg, Herbert. "Brief eines Vaters unserer Zeit." *Pan* 1, no. 11 (1 Apr. 1911): 358–63.

———. "Ein Protest." *Pan* 1, no. 12 (16 Apr. 1911): 393–95.

Ewald's Polizei-Verordnungen für Frankfurt am Main. Frankfurt, 1906.

Feldman, Siegmund. "Die Dirne Elisa." *Freie Bühne* 2, Heft 3 (1891): 68–70.

Feuchtwanger, Edgar. *Imperial Germany 1850–1918.* London and New York, 2001.

Fischer, Ernst. "Der 'Schutzverband deutscher Schriftsteller' (1909–1933)." *Archiv für Geschichte des Buchwesens* 21 (1980): 1–666.

Fischer, Heinz-Dietrich, ed. *Deutsche Kommunikationskontrolle des 15. bis 20. Jahrhunderts.* Munich, 1982.

Flatz, Roswitha. *Krieg im Frieden. Das aktuelle Militärstück auf dem Theater des deutschen Kaiserreichs.* Frankfurt, 1976.

Fosdick, Raymond. *European Police Systems.* 1915. Reprint: Montclair, NJ, 1972.

Foucault, Michael. *Discipline and Punish: The Birth of the Prison.* Alan Sheridan, trans. New York, 1977.

———. *The History of Sexuality. Volume I: An Introduction.* Robert Hurley, trans. New York, 1978.

Fowell, Frank and Frank Palmer. *Censorship in England.* 1913. Reprint: New York, 1969.

Frank, Reinhard, ed. *Das Strafgesetzbuch für das Deutsche Reich, nebst dem Einführungsgesetze.* 8.–10. rev. Aufl. Tübingen, 1912.

Fritz, Horst. "Die Dämonisierung des Erotischen in der Literatur des Fin de siècle." In *Fin de Siècle. Zur Literatur und Kunst der Jahrundertsend,* Roger Bauer, et al., eds. Frankfurt, 1977: 442–64.

Freshwater, Helen. "Towards a Redefinition of Censorship." In *Censorship and Cultural Regulation in the Modern Age,* Beate Müller, ed. Amsterdam and New York, 2004: 224–45.

Fügen, Hans Norbert. "Zensur als negativ wirkende Institution." In *Lesen—Ein Handbuch,* Alfred C. Baumgärtner, ed. Hamburg, 1974: 623–62.

Fuld, Ludwig. "Majestätsbeleidigung." *Neue Deutsche Rundschau* 4, no. 1 (1898).

Funk, Albrecht. *Polizei und Rechtstaat. Die Entwicklung des staatlichen Gewaltmonopol in Preussen 1848–1914.* Frankfurt, 1986.

"Für Frank Wedekind." *Die Aktion* 1/17 (12 Juni 1911): 531–32.

Füssel, Stephan. "Thomas Mann's 'Glaudius dei' (1902) und die Zensurdebatte der Kaiserzeit." In *Zwischen den Wissenschaften: Beiträge zur deutschen Literaturgeschichte,* Gerhard Hahn and Ernst Weber, eds. Regensburg, 1994: 427–46.

Gafert, Karin. *Die soziale Frage in Literatur und Kunst des 19. Jahrhunderts. Ästhetische politisierung des Weberstoffes.* Kronberg, 1973.

Gerstmann, Adolf. "Zur Frage der Theater-Zensur." *Deutsche Schriftsteller Zeitung* 1, no. 23 (1 Dec. 1885): 537–42.

Gesetz- und Verordnungsblatt für den Freistaat Bayern. Munich: 1874-1918

Ghirardini-Kurzweill, Susanne. "Das Theater im den politischen Strömungen der Revolution von 1848." Inaugural-Dissertation, Ludwig-Maximilians-Universität, Munich, 1960.

Gibbs, Jack P. *Norms, Deviance, and Social Control: Conceptual Matters.* New York, 1981.

Giesing, Michaela. "Theater, Polizei und Politik in Hamburg um 1900." *Maske und Kothurn* 42, no. 2–4 (1996): 121–63.

Gilbert, Felix and David Clay Large. *The End of the European Era: 1890 to the Present,* fifth ed. New York, 2002.

Gillon, Steven M. *That's Not What We Meant To Do: Reform and its Unintended Consequences in the 20th Century.* New York, 2000.

Glasenapp, Helmuth von. *Meine Lebensreise.* Wiesbaden, 1964.

Glossy, Karl. *Vierzig Jahre Deutsches Volkstheater. Ein Beitrag zur deutschen Theatergeschichte.* Vienna, 1929.

Göpfert, Herbert G. and Erdmann Weyrauch, eds. *"Unmoralisch an sich ... " Zensur im 18. und 19. Jahrhundert.* Wiesbaden, 1988.

Goldbaum, Wenzel. *Theaterrecht.* Berlin, 1914.

Goldstein, Robert J., ed. *The Frightful Stage: Political Censorship of the Theater in Nineteenth-Century Europe.* New York and Oxford, 2009.

———, ed. *The War for the Public Mind: Political Censorship in Nineteenth-Century Europe.* Westport, CT, 2000.

Gordon, Harold J. *Hitler and the Beer Hall Putsch.* Princeton, NJ, 1972.

Gorsen, P. *Das Prinzip Obszön. Kunst, Pornographie, und Gesellschaft.* Reinbeck, 1969.

Gove, Walter R. "The Labeling Perspective: An Overview." In *The Labeling of Deviance: Evaluating a Perspective,* second edition, Walter R. Gove, ed. Beverly Hills, CA, 1980: 9–26.

Grelling, Richard. "Die Maßregelung der Freien Volksbühne." *Das Magazin für die Literatur des In- und Auslandes* 61, nos. 6 and 7 (6 and 13 Feb. 1892): 92–93, 108–10.

———. "Die Theater-Zensur." *Das Magazin für die Literatur des In- und Auslandes* 59, no. 44 (1 Nov. 1890): 681–83.

———. *Streifzüge. Gesammelte Aufsätze.* Berlin, 1894.

Gritschneider, Otto, ed. *Angeklagter Ludwig Thoma. Unveröffentlichte Akten.* Rosenheim, 1978.

Grundberg, Andy. "Art Under Attack: Who Dares Say That It's No Good?" *New York Times,* Sunday, November 25, 1990, Section 2: 1, 39.

Gumppenberg, Hanns von. *Lebenserinnerungen. Aus dem Nachlaß des Dichters.* Berlin and Zurich, 1929.

Hadamansky, Franz. "Der Kampf um *Die Weber* in Wien." *Phaidros* 2 (1947/48): 80.

Halbe, Max. *Jahrhundertwende. Geschichte meines Lebens 1893–1914.* Danzig, 1935.

Hall, Alex. "By Other Means: The Legal Struggle Against the SPD in Wilhelmine Germany 1890–1900." *Historical Journal* 17, no. 2 (June 1974): 365–86.

———. "The Kaiser, the Wilhelmine State, and Lèse Majesté." *German Life and Letters* 27 (1973–74): 101–15.

————. *Scandal, Sensation and Social Democracy: The SPD Press and Wilhelmine Germany 1890–1914.* Cambridge, 1977.

Halliday, John D. "Censorship in Berlin and Vienna During the First World War: A Comparative View." *The Modern Language Review* 83, no. 3 (July 1988): 612–29.

Hamann, Richard and Jost Hermand. *Naturalismus.* Frankfurt, 1972.

Hamerow, Theodore S., ed. *The Age of Bismarck: Documents and Interpretation.* New York, 1973.

Handbuch über den Königlichen Preußischen Hof und Staat. Berlin, 1872–1918.

Hanstein, Adalbert von. *Das jüngste Deutschland. Zwei Jahrzehnte miterlebter Literaturgeschichte.* Leipgiz, 1901.

Harden, Maximilian. "Auf der Anklagebank." *Die Zukunft* 25 (12 Nov. 1898): 273–85.

————. *Berlin als Theatershauptstadt.* Berlin, 1888.

————. "König Otto," *Die Zukunft* VI Jg., no. 29 (16 Apr. 1898): 97–102.

————. "Landesgererichtsdirektor Schmidt." *Die Zukunft* 7, no. 37 (16 Jun. 1894): 483–90.

————. "Prozeßbericht." *Die Zukunft* 9, no. 3 (20 Oct. 1900): 95–109.

————. "Das Urtheil im Fall Harden." *Die Zukunft* 6, no. 33 (14 May 1898): 312–17.

Harms, Kathy. "Writer By Imperial Decree: Ernst von Wildenbruch." In *Imperial Germany,* Volker Dürr, Kathy Harms, and Peter Hayes, eds. Madison, WI, 1985: 134–48.

Harston, Barnet. "Reluctant Justice: Government Legal Intervention on Behalf of Jews in Imperial Germany." *German Studies Review* 27, no. 1 (Feb. 2004): 81–102.

Hart, Julius. "Die Entstehung der 'Freien Bühne.' Persönliche Erinnerungen von Julius Hart." *Velhagen und Klasings Monatshefte* 24, Bd. 1 (1909/10): 289–94.

Hartl, Rainer. *Aufbruch zur Moderne. Naturalistisches Theater in München, Teil I.* Munich, 1976.

Hatzipetros, Nicolaus. "Begriff der unzüchtigen Schrift und ihrer Verbreitung (Str. G. B. § 184)." Diss., Univ. Göttingen, 1896.

Hawkins, Richard and Gary Tiedeman. *The Creation of Deviance: Interpersonal and Organizational Determinants.* Columbus, OH, 1975.

Heindl, Robert. "Die Theaterzensur." Diss. Jur., Univ. Erlangen, 1907.

Heine, Wolfgang. "Das Leipziger Autodafé. Unjuristischen Gloßen eines Juristen." *Moderne Dichtung* 1 (1890): 565–68.

Heinrichs, Heinz-Dieter. "Das Rose-Theater. Ein volkstümliches Familientheater in Berlin von 1906 bis 1944." Diss., F.U. Berlin, 1965.

Heinzmann, Kurt. *Deutsches Theaterrecht.* Munich, 1905.

Hellge, Manfred. *Der Verleger Wilhelm Friedrich und das "Magazin für die Literatur des In- und Auslandes." Ein Beitrag zur Literatur- und Verlagsgeschichte des frühen Naturalismus in Deutschland.* Sonderausgabe aus dem *Archiv für Geschichte des Buchwesens,* Bd. 16, Lieferung 4. Frankfurt, 1976.

Hellwig, Albert. "Die Filmzensur in Württemberg. Ihre Notwendigkeit, ihre rechtliche Grundlagen und ihre zweckmäßigste Gestaltung." *Zeitschrift für die Freiwillige Gerichtsbarkeit und die Gemeindeverwaltung in Württemberg* 55 (Jan. 1913): 18–30.

————. *Rechtsquellen des öffentlichen Kinematographenrechts. Systematische Zusammenstellung der wichtigsten deutschen und fremden Gesetze.* Mönchen-Gladbach, 1913.

Henning, Adolf. *Die öffentliche Sittenlosigkeit und die Arbeit der Sittlichkeitsverine: Eine Denkschrift.* Berlin, c. 1898.

Henschke, Alfred [Klabund]. *Briefe an einen Freund,* Ernst Heinrich, ed. Cologne, 1963.

Herrmann, Wilhelm. "Mannheimer Theaterzensur im 19. Jahrhundert." *Mannheimer Hefte* 1976, no. 2: 74–78.

Herzog, Wilhelm. "Der denunzierte Dichter." *Pan* 1, no. 12 (16 Apr. 1911): 396–98.

———. "Die unzüchtige No. 7." *Pan* 1, no. 18 (15 Jul. 1911): 587ff.

———. *Menschen, denen ich begenete.* Bern, 1959.

Hesse, Hermann. "Der Beruf des Schriftstellers," *Wissen und Leben* (1910): 48.

Hett, Benjamin Carter. "The 'Captain of Köpenick' and the Transformation of German Criminal Justice, 1891–1914." *Central European History* 36, no. 1 (2003): 1–43.

Hilscher, Eberhard. *Gerhart Hauptmann: Leben und Werk. Mit bisher unpublizierten Materialen aus dem Manuskriptnachlaß des Dichters.* Frankfurt, 1988.

Hirschamann, Lothar. "Das Berliner-Residenz-Theater und das Neue Theater unter der Leitung von Sigmund Lautenberg, dargestellt aus der Publizistik der Zeit." Diss. phil., F.U. Berlin, 1960.

Holm, Korfiz. *Farbiger Abglanz. Erinnerungen an Ludwig Thoma, Max Dauthenden, und Albert Langen.* Munich, 1940.

———. *ich, kleingeschrieben. Heitere Erlebnisse eines Verlegers.* Munich, 1932.

Holmquist, Michael. "Corrupt Originals: The Paradox of Censorship." *PMLA* 109, no. 1 (1994): 14–25.

Horváth, Ödön von. *Gesammelte Werke.* 8 vols. Traugott Krischke and Dieter Hildebrandt, eds. Frankfurt, 1972.

Houben, Heinrich H. *Hier Zensur—Wer dort?* Leipzig, 1918.

———. *Polizei und Zensur. Längs- und Querrschnitt durch die Geschichte der Buch- und Theaterzensur.* Berlin, 1926. Reprinted as: *Das ewige Zensor.* Kronberg, 1978.

———. *Verbotene Literatur. Von der klassischen Zeit bis zur Gegenwart. Ein kritisch-historisches Lexikon über verbotene Bücher, Zeitschriften und Theaterstücke, Schriftsteller und Verleger.* 2 vols. Berlin, 1924. Reprint: Hildesheim, 1965.

Huber, Gerdi. *Das klassische Schwabing: München als Zentrum der intellektuellen Zeit- und Gesellschaftskritik um 1900.* Munich, 1973.

Hülsen, Hans von. "Der Kaiser und das Theater." *Die Tat* 5, Heft 6 (Sept. 1913): 587–95.

Ingraham, Barton L. *Political Crime in Europe: A Comparative Study of France, Germany and England.* Berkeley, CA, 1979.

Jäger, Georg. "Der Kampf gegen Schmutz und Schund. Die Reaktion der Gebildeten auf die Unterhaltungsindustrie." *Archiv für Geschichte des Buchwesens* 31 (1988): 163–91.

Jansen, Sue Curry. *Censorship: The Knot That Binds Power and Knowledge.* New York, 1988.

———. "The Censor's New Clothes: Censorship in Liberal Societies." In *Patterns of Censorship Around the World,* Ilan Peleg, ed. Boulder, CO, 1993: 189–202

Jelavich, Peter. "Literature and the Arts." In *Imperial Germany: A Historiographical Companion,* Roger Chickering, ed. Westport, CT, 1996: 377–408.

———. *Munich and Theatrical Modernism: Politics, Playwriting, and Performance, 1890–1914.* Cambridge, MA, 1985.

———. "Paradoxes of Censorship in Modern Gemany." In *Enlightenment, Passion, Modernity: Historical Essays in European Thought and Culture.* Mark S. Micale and Robert L. Dietle, eds. Stanford, CA, 2000: 265–85.

John, Michael. "Constitution, Administration, and the Law." In *Imperial Germany: A Historiographical Companion,* Roger Chickering, ed. Westport, CT, 1996: 185–214.

Jones, Derek, ed. *Censorship: A World Encyclopedia.* 4 vols. London and Chicago, 2001.

Just, Harald. "Wilhelm Busch und die Katholiken. Kulturkampfstimmung im Bismarck-Reich." *Geschichte in Wissenschaft und Unterricht* 25 (Feb. 1974): 65–78.

Kanzog, Klaus. "Textkritische Probleme der literarischen Zensur. Zukünftige Aufgaben einer literaturwissenschaftlichen Zensurforschung." In *"Unmoralisch an sich ..." Zensur im 18. und 19. Jahrhundert.* Herbert G. Göpfert and Erdmann Weyrauch, eds. Wiesbaden, 1988: 309–31.

———. "Zensur, literarische." In *Reallexikon der deutschen Literaturgeschichte,* 2 Aufl. W. Kohlschmidt, et al., ed. *Band IV,* ed. K. Kanzog and A. Masser. Berlin, 1984: 998–1049.

Kellermann, Bernhard. "Der Schriftsteller und die deutsche Republik." In *An Alle Künstler!* [Berlin: 1919], in *Weimarer Republik. Manifeste und Dokumente zur deutschen Literatur 1918–1933,* Anton Kaes, ed. Stuttgart, 1983: 30–31.

Kerr, Alfred. "Ballade vom Alexanderplatz." *Pan* 1, no. 8 (16 Feb. 1911): 255–56.

———. "Jagow, Flaubert, *Pan.*" *Pan* 1, no. 7 (1 Feb. 1911): 217–23.

———. "Den Richtern." *Pan* 3, no. 31 (23 Dec. 1913): 715–25.

———. "Freisprechung." *Pan* 2, no. 1 (1 Oct. 1911): 34.

———. "Nachlese." *Pan* 1, no. 10 (15 May 1911): 321–26.

———. "Vorletzter Brief an Jagow." *Pan* 1, no. 9 (1 Mar. 1911): 287–90.

Kessler, Jascha. "The Censorship of Art and the Art of Censorship." *The Literary Review* 12, no. 4 (Summer 1969): 409–31.

Kienzle, Michael and Dirk Mende, eds. *Zensur in der BRD. Fakten und Analysen.* Munich, 1980.

Kirchner, Friedrich. *Gründeutschland, ein Streifzüg durch die jüngste deutsche Dichtung.* Vienna, 1893.

Kirstein, Gustav, Walter Tiemann, and C. R. Weiss, eds. *Richard Dehmels Tagebuch: 1893–1894.* Leipzig, 1921.

Klabund. See: Henschke, Alfred.

Klee, Siegbert. "Macht und Ohnmacht des Zensurspielers Carl Sternheim." In *Zensur und Kultur/Censorship and Culture. Zwischen Weimarer Klassik und Weimarer Republik mit einem Ausblick bis heute/From Weimar Classicism to Weimar Republic and Beyond.* John A. McCarthy and Werner von der Ohe, eds. Tübingen, 1995: 134–48.

Klinger, Charlotte. "Das Königliche Schauspielhaus unter Botho von Hülsen, 1869–1886." Diss. phil., Berlin, 1954.

Knoche, Michael. "Einführung in das Thema." In *Der Zensur zum Trotz. Das gefesselte Wort und die Freiheit Europa,* Paul Raabe, ed. Wolfenbüttel, 1991: 23–39.

Knudsen, Hans A. *Deutsche Theatergeschichte,* 2. Aufl. Stuttgart, 1970.

Kohut, Thomas. *Wilhelm II and the Germans: A Study in Leadership.* New York, 1991.

Kosch, Wilhelm, ed. *Biographisches Staatshandbuch,* Bd. I. Bern, 1963

Koszyk, Kurt. *Deutsche Presse im 19. Jahrhundert.* Berlin: 1966.

———. "Entwicklung der Kommunikationskontrolle zwischen 1914 und 1918." In *Pressekonzentration und Zensurpraxis im Ersten Weltkrieg. Text und Quellen.* Heinz-Dietrich Fischer, ed. Berlin, 1973: 152–93.

Krais, G. "Über Theaterzensur. Vom Standpunkte des Zensors." *Die Gesellschaft* 18, no. 1 (1902): 7–14.

———. "Über Theaterzensur." *Blätter für administrative Praxis* 51 (1901): 23–43.

Kron, Friedhelm. *Schriftsteller und Schriftstellerverbände. Schriftstellerberuf und Interessenpolitik 1842–1973.* Stuttgart, 1976.

Krug, Marven H. "Civil Liberties in Imperial Germany." Ph.D. diss., University of Toronto, 1995.

Kuhn, Annette. *Cinema, Censorship and Sexuality, 1900–1925.* London and New York, 1988.

"Kunst und Polizei." *Das Magazin die für Literatur des In- und Auslandes* 61, no. 50 (10 Dec. 1892): 816–17.

"Kunstpolizei." *Die Gesellschaft* 16, Bd. 1, Heft 2 (1900): 129.

Kutscher, Artur. *Frank Wedekind. Sein Leben und sein Werke.* Munich, 1922–1931.

Kutzbach, Karl A. "Paul Ernst, Früheste dichterischen Arbeiten." *Der Wille zur Form* 7 (Oct. 1961): 261–70.

L'Arronge, Adolph. *Deutsches Theater und deutsche Schauspielkunst.* Berlin, 1896.

———. "Das Theater und die Gewerbefreiheit." *Nord und Süd* (Oct. 1881).

Landmann, Robert von and Gusta Rohmer. *Kommentar zur Gewerbeordnung für das Deutsche Reich.* 5. Aufl. Munich, 1907.

Lange, Annemarie. *Berlin zur Zeit Bebels und Bismarcks. Zwischen Reichsgründung und Jahrhundertwende.* Berlin, 1972.

Lautensack, Heinrich. "Offener Brief an Herrn Regeirungsrat Klotz von der Abtheilung für Theatersachen des Königlicher Polizeipräsidiums zu Berlin." *Die Schaubühne* 6, Bd. 2 (1910): 1103–5.

Le Bon, Gustav. *Psychologie der Massen.* Rudolf Eisler, trans. Stuttgart, 1982.

Ledford, Kenneth F. "Formalizing the Rule of Law in Prussia: The Supreme Administrative Law Court, 1876–1914," *Central European History* 37, no. 2 (2004): 203–24.

———. *From General Estate to Special Interest: German Lawyers 1878–1933.* Cambridge, 1996.

Lees, Andrew. *Cities, Sin and Social Reform in Imperial Germany.* Ann Arbor, MI, 2002.

Lehmann, P. *Polizei-Handlexikon. Ein Auszug aus sämmtlichen in das Gebiet der polizeilichen Thätigkeit einschlagenden Gesetzen, Verordnungen, Bekanntmachungen, etc. mit besonderer Berüchsigtigung der für Berlin erlassenen Specialbestimmungen.* Berlin, 1896.

Lehnert, Herbert and Wulf Segebrecht. "Thomas Mann im Münchener Zensurbeirat (1912/13). (Ein Beitrag zum Verhältnis Thomas Mann zu Frank Wedekind.)" *Jahrbuch der deutschen Schillergesellschaft* 7 (1963): 190–200.

Leiss, Ludwig. *Kunst im Konflikt. Kunst und Künstler im Widerstreit mit der 'Obrigkeit.'* Berlin, 1971.

Lenman, Robin J. V. "Art, Society and the Law in Wilhelmine Germany: the Lex Heinze, *Oxford German Studies* 8 (1973): 86-113.

———. "Censorship and Society in Munich, 1890–1914, With Special Reference to Simplicissimus and the Plays of Frank Wedekind." Ph.D. diss., Oxford, 1975.

Leppmann, Wolfgang. *Gerhart Hauptmann. Leben, Werk und Zeit.* Bern, 1986.

Lessing, Theodor. *Der Fall Panizza. Eine kritische Betrachtung über 'Götteslästerung' und künstlerische Dinge vor Schwurgericht.* Munich, 1895.

———. *Einmal und nie Wider. Lebenserinnerungen. Gesammelte Schriften in Zehn Bänden, Band 1.* Prague, 1935.

Leutenbauer, Siegfried. *Das Delikt der Götteslästerung in der Bayerischen Gesetzgebung.* Cologne, 1984.

Leuthold, Dr. "Theaterpolizei." In *Wörterbuch des deutschen Verwaltungsrechts,* Karl Freiherr von Stengel, ed. Freiburg, 1890: 2: 625–26.

Levine, Michael. *Writing Through Repression.* Baltimore, 1995.

Lewinsky, J. "Über Theaterzensur." *Deutsche Revue* 26, no. 4 (1901): 157–66.

Lewis, Ward B. *The Ironic Dissident: Frank Wedekind in the View of His Critics.* Columbia, SC, 1997.

Lidtke, Vernon L. *The Alternative Culture: Socialist Labor in Imperial Germany.* New York, 1985.

———. "Naturalism and Socialism in Germany." *American Historical Review* 79 (Feb. 1974): 14–37.

———. *The Outlawed Party: Social Democracy in Germany, 1878–1890.* Princeton, NJ, 1966.

Lier, Leonhard. "Künstlerische, nicht polizeiliche Zensur." *Der Kunstwart* 11, Heft 6 (Zweiter Dezember Heft, 1897): 186–88.

Linke, Manfred. *Carl Sternheim in Selbstzeugnissen und Bilddokumente.* Reinbeck bei Hamburg, 1979.

Lippert, Freidrich and Horst Stobbe. *Im memoriam Oskar Panizza.* Munich, 1926.

Lizst, Franz Eduard von. *Das deutsche Reichs-Preßrecht, unter Berücksichtigung der Literatur und der Rechtsprechung.* Berlin and Leipzig, 1880.

———. *Lehrbuch des deutschen Strafrechts,* 9 Aufl. Berlin, 1899.

Litzmann, Berthold. *Ernst von Wildenbruch. Zweiter Band: 1885–1909.* Berlin, 1916.

Lotze, Dieter. *Wilhelm Busch.* Boston, 1979.

Lougee, Robert W. "The Anti-Revolution Bill of 1894 in Wilhelmine Germany." *Central European History* 15 (Sept. 1982): 224–40.

Löwe, Ewald, ed. *Die Strafprozeßordnung für das Deutsche Reich mit Kommentar.* 12 Aufl. Berlin, 1907.

Mandel, E. "Gerhart Hauptmanns "Weber" in Rußland." *Zeitschrift für Slawistik* 12 (1967): 5–19.

Mann, Heinrich. *Essays.* Hamburg, 1960.

Mann, Thomas. *Briefe 1889–1936.* Erika Mann, ed. Frankfurt, 1961.

———. *Letters of Thomas Mann 1889–1955.* Richard and Clara Winston, eds. and trans. New York, 1970.

Martens, Kurt. "Das neueste Zensurverbot," *Münchener Neueste Nachrichten,* 28 May 1913.

Marx, Gary. "Ironies of Social Control: Authorities as Contributors to Devicance Through Escalation, Nonenforcement and Covert Facilitation." *Social Problems* 28, no. 3 (Feb. 1981): 221–46.

Mast, Peter. *Künstlerische und wissenschaftliche Freiheit im Deutschen Reich 1890–1901.* Rheinfelden, 1980.

Masur, Gerhard. *Imperial Berlin.* Devon, UK, 1973.

M[authner], F[ritz]. "Das Obscöne vor Gericht." *Deutschland* 1, no. 41 (12 July 1890): 683–84.

———. "Die freien Bühnen und die Theaterzensur." *Das Magazin für die Literatur des In- und Auslandes* 60, no. 51 (19 Dec. 1891): 801–3.

Mayer, Arno. *The Persistence of the Old Regime: Europe to the Great War.* New York, 1981.

Matza, David. *Becoming Deviant.* Englewood Cliffs, NJ, 1969.

McCarthy, John A. and Werner von der Ohe, eds. *Zensur und Kultur/Censorship and Culture. Zwischen Weimarer Klassik und Weimarer Republik mit einem Ausblick bis heute/From Weimar Classicism to Weimar Republic and Beyond.* Tübingen, 1995.

Mechtenberg, Theo. "Vom poetischen Gewinn der Zensor." *Deutschland Archiv* 9 (Sept. 1985): 977–84.

Mehring, Franz. *Gesammelte Schriften. Bd. 12: Aufsätze zur ausländischen Literatur. Vermischte Schriften.* Thomas Höhle, Hans Koch, and Josef Schleifstein, eds. Berlin, 1976.

———. "Proletärische Ästhetik." *Die Volksbühne, 2 Jg., 1893/94, H. 2 (Oct. 1893)*: 8–9.

Meissner, Heinrich. "Monarchisches Prinzip und Theaterzensur. Eine Skizze nach den Akten." *Preußische Jahrbücher* 206 (Dec. 1926): 316–26.

Merton, Robert K. *Social Theory and Social Structure.* Enlarged edition. New York, 1968.

———. "The Unanticipated Consequences of Purposive Social Action." *American Sociological Review* I (1936): 894–904.

Meyer, F. Hermann. "Bücherverbote im Königreich Preußen von 1834 bis 1882." *Archiv für Geschichte des deutschen Buchhandels* 14 (1891): 317–49.

Meyer, Michael. *Theaterzensur in München 1900–1918. Geschichte und Entwicklung der polizeilichen Zensur und des Theaterzensurbeirates unter besonderer Berücksichtigung Frank Wedekinds.* Munich, 1982.

———. "Zur Rezeptionsgeschichte von Sternheims Komödie 'Die Hose' (1911–1926)." In *Carl Steinheims Dramen. Zur Textanalyse, Ideologiekritik und Rezeptionsgeschichte,* Jörg Schönert, ed. Heidelberg: 1975: 191–206.

Mieruch, Margaret. "Die Stellung der Berliner Theaterzensur zu den deutschen Naturalisten." Maschinschriftliche Hausarbeit zur Magisterprüfung, F.U. Berlin, c. 1975.

Miller, Henry. *Obscenity and the Law of Reflection.* New York, 1948.

Mommsen, Wolfgang. *Bürgerliche Kultur und künstlerische Avantgarde. Kultur und Politik im deutschen Kaiserreich 1870 bis 1918.* Frankfurt, 1994.

Mühsam, Erich. "Der Münchener Zensor. Offener Brief an den Herrn Kgl. Staatsanwalt beim Landgericht I zu München, Justizpalast." *Kain* 3, no. 3 (June 1913): 40–44.

———. "Polizeidiktatur." *Kain* 2, no. 11 (Feb. 1913): 161–64.

———. "Der Zensurskandal." *Kain* 3, no. 4 (Jul. 1913): 56–63.

Müller, Beate, ed. *Censorship and Cultural Regulation in the Modern Age.* Amsterdam and New York, 2004.

———. "Censorship and Cultural Regulation: Mapping the Territory." In *Censorship and Cultural Regulation in the Modern Age,* Amsterdam and New York, 2004: 1–31.

Münchhausen, Börries von. "Dalldorfer Lyrik." *Die Gegenwart* 25 (18 June 1898): 393–94.

Münchow, Ursula, ed. *Aus den Anfängen der sozialistischen Dramatik, I.* Berlin, 1964.

Natter, Wolfgang G. *Literature at War, 1914–1940: Representing the 'Time of Greatness' in Germany.* New Haven, CT, 1999.

Nestriepke, Siegfried. *Geschichte der Volksbühne Berlin. I. Teil: 1890–1914.* Berlin, 1930.

Nestroy, Johann. *Komödien.* 3 vols. Franz H. Mautner, ed.. Frankfurt, 1970.

Nichols, J. Alden. *Germany After Bismarck: The Caprivi Era, 1890–1894.* Cambridge, 1958.

Nikitenko, Aleksandr. *The Diary of a Russian Censor.* Helen Galtz Jacobson, ed., and trans. Amherst, MA, 1975.

Nipperydey, Thomas. *Deutsche Geschichte 1866–1918. Band I: Arbeitswelt und Bürgergeist.* Munich, 1990. *Band II: Machtstaat vor der Demokratie.* Munich, 1992.

Nordau, Max. *Entartung.* Berlin, 1892

Oboler, Eli. *The Fear of the Word: Censorship and Sex.* Metuchen, NJ, 1974.

Ohles, Frederik. *Germany's Rude Awakening: Censorship in the Land of the Brothers Grimm.* Kent, OH, 1992.

Olshausen, Justus. *Kommentar zum Strafgesetzbuch für das Deutsche Reich.* 8 Aufl. Berlin, 1909.

Opet, Otto. *Deutsches Theaterrecht.* Berlin, 1897.

Orlowski, Hubert. *Polnisches Schrifttum unter Zensur. Wilhelminische und nationalsozialistische Zensurpolitik im Vergleich.* Frankfurt, 1988.

Otto, Rudolf. *The Idea of the Holy: An Inquiry into the Non-Rational Factor of the Idea of the Divine and its Relation to the Rational.* John W. Harvey, trans. London, 1923.

Otto, Ulla. *Die literarische Zensur als Problem der Soziologie der Politik.* Stuttgart, 1968.

———. "Zensur—Schutz der Unmündigen oder Instrument der Herrschaft?" *Publizistik* 13 (1968): 5–15.

"Owing to the Complex Rules as to Religious Subjects and the Deference Due to Royalty the Berlin Censor Has His Hands Full," *New York Times,* 27 Sept. 1908, SM8.

Panizza, Oskar. "Dialog im Geiste Huttens" in *Das Liebeskonzil und andere Schriften,* Hans Prescher, ed. and intro. Neuwied, 1964: 187–224.

———. "Ein Jahr Gefängnis. Mein Tagebuch aus Amberg." In *Das Liebeskonzil und andere Schriften,* Hans Prescher, ed. and intro. Neuwied, 1964: 169–86.

———. *Das Liebeskonzil und andere Schriften.* Hans Prescher, ed. and intro. Neuwied, 1964.

———. *Der Illusionismus und die Rettung der Persönlichkeit. Skizze einer Weltanschauung.* Leipzig, 1895.

———. *Genie und Wahnsinn.* Munich, 1891.

———. *Meine Verteidigung in Sachen 'Das Liebeskonzil.'* Zurich, 1895.

———. *Parisjana. Deutsche Verse aus Paris.* Zurich, 1899.

———. *Psichopatia Criminalis.* Zurich, 1898.

———. "Selbstbiographie [17. Nov. 1904]." *Tintenfisch* 13 (1978): 13–22.

Paret, Peter. "The Artist as Staatsbürger: Aspects of the Fine Arts and the Prussian State Before and During the First World War." *German Studies Review* 6 (Oct. 1983): 421–37.

———. *The Berlin Secession: Modernism and its Enemies in Imperial Germany.* Cambridge, MA, 1980.

Pareto, Vilfredo. *The Mind and Society: A Treatise on General Sociology.* Andrew Bongiorno and Arthur Livingston, trans. New York, 1935.

Parmod, Maximilian [Max Apt]. *Antisemitismus und Strafrechtspflege.* 3 Aufl. Berlin, 1894.

Pascal, Roy. *From Naturalism to Expressionism: German Literature and Society 1880–1918.* London, 1973.

Patterson, Annabel. *Censorship and Interpretation: The Conditions of Writing and Reading in Early Modern England.* Madison, WI, 1984.

Patterson, Michael. *The Revolution in German Theatre 1900–1933.* Boston, 1981.

Pechstedt, E. "L. N. Tolstojs Drama 'Macht der Finsternis' und die deutsche Theaterzensur." *Zeitschrift für Slawistik* 13, no. 4 (1968): 558–64.

Penzler, Johannes, ed. *Die Reden Kaiser Wilhelms II. in den Jahren 1901—Ende 1905.* Leipzig, 1907.

Perrine, Laurence and Thomas R Arp. *Literature: Structure, Sound, and Sense.* Sixth ed. Ft. Worth, TX, 1993.

Pflanze, Otto. *Bismarck and the Development of Germany.* Volume 2: *The Period of Consolidation, 1871-1880.* Princeton, NJ, 1990.

Pilgrim, H. von. "Die Bühne und ihre Zukunft." *Das Magazin für die Literatur des In- und Auslandes* 3 (1887).

Polenz, Wilhelm von. "Über die Grenzen des Unanständigen in der Kunst." *Das Magazin für die Literatur des In- und Auslandes* 62, no. 24 (17 June 1893): 383–85.

Pöllinger, Andreas. *Der Zensurprozeß um Paul Heyses Drama "Maria von Magdala" (1901–1903)*. Frankfurt, 1989.

Post, Robert C., ed. *Censorship and Silencing: Practices of Cultural Regulation*. Los Angeles, 1998.

Praschek, Helmut, ed. *Gerhart Hauptman's "Weber". Eine Dokumentation*. Berlin, 1981.

Prescher, Hans. "Hinweise auf Leben und Werk Oskar Panizza." In *Das Liebeskonzil und andere Schriften*, Hans Prescher, ed. and intro. Neuwied: 1964: 247–62.

Protokoll der Delegierten Versammlung der Genossenschaft Dtr. Bühnenangehöriger zu Berlin am 11. Dec. 1902.

Quidde, Ludwig. *Caligula. Schriften über Militarismus und Pazifismus*. Hans-Ulrich Wehler, ed. Frankfurt, 1977.

———. "Erinnerungen. Im Kampf gegen Cäsarismus und Byzantinismus im Kaiserlichen Deutschland." In *Caligula. Schriften über Militarismus und Pazifismus*. Hans-Ulrich Wehler, ed. Frankfurt, 1977: 19–32.

Raabe, Paul, ed. *Der Zensur zum Trotz. Das gefesselte Wort und die Freiheit Europa*. Wolfenbüttel, 1991.

Ragins, Sanford. *Jewish Responses to Anti-Semitism in Germany, 1870–1914: A Study in the History of Ideas*. Cincinnati, OH, 1980.

Rajch, Marek. *Preußische Zensurpolitik und Zensurpraxis in der Provinz Posen 1848/49 bis 1918*. Frankfurt, 2002.

Reiner, Inge. "Die Stellung der deutschen Sozialdemokratie zur Volksbühnenbewegung (1890–1896)." Magisterarbeit, F.U. Berlin, March 1976.

Reisinger, Hedwig. "Michael Georg Conrad. Ein Lebensbild mit besonderer Berücksichtigung seiner Tätigkeit als Kritiker." Inaug. diss., U. Munich, 1939.

Retallack, James. *Germany in the Age of Kaiser Wilhelm II*. New York, 1996.

Richter, Dieter. "Literaturfreiheit und Zensur." *Buch und Bibliothek* 31, H. 4 (Apr. 1979): 323–30.

Riess, Kurt. *Erotica! Erotica! Das Buch der verbotenen Bücher*. Hamburg, 1967.

Riley, Thomas A. *Germany's Poet-Anarchist John Henry Mackay: A Contribution to the History of German Literature at the Turn of the Century, 1880–1920*. New York, 1972.

Roeren, Hermann. *Die öffentliche Unsittlichkeit und ihre Bekämpfung. Flugschrift des Kölner Männervereins zur Bekämpfung der öffentlichen Unsittlichkeit*. Cologne, 1904.

Röhl, John. *Germany Without Bismarck: The Crisis of Government in the Second Reich 1890–1900*. Berkeley, CA, 1967.

Rollka, Bodo. *Die Belletristik in der Berliner Presse des 19. Jahrhunderts. Untersuchungen zur Sozialisationsfunktion unterhaltender Beiträge in der Nachrichtenpresse*. Berlin, 1985.

Rößler, Walter. "Ein Bißchen Gefängnis und ein Bißchen Irrenhaus. Der Fall Oskar Panizza. *Sinn und Form* 32, Heft 4 (Jul/Aug 1980): 840–55.

Rüden, Peter von. *Sozialdemokratisches Arbeitertheater (1848–1914). Ein Beitrag zur Geschichte des politischen Theaters*. Frankfurt, 1973.

Rürup, Reinhard. "Ludwig Quidde." In *Deutsche Historiker, Band III*. H-U. Wehler, ed. Göttingen, 1972: 124–47.

Schauer, Frederick. "The Ontology of Censorship." In *Censorship and Silencing: Practices of Cultural Regulation.* Robert C. Post, ed. Los Angeles, 1998: 147–68.

Schauer, Rudolf. *Zum Begriff der unzüchtigen Schrift. Ein Beitrag zur Erläuterung des §184 R.St.G.B.* Leipzig, 1893.

Scherer, Herbert. *Bürgerliche-oppositionelle Literaten und sozialdemokratische Arbeiterbewegung nach 1890. Die "Friedrichshagener" und ihr Einfluß auf die sozialdemokratische Kulturpolitik.* Stuttgart, 1974.

Schiller, Friedrich. "Die Schaubühne als eine moralische Anstalt betrachtet." In *Sämtliche Schriften.* 5 vols. Munich, 1968: 5: 92–101.

Schettler, Paul. "Heinz Tovote." *Die Gesellschaft* 9 (March 1893): 290–95.

Schinnerer, O. P. "The Suppression of Schnitzler's *Grüne Kakadu* by the Burgtheater: Unpublished Correspondence." *Germanic Review* 6 (1931): 183–92.

Schlesinger, Maximilian. "Das jüngste Deutschland vor Gericht." *Monatsblätter. Organ des Vereins Breslauer Dichterschule* 16, no. 10 (Oct. 1890): 156–58.

Schmid, Dr. "Theaterzensur." *Zeitschrift für die freiwillige Gerichtsbarkeit und die Gemeindeverwaltung in Württemberg* 51 (1909): 144–52.

Schmidt, Lothar [Lothar Goldschmidt]. "Polizei und Bühne." *Die Aktion [Berlin]* 1, no. 38 (6 Nov. 1911): 1187–90.

Schneider, Gerd K. *Die Rezeption von Arthur Schnitzlers Reigen 1897–1994.* Riverside, CA, 1995.

Schneider, Louis. "Ironic Perspective and Sociological Thought." In *The Idea of Social Structure: Papers in Honor of Robert K. Merton,* Lewis A. Coser, ed. New York, 1975: 323–37.

Schnitzler, Arthur. *Briefe 1875–1912.* Therese Nickl and Heinrich Schnitzler, eds. Frankfurt, 1981.

Schöndienst, Eugen. *Geschichte des deutschen Bühnenvereins. Ein Beitrag zur Geschichte des Theaters 1846–1935.* Frankfurt, 1979.

Schorer, Hans. *Das Theaterleben in Münster in der zweiten Hälfte des 19. Jahrhunderts.* Emsdetten, 1935.

Schulz, Gerhard. "Naturalismus und Zensur." In *Naturalismus. Bürgerliche Dichtung und soziales Engagement,* Helmut Scheuer, ed. Stuttgart, 1974: 93–121.

Schulze-Olden, Wolfgang. "Die Theaterzensur in der Rheinprovinz (1819–1918)." Inaug. diss., Cologne, 1965.

Schwab-Felish, Hans. *Gerhart Hauptmann. Die Weber. Vollständiger Text des Schauspiels. Dokumentation.* Frankfurt, 1973.

Scott, George R. *"Into Whose Hands": An Examination of Obscene Libel in its Legal, Sociological, and Literary Aspects.* London, 1945.

Seehaus, Günter. *Frank Wedekind und das Theater.* Munich, 1974.

Seidel, Paul, ed. *Der Kaiser und die Kunst.* Berlin, 1907.

Sendach, Ludwig. "Erinnerungen und Gedanken eines ehemaligen k. u. k. Wiener Zensors." *Bühne und Welt* 4, pt. 1 (1902/03): 779–85.

Siemann, Wolfram. "Ideenschmuggel: Probleme der Meinungskontrolle und das Los deutscher Zensoren im 19. Jahrhundert." *Historische Zeitschrift* 245 (1987): 71–106.

Sittenfeld, Konrad. [Conrad Alberti]. *Was erwartet die deutsche Kunst von Kaiser Wilhelm II? Zeitgemäßige Anregungen von ***.* Leipzig, 1888.

———. "Eine Majestätsbeleidigung." In *Plebs. Novellen aus dem Volke.* Leipzig, 1887.

———, ed. "Der Realismus vor Gericht. Nach dem stenographischen Bericht über die Verhandlungen am 23., 26., und 27. Juni 1890 vor der Strafkammer I des

Königlichen Landesgerichts zu Leipzig gegen Conrad Alberti, Hermann Conradi, Willi Walloth, und deren Verleger (§184 und §166 des Reichstrafgesetzbuches)." *Die Gesellschaft* 6 (August 1890): 1141–232.

———. "Die vernagelte Litteratur." *Die Gesellschaft* 6 (August 1890): 1137–40.

Skriver, Ansgar. *Gotteslästerung?* Hamburg, 1962.

Soergel, Albert and Curt Hohoff. *Dichtung und Dichter der Zeit. Vom Naturalismus bis zur Gegenwart.* Düsseldorf, 1961.

Sommer, Maria. "Die Einführung der Theaterzensur in Berlin." *Kleine Schriften der Gesellschaft für Theatergeschichte,* Heft 14 (Herbst 1955/Sommer 1956): 32–42.

Spreizer, Christa. *From Expressionism to Exile: The Works of Walter Hasenclever (1890–1940).* Rochester, NY, 1999.

Ssymank, Paul. "Leben Hermann Conradis." In *Hermann Conradis Gesammelte Schriften,* Paul Ssymank and G. W. Peters, eds. Munich, 1911–1912: 1: xix–ccliv.

Stark, Gary D. "All Quiet on the Home Front: Popular Entertainments, Censorship, and Civilian Morale in Germany, 1914–1918." In *Authoritiy, Identity and the Social History of the Great War: Essays in Comparative History.* Frans Coetzee and Marilyn Shevin-Coetzee, eds. Providence, RI, 1995: 57–80.

———. "Cinema, Society, and the State: Policing the Film Industry in Imperial Germany." In *Essays on Culture and Society in Modern Germany,* Gary D. Stark and Bede K. Lackner, eds. College Station, TX, 1982: 122–86.

———. "Diplomacy By Other Means: Entertainment, Censorship, and German Foreign Policy, 1871–1918." In *Zensur und Kultur/Censorship and Culture. Zwischen Weimarer Klassik und Weimarer Republik mit einem Ausblick bis heute/From Weimar Classsicism to Weimar Republic and Beyond,* John McCarthy and Werner von der Ohe, eds. Tübingen, 1995: 123–33.

———. "Pornography, Society and the Law in Imperial Germany." *Central European History* 14 (Sept., 1981): 200–229.

———. "Trials and Tribulations: Authors' Responses to Censorship in Imperial Germany, 1885–1914," *German Studies Review* 12, no. 3 (October 1989): 447–68.

St. John-Stevas, Norman. *Obscenity and the Law.* London, 1956.

Stauf von der March, Ottokar [Ottokar F. Chalupka] *Zensur, Theater, und Kritik.* Dresden, 1905.

Steinke, Gerhardt. E. *The Life and Work of Hugo Ball: Founder of Dadaism.* The Hague, 1967.

Stengel, Karl M. J. L. von, and Max Fleischmann, eds. *Wörterbuch des deutschen Staats- und Verwaltungsrechts.* 2 Aufl. Tübingen, 1911–1914.

Stephens, John Russell. *The Censorship of English Drama 1824–1901.* New York, 1980.

Stern, Ernst. *Bühnenbilder bei Max Reinhardt.* Berlin, 1955.

Stümke, Heinrich. *Hohenzollernfürsten im Drama.* Leipzig, 1903.

———. *Theater und Krieg.* Oldenburg and Leipzig, 1915.

Sudermann, Hermann. *Drei Reden, gehalten von Hermann Sudermann.* Stuttgart, 1900.

Tannenbaum, Frank. *Crime and the Community.* Boston, 1938.

Tenner, Edward. *Why Things Bite Back: Technology and the Revenge of Unintended Consequences.* New York, 1997.

Die Theaterzensur. Fünf Vorträge, gehalten in der Versammlung des Berliner Goethebunds in den Philharmonie am 8.III.1903. Berlin, 1903.

"Die Theaterzensur in der Reichstagkommission." *Vossische Zeitung,* 1905, Nr. 113 (8 March 1905).

Thoma, Ludwig. *Ausgewählte Briefe.* Josef Hofmiller and Michael Hochgesang, eds. Munich, 1927.

———. *Erinnerungen.* In *Gesammelte Werke, Band 1.* Munich, 1956.

———. "Gegen die Staatsanwälte." (1907) In *Gesammelte Werke.* Munich, 1932: 7: 358–73.

———. *Gesammelte Werke.* Munich, 1932.

———. *Gesammelte Werke.* Munich, 1956.

Townsend, Mary Lee. *Forbidden Laughter and the Limits of Repression in Nineteenth-Century Prussia.* Ann Arbor, MI, 1992.

Treitel, Richard. *Bühnenprobleme der Jahrhundertwende in Spiegel des Rechts. Theaterrechtlichen Aufsätze.* Manfred Rehbinder, ed. Berlin, 1990.

Trojan, Johannes. *Zwei Monate Festung.* 3 Aufl. Berlin, 1899.

Türk, J. "Die Tätigkeit der Freien Volksbühne." *Volksbühne* 2, no. 8 (Apr. 1894): 10–13.

Umlauff, Ernst. "Zur Struktur der europäischen Kulturwirtschaft. Der deutsche Buchhandel bis 1930." *Europa-Archiv* 2 (Sept. 1947): 889–902.

Ungar, Frederick, ed., *Friedrich Schiller: An Anthology for Our Time.* New York, 1959.

Urban, Josef. "Von der Notwendigkeit und dem Inhalt eines Reichstheatergestezes. Die privatrechtlichen Probleme des Bühnenrechts nach geltenden Rechte und den deutschen und österreichischen Gesetzentwürfen." Inaug. diss., Greifswald, 1915.

Ussel, J. M. van. *Sexualunterdrückung. Geschichte der Sexualfeindschaft.* Reinbeck, 1970.

Verwaltungsbericht des königlichen Polizei-Präsidiums zu Berlin für die Jahre 1871–1880. Berlin, 1882.

Verzeichnis der im Gebiete des Preußischen Staates auf Grund des §56 Nr. 10 der Reichs-Gewerbeordnung vom Feilbieten im Umherziehen ausgeschlossenen Druckschriften, andere Schriften und Bildwerke, herausgegeben im Ministeriums des Inneren zu Berlin. Berlin, 1897–1898.

Verzeichnis derjenigen Druckschriften und anderen Schriften und Bildwerke welche von preußischen Behörden (der einzelnen Bezirksausschüßen, in Berlin von dem Polizeipräsidenten) zum Feilbieten im Umherziehen nicht zugelassen worden sind, herausgegeben im Ministeriums des Inneren zu Berlin. Berlin, 1908–1914.

Victor, Paul. "Execution an einem Buch." *Berliner Börsen-Courier,* 9 Jan. 1898.

Vizetelly, Henry. *Berlin Under the New Empire: Its Institutions, Inhabitants, Industry, Monuments, Museums, Social Life, Manners.* London, 1879. Reprint: New York, 1968.

Wahnrau, G. *Berlin. Stadt der Theater. Der Chronik. I. Teil.* Berlin, 1957.

Walach, Dagmar. "Das doppelte Drama oder die Polizei als Lektor. Über die Entstehung der preussischen Theaterzensurbibliothek." In *Die besondere Bibliothek, oder, die Faszination von Büchersammlungen.* Antonius Jammers, et al., eds. Munich, 2002: 259–74.

Weber, Ludwig. *25 Jahre der Sittlichkeitsbewegung.* 1911.

Webster, Huston. *Taboo: A Sociological Study.* Stanford, CA, 1942.

Wedekind, Frank. *Gesammelte Briefe.* Fritz Strich, ed.. Munich, 1924.

———. *Gesammelte Werke.* 9 vols. Munich, 1924.

———. "Herr von der Heydte." *Die Aktion* 2, no. 8 (19 Feb. 1912): 239.

———. "Torquemada. Zur Psychologie der Zensur." In *Gesammelte Werke.* Munich: 1924: 9: 391–95.

———. "Vorrede zu 'Oaha.' In *Gesammelte Werke.* Munich: 1924: 9: 449–51.

———. "Wer, Was, Warum," *Münchener Neueste Nachrichten,* 24 Nov. 1911.

———. *Werke in drei Bänden.* Manfred Hahn, ed. Berlin, 1969.

————. *Die Zensur. Theodizee in drei Szenen.* [1907]. In *Frank Wedekind, Werke in drei Bänden,* Manfred Hahn, ed. Berlin: 1969: 2: 59–89.

————. "Zensurbeirat." *Der Komet* 1, no. 4 (22 Mar. 1911).

Wehler, Hans-Ulrich. *Deutsche Gesellschaftsgeschichte. Dritter Band: Von der 'Deutschen Doppelrevolution' bis zum Beginn des Ersten Weltkriegs 1849–1914.* Munich, 1995.

————. *The German Empire 1871–1918.* Kim Traynor, trans. Dover, NH, 1985.

Weller, Bruce Uwe. *Maximilian Harden und die 'Zukunft.'* Bremen, 1970.

Wendelberger, E. "Das epische Werk Wilhelm Walloths. Ein Beitrag zur Geschichte des Frühnaturalismus." Diss., U. Munich, 1953.

Widman, Hans. *Geschichte des Buchhandels. Von Altertum bis zur Gegenwart.* rev Aufl. Wiesbaden, 1975.

Wilcke, Joachim. "Das Lessingtheater in Berlin unter Oscar Blumenthal (1888–1893). Eine Untersuchung mit besonderer Berücksichtigung der zeitgenössischen Theaterkritik." Diss. phil. F.U. Berlin, 1958.

Wildenbruch, Ernst von. "Theater und Zensur. Ein Mahnwort (1900)." In *Gesammelte Werke,* Berthold Litzmann, ed. Berlin, 1924: 16: 182–89.

Wille, Bruno. "Aufruf." *Berliner Volksblatt* (23 March 1890).

————. "Die Freie Volksbühne und der Polizei-Präsident." *Freie Bühne* 2, no. 2 (1891): 673–77.

————. "Die Justiz als Kunstrichterin. Gloßen zum Urteil des Oberverwaltungsgerichts über die 'Freie Volksbühne.' *Allgemeine Theater-Revue für Bühne und Welt* 1, no. 3 (8 May 1892): 1–5.

Wolf, Eva. *Der Schriftsteller im Querschnitt: Außenseiter der Gesellschaft um 1900? Eine systematischer Vergleich von Prosatexten.* Munich, 1978.

Wolff, Arthur. "Theater Recht." In *Wörterbuch des Deutschen Staats- und Verwaltungsrechts,* 2 Aufl. Karl von Stengel and Max Fleischman, eds. Tübingen, 1914: 3: 589–94.

Worchel, Stephen and S. E. Arnold. "The Effects of Censorship and the Attractiveness of the Censor on Attitude Change." *Journal of Experimental Social Psychology* 9 (1973): 265–77.

Worchel, Stephen, S. E. Arnold, and M. Baker. "The Effect of Censorship on Attitude Change: The Influence of Censor and Communicator Characteristics." *Journal of Applied Social Psychology* 5 (1975): 222–39.

Young, Harry. *Maximilian Harden, Censor Germaniae: The Critic in Opposition from Bismarck to the Rise of Nazism.* The Hague, 1959.

Zedlitz, Konstantin von. "Die Theaterzensur in England." *Die Zeit. Wiener Wochenschrift für Politik, Volkswirtschaft, Wissenschaft, und Kunst* 34, no. 443 (28 Mar. 1903): 153–54.

Ziegler, Edda. *Literarische Zensur in Deutschland 1819–1848. Materialien, Kommentare.* Munich, 1983.

Zils-München, W., ed. *Geistiges und künstlerisches München in Selbstbiographien.* Munich, 1913.

Zmegac, Viktor, ed. *Geschichte der deutschen Literatur vom 18. Jahrhundert bis zur Gegenwart, Band II.* Königstein, 1985.

Die Zukunft der deutschen Bühne. Fünf Vorträge und eine Umfrage. Reichsverband deutscher Schriftsteller, ed. Berlin, 1917.

[*Zweiter*] *Verwaltungsbericht des königlichen Polizei-Präsidium von Berlin für die Jahre 1881–1890.* Berlin, 1892.

Index of Censored Authors, Titles, Periodicals, and Publishing Firms

GENERAL INDEX

Jagow, Traugott von, 49–50, 82n27, 104,
207–9, 215–16, 239, 242–43, 265
Jesus Christ, 151, 157–58, 173–74, 177,
179–81, 235
Jews, 4, 6–7, 70, 121, 163–68
Jugendstil, 190, 203, 269

Kassel, 213, 231n24
Kellermann, Bernhard, xv, 256, 270
Kiel, 126, 179, 231n115
Köller, Ernst von, 128, 140
Königsberg, 104, 141, 218, 221, 231n124
Kulturkampf, 7, 150–51, 155, 162, 166,
171, 262, 267

League for the Elevation of Public Morality
(Verein zur Hebung der öffentlichen
Sittlichkeit), 61, 195
LeBon, Gustave, 11–12
Left Liberal party (Freisinnige Volkspartei)
11, 88–89, 178
legal/judicial system, plays about, 103–04
Leipzig Realists, 87, 166, 201, 203, 210,
235, 237, 244, 247, 267
trial, 196–200
Leipzig, 5, 16, 19, 40, 47, 92–93, 96, 109,
141, 158, 179, 196–97, 199, 210,
219, 224, 270
lèse majesté, xviii, 2, 5–6, 87–95, 110n2,
153, 157, 159, 196, 241, 244,
248–49
and Paragraph 95, 87–95
Lessing Theater (Berlin), 125, 210, 213,
220, 229n80
Lessing, Gotthold E., 125, 197
Lessing, Theodor, 169, 275
Lex Heinze bill, 21–24, 26–27, 62–63, 65,
104, 195, 202, 204, 252–53, 262–65
Liberal (National Liberal) party, 22, 27, 89,
140, 155, 170, 195, 169
literary life, xix, xxi, 1, 24, 30–31, 66,
109–10, 117, 144, 151, 235, 248,
266, 280
Lübeck, 15, 47, 96, 176
Lüchow, 108
Ludendorff, Erich von, 108–9, 223
Luise of Tuscany, Crown Princess of Saxony,
94
Luise, Queen of Prussia, 97–99
Luitpold, Prince Regent of Bavaria, 6, 94

Mann, Heinrich, 207, 253–55
Mann, Thomas, 84n76, 233–34, 256
and Censorship Advisory Board, 72–79,
217, 255
Mannheim, 18, 133, 161
Martens, Kurt, 76–77
Mauthner, Fritz, 58, 237
Mehring, Franz, 124–25, 128–29, 146n37
Men's League for the Suppression of
Public Immorality (Männerverein
zur Bekämpfung der öffentlichen
Unsittlichkeit), 61, 71, 214, 224,
273
military, military authorities, 2, 7–9, 29–30,
32, 58, 63–65, 81n18, 83n51,
99–105, 108, 112n42, 118, 130,
148n73, 161, 218, 238, 249–50,
262, 266–67, 270–72, 276
portrayed on stage, 99–103
and wartime censorship of immoral
dramas, 223–226, 232n138
Minden, 141
Ministry/Minister of Interior
Bavarian, 69, 83n50, 157, 219
and *Die Weber,* 139–41
Prussian, 21, 29, 43, 67–68, 111n29,
127–28, 156, 176–82, 212, 219
Modern Life Society (Gesellschaft für
modernes Leben), 202, 244
modernism, artistic, xvii, 11, 24, 68–69, 79,
120, 196, 200, 202–3, 267
moral entrepreneurs, 60–65
Mühsam, Erich, 75–77
Müller-Meiningen, Ernst, 11, 74, 112n36
Münchhausen, Börries von, 160, 204
Munich, 3, 5, 6, 10, 11, 14, 16–19, 23, 58,
65, 80n16, 83n45, 85n76, , 236–41,
243–44, 246–47, 249, 251, 255,
258n37, 265, 269–70, 273
and Censorship Advisory Board, 68–79
moral issues in, 193, 195–96, 202–10,
213–24, 228n41, 229n77,
230n97, 230n101, 231n117,
231n124
police force in, 40–44, 46–47, 50–52
political issues in, 90–93, 102–4
religious issues in, 157–61, 166, 171,
175–79, 186n85, 186n87
social issues in, 129–30, 134, 141–42
Münster, 18